D1221501

The Risk Controllers

Further praise for *The Risk Controllers*

"The fallout from the 2008 financial crisis is forcing the world of clearing and settlement out of its traditional back-office obscurity into the limelight. Peter Norman's book presents an invaluable view of the history, operations and strategic issues relevant to this world. At a time when market infrastructure is undergoing the most fundamental change in living memory, his book is an essential companion to anybody involved in helping to shape the new landscape."

—Richard Berliand, former Head of Prime Services and Market Structure at J.P. Morgan

"The Risk Controllers *is an invaluable historical and investigative work about one of the more arcane, yet critical parts of the financial industry. As a result of the financial crisis, Central Counterparty Clearing is now full square at the centre of the global financial repair agenda, especially for derivatives markets, which makes this book particularly timely and welcome. This book will be the reference work on this subject for years to come."*

—David Wright, Deputy Director General, Internal Market, European Commission (2007–2010)

"A must-read for all involved in the development, implementation and oversight of new clearing regulations following the recent financial crisis. Peter has presented a rich history of clearing in a concise and significant manner for those who must seize the successes of the past in putting today's new clearing regimen in place. All should thank Peter for creating this important work which is so relevant in today's world."

—Dennis Dutterer, Retired CEO, President and Director of The Clearing Corporation; former General Counsel of the CFTC

"The Risk Controllers *provides a welcome insight into the world of central clearing. A timely exercise as legislators around the world pin their hopes on CCPs to plug the deficiencies in risk management identified in the global derivative markets. By explaining the history, exposing the limitations and describing the myriad of vested interests involved in central clearing, Peter Norman has clearly outlined the possible pitfalls we must all now try to avoid. A very concise and engaging book on a complex topic."*

—Dr Kay Swinburne, Member of the European Parliament, ECR Coordinator for Economic and Monetary Affairs

The Risk Controllers

Central Counterparty Clearing in Globalised Financial Markets

Peter Norman

A John Wiley and Sons, Ltd., Publication

This edition first published in 2011

Registered office
John Wiley & Sons Ltd, The Atrium, Southern Gate, Chichester, West Sussex, PO19 8SQ, United Kingdom

For details of our global editorial offices, for customer services and for information about how to apply for permission to reuse the copyright material in this book please see our website at www.wiley.com.

A catalogue record for this book is available from the British Library.

ISBN 978-0-470-68632-4 (Hardback)
ISBN 978-1-119-97655-4 (ebk)
ISBN 978-1-119-97794-0 (ebk)
ISBN 978-1-119-97795-7 (ebk)

Typeset in 10/12pt Times by Aptara, New Delhi, India
Printed in Great Britain by CPI Antony Rowe, Chippenham, Wiltshire

To Janice
and in memory of Frank Norman

Contents

Preface

This history and account of central counterparty clearing is my second book dealing with an important financial infrastructure and covers a business that has shot to prominence since the bankruptcy of Lehman Brothers.

The Risk Controllers was conceived before the cataclysmic events of September 2008. As with my previous book – *Plumbers and Visionaries: Securities settlement and Europe's financial market* – the present volume is the result of a three-way collaboration between Chris Tupker, the former chairman of LCH.Clearnet, John Wiley & Sons, Ltd and myself.

Like the previous book, the origins of *The Risk Controllers* can be traced back to a lunch – this time in March 2008 – when I met Chris Tupker to chew over our experiences that resulted in the publication of *Plumbers and Visionaries* a few months before.

He suggested that I prepare a synopsis for a companion volume that would deal with the little known and rather abstruse business of CCPs, which ensure that trades in derivatives and securities markets will be completed in cases where one of the parties to a trade defaults.

As with the previous book, Chris Tupker's ambition was to have a book that would explain the business of clearing and how it worked to a wider audience and how an important but little known part of the financial world had developed over time in the context of society, politics and regulation.

After some hesitation, prompted mainly by a non-specialist's concern that clearing involved some highly technical issues, I agreed. On balance, we both thought that writing *The Risk Controllers* would be a relatively easy task, given that it would build on insights gained writing the earlier book.

That was six months before the bankruptcy of Lehman Brothers, which turned the financial world upside down and propelled the business of clearing from the back office to the front pages.

The Lehman bankruptcy and its aftermath made the subject of clearing topical but added greatly to the complexity of this book. The result is a work that is much bigger than originally envisaged, with a case study of how clearing houses in general and LCH.Clearnet in particular handled the Lehman default in Chapter 3. Part V of the book deals with the political, regulatory and corporate developments since September 2008, which will shape the business of clearing for years to come. The book covers developments up to the middle of October 2010, with some late updates inserted in March 2011. It therefore takes into account the post-crisis legislative initiatives to reform the US, EU and global financial systems.

While paying due attention to the events of the past three years, the book has tried to stay true to its original goal of providing a description and history of clearing. This too has made for an ambitious project as the subtitle 'Central Counterparty Clearing in Globalised Financial Markets' implies. As the reader will discover, CCPs are complex businesses, deeply rooted in history and in several continents.

As far as I can tell, this is the first attempt in many years to write a general account and empirical history of clearing. Clearing houses attracted a good deal of attention during the two decades after they were introduced in Europe in the 1880s. Attention waned for much of the 20th century, however, as they shrank in importance with the global economy under the impact of two World Wars and the Great Depression. A considerable literature on CCPs and clearing has built up since the early 1980s, but this appears largely to consist of official reports and specialist studies of aspects of clearing rather than any general history.

Although I hope that this book will appeal to specialists, I especially hope it will bring the world of the CCP to a wider audience, including readers with a general interest in economics, finance and business and how these interact with politics and regulation.

The book itself cannot possibly claim to be the definitive account of CCPs and central counterparty clearing. Wars, technological advance and office relocations have conspired against the retention of the records necessary to produce such a work, if ever one were possible. CCPs, like many other IT-related businesses, have tended to show scant regard for their roots or history. In my experience, the first thing to disappear into a skip, if space is in short supply or an office is being moved, is the company archive.

Yet, I am convinced there is much more to be discovered about the history of clearing, in archives that may be half forgotten or are waiting to be catalogued. It is encouraging that some companies, such as ICE Futures in Canada, have donated historical material obtained through corporate acquisitions to university archives. If such acts, or indeed this book, encourage other companies to follow suit or researchers to take up the history of financial infrastructures, it will be all to the good.

This book has been made possible by the support of LCH.Clearnet Group, which provided financial backing without which the research would have been impossible. The story of the clearing houses that eventually merged to form LCH.Clearnet forms part of the narrative. But the book is not an official history of LCH.Clearnet or any other clearing house. My relationship with the LCH.Clearnet Group has been at arm's length throughout.

Books are never written without the assistance of many people and this is especially true of *The Risk Controllers*. The list of individuals and institutions who helped me research this book is long. They are mentioned, with thanks, in the following Acknowledgements.

However, there are some without whom this book could not have been produced. Special thanks go to Chris Tupker, whose patience, encouragement and guidance proved a great support at all times. I am also grateful to Rory Cunningham, who helped me understand, if not master, some of the technicalities of modern day clearing. Dennis Dutterer unselfishly shared documents from his own collection of papers covering the early history of the Board of Trade Clearing Corporation, read some of the early draft chapters and provided valuable insights into the development of clearing in the US. Michael March, Natasha de Terán, Rory Cunningham, Ed Watts, Andrea Schlaepfer, Peter McLaren, David Wright and Ben Norman took the time and the trouble to read parts of the text and made helpful comments. After all that input, it goes without saying that any errors in the pages that follow are mine as are the judgements.

Finally, there would be no *The Risk Controllers* without Janice, my wife, whose patience, good humour and support sustained me as I researched and wrote this book.

Acknowledgements

I am indebted to many people who helped me research and prepare this book. Some I have already thanked in the Preface. There are many more whom I met and who gave generously of their time and wisdom. Others responded helpfully to e-mailed queries, shared their thoughts over the telephone or swapped ideas on the margins of conferences and seminars. Some were happy to be quoted in the text. Others preferred to discuss matters on a background basis. Without their help *The Risk Controllers* would never have been written.

My thanks go to: Jacques Aigrain, Will Acworth, Valerie Bannert-Thurner, John Barneby, Robert Barnes, Jan Bart de Boer, Anthony Belchambers, Richard Berliand, Jim Binder, Michael Bodson, Thomas Book, Bill Brodsky, Phil Bruce, Maurice Buijsman, John Burke, Didier Cahen, Michael E Cahill, Diana Chan, Ignace Combes, Tom Costa, John Damgard, Godfried De Vidts, Diana Dijmarescu, Athanassios Diplas, Don Donahue, Oliver Drewes, Wayne Eagle, Peter Elstob, David Farrar, Rudolf Ferscha, Werner Frey, Piet Geljon, Phupinder Gill, Daniel Gisler, Victorien Goldscheider, Stuart Goldstein, Jeremy Grant, Carol Gregoir, Owen Gregory, Catherine Gully, Claire Halsall, François-Guy Hamonic, John Harding, David Hardy, Judith Hardt, Tina Hasenpusch, Daniel Heller, Christophe Hémon, Richard Heyman, Michael Hofmann, Thomas Huertas, Paul-André Jacot, Hans-Ole Jochumsen, Christopher Jones, Alexander Justham, Pen Kent, Cherelt Kroeze, Jacques de Larosière, Olivier Lefebvre, Iona Levine, Roger Liddell, Kelly Loeffler, Walter Lukken, Wayne Luthringshausen, Gina McFadden, Ian McGaw, John McPartland, David Marshall, Gérard de la Martinière, Susan Milligan, James Moser, Mario Nava, John Nordstrom, Patrick Pearson, Nils-Robert Persson, Denis Peters, Martin Pluves, Martin Power, Peter Praet, Alberto Pravettoni, Wal Reisch, Pierre-Dominique Renard, Scott Riley, Daniela Russo, Ulrike Schaede, Heiner Seidel, John Serocold, Martin Spolc, Robert Steigerwald, Marco Strimer, Paul Swann, Kim Taylor, Marc Truchet, Paul Tucker, Steven Van Cauwenberge, Paul Watkins, Martin Wheatley, Justin Wilson, Colin Woodley, Eddy Wymeersch and Marcus Zickwolff.

One of the challenges of this book was to keep up with unfolding events at the same time as researching the past. It helped greatly to attend some of the more important conferences that bring clearing professionals, regulators and policy makers into contact. I am especially grateful to the CSFI; Eurofi; FESE; the FIA; the Financial Markets Group of the London School of Economics; the FOA; Forum Europe; ICBI, Mondo Visione and the SFOA for making me welcome at their events.

To build a picture of clearing before modern times meant rediscovering the delights of digging around in libraries and archives. The British Library, the Library of Congress, the

New York and Chicago Public Libraries yielded valuable background and source material. London's Guildhall Library, with its helpful staff, was an important source of information about LPCH.

I gained access to other information because several organisations kindly allowed me to study material in their possession. These included the Archives municipales du Havre; the Bank of England; Czarnikow in London; the CFTC and Federal Trade Commission in Washington DC; the Museum of American Finance, New York; The National Agricultural Library, Beltsville, Maryland; the Special Collections Department of the Richard J Daley Library of the University of Illinois at Chicago and the Stichting Vereniging voor de Effectenhandel (VvdE) of Amsterdam.

There were some collections and archives that I was unable to visit but which responded helpfully to e-mailed requests for assistance. I am especially grateful to Brian Hubner of the University of Manitoba Archives & Special Collections in Winnipeg; Alison Purgiel of the Minnesota Historical Society Library in St Paul, and Rita Maloney and Eric Grover of MGEX in Minneapolis. My thanks go also to David Boutros of the Western Historical Manuscript Collection-Kansas City and Heather Paxton in Kansas City, Missouri.

Helping inform this book have been insights and contacts gained over 40 years in journalism, many of them writing on economic and financial affairs, with 22 of those years based on the European mainland. This book has also benefited from work I did for *Plumbers and Visionaries*, my book on securities settlement in Europe, which was published in December 2007.

The Internet was also an essential tool for researching this book. Quite apart from making 'on the record' announcements of companies, regulators and policy makers instantly accessible, the web has made available a phenomenal and ever growing amount of historical and archive material. In researching this book two services were especially useful: the WorldCat online library catalogue service and the San Françisco-based Internet Archive.

Preparing the Risk Controllers necessitated learning some new skills: my thanks go to Vida Yirenkyi at LCH.Clearnet in London for giving me a crash course on how to create graphics using a computer. I am also grateful to Kate McAusland, who as assistant to Chris Tupker was always helpful.

Finally, my thanks go to John Wiley & Sons, Ltd the publisher of this work, and in particular to Aimee Dibbens, Caitlin Cornish, Pete Baker, Viv Wickham and Lori Boulton for their guidance and help through the gestation of *The Risk Controllers*, and also to Andy Finch, who as copyeditor helped clean up and prepare my text ready for typesetting.

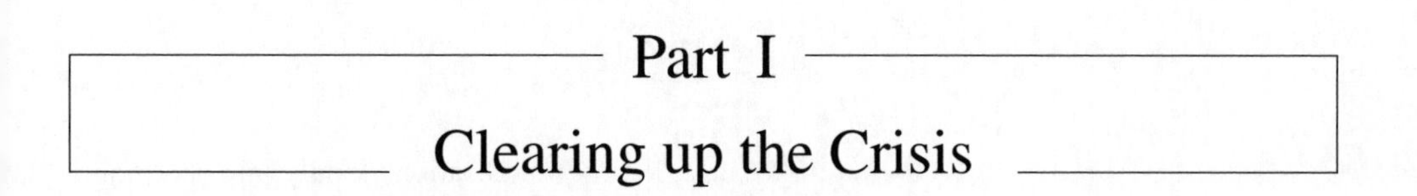

Part I

Clearing up the Crisis

1
Unlikely Heroes

Crises create unlikely heroes. The bankruptcy of Lehman Brothers on 15 September 2008 was no exception.

When Lehman sought protection from its creditors in the US that day, a small number of specialist financial institutions sprang into action to keep the world's securities and derivatives exchanges at work.

First in Europe, and later around the globe, central counterparty clearing houses (known as CCPs) stepped in to rescue trillions of dollars worth of trades caught up in the Lehman collapse. Without their action, the global financial meltdown threatened by the failure of the 158 year old investment bank would have been an instant reality.

These little known organisations fulfilled their emergency role of successfully completing trades for which they had assumed responsibility. Therefore they ensured that the world's securities and derivatives exchanges could continue to function and handle trading volumes that leapt into the stratosphere as prices for shares, bonds and other exchange-traded instruments gyrated wildly in the crisis.

The collapse of Lehman Brothers changed the world in many ways. The petition for Chapter 11 protection, filed by Lehman Brothers Holdings Inc. with the US Bankruptcy Court for the Southern District of New York, turned a steadily escalating international financial crisis into a global economic cataclysm. The investment bank's failure put paid to any prospect of orderly management of the financial turmoil that started during the summer of 2007 as a result of growing losses in the subprime sector of the US housing market. The bankruptcy shattered confidence in market-based finance. The lending between banks that lubricated transactions in the global economy jammed as trust drained away. Money became scarce. Its cost soared.

The decision of the US authorities to let Lehman fall shattered a widespread belief that large institutions of importance to the global financial system were simply too big to fail. That the same authorities decided within 24 hours to prop up the crippled AIG insurance group only added to the convulsions. No-one was left with a clear idea of what would or would not be saved. The issue of 'counterparty risk' – whether it was safe or not to do business with another financial institution, no matter how great or low its standing might be – assumed an overwhelming importance.

In the following weeks, governments in the US, Britain and continental Europe were forced to prop up banking and financial systems with rescue packages costing billions of dollars, pounds and euros. Interest rates tumbled. Budget deficits soared. Many leading banks survived solely because taxpayers' funds were committed to their recapitalisation. In a few frantic weeks mighty financial structures created over the previous three decades either crumbled away or sought to survive as subsidiaries of stronger rivals or wards of the state. The market-based financial systems that had spread from the US around the world since the early 1980s now hosted banks that were either partly or wholly state-owned.

Lehman's bankruptcy placed in jeopardy trillions of dollars worth of transactions conducted by and through the investment bank and its many subsidiaries. Assets were caught in limbo, spreading financial hardship, and in some cases collapse, to companies at the other end of these trades. As became clear when bankruptcy administrators on both sides of the Atlantic tried to make sense of the wreckage, assets worth many billions of dollars would be out of reach for creditors for months if not years.

But the story was very different for those trades transacted on derivatives and stock exchanges and even for a minority of the huge volume of specialised transactions negotiated among financial institutions bilaterally on the 'over-the-counter' (OTC) markets between buyers and sellers. These trades escaped the Lehman catastrophe for the simple reason that they were cleared by central counterparty clearing houses. The CCPs covered for losses after Lehman's default, having stepped in as the buyer to every seller and the seller to every buyer in the markets that they cleared.

Within a week of the Lehman bankruptcy, most outstanding open positions relating to these trades had been neutralised or 'hedged' so that they no longer threatened further losses to creditors or to add more chaos to the world financial system.

Within two weeks, most of Lehman's customer accounts were transferred to other investment companies.

By late October 2008, CCPs in most leading financial markets had reported success in managing the biggest default in financial history without cost to their member companies.

The performance of these unglamorous institutions permitted some rare outbursts of satisfaction in a business where sober understatement is the norm.

In New York, Don Donahue, the Chairman and Chief Executive of the Depository Trust and Clearing Corporation of the US, reported that DTCC was 'able to ensure reliability and mitigate risk across the industry' despite 'unprecedented volatility and shaken confidence' in the financial services sector.[1]

Terrence A. Duffy, Executive Chairman of the Chicago-based CME Group of derivatives exchanges, declared that 'no futures customer lost a penny or suffered any interruption to its ability to trade' when Lehman Brothers filed for bankruptcy. 'The massive proprietary positions of Lehman were liquidated or sold, with no loss to the clearing house and no disruption of the market. This tells us that our system works in times of immense stress to the financial system,' Duffy told a Senate committee.[2]

In London, where LCH.Clearnet Ltd, the UK operating subsidiary of the multinational LCH.Clearnet Group, declared Lehman in default shortly after the start of trading on 15 September 2008, Group Chairman Chris Tupker recalled how: 'At the moment Lehman sought Chapter 11 protection, every exchange in London was clearing through us. No other CCP had the variety and size of positions on its books that we did. I shudder to think what might have happened to the marketplace if we had failed.'[3]

The ability of LCH.Clearnet and other clearing houses successfully to manage the Lehman default helped enable the City and other leading financial centres to survive one of the darkest chapters in the global economic crisis. Thanks to CCPs, the world's securities exchanges have continued to raise capital for enterprises while futures and options exchanges

[1] DTCC (29 October 2008), Addressing the DTCC Executive Forum 2008. DTCC provides clearing, settlement and other post-trade services for companies trading on US stock markets and other financial markets.

[2] Testimony before the Senate Committee on Agriculture, Nutrition and Forestry, 14 October 2008.

[3] Conversation with the author, 12 January 2009.

continue to provide investors, traders and entrepreneurs with the means to protect themselves against risk.

The events of September 2008 changed fundamentally the status of CCPs in financial markets and the priority they are accorded on the agenda of policy makers. After years spent in obscurity, central counterparty clearing houses emerged from the days of chaos among very few organisations in the global financial system with a good story to tell.

This book takes up the story of central counterparty clearing by examining in detail how CCPs functioned in the emergency that followed Lehman's bankruptcy petition.

Chapter 3 places special emphasis on the successful responses of the LCH.Clearnet Group despite serious, unexpected problems faced by its CCPs in London and Paris. The multinational CCP operator was the first big clearing house to declare Lehman companies in default on 15 September. It cleared for a wider range of markets and asset classes than any other CCP. It broke new ground in closing down very large open positions in the interest rate swap market, where over the previous 10 years SwapClear, its specialist clearing service, had built up unique experience in clearing these OTC instruments.

Having demonstrated the value of CCPs in a crisis, the book explores how central counterparty clearing houses grew out of techniques rooted in antiquity and developed from the late 19th century into the institutions on which many hopes are pinned today.

Part II of the book shows how clearing house pioneers in the globalising world of the late 19th and early 20th centuries adopted different systems of governance and ownership, strung along a spectrum from mutualised utility to for-profit, listed corporations, and faced challenges that would be familiar to some of today's CCP managers. Then, as now, technological change – notably in the field of communications – and political developments shaped their decisions.

Part III tells of the emergence of modern CCPs amid the turmoil of the late 20th century and their increased interaction with policy makers and regulators.

Part IV brings the story of CCP clearing to the point of Lehman's default in September 2008 as the optimism engendered by economic globalisation gave way to the global financial crisis.

Part V examines how clearing and CCPs have shot up the public policy agenda as a result of their successes in dealing with the Lehman default and some of the lessons learned from the crisis.

The final part of the book reviews the initiatives by industry and governments to use CCPs to bring transparency and mitigate risks in financial markets and so help ensure that the worst global economic crisis since the Great Depression of the 1930s is not repeated. These include a central role for CCPs in the markets for OTC derivatives, the financial instruments that caused massive losses at AIG, the US insurance group rescued by the US taxpayer immediately after the Lehman bankruptcy. Great hopes are being pinned on CCPs. The big question is whether too much is being expected of institutions that concentrate as well as mitigate risk.

The story of central counterparty clearing in globalised financial markets is a story of constant change, made difficult at times by the absence of a common vocabulary. The terminology of clearing has changed as the business has developed over the past century and a quarter. The terms 'central counterparty clearing' and 'CCP' are relatively recent, and only in common use since the early 1990s.

In examining CCPs and their history, this book covers institutions which existed before the phrase 'central counterparty clearing' and the abbreviation 'CCP' were invented and which nonetheless performed similar functions. It also provides a review of earlier forms of clearing to provide some context for the eventual emergence of CCPs. But it does not claim to be a comprehensive history of all forms of clearing.

CCP-type institutions first existed in 18th century Japan, where they were part of the infrastructure of the Dojima rice market of Osaka. However, today's CCPs trace their lineage back to clearing systems that guaranteed against counterparty risks in commodity futures trading in late 19th century Europe.

During the 1880s, in the historic trading cities of continental Europe and the UK, techniques foreshadowing central counterparty clearing appeared in support of traders who were developing futures and options to manage and exploit the vagaries of the seasons and the cycles of investment, production and trade in markets for agricultural commodities and raw materials.

Soon afterwards, new style clearing practices appeared in North America, where 'complete clearing' houses took on the role of buyer to every seller and seller to every buyer in the nation's commodity exchanges. After a slow start, partly reflecting anti-gambling sentiment, complete clearing became firmly established as the norm for US commodity exchanges in the years of rapid growth between the end of the First World War and the Great Depression.

The importance of central counterparty clearing has grown exponentially in the past 40 years. Human-made uncertainty arising from the shift to floating exchange rates in the early 1970s gave a huge boost to derivatives trading – and by extension to CCPs. The invention of financial futures that facilitated speculation and the management of risks inherent in currencies, securities and interest rates created markets that dwarf the commodities exchanges that CCPs were originally created to serve.

Ever greater computer power has supported the development of CCPs. An important influence was the Wall Street Crash of 1987, which highlighted the growing importance of clearing houses and the risks that attached to them and brought in its wake greater regulatory involvement with CCPs.

Also crucial has been the realisation, during the past two decades, that CCPs have a capacity to add value in the chain of transactions between the buyers and sellers of securities and futures contracts. This gave an impetus to the drive to demutualise exchanges and the infrastructures that support them.

Until recently, it was axiomatic that CCPs dealt only with standardised commodities or financial instruments. CCPs are still used mainly in support of transactions in bonds, shares and futures and options contracts that are listed and traded on regulated exchanges. As initiatives to create CCPs for credit instruments traded over-the-counter show, the role of central counterparty clearing in financial markets stands on the threshold of a new era.

But before exploring the role of CCPs in the past, present and future, the following chapter offers an overview of the modern CCP, how it works and the special features that define central counterparty clearing and its place in today's financial markets.

2
The Modern Central Counterparty Clearing House

2.1 THE CCP's UNIQUE SELLING POINT

The near meltdown of the global financial system following the bankruptcy of Lehman Brothers refocused the attention of markets and policy makers on the original and unique purpose of CCPs.

Just as the forerunners of today's CCPs were set up in the 19th century to neutralise counterparty risk in commodity markets, the core responsibility of today's central counterparty clearing house is again to ensure that a security or derivatives trade between two of its users will not fail because the buyer or the seller are unable to fulfil their side of the bargain. By becoming the buyer to every seller and the seller to every buyer, the CCP assures completion of the trade if a trading partner defaults.

The trade might take place on an exchange, an alternative electronic trading platform or be bilaterally negotiated in an OTC trade. The legal substitution of the clearing house as the counterparty in two new trades, in which the seller sells to the clearing house and the buyer buys from the clearing house, is generally known as *novation*.

Thanks to advanced technology, modern CCPs clearing for exchanges novate and become counterparties to trades instantaneously at the time of their execution. Under traditional methods – still used for OTC trades – novated trades are registered on the CCP's books just after the trade and the details of the original bargain have been verified or matched. Novation takes place before the completion or settlement of trades, which in many cases is handled by a different institution.

Counterparty risk was relatively low among the concerns of financial markets in the decade and a half before Lehman's collapse. Most users in those years probably placed more value on the ability of CCPs greatly to minimise costs and maximise efficiency by netting the positions of counterparties to trades and to provide anonymity for their trades.

If users valued the guarantee function of a CCP it was probably because it also reduced their costs. Under internationally agreed bank capital rules, the substitution of a CCP, with its high credit rating, meant the original counterparties to a trade no longer had to hold capital in respect of their open positions.[1]

Before the Lehman weekend, CCPs appeared worthy at best: little known companies that combined some of the attributes of a bank, a post office and an insurer. In fact, after computers began to take over the processes of registration, novation and netting in the 1960s, the capacities

[1] For details, see Section 2.5.

of CCPs increased exponentially in scope as well as scale so that today, for example, the LCH.Clearnet Group clears more than 2 billion trades a year.[2]

Thanks to their technical capabilities and risk-management techniques, CCPs were the circuit breakers that stemmed financial rout and stopped the crisis of 15 September 2008 turning into a wholesale collapse of the global economy.

2.2 TRADING VENUES AND CLEARING MARKETS

Modern day clearing houses are therefore vitally important participants in the complex network of institutions, intermediaries and regulators that interact in today's wholesale financial markets.

'We allow the City to sleep at night,' was how Chris Tupker once described the job of LCH.Clearnet and other clearing houses. It is a sentiment now echoed in financial markets around the world.

In order to function, CCPs must have very close relationships with the exchange, trading platform or other venue where the trades they clear take place. A central counterparty clearing house will be contracted to register and novate the trades agreed by buyers and sellers on the given trading venue and rely on a 'feed' of trade information from there to be able to carry out its tasks.

The CCP will provide the services of guaranteeing and netting trades to a relatively small group of financial companies among the trading venue's users. For the most part, these 'clearing members' of the modern CCP are large investment banks or commercial banks. Only market participants approved by the CCP have a contractual relationship with the clearing house.

There are two broad categories of clearing member licensed by CCPs to be their counterparties: general clearing members (GCMs) and direct clearing members (DCMs). A GCM is able to clear its own trades, those of its clients and the trades of non-clearing member firms (NCMs), which are market participants of the trading venue where the GCM trades but which do not have direct access to the CCP.

The definition of a DCM is less straightforward and depends on the rules of the individual clearing house or exchange. According to some definitions, a DCM clears only its own trades with the CCP.[3] In the case of Eurex Clearing AG, by contrast, a direct clearing member may clear trades with the Frankfurt-based CCP on its own account, for its customers and for clients of NCMs that are affiliated to the DCM.

The banks or brokerages that choose, as clearing members, to clear for other firms act as a conduit between the clearing house and a far greater population of banks, brokerages and financial intermediaries – which in the case of some big GCMs may run into hundreds. A clearing member's clients may trade on their own account or act for end-investors when buying or selling the securities or derivatives contracts that are cleared by the CCP.

Significant shifts have taken place in the make-up and interests of clearing members and investors during the history of clearing and these have been reflected in the business of CCPs.

The explosive growth of financial futures from the 1970s onwards turned banks and investment banks into the dominant group among clearing members – even in commodity markets

[2] 2 023 838 000 transactions in 2008, consisting of exchange traded derivatives, energy, freight, interbank interest rate swaps, equities, commodities, and euro and sterling denominated bonds and repos.

[3] This definition appears, for example, in the glossary of the March 1997 Bank for International Settlements report 'Clearing Arrangements for Exchange Traded Derivatives'.

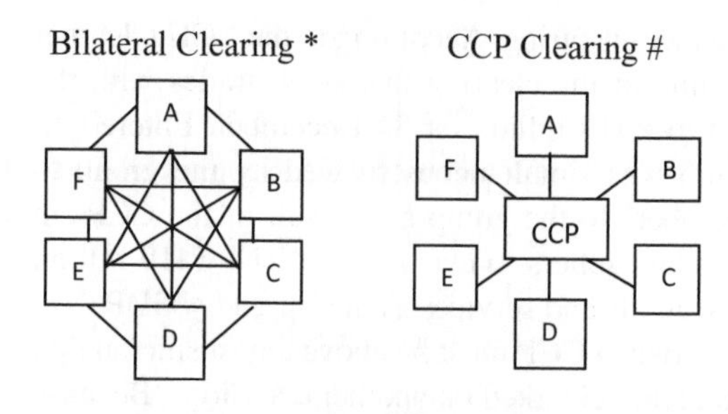

Boxes A to F represent counterparties

* Bilateral clearing can involve a complex web of multiple exposures; complicated collateral movements; risk of failed trades and contagion should one of the counterparties default.

CCP acts as buyer to every seller and seller to every buyer and ensures completion of trades if a counterparty defaults.

Figure 2.1 Bilateral versus CCP clearing

where they displaced traditional traders and merchants. In the early years of this century, hedge funds emerged as major clients of clearing members and in some cases, as they grew in size, became clearing members in their own right. In more recent years, specialist, high volume algorithmic traders and liquidity providers have become increasingly important at the trading level and as clients of clearing members.

It is the duty of the clearing member to meet the outstanding obligations of its customers if they default. But if client defaults are so big that they put the clearing member into default, the CCP steps in.

The clearing house is therefore the backstop for the failure of its clearing members. It is because CCPs manage and, if necessary, absorb these risks that they have become of such interest to policy makers and regulators following the Lehman bankruptcy.

According to Andrew Haldane, Executive Director for Financial Stability at the Bank of England, CCPs can hinder the spread of a financial crisis as effectively as targeted vaccination programmes can curtail epidemics or firebreaks restrict forest fires.[4]

Applying to finance, lessons from network disciplines such as ecology, epidemiology, biology and engineering, Haldane has argued that CCPs can deal 'at a stroke' with the complexity that has contributed to the fragility of modern financial systems. By interposing CCPs in every trade, 'a high-dimension web is instantly compressed to a sequence of bilateral relationships with the central counterparty – a simple hub-and-spokes. The lengthy network chain is condensed to a single link.' Provided the hub's resilience is beyond question, 'counterparty uncertainty is effectively eliminated'. Figure 2.1 illustrates this situation.

2.3 MANAGING RISK

CCPs lower risk in markets by cutting the danger of defaults leading to a chain reaction. But in so doing, they concentrate risk in themselves, becoming potentially a single point of failure in a financial system.

This 'CCP paradox' means they are systemically important, of growing public policy concern and subject to very strict regulation, which will get stricter as policy makers require CCPs to mitigate risks in a growing number of financial market places.

[4] Bank of England (April 2009a), 'Rethinking the Financial Network', speech delivered at the Financial Student Association, Amsterdam. Global finance in this analysis constitutes 'a complex adaptive system' in which 'interconnections serve as shock-amplifiers, not dampeners, as losses cascade'.

The value of trades on a CCP's books can be awe-inspiring. According to the LCH.Clearnet Group's annual accounts for 2009, the fair value of the clearing members' trades with the group's CCPs in London and Paris amounted to €419 billion on 31 December. Entered on both sides of the balance sheet, this huge sum was simultaneously owed by the group to the clearing members and by the clearing members to the group as a result of the CCPs in London and Paris being buyers to every seller and sellers to every buyer. The €419 billion were equivalent to three months' output of UK goods and services as measured by GDP.

To be an effective neutraliser of counterparty risk, a CCP must be above any suspicion that it might itself default on its obligations. As Haldane remarked on another occasion: 'Because a CCP represents a single point of failure, it needs to be bullet proof.'[5]

Achieving this objective involves a cooperative effort with the clearing members, which mutualise the risk of a default of one of their number and so accept responsibilities that go well beyond the payment of fees to the CCP for its services.

Clearing members must help to provide and finance the resources and instruments needed by the CCP to manage risk. The CCP then deploys a cascade of tools and measures to make its activities as secure as possible in the face of any conceivable market crisis. Its armoury includes the following:

- Marking to market, so that each day – and increasingly during the trading day as well – the clearing house can take account of changes in the value of the trades on its books.
- Margining, or the process of taking and holding a portion of the value of the trade from buyer and seller as collateral against one or the other failing to complete the deal.
- Setting criteria to ensure that clearing house members have the financial solidity needed to enable the CCP and the market or markets that it serves to function.
- Setting strict rules for clearing members that include sanctions such as the compulsory closure by the clearing house of any open trades in the event of default.
- Prudent governance: for example, at LCH.Clearnet the risk-management staff are separated completely from the clearer's commercial division and take no instructions from it.
- A default fund to which clearing members contribute and which can be drawn upon by the CCP if it uses up a defaulting member's margin when closing out its positions. In some cases, CCPs contribute to the default fund on the grounds that having 'some skin in the game' underlines the shared responsibility of a clearing house and its members for its successful operation.[6]
- Specified powers giving the CCP rights to liquidate, transfer or otherwise safeguard its exposures in the event of a default.
- Insurance to cover against further losses, although this form of protection is now less prevalent because of the withdrawal of providers from the market.
- Other lines of financial support, such as a guarantee from a parent company or contractual rights to tap clearing members for additional capital.
- Its own capital as a final financial backstop.

Margins are the CCP's first line of defence in case of a default. When responsibility for a trade is accepted by the clearing house, clearing members provide the CCP with 'initial'

[5] Haldane, Andrew (8 May 2009), 'Small Lessons from a Big Crisis', Remarks at the Federal Reserve Bank of Chicago 45th Annual Conference, *Reforming financial regulation*.

[6] For example, ICE, an operator of trading platforms and clearing houses, contributes to the default funds of ICE Clear Europe, its London-based CCP, and ICE Trust, its CCP for Credit Default Swaps, which it began clearing in 2009. See Sections 17.4 and 19.2.

margin, or a portion of a trade's value, to cover its risks until the contract is completed or closed out. The actual sum deposited will vary according to what is traded, the length of time a trade remains open and the clearing house's own margin methodology. The initial margin required to manage a futures contract will generally be greater than that required for clearing an equity which on most stock exchanges is settled on the third day after the bargain is agreed.

The CCP will also pay and collect 'variation' margins. As the name implies, variation margin changes with the value of the trades that the CCP has registered and which remain open. The idea of variation margin is to compensate for all losses and gains of the CCP's counterparties to ensure that none runs up losses that it cannot cover before its trade is settled or closed. Variation margins will be levied on clearing members on a daily basis if prices move adversely against them. On the other hand, CCPs will credit a clearing member with variation margin should the price of the security or futures contract move in the member's favour.

During volatile trading, the CCP may call for additional variation margin to protect itself against sudden and adverse price movements during the business day. Additional intra-day variation margin calls can come frequently during the trading day and woe betide any clearing member or investor who fails to meet them. The CCP will not hesitate to declare the offender in default and liquidate or transfer its remaining open positions. The CCP's clearing members will in turn usually be entitled to take similar action when their own clients fail to produce additional funds.

Margin calls by CCPs increased sharply in the final quarter of 2008 after the bankruptcy of Lehman Brothers. This was reflected at the LCH.Clearnet Group by a jump in the daily average of assets managed by its treasury teams to €48 billion in October against €26 billion throughout the year.[7]

In November 2010, a margin call gave a new twist to the eurozone sovereign debt crisis, when LCH.Clearnet Ltd increased the margin required for Irish government bonds cleared through its RepoClear service by 15% of net exposure. From being of interest only to financial professionals, margins suddenly became headline news.

To be allowed to join a CCP, potential clearing members must demonstrate that they have sufficient financial strength and technical capacity in their back offices to conduct their business without risk of default. The CCP will stipulate robust capital requirements for clearing members reflecting the riskiness of the business that the clearing member undertakes. So a company that does equity trades, which settle within three days, needs a much lower level of capital than one engaged in interest rate swap transactions, where the notional sum at risk runs to trillions of dollars and there may be many months or years before the position expires.[8]

The trading positions and broader business activities of clearing members will also be subject to close monitoring so that the CCP can discover at the earliest possible time any development that may threaten the ability of a member firm to meet its obligations.

In return, CCPs must ensure that the services they provide are attractive enough to win the support of their clearing members which in turn are competing for investors' business. While taking responsibility to complete trades and preserve the marketplace from the risk of counterparty default, clearing houses do everything in their power to protect the margins and default monies of their members and, indirectly, of their members' clients.

[7] According to the LCH.Clearnet Group annual report for 2008.

[8] The Committee on Payment and Settlement Systems of the Bank for International Settlements reported in March 2007 in 'New developments in clearing and settlement arrangements for OTC derivatives' that SwapClear members must have US$5 billion of Tier 1 capital and a swap portfolio of US$1 trillion outstanding. By contrast, Eurex in the final quarter of 2008 stipulated that a company applying for a licence to act as a general clearing member on the Frankfurt Stock Exchange required a minimum capital of €25 million.

In the case of Lehman, where subsidiaries of the investment bank were clearing members of CCPs around the world, the margins provided by the subsidiaries proved sufficient to protect nearly all the clearing houses from the effects of Lehman's default. As will be discussed in the next chapter, only in one known case – a clearing house in Hong Kong – was a CCP obliged to dip into the guarantee fund provided by its members.

2.4 CLEARING DERIVATIVES AND SECURITIES

CCPs have evolved over the past century and a quarter to provide security and transparency in futures and options markets. They are essential for safe and efficient trading of derivatives contracts listed on exchanges. Thanks to computer technology, CCPs have been instrumental in the rapid growth in size and numbers of derivatives exchanges around the globe and the proliferation of contracts that investors can trade.

Following the Lehman collapse, the world's leading legislatures are mandating an increasingly important role for CCPs in the world of OTC derivatives.[9]

Long ubiquitous in derivatives markets, CCPs are a relatively recent innovation in markets for cash securities such as stocks or bonds. They became established in US stock markets in the 1970s following a major reform of financial markets. It is only since the 1990s that they have played a significant role in European stock markets, following the introduction of an equities CCP for the Paris stock exchange.

These contrasting histories reflect some important differences between derivatives and securities in terms of what they represent and how they are traded and cleared.

As the name implies, a derivative derives its value from some other product, asset or price. It may relate to any one of a vast number of underlying assets or instruments, including commodities such as oil or sugar, foreign currencies, company shares, government bonds or the price of money as expressed by interest rates.

A derivative might be a future, which is a legally binding agreement to buy or sell a specified amount of a pre-defined asset at an agreed price at or by a set date in the future. It may be an option giving the holder the right, but not the obligation, to buy or sell a specified underlying asset at a pre-arranged price at or by a fixed point in the future. It could be a swap agreement by which two counterparties agree to exchange one stream of income against another arising from the same principal amount of two financial instruments.[10] It might be a hybrid: for example, an option on a future.

Derivatives vary greatly in complexity. One characteristic shared by all derivatives is that they are contracts, created to meet demand, in which seller and buyer agree detailed commitments. They are traded on an exchange in the case of standardised, listed derivatives or negotiated bilaterally among counterparties in the case of OTC derivatives. Another important characteristic of derivatives contracts is that they are margined instruments requiring the investor to pay only a small portion of the value of the trade to the clearing house at the time of registration.

Unlike stocks – where trades to buy or sell are 'settled' with delivery versus payment within days – it may be weeks, months, years or even decades before a derivatives contract is due

[9] See Part V of this book.

[10] A simple example of a swap involves the exchange between counterparties of income at a fixed interest rate for income at a floating rate.

to expire.[11] Few derivatives contracts run to maturity and have to be settled, however. Instead they are typically closed out at the time of the investor's choosing usually by engaging in an equal and opposite trade to offset the position taken.

By registering and netting offsetting trades, clearing houses facilitate early closure of contracts and so provide an essential function for derivatives investors. Hedging strategies and speculation work better if investors have the ability to close out derivatives transactions at will before maturity.

Where there is settlement of derivatives contracts, it can take two forms. Cash settlement entails the exchange of the net value of contracts and is essential if the asset underlying the contract is intangible, as are interest rate or stock index futures. Physical delivery of the product underlying the derivative can happen in the case of securities and commodities contracts, but is rare. At Eurex, for example, only about 2% of all derivatives transactions (measured in terms of notional amount) are settled physically against payment of the agreed price.[12]

The potentially lengthy period of time that derivatives trades can remain open, combined with the margined character and huge variety of cleared derivative contracts, explain their enormous appeal. They offer possibilities of low cost protection of investments to hedgers and large gains from leveraged positions for speculators trading on the same markets.

These characteristics also highlight the desirability – indeed the need – for the intervention of a CCP. Markets would be very restricted and illiquid without a clearing house to limit counterparty risk and to manage contracts as long as they stay open.

A security differs significantly from a derivative. An investor holding an equity share or corporate or government bond has rights of ownership, defined by the issuer of the instrument. A stock or equity is a share of the ownership of a company,[13] whereas a corporate or government bond confers ownership of the income stream from a credit relationship between the issuer and investor for specified period of time. A securities trade transfers ownership definitively from one holder to another in return for payment. Once transacted, the trade is best settled as quickly as possible.

Over the past 20 years, there has been convergence internationally towards settlement of equities trades on the third day after a trade. Known as T+3, this three day settlement interval has sharply reduced risks in stock markets. The transfer and custody of stocks and bonds is entrusted to other specialist financial infrastructure providers, which may be custodian banks, central securities depositories (CSDs) and international central securities depositories (ICSDs).[14]

CCPs in Europe novate equity trades as soon as they have been conducted and received by their systems, whereas in the US they are novated after execution and before netting outstanding positions and settlement. Historically CCPs have guaranteed equity trades after a market has closed, often overnight following the day of the trade or even later. National

[11] LCH.Clearnet announced in May 2010 that its SwapClear service had cleared its first 50 year interest rate swaps (LCH.Clearnet Group,12 May 2010). SwapClear can clear interest rate swaps with maturities up to 50 years in US dollars, euros and sterling and up to 30 years in Australian and Canadian dollars, Japanese yen, Swiss francs and Swedish krona.

[12] Deutsche Börse Group (2008), *The Global Derivatives Market: An Introduction*, based on figures for the first quarter of 2008.

[13] The word 'stock' can mean different things depending in the jurisdiction in which it is used. In the US, for example, a stock is an equity share and the term 'stock exchange' is generally taken to mean an exchange on which the main instruments traded are equities. However, in the UK, 'loan stock' is a type of bond (that can also be traded on a stock exchange). Unless otherwise specified, the terms 'stock' and 'equity' are interchangeable in this book.

[14] For a detailed account of the role and development of ICSDs and CSDs in modern financial markets, see the author's work: Norman, Peter (2007), *Plumbers and Visionaries: Securities settlement and Europe's financial market*.

Securities Clearing Corporation (NSCC), the monopoly clearer of stocks in the US, has, for example, assumed responsibility for guaranteeing trades at midnight on the day after the trade is agreed (between T+1 and T+2).[15] However, with the spread of algorithmic and high frequency trading and the greater concern of regulators about risk exposures, pressure has grown for earlier settlement and to bring novation, when trades are guaranteed, nearer to the time of trading.[16]

The comparatively short period in which equities trades are open has meant a rather different approach to managing risk in the operations of an equities CCP than one clearing derivatives.

Although CCPs in Europe, such as LCH.Clearnet and Eurex, take margin from clearing members to cover risks in respect of equity trades, the amount of margin they collect and hold is much less than for clearing derivatives. In the US, there is no direct collection of margin by NSCC to manage risk. The CCP guarantees the payment and delivery of securities trades on the strength of clearing funds based on contributions from clearing members which are calculated as a percentage of each firm's average daily business.

Equities CCPs have helped support the dramatic transformation of stock markets from dozy traders' clubs to aggressively competitive, high tech IT driven businesses over the past two decades. By acting as the buyer to every seller and seller to every buyer, they not only neutralised counterparty risk but provided anonymity for the participants in a trade or series of trades. This helped promote the spectacular growth and spread of electronic trading platforms that enable stocks to be traded, often across national frontiers, in tiny fractions of a second.

2.5 CCPs AS A BUSINESS

Clearing trades costs money. A CCP covers the costs of its services in two main ways. It charges fees for every trade processed and derives net interest income from managing the funds it holds in the margin accounts and default fund contributions of users.

The relative importance of these sources of income will depend on market conditions and the types of markets the CCP serves. An equities clearing house may be more reliant on fee income because of low levels of margin for equities trades and the short period of time between novation and settlement. Because CCPs charge fees for every trade they clear, equity clearing houses can also expect to benefit from the much larger volumes of equities traded each business day, especially at times of heightened volatility.[17]

Derivatives clearers tend to rely more on net interest income arising from the margin and collateral they hold for clearing members. In general, the sum of margin monies managed by a derivatives clearing house will be greater than that managed by a comparable equities CCP, reflecting the longer period that derivatives contracts stay open and the higher margins paid for all except the most liquid derivatives contracts. The clearing house profits from the difference between the interest income it derives from the default fund and cash and collateral margin balances and its payments of interest to clearing members in respect of the deposits they have made.

---

[15] Morris, Virginia B. and Goldstein, Stuart Z. (2009), *Guide to Clearance & Settlement: An introduction to DTCC*.

[16] NSCC guarantees trades in equities, corporate and municipal bonds. According to its annual report for 2009 (DTCC, 2010), DTCC is working to bring forward the guarantee to the point of trade validation on trade date (T) for its NSCC, FICC (Fixed Income Clearing Corp) and planned NYPC (New York Portfolio Clearing) CCPs. NSCC nets the trades to which it is counterparty on T+2.

[17] Fee tariffs can be complex, however, and are difficult to compare among CCPs. In some cases, where fees might appear low, a CCP will boost its income by imposing fines on clearing members whose trades fail. The treatment of fails also varies among clearing houses.

Both types of income can be subject to sudden change. Fees can come under pressure if markets are made more open to competition. This happened in European equity markets in 2008–10 when deregulation through implementation of the Markets in Financial Instruments Directive (MiFID) triggered sharp falls in trading and clearing fees.[18]

Interest income is vulnerable to changes in the wider economy. When the world's monetary authorities loosened policy in response to the global financial crisis of late 2008, the resulting sharp fall in interest rates hit clearing house revenues.

In one important respect, public authorities support the business model of the CCP. Bank regulators and supervisors give favourable treatment to trades transacted by clearing members and guaranteed by CCPs under internationally agreed rules on bank capital.

According to the so-called Basel II framework, agreed in 2004 by the Basel Committee on Banking Supervision at the Bank for International Settlements: 'An exposure value of zero for counterparty credit risk can be attributed to derivative contracts or STFs[19] that are outstanding with a central counterparty (e.g., a clearing house)' and also to banks' credit risk exposures resulting from such transactions outstanding with a CCP.[20]

This Basel rule is not an automatic right and supervisors can and do require that capital is maintained for some CCP exposures.[21] Moreover, at the time of writing, the Basel Committee on Banking Supervision has proposed strengthening banks' capital requirements for counterparty credit risk exposures to include a modest risk weighting of 1–3% for banks' mark-to-market and collateral exposures to CCPs in recognition that they are not risk free.[22]

2.6 NETTING TRADES AND OPEN INTEREST

From the preceding sections, a picture is beginning to emerge of CCPs acting as more than mere facilitators in a transaction chain. The costs and obligations that CCPs impose on clearing members are tempered by important benefits that profit their members and the trading platforms for which they clear.

As CCPs serve extremely competitive businesses, there are very real pressures on them to perform well commercially. They are expected to lower costs for their members while at the same time maintaining their risk-management standards, covering their operating costs and ensuring they have the necessary finance for often heavy investments in advanced computerised systems.

The most commercially significant of the benefits that a CCP provides for its members is the netting of positions concentrated in the clearing house. Netting has many attractions. It makes markets safer and more efficient. It concentrates liquidity, reduces complexity and lowers the cost of margining derivatives trades and settling equities transactions.

Netting is not unique to CCPs. Any entity trading with another can net the amounts owed between the two counterparties to a single sum payable from one party to the other by cancelling out claims against each other. Such bilateral netting is common in OTC markets.

[18] See Sections 20.1 and 20.2.

[19] STFs are 'securities financing transactions'.

[20] Bank for International Settlements (June 2006), 'International convergence of capital measurement and capital standards: A revised framework', Comprehensive Version, Basel Committee on Banking Supervision.

[21] According to EACH, the European Association of Central Counterparty Clearing Houses (28 August 2009), in comments about the European Commission communication, 'Enhance the resilience of OTC derivatives markets', of July 2009.

[22] Bank for International Settlements (26 July 2010), 'The Group of Governors and Heads of Supervision reach broad agreement on Basel Committee capital and liquidity reform package', Basel Committee on Banking Supervision, press release plus Annex. See also Section 21.3.

But as the counterparty to a vast number of transactions, a CCP is able to provide multilateral netting. To illustrate the beneficial impact of multilateral netting, consider a market with 10 participants. Organised bilaterally, there will be 90 counterparty relations. Put a CCP in the centre and the number of counterparty relations shrinks to 10, each of which is between the CCP and a clearing member.

Multilateral netting allows the CCP to offset the amounts it owes and is owed by market participants resulting in what are usually small residual amounts that become single debits or credits between the CCP and each of its clearing members. Netting reduces the gross risk exposures of the CCP and its members. It can also cut hugely the clearing member's transaction costs of closing out or settling trades, and reduce the complexity of its back office and the risk of failed deliveries.

The more clearing member firms that use a CCP, the more beneficial is the impact of netting, either by reducing the net counterparty risk exposure of a derivatives clearing house or the number of trades remaining to be settled in the case of an equities CCP.

With equities clearing, netting by a CCP can reduce the volume of stocks that need to be transferred from seller to buyer in return for payment by up to 99%.[23]

By offsetting risk exposures, netting permits a derivatives clearing house to require appreciably less collateral from its members in the form of margin, cutting their costs and increasing the liquidity of the exchange where they trade.

These advantages are central to the economics of clearing. All things being equal, a clearing house with a large volume of business will be more competitive than one which clears few transactions. Should there be a choice of CCP, liquidity will gravitate to that which has the biggest number and volume of open transactions against which it can offset long and short positions.

The total number of outstanding trades on the books of a CCP is its 'open interest'. For decades after the first clearing houses opened for business, open interest was an uncontentious and uncontested quantity. Markets and 'their' CCPs were mutually owned and often monopolies operating usually within national frontiers. Insofar as open interest attracted attention, it was as a statistic often used by investors to judge the liquidity of a given trading venue or contract.

Today, open interest is perhaps the most important measurement in the business of clearing because the amount of open interest on a CCP's books determines how far it can provide offsets and so influences the amount of margin the CCP will call from clearing members.

Open interest became more important for the business strategies of exchanges from the late 1990s onwards as they were transformed from mutually-owned to for-profit businesses and globalisation increased competition among exchanges and other trading venues. At derivatives exchanges in particular, the realisation grew that the open interest on the books of a CCP could play a crucial role in securing the economic prosperity of an exchange and its owners.

The open interest that accumulates on the books of derivatives clearing houses is large compared with that of equities CCPs because in general positions at derivatives CCPs stay open far longer. In the futures business, the open interest on the books of an established CCP can reinforce the attractions of the exchange for which it clears and create barriers to companies seeking to establish new trading venues for the same product.

Take the case of a hypothetical exchange where trades are cleared by an established CCP with a large open interest. The exchange can derive a big competitive advantage from the open

[23] According to DTCC's 2009 annual report (DTCC, 2010), DTCC's NSCC subsidiary reported a 'netting factor' of 99% in 2008 when the value of trades requiring settlement was reduced to US$2.9 trillion from US$315.1 trillion. In 2009 netting reduced financial settlement by 98%, to US$5 trillion from US$209.7 trillion.

interest of the CCP so long as it prevents access to 'its' CCP by companies trading on other platforms. This is commonly achieved by creating a 'vertical silo', where exchange and CCP are integrated and access to clearing is denied to trades not executed on the exchange.

A rival exchange trying to compete with an incumbent by offering copy-cat contracts would find this difficult so long as its trades could not be offset against the open interest on the books of the established exchange's clearing house. Another CCP, if new to the market, would have to gather margin from scratch and be unable to provide the offsets and lower margins of the established CCP and would therefore be more expensive to use.

The dangers to free competition from this state of affairs are evident. The traders on the exchange using the established CCP benefit from lower margins that come with the greater scale of the CCP's operations. But they run the risk of being at the mercy of a monopoly provider of exchange and clearing services which may abuse its position by levying inappropriately high dealing and/or clearing fees.

Such concerns have prompted a lively debate about who 'owns' or 'controls' the open interest on the books of a CCP and therefore derives economic benefit from it.

Is it the exchange, where the trades take place; the CCP where the open interest is booked; or is ownership or control determined by a contractual arrangement between the CCP and its members?

It is a measure of the complexity – and the relative novelty of the controversy – surrounding open interest that in the UK, a mature democracy with a centuries' old tradition of the rule of law, there appears to be no legal clarity on the issues of ownership and control.

One logical response is to say that the trades cleared by a CCP and on the books of the clearing house belong to the counterparties. In that case, the exchange or trading platform where the trades took place has no ownership of the trades.

But twice in recent years, futures exchanges have demonstrated that they can move open interest from one CCP to another if they so wish, and overcome the resistance of the incumbent clearing house in the process.

This was the case in 2003–4 when the Chicago Board of Trade (CBOT) decided to move the clearing and open interest of its trades from the Board of Trade Clearing Corporation (BOTCC), its clearing house for nearly 80 years, to the clearing division of the Chicago Mercantile Exchange (CME). In 2008, ICE, an Atlanta-based exchange and clearing group, moved the clearing and open interest of its OTC derivatives contracts and energy futures traded on ICE's London exchange from LCH.Clearnet to ICE Clear Europe, a new London-based clearing house owned by ICE, against opposition from LCH.Clearnet and – initially at least – from the counterparties to the trades.[24]

Both these migrations happened without opposition from regulators or competition authorities and so established the precedent that futures exchanges could control the open interest arising from their trades. These events in turn hardened the demarcation line between two very different structures for central counterparty clearing that had grown up over the previous 120 years. These different models are

- *Vertically-structured CCPs*, which are integrated as part of a corporate entity or group that provides services along a chain from trading to the closure or settlement of transactions. The vertical integration of exchange and CCP has become the dominant pattern for futures exchanges around the world, with the resulting groups usually operating as for-profit entities.

[24] For details, see Sections 13.4 and 17.4.

- *Horizontally-structured CCPs*, which serve multiple markets and may process several asset classes. Horizontal clearing houses are institutionally separate from trading platforms. Today's horizontally-structured CCPs tend to be user-owned, user-governed companies that fix their fees on an at- or near-at-cost basis.

The emergence of the vertical and horizontal models of clearing is a recurring feature in the chapters that make up Parts II to V of this book. The divide is important for understanding the business and history of central counterparty clearing. For this reason, brief summaries of vertical and horizontal clearing developments in the US and Europe follow in the next two sections.

2.7 VERTICAL AND HORIZONTAL CLEARING SYSTEMS IN THE US

Although the forerunners of today's CCPs emerged in Europe in the 1880s, today's sharp divide between the vertical and horizontal has its roots in the financial revolution of the 1970s, when financial futures were invented in the US, and in the way that regulators responded to this.

The vertical integration of exchange and CCP was already the preferred model for commodity futures exchanges in the US before the 1970s when the rival Chicago commodity exchanges, the CBOT and CME, invented financial futures. They adapted tried and tested methods for clearing their new financial products, which sowed the seeds of a massive global expansion of derivatives trading on exchanges. Vertical integration was the model in operation when the Commodity Futures Trading Commission (CFTC), the futures market regulator, took on the job of policing US futures markets in 1975.

The present dominance of the vertical silo in futures trading has been reinforced by the success of the Chicago-based CME Group and the support given by regulators and US competition authorities to its model of integrated trading and clearing of futures to provide a single product offering for investors.

The CME Group has been vertically integrated since its forerunner, the CME, first set up its clearing house division in 1919.[25] Since the CME demutualised in 2002, the US Department of Justice has acquiesced in the CME Group's acquisition of rival and complementary exchanges in Chicago and New York and its resulting domination of the US futures business.

The vertical integration of US futures exchanges enables them to protect their contracts and open interest. They defend this business model with the argument that the contracts are created by exchanges and contain their intellectual property. The CME Group points out that its major innovations such as the invention of financial futures in the 1970s required research, development and investment to become established.[26]

Futures exchanges such as the CME also insist they are subject to competitive pressures because at the global level other exchanges in other jurisdictions offer competing products.

Supporters of vertical integration claim that the structure benefits users. For example, at board level, there is only one set of decisions when the clearing house is integrated with the exchange. In an increasingly competitive environment, a vertically-structured pairing of

[25] Unlike the CME's clearing house, the clearing house of the CBOT, the Board of Trade Clearing Corp (BOTCC), was not an integrated part of the exchange. But although a separate corporation, BOTCC was effectively vertically integrated with the CBOT throughout the 20th century. See Sections 7.4 and 7.5 and Chapter 13.

[26] For example, in Craig Donohue's (CEO of the CME) speech: 'Efficient clearing and settlement systems: the case for market-driven solutions' (CME Group, June 2006) at the *10th European Financial Markets Convention*, Zurich.

exchange and clearing house should be able to take decisions more quickly than the pairing of an exchange and non-integrated clearing house. Vertically integrated exchanges say their CCP services can help bring new products to market faster than horizontally-structured CCPs which have to weigh and prioritise the merits of different projects put forward by the different exchanges and types of user that they serve.

Although US competition authorities have effectively supported these arguments by approving the acquisitions of the CME Group in recent years, the success of the vertical model has not silenced critics who condemn silo arrangements as anti-competitive.

In contrast, say, to the pharmaceutical industry, where the patents protecting intellectual property in new drugs run out over time, there appears in the US to be no provision to open up futures markets or the open interest of their CCPs to competition once contracts become routine and commoditised.

The development of the infrastructure for trading and clearing securities was very different. The clearing of equities and equities options in the US is handled by horizontally-structured CCPs serving multiple markets because of a regulatory framework mandated by Congress in the 1970s and enforced by the Securities and Exchange Commission (SEC).

NSCC, which is a subsidiary of the New York-based Depository Trust and Clearing Corporation (DTCC), is the sole CCP for more than 50 US exchanges and other platforms for trading cash equities and other securities. The Options Clearing Corporation (OCC), based in Chicago, provides CCP services for all equity options markets in the US.[27] Both DTCC and OCC are user-owned, user-governed companies that fix their fees on an at- or near-at-cost basis. They are the largest CCPs of their type in the world.

This structure, known as the 'National Market System' (NMS), emerged as a result of the Securities Acts Amendments of 1975, which encouraged competition at the level of exchanges and trading platforms while prescribing an efficient, robust, national infrastructure for clearing and settling equities. Even before NMS was formally operational, the SEC brokered horizontal clearing for US equity options trades through the OCC. Meanwhile, it was with the strong encouragement of the SEC that NSCC emerged as the sole clearing house for US stock markets through a process of competition and consolidation during the last 25 years of the 20th century.[28]

The way NMS operates, there can be no question of an exchange or CCP deriving revenues from any intellectual property in securities. The intellectual property represented by a stock or bond resides with the issuer. The at- or near-at-cost clearing fees charged by DTCC for its clearing and settlement services have created a level playing field for rival trading platforms to compete with one another on the quality of their service. Because equities are tradable on multiple platforms, a market participant can invest on one venue and divest on another.

The system is somewhat different for equity options in the US because contract terms are generally set by the OCC. But the effect is the same: options contracts traded on one exchange are completely interchangeable with those traded on another.

This interchangeability of stocks and equity options in their respective market sectors in the US allows clearing to be centred in one CCP for each asset class. Known as 'fungibility', it is the bedrock of a highly competitive culture among trading venues which has seen spreads narrow and volumes soar to the benefit of investors and those trading platforms that can outpace their competitors.

[27] Seven options markets and five futures exchanges at the end of 2009, according to the OCC's 2009 annual report (OCC, 2010).

[28] For details, see Sections 8.6 and 8.7.

It says much for the power of the different regulatory regimes in the US – as well as the inaction of its competition authorities – that the two systems of clearing have continued alongside each other without great friction for the last 40 years in spite of a progressive blurring of boundaries between markets and asset classes.

There have, however, been several attempts since the turn of the century by new trading platforms to challenge the dominance of the CME Group and its vertical model. Although unsuccessful, successive challenges have prompted trading and clearing fees at the CME Group to fall at least temporarily, suggesting that there is room for more competition in futures trading.

At the time of writing, there are two new challengers, one of which – ELX Futures – is trying to gain access to the open interest of the Chicago-based behemoth. The other – a joint venture between NYSE Euronext and DTCC called New York Portfolio Clearing – is seeking to cut into the CME Group's near monopoly as the trading venue for US Treasury futures by reaching across traditional demarcation lines to extract advantages for users who trade in both cash and futures markets.[29]

2.8 VERTICAL VERSUS HORIZONTAL IN EUROPE

As a consequence of globalisation, the vertical and horizontal models developed in the US have influenced clearing across the world. But because of different systems of regulation, the complexities of competition policy and the varying structures of trading and clearing that have emerged for different asset classes in different regions, the result is an unlevel playing field with differing rules, depending on the location of the CCP, whether it clears derivatives or equities trades and how and by whom it is regulated.

Nowhere is this more true than in Europe, where much of the action described in this book takes place. It is in the European Union that the contest between vertical and horizontal methods of clearing is most intense and wide ranging, extending to both derivatives and equities clearing.

After a delay, financial futures reached Europe in the late 20th century but some years before the introduction of the euro and the development of plans for a single market for financial services in the EU.

Most of the new futures exchanges set up in Europe's nation states adopted the vertical silo model of the CME. The commercial success of the CME Group since its demutualisation has emphasised the attractions of the vertical silo structure for its rivals around the globe.

Europe's futures exchanges have responded by ensuring that the open interest resulting from their trades is either held in wholly owned clearing houses or is otherwise protected. Futures exchanges that own their clearing houses in vertical silos refuse to allow other trading platforms access to their CCPs. Where a clearing house is not exchange owned, as in the case of LCH.Clearnet, the futures exchanges for which it clears trades now insist that access to their open interest is protected by contract to prevent competition from rivals attempting to offer better or cheaper services that otherwise might attract liquidity from the old trading platform to the new.

Exchange owned clearing houses are increasingly the norm for European stock markets. Equities clearing was not widely established in European countries until the 21st century and, when introduced, CCPs for equities were often bolted on to existing derivatives clearing houses. Whereas the horizontal model of clearing stocks and equity options in the US is

[29] See Chapter 20.

anchored in regulation, regulators had little bearing on the structure of clearing in the EU until 2006 when the European Commission brokered an industry Code of Conduct to bring competition to the trading, clearing and settlement of equities trades in Europe.

The Commission allowed vertical and horizontal structures to coexist but with provisions for interoperability between them in the case of equities clearing. The code did not apply to the much larger and riskier derivatives markets, enabling vertically-structured incumbents to maintain their profitable business models in these markets.

The interoperability provisions of the code have proved difficult to implement, not least because the regulators of CCPs in countries such as Germany and Italy adopted positions supportive of their own vertical structures.

As a result, the Commission proposed that this step towards the competitive cross-border trading of equities in the EU be underpinned by EU-wide legislation that will leave untouched the vertical silo structure for the trading and clearing of exchange traded derivatives at least until 2014.[30]

Occupying a unique place at the centre of cross currents created by competing commercial interests and diverse regulatory agendas is the LCH.Clearnet Group, the only CCP that can trace a continuous history back to the 1880s, when several horizontally-structured clearing houses were set up in Europe as for-profit, limited liability companies to serve commodity futures markets.

At present user-owned and user-governed, LCH.Clearnet has undergone many a transformation in its history. Multinational and structurally horizontal, because it is not part of an exchange or settlement group, LCH.Clearnet clears a wide range of assets including equities, exchange traded derivatives, energy, freight, interest rate swaps, government bonds and repos (securities repurchase agreements), which are traded in a multitude of markets. Its relationships with the trading venues that it serves vary according to contracts it has signed and the regulatory environment for the market in question from interoperability with other clearing houses to quasi-vertical where no competing clearing house exists.

LCH.Clearnet's story is prominent in the pages that follow, the challenges it has faced often putting into sharp relief the complexities confronting the clearing sector as a whole.

2.9 RISK AND RESPONSIBILITY

Although CCP structures may differ, the responsibilities borne by CCPs set them apart from other financial institutions. Although CCPs form part of the high tech infrastructure of modern financial markets and compete fiercely for business where conditions allow, the relationship between the clearing house and its members still carries echoes of the mutual tradition that played an important part in finance until the 1980s.

Clearing members will grumble about the costs of a CCP arising from fees and margin calls. But CCPs exist because market participants realise that sharing the mitigation of risk can yield offsetting and greater benefits that justify acting together rather than for themselves.

CCPs must walk a fine line between cost and benefit and risk and reward. The need to balance these conditions maintains standards of probity. Because clearing members have their capital at risk in the default fund of a clearing house as well as being obliged to pay fees and margins in the course of trading, CCPs tend to have austere business ethics. They tend not to court headlines. The executives interviewed for this book made a virtue of a deliberately low

[30] See Section 21.2.

key approach to running businesses with a huge responsibility for the successful functioning of the world economy.

CCP set themselves high standards. During a crisis such as Lehman, for example, any use of back-up facilities such as the guarantees or the default funds provided by their members was perceived as failure, no matter how small the loss might be.

Although clearing can be a competitive business, the thought of a 'race to the bottom' on margining has remained a taboo – so far. In crises such as the Lehman bankruptcy, CCPs put aside long standing rivalries to cooperate and overcome the threats posed to financial markets.

The lack of ostentation among clearing houses and their tradition of mutual support in a crisis are signs that they operate close to the borderline between private enterprise and public policy. CCPs have a strong sense of commitment and responsibility to the markets that they serve. As systemically important concentrators of risk, they are also heavily regulated to keep them on the straight and narrow.

The LCH.Clearnet Group, which provides CCP services from offices in the UK, France, Belgium, the Netherlands and Portugal, has more than a dozen regulators. Its role in payment systems is also subject to oversight by the Bank of England, The European Central Bank and the central banks of the individual eurozone countries in which it is based.

Until now, strict regulation has not meant regimentation. Although CCP techniques are similar, there are no uniform rules for risk management. Some countries – Germany and France are examples – insist that CCPs must be banks and regulated as such. Others, such as the UK, do not.

Although international regulators, grouped in organisations such as CPSS-IOSCO or the European Union's CESR and ESCB,[31] have set recommendations for the conduct of CCPs, there has so far been insufficient political consensus for such bodies to prescribe internationally binding standards.

It remains to be seen how far this changes in the light of the wave of financial regulation in the US, EU and other members of the G20 following the crisis.

It is a matter of pride among CCPs that in normal times they allow their customers to sleep peacefully at night. However, in a crisis, occasioned by the default of a clearing member, the CCP becomes a trader and auctioneer. It has to act decisively at high speed as it squares the interests of clearing members and society at large with the dictates of self preservation.

2.10 CLEARING UP A CRISIS

So how does a CCP meet these different objectives in a crisis? Four goals set by LCH.Clearnet SA, the Paris-based operating subsidiary of the LCH.Clearnet Group, provide one answer:

1. Prevent a default getting out of control and posing a risk to the financial system.
2. Ensure that any losses arising from managing a default are covered by the margin payments made by the defaulting clearing member in order to minimise, and ideally avoid, accessing the contingent resources provided by other members in the form of default fund or guarantees.

[31] CPSS-IOSCO brings together the Committee on Payment and Settlement Systems (CPSS), based at the Bank for International Settlements in Basel, and the Technical Committee of the International Organisation of Securities Commissions (IOSCO), based in Madrid. The European System of Central Banks (ESCB) and the Committee of European Securities Regulators (CESR) produced the EU recommendations.

3. Minimise adverse market effects, such as wild price movements, from the CCPs operations in clearing up the defaulting member's positions.
4. Preserve as far as possible the financial interests of the clients of the defaulting clearing member. The preservation required by this important, but often unwritten, rule is vital for the reputation of the financial system and explains why clearing houses go to considerable lengths in a crisis to transfer client accounts from a defaulted clearing member to other members of the CCP.

When Lehman's collapse unleashed the world's biggest default on financial markets on 15 September 2008, the CCPs of the world had years of drill but little direct experience to fall back on. 'We were the soldier that finally got to go to war,' was how Richard Heyman, Head of Customer Management for the UK arm of LCH.Clearnet, remembered that day. 'We do a routine process, day in day out, guaranteeing all this business. Well guess what, we actually proved that we could deliver when we were required to.'[32]

How LCH.Clearnet and other central counterparty clearing houses 'delivered' and safeguarded the world economy from the disaster of a collapse of the world's securities and derivatives markets is the subject of the next chapter.

[32] Conversation with the author, 7 October 2008.

3
The Biggest Bankruptcy

3.1 AN INAUSPICIOUS START

For Daniel Gisler, it was an inauspicious start to the biggest day of his career. A clearing professional with 14 years experience as a senior manager for leading CCPs in Europe, the Managing Director of Risk and Operations for the LCH.Clearnet Group was being denied access to the headquarters of Lehman Brothers International Europe (LBIE) in London's Canary Wharf.

Gisler was despatched early on Monday, 15 September 2008, from LCH.Clearnet's offices in the City to the imposing 150-metre-tall glass and steel tower block which had been the humming centre of Lehman Brothers' European investment banking operations until that morning. Gisler and his team were the financial fire brigade who had rushed the five and a half kilometres to 25 Bank Street in London's mini-Manhattan after LCH.Clearnet's UK CCP declared LBIE in default. His brief was to work with Lehman staff to manage and neutralise open trades worth trillions of dollars and so help prevent the investment bank's collapse turning into a catastrophe that could overwhelm global financial markets. But instead of being welcomed into the building, Gisler and his colleagues found their way inside barred after court-appointed administrators had taken command of LBIE just hours before.

It was a messy twist in a drama that had turned overnight into a full blown crisis. As news spread that Lehman Brothers Holdings Inc. was filing for Chapter 11 protection under US bankruptcy law, LBIE's directors concluded that their company, the principal UK and European trading company in the Lehman group, was no longer a going concern.

In the early hours of 15 September, they appointed four partners of insolvency practitioners PricewaterhouseCoopers (PwC) UK as administrators of LBIE. The partners with lawyers from Linklaters, one of London's 'Magic Circle' of elite law firms, hastily assembled the papers required to obtain a High Court order for administration under UK insolvency law. At 7.56 A.M., just minutes before London's financial markets opened, a judge who had been on standby during the night, placed LBIE and three other group companies in administration[1] and put the PwC partners in full executive control.

At first sight, there appear to be many similarities between Chapter 11 in the US and administration under UK law. Both procedures are intended to protect the assets and maximise the value of the stricken company to allow it to continue with its operations. But there were general and specific differences between US and UK practice in the Lehman Brothers case that had a profound effect on how CCPs responsible for Lehman's trades responded on either side of the Atlantic.

---

[1] PricewaterhouseCoopers UK said the three other companies were: Lehman Bros Ltd, the service company for the UK, employing all staff; Lehman Brothers Holdings PLC, an intermediate holding company owning shares in investment banking and asset management subsidiaries; and LB UK RE Holdings Ltd, an intermediate holding company with many real estate investment special purpose vehicles.

Chapter 11 in the US is strongly focused on maintaining the stricken company as a going concern. Administrators in the UK, by contrast, have a fiduciary responsibility to protect and realise a company's assets for the benefit of all creditors, who have to be treated equally. In the Lehman Brothers case, the Chapter 11 filing only applied to Lehman Brothers Holdings and specifically excluded its US registered broker-dealer and investment management subsidiaries which continued to trade, using clearing houses in the US and elsewhere.

When LBIE went into administration in the UK, its trading activities and the activities of numerous LBIE branches and representative offices abroad became the responsibility of PwC, exercising full executive control. An added complication under UK law was that the partners handling the administration were personally liable for its outcome.

Unlike the Lehman operating companies in the US, LBIE had no resources to continue trading. As part of a rigorous cash management system, Lehman Brothers in New York swept up all the cash from its foreign subsidiaries each night and released the funds the following day. Having decided to seek Chapter 11 protection, Lehman management in New York did not transfer to the UK any of US$8 billion cash sent to the US at the weekend, which was needed by the bank's London operations in order to start trading on Monday.[2]

As Tony Lomas, the senior licensed insolvency practitioner appointed by the court to wind down LBIE's affairs, later noted: 'There was a central treasury function in the Lehman group so that every subsidiary, every morning, was dependent upon money coming from the US to fund the outgoings of that day.'[3] The UK company had more than US$3 billion of outgoings due on the morning of 15 September and the money was not there.

At LCH.Clearnet, managers had heard rumours about the Lehman 'sweep'. Once LBIE went into administration it was clear that it and Lehman Brothers Special Financing Inc. (LBSF), a subsidiary of the US holding company that dealt in specialised derivatives products including interest rate swaps, would fail to make margin calls due on trades left open from Friday. LCH.Clearnet Ltd, the group's London-based UK CCP, declared both LBIE and LBSF in default at around 9.15 A.M. in London. LCH.Clearnet SA, the Paris-based CCP, declared LBIE in default around the same time.

3.2 LCH.CLEARNET IN THE FRONT LINE

The biggest and most complex bankruptcy in the history of finance was just beginning. For LCH.Clearnet Group's CCPs, the default declaration marked the start of a frantic race against time to manage and neutralise open positions with a notional value of US$10 trillion. Although other CCPs outside the US followed with similar decisions, LCH.Clearnet was the central counterparty with the biggest and widest range of Lehman exposures on its books. The US investment bank was active in all of LCH.Clearnet's business segments apart from freight.

LCH.Clearnet had a long history. Created from the merger in December 2003 of the London Clearing House of the UK and France's Clearnet SA, it could trace its roots back to 1888 when the London Produce Clearing House was established to guarantee the completion of futures trades in the London coffee and sugar markets. But the group had gone through some difficult years since the merger. Promised synergies had not materialised. A multi million euro

[2] According to Andrew Gowers, former head of corporate communications for Europe and Asia at Lehman Brothers, writing in the *Sunday Times*, 21 December 2008.

[3] In remarks on 19 January 2009 to a conference in London organised by the London School of Economics.

investment in a new clearing system had failed, triggering the enforced departure of its Chief Executive and the installation of a new Chairman and CEO in 2006.

There was discontent among some of LCH.Clearnet's customers, who complained about high fees. The group was losing business. Following recent European legislation to liberalise securities markets, a new breed of small, single-purpose CCP had begun competing for the business of clearing European equity trades. As the storm clouds gathered around Lehman, ICE[4], an Atlanta-based operator of futures exchanges and clearing services, was preparing to move the CCP services for its energy futures markets from Ltd[5] to its own newly established clearing house, ICE Clear Europe. A tricky operation in any circumstances, the migration to ICE Clear Europe was due to take place against a background of extreme turbulence on oil markets with crude oil futures poised to plunge in price below US$100 a barrel to their lowest levels for seven months. NYSE Liffe, the international derivatives business of the NYSE Euronext exchange group and a partner and client of LCH.Clearnet since the LIFFE futures market was founded in London in the early 1980s, was also preparing to bring its technical clearing functions for London-based contracts in-house, leaving just the management of risk and margins outsourced to LCH.Clearnet Ltd in the future.[6]

LCH.Clearnet was already in the process of redefining its future. It was negotiating a merger with Depository Trust and Clearing Corp (DTCC), the much bigger US post-trade group. Provisional agreement on the deal, which would leave DTCC the dominant partner, was announced a little over a month later on 22 October 2008.

So when LBIE was placed in administration, a lot was riding on LCH.Clearnet rising successfully to the challenge. Its own future was at stake as much as that of the financial markets that it cleared.

It went into the crisis in a state of heightened alert. As rumours of Lehman's impending demise flew around the world's financial centres on Friday 12 September, Ltd's senior risk managers in London contacted colleagues at Lehman and obtained mobile phone numbers for key Lehman Brothers staff. On the following day, Saturday, teams of operations and risk-management and legal staff were on hand in LCH.Clearnet's London headquarters. They were already scheduled to be in the office to manage a long arranged migration of open positions in energy futures and OTC derivatives to ICE Clear Europe.

Also preparing for the worst that weekend were officials of Britain's regulator, the Financial Services Authority (FSA). On Saturday, they informed Roger Liddell, LCH.Clearnet Group Chief Executive, of serious concerns about Lehman's viability and suggested Lehman might not open for business on Monday. Liddell contacted Christopher Jones, head of risk management at Ltd to warn him that the picture was 'extremely serious'.

Jones called his risk managers into work the following day. 'We had six people in on Sunday, covering the major products,' he said later.[7] They slipped into a well rehearsed routine. At least once a quarter, LCH.Clearnet's managers practised for a default at a major counterparty. The rehearsals, Jones said, involved 'stress testing, war gaming, that sort of stuff'. As Sunday

---

[4] The abbreviation for IntercontinentalExchange, Inc.

[5] When appropriate, the abbreviations 'Ltd' and 'SA' may be used respectively for further references to LCH.Clearnet Ltd and LCH.Clearnet SA, the two CCPs in the LCH.Clearnet Group.

[6] LIFFE, originally the abbreviation for the London International Financial Futures Exchange, was written in capital letters until the exchange's acquisition by Euronext, which took effect in January 2002. Although 'LIFFE' in capitals was retained for regulatory purposes, Euronext's international derivatives markets then took the name Euronext.liffe. After Euronext's merger with the New York Stock Exchange in 2007, the name of the markets changed again to NYSE Liffe.

[7] Conversation with the author, 7 October 2008.

progressed and the reports and rumours about Lehman grew grimmer, Jones's team consulted spreadsheets and pulled together all available information and waited... and waited for an announcement from the US.

In Paris, Christophe Hémon, Chief Executive of LCH.Clearnet SA was also making preparations. He had a long conference call on Sunday with Liddell and with the risk, operations and legal departments at LCH.Clearnet in London. 'We were organising ourselves so that we could be ready.'[8]

Back in London, SwapClear, a specialised service of LCH.Clearnet Ltd, was preparing for the worst. LCH.Clearnet was unique among the world's CCPs in providing a clearing service for interest rate swaps, financial instruments that are bilaterally negotiated and traded 'over-the-counter' among banks in small trade volumes but with eye-watering values. SwapClear includes some of the world's biggest banks and dealers among its members, with a subgroup sharing in its governance through a company called OTCDerivNet. The 20 SwapClear members in September 2008 included Lehman and had special rules agreed with LCH.Clearnet in case one of them defaulted.[9]

The LCH.Clearnet Group's clearing businesses in London, Paris, Brussels, Amsterdam and Lisbon would take responsibility for managing those open derivative, bond, option and equity positions where they acted as Lehman's counterparty when Lehman failed. By contrast, SwapClear's default management process would be a partnership of Ltd and the remaining 19 SwapClear members. Late on Sunday, managers at LCH.Clearnet in London contacted the SwapClear banks to warn them that Ltd might invoke the process. They should be ready on Monday to send experienced traders to LCH.Clearnet to hedge its interest rate exposure to a nominal US$9 trillion of outstanding trades of LBSF.

At around 7 P.M. on Sunday, the FSA, LCH.Clearnet and ICE Clear Europe agreed not to go ahead with the migration of the ICE positions. On Monday, Ltd continued to clear trades on the London markets operated by ICE. This late decision helped LCH.Clearnet manage the crisis. Other developments – at that point unforeseen – made the job of closing out the positions of LBIE far more difficult than anyone could have expected.

3.3 LBIE – A DIFFICULT DEFAULT

For Jones and his colleagues, Monday morning meant an early 5.30 A.M. start after working late the night before. Lehman's position had worsened, but the situation in the US was still unclear. Lehman paid margin it owed to SA at 7 A.M. in Paris (6 A.M. London time). But 'there was more and more noise saying that this was bad,' Jones remembers. 'The banks we were talking to effectively said they were not paying.'

At 2 A.M. Eastern Standard Time in the US (7 A.M. London time), the Lehman holding company filed for bankruptcy protection. LCH.Clearnet's top management took the decision to put both LBIE and LBSF into default, knowing there would be no payments of margin from either Lehman subsidiary by way of LCH.Clearnet's Protected Payments System (PPS) of direct debits used to transfer funds to and from its clearing members.

Because of market holidays in Japan, Hong Kong and China on that Monday, Europe felt the full brunt of the Lehman collapse. Two weeks of frantic activity followed at LCH.Clearnet versus fearsome odds. Against a background of turmoil and extreme volatility on financial

[8] Conversation with the author, 9 December 2008.

[9] Both SwapClear and OTCDerivNet have grown in membership since the crisis but still remain comparatively small. See Chapter 19.

markets, with the crisis on Wall Street spreading like wildfire to AIG, the insurance and financial services group, and other US banks, the clearing house's managers had to contend with obstacles and operational problems for which no amount of rehearsal could prepare them.

In the event of a default, the textbook response of a CCP is to move swiftly to ensure that the financial position of the afflicted institution gets no worse. The clearer's first duties are to use the collateral that it holds on behalf of the defaulting institution to close out open positions and, if possible, transfer the accounts of the defaulter's clients to other clearing members to minimise the clients' losses. When Lehman went into administration, LCH.Clearnet held about US$2 billion of initial margin deposited by the investment bank to cover the CCP for losses liquidating its portfolio.[10]

Handling a default does not happen in a vacuum, however. In the pandemonium of a large scale financial failure, countless other businesses are striving to save what they can from the wreckage with scant regard to the overall good. Without active management, the value at risk in the many trading books of an investment bank of Lehman's size could soar into the stratosphere from hundreds of millions of dollars one day to billions the next as counterparties took action to safeguard their own positions.

CCPs do not employ their own trading staff. The best approach after a default is for the clearing house to work with the staff of the failed entity to manage down the risk. To help CCPs do this, clearing houses in the UK are exempted from the normal rules of insolvency under Part VII of the UK Companies Act 1989, as they relate to actions under their default rules, including the collection or realisation of collateral.

However, in dealing with LBIE in administration that Monday, Ltd found that PwC, Lehman's administrator, was not cooperating, as if unaware of the support clearers should be given under Part VII of the Companies Act.

LCH.Clearnet had been unable to reach any person of responsibility from PwC or LBIE, either before or after the default announcement.

Although Gisler and his team were allowed entry to 25 Bank Street after about 30 minutes, they were not permitted to talk to any Lehman staff on the trading floor. The Lehman staffers were under instructions from the administrator not to share any information.

After about five hours, Gisler was able to make his case in person. Along with Jones, Iona Levine, General Counsel of LCH, and Paul Watkins, another lawyer at LCH, he attended a meeting with Mike Jervis, one of the three administrators, Darren Ketteringham of PwC, Peter Barrowcliff, who had been Head of Compliance at LBIE, and Michael Kent of Linklaters, in the executive dining suites at 25 Bank Street. LCH's lawyers emphasised the requirement for assistance from the administrators, as provided for in the legislation. LCH explained why it needed the information for it to transfer the positions of clients, not just for the clients' benefit, but also for the benefit of the market as a whole.

Once back in LCH's office, however, the team found there was still no cooperation.

The frustration of that day is etched on Jones's memory:

> Monday we spent a lot of time talking to the administrators, saying: Give us access to the traders. They refused. We asked for access to the books and records, so we could trace clients and work with them to reduce positions. We were told we could not have that access. We went to their offices, explained the powers we have under insolvency, because we are carved out of insolvency law. And it fell on deaf ears.

[10] According to Roger Liddell, LCH.Clearnet Group Chief Executive, in evidence to the House of Lords European Union Committee on 9 February 2010 (House of Lords, 2010), 'The future regulation of derivatives markets: Is the EU on the right track?'.

It took until 7 P.M. on Tuesday evening before PwC gave Ltd access to client records and that was only after the FSA had intervened on behalf of the clearing house. By then, LCH.Clearnet would normally have managed down the exchange traded risk of a defaulted clearing member such as Lehman. Instead, it had to extend the process and extemporise, incurring considerable risk to itself, when it also had an unusually large day-to-day business to attend to.

During the week of 15 September 2008, trading volumes were very high and prices gyrated wildly. Further adding to the challenges facing Liddell, Jones and senior LCH.Clearnet managers were problems on the listed derivatives side of Lehman's business for which no standardised default procedures or any amount of preparatory drilling could have prepared it.

The problems centred on the records of customer and proprietary trading accounts relating to exchange traded derivatives supplied by Lehman before the crisis weekend. These added to Ltd's difficulties when dealing with some LBIE customer and 'house' accounts that were 'commingled', creating the risk that clients' investments could be accidentally sold off when the clearing house closed out Lehman's own positions.

The difficulties with the commingled accounts surfaced on Monday afternoon as managers of Ltd in London looked at the size of Lehman's listed derivatives positions on futures markets such as Euronext-Liffe, ICE and the London Metal Exchange.

'We were struck that their client account looked too small. We had a difference in the size of the portfolio between house and client that just had alarm bells all over it. We knew Lehman had a big client business and that they were big in proprietary trading too. But it was so imbalanced in those markets that we began to smell a rat,' Richard Heyman, Ltd's London-based Head of Customer Management, recalled.[11]

One underlying problem was a difference in US and UK law. In the US, clearing member firms must maintain separate accounts for the funds and positions of clients and clearing members. Dubbed 'customer segregation', the requirement is intended to protect the clients' assets in the event of insolvency of a clearing member and aid the transfer of customer accounts to another viable clearing member. In the UK, however, a client could opt out of 'client money rules' and have its positions commingled with those of the member firm to save administrative costs.

But when clients opt out, a clearing member such as Lehman would be expected to keep accurate records of segregated and non-segregated customer positions, with the latter usually grouped in a special omnibus account. What Ltd discovered in the records of LBIE were about100 non-segregated accounts, all called Lehman Brothers Inc., which actually represented the business of segregated customers in the US.

Unravelling this confusion entailed a good deal of detective work. The administrator, when approached during trading hours on Tuesday, continued to deny Ltd access to the staff and records of LBIE. In the meantime, LCH.Clearnet was having to deal with requests from clearing members asking for the transfer to them of positions of clients of LBIE.

Although Ltd would have been legally entitled to liquidate these client positions at Lehman without hesitation, Liddell took a conscious business decision to continue to run the market exposures on LBIE's derivatives book using the margin that was available while the clearing house's staffers tried to sort out which positions belonged to clients. It was a pragmatic approach that took account of the principle, applied in UK defaults, of giving a higher priority to protecting the money of clients over the capital of the member firms.

[11] Conversation with the author, 7 October 2008.

The wisdom of pausing emerged during Tuesday afternoon when Ltd contacted Lehman's New York office, which was still trading under US Chapter 11 bankruptcy protection. Ltd managed to obtain insight into which positions in the commingled accounts were client positions, even though technically its counterparty was LBIE in London.

Armed with this information, Liddell began transferring Lehman's client positions to other clearing members when requested. It was a course that entailed some legal risk, because there was no possibility of Ltd independently verifying the information on which the transfers were based. But he took the view that it was better to get the transfers moving than sell off or keep the positions frozen in the midst of highly volatile markets.

There was still friction with the administrator, who by this time was demanding an indemnity from LCH.Clearnet as a condition for access to client records. This LCH.Clearnet refused. When PwC finally released data on Tuesday evening, it warned LCH.Clearnet that it was on its own as far as legal issues were concerned. This was something Liddell and Jones could live with. They took the information and pulled staff members who had been trying to liaise with PwC officials back from the former Lehman headquarters at Canary Wharf.

Ltd began the systematic transfer of client accounts, helped by an unconventional decision taken earlier on Tuesday. 'We had tried to restore communication links but Lehman's back-office staff said basically that they were not getting paid. They were experiencing an enormous amount of grief; they did not have a job; so they were going. They were about to walk out, so we offered them £1000 a day each to stay and they did,' Jones recalls. 'We needed to keep these people so that the clients would have their records and be able to get their money back.' Altogether Ltd paid £18 000 to Lehman staff.

Moving the client accounts so as to avoid any increase in Ltd's exposure was 'a complicated puzzle,' Jones says. On Wednesday, senior LCH.Clearnet management reviewed whether further client transfers were possible. Conditions in financial markets had been chaotic since Lehman's collapse. But the clearing house's net positions across all asset classes regarding collateral and risk remained broadly unchanged. In the meantime, it had safeguarded the positions of those Lehman clients at LBIE – mainly US money managers – who had come forward via their clearing members to request transfers. Following the review, the clearing house stepped up the shifting of client accounts by proactively approaching clearing members to see whether they would accept transfers.

The problems encountered by Ltd meant it had reduced the risk in the Lehman positions only modestly during the first two days of the default. But at least the risk had declined at a faster rate than the Lehman collateral held by the clearing house.

'On Wednesday, things really did accelerate and we started transferring clients very, very quickly,' Jones recalls. 'Over the period of the next couple of days, I think we transferred 77 clients to solvent clearing members.' By the end of the week, Jones's team was able to report that only a very small fraction of positions in the LBIE client account remained to be solved.

The client accounts were just one of the issues to be addressed in that first week of the default. Ltd also had to shrink the risk on LBIE's proprietary trading books. The different asset categories needed different treatment. In some cases Ltd found it was on a steep learning curve. As John Burke, Director for Fixed Income at Ltd, pointed out, the company 'had never experienced a proper default before in bonds or repos'.[12]

[12] Conversation with the author, 7 October 2008.

The risk managers opted to hedge the market exposures in Lehman's bond portfolio through bilateral deals with various investment houses. The portfolio of repos[13] required a different approach. According to Jones: 'We managed the market risk of the repo portfolio by transacting a series of large bond trades and we then set about managing the forward settlement risk of the repos in a separate phase.'

Ltd's commercial services department took the lead in planning blind auctions of some of Lehman's energy portfolios traded on ICE's London market and equity derivatives positions traded on Liffe for the Thursday following the default. Each proved successful, having attracted seven or eight major players as participants. In consequence, Jones could report that the outstanding risk on LBIE's proprietary trading and client derivatives books relative to collateral was 'significantly positive' in Ltd's favour. On Friday – after five days of crisis management – about £100 million were still at risk in the two accounts, but this compared with about £500 million of collateral in Ltd's possession.

For the operations and risk-management teams handling the Lehman default, the crisis meant 17 or 18 hours work a day for several days running. The commercial services department was also fully engaged, dealing with front- and back-office contacts and taking some of the pressure of communicating with clients and counterparties away from the risk and operations staff. Key employees were billeted in hotels around the City to be better able to cope with the volume of work.

'By Thursday, we were starting to be significantly stretched at a department level and at company level,' Jones recalls. 'We had to significantly reduce the burn on people. People were incredibly wired, incredibly tired. These were unprecedented market conditions. What we needed were people who were fresh and ready to go.'

Jones started sending people home – a decision that enabled Ltd's staff to recharge their batteries in readiness for the next stage of the financial tsunami that swept through the world financial system after Lehman's collapse. Within just a few days, it threatened to topple such elite Wall Street institutions as Morgan Stanley and Goldman Sachs.

But on 23 September, eight days after putting Lehman into default, LCH.Clearnet could announce that the default was being successfully managed and that risk exposure had fallen more than 90%. Remaining exposure was well within the margin held. A few days later, on 26 September, Ltd made the first interim payment of collateral to PwC, the administrator. By this time, LCH.Clearnet staffers had also been working for several days to help LBIE reconstruct its trading books and records.

3.4 SWAPCLEAR IN FOCUS

Although unprecedented in scope and complexity, the Lehman default was not the first such experience for LCH.Clearnet's London operation. It had coped with four defaults previously, of which two – Drexel Burnham Lambert in 1990 and Baring Brothers & Co in 1995 – were big events of international significance.

However, before 15 September 2008 the group never had to deal with the repercussions of a default in an off-exchange market traded 'over the counter' among financial institutions. The Lehman default was the first test in a crisis for Ltd's SwapClear service, set up in 1999 to provide central counterparty clearing facilities for interbank interest rate swaps.

[13] Sale and repurchase agreements.

Interest rate swaps come in all sizes, currencies and maturities. In a typical case, the purpose is to enable counterparties to exchange the income stream from a fixed rate of interest on a given security for a floating rate income stream on the same notional amount of another security. Such swaps form a huge market with much of the activity concentrated in large banks. The notional amount of interest rate swaps outstanding at around the time of Lehman's bankruptcy was more than US$350 trillion.[14]

Through London-based SwapClear, LCH.Clearnet provided central counterparty services for 20 big banks, one of which was Lehman Brothers. The SwapClear portfolio exceeded US$100 trillion of notional value, spread across 14 currencies, in 2007.[15] SwapClear cleared about half the global interbank OTC interest rate swap market.

Lehman Brothers Special Financing Inc. was a big player in this market. Like all member banks it had demonstrated it had capital of several billion dollars to be able to join SwapClear. LBSF's US$9 trillion interest rate swap portfolio handled by SwapClear was spread over 66 390 trades and divided among five leading currencies. The notional value of this business dwarfed the exchange traded portfolios caught up in Lehman's default.

Managing down such a large portfolio would not be easy. The high total value of trades implied big operational risks. But whereas all CCPs mutualise their members' risks, SwapClear had taken the idea of partnership to a higher level. Ltd and the participating banks had worked out in advance a default management process with robust legal arrangements: first, to work together in hedging the risks of a defaulting SwapClear member and then in auctioning its portfolios to the remaining SwapClear participants.

Nonetheless, it was still with some trepidation that Chris Jones waited on Monday morning after the Lehman default to see whether the SwapClear member banks would follow the rules and send experienced traders to LCH.Clearnet in London to help manage LBSF's portfolio rather than keep them back to manage their own positions during the crisis.

He need not have worried. Six SwapClear banks, selected according to a pre-arranged rota, sent traders, including some very senior individuals, to help manage down the risks arising from the default. By a happy coincidence, Ltd had staged its annual rehearsal for a SwapClear default just the week before Lehman's bankruptcy. The traders – from Barclays, UBS, Goldman Sachs, Merrill Lynch, HSBC and Deutsche Bank – had already worked together with members of LCH.Clearnet's swaps team. They were sent to a special crisis centre and got to work.

Unlike the LCH.Clearnet staffers dealing with Lehman's exchange traded derivatives, the SwapClear dealers had no difficulties with the Lehman administrators. LBSF, as a US entity, continued operating under Chapter 11 bankruptcy rules. The traders got to work quickly using the margin payments that had been deposited by Lehman to apply hedges that would neutralise risk in the defaulted investment bank's swaps portfolio. 'They were pretty well done after Tuesday,' Jones recalled. 'You could see the risk just come flying down. At that point there was very little that could hurt us.'

Supervising the hedging was Christian Lee, LCH.Clearnet's risk manager of interest rate products. It was his job to lead SwapClear traders – powerful personalities and market rivals all – through the unfamiliar exercise of cooperating with one another.

[14] US$356.8 trillion at the end of June 2008 according to the Bank for International Settlements, A trillion is a million-million. The notional total was published in Bank for International Settlements (13 November 2007), 'Triennial and semiannual surveys on positions in global over-the-counter (OTC) derivatives markets at end June 2007'.

[15] According to LCH.Clearnet's annual report for 2007.

John Burke, meanwhile, let the traders get on with their job. An eminently unflappable man with a dry sense of humour, Burke stayed in touch by phone on the first day and called by the crisis centre at about 4 P.M. in the afternoon of Tuesday to offer assistance. Amid the debris of takeaway meals and coffee cups, he found 'quite a lot of tension'. Despite the near meltdown of financial markets around the globe, Burke decided to be understated and appear calm. The tactic paid off.

> At the beginning there was a level of excitement, fear, giddiness, a little bit of craziness in the market. But the flatter and more monotone we became, and the more we said we would do things and then did them, the more they really learned to trust. The whole thing calmed down. It took about three days. On the third day, things became really calm. This was also true of the calls we were getting from senior members of staff.

On Wednesday, the SwapClear hedging operation was virtually complete and the traders from the six member banks making up the default management group suspended their activities.

At this point, Burke began to plan the next stage of the process: a novel competitive auction system to sell the Lehman SwapClear portfolios to new owners among the remaining 19 SwapClear members. He scheduled five SwapClear auctions – one for each major currency – to dispose of the Lehman portfolios between Tuesday 23 September and Friday 3 October 2008. As with the hedging, the remaining SwapClear members were obliged under the system's rules to help ensure that the auctions would be a success.

The SwapClear members had agreed in 2006 to rules that gave LCH.Clearnet added leverage in managing auctions. The clearing house was empowered to allocate portfolios of a defaulting member unilaterally and pro rata to SwapClear members should an auction fail. This rule was designed to encourage SwapClear members to bid for portfolios they would not normally want in times of constrained liquidity. An example of the subtle thinking behind the SwapClear arrangements, the provision played on market psychology by giving member firms the option to bid for positions where they could have some control over composition and price, rather than have an unwanted portfolio foisted on them through a process of allocation.

Even so, the mechanics of the auctions took some working out.

'It was all new,' Burke recalled later:

> We hadn't prepared any of the minutiae such as working out how it would work in practice. We did it by having 19 dealers bidding and 19 people on desks here. We got two people from other departments. One was an IT guy to manage anything needed to support the auction, such as power and IT equipment. We relied on email and telephone bids, all of which had to be recorded on a form, to make sure they were recorded correctly. We got someone from finance to receive the bids and record them on a board in a very calm way, so that the preferred bid could be decided.

Each auction required about 50 staff, with about 35 involved in the operation itself and another 15 providing IT and behind the scenes backup.

The procedure had 'to be very measured,' Burke explained. The incoming bids were very large, running into hundreds of millions of dollars or euros. 'It was very easy to mix up buy and sell or mis-record a trillion or billion. We had to prepare a structure that protected the staff from themselves.' That meant reading back bids to the bidder as a matter of routine, insisting that incoming emails followed a prescribed format, discreetly double-checking if any bid appeared wildly out of line with market conditions, and banning any distracting noise from the room where the incoming bids were received.

> We didn't allow people to move, because when people move they make a noise and that could distract other people on the phone to another dealer. When a bid was written down, the person taking it would put up a hand. We had three walkers – as opposed to runners – to take the paper to the door of the room where the member of the LCH.Clearnet finance staff was recording the bids. Another person would hand the paper to the guy in the office – dubbed the 'Big Brother' room. He'd take the bid and write it on the grid.

Burke and his staff did dry runs for each auction and with each dealer to ensure they knew what they were bidding for and which way round the bidding process worked: 'whether it was we pay them or they pay us'. One error could cost a great deal. Not only did the instruments being auctioned change in value every day, but the bigger portfolios – for euros and dollars – were very large in terms of the number of trades they contained and compared with the existing portfolios of some of the bidders.

The auctions were categorised by currency and sequenced by complexity, starting with easiest. The first two SwapClear portfolios – for Swiss francs and sterling respectively – were sold on Wednesday and Thursday, 24–25 September. The yen, euro and dollar portfolios were auctioned on the Monday, Wednesday and Friday of the following week.

There were some moments of stress. Selected dealers from the default management group that had hedged the Lehman interest rate swap portfolio were asked to observe the operation in order to assist LCH.Clearnet staff judge whether the bids properly reflected the intentions of the bidders. This prompted some concern among firms outside that their rivals would discover the identity of the bidders. 'It became quite tense. The whole cooperation thing began to wobble,' Burke admitted. 'However, we got round that by allocating numbers to bidding banks and desks with a different number for each bank for each auction. That worked beautifully.'

There was also the unexpected, as on 30 September, the day between the yen and euro SwapClear auctions, when an excavator cut though a power line outside LCH.Clearnet's main office in the City. The power cut – the first that Burke had experienced in 10 years of working for the group – meant shifting some of the work to a backup site for some hours.

But the auctions functioned well. Only once did the Ltd staffers organising the process have to check whether a bid reflected the bidder's true intent – it did. Burke reported that 16 of the 19 remaining SwapClear members took part in the auctions. The interest they generated was reflected in 'hundreds of calls about each auction' from around the world reflecting SwapClear's global membership. Some three weeks after putting LBSF into default, LCH.Clearnet announced that it and OTCDerivNet had successfully wound down Lehman Brothers' OTC interest rate swap portfolio.[16]

3.5 THE PICTURE IN PARIS: LCH.CLEARNET SA

For Christophe Hémon, Chief Executive of LCH.Clearnet SA in Paris, the payment by Lehman of its early morning margin call on 15 September was a mixed blessing. He remembers checking the CCP's account with the Banque de France: 'We were relieved to see the payment, but it

[16] LCH.Clearnet (8 October 2008), '$9 trillion Lehman OTC interest rate swap default successfully resolved'.

was a bit tricky too – we were not able to declare Lehman in default at this time because they had paid their margins.'[17]

His dilemma disappeared with the news of the default declaration in London. SA declared LBIE in default at the same time as LCH.Clearnet Ltd. It immediately advised its main regulators in Paris and Amsterdam and the 'college' representing all 10 regulators that dealt with LCH.Clearnet on the continent.[18]

On paper, managing the Lehman default should have been relatively straightforward for SA. It had only one Lehman counterparty – LBIE – and cleared far fewer derivatives than Ltd.

But as with Ltd in London, SA had to cope with an uncooperative administrator, while steps taken by the CCP's business partners added to the complexity of the closing out operations.

Hémon decided that SA's by-laws took precedence over any of PwC's scruples. 'Our rulebook is very clear,' he said later. 'We need to make sure that we protect the CCP's interest, the customer's interest and the market overall.' To do so, he started organising auctions to liquidate LBIE's positions. 'This was quite an exciting and difficult exercise given the market volatility and the market circumstances, especially with rumours about AIG's possible default the next day.' The company had practised for such an eventuality with some of its banking partners, but 'that was like a military exercise: we had never done things on a real live basis'.

Hémon and his colleagues started with the small portfolios first, beginning with those traded on Powernext, an energy marketplace, and the commodities contracts. Equities and index derivatives portfolios followed. Cash equity business was no problem for the CCP because in this business sector, LBIE subcontracted its clearing business with SA through BNP-Paribas, the large French bank, which was one of SA's general clearing members.

When it came to LBIE's bond and repo positions, theory and practice began to diverge. This was the biggest chunk of the Lehman's business in SA. The business model for this asset class was very different from other asset classes, in particular for Italian debt. SA used BNP-Paribas in Milan as settlement agent in Italy and was in a contractual and operational relationship with CC&G, the Italian CCP, as an 'allied clearing house' in an example of interoperability among CCPs. The trades were settled at Monte Titoli, the Italian central securities depository (CSD).

Each entity had to deal with the default according to its own default management procedures and this created complexity and confusion in the marketplace. When, for example, Monte Titoli cancelled all the trades related to Lehman's activities in line with Italian default management rules, it resulted in an operational overload that added to the default management burden of SA. Monte Titoli's action meant SA was unable to keep track of its trades on the Italian market and had to ask BNP-Paribas in Milan to key the trades manually into the system to restore the settlement entries before it could continue.

The Paris CCP cleared large numbers of trades in Italian government debt for LBIE which were settled afterwards at SA's account in Monte Titoli. The two sides of each trade would be settled on the same day, but perhaps not at the same time, so even though the net cash requirement for a given day would be zero there could be huge intraday swings in exposures.

These circumstances caused a liquidity shortage for SA in the very difficult conditions following Lehman's default. 'People were under huge stress because markets were very bad. Companies were uncertain about what they would end up with from Lehman trades and regulators were getting very nervous because they knew Lehman was a very big customer and they were wondering whether the whole process would end in fiasco,' Hémon said later.

[17] All quotes by Hémon in this chapter are from a conversation with the author, 9 December 2008.

[18] See Section 16.1 for details of the regulatory arrangements of LCH.Clearnet Group and its subsidiaries.

The Lehman positions liquidated at the beginning of the week had to be settled on Thursday and Friday. SA calculated that it needed to settle securities worth a net €1 billion and knew it would have to put cash through the European Central Bank's Target2 high value payments system into its Monte Titoli account to kick-start the whole process.

However, on Thursday, the peak settlement day, SA needed €3.5 billion to facilitate the settlement process. About two thirds, between €2 billion and €3 billion, were needed to complete purchases of securities from Monte Titoli that had been initiated by Lehman or its clients and caught up in the default. The rest was to settle positions at Euroclear France, the French CSD for LBIE operations on French debt. As Hémon explained: 'It was a large amount of cash. Normally we don't have to fund so much on an overnight basis. The difficulty for us was to be sure that we would be paid back at the end of the day.'

The positions with Euroclear were not a serious problem. 'Euroclear was quite cooperative – we have good relationship with Euroclear Bank [the Brussels-based international central securities depository, or ICSD, that handles international securities] and Euroclear France. We agreed with the Chief Executive of Euroclear France that he would put extra resources into this part of their business.'

'The settlement process at Monte Titoli seemed very different from that of Euroclear,' Hémon said later. 'Our feeling was that Monte Titoli was settling all our buys first and settling all our sells later in the day. That was why we needed quite a lot of cash, either to inject liquidity or prefund settlements in a crisis mode.'

'Just one example: we had to settle €1.3 billion at a particular moment in the day. We had to inject €1 billion in order to settle. That was almost one euro for one euro. That was clearly a very expensive way of doing things.'

Hémon had to take unprecedented steps:

> We had to test on a live basis a procedure that we had never tested before. We had a large amount of collateral in our account at Euroclear Bank which we transferred back to the Banque de France just in case, to facilitate the cash transfer to the Bank of Italy, in order to settle the trades. At the same time, we also borrowed from the market which SA seldom does, as the CCP is cash-long.

Without these emergency actions, SA could have been exposed to the risk of a liquidity shortfall.

Looking back, a big lesson for SA was the importance of readily available liquidity. Managing Lehman's default showed there were advantages in SA being a bank, as required under French law. The CCP had access to the Banque de France for funds against collateral and was able to use the ECB's Target2 payments system to move payments quickly to Italy.

As Hémon admitted afterwards:

> As always in a crisis of such magnitude, there are things that go according to plan and unexpected events that do not. This real case of default emphasised the need for us to gain rapid access to liquidity. I have wondered what would have happened if this was not possible.

3.6 RESPONSES ELSEWHERE

LCH.Clearnet Group's CCPs were not the only European clearing houses handling the Lehman default. PwC, LBIE's administrator, later identified three other CCPs, recognised as clearing houses by the UK's FSA, as having been involved in closing out positions with LBIE.[19] These were Eurex Clearing AG, the CCP of the Deutsche Börse group; EMCF[20], a subsidiary of Fortis Bank; and EuroCCP[21], a London-based subsidiary of DTCC.

At the end of September 2008, Eurex announced that it too had successfully wound down the proprietary trading positions and transferred the customers' positions with LBIE that were on its books when the US investment bank failed. Like LCH.Clearnet, Eurex managed to complete the operation by using the collateral deposited by LBIE. At no point did it require recourse to deeper assets – such as the default fund – provided by its members for its defence.

The clearing house was under heavy time pressure because Friday 19 September was a large contract expiry date. 'It took some discussions with the administrator to convince them that there was a need for action,' recalled Marcus Zickwolff, Executive Director and Head of System Design department of Eurex in Frankfurt.[22]

Eurex had some staff members in Lehman's premises in Canary Wharf after the administrator released data on Tuesday evening following the default. There they worked with the LBIE staff, who assisted with winding down proprietary positions and placing customer accounts with other clearing members.

In the European equities market, the default provided an early test of infrastructures put in place in response to MiFID, the European Union's Markets in Financial Instruments Directive, that took effect in November 2007. MiFID, launched with the aim of opening up Europe's financial markets to greater competition, authorised new-style trading platforms known as multilateral trading facilities (MTFs). Two of these were established in London by the time of Lehman's default and each had chosen new contenders to provide CCP services: Chi-X had its trades cleared by EMCF; Turquoise, which had begun trading equities only in August, used EuroCCP, which had been reactivated after several years of lying dormant to act as its clearing house.

Clearing for equity markets entails few of the difficulties faced by CCPs handling derivatives. In the case of equities, the settlement or completion of the transaction takes place only three days after a trade (T+3). With futures and other derivatives, closing out or settlement of a contract may be months or even years after the trade, giving rise to the need for sophisticated margining and risk-management systems at CCPs that handle such business.

Nonetheless, given the circumstances, it was probably understandable that on the day after the default, there should be a look of satisfaction on the face of Jan Bart de Boer, chairman of the supervisory board of EMCF.

EMCF, De Boer disclosed, was out of its Lehman position by 8 A.M. on the morning of Tuesday, 16 September: 'We passed our test. Lehman was a DCM [direct clearing member]. It worked. So we informed our clearing members this morning that the positions are gone, that the clearing funds didn't take a hit and that it's business as usual at EMCF.'[23]

On the day before, EMCF sent LBIE a formal default notification advising that it would act to close out its positions. Although on a much smaller scale, its procedures were similar to those followed at LCH.Clearnet.

---

[19] Notice about exchange and clearing house communications relating to LBIE in administration. PwC website (www.pwc.co.uk), 25 September 2008 (accessed 10 December 2010).

[20] European Multilateral Clearing Facility NV. At the time, Fortis was still functioning as a private sector Belgo-Dutch financial conglomerate. Some weeks later, Fortis had to be rescued by the Dutch, Belgian and Luxembourg governments and was subsequently broken up along national lines. The Dutch part, with the majority stake in EMCF, was later reconstituted as ABN AMRO Bank NV.

[21] European Central Counterparty Ltd.

[22] Conversation with the author, 3 December 2008.

[23] In conversation with the author, 16 September 2008.

'We had an auction where we sent the positions out to a number of broker-dealers,' de Boer recalled. 'We got the quotes in, picked the best and sold the positions to that firm.' There was more than enough margin. The rest went back to the administrator.

It helped that EMCF had rehearsed the event. 'We prepared at the weekend – just for the eventuality,' de Boer explained. 'It is something you test once a month. But normally all these tests about a default situation are always a bit geeky . . . until it is really happening.'

Taking long and short positions combined, the LBIE position with EMCF was worth nearly €500 million involving some 600 to 700 named securities or ISINs.[24] 'That was a big position – sizeable,' he said.

As the clearing house for a more recent start-up, EuroCCP had correspondingly smaller trading positions to close out. According to DTCC, its EuroCCP subsidiary was faced with open Lehman trades worth nearly €21 million in 12 markets and in six currencies on 15 September.[25] EuroCCP suspended Lehman from new trade input that day but managed, with Lehman's agent banks, to deliver trades worth about €5 million to other financial institutions before ceasing to act for Lehman on 16 September. EuroCCP then engaged a broker to close out the remaining €16 million worth of trades, settling them after an interval of one day (T+1) rather than the usual three days. Lehman's margin deposits proved sufficient to cover the costs of the operation. The London-based clearing house had no need to draw on the guarantee fund provided by its members.

EuroCCP's involvement with the Lehman default was tiny compared with that of the DTCC group as a whole. But it was a test nonetheless. The Lehman bankruptcy happened a week before EuroCCP was due to operate at full capacity. EuroCCP also had to close out its Lehman positions several days before CCPs in the US, including those of its parent group.

Lehman's US broker-dealer did not go into default until after agreement on the sale of its North American investment banking operations to Barclays of the UK. This was during the week after the default in Europe, by which time US CCPs could make preparations.

'There was some stability injected into the system when there were arrangements made over the first weekend to ensure that the broker-dealer would have sufficient resources to continue to operate in the US,' noted Kim Taylor, Managing Director and President of CME Clearing in Chicago. Speaking 10 days after Lehman Brothers Holdings (LBH) filed for bankruptcy protection in New York, she recounted how the CME Group 'had a clearing member that was functioning and meeting all its obligations for that week. [. . .] So we've never had a case where someone has defaulted to us and where we had to put a member in default and put them out of business in the way that LCH did.'[26]

On the other hand, coping with Lehman's collapse was far from easy for the CME Group. It emerged 18 months later that the Lehman bankruptcy prompted CME's clearing division to carry out the first forced sale of a clearing member's positions in its history.

Details surfaced in a 2200 page report on the failure of the investment bank by Anton Valukas, a distinguished lawyer appointed by the US Trustee as 'examiner' in the LBH bankruptcy.[27] CME held around US$4 billion of margin funds on behalf of Lehman Brothers Inc. (LBI), a main operating subsidiary of LBH and a CME clearing member, as surety for its open positions with the CME Group's exchanges. The deposits, which were a significant chunk of the US$95 billion margin deposited by all clearing members with CME, consisted of

[24] International securities identification number. An ISIN is a 12 digit securities identification code unique to each security.

[25] DTCC (30 October 2008), 'DTCC successfully closes out Lehman Brothers bankruptcy', press release.

[26] Conversation with the author, Chicago, 25 September 2008.

[27] Valukas, Anton R. (2010), 'Examiner Report re Lehman Brothers Holdings Inc. to the US Bankruptcy Court Southern District of New York'. Published in redacted form 12 March 2010 and unredacted 14 April 2010.

about US$2 billion as collateral for LBI's proprietary or 'house' positions and US$2 billion for LBI customers' positions.

After LBH entered bankruptcy proceedings on 15 September 2008, CME decided that LBI's house positions should be held ready for liquidation and authorised the exchange's clearing house division to sell or transfer these positions in bulk. With Lehman's consent it had earlier selected six firms to submit contingent bids for the house positions. It also put LBI on 'liquidation only' status for its proprietary positions, meaning all LBI's open trades were to be liquidated. However, it set no deadline for this.

Instead of liquidating its house positions at the CME, 'LBI modestly added to its positions over the next two days'. This, Valukas reported, reflected 'confusion and chaos at LBI'. Meanwhile concern was growing at CME. The exchange thought it just a matter of time before positions had to be liquidated and was worried that JP Morgan might cease to be LBI's settlement bank with the CME Clearing Division, which (if it happened) would make liquidation much more difficult.

On the evening of Wednesday 17 September, the CME sought new bids from five of the six firms approached earlier for five baskets of LBI house positions. The five baskets contained: energy derivatives, foreign exchange derivatives, interest rate derivatives, equity derivatives, and agricultural and alternative investment derivatives. The five chosen bidders were Barclays, Goldman Sachs, JP Morgan, Citadel LP and DRW Trading.

The bids were evaluated on Thursday morning and the house positions transferred in bulk to three of the companies: Barclays, Goldman Sachs and DRW Trading. According to Valukas's report, all the bids involved substantial losses to LBI in the form of the transfer to the bidders 'of the majority (and in several cases all) of the CME margin posted in connection with the positions'. The forced transfer caused LBI to lose more than US$1.2 billion over the close-of-business liabilities associated with the positions. When the Valukas report was written, the CME was holding roughly US$150 million of former LBI margin collateral.

The financial details of the liquidation and the names of the successful bidders were concealed in the redacted version of Valukas's report published in March 2010. When the bankruptcy judge allowed release of the unredacted report a month later, blogs and news reports[28] that the bidding companies made huge profits from an apparently untransparent procedure at the expense of the creditors of Lehman Brothers triggered a furore.

The Valukas report made for uncomfortable reading. It brought to public attention difficulties that CCPs could face when handling the default of a large clearing member. Even allowing for chaos on financial markets following Lehman's collapse, the losses from the forced sales raised questions about the effectiveness of the CME's auction process. The CCP suffered no loss. But how, people wondered, would the CME or other CCPs have fared if, as well as Lehman Brothers, other major market players had been allowed to fail during that week?

To be sure, the size and scope of Lehman Brothers' activities made liquidation of its trades a complex process for US CCPs. This was true too of the DTCC, which had to close out exposures of market participants totalling more than US$500 billion, making it the biggest such task in its history.

On 22 September, DTCC announced that it would work to bring about an orderly winding down of all LBI open trades not acquired by Barclays. More than five weeks passed before it

[28] For example: Reuters (2010), 'Firms reaped windfalls in Lehman auction: examiner', 14 April 2010 among others.

reported that the close out was a success and it had not needed clearing funds provided by its member firms.[29]

During that time, the US post-trade giant – which provides clearing, settlement and other services for equities; corporate, municipal and government bonds; mortgage backed securities; money market instruments and over-the-counter derivatives – also had to process four consecutive days of record high equity trading volumes. These peaked on Friday, 10 October 2008, when 19.3 billion shares worth nearly US$3.3 trillion were traded. That day, DTCC's National Securities Clearing Corporation (NSCC) subsidiary processed a record 209.4 million transactions – more than double the highest volume of 2007 – netting them down by 98% to leave an actual settlement value of 'only' US$57.5 billion.

NSCC clears equities, municipal debt and other securities traded on US exchanges and alternative trading platforms. DTCC's Depository Trust Company (DTC) unit provides securities settlement functions for the same markets. This structure yielded dividends in the Lehman case. NSCC had to manage an exposure of US$5.85 billion inherited from Lehman. But, with the help of DTC, it was able to gain access to US$1.9 billion of securities deposited with banks as collateral to settle open trades.

As with some European infrastructure providers, DTCC had conducted scenario planning for worst case market events. 'However, in 2005, we began asking ourselves, how would we handle the possible failure of one of the top 10 financial firms?' said Don Donahue, DTCC's chairman and CEO.[30] 'We began a programme then of running the whole organisation through drills, assuming we were going to lose a major firm. We asked: what happens? How do we deal with it? What are the issues? Are our systems capable of handling something of that magnitude?'

The drills showed there were scale limits on the number of positions DTCC could handle in a liquidation, prompting it to change its systems during 2006. The result, according to Donahue, was that DTCC began preparing for the worst, using systems that were 'totally scalable' for the 'most unimaginable scenario you can think of'.

'So when Lehman Brothers failed, with half a trillion US dollars worth of open positions that we inherited there was no issue of the system's ability to be able to handle a liquidation of that magnitude,' Donahue recalled. 'We had in fact done what we needed to do.'

DTCC carried out two internal exercises simulating a major firm or Lehman-type failure during the 12 months before September 2008. The second of these, in June 2008, actually used Lehman data in the scenario and had members of DTCC's board and representatives of its regulators taking part. The drills 'were incredibly invaluable in identifying problems and possible solutions,' Donahue observed. 'And because of that, and the talent of our risk-management staff, the liquidation went through in those few weeks remarkably smoothly.'

But some improvisation was still necessary. DTCC provided clearing services for mortgage backed securities through its Fixed Income Clearing Corp (FICC) subsidiary, but there was no central counterparty clearing facility in operation for this market at the time of the Lehman bankruptcy. One was being constructed with a targeted completion date of mid-2009.

Lehman's book of forward mortgage backed securities with DTCC amounted to a daunting gross US$329 billion when the investment bank defaulted. As Donahue told industry leaders shortly afterwards,[31] DTCC's customers and SIFMA – the Securities Industry Financial

[29] DTCC (30 October 2008).

[30] Conversation with the author, London, 12 January 2009.

[31] In a presentation to the DTCC Executive Forum (DTCC, 29 October 2008).

Markets Association – suggested that the company 'play CCP for a day' and work with the dealers, banks and securities firms with which Lehman had traded to net down Lehman's open positions. DTCC followed the advice. It reduced the forward positions in the mortgage backed market to about US$30 billion, and, as Donahue noted, 'immediately erased a lot of pain and concern from many balance sheets'.

It appeared in the months following the Lehman bankruptcy that CCPs around the world had managed the fall-out from the Lehman default, without drawing on their members' default fund contributions. But in December 2008, Hong Kong Exchanges and Clearing Ltd (HKEx) disclosed the loss of HK$157 million,[32] including costs and expenses, as a result of the Hong Kong Securities Clearing Company (HKSCC) closing out Lehman Brothers Securities Asia (LBSA). The disclosure had a particular resonance, because Hong Kong was the scene of significant losses linked to its futures exchange and its clearing arrangements some 21 years before.[33]

HKEx said the loss followed a decision by the Securities and Futures Commission (SFC), Hong Kong's regulator, to issue a restriction notice on LBSA which 'effectively prohibited LBSA from settling any of its positions in HKSCC's Central Clearing and Settlement System (CCASS) and completing settlements with its customers (excepting returning fully paid shares to customers)'.[34]

Following the restriction notice, HKSCC declared LBSA a defaulter on 16 September 2008 and took action to close out defaulted positions totalling HK$3.5 billion in accordance with its rules.[35] According to the accounts published by CCP12 and HKEx, the loss arose when HKSCC had to make on-market purchases and, as HKEx put it, 'fill a [HK]$2.5 billion funding gap in a very tight credit market to fulfil its settlement obligations as the central counterparty'.

HKSCC had to sell a large number of securities in a falling market while the amount of collateral provided by LBSA was relatively small. Rather than impose collateral requirements to cover the potential price risks of unsettled positions of clearing participants in the securities market, HKSCC had required participants to post collateral mainly when their unsettled positions were large relative to their liquid capital.

HKSCC announced it would seek recovery of the closing-out loss from the Lehman liquidator and draw on other resources including HK$394 million held in the HKSCC guarantee fund. To protect itself and the guarantee fund from any further Lehman-like default, HKSCC subsequently called for extra collateral from its most active clearing members that amounted to 10% of whichever was higher of the daily gross short or long positions of each participant. It also signalled its intention to develop 'comprehensive long term solutions' to the problems that had surfaced during the second half of 2008.

3.7 IMMEDIATE LESSONS FROM THE DEFAULT

Although most CCPs dealt successfully with the biggest financial default in history, the Lehman bankruptcy inevitably yielded a crop of lessons to be learned.

An overarching problem – with ramifications extending far beyond the scope of this book – was the way a group like Lehman Brothers, which consisted of 2985 entities globally[36] with a

[32] Worth US$20.14 million at the 15 September exchange rate of HK$7.7937 to US$1.

[33] See Section 9.4.

[34] HKEx (January 2009), *Exchange*.

[35] CCP12 (April 2009), 'Central counterparty default management and the collapse of Lehman Brothers'.

[36] According to CESR (23 March 2009), 'The Lehman Brothers default: An assessment of the market impact'.

vast number of intercompany balances, was multinational in life but national in death. Different bankruptcy regimes in the jurisdictions where Lehman operated meant the group's subsidiaries fell into the hands of different administrators working to different rules and regulations with the aim, first and foremost, of satisfying the needs of their local creditors.

In the UK, where CCPs faced the biggest challenges, the crisis cast doubt on the suitability of the bankruptcy regime for dealing with the failure of an investment bank. Whereas the US system of Chapter 11 protection enabled Lehman's operating subsidiaries to keep running until a buyer for most of the assets was in place, the UK bankruptcy system recognised no difference between a financial firm and a factory. As Chris Jones of LCH.Clearnet Ltd observed: 'Factories shut down production and when the administrators are ready, they reopen production. But you can't do that with investment banks. The mere fact of doing that would mean any hope of salvaging the thing is gone.'

Ltd had no option but to declare LBIE and LBSF in default and try and seize control of the situation. 'The US clearers were able to manage down their risk [and] transfer clients in a much more orderly manner than we did,' Jones noted.

LBIE was in any case vulnerable because of the absence in the UK of any regulatory requirement for minimum holdings of liquidity for large, international banking institutions. Lehman's central treasury function in New York was able to conduct its nightly 'sweep' of subsidiaries' cash holdings unimpeded. Only after Lehman's collapse, did the UK's FSA prescribe liquidity requirements.

A further problem concerned the commingled client accounts. Part of the fault lay with the record keeping practices of Lehman Brothers and its subsidiaries. But with hindsight, the UK opt out from US-style customer segregation will probably be judged a false economy.

This difference might not have mattered had the administrator winding down LBIE shown a better understanding of the clearing houses' carve-out from British insolvency law through Part VII of the UK Companies Act 1989. Instead, the obstruction of the clearing houses' operations in the important first two days after the default added potentially damaging complications to an already grave situation.

To be sure, administrators in the UK and around the world faced unprecedented challenges. Nothing as big as the Lehman collapse had ever happened before. The previous big bankruptcy handled by the head of PwC's restructuring and insolvency practice, who was appointed to manage the winding down of LBIE, was that of a car company. 'Bear in mind, I'm not an investment banker,' Tony Lomas told an audience of financiers and academics four months later. 'The last significant insolvency I dealt with was MG Rover.'[37]

Lomas and his colleagues had to leap into action at very short notice. 'We got our phone call about this on Saturday night and attended a board meeting on Sunday morning and we were appointed the next morning,' he told the same conference in January 2009.

> We had half a day basically and the company had made no contingency plan to deal with this sort of eventuality. [...] I deal with lots of distressed situations and in the ordinary course of events there is some warning. That allows me to plan. Half a day was no time at all. When we did the Enron insolvency in the UK we did at least have a two-week window to plan.

The structure of LBIE's unsettled transactions may also have diverted the administrators from paying sufficient heed to the requests of LCH.Clearnet and other CCPs to have their rights under Part VII of the Companies Act 1989 respected.

[37] In remarks on 19 January 2009 to a conference in London organised by the London School of Economics.

PwC estimated later that there were approximately 142 000 unsettled securities transactions to which LBIE was a counterparty at the time of its appointment as administrator.[38] Of these, 83 500 were trades to be settled in Europe, 45 000 in Asia and 12 500 in the US. According to PwC, the majority of the unsettled cash trades in Europe were executed off-exchange. Although about 65% were settled through the settlement systems of Denmark, France, Italy, Norway, Switzerland and the UK, plus Brussels-based Euroclear, only 'a small number' were executed on exchanges cleared through CCPs.

The fact that the administrators were personally liable for the decisions may have encouraged them to err on the side of excessive caution. In December 2008, a study commissioned by the Mayor of London, produced by a high-level panel and chaired by Bob Wigley (then chairman for Europe, Middle East and Africa of Merrill Lynch), highlighted this quirk of UK insolvency law when it concluded that

> The [UK] government must urgently review the UK's administration laws to restore trust in London-based financial subsidiaries of overseas firms. The process the Lehman Brothers London subsidiary administrators have had to go through – and the fact that they carry personal liability – is inconsistent with a rapid release of assets and settlements to creditors and therefore stands in the way of rapid resolution of the insolvency.

According to Wigley's panel, global firms' UK operations fared materially worse in relation to Lehman's insolvency than in other financial centres.[39]

But there was no getting away from the difficulties experienced by LCH.Clearnet and other CCPs in establishing communications with the administrators and in obtaining accurate client position data immediately after the Lehman Brothers' bankruptcy. These issues were raised in sometimes heated conference calls with the FSA during the crisis, and in 'lessons to learn sessions' with the regulators after the CCPs had completed their task.[40]

'Together with LCH we said afterwards it would be useful if we had administrators with a base knowledge of derivatives,' Eurex's Marcus Zickwolff commented.

The Bank of England also attached a high priority to improving procedures, as became clear a few months later when it delivered a thinly veiled rebuke to the administrators of LBIE.

Writing in April 2009, the Bank observed that events surrounding the Lehman default 'highlighted the importance of market participants having a clear understanding of the application of systems' default arrangements to all types of transaction and exposures that they are involved in, including an understanding of the relevant legal protections, such as Part VII of the Companies Act 1989 and the UK Financial Market and Insolvency (Settlement) Finality Regulations 1999'.[41]

With the support of the Bank and the FSA, the UK's recognised clearing houses and insolvency practitioners began in 2009 to work on a document setting out 'cooperation guidance' to minimise conflicts over the application of Part VII of the Companies Act.

The guidance was to be nonbinding and this proved a problem when draft texts were circulated for consultation. The drafts did nothing to allay deep seated doubts among clearing

---

[38] PwC (7 November 2008), 'Unsettled trades – market update', communication regarding LBIE (in administration).

[39] Merrill Lynch Europe Ltd (12 December 2008), 'London: Winning in a changing world – Review of the competitiveness of London's Financial Centre'.

[40] The author has been at pains to be even-handed in the account of the administrator's handling of Part VII of the Companies Act 1989. He approached Tony Lomas for an interview at the LSE conference mentioned in the text and Mr Lomas agreed to the request. However, Mr Lomas's office replied to a follow up email and telephone calls with the information that he was 'unable to commit to a meeting'. A further email repeating the author's request for a meeting went unanswered.

[41] Bank of England (April 2009b), 'Payment systems oversight report 2008', Issue No. 5.

houses about the effectiveness of a nonbinding accord to change anything in future Lehman-type crises. With little sign of progress by the summer of 2010, there seemed growing support among clearing house professionals for the law to be changed in order to provide legal certainty that the operation of clearing house default rules under Part VII of the Companies Act 1989 would take precedence over the insolvency procedures of administrators.

3.8 LCH.CLEARNET STANDS THE TEST

LCH.Clearnet used only 35% of the US$2 billion of the initial margin provided by Lehman to clear up the default.[42] That it was able to overcome the obstacles of the first days and deal with the proprietary and client positions at LBIE without using other clearing members' funds or Lehman's contribution to the default fund owed much to its structure.

LCH.Clearnet's multi-asset class clearing model gave CEO Roger Liddell the freedom of manoeuvre to hold back from liquidating the positions of LBIE clients during the first two days of the default while the clearing house was hammering fruitlessly on the administrator's door and having to sort out the riddle of the non-segregated client accounts.

As the company liquidated positions elsewhere, the amount of cover – that is the surplus of margin it held against risks on a day-by-day basis – increased. The clearing house became more secure each day as value at risk declined. As a result, Liddell could safely take the decision, repeatedly, to seek the transfer of the non-segregated positions which otherwise would have been liquidated:

> We always thought that a common default fund would be the main benefit from being a multi-asset CCP,' Liddell recalled later. In fact, the big and far more valuable discovery during Lehman was that the initial margin in each market was completely fungible. With all the risk on our books, we had the benefit of the portfolio effect. There were inverse correlations with prices moving one way in some markets, another way in others. As we managed to liquidate some of the portfolios more quickly than others, it meant that the margin that was left after some had been liquidated was available to cover risk somewhere else. That was a massive, massive benefit.
>
> We would never have run out of margin in any of the silos. But it meant we had a much bigger cushion all the time. And the effect of a bigger cushion was that we could be much more diligent in identifying client positions. We didn't have the same sort of urgent need to get rid of everything straight away.[43]

'It's a story of a model which has been totally vindicated,' Chris Tupker, LCH.Clearnet Group chairman, said afterwards. 'It is the model of having many asset classes in one clearing house so that there is collateral from one user spread over a wide range of assets, and yet all of that collateral can be allocated against one asset class.'

LCH.Clearnet's multi-asset class model helped Chris Jones and his team to manage the risk in extremely volatile markets:

> We knew that because we were so diversified – we were losing money on oil, making money on gas; losing money on equities, making money on repos – the balance of our portfolio was not losing a lot of money. We were able to balance these things up and so bought ourselves some time. And that was part luck, part judgement.

---

[42] According to Roger Liddell in his testimony to the House of Lords European Union Committee on 9 February 2010 (House of Lords, 2010).

[43] Conversation with the author, 22 December 2009.

LCH.Clearnet would have had less manoeuvring room if the planned migration of the oil futures from Ltd to ICE Clear Europe had gone ahead during the weekend before Lehman sought Chapter 11 protection.

As it was, LCH.Clearnet had the experienced personnel and contacts in place to deal with the emergencies that arose after the Lehman default. Experience and structure paid off when the problem of Lehman's commingled client accounts surfaced. Because the group cleared a broad range of asset classes, the company could win time and hold back from liquidating the LBIE client positions. These would otherwise have been sold, resulting in the potentially costly destruction of hedged positions and, in the process, doing perhaps irreparable damage to the confidence of global investors in the City of London.

At LCH.Clearnet SA in Paris, Christophe Hémon had reason to reflect on another piece of good fortune. Although the Lehman default presented SA with its biggest corporate bankruptcy to date, LBIE was not the most technically complex entity on its books. How, asked Hémon afterwards, might his CCP have fared if, as well as trading on its own account and for clients, LBIE had also been a general clearing member (a GCM), one of those banks that specialised in clearing the trades of other financial institutions through the CCP?

The question became acute about two weeks after the Lehman default, when Fortis, the Belgian-Dutch bank, suffered a collapse of investor confidence and had to be rescued by tripartite action of the Belgian, Dutch and Luxembourg governments. Although the rescue turned out to be only the first step in a long drawn out saga that has involved multiple legal actions and the fall of a government in Belgium, the governments' action removed the risk of a Fortis default. This was just as well. Fortis was not only a very big customer for the derivatives clearing services of LCH.Clearnet SA; as a GCM, the Belgo-Dutch financial group cleared for 120 trading members.

That, according to Hémon, was a huge business:

> And the impact would not only have been on us. Transferring those positions would have been a very big enterprise. You would have to transfer them to another entity or global clearing member. That would have impacted the market a lot because these companies would not have been able to trade or flatten their positions on the Monday, if a Fortis scenario had arisen over a weekend. The transfer process would still be going on. If that had been the situation, there would have been a significant impact on NYSE Liffe's European markets, for example, and market volatility would have been very significant.[44]

The alarm surrounding Fortis was a reminder that CCPs must be ready to deal with any kind of crisis. 'When you consider a big customer like Lehman or a GCM like Fortis, the impacts are totally different and the organisation has to be adapted accordingly as far as default procedures are concerned.'

Regulators too have been drawing lessons from the default. The liquidity difficulties between SA and Monte Titoli were followed up three months after the default in four-party post-mortem discussions involving the two companies and Banque de France and Bank of Italy.

That episode appeared to demonstrate some advantages in a CCP having banking status and maintaining a very close relationship with its national central bank at all levels. SA's French banking licence provided access to central bank money. As Hémon reported afterwards:

> SA had to face a liquidity crisis during the week. That was because all the banks were being very cautious in the market. They were ending up with big balances at the end of the day, but preferred

[44] All quotes by Hémon are from a conversation with the author, 9 December 2008.

to keep the money with the Banque de France rather than lend to other banks. So direct access to the central bank was useful, and also being a bank enabled LCH.Clearnet SA to get access to the European Central Bank.

Access to the ECB allowed SA to use the Target2 payments system to shift money to where it was needed in Italy.

But the problems encountered might have been better monitored if Monte Titoli terminals had been installed in the office of SA in Paris allowing the CCP to follow movements of securities and predict how much cash was needed. Screens have since been installed as one of several measures to improve liquidity operations in a crisis.

SA has also taken the following actions:

- Increased credit lines with ICSDs.
- Established reciprocal credit lines with Ltd in London.
- Arranged to use CCBM, the 'correspondent central banking model' of the European System of Central Banks, which allows participants to use foreign securities as collateral to obtain cash from their own national bank.
- Set up procedures with CSDs and ICSDs to repatriate securities within half a day and turn them into cash at the Banque de France using a facility known as 3G (*Gestion Globale de Garanties*).

As far as managing the financial crisis was concerned, the Lehman episode confirmed that CCPs had become the 'must-have' accessory for treasury ministers and financial policy makers on both sides of the Atlantic.

In particular, the successful closing out of trillions of dollars worth of OTC interest rate swaps by Ltd's SwapClear service and DTCC's successful netting down of forward positions in the US mortgage backed securities market through its 'CCP for a day' exercise showed how effectively CCPs could operate in an off-exchange environment in an emergency, especially when they harnessed the expertise of market players.

The success of the LCH.Clearnet Group and other clearing houses in the aftermath of the Lehman bankruptcy made clearing OTC trades a high priority for policy makers in their efforts to learn from the financial crisis. This book will return to the policy makers' demands, the industry's response and the future of central counterparty clearing in Part V.

The weeks after Lehman's collapse put CCPs through a most rigorous test. How central counterparty clearing developed so that today's CCPs could cope with those challenges is the subject of Parts II, III and IV of this book.

Part II

The Road to Central Counterparty Clearing

4 Early Clearing

4.1 THE FIRST TRADERS AND POST-TRADE PRACTICES

Centuries before the emergence of today's CCPs, humans developed techniques that would become part of the practice of clearing trades.

Archaeological discoveries suggest the first futures and options were traded around 1750 BC in the ancient city states of Mesopotamia. As soon as three or more people gathered to trade goods or services, there was a need to make sense of deals struck and payments to be made. One writer has speculated that temples, which facilitated trade in what is now Iraq, may have functioned as clearing houses nearly 4000 years ago.[1]

As far as this author can tell, no scholar has yet constructed a picture of post-trade activities in Assyria from the thousands of cuneiform texts on baked clay tablets that provide details of the early trading, banking and accountancy practices in and among the cities of the region. Fast forward a few centuries, however, and there is evidence of techniques and practices that form part of the DNA of today's CCPs.

Netting has existed since antiquity. The principle of *compensatio* in Roman law recognised the setting-off of payments due when settling disputes between debtors and creditors. It was resurrected after the decline and fall of the Roman Empire in the West to form the legal basis for netting in Medieval Europe.

European traders in the Middle Ages developed increasingly sophisticated netting techniques to handle bills of exchange, which were the main form of cashless payment among merchants until the 20th century. Such bills enabled merchants to overcome a general dearth of specie and the risk of robbery when trading in distant lands. Europe's trade fairs, which attracted participants from far and wide, created facilities that allowed traders to clear the bills of exchange when settling their trades.

The fairs of Champagne, which were held from the 12th century in different parts of the region at different times of the year, set aside time for settling accounts among participants after trading finished. Traders from Flanders, England, Germany and other parts of France used an early version of the bill of exchange – the *lettre de foire* – for transactions. At their height, each of the fairs lasted 49 days with the first week devoted to receiving goods, the next four weeks to trading and the final two weeks to settling accounts. Indicating a fairly sophisticated financial infrastructure, there was a commercial 'court of the fair' to resolve disputes.[2]

By the 15th century the fairs of Champagne were in decline, damaged by the 100 Years War between France and England. In 1463, about 10 years after the war's end, Louis XI of France

[1] Swan, Edward (2000), *Building the Global Market: A 4000 year history of derivatives.* For the development of cities in the Fertile Crescent, see Leick, Gwendolyn (2002), *Mesopotamia. The Invention of the City.*

[2] Teweles, Richard J., Harlow, Charles V. and Stone, Herbert L. (1974), *The Commodity Futures Game.*

authorised four fairs a year at Lyons to fill the gap that they left. Each fair was followed by a day of settlement when bills of exchange were presented and outstanding debts cleared. The Lyons settlement procedures cancelled out offsetting claims, giving traders the opportunity to settle outstanding balances with cash, of which, according to one economic historian, 'very little was ultimately required'.[3]

Netting lowered costs, making the fairs attractive as a place for business and helping Lyons grow as a financial, commercial and industrial centre.

Lyons remained an important centre for fixing exchange rates among European currencies until the late 16th and early 17th centuries. By then, however, innovation in processing bills of exchange had shifted to the trading cities of northern Italy. Among these was Genoa where the Banco di San Giorgio cleared *cambi* or bills of exchange at special 'exchange fairs', established specifically for that purpose.

The bank's clearing activities, which flourished between 1580 and 1630, facilitated the cashless settlement of commercial business, loans and payments for merchandise in distant lands, reducing the risk of transporting of cash over long distances. Drawing on the bank's archives, two scholars – Giuseppe Felloni and Guido Laura – have described clearly defined procedures for exchange fairs held every quarter in different locations.[4]

The fairs lasted eight days, during which participants could accept bills of exchange that had been issued in other cities and were due to expire at the fair, negotiate new bills and settle previous transactions by way of 'reciprocal compensation and payment in cash of outstanding balances'.

The proceedings followed a routine. Participants and expiring bills of exchange were registered on the first day. The differences between the existing debits and credits of participants were calculated and totalled up on the second. These were verified on the third day when agreement was also reached on the reciprocal debits and credits which could be cancelled and the outstanding payments that needed to be made. The next day, exchange rates were agreed for the other cities and new bills issued and sold. The positions of the participants were then updated. The results of all this activity were then gathered together in a final 'balance sheet of payments', which recorded the sums owed and expected from each participant. After further verification, the balance sheets were countersigned by the bankers and delivered to an official, the Consul of the Fair, who fixed his seal to the document and closed the proceedings.

Although conducted at a leisurely pace, the procedures of registration, matching, verification and netting used by the Banco di San Giorgio would be familiar to today's clearing house managers.

4.2 CLEARING IN THE DUTCH GOLDEN AGE

While the Genoese exchange fairs specialised in clearing bills of exchange for merchants, post-trade techniques were being developed in the Netherlands to facilitate investment business, which was often of a highly speculative nature.

The 17th century was the Dutch 'Golden Age' when the Netherlands was a hot bed of financial innovation. Although the Dutch Tulip Mania of 1636–37 has gone down in history

[3] Conant, Charles A. (1905), *Principles of Money and Banking*, Vol. II.

[4] These included Piacenza, Novi Ligure and Sestri Levante: Felloni, Giuseppe and Laura, Guido (2004), *Genoa and the History of Finance: A series of firsts?* at www.giuseppefelloni.it (accessed 3 December 2010). For a condensed account of their work, see Boland, Vincent (2009), 'Banking: The first chapter', *FT Weekend Magazine*, 18–19 April 2009.

as one of the most egregious speculative bubbles ever, the mania in which enthusiasts and speculators bid up the price of prized bulbs while still in the ground also gave rise to progress in clearing.

Inn-based trading clubs emerged to clear trades in tulip bulbs. The sessions were well organised, according to two Dutch economic historians:

> On entering the inn, customers wishing to participate had to introduce themselves to the book-keeper, who then gave them a slate with their name written on it for the bidding. The book-keeper also tracked all transactions in a ledger for settlement through clearance at the end of the evening.[5]

Settlement followed the cancelling out of mutual claims so that the traders had only to pay each other the 'differences' or balances left owing to buyers and sellers as a consequence of the different prices agreed for bulbs in the course of the trading session. A small charge was levied on sales to cover expenses.

The trading clubs were rudimentary clearing houses in a country that by this time was home to the world's first company to attract a large pool of private investors. The Dutch East India Company, or VOC,[6] was founded in March 1602 and granted a monopoly by the Dutch government to trade with Asia. From 1641, it was the only European entity allowed by the Japanese to trade with Japan, which it did through a base on Dejima island, at the port of Nagasaki.

VOC shares were traded on the Amsterdam Stock Exchange and were a favourite of speculators because of fluctuations in the company's dividends.[7] The methods of trading VOC shares in the late 17th century were recorded by Joseph de la Vega, a Portuguese businessman and poet, whose book, *Confusión de Confusiones*, is the first guide to the business of stock markets.[8] De la Vega's account, completed in 1688, just three months before a serious crash in VOC shares, described how they were cleared and settled.

Fully paid up ordinary VOC shares that were traded would be delivered on the 20th of the month and paid for on the 25th. But because units of stock were traded several times during a month, delivery and payment were liable to upset. As de la Vega put it, 'negligence, disorder and confusion have gained ground in the settlement process, for one [investor] neither takes delivery nor pays when one should'. Special brokers or 'rescounters' dealt with this problem. Their business was 'to balance out or rescounter the commitments and to pay and to receive the differences' that arose from the traders' deals.

De la Vega also described a lively trade in small denomination 'ducaton shares' that were created when holders of the large-value shares split them into tenths to offer a form of participation right to small investors. Ducaton trading was highly speculative, attracting 'both sexes, old men, women, and children' who formed a market which was 'as boisterous as it is quick witted'.

The ducaton trades were cleared by an official called the General Cashier who recorded the transactions in a book for a small fee from buyers and sellers. On the first of every month,

---

[5] Gelderblom, Oscar and Jonker, Joost (2005), 'Amsterdam as the cradle of modern futures and options trading, 1550 to 1650'. Also see Chancellor, Edward (1999), *Devil Take the Hindmost*.

[6] VOC is the acronym for Verenigde Oost-Indische Compagnie, the company's name in Dutch.

[7] Den Heijer, Henk (2002), *The VOC and the Exchange*.

[8] The author has drawn on the 'Marketplace Book' edition of *Confusión des Confusiones*, published in 1996 by John Wiley & Sons Inc., in which a translation of de la Vega's text is coupled with an edited version of Charles Mackay's *Extraordinary Popular Delusions and the Madness of Crowds*. This edition includes a very useful introduction to de la Vega's work by Hermann Kellenbenz from 1957.

when the stock exchange clock struck 1.30 P.M., he would calculate a price for the shares on the basis of the traded value of the large VOC shares so that any outstanding transactions could be settled in cash.

These procedures foreshadowed later practices. By calculating and arranging the payment of differences, the Dutch inn-based trading clubs and de la Vega's 'rescounters' developed services similar to those provided by the first commodities clearing houses in the 19th century. When referring to the stock exchange clock, the General Cashier for ducaton share trades fixed a reference price, which is an essential part of any clearing operation.

4.3 THE SPREAD OF CLEARING HOUSES

The Amsterdam Stock Exchange was set up to meet VOC's large appetite for new capital. Its foundation followed the gradual spread in the 16th century of exchanges as permanent meeting places for commercial and financial transactions in other northern European cities. An exchange opened in Antwerp in 1531; London's 'Royal Exchange' followed in 1567.

Once traders concentrated their activities in one place, clearing infrastructures eventually followed suit. The first known clearing house building was the *loge des Changes*, built in Lyons around 1630.

It was in London – with its thriving 18th century banking community – that clearing at a clearing house became an everyday event. In 1773, bankers hired a room in the Five Bells tavern off Lombard Street where their clerks could meet to exchange notes, bills and cheques and settle debts among the City's banks.[9]

The move eliminated the need for the bankers to send clerks to all of each other's premises to collect sums owing to them. Initially, The London Clearing House[10], as the institution became known, seems to have operated like a private club. A permanent committee of bankers was formed to regulate its activities in 1821. Having moved twice to larger rented premises, its first building was constructed in 1833.

For many years membership of the clearing house at Post Office Court, Lombard Street, was restricted to the City's private bankers. After resisting for more than 20 years, it admitted London's corporately owned joint stock banks in 1854 and four years later, in 1858, started clearing cheques drawn on England's country banks.

In 1854, the Bank of England also became a member so that balances between participating banks were settled by transfers among accounts held at the central bank. This development marked an important advance in the organisation of clearing and payments and presaged the very active role that the Bank and other central banks would play in clearing to the present day.

When the economist and philosopher William Stanley Jevons visited the London Clearing House in the 1870s, cheques had become the most popular means of payment in Britain and the largest part of its operations.[11]

Jevons found there were three clearings daily in a plain oblong room in the Lombard Street building. The clearing house settled 'the reciprocal claims of the 26 principal City banks' while 'debts to the average amount of nearly twenty millions sterling per day' were liquidated

[9] According to information from the Cheque & Credit Clearing Company: www.chequeandcredit.co.uk (accessed 3 December 2010).

[10] And as such not to be confused with the 20th century company of that name that now forms part of LCH.Clearnet.

[11] Jevons, William Stanley (1875), *Money and the Mechanism of Exchange*. Jevons gave some examples showing that cheques and bills accounted for 68–97% of banks' payment transactions.

'without the use of a single coin or bank-note'. Some participating banks sent as many as six clerks to the clearings to cope with workplace pressure that, according to Jevons, was 'very great at times'.

His concern was palpable as he described conditions reminiscent of a modern City dealing room:

> The facility which these clerks acquire by practice in making and adding up entries is very great, but the intense headwork performed against time, in an atmosphere far from pure, and in the midst of bustle and noise arising from the corrections shouted from one clerk to another across the room, must be exceedingly trying. Brain disease is occasionally the consequence.

Other clearing houses sprang up in regional cities in the UK to clear cheques and payments. Drawing on the London experience, The New York Clearing House Association was set up in October 1853 to bring order to chaotic payment and settlement procedures among the city's 57 banks. It became a model for bank clearing houses in city after city as the US frontier moved westwards.

But clearing, Jevons noted, did not have to remain the preserve of bankers. 'Wherever a set of traders have numerous reciprocal claims, they may find it desirable to set up their own clearing house,' he observed. One such case was the Railway Clearing House, established in 1842, to settle the work – 'vastly more complicated and various than that of a bankers' clearing house' – that resulted from the multitude of early 19th century British train operating companies running rolling stock over each others' tracks. A 'great house full of accountants at Euston Square' in London settled and adjusted the receipts from through traffic of passengers and goods between stations in regions where different railway companies held sway.[12]

The London Stock Exchange set up a clearing house for brokers in 1874, which in Jevons's words undertook to clear 'not sums of money, but quantities of stock'. Because brokers on the exchange settled their accounts once a fortnight – and monthly in the case of UK government consolidated stock – it followed that they often bought and sold the same stocks many times over in the interval. The clearing house eliminated the need for numerous bilateral stock transfers by obliging each of its members to prepare a statement of the net amount of each stock he[13] should receive from or deliver to each other member. The clearing house manager would then direct debtor members to transfer the necessary stocks to creditor members to close all transactions. The transfers were made from broker to broker rather than to the clearing house. The overall effect was to net the volume of transactions so that 'the quantities actually transferred do not exceed 10% of the whole transactions cleared' bringing significant reductions in payments made on settlement days.

In his book, Jevons made passing reference to the adoption of clearing by the Cotton Brokers' Association of Liverpool to simplify the settlement of forward trades in cotton. This, at the time, was the latest innovation in clearing in Britain. However, unbeknown to Jevons, clearing houses had played an integral role in futures trading for more than a century in a country that was half a world away and which in 1640 isolated itself – economically, culturally and diplomatically – from the West for more than 200 years. That country was Japan.

[12] The Railway Clearing House is reasonably well documented because it soon came under the watchful gaze of parliament and was regulated by the Railway Clearing House Act of 1850.

[13] This was 99 years before the admission of women to the stock exchange on 26 March 1973.

4.4 THE DOJIMA RICE MARKET

In 1730 the Shogunate, which ruled Japan on behalf of its emperor through a succession of military governors, published a decree that turned the Dojima rice market[14] of Osaka into an official exchange.

Largely cut off from outside influences, Japan was at that time a society where prestige resided with the rural, feudal Samurai class but merchants and artisans in the towns were growing more prosperous in an increasingly money-based economy.

Rice was the main crop. Japan's land owners and feudal lords collected a percentage of the crop each year from their tenant farmers as rent and tax. Because they needed money for supplies, weapons and to maintain a presence at court, they would ship surplus rice to Osaka and Edo (modern Tokyo) to raise cash. Land owners began to sell tickets or warehouse receipts (*cho-ai-mai*) to raise ready money against rice that was stored either in the country or in town. Because of the vagaries of the seasons, fluctuations in the harvest and a tendency – shared by nobility throughout the ages – to live beyond their means, the Samurai landlords were soon offering warehouse receipts against future deliveries of rice. These receipts were traded, giving rise to a market for future deliveries of rice centred on Osaka.

The decree of 1730 laid down rules for trading rice warehouse receipts (*cho-ai-mai-kaisho*) that were similar to those of a modern futures exchange and included clearing houses as an integral part of the market infrastructure.[15] They stipulated the following:

- contracts should be of limited duration;
- they should be standardised within that term;
- there should be an agreed grade of rice for each contract period;
- no contract could be carried over into a new contract period.

In addition, all trades were to be cleared through a clearing house with which each trader must have a line of credit.

Thus organised, the market enabled traders and producers to hedge their positions and appears to have been a success. There were 1300 traders registered on the Dojima rice market by 1732, of whom 500 were wholesalers and 800 brokers.[16] There were between 50 and 60 clearing houses and more than 1000 people employed in settling transactions between rice buyers and brokers.[17]

According to Ulrike Schaede, associate professor at the University of California, San Diego, the clearing houses existed originally to change rice into money and keep the deposits of rice merchants. But they started settling transactions as the exchange's business grew. The clearing houses were not allowed to trade on their own account. Instead they took fees and margin on open positions and on receiving margin took responsibility for fulfilling the contract. Thus,

[14] Named after its location in the Dojima River area. Not to be confused with Dejima island in Nagasaki, the base of VOC in Japan from 1641 (see Section 4.2), which was the outside world's only point of access to Japan. Whether the clearing houses of Dojima learned anything about clearing from Dutch traders using Dejima is unknown.

[15] Poitras, Geoffrey (2000), *The Early History of Financial Economics, 1478–1776*, and Teweles, Richard J., Harlow, Charles V. and Stone, Herbert L. (1974), *The Commodity Futures Game* have very similar accounts of the Dojima rice market's rules.

[16] Poitras (2000).

[17] Figures for the scale of clearing activity are drawn from Poitras (2000), and also from Miyamoto, Matao (1999). 'The Dojima Rice Exchange, the world's first commodity futures market', *Journal of Japanese Trade and Industry*; and from remarks by Moscow, Michael H., President and CEO of the Federal Reserve Bank of Chicago to a Joint Conference of the European Central Bank and Chicago Fed on *Issues Related to Central Counterparty Clearing*, Frankfurt.

Schaede says, the merchants could 'settle their positions at the clearing house without regard to the creditworthiness of the ultimate counterparty'.[18]

The Dojima rice market ran into difficulties in the 19th century. The number of clearing houses shrank dramatically to just four: probably, Schaede suggests, because they were very labour intensive and suffered losses accordingly. Between 1830 and 1843, Japan experienced an economic downturn with bad harvests, rice riots and mounting indebtedness. Schaede tells how clearing houses raised commissions and margin requirements to minimise the risk of guaranteeing futures during these years.

Japan's policy of seclusion effectively ended on 8 July 1853 when the 'Black Ships' of US Commodore Matthew Perry entered Tokyo Bay. The Dojima rice market was disrupted by the upheavals that accompanied the ebbing of the Shogun's power and the opening of Japan to the outside world. It survived until 1869, the year after the emperor regained political control of Japan in the Meiji Restoration, when the imperial government suppressed as gambling trading in contracts solely to profit from differences in their price.[19]

The government ordered all exchanges in Japan to be closed while still permitting spot trading in rice. Two years later, the Dojima rice market reopened but its glory days were over. Although fixed term trades were legalised, they were made conditional on the actual delivery of goods in settlement.

Yet, on the evidence available, it seems that the rice market in Osaka had created clearing houses that fulfilled the role of a modern CCP by taking over the counterparty risks of the participants to a trade and so undertaking to complete open trades. This was unknown in Western capitalist countries for nearly three decades after the opening of Japan in 1853.

However, commodities trading was changing in the UK, other parts of Europe and the US, with the gradual emergence of forward trading in contracts 'to arrive', followed later by futures. After a lag, these developments encouraged further progress in clearing.

4.5 FORWARDS AND FUTURES

Britain in the middle of the 19th century was the 'workshop of the world'. As the first country to industrialise, it depended increasingly on imports of raw materials for its mills and factories and food for its expanding urban workforce. The US by this time was an emerging economic power. As it pushed the frontier of settlement and economic development westwards, the US produced all manner of commodities, including grain, cotton, gold and (later) oil, which supplied the cities and factories of its eastern seaboard and export markets in the UK and elsewhere.

In Europe, the industrial revolution and the rapid growth of towns and cities spread outwards from the UK, first to Belgium and then to other countries. Demand for commodities grew. So too did sensitivity in farming communities and among the urban masses to the sharp price movements to which commodities were prone.

[18] Schaede, Ulrike (1983), 'Forwards and futures in Tokugawa-period Japan: A new perspective on the Dojima rice market', *Journal of Banking and Finance*. Also reproduced in Smitka, Michael (ed.) (1998). *The Japanese Economy in the Tokugawa Era, 1600–1868*. Professor Schaede, who made her study of the Dojima rice market and clearing system in the 1980s when a visiting researcher at the Institute for Monetary and Economic Studies at the Bank of Japan, provided additional insights in an email exchange with the author.

[19] Sano, Zensaku and Iura, Sentaro (1931), 'Commodity exchanges in Japan', *The Annals of the American Academy of Political and Social Science*. There is a subtle distinction between trading for differences without intending to deliver the commodity as here, and paying out differences in settlement of a trade as a result of netting, as described earlier in the case of the inn-based trading clubs of 17th century Holland.

It took some time before advances in technology and communications produced changes in the techniques of trading to cope with these challenges. Most commodities and raw materials in Britain were sold 'on the spot' until well into the 19th century, with auctions the most common means by which goods changed hands.[20]

Unreliable transport and the uneven quality of goods were obstacles to purchasing in advance. Moreover, supply chains – from the pioneer farmer sending surplus grain from the US Midwest to the American east coast, or from the cotton plantation in the pre-Civil War south to the factory making cloth in northwest England – sustained a large and varied population of merchants and other middle men with a vested interest in the status quo.

But forward trading, known also as the sale and purchase of commodities 'to arrive', gradually became more established and this, after some delay, led to the development of more organised futures markets and, eventually, clearing houses.

Forward transactions in the European and US economies emerged for much the same reason as did the Dojima rice market in 18th century Japan. Producers and purchasers of agricultural commodities sought to escape the constraints of the seasons through trading methods that enabled protection against price changes by hedging.

Forward trading in commodities was an interim phase in the development of markets from auction houses, where only goods changed hands, to futures markets, where trading in standardised contracts offers the economic benefits of price discovery and risk control as well as abundant opportunity for speculation without participants to a trade having to take delivery of any produce.

As forward markets developed, traders learned to use them as they would later use futures: to hedge positions by entering into offsetting transactions against spot deals and so obtain protection against price swings. However, these markets had drawbacks. Forward markets were designed for the ultimate delivery of specific parcels of physical commodities. There was only limited standardisation of contracts and so the markets were relatively illiquid. Forward trading was prone to market abuse. There were frequent 'corners' and attempted corners, in which a trader would acquire all available stocks of a commodity and hold to ransom all other market participants who had to acquire supplies from the person who had cornered the market in order to settle their trades.

Futures markets were based on more standardised products and general contracts and governed by increasingly well defined rules. Sometimes described as markets in promises, futures markets were more liquid than forward markets, enabling traders to dispose more easily of an obligation arising from a buy or sell contract for a future date by carrying out an opposite transaction for the same date in the future. Liquidity of futures markets improved still further once the markets were supported by clearing houses.

The development of futures trading was aided by improvements in communications, which meant goods could be bought for future delivery with greater confidence. The spread of railways, steam ships and postal services enabled samples to be sent from producer to market in advance of cargos, which also moved much faster than in the days of sail. Purchasers no longer needed to inspect consignments of commodities in their place of arrival before buying them. The development of the electric telegraph quickened the flow of instructions back and forth between markets and producers, with communications between Europe and the US cut to a matter of hours after the successful laying of the transatlantic cable in 1866.

[20] Rees, Graham L. (1972), *Britain's Commodity Markets*.

During the final quarter of the 19th century, futures markets evolved from forward markets on both sides of the Atlantic and gradually eclipsed them.

There is relatively little detailed information about the emergence of early futures markets and their clearing practices. But two 19th century markets – the cotton market in the UK port of Liverpool and grain trading on the Chicago Board of Trade – have left sufficient material to give an idea of how clearing houses developed to meet market needs. In each case, the methods adopted stopped short of CCP-type clearing. But they highlight the emergence of clearing as a vital support for organised futures markets, which was where the first CCPs flourished.

4.6 TRADING AND CLEARING COTTON IN LIVERPOOL

In Britain, the Liverpool cotton trade took the lead in developing trading techniques from spot through forward to futures trading in the second half of the 19th century, helped in part by the creation of a clearing house. It is mainly through the writing of Thomas Ellison,[21] a participant in that market, that we have an idea of how trading and clearing systems emerged.

Until the American Civil War of 1861–65, cotton trading in Liverpool mainly concerned shipments that had already arrived in the port. The trade functioned according to a clearly defined but unwritten code. The merchants who imported the cotton would sell it through selling brokers, while the spinners of Lancashire who used the cotton bought it through buying brokers. Brokers very rarely acted as buyers and sellers. Looking back from the 1880s, Ellison noted there was very little trading in cotton 'to arrive' in Liverpool before the American Civil War.

The war disrupted the cash trade in cotton between the seceding states and England, giving rise to violent price movements. This encouraged the development of a 'to arrive' or forward market to give importers the means of protecting their positions. The forward market thrived on a rich diet of uncertainty and speculation so that by the end of the conflict, forward contracts had, according to Ellison, 'almost entirely superseded speculative transactions in cotton on the spot'.

However, trading in forwards was handicapped by the inherent limitations of forward contracts. Futures contracts enabled cotton importers to hedge their dealings in cotton more effectively. Encouraging the market for futures in Liverpool were the well developed groups of buyers and sellers that generated sufficient speculative interest to provide counterparties for the importers' hedging activities.

For speculators, an attraction of futures trading was the ability to use techniques that avoided any commitments to take in or dispose of actual produce. But such transactions meant that importer and speculator alike would usually be left owing or owed a 'difference' in price between the contracts that they had traded. This difference would be just one of many differences to be settled among the participants in the market.

Sorting out these differences was a serious problem. Contracts changed hands many times and had to be settled between the original parties along a chain. This system of bilateral clearing caused delays and inconvenience, or as Ellison put it, 'wranglings and heart burnings' and 'imprecations'. The result was a movement to reform the market, headed by Joseph B. Morgan, a prominent local broker, who proposed a clearing house. The idea met with resistance from those who feared it could lead to an excess of speculation. Others worried that the clearing

[21] Ellison, Thomas (1886), *The Cotton Trade of Great Britain.*

house managers would gain an insight into the business of the participating firms. But Morgan got his way and the Cotton Market Clearing House went ahead in 1876.

Each day, a member of the clearing house committee would receive in cash all payments or 'differences' for cotton due from those who owed money. Having taken in the money, he then proceeded to pay cash out to those who had 'differences' or payments to receive. The clearing house was structured in such a way as to deny members of the clearing house committee any insight into the business of other companies. 'Barring mistakes, which very rarely occurred, and which were promptly found out, the tills were as empty at the end of each day as at the beginning,' Ellison wrote.

The clearing house was followed by other infrastructure developments. The Cotton Brokers' Bank opened for business on 14 April 1878. Another of Morgan's ideas, the bank eliminated the risk of having cash balances of between £100 000 and £150 000 slopping around the market each day.

According to Ellison, a buying broker who had several payments to make would deposit a sum for the total in the 'Brokers' account'[22] at the Bank of England branch in Liverpool. He would then issue credit vouchers to the selling brokers to whom he owed the payments. The selling brokers would deposit these vouchers with the Cotton Bank and could draw against these deposits either by issuing new credit vouchers to pay other traders or, at the close of clearing, by a cheque on the Bank of England. A credit voucher started by one broker could pass through many firms and settle several accounts during a day, so cutting down the use of cash. At the close of the day, the cash remaining in the Bank of England branch would be transferred by cheque to the last receivers of the credit vouchers.

The system was extended so that spinners and other end-users of cotton could pay money into the Manchester branch of the Bank of England to the credit of the 'Brokers' account' in the Liverpool branch and get their buying brokers in Liverpool to issue credit vouchers to the selling brokers. This cut the need for cash transfers between Manchester and Liverpool. The clearing house and the Cotton Brokers' Bank eventually amalgamated so that, according to Ellison, 'the whole of the payments in connection with "futures" were paid through the Bank, and distributed by "credit vouchers", instead of in cash, over the counter of the clearing house.'

The clearing house had some far-reaching consequences. The Liverpool based merchants, who had managed the supply chain for spot contracts in cotton, were already losing business to brokers who dealt directly with traders in the US after the laying of the transatlantic telegraph cable. The clearing house led to a fall in brokers' fees and sharply increased competition between brokers and merchants. Ellison reported how the merchants were put at a further disadvantage 'when it became absolutely necessary for all "futures" to go through the clearing house, and when the right of using that institution was refused to others than members of the Cotton Brokers' Association'.

Importing merchants wanting to hedge their trades had to pay 1% in commission to the brokers. They reacted by setting up a rival institution: the Liverpool Cotton Exchange in 1881. Rather surprisingly, given the tendency of breakaway trade bodies to spawn long lasting disputes, the brokers' association and the merchants' exchange settled their differences a year later and together formed The Liverpool Cotton Association in which both classes of trader were represented.

---

[22] Ellison refers consistently to a 'Brokers' account', with the apostrophe after the 's' in Brokers, suggesting that the Bank of England operated one account for many brokers.

The cotton association further refined the Liverpool clearing and settlement system by introducing settlement of contracts on fixed dates: first fortnightly and later weekly. This step, pioneered by a voluntary 'Settlement Association' of some 60 brokers and merchant firms in December 1882 and adopted by the cotton association in 1884, followed a number of business failures that were attributed to speculation.

The original rules of the Liverpool clearing house left the collection of brokers' fees and 'differences' until a contract matured by which time speculators could have accumulated significant liabilities. By imposing a limit of one week on the time of contracts to settlement and the introduction of official settlement prices, the new system of 'periodic settlement' amounted to 'marking to market' once a week. The official prices enabled members to draw up statements with details of all contracts whether closed or still open. Association members would give these statements to each other on the day before settlement day and, in this way, keep tabs on contracts that were still open and so avoid becoming over-exposed.

The Liverpool system of clearing marked a significant step towards the development of the modern clearing house that limited counterparty risk. But there were some omissions. There was no system of guaranteeing the execution of contracts to seller or buyer. Although periodic settlement allowed an overview of 'differences' and so created some transparency about speculative positions in the market, it provided less protection than margining. However, the Liverpool system may be seen as an interim step towards central counterparty clearing.

4.7 FUTURES AND CLEARING IN CHICAGO

Just as the American Civil War boosted the forward trade in cotton in Liverpool, so it also gave a huge impetus to the trading of grain and other farm products such as hogs from the American Midwest among the northern states of the Union.

Trade between the west and east of the US was already growing rapidly. Exchanges and forward markets emerged in both northern and southern states between the 1820s and the Civil War as the country grew and the frontier moved westwards. A key event was the completion in 1825 of the Erie Canal, which linked the Great Lakes at Buffalo via the Hudson River to New York City and accelerated the spread of grain cultivation west of the Appalachian mountains.

The canal transformed the western New York state from a frontier zone into a prosperous farming community, which for 20 years was the wheat and milling centre of the US. The canal made the Great Lakes region part of New York City's hinterland, diverting commerce of the northern Midwest states away from the Mississippi and the south in the process.[23] Just as importantly, it opened a route for settlers from the eastern states and abroad to reach the Great Lakes and move further west into fertile prairie country. By the 1850s, nearly four million people, or just under a fifth of the US population, lived in the north central states of the Union.

The success of the Erie Canal triggered a boom in canal building around the Great Lakes region. Railroads followed canals, further opening up the prairies to settlers and grain in the 1850s. New financial and commercial infrastructures followed the canals and railroads.

A 'Board of Trade' or exchange was set up in Buffalo, New York, in 1844[24] to trade grain and this appears to have become a centre for forward sales within three years. Other exchanges

[23] By 1836, more grain was shipped via the Great Lakes and via Buffalo through the Erie Canal to the east than south along the Mississippi to New Orleans according to Santos, Joseph (2008), 'A History of Futures Trading in the United States', *EH Net Encyclopaedia*, Whaples, R. (ed.); http://eh.net/encyclopaedia/article/Santos.futures (accessed 3 December 2010).

[24] Moser, James T. (1994), 'Origins of the modern exchange clearinghouse', Working Paper Series, *Issues in Financial Regulation*.

were set up in transport hubs such as Cleveland, Detroit, Chicago and Milwaukee as grain cultivation moved west. The most important of these was the Board of Trade in Chicago, founded in 1848.

When Chicago obtained city status in 1837 it had a population of little more than 4000. Although built on a swamp, geography predestined Chicago for greatness. The city was located at the Lake Michigan end of a short portage between a tributary of the Mississippi and the Great Lakes water system. A year after its incorporation as a city, the first ship with a cargo of grain set off from Chicago to take the Great Lakes route to Buffalo. By the late 1850s, after the city had been linked to the Illinois Central Railroad and routes to the east, Chicago became the premier grain hub of the Midwest. In 1860 its population exceeded 100 000 and it was shipping east the equivalent of 20 million bushels of grain a year.[25]

The Midwest boards of trade performed a variety of functions. They initially focused on resolving local commercial disputes but soon established a system of grades, standards and inspections which made stores of grain fungible. This was an important pre-condition for the development of forward, and eventually, futures trading.

The first known 'time contract' in Chicago dates from 13 March 1851 when a deal was sealed for 3000 bushels of corn to be delivered to Chicago in June at one US cent below the cash market price.[26] An important step towards regulating the market came in 1859 when the state of Illinois recognised the Chicago Board of Trade (CBOT) as a state chartered private association, which meant it could set rules for business conduct and arbitrate and settle disputes as if it were a circuit court.[27]

In March 1863, the CBOT's members adopted the first rules for trade in forwards on the exchange, which included suspension for failing to comply with the terms of a contract. In the following years, the CBOT introduced more rules to protect against counterparty defaults. These included margin requirements from May 1865, which at this stage were not mandatory,[28] and in 1873 a requirement that any member failing to meet a contract must make a declaration of 'his financial condition on oath to the Directory of the Board' on pain of expulsion from the association.

These were important steps in the transformation of forward 'to arrive' contracts into standardised contracts that could be regarded as futures. The developments in Chicago coincided with improvements in rail links, telegraph communications and grain storage. Although the date of the first US futures contract is a matter of dispute among academics, there is a consensus that the CBOT could be considered a futures exchange by the mid-1870s.

However, the CBOT lacked one of the key supports of a modern futures exchange – an effective system of clearing. That changed in September 1883: following a big contract dispute, the exchange required trading firms to make a daily statement of their debits and credits on deliveries and other settlements and pay over or receive the balance due. The CBOT created a clearing house to make sure the counterparties realising gains or losses received the appropriate credits and debits.

The CBOT's clearing house was not a forerunner of today's CCPs, unlike the European clearing houses described in Chapters 5 and 6 and the later 'complete clearing houses' of the US covered in Chapter 7. It had no capital stock or assets of any kind. It played no part in

[25] Thistlethwaite, Frank (1955), *The Great Experiment*.

[26] Teweles, Richard J., Harlow, Charles V. and Stone, Herbert L. (1974).

[27] Lurie, Jonathan (1979), *The Chicago Board of Trade 1859–1905*. The author is indebted to Dennis Dutterer for pointing out that the procedures of the CBOT are often cited as the forerunner of the concepts of self regulation embedded in US law.

[28] See Section 7.1.

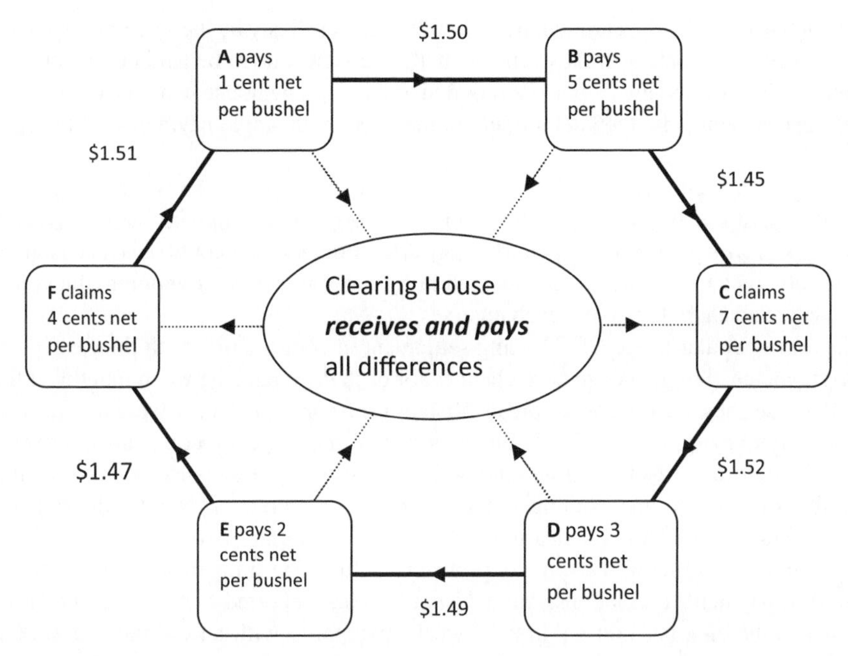

Figure 4.1 Ring Settlement in Chicago: A, B, C, D, E and F are Clearing House Member Firms. The dollar amounts are the selling prices per bushel of the preceding clearing house members and the buying prices of the following clearing house members in the Ring. The payments to and from the clearing house follow the dotted lines

(Based on The Federal Trade Commission Report on the Grain Trade, 1920.)

the physical delivery of a commodity if a futures contract matured. It was a department of the CBOT and viewed by some commentators as little more than a 'post office' that handled the exchanging of cheques and margin certificates among exchange members.[29]

But it facilitated netting, clearing and settlement of offsetting trades. At the simplest level it provided an infrastructure for 'direct settlement', which was where two exchange members would find at the end of a day's trading that they had offsetting positions with each other as buyers and sellers of the same amount of the same contract. In this case, as members of the clearing house, they would use the clearing house to settle any differences owing and owed between them that arose from variations in the prices at which the trades were made.

The existence of the clearing house also encouraged the development of 'ring settlement', where three or more clearing house members that were buyers and sellers of the same amounts of the same contract would use the clearing house to pay the differences due or collectible between the participants of the ring.

Rings would be formed if a chain of buyers and sellers could form a loop. They would be put together after the close of trading by settlement clerks employed by the various trading firms. The clerks would note the quantities bought and sold and, after checking with their firms, congregate in noisy groups the following morning to work out the offsetting contracts and differences due for settlement. The differences were calculated with reference to a settlement

[29] Boyle, James Ernest (1920), *Speculation and the Chicago Board of Trade*.

price, which was established around the close of trading each day by the secretary of the CBOT and 'conspicuously posted' in the exchange hall. The sums due to be paid or collected by the members of the various rings would be reported to the clearing house, which would receive all the differences owing and then debit or credit members with single payments for the amounts due.[30]

The rings were entirely voluntary groups and some companies chose not to participate. Those firms that did participate would in practice form many rings in one day. The trades cleared by a ring may have been open for many days. Equally they could have been agreed the previous day. As a result, the amount cleared in a given day bore no relation to the volume of trades conducted each day on the exchange.

Rings were popular at the CBOT. Ring settlement in coordination with the clearing house eliminated the need to give or receive cheques for each difference between individual trading firms. Because they enabled widespread offsetting of contracts, rings were set up to avoid having to put up margins on trades.[31] But a successful ring depended on counterparties being able to substitute and offset positions among themselves using the same contracts to minimise the number of transactions resulting in the payment of differences. Neither the ring system nor the structure of the CBOT's clearing house mitigated counterparty risk.

That said, the clearing house quickly proved of value. One immediate consequence was a sharp fall in payment transactions. The *Chicago Tribune* reported that 26 986 cheques were processed in the clearing house's first 14 weeks compared with an estimated 260 000 that would have been needed previously. This was no one-off: in its first nine months the clearing house processed 76 500 cheques compared with around 740 000 under the old system.[32]

In 1884, the clearing house took over responsibility for registering trades, performing this task when trades were executed rather than a day later as previously.

But although such innovations added to the efficiency of the market and lowered costs, the ring system had drawbacks. The chain of buyers and sellers in a ring was only as strong as its weakest link. In 1902, the bankruptcy of George Phillips, a CBOT member, impacted on the accounts of 748 CBOT members or more than 42% of the membership of the exchange.[33]

Ringing was by this time the method of clearing used in most US commodity exchanges. Its failings in the Phillips case highlighted the benefits of alternative methods. One such method was 'complete clearing' where a clearing house set up with adequate funds to protect traders stepped in as the buyer to every seller and the seller to every buyer, thus eliminating the risk that a trader could suffer loss through the default of a counterparty, while establishing levels of margin that protected the clearing house from default.

Complete clearing is known as central counterparty clearing today. Its adoption in the US came some years after the development in Europe of clearing houses that performed the same function by guaranteeing trades against counterparty risk.

As described in Chapter 7, complete clearing began with a whimper rather than a bang in the US when traders at the Minneapolis Chamber of Commerce, the city's grain exchange, set up a clearing association separate from the exchange in 1891. In North America, the practice spread slowly and largely unnoticed by contemporaries as other clearing associations were established to handle grain trading in Kansas City, Missouri, in 1899; in Winnipeg, Canada, in 1901; and in Duluth, Minnesota, in 1909.

---

[30] Federal Trade Commission (1920), 'Report of the Federal Trade Commission on the grain trade, Volume 5'.

[31] Federal Trade Commission (1920).

[32] CCorp (2006), *A History: Trusting, Growing, Leading, Clearing*.

[33] Moser (1994).

Table 4.1 Trading in the main cereals on US futures markets: Estimated volumes, in millions of bushels, in five year periods

	Chicago	Minneapolis	Kansas City	St Louis	Other
1884–1888	108 500	n.a.	500	1100	7900
1889–1893	81 000	500	600	700	7000
1894–1898	98 000	2000	800	500	6300
1899–1903	81 900	3000	1500	1200	9600
1904–1908	72 200	5500	2200	1500	13 000
1909–1913	65 000	5000	2900	1600	5300
1914–1918	83 400	4900	3300	1200	4200

Source: FTC (1920). Report of the Federal Trade Commission on the Grain Trade, Washington DC.

These were small exchanges compared with the CBOT, which accounted for 80% of futures trading in the US. It would be 1926 before the CBOT used a modern CCP. One reason was the fear that complete clearing could contravene the state of Illinois' strict anti-gambling legislation.

4.8 ANTI-GAMBLING SENTIMENT IN THE US

Gambling was a contentious and emotionally charged political issue in the US and Europe in the later 19th century. The opposition to gambling among moral reformers may not have won universal support, but it resonated sufficiently among the increasingly educated and enfranchised, aspiring working and middle classes to emerge as a powerful political force in times of economic hardship in the US and Germany and, to a certain extent, in Britain.

Chicago was a boisterous city. But large swathes of the Midwest were settled by god-fearing folk from Protestant northern Europe and Puritan New England. They and many of the people they elected to public office looked askance at practices on the Chicago futures market.

Attempts to corner the market were legion. No fewer than seven corners or attempts were reported on the grain market in 1868. It was a particularly egregious corner in the market for lard that triggered the 1883 CBOT reforms that resulted in ring clearing. Bucket-shops proliferated in the shadow of the exchange. These were venues for making illegal bets based on prices quoted on the exchange without any intention to acquire or deliver the underlying commodity. Until coded messages were permitted, there were attempts by unscrupulous traders to gain information and manipulate markets by bribing the operators of the telegraph system and the transatlantic cable.

It is doubtful whether, as individuals, many farmers in Chicago's hinterland were averse to speculation. But it was axiomatic among farming communities that gambling on the nation's commodity exchanges was the source of many of their ills. Western farmers were chronically burdened with debt, made worse by declining grain prices from the 1880s and a severe economic depression in the US in the 1890s. Sharp downwards movements in price were invariably ascribed to the nefarious activities of 'plungers' on the nation's grain exchanges.

The *Farmers Voice*, a Bloomington, Illinois, newspaper, captured the mood in its edition of 21 March 1896: 'It is not too much to say that our Boards of Trade are the worst nest of gamblers that there is in this country. They are the most subtle, the most infamously designing crowd, the most audacious robbers of the farmers that this country has ever produced.'[34]

[34] As quoted by Lord Stanley of Alderley in a debate on futures markets in the British House of Lords on 1 May 1896 and reported by Hansard of that date.

The hostility towards futures trading in the US was reflected in numerous, failed attempts to pass anti-gambling legislation in the US Congress as well as in Illinois' anti-gambling laws that made illegal all trading without intent to receive or make delivery of goods.

The Illinois laws prompted fears as to the legal validity of the CBOT's ring system of clearing. There was concern that the courts might take ring settlement as proof that trading on the exchange was 'simply a gambling in differences'. So long as the ring system of clearing operated under a cloud, the prevailing view was that complete clearing would be impossible in Chicago.

In May 1905 – more than 20 years after the establishment of the CBOT's clearing house – the legality of futures trading and clearing came before the US Supreme Court in the case of the 'Board of Trade versus The Christie Grain and Stock Company'.

By a majority, the court backed futures contracts and the Chicago method of ring clearing as legitimate business activities. As spokesman for the majority, Justice Oliver Wendell Holmes, was unperturbed that a futures contract made in good faith for actual delivery might commonly be closed out and settled by the payment of differences. He wrote: 'It is nonetheless a serious business contract for a legitimate and useful purpose that it may be offset before the time of delivery in case delivery should not be needed or desired.' He noted: 'Set-off has all the effects of delivery. The ring settlement is simply a more complex case of the same kind.'[35]

But although futures contracts were judged to differ from wagers, it would take another 20 years, five votes by the CBOT membership and heavy pressure from the US federal government before the CBOT finally introduced a CCP.

The lost votes reflected members' fears that complete clearing could result in a leaking of confidential commercial information to rivals as well as a feeling that it was safer to stay with a system explicitly approved by the Supreme Court. Even after the Board of Trade Clearing Corp (BOTCC) began operating on 4 January 1926, Illinois gambling laws would impinge on the activities of Chicago's exchanges and clearing houses until the 1980s.

In the often difficult boom and bust conditions of the late 19th century, anti-gambling sentiment also posed problems for nascent futures markets and their clearing houses in many European countries.

France had fewer scruples than most. Futures trading in coffee and cotton developed quickly from the 1870s onwards in the French port city of Le Havre, where a clearing house that performed the same risk-management functions as today's CCPs was launched in 1882.

[35] Board of Trade v Christie Grain & Stock Co, 198 US 236, decided 8 May 1905.

5
Innovation in Europe

5.1 BREAKTHROUGH IN LE HAVRE

The founding of the *Caisse de Liquidation des Affaires en Marchandises* in Le Havre in November 1882 marked a revolutionary departure in the way clearing was conducted and managed as a business.

Set up to support the city's recently established commodity futures markets, the *Caisse* in Le Havre established a commercial lead over all European rivals by guaranteeing the contracts that it registered. Within a decade the other leading commercial centres of northwestern Europe had been forced to follow Le Havre's example and create clearing houses that supported futures exchanges with a guarantee function, often in the teeth of fierce opposition from established trading interests.

In the 1880s, the world was in a phase of development with similarities to that a century later. Its leading economies were experiencing an early form of globalisation, spurred on by industrialisation, international trade and faster and more effective communications. The absence of major wars in Europe between 1871 and 1914 helped.

Le Havre was a fast growing and busy port.[1] The Paris basin was its immediate hinterland and it had well developed trade links to the Americas and the Pacific. It was one of Europe's leading importers of coffee, reflecting France's position as the world's third largest consumer of coffee before the First World War. It was also continental Europe's main port for importing US cotton – a legacy of France's role in the American War of Independence when it helped American exporters circumvent a British embargo. By the 1830s, Le Havre imported around 15% of each year's American cotton crop.

But from the middle of the 19th century, the established methods of importing these commodities were increasingly problematic for the port's closely knit community of merchants, who imported the goods, and its brokers, who bought them from the merchants for selling on to consumers inland. The difficulties led them to develop futures trading and a revolutionary method of clearing.

Traditionally, Le Havre's importers bought specific consignments of coffee from merchants in Brazil and Haiti, which the importers paid for with money borrowed from banks. By the 1860s, this practice was coming under strain. Rising import volumes to satisfy the French consumers' appetite for coffee required a greater commitment of capital. Moreover, prices became more volatile, reflecting the faster reactions of speculators to the greatly increased flow of news about commodities that resulted from improved communications. These developments exposed importers to greater risk.

[1] The city's population more than doubled from 56 500 inhabitants in 1853 to 130 200 in 1901.

One solution adopted by the port's coffee importers was to make the merchants in the exporting countries accept forward contracts with a fixed price 'to arrive' at the port. The importer would hope to take profitable delivery or else minimise the risk of adverse price movements by selling the 'to arrive' contracts before the coffee was unloaded in Le Havre. Around the 1870s, these 'to arrive' coffee contracts became sufficiently standardised to be considered as futures. The appearance of tradable futures contracts allowed the importer to buy coffee once more in the exporting country and hedge the purchase in Le Havre, thus transferring the risk of adverse price movements to speculators.

In the case of cotton, the American Civil War confronted the merchants of Le Havre with the same sharp price fluctuations as their competitors in Liverpool, causing the ruin of many trading houses and spinners.

As in Liverpool, the cotton importers of Le Havre adopted 'to arrive' contracts to provide some protection against price fluctuations and began to trade these. They immediately ran into problems of quality.

The cotton making up the 'to arrive' contracts varied too much to guarantee a consistent quality for the spinners. Consequently the merchants and spinners were unwilling to set too precise standards for fear that the resulting market would be too narrow and illiquid. They overcame this difficulty in the 1870s by agreeing a standard quality of cotton as a basis for futures trading and a scale of price differentials to encompass different grades of cotton on delivery.

After these changes, trading in the two commodities for future delivery grew, helped in the case of cotton by the adoption in 1877 of a first set of rules for a futures market in France. The regulations fixed the number of bales per contract at 50 and were thus a step towards the substitutability or 'fungibility' of contracts.

By 1880, the brokers and merchants of Le Havre were looking for ways to strengthen the city's trade in futures. They came up with the idea of a clearing house that would guarantee the fulfilment of contracts. On 6 November 1882, the *Caisse de Liquidation des Affaires en Marchandises* was incorporated as a limited company with a capital of 2 million francs, with many of the port's leading traders among its owners.

Quite why Le Havre pioneered this development is unclear. Given their long history of financial innovation and their role in the evolution of clearing, one might have expected markets in London or Amsterdam to take the lead. Instead the traders and merchants of these cities were forced to react to the developments in the French port city, just as were their counterparts in Paris, Marseilles, Antwerp and Rotterdam, where new-style clearing houses were created in the 1880s.

According to Robert Lacombe, who wrote a history of Le Havre's futures markets and clearing house just before the Second World War, the creation of the *Caisse* followed a visit to the US by one of Le Havre's leading traders, a Mr Le Normand. Le Normand was inspired by a visit to the New York Coffee Exchange, which was founded in 1882 and had a clearing house. Le Normand returned to France and the result was the *Caisse*, 'an organism even more perfect than the American equivalents of the time,' according to Lacombe.[2]

[2] Lacombe, Robert (1939), *La Bourse de Commerce du Havre (Marchés de Coton et de Café)*. Lacombe was a Banque de France official based in Le Havre. He drew not only on his own expertise but a large number of documents that appear not to have survived the 80% destruction of the city and port areas by German and allied bombardment during the war. A copy of Lacombe's book is preserved in the Le Havre City Archives.

Several European commentators in the 1880s and early 1890s wrote that the New York Coffee Exchange clearing house had a guarantee function.[3] There is strong evidence, however, that this was not the case.[4] This author's researches suggest that it was not until 1916 that complete clearing was adopted for coffee trading in New York.

If the US was not the intellectual source of Le Havre's clearing house, could the inspiration have come from Japan? There is circumstantial evidence – but no more – to allow the hypothesis that the clearing practices of the Dojima rice market may have influenced the foundation of futures trading and the clearing house in Le Havre.

Relations between Japan and France grew close after the US forced Japan to open up to the outside world. In October 1858, France and Japan signed a treaty of 'peace, friendship and commerce'.

With the US embroiled in its Civil War, in the 1860s France exercised more influence over Japan than any other foreign power.[5] It gave military support to the Shogunate in its declining years and managed to maintain an influential position after the Meiji restoration.

Economic links flourished. France became the biggest importer of Japanese silk and relied on Japanese silk worms to revive its industry after disease ravaged its own production. Japan participated in the Paris World Fair of 1867, which was visited by the Shogun's younger brother. The links continued to grow through the 1870s, with France exporting silk making machinery to Japan and Japan exhibiting at the 1878 Paris World Fair. In addition, Japanese art influenced the French Impressionists.

In these circumstances, the possibility that clearing house techniques filtered through to France from Japan cannot be ruled out, although equally traders in Le Havre could have come up with the idea of adding guarantees to existing practices without external prompting.

Whatever its origins, the *Caisse de Liquidation* in Le Havre became a great success. The introduction of its special type of clearing for coffee and cotton futures was followed by new rules and laws that helped bring greater standardisation and legal certainty to those markets.

In January 1883, Le Havre's cotton traders agreed rules specifying a weight of 11 000 pounds of cotton per contract. In August that year the first rules for a coffee futures market were drawn up for contracts of Santos beans. Regulations for futures trading in coffee from Haiti followed 15 months later.

In March 1885 a law was passed that gave strong support to futures trading and clearing houses by specifying that futures contracts could not be challenged under the anti-gambling provisions of Article 1965 of the French Civil Code, which prohibited the recovery in the courts of debts arising from gaming or wagering. The act stated that all organised securities or produce exchanges were assumed to be legal, adding that: 'No individual may escape from an obligation incurred on such an exchange by availing himself of Article 1965 of the Civil Code, even when the obligation is determined solely by the difference between two prices.'[6]

For good measure, France's final court of appeal, the *Cour de Cassation*, ruled in 1898 that the law prevented judges from enquiring into the intentions of parties to a trade and that all cases of speculation on organised exchanges should be considered legal.

[3] Not least the *Financial Times* in its first ever edition, of 13 February 1888, in a front page article headlined 'Mincing Lane in feeble form'.

[4] See Section 7.3.

[5] Storry, Richard (1960), *A History of Modern Japan*.

[6] De Lavergne, A. (1931), 'Commodity Exchange in France', *The Annals of the American Academy of Political and Social Science*.

5.2 THE FUNCTIONING OF THE *CAISSE*

The *Caisse*, as constituted in Le Havre, was close to the markets that it served but theoretically independent. Set up as a private limited company, it drew its income from fees that it levied on the contracts that it registered and guaranteed. It played no part in the negotiation and conclusion of futures contracts. There was no mandatory regulation for traders to register their trades with the *Caisse* and, in its turn, the *Caisse* was free to refuse to register contracts put to it.

The system had an effect similar to that of a modern CCP and worked as follows. The *Caisse* would register contracts, setting down all the details, at which point it would accept deposits from the buyers and sellers alike. These would be the equivalent of initial margin in a modern CCP. The deposits would be paid into a bank account opened by the *Caisse* in the traders' names. On opening the account, the trader would undertake to transfer deposits requested by the *Caisse*, which could be altered by a decision of its board of management. Once the initial deposit was accepted, the contract would be guaranteed by the *Caisse*. The *Caisse* would inform the traders by sending them copies of the registration and guarantee which served as proof that it had assumed responsibility for the trade.

To protect itself, the *Caisse* insisted that any person or company opening an account must be registered with the city's Chamber of Commerce and approved by the *Caisse's* managing board. The board reserved the right to order certain traders to pay more than the standard rates of initial deposit.

To further cover the *Caisse* against risk, it could order traders whose positions showed losses to pay on a daily basis an additional margin that would reflect the difference between the price agreed by the trader and the prevailing official price posted on the exchange. Although the *Caisse* could take in the equivalent of variation margin in this way, it was not obliged to transfer in cash any credits accruing to traders whose positions were making profits.

The *Caisse* took no initial deposit where a trader registered offsetting buy and sell contracts for the same month. It levied a reduced initial deposit for buy and sell contracts in the same commodity for delivery in different months. It allowed no margin offset for clients who were long in one commodity and short in another.

In principle, the *Caisse* expected the margins to be paid in cash. But when Lacombe wrote his history of the *Caisse*, its managing board could approve the use of listed securities as collateral at 75% of their value. It was also prepared to accept warrants for the delivery of a commodity that had been endorsed in the *Caisse's* favour, and even guarantees, although in such cases it reserved the right to call for cash at any time.

A trader with buy and sell contracts for the same commodity with the same month of delivery could liquidate these at any time before maturity for a fee, thus realising profits or stemming losses.

When a contract ran to maturity, the seller of the contract would provide the *Caisse* with an endorsed transfer document. The *Caisse* would then run through the list of buyers of the commodity that remained on its books for the month of delivery until it found one that wanted to take the goods in question. The acquirer of the goods – who would almost certainly not be the buyer in the original futures trade – would then get in touch with the seller to arrange delivery. The guarantee of the *Caisse* would remain in place until the operation had been concluded with delivery and payment completed.

At this point, another institution, Le Havre's Chamber of Arbitration, might get involved if there was a dispute or a need to determine any adjustments in payment to reflect deviations from the standard quality of the contract of the goods delivered. *In extremis*, the *Caisse* might

Table 5.1 Shipments of Santos coffee (in 60 kg bags)

Year	To Hamburg	To Le Havre
1876–81	321 200	181 900
1881–85	359 500	520 900
1886–91	649 000	489 600

Source: Brockhaus Konversationslexikon, 14th edition, 1892–95

find itself having to supply the goods if the consignment provided by the seller was not up to scratch. Similarly, if the acquirer of the goods was unable to find the money to pay for the delivery, the *Caisse* might step in at this stage as buyer and take the goods into one of its own warehouses.

In the event of a default, the *Caisse* could liquidate all positions in the defaulter's account without formality or delay. If necessary it could take on an administrator's role and manage the affairs of the defaulter in Le Havre and even abroad in order to reduce its liabilities and liquidate its positions.

In legal terms, the *Caisse* did not see itself as a buyer to every seller and a seller to every buyer and in this respect it differed from later US clearing houses. Its statutes, as reported by Lacombe, stated that it did not substitute itself for the counterparties in a trade. Instead, and despite its sweeping powers in the event of a default, it saw itself as acting on its clients' behalf as an agent or proxy.

The *Caisse's* early success encouraged the establishment of a rival organisation in the city in 1884.[7] Happily for the *Caisse's* owners, this proved a short lived venture and the newcomer soon merged with the original *Caisse*, which modified its name slightly to *Caisse de Liquidation des Affaires en Marchandises au Havre*.

In 1883, its first year of operations, the *Caisse* registered contracts worth 185 million francs.[8] Four years later in 1887, its registrations were valued at 2478 million francs and its capital was doubled to 4 million francs.

By this time, the Le Havre model of a *Caisse de Liquidation* was being copied in trading centres throughout western Europe. The city's pioneering clearing house and futures exchange helped Le Havre replace Hamburg as Europe's leading market for coffee for some years in the 1880s[9] (see also Table 5.1) and become a supplier of coffee to much of continental Europe: a position it held until the First World War.[10] During this period, the *Caisse* also took to clearing other commodities including indigo, wool, pepper and copper.

5.3 EUROPE FOLLOWS LE HAVRE'S LEAD

It took about five years before other European centres set up their own versions of the *Caisse de Liquidation* pioneered in Le Havre, whereupon the rivals came thick and fast.

Paris created its own *Caisse de Liquidation* in 1887 to guarantee bargains in futures markets, with a strong focus on sugar. Similar clearing houses were set up in that year to guarantee

[7] This may have been based on an earlier clearing house, that was founded in 1867 to register and keep track of trades in cotton and other commodities in the city's cash produce markets, before futures trading was established.

[8] In the years before the First World War, there were 25 Francs to the British Pound, the main international trading currency.

[9] Becker, Ursula (2002), *Kaffee Konzentration: Zur Entwicklung und Organisation des Hanseatischen Kaffeehandels.*

[10] Rufenacht, Charles (1955), *Le Café et les Principaux Marchés de Matieres Premieres.*

coffee futures transactions in Marseilles and Antwerp as well as in Hamburg, where the new-style clearing house, known as a *Warenliquidationskasse*, also began clearing beet sugar early in 1888.

In February 1888, the London Produce Clearing House (LPCH) – the forerunner of LCH – was incorporated and began clearing coffee futures on 1 May 1888 and sugar contracts 11 weeks later. On the day LPCH opened for business, so too did the *Amsterdamsche Liquidatiekas* (ALK).

The long standing commercial rivalry between Amsterdam and Rotterdam ensured that the Netherlands would have two new-style clearing houses albeit with the functional part of their names spelt differently. Two weeks after ALK cleared its first coffee contracts on 1 May 1888, the *Rotterdamsche Likwidatiekas* opened its doors. In September 1889, Germany's second largest sugar market in Magdeburg followed Hamburg's lead and set up its own modern clearer with share capital of 3 million marks.

From the evidence that survives,[11] it appears that the techniques adopted by the various European clearing houses set up in the late 1880s to guarantee trades against counterparty risk differed little from those developed in Le Havre. The early by-laws and regulations of LPCH were modelled closely on those of the original French *Caisse* and the *Warenliquidationskasse* in Hamburg. LPCH guaranteed the contracts that it registered for a fee.

But although the new European clearing houses operated in much the same way, the motives for creating them differed, as did their ownership structures and governance.

Most, including LPCH and the Hamburg *Warenliquidationskasse*, were created to combat the competitive threat from Le Havre once it had proved successful. By contrast, the decision to set up the *Magdeburger Liquidationskasse* came after a speculative price bubble burst in the summer of 1889, ruining many companies.[12] The 'Magdeburg Sugar Crash' prompted the town's surviving brokers to seek the greater security against risk in a clearing house.

The new-style clearing houses were not popular with all traders. In Amsterdam and Hamburg, for example, the backers of futures markets with clearing houses had to overcome resistance from established traders and existing trade bodies.

The ALK in Amsterdam was set up only after a split between the founders and the majority of members of the city's recently created coffee traders' association.[13] On 22 December 1887, the association rejected a proposal to set up a futures market and new-style clearing house. Undeterred, the main promoter of the plan – an energetic trader called Ernst Alexander Bunge – sent a circular to 22 like-minded traders on Christmas Eve, inviting them to a meeting on 29 December in 'Tot Nut van't Algemeen', a well known hostelry. Even though it was the middle of the festive season, he was able to rally sufficient support to re-launch the project for

[11] Clearing house regulations and by-laws give the best insight into the operations of the European clearing houses in the late 19th century. Copies of LPCH's *Regulations for Coffee Future Delivery Business*, May 1888, and *Regulations for Future Delivery in Rio Coffee*, July 1893, have survived. The methods of the *Caisse* and *Warenliquidationskasse* were also described in the 1896 US work, *Speculation on the Stock and Produce Exchanges of the United States* by Henry Crosby Emery and in the German encyclopaedia *Brockhaus Konversationslexikon*, 14th edition, published 1892–95.

[12] Eberhardt, Jörg and Mayrhofer, Thomas (2002), 'Die Entwicklung der Magdeburger Börse', in *Jahresbericht, Studentischer Börsenverein Magdeburg e V*, 2001–2.

[13] Geljon, P.A. (1988), 'Termijnhandel in Nederland', published in *Termijnhandel en termijnmarkten*, Deventer, Kluwer. This account of clearing house developments in the Netherlands also draws on a telephone conversation with Piet A. Geljon on 4 June 2009 and the following additional documentary sources: the 50th annual report of ALK for the year 1937; the 1987 Annual Report of Bank Mees & Hope NV. In the latter, Geljon wrote a summary of events in 1887–8 to mark the centenary of the Amsterdam and Rotterdam clearing houses, which later became part of the Mees & Hope banking group.

a coffee futures market with a separately capitalised, for-profit clearing house independent of the coffee association.

The ALK was formally established in April 1888 with a nominal capital of one million florins of which 300 000 florins was placed, mainly with its founding directors. Relations were quickly repaired between ALK and the coffee association. The clearing house was soon clearing other products – cotton in 1890, tin in 1891 and pepper in 1892 – and developing bigger ambitions.

From the beginning, the ALK demonstrated an independent and strongly entrepreneurial streak – in contrast to its neighbour, the *Rotterdamsche Likwidatiekas*, which was set up on the initiative of the Rotterdam Commodity Trade Association.

The Rotterdam clearer avoided competing with the country's banks. In 1894, by contrast, the ALK allowed traders using it to have overdraft facilities and began to provide loans. This proved to be the first step towards ALK becoming a bank that specialised in commodity-based financing alongside clearing. In 1895, ALK increased its paid up capital to 500 000 florins before doubling this to 1 million florins the following year. Further capital increases followed.[14]

The examples of Amsterdam and Rotterdam show how the business practices of the new European clearing houses could vary according to local laws and circumstances within a small area.

Some features were shared by all the new clearing houses, however. They all needed relatively strong financial backing because they were in the business of guaranteeing against risk. They also required clearly defined contractual relationships with the markets they served and the traders who operated on those markets. In general, the clearing house would only register trades transacted by a broker authorised to operate on the market in question. The broker, in turn, would normally be obliged to conduct all his trades with the clearing house.

Many long established traders found such conditions onerous. Contemporaries described how Hamburg's inherently conservative coffee traders embraced only with considerable reluctance the idea of a futures market backed by a clearing house that guaranteed trades.[15]

But they felt they had no choice. The spread of Le Havre-style clearing houses in Europe in the 1880s reflected the realisation among competitors that the French port had established a powerful comparative advantage through the *Caisse* taking over counterparty risk from futures traders. The coffee futures market in Le Havre – backed by its clearing house – increased its turnover to such an extent in its first years of operation that Hamburg's traders feared their market might decline into a mere centre for trans-shipping consignments of coffee.

Others found the economic arguments in favour of the new-style clearing houses compelling. In 1894, Max Weber, the German political economist and sociologist, described in an essay how clearing houses that guaranteed trades against counterparty risk triggered a virtuous circle of growth.[16] According to Weber, the removal of counterparty risk for speculators led to 'an enormous widening of the market' in terms of turnover of futures traded and the number of participating investors. Increased futures trading in turn promoted growth of the financial centres in which futures markets were based and attracted more spot trading in

[14] ALK's paid up capital was increased in stages from 500 000 florins in 1895 to 3 million in 1912 and 8 million in 1926. Although it later cleared other products, ALK eventually evolved into a bank. It changed its name to Amsterdamsche Goederen-Bank in 1940 after the German occupation of the Netherlands in the Second World War and the related closure of Dutch commodity markets.

[15] Becker (2002).

[16] Weber, Max (1988), 'Die Börse', in *Gesammelte Aufsätze zur Soziologie und Sozialpolitik.*

the physical commodities or underlying securities to these centres. Finally, the growth of such financial centres increased the political clout of the countries in which they were located to the detriment of competitors that had not embraced futures markets supported by the new breed of clearing house.

It needs to be remembered that Weber made his case in difficult political circumstances: he was pushing against the *Zeitgeist*. He lived in a society prone to boom and bust – as evidenced by the 'Magdeburg Sugar Crash'.

Two years after Weber's essay was published, charges that futures markets and clearing houses fostered gambling and speculative excesses acquired sufficient political momentum in Germany to result in the passing of a wide ranging *Börsengesetz* or exchange law, which included a ban on futures markets for grains and flour. The 1896 *Börsengesetz* remained the cornerstone of German legislation covering exchanges during the 20th century and some of its restrictive regulations stayed in force for more than 90 years.

5.4 ANTI-GAMBLING SENTIMENT IN EUROPE

Just as in America, opposition to the evils of gambling would stoke up a significant head of steam among European politicians and the public in the late 19th century.

In the Netherlands, where futures trading was linked in the popular mind with the Tulip Mania of the 1630s and later 18th century speculative excesses, known as the *windhandel*, Ernst Alexander Bunge's plans for a futures market and clearing house prompted some notably hostile press comment. *De Economist*, a well known periodical at the time, attacked his proposal by arguing that futures trading 'when reduced to the simplest terms boils down to a wager being made' in which 'the butcher bets that coffee will go up and the barber bets that it will go down'. It appealed – without success – to the King to withhold approval for Bunge's new venture on the grounds that it was 'an offence against common decency'.[17]

In neighbouring Germany in the 1890s, an ad hoc coalition of concerned citizenry and hostile farmers secured the approval of the Reichstag, the German parliament, for the draconian *Börsengesetz*.

Imperial Germany was the home to some important futures markets at the time, including the markets for coffee and sugar in Hamburg. But, then as now, markets were viewed with suspicion in Germany and none more so than the grain futures market in Berlin. The unification of the country in 1871 was followed by a powerful financial boom and then a bust which segued into a long agricultural depression.

Germany's politically powerful grain growers – the Junkers of Prussia – suffered from falling prices. They whipped up concern in the Reichstag and among the population at large about the morality of futures markets and of the Berlin grain market in particular, arguing that falling prices could threaten the nation's ability to feed and arm itself in event of war. Paradoxically, their campaign won extra support after grain prices spiked upwards in the early 1890s as a result of bad harvests and when Germany was in recession. The outcome was the exchange law of 22 June 1896 with its ban on grain and flour futures and on forward trades in stocks of mining and manufacturing companies[18] and firms with a capital of less than 20 million marks.

---

[17] As recounted in the 1987 annual report of Bank Mees & Hope NV.

[18] Baehring, Berndt (1985), *Börsen-Zeiten*.

The *Börsengesetz* created hurdles before futures trading in any other commodities could take place on any exchange. There had to be a hearing of stakeholders with an interest in the commodity after which final admission to the exchange required the approval of the Imperial Chancellor no less. Only registered professionals were allowed to trade on the futures markets that remained in Germany. All contracts involving an unregistered counterparty were void.[19]

The German law forced much futures trading into unregulated channels and stunted the development of clearing infrastructures.[20] It did nothing to support farm prices. The ban was partly rescinded in 1908 but many restrictions remained.[21] Although Germany's coffee and sugar markets recovered somewhat in the years up to 1914, most subsequent attempts to revive futures markets in Germany proved short-lived as two World Wars and political and economic upheavals took their toll. It was only in 1989 that the Bonn government revised the German exchange law to permit a modern futures market and clearing infrastructure as part of its programme to modernise Germany's financial services sector.

Politics and the national interest in Britain were very different to those in Germany or the US. The UK had embraced free trade in 1846 with the repeal of the Corn Laws. As the world's first industrial power, Britain had a vested interest in cheap food and raw materials. The percentage of Britain's population living in towns was far higher than in Germany and the US, even though Germany and the US were industrialising rapidly.[22] But there was widespread suspicion of futures trading, rooted in the belief that it was gambling. As already noted, concern about speculation in the Liverpool cotton market was one factor behind the 1882–4 settlement reforms in that market.

On 1 May 1896, shortly before the Berlin Reichtag passed the *Börsengesetz*, the British House of Lords debated futures trading and clearing. Lord Stanley of Alderley rose to condemn the fall 'in the prices of wheat, cotton, wool, silver, coffee and other agricultural products [sic]', which he blamed on 'the international system of trading in "Options and Futures", representing fictitious or non-existing produce'.[23]

After noting that the average price of wheat per bushel in the US had fallen from 119 cents in 1881 to 53 cents in 1893, he complained that UK wheat prices were depressed by the activities of the LPCH set up eight years earlier. But, being a peer of no party affiliation and with a reputation for eccentricity, he failed to persuade the UK's Conservative government to back his opposition to futures. In reply, the Earl of Dudley, secretary to the UK Board of Trade, cited expert opinion 'that this system of dealing in futures instead of deteriorating prices, rather tends to equalise them and to counteract the fluctuations that always must exist'.

The issue of whether forward commodity contracts were in breach of UK Gaming Acts came before the UK courts on several occasions in the 19th century and the judgements oscillated between for and against. Although by the 1880s case law upheld bargains where counterparties might gain or lose according to what happened in the future, it was not until

[19] Emery, Henry Crosby (1896) *Speculation on the Stock and Produce Exchanges of the United States*, Studies in History, Economics and Public Law, volume 7, number 22, which also contains a lucid account of the *Börsengesetz*.

[20] For example, the cash balance of the *Magdeburger Liquidationskasse*, the clearing house serving the Magdeburg sugar market, fell from 5.5 million marks in 1895 to 1.3 million marks in 1903: Eberhardt and Mayrhofer (2002).

[21] Remaining restrictions included a rule that futures contracts involving private investors counted as gambling, which meant liabilities arising from them were void. Deutsche Bundesbank (2003), 'Role and importance of interest rate derivatives', Monthly Report.

[22] Britain's urban population of 11.2 million in 1890 was 29.9% of the total UK population. The 9.6 million Americans living in towns and cities in 1890 accounted for 15.3% of the US population. The urban population of Germany was 5.6 million or 11.3% of the total: Kennedy, Paul (1988), *The Rise and Fall of the Great Powers*.

[23] Hansard, 1 May 1896.

1925 that the English Court of Appeal ruled that futures trades were real transactions, with real counterparties and were gambling only in a loose or colloquial sense.[24]

These circumstances help explain why, when a group of merchants, brokers and banks – many of which were of German origin (see Box 5.1) – registered the LPCH as a joint stock company on 22 February 1888, their initiative provoked an outburst of hostile comment in the English press.

Box 5.1 Underwriters of LPCH[25]

• André, Reiners and Co.	Merchants
• Arbuthnot, Ewert and Co.	East India merchants
• Arbuthnot, Latham and Co.	Merchants
• Baring Brothers and Co.	Merchants
• Blyth, Greene, Jourdain and Co.	Merchants
• Wm Brandts Sons and Co.	Merchants
• Carey and Browne	East India and Colonial brokers
• Chalmers, Guthrie and Co.	Merchants and bankers
• W.H. Cole and Co.	Merchants
• C. Czarnikow	Colonial broker
• Frühling and Goschen	Merchants
• Antony Gibbs and Sons	Merchants
• C.J. Hambro and Sons	Merchants
• Hardy Nathan and Sons	Merchants
• Fred. Huth and Co.	Merchants
• Ed. Johnston Son and Co.	Merchants
• Kleinworth, Sons and Co.	Merchants
• Knowles and Foster	Merchants
• Maclaine, Watson and Co.	Merchants
• Megaw and Norton	Brazilian merchants
• Rösing Bros and Co.	Merchants
• N.M. Rothschild & Sons	Merchants
• I.A. Rücker and Bencraft	Tea, coffee, cocoa, sugar, bark and Colonial produce brokers
• J. Henry Schroder and Co.	Merchants
• A. Tesdorpf and Co.	Merchants
• Wallace Bros	Merchants and East India agents
• Wogau and Co.	Merchants

The *Daily News* acknowledged that some of the City's big names supported the project. But any admiration this might imply was tempered by dislike and suspicion of the clearing house's purpose and the fact that so many of LPCH's backers had German sounding names.

'The Company is to be most powerfully sponsored,' the newspaper noted with an almost audible sniff:

> Upwards of two dozen firms, containing among them the first houses in London, have been found willing to figure on the prospectus as 'founders' or underwriters of the half million of capital to be

[24] Cranston, Ross (2007), 'Law through practice: London and Liverpool commodity markets c. 1820–1975'.

[25] The companies are categorised as they described themselves in the *1888 Post Office London Directory*, published by Kelly and Co. Baring Brothers and N.M. Rothschild also appear as 'private bankers' in the *Banking Almanac* for 1888. Among the companies are some, such as Hambros and Schroders, which would more commonly be thought of as banks.

> offered to the public next Monday. Barings are there, and the Rothschilds, and the Frühling and Goschen, and the Hambros, and the Huths, and the Schröders – as imposing an array of names as ever propped a foreign State or launched a Brewery.[26]

The newspaper's underlying message was that the clearing house would be up to no good and would undermine London's historic commodity trading houses in Mincing Lane: 'The true function of the new Company is that of stake-holder in a gamble. It is designed to open the markets of Mincing Lane to the man in the street, the loafer in the Clubs, the frequenter of City taverns – anybody and everybody able to command a five pound note.'

Although avoiding the xenophobic overtones of the *Daily News*, the *Financial Times* – at this point a newcomer among UK newspapers – went even further. The new company would turn the produce markets and Mincing Lane into 'one vast gambling house'. Commenting under the headline 'The Produce Gamble', the FT, in its edition of 25 February 1888, found it difficult to reconcile the eminence of the backers of the clearing house, for whom it obviously had some respect, with its belief that LPCH would be a 'gambling company' of benefit to speculators but 'an unmitigated injury to others' and 'in a number of respects highly detrimental to the best interests of the public at large'.

Nor had the FT softened its tone by 1 May 1888, the day LPCH opened for business. It commented that the clearing house's newly published regulations for the market in coffee futures 'confirm all our predictions as to the gambling spirit in which this enterprise has been conceived and is to be carried on'.[27]

[26] The *Daily News* quotations are taken from newspaper clippings reproduced in '100 Years of ICCH', a brochure published in 1988 to mark the 100th anniversary of the founding of LPCH. The author is grateful to Michael March of LCH.Clearnet for the information that these comments appeared in the *Daily News* during February 1888.

[27] One of the few newspapers to report on the plans for LPCH in less than hysterical tones was the *Liverpool Mercury*. No doubt reflecting that city's experience of futures trading, it commented in its edition of 27 February 1888 that 'a clearing house for the London Produce Markets has been deemed desirable for a long time past by all those interested in these trades'.

6 The London Produce Clearing House

6.1 CLEARING FOR PROFIT

Mincing Lane in the City of London exuded an air of quiet competence in the 1880s. Then and for decades afterwards it was the centre of London's commodity trade.

The narrow street eschewed celebrity and notoriety. Mincing Lane was, the *Financial Times* observed in its first edition, 'one of the most unassuming business centres of the City' and yet had 'an air of solidity, peculiar to itself'.[1]

But, as the newspapers of the time suggest, Mincing Lane was in a state of considerable agitation early in 1888 because of plans to set up the London Produce Clearing House (LPCH).[2]

Warning that the venture would benefit 'those who gamble pure and simple,' the FT reported with some relish that: 'The oldest and best established firms in Mincing Lane are up in arms against any such scheme.' Its correspondent advised the newspaper's readers to 'look out for some fun' should the plan go ahead.

For some established traders of Mincing Lane, the idea of LPCH was no source of amusement. They were not so much concerned about gambling, as the fact that the business plan for LPCH would change the way they had traded commodities for decades.

Adopting the methods pioneered in Le Havre, the clearing house planned to guarantee the completion of futures contracts in a variety of commodities starting with coffee and sugar as an entrepreneurial, for-profit venture.

LPCH's shares were to be offered to a broad public and listed on the London Stock Exchange. The company made very clear promises at the outset to pay dividends to its shareholders.

LPCH differed from the clearing infrastructures that evolved to support the emerging trade in cotton futures in Liverpool in that it was constituted *before* the futures markets it was set up to serve.

Unlike the *Caisse* in Le Havre, which by the late 1880s was well supported by that city's commodity traders, LPCH evidently represented the 'new' versus the 'old' in Mincing Lane.

In this respect, its position vis-a-vis established trading interests was similar to that of the *Warenliquidationskasse* in Hamburg or the ALK in Amsterdam. But although the ALK later

---

[1] *Financial Times* (13 February 1888), 'Mincing Lane in feeble form: A proposed innovation'.

[2] Piecing together the early history of LPCH is no easy task. Information about its early years is patchy. Five volumes of board minutes from 1888 until 1932 have survived and are kept in London's Guildhall Library. So too have the annual reports for the period up to 1950 when LPCH was listed on the London Stock Exchange. These, however, stick very much to the bare facts and figures. The LPCH Prospectus and company 'Memorandum of Association' of February 1888 have also been preserved on microfiche by the Guildhall Library. The minutes record how the board resolved in October 1930 that all old books and papers up to 1914 should 'be destroyed with the exception of the minute books and share registers'. Two old ledgers and an early share register were discovered during 2008 in LCH.Clearnet's London office. The ledgers are charred at the edges, indicating fire damage in the Second World War Blitz on London. Some copies of early regulations have survived. The author located a copy of the *Regulations for Coffee Future Delivery Business* (May 1888) in the British Library. *Regulations for Future Delivery in Rio Coffee*, July 1893 and *Regulations for '88 degree' Beetroot Sugar* dating from June 1913 have been pasted into the board minutes.

proved to be even more entrepreneurial than LPCH – as when it morphed into a bank – the Dutch clearer nonetheless took the trouble quickly to restore good relations with Amsterdam's coffee traders' association and to cooperate with the *Likwidatiekas* in Rotterdam. LPCH, by contrast, would have a difficult relationship with parts of the London sugar trade for many years.

6.2 ESTABLISHMENT OF LPCH

The underwriters of the LPCH share offering presented their continental-style clearing house as a for-profit venture that would bring wider benefits. 'The *Caisse de Liquidation* in Havre and a similar institution recently established in Hamburg have proved very profitable undertakings, and have at the same time given important and safe development to local trade', the prospectus for the public offering of LPCH shares on 27 February 1888 declared.

It noted how

> The want of such a system here causes a considerable portion of English business to be transferred to foreign markets, where safer methods prevail, and this diversion of trade is rapidly growing, to the injury of British commerce, and at a heavy charge to our traders, in the increased commissions and brokerages thereby incurred.

If the planned London clearing house went ahead, its hoped-for success 'must lead to an extension of business in other directions, as well as to an actual increase in imports, and thereby benefit the trading, shipping and dock interests of London'. As the prospectus noted: 'The chief depot of any article of commerce will always be found where the transactions are of the greatest magnitude, and for distribution London has exceptionable advantages.'

The underwriters launched LPCH with a nominal capital of £1 million, made up of 99 900 ordinary shares of £10 each and 100 Founders' shares of the same nominal value. The 100 Founder's shares were placed privately and fully paid up among the directors and backers of the clearing house, while 50 000 ordinary shares were offered for public subscription partly paid at £2/10 shillings (£2.50) each.[3]

The flotation raised £126 000 in capital easily. The ordinary shares were oversubscribed and appear to have been widely placed. There were plenty of individuals who bought just £5 worth of shares. The company's share register suggests that a goodly proportion of the small shareholders 'stagged' the issue, selling their newly acquired shares by May or June 1888.

In future years, LPCH's capital structure with its large amount of callable capital would act as a brake on the company's share price. It was so structured because LPCH had no default fund at the time. The large uncalled liability borne by investors was one way of reassuring customers that it could deal with the 'direst extremity'.[4]

Until that time came, investors would be remunerated. LPCH was in the business to make money for its shareholders. The prospectus promised that ordinary shareholders would receive a cumulative dividend of at least 6% on their paid-up capital. The Founders' shares would then receive 25% of the remaining profits after which the ordinary shares could qualify for a further pay-out.

On 25 February 1888 – the day the FT criticised LPCH as a 'produce gamble' – the clearing house's 10 directors held their first board meeting in temporary rented offices in Mincing Lane.

[3] The UK operated a duo-decimal currency system until 15 February 1971. One pound comprised 20 shillings, which in turn were worth 12 pennies each. One pound was therefore worth 240 old pence. £2/10/-shillings would be £2.50 in today's money.

[4] *The Times* (31 January 1914).

The minutes of that meeting do not record whether the directors were at all perturbed by the hostile press that greeted the registration of their company three days earlier. Instead, they set up committees to draw up rules for guaranteeing futures trading in coffee and sugar, and elected Francis J. Johnston, a director of the company's main bank, as chairman and Caesar Czarnikow as deputy chairman.[5]

Of the two, Czarnikow was to play a more high profile role in the development of the clearing house. He was a prominent sugar broker and, like many of his fellow founders, German-born. He took British nationality in 1861, the year he founded Czarnikow & Co.

Czarnikow would have fitted many a modern City stereotype. Remembered as a short, stocky individual with a penchant for large Cuban cigars, he was, according to one biographer, an autocratic, impulsive and short-tempered businessman who was 'capable of sacking and re-employing the same person on the same day'.[6]

The combative side of Czarnikow's character was tempered by a passion for flowers and animals that led him to own, at various times, monkeys, emus, eagles and even a bear.[7] Among the mourners who attended his funeral at his country home in Effingham, Surrey, in 1909 were the secretary of the London Zoological Society, the assistant superintendent of the Zoo in Regent's Park and six zoo keepers, as well as four Kleinworts and a Huth and other members of the City's Anglicised German banking families.[8]

Czarnikow described himself as a 'colonial broker'. But his company retained a distinctly German character until his death. And it was to Germany that Czarnikow and the other founders of LPCH turned when recruiting talent for the new London clearing house.

Shortly after LPCH was incorporated, Czarnikow and Hermann Fortlage, a fellow director, visited Hamburg. There, as they reported back to the board on 28 March 1888, they engaged two clerks 'acquainted with the routines of the Hamburg Produce Clearing House'. They also entered into negotiations with one Wilhelm Schultz about his becoming second manager of LPCH. Three weeks later, on 18 April, Schultz was hired on a salary of £800 a year and a share of at least 2.5% of net profits. The board also approved the renting of offices at 21 Mincing Lane, in the heart of the City's commodity trading area.

A few months later – on 1 November – Schultz was appointed manager for an initial period of three years on a salary of £1000[9] plus a share of 5% of the first £50 000 of net profits and 2.5% thereafter. Another German, Hermann Schumann, was appointed company secretary at £500 a year and 1% of net profit. Schumann stayed only briefly with the firm, but Schultz would remain LPCH's manager until the First World War.

Although LPCH turned to Hamburg for staff and know-how, its method of clearing contracts was very similar to that of the *Caisse* in Le Havre, suggesting that Hamburg's *Warenliquidationskasse* also copied the French model.

Like the *Caisse*, whose methods are described in Chapter 5, LPCH fulfilled its obligations to buyers and sellers of futures in London through a process of registering contracts and issuing certificates of guarantee. This technique was adopted in the 'Regulations for Coffee Future

[5] According to the minutes of the LPCH board, which survive for the period from 1888 to 1932. The other directors were Francis Augustin Browne, Alexander Patrick Cameron, Hermann Fortlage, Charles Seton Sinclair Guthrie, Henry John Jourdain, Edward Augustus Rucker, Robert Ryrie and Benjamin Dixon Tabor.

[6] Orbell, John (2004), 'Czarnikow, (Julius) Caesar (1838–1909)', *Oxford Dictionary of National Biography*.

[7] The bear's presence in Czarnikow's menagerie was short-lived. Acquired around 1877, it was disposed of soon after disgracing itself by gnawing at the door of a four wheeler cab when travelling with its master to London Bridge: Janes, Hurford and Sayers, H.J. (1963), *The Story of Czarnikow*.

[8] *The Times*, 21 April 1909.

[9] Worth £93 670 in terms of end-2007 pounds sterling, according to the Bank of England's Inflation calculator.

Delivery Business', published by LPCH when it started clearing coffee futures in London in May 1888 and retained with minor modifications for other contracts until computerisation in the 1960s.

LPCH took deposits or initial margin when it accepted and registered the contracts for guarantee and called for margin payments on contracts in the event of a fall in their book value. But LPCH was not the legal counterparty to any trade. In the event of default by a member, for example, it would guarantee fulfilment of that member's contracts by instructing another member to trade out all or some of the defaulter's outstanding contracts. If the clearing house held insufficient deposit and margin funds to cover the defaulter's closed out positions, it suffered a loss.

In its early days, LPCH had two types of members: ordinary and authorised brokers. Ordinary members were akin to non-clearing members in today's CCPs. The admission of all members was 'in the absolute discretion of the Board of Directors'[10] and the minutes show the board took this duty seriously and rejected some applicants. Members had to have an office or place of business in the City.

When starting up its coffee futures business, LPCH was 'prepared to admit as members a certain number of duly authorised brokers' who had the sole right to register futures contracts with the company.[11] These authorised brokers were the equivalent of today's general clearing members and it was through them that the ordinary members' contracts were registered and guaranteed.

Whereas ordinary members paid an annual subscription of 'not less than one guinea' (£1/1/0d or £1.05), the authorised brokers paid an additional subscription of not less than 5 guineas. The brokers had to be 'elected' by the board and agree to special conditions and obligations. For example, authorised or privileged brokers were not allowed to engage in coffee futures business 'for principals not residing within the United Kingdom'. Also, if a broker's client (who would be an LPCH member) was based further than a mile away from the clearing house, the broker had to assume all the obligations and duties of a principal. The special brokers were also liable for service on a five-strong brokers' committee that was charged, under the watchful eye of LPCH managers, with fixing the daily price that was used for setting margins.

LPCH accepted its first 59 members towards the end of April 1888, shortly before it began registering and guaranteeing forward coffee contracts on 1 May. Membership grew quickly. When the board met on 16 May, it accepted the 50th application to be an authorised coffee broker and considered applicants 244 to 256 to be ordinary members.

There was a certain amount of trial and error in LPCH's start up phase, especially when it tried to establish the right level of control over counterparty risk. Its May 1888, the coffee future regulations stated that the clearing house would only register contracts 'for firms, members of the Company [LPCH], domiciled in London within one mile of the Clearing House'. This was clearly too restrictive and quickly modified so that contracts would be registered for firms, '*one or more of the partners of which* are members of the Company, domiciled in London within one mile of the clearing house'.[12] This clause was included in the July 1888 regulations for sugar futures but also proved to be too restrictive. It was no longer in the rules five years later.

[10] LPCH (London Produce Clearing House Ltd) (April 1888a), *Preliminary General Rules as to Membership*.

[11] LPCH (April 1888b), *Preliminary Regulations for the Admission of Brokers authorised to deal with the London Produce Clearing House Ltd in Coffee Business for Future Delivery*.

[12] According to an amendment, included with the board minutes for 16 May 1888. Author's italics.

LPCH became more international in outlook as time passed. In 1896 it accepted shareholders with addresses outside the UK. The board minutes show that a growing number of foreign-based firms became members of LPCH during the 1890s and 1900s. Several new members with German names were accepted in 1896, the year of the *Börsengesetz*.[13] In June 1908 alone, new members included three firms based in Prague, two in Hamburg, two in Antwerp and one in Amsterdam.

For the most part, however, the regulations produced by LPCH changed little after its first few months until June 1913 when the rules for registering, guaranteeing and, where necessary, delivering '88 degree' beetroot sugar were expanded to include a clause relating to the possibility of war between the UK and Germany.

The system of guarantees developed by the *Caisse* and other European clearing houses only ended at LPCH about the time that financial futures trading came to London in the 1980s, when it adopted the US system where clearing houses were described in their regulations as being the buyer to every seller and the seller to every buyer.

Although different, the two approaches had practically the same effect of mitigating traders' counterparty risk and came close to convergence when a counterparty of LPCH wanted to close out two contracts for the same delivery as both a buyer and a seller. Then the counterparty presented the clearing house with the two certificates of guarantee. LPCH made up the accounts and offset and terminated the contracts, paying to the contracting party any balance due. In this case, according to rule 13 in the 1913 version of LPCH's regulations for clearing sugar futures, 'all rights and liabilities of the contracting party as regards the respective contracts' would devolve upon LPCH. However, in contrast to the system of 'complete clearing' adopted gradually in the US after 1891, LPCH was not and did not become the counterparty to the other participants in the two trades. Instead, buyers and sellers of the oldest open contracts, in the numerical order of LPCH's register, took the place of the counterparty whose contracts were liquidated.

These subtleties were easily overlooked. In 1916, a UK court conflated LPCH's clearing methods with the US method of clearing when describing the functioning of LPCH. It also brought the word 'novation' into the vocabulary of clearing to describe the substitution by the clearing house of the obligations of the original counterparties when LPCH provided certificates of guarantee to the two parties in a commodity futures contract.[14]

In Jager vs Tolme & Runge and LPCH Ltd, a case concerning the effect of the First World War on a sugar contract, the UK Court of Appeal observed that: 'Under the rules and regulations both vendors and purchasers of sugar register their contracts with the London Produce Clearing House Ltd and a novation follows under which the clearing house becomes the purchasers from the sellers and the sellers to the buyers.'[15]

6.3 LPCH: SUGAR AND THE GERMAN CONNECTION

When Hamburg set up its futures markets and a clearing house for coffee and sugar in 1887–88 it was logical that London should follow suit. Coffee was an important commodity in

[13] The same minutes also show that LPCH had a considerable membership by 1896. Mr C. Meyer of Fr Meyer's Sohn was accepted as member number 707 in March 1896; Fr Lehmann, a silver broker, as member 719 in July 1896; and C.W. Engelhardt, a sugar broker, became the 725th member in October 1896.

[14] The word 'novation' appears not to have been used by LPCH itself until 1921 when a board meeting on 25 July discussed new rules for the sugar market and the minutes noted that 'the wording of the clause re "novation" was approved'.

[15] *The Times*, 5 February 1916, Law Report.

international trade while sugar was big business in tea-drinking Britain. During the spring of 1888, LPCH opened negotiations with representatives of the London sugar trade and started handling sugar contracts on 16 July 1888.

The UK occupied a unique position in the world sugar trade before 1914. The British, then as now, were noted for having a sweet tooth and the UK consumed more sugar per head than anywhere else in the world.[16] The German Empire catered to this demand and was the UK's biggest single supplier of sugar from around the time of LPCH's foundation until 1914.

The manufacture of sugar from beet was an 18th century German discovery. It gave rise to a refining industry in continental Europe that grew rapidly, while German immigrants played an important role in sugar refining in Britain until well into the 19th century. The continental beet sugar industry prospered partly because of UK government actions and policies, including the UK's blockade of Europe in the Napoleonic Wars; Britain's early 19th century abolition of the slave trade (which upset the economics of West Indies sugar production); and Britain's free trade policies which eliminated sugar duties from 1874. Until the early 1900s, continental production also benefited from export subsidies in France and Germany.

By the end of the 19th century, two thirds of world sugar production was beet sugar and two of the biggest sugar markets were in Hamburg and Magdeburg, near areas of beet cultivation on the north German plain.

Britain grew no beet. Instead, true to its free trade ideals, it depended on imports of raw and refined sugar. The UK was heavily dependent on Germany and Austria-Hungary, Germany's neighbour and ally, for supplies of both.

The dependence was mutual. Germany's share of UK sugar imports rose dramatically from just 3% in 1875 to 65% in 1903 before declining to 33% in 1910. Britain absorbed about half of German sugar exports at the end of the 19th century and as much as 77% in 1907.[17] In 1911–13, Britain imported sugar with 1.99 million metric tonnes raw value, of which 767 200 tonnes came from Germany and 302 300 tonnes from Austria-Hungary.[18]

Beet sugar was very well suited for futures trading. It was a standardised product: its quality was easily and scientifically verifiable. The Hamburg sugar market provided the international benchmark price, reflecting the port's position as the leading sugar trading centre in Europe's largest producer country. The contract unit for sugar futures trading in London was 500 bags of 88 degree white beet sugar, free on board Hamburg.

The prospects for trading and guaranteeing sugar futures contracts in London must have appeared bright to the founders of LPCH in 1888. As its deputy chairman, the company had Caesar Czarnikow, a leading figure in the London and international sugar trade. The large community of German sugar traders in Mincing Lane could draw on Hamburg's experience to build up a futures markets backed by a clearing house.

But although LPCH's coffee futures business appeared to launch smoothly, clearing futures in sugar ran into problems which clouded the clearing house's first two decades.

---

[16] In 1899–1900 the citizens of Great Britain consumed an estimated 91.65 pounds of sugar per head, according to figures from the German sugar company F.O. Licht (Hutcheson, John M. (1901), *Notes on the Sugar Industry*. The next highest per capita consumption was in the US with 65.21 pounds per head. The average for the 19 main consuming countries was 33 pounds per head.

[17] Chalmin, Philippe (1990), *The Making of a Sugar Giant*.

[18] Rees, Graham L. (1972), *Britain's Commodity Markets*.

6.4 A DIVIDED MARKET AND A CLEARING COMPETITOR

LPCH board minutes record how, in its early months, the clearing house was threatened with legal action for alleged copyright infringement by London's Beetroot Sugar Association, a trade body, over the form of contract it had adopted. Relations between the two bodies remained fraught until 1893 when they settled their differences.

Meanwhile, just weeks after LPCH began operating, a row broke out between Czarnikow and other board members over who should be entitled to register sugar futures contacts with the clearing house.

The minutes give only a partial insight into the dispute, but it was evidently intense. It centred on Czarnikow's objection to a proposal that none other than brokers should be allowed to register sugar contracts with LPCH. Only brokers were allowed to register coffee futures contracts with the clearing house and a majority of the board wanted the same rules to apply to the sugar trade. Czarnikow was in a minority and, although other directors expressed their 'extreme regret' at having to oppose their deputy chairman, they nonetheless forced him to vacate the chair on occasions.

When on 27 June 1888, the board agreed to admit sugar brokers on the same terms as coffee brokers, it was by a majority vote with Czarnikow and one other board member dissenting.

This particular quarrel was soon patched over. A fortnight later the board ruled that 'authorised agents'[19] should channel all their business through the clearing house. Czarnikow was again chairing board meetings from the autumn of 1888 and continued to do so until his sudden death, aged 72, in 1909.

But the business of sugar continued to engender disputes. LPCH's board may have leaned in Czarnikow's direction in February 1889 when it created a new special 'privileged' group of sugar brokers and agents with exclusive rights to present the contracts for registration by the clearing house. In return, these privileged brokers had to channel all their London futures delivery business through LPCH; ensure they liquidated business conducted in foreign markets through merchants or agents resident in the UK; and register all dealings among themselves with the clearing house.

The new rules were no doubt intended to prevent companies internalising trade in sugar futures and stop business leaking to foreign centres such as Hamburg. But they left a sour taste in the London market. In March 1889, dissident brokers and members of LPCH, representing small companies, submitted a 'memorial' specifically protesting the admission of authorised agents to the sugar business. They formed a brokers' association to organise 'concerted action' against the clearing house.

Nonetheless, LPCH's business grew. After the first week of trading in May 1888, the board was told that the clearing house's clients had made deposits and margin payments of just £8435/7/6d. Towards the end of October that year, LPCH held £46 520 in cash and securities worth £38 065 for customers as deposits and margin payments. A year later, at the end of October 1889, cash totalling £94 016 and securities valued at £191 655 were credited to clients of the clearing house as initial deposits and margin payments.[20]

The directors were upbeat when they published LPCH's first annual report on the 12 months to 30 April 1889: 'The advantage of the Clearing-House to trade in giving facility of sale with

[19] The exact status of the authorised agents is not clear from the minutes. However, the protest of the dissident brokers in March 1889 would suggest they were most likely representatives of large trading firms.

[20] Figures drawn from LPCH board minutes.

Table 6.1 Registrations of contracts in the three main sugar markets (in numbers of bags)

	1892	% share	1893	% share	1894	% share
London	4 382 500	27	8 288 500	34	4 452 000	27
Hamburg	7 503 000	46	10 291 500	42	8 510 000	52
Magdeburg	4 357 500	27	5 906 500	24	3 492 000	21
Totals	16 243 000	100	24 486 500	100	16 454 000	100

Source: A special report on the sugar market in the LPCH board minutes of April 1895. Percentage shares, rounded to the nearest whole number, were calculated by the author.

security of contract, and thereby attracting business to London, is every day becoming more recognised,' they said. Although the first year of business was 'to a large extent initiatory', the company had started to grow: more than half the 2.27 million bags of coffee and two thirds of the 1.28 million bags of sugar that LPCH guaranteed and cleared in 1888–89 were registered in the final four months of the business year. By the time the report was published, LPCH had started to clear tea and was in negotiations to handle other imports. It reported a net profit of £5742 in 1888–89, which it carried forward.

When LPCH issued its second annual report for a short eight-month business year to the end of 1889,[21] the directors' optimism seemed justified. It registered contracts for 4.51 million bags of sugar in the eight months, well up on the 1888–89 total, and 2.59 million bags of coffee. LPCH was guaranteeing and clearing contracts for tea, silk, wheat and maize.[22] By the year's end, its balance sheet showed assets and liabilities of £222 761, equivalent to £20.63 million in end-2007 money. The board reported a net profit, after expenses, of £14 785 and declared a dividend of 5 shillings (or £0.25) on the 50 000 partly-paid ordinary shares. The other component in the company's paid in capital – the 100 Founders' shares – did not qualify for a dividend at this stage.

But worries about the company's sugar business continued to surface in LPCH board meetings. In 1895 the board was concerned that the London sugar trade was losing ground to German competition. Although the directors' worries were eased somewhat when a specially commissioned report showed that by the early 1890s LPCH had moved ahead of Magdeburg in terms of bags registered and cleared while ranking second to Hamburg (see Table 6.1), the world's leading centre for trading sugar, problems still lurked closer to home.

The German connections of LPCH and many of its member companies should have helped secure business for the clearing house after Germany's futures markets were more tightly regulated by the 1896 *Börsengesetz*. But unlike the Liverpool cotton traders and ALK in Amsterdam in the 1880s, which made peace in their own markets, LPCH failed to heal the divisions in the London sugar market. English sugar refiners preferred to deal directly with Hamburg or Magdeburg for many years.[23] Symptomatic of continuing discontent, a suggestion was made to the LPCH board in early 1897 for a so-called 'open sugar market' with weekly margin calls. This the board rejected.

In June 1897, a rival clearing house – the Contract Association – was formed with a capital of £50 000 to register and clear contracts in 'colonial and other products'. Reporting that

[21] The eight-month accounting period was to bring LPCH's business year into line with the calendar year.

[22] It registered 572 000 half chests of tea, 2660 bales of silk, 55 000 quarters of wheat and 3 000 quarters of maize between 1 May 1889 and 31 December 1889.

[23] Chalmin, Philippe (1990).

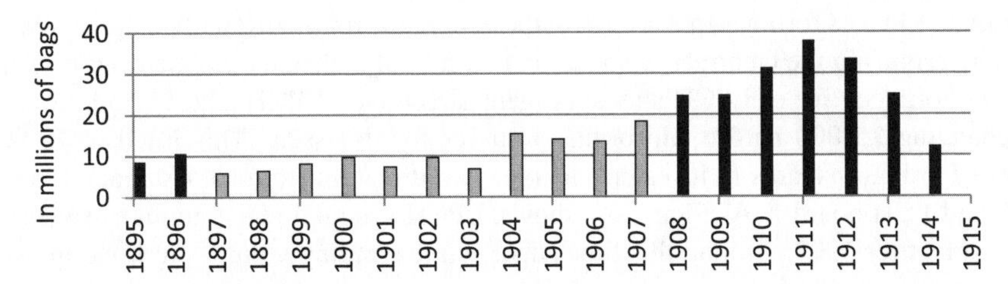

Figure 6.1 LPCH: Registrations of London sugar futures, 1895–1915 (contract unit: 500 bags, white beet sugar 88 degrees, FOB Hamburg). The Contract Association also cleared sugar futures in London from 1897 to 1907.

Source: LPCH figures as reproduced in Rees, G.L. (1972). *Britain's Commodity Markets*, Paul Elek Books, London.

the Association would begin clearing beet sugar, the *Daily News*[24] disclosed that five of its directors came from 'leading Mincing Lane firms'. Each subscribed £5000 of its capital.

Like LPCH, the new clearing house had German firms among its members. The Contract Association operated with weekly rather than daily margin calls and appears to have been less profit-oriented than LPCH. The number of sugar contracts registered at LPCH fell sharply in 1897 – the year the Association was launched – as Figure 6.1 shows.

Reacting to the Contract Association, LPCH sought to broaden the range of contracts that it cleared. But its success was limited. LPCH cleared silk until 1898, and indigo was another short-lived venture, lasting from 1900 until 1905. LPCH also had an on-off history of clearing grain contracts. It cleared wheat futures contracts for five years from 1889 and maize contracts for just three years. Although the London grain trade persuaded LPCH to resume clearing wheat and maize futures contracts in 1897, the business ceased after only eight years. The Liverpool Corn Exchange was the major beneficiary of the closure of Germany's grain futures markets following the *Börsengesetz*. The London Corn Trade Association eventually took over clearing grain futures in London.

The early years of the new century were not particularly easy for commodity traders and their clearers. Cementing its reputation as one of Europe's less serious markets, the Paris sugar market suffered the effects of a drought-induced speculative bubble and crash in 1905. This led to the suicide of a prominent local speculator, a slight reduction in LPCH's registrations of sugar futures and a flurry of rumours of heavy losses at Czarnikow, estimated by some at a quarter of a million pounds.[25]

In 1907–8 the world was in the grip of a major financial crisis with some similarities to that which began in 2007.[26] In the commodity markets, producer countries started to question the prevailing system by which markets in the industrialised world set the price for their products. Following a record coffee crop, Brazil began buying futures and stockpiling physical coffee in 1906–7 in a bid to support the price. Its policy of intervention benefited Le Havre more than other European centres.

[24] Of 25 June 1897.

[25] A huge sum in those days. When asked about the alleged losses by a journalist, Czarnikow replied that he could still afford to light one of his trademark cigars with a £5 note. The actual loss turned out to be 'short of £55 000': Janes, Hurford and Sayers, H.J. (1963).

[26] Czarnikow's comments on 'the far reaching effects of the financial crisis in the USA' to the LPCH annual meeting in February 1909 would not have been out of place a century later. *The Times* of 12 February 1909 reported that in commenting on the failure of cheap money to stimulate a recovery, Czarnikow observed that the 'shock to credit was too severe' and that 'capitalists showed a marked disinclination to embark on any ventures containing the least element of risk'.

However, LPCH's fortunes took a turn for the better in 1907 when it unified the London sugar market by acquiring the Contract Association in a friendly takeover initiated and brokered by Hermann Fortlage, one of LPCH's most diligent directors.[27] LPCH paid £62 500 for its rival by exchanging 25 000 partly paid ordinary shares for its assets. This lifted to 75 000 the number of ordinary shares in investors' hands. Two directors from the Contract Association joined the LPCH board.[28] As Figure 6.1 shows, LPCH's annual registrations of sugar futures rose sharply after 1907. Around this time sugar futures trading volumes in London overtook those in Hamburg.

But although important for the London coffee and sugar trades, LPCH could hardly be considered a dominant force in the City – especially when measured against its early ambitions. The clearing house remained heavily dependent on the beet sugar trade. In 1913, the last full year of peace, the only other products that it cleared were coffee, granulated sugar, pepper and silver.

However, it continued to pay dividends year in year out. It rewarded its directors reasonably well, paying £200 a year to each for many years. They in turn attended board meetings faithfully although they switched from weekly board meetings in February 1897 to a fortnightly routine.

The clearing house's working methods entailed much paper and copying. At times it appeared to be running close to full capacity, as in October 1910 when the issue of clerks' overtime was taken up by the board, which agreed that the company's clerical staff should be entitled to 1s/6d if working after 7 P.M. and 3 shillings after 8:30 P.M. on weekdays. On Saturdays, overtime pay was 1s/6d after 4 P.M. and 3/- after 5:30 P.M..

An idea of working life at LPCH in Edwardian times has been handed down by J.P. Kimmins who began with the firm as a 22-year-old registrations clerk on 17 March 1923. Interviewed in a publication commemorating the centenary of the foundation of the clearing house,[29] Kimmins passed on reminiscences of Henry Pute, who was a clerk working under Wilhelm Schultz before the First World War and who later rose to be company secretary:

> Pute used to describe his early days as very disciplined. There was no talking at desks. At five o'clock they prepared to go home by placing their coats and bowler hats on their high clerks' desks. On the stroke of five Schultz would walk out, announce 'Goodnight Gentlemen', and that was the signal to go.

When war broke out in 1914, the board minutes recorded a workforce of just 23 people, ranging from the humblest clerk to Schultz, the manager. These would have been seen as jobs for life. When 'Honest John' Culbertson retired as company secretary in January 1930, he had been with LPCH for 40 years. In October 1937, William Matt, who took over as manager after the First World War, retired after 49 and a half years.

LPCH's clearing methods and formality in the workplace survived two world wars until the 1950s. What could not survive the First World War was the company's strongly Germanic character and the very close ties between the British and German sugar trades.

[27] Fortlage was one of LPCH's most active directors from the time the company was founded. With Czarnikow, he negotiated the hiring of Schultz in Hamburg in 1888 and, also with Czarnikow, secured LPCH's first office in Mincing Lane. Fortlage requested leave of absence in February 1913, explaining that he had been ordered abroad for health reasons, after which his leave of absence was prolonged several times. In August 1915, the board accepted Fortlage's letter of resignation 'with great regret' and requested the chairman 'to write to Mr Fortlage to that effect'. It is unclear whether Fortlage was a German citizen during his time as a director of LPCH.

[28] John Ramsay Drake and Charles Herman Runge. In 1907, Francis J. Johnston stepped down as chairman of LPCH.

[29] International Commodities Clearing House (1988) *100 Years of ICCH*. The International Commodities Clearing House (ICCH) changed its name from LPCH in 1973.

6.5 LPCH AND THE FIRST WORLD WAR

On New Year's Day 1913, *The Times* ran a special article on LPCH, highlighting its consistent profits and satisfactory dividend payments since the end of the 19th century. Noting poetically how 'in the quiet, unobtrusive byways of commerce, unaffected by the feverishness of the Stock Exchange, there are companies making large and regular profits without any blare of trumpets or financial stir', the newspaper commented that LPCH was 'perhaps unique' in that it had 'never made a bad debt'. In this respect, 'it must stand almost alone amongst London joint-stock enterprises'.[30]

However, the gentleman from *The Times* failed to report that storm clouds were gathering and had been for some time. LPCH minutes note how, as early as June 1910, the company's board was considering how it should deal 'with the event of possible war in Europe'.

In August 1912, a specially convened LPCH board meeting agreed unanimously to amend the clearing house's own rules 'for the contingency of a war between Germany and Great Britain'. They should include a 'war clause' so that official notification or proclamation of war would result in compulsory liquidation of all contracts registered in the clearing house, based on one price only for each month of delivery and for all buyers and sellers.

On 18 January 1913, LPCH published the war clause to be included in its regulations for sugar and other futures contracts. It pinpointed Germany as the likely aggressor:

> In the event of Germany being involved in a war with either [sic] England, France, Russia and/or Austria, this contract, unless previously closed, shall on official notice being given that such a state of war exists, be deemed to be closed at the average quotation of the official calls held on the sixth working day counted backwards from the day when such notice is given . . . and accounts shall be made up with and between the contracting parties who shall accept such settlement as complete and final; all differences arising there from shall be due immediately.

The board met on 4 August 1914, the day the UK entered the First World War, and twice more before 14 August, when steps were initiated for liquidating open positions in the coffee and sugar markets.

Despite the prescience of the war clause, the first days of conflict witnessed a good deal of confusion and concern that LPCH could incur large losses. William Matt, at that time LPCH's sub-manager, told the board on 17 August of a 'great danger' that the clearing house might have to accept large amounts of coffee on 1 September as a consequence of 'open bull engagements' in the commodity. LPCH issued a circular two days later stating that the market would remain closed and the clearing house would not accept any new business until further notice.

The company's dependence on clearing sugar futures was a bigger problem. On 31 August, LPCH's chairman wrote to *The Times* to urge clarification of the status of open sugar contracts put in store in Hamburg before the war. 'Great confusion prevails as to the obligations of parties . . . in a very large number of contracts entered into before the war, but maturing after the declaration of war, which cannot be carried out because of the conditions which are prevailing', he wrote. The problem of German sugar warrants, which had been accepted by LPCH before August 1914 as cover against forward sales registered with the company, would be reflected in the company's balance sheet for some years after the war.

On 28 September, the board heard of defaults in certain white pepper contracts. Two weeks later, the conflict ended the career of Wilhelm Schultz, who appears to have remained a

[30] *The Times*, 1 January 1913.

German citizen during his 26 years as LPCH's manager. The minutes record how the board on 12 October agreed that Schultz's position 'be terminated as from this date'. Whoever was writing the minutes then had second thoughts because the word 'terminated' was crossed out and replaced by 'determined'. It was agreed that Schultz should be credited with six month's salary but 'any question of the grant of a pension be left until a later date'.

Schultz's name appears twice more in the board's minutes – on both occasions after the war. In February 1920, an extract from a letter dated 4 January to Matt from Schultz was read to the board and 'it was agreed to do nothing at present'. Could Schultz have been asking for a pension? If so, the issue soon became academic. He died soon after. On 7 April 1921, the board agreed that a commission payment due on £7808 of profit from a Reichsmark transaction held in suspense during the war 'be passed to the credit of the late Wm Schultz'.

The war forced LPCH to retrench. In December 1914, it drew up an austerity budget for 1915, having already cut its headcount by seven. Salary cuts and staff cuts reduced the company's pay bill from £7154 in 1914 to £3281 in 1915. The departure of Schultz, who earned more than double any other staff member, saved LPCH £2130 in 1915.

Hostilities produced a catastrophic fall in its sugar business as the UK government took control of supplies. LPCH registered just 9500 bags of sugar in 1915 and no more during the war. In February 1917, LPCH repealed its regulations concerning privileged sugar members because trading sugar futures in London had effectively ceased.

Sugar became the first foodstuff to be rationed in Britain in 1917. Records show LPCH cleared some coffee trades throughout the war, but activity was erratic and subject to interruptions. LPCH suspended dividend payments in July 1915. Its board met less often – roughly once a month after March 1916 and only four times in 1918.

The Hamburg sugar exchange was also closed during the war. The closure of Europe's commodity markets, however, created opportunities in the US. Trading in sugar started on the New York Coffee Market in 1914 and grew rapidly so that in 1916 the market changed its name to the New York Coffee and Sugar Exchange. Although the New York market also closed in 1917 when the US entered the war, it reopened in February 1920, ahead of London and Hamburg, which resumed futures trading in 1921 and 1925 respectively. By this time, Cuba – on the US's doorstep – had emerged as the biggest sugar producing country.

The New York market soon became the most important sugar exchange in the world, just one of many indicators of the shift of economic power from the old world to the new as a consequence of the First World War.

6.6 LPCH: AN AWKWARD RECOVERY

The war shattered long established trade relations. It undermined the pre-war international monetary system based on the gold standard, which before 1914 had created the framework for an early version of a globalised economy. Capital no longer moved freely around Europe. Markets became nationally focused. Protectionism grew and countries acted to promote domestic production of commodities where possible. Economic recovery in the 1920s was correspondingly uneven and fragile. The Wall Street Crash of 1929 and the ensuing slump created difficult conditions for markets and clearing houses alike.

LPCH scaled back its ambitions before the war's end. During the summer of 1918 the board decided to reduce the company's uncalled capital. In 1919, it petitioned the High Court to cut the nominal value of its 99 900 ordinary shares from £10 to £5 each, reducing its total authorised and issued capital to £500 500 from £1 million previously. The number of ordinary shares issued remained at 75 000, partly paid to a value of £2/10/0 each.

In 1919, LPCH's assets and liabilities amounted to £326 089, which included investments in securities worth £106 000. But on the balance sheet were £151 058 worth of advances (including accrued interest) to German clients, made against collateral under German control. Moreover, UK clients owed the clearing house £58 571, which partly represented pre-war advances against sugar stored in Germany.

Late in 1919, the LPCH board decided that all claims against the German clients should be settled by a foreign claims sugar committee in London. But in April 1921, the board minutes record that Matt, who succeeded Schultz as manager, travelled to Berlin to press for settlement against the Mitteldeutsche Privat Bank, a leading business partner in pre-war Germany. Matt visited Berlin and Hamburg frequently in the early 1920s for debt negotiations. The state of legal cases to recover monies owed by other companies was a recurrent subject of discussion in the LPCH board in these years.

Normality of a sort was restored in 1921 when the London sugar terminal market reopened. But the sugar trade had changed out of all recognition. Futures trading was no longer based on 88 degree beet sugar, FOB Hamburg. Instead, the contract unit was 50 tons of white sugar, ex-bonded warehouse in London, of which LPCH cleared 61 050 tons in that year.

The UK had expanded its own beet sugar production during the war and with other – mainly cane-based – suppliers in the dominions and colonies filled the gap left by Germany after 1914. Rationing and the closure of markets during the war had strengthened the position of UK sugar refiners vis-a-vis the traders of Mincing Lane. The shift in power was confirmed in 1926 when Julius Joseph Runge, a high profile director of Tate & Lyle, joined the LPCH board.[31]

The war appeared to create other opportunities, however. It had greatly increased the use of motorised vehicles, producing in turn booming demand for rubber. Trading in natural rubber futures was launched in Rotterdam with some success in 1913 and resumed after suspension during the war in both Rotterdam and Amsterdam in 1919 with the *Rotterdamsche Likwidatiekas* and the ALK in Amsterdam clearing the contracts.

LPCH was less successful. It began guaranteeing rubber contracts from 1 November 1921 – having secured the business after rubber brokers suffered heavy speculative losses the year before.[32] But this proved a short-lived diversification because the Rubber Trade Association set up a rival settlement scheme around the same time.

LPCH reported a net profit for 1921 and paid 6 shillings per part-paid ordinary share – its first dividend since 1915. In January 1922, the board raised the annual salaries of Matt and John Culbertson, the company secretary, to £750 each and paid each a bonus of £300. This brought their salaries back to around 1914 levels. But their incomes, including bonuses, were well below those of Schultz before the war.

The clerical staff of LPCH also had to accept less generous conditions. When J.P. Kimmins joined the clearing house in 1923, he was paid £120 a year – less than the going rate in 1914.

[31] Runge, a scion of the sugar trading house Tolme & Runge, was secretary and manager of the UK government's Royal Commission on Sugar Supply during the First World War. In 1921 he joined the board of the sugar refining company Abram Lyle and Sons, which merged with Henry Tate and Sons to form Tate & Lyle.

[32] *The Times*, 25 October 1921. LPCH cleared 495 tons of rubber in 1922 and 450 tons the following year.

Kimmins's reminiscences, published in 1988, point to a male-dominated world of work where little changed from one year to the next:

> The day started around 9:30 [and] normally finished about 5:30. The pace was 'hell for leather' all day. We had to write and copy everything by hand. Contracts were prepared by the brokers and we came in Saturdays to check the week's work.
>
> It was unusual to see ladies working in the City in the 1920s. Our office was staffed by men until quite late and routines hardly changed from 1923 to the 1950s.

Great events came and went. During the week of the General Strike of 1926, Kimmins cycled into work in Mincing Lane from Chiswick and was rewarded with £5 extra. He recalled how three years later: 'Business wasn't much affected by the Great Crash. We carried on at nearly the same turnover, although we clerks suffered!' The manager declared that clerks were 'two a penny' and ordered their wages cut.

From the early 1920s onwards, LPCH filled a steady but unspectacular niche in the City. By 1926, the German problems were in the past. Its main business was clearing contracts traded on the sugar futures market where, between 1928 and 1931, contracts for raw sugar gradually supplanted white sugar.

After a brief post-war revival, the Santos coffee business declined, fizzling out in 1927 because the Brazilian government took over marketing its crops. Instead, LPCH cleared cocoa futures from 1928. The size of LPCH – as measured by its balance sheet – fluctuated around £700 000 from 1926, the year of the General Strike, into the 1930s.

The company's five-member board decided to pay what became regular dividends of 7s/6d (15%) per ordinary share from 1925 onwards and £56/5/- from 1926 on each of the 100 founders' shares with a nominal value of £10 each. In March 1927, the company's 40th annual general meeting heard that all arrears on the 6% cumulative dividends had been paid to shareholders. The payments of 15% and £56/5s on LPCH's paid-up ordinary capital of £187 500 and £1000 nominal of Founders' shares remained unchanged through good years and bad until January 1940, when the company cut its dividends for 1939 to 10% and £25 respectively.

The nominal paid up capital of LPCH stayed unchanged at £188 500 throughout the interwar years although the terms were adjusted twice. In 1930, all ordinary shares, whether issued or not, were given a nominal value of £2/10s each, making them fully paid up. In 1937, the £187 500 of paid-up ordinary shares were converted into 187 500 units of loan stock with a nominal value of £1 each with a promise to pay at least 6% a year.

Before the First World War, LPCH relied on uncalled capital to support its guarantees in a crisis. Between the wars, a prudent dividend policy enabled it to accumulate investments as an informal guarantee fund. These were valued at £488 810 at the end of 1939.

Raw sugar and cocoa were the only products cleared by LPCH during most of the 1930s. Volumes slumped in 1931 as the Great Depression took hold and again in 1935. The AGM in February 1936 heard how 'government interference in production and consumption in nearly all producing countries' was stifling speculative trading.

Activity picked up strongly in 1937 when, on the eve of its 50th anniversary, LPCH cleared contracts for 3.93 million tons of raw sugar and 352 250 tons of cocoa – more than in any previous year.

Business sagged again before the Second World War although by this time, the clearing house had begun to handle other products. In 1937, LPCH helped create a new futures market for pepper following an attempt by speculators to corner the market. In February 1938, it defended its policy of paying 'steady and adequate dividends' on the grounds that it was hoping to expand and needed finance on hand.

Instead war intervened. When the UK declared war on Germany in September 1939, LPCH registered and cleared futures transactions in raw sugar, cocoa and shellac and small quantities of white and black pepper (see Box 6.1).

Box 6.1: LPCH contracts registered in 1939

- raw sugar: 1 221 300 tons (as against 2 690 700 tons in 1938);
- cocoa: 80 280 tons (as against 226 160);
- white pepper: 30 tons (as against 85);
- black pepper: 50 tons (as against 35);
- shellac: 23 250 bags and/or cases (no comparison).

The company had recovered somewhat from its depressed state of 1918 but it never regained its pre-First World War stature during the interwar years.[33]

6.7 FORCED INACTIVITY AND THE SALE OF LPCH

The Second World War had a far more drastic effect on LPCH than the First World War. The UK government took control of the economy, closing commodity markets and putting an end to LPCH's clearing activities.

LPCH ran on a care and maintenance basis. It continued to collect interest and dividends on its investments and paid dividends totalling 6% a year on its ordinary stock throughout the war. The energies of its directors were deployed in the war effort. LPCH's annual report for 1944 showed two of them had been awarded the Military Cross.

Published early in 1945, the 1944 report broke with the company's previous taciturn tradition and carried a brief statement from Geoffrey Swann, the chairman. It struck a hopeful note. The directors, Swann said, were eagerly awaiting the day when produce markets would re-open for trading and the company could 'resume its normal function of financing and guaranteeing the exchange and distribution of commodities'.

Britain's post-war Labour government took no notice. It kept controls and rationing in place and markets closed, relying on centralised agencies to purchase commodities in bulk from abroad. By 1949, the government's policies were causing real problems for LPCH. Its continued inactivity combined with increased taxes on profits forced a cut in its overall annual dividend for 1948 to 5%.

On 11 February 1949, the directors wrote to shareholders. They had given serious thought to the company's future. It had built up significant reserves of £121 954 by retaining part of its profit each year and also had a surplus of about £157 934 because of the difference between the book value of its investments, at £316 402/5/5d, and their market value of £474 336.[34]

[33] The assets and liabilities on LPCH's balance sheet amounted to £461 123 at the end of 1939. This was the equivalent of £21.72 million in 2007 terms and not much more in real terms than the total 50 years before when LPCH had operated for less than two years. Expressed in 2007 pounds, its balance sheet was worth £12.7 million at the end of 1918, £59.49 million at end-1913 and £20.63 million at end-1889. LPCH's investment portfolio, also expressed in 2007 pounds, was worth £14.34 million at the end of 1913, £4.23 million at the end of 1918 and £21.14 million at the end of 1939.

[34] Worth £12.43 million in 2007 terms.

However, they were uncertain about the value of the company's shares, and especially the Founders' shares, in the event of any distribution of the surpluses or a liquidation of LPCH. The directors did not know whether holders of Founders' shares were entitled to more than their £10 nominal value. They therefore presented three hypotheses, which valued the Founders' shares respectively at £10, £23 and £654 and LPCH's ordinary stock at £2/7/6d, £2 and £1. Holders of each type of share were invited to appoint representatives to committees to consider the problem.

A year passed in which the committees made no progress. The clearing business was still moribund while investment income was falling because of still higher taxes on distributed profits. An unchanged 5% dividend for 1949 left LPCH's ordinary stock dividend a cumulative 2% in arrears. The only bright spot was a recommendation by the House of Commons Select Committee on Estimates to reopen the UK's tea, cocoa and grain markets to revive the UK's entrepot trade and invisible earnings. Swann commented gloomily that the damage caused by five years of socialist government policy was only being noticed after foreign locations had taken trade formerly held by London and Liverpool.

In May 1950, the directors decided to sell LPCH. Writing to shareholders, the company reported that the cocoa market was still under government control 'although it hopes for some freedom shortly – while the sugar market believes that control of its operations must continue for at least five years'. As sugar was LPCH's main business line before the war, the directors could see no prospect for trading profitably without it.

The board had received an offer from United Dominions Trust (UDT), a fast-growing finance company, of £2/1/3d for each £1 of ordinary LPCH stock compared with the most recent London Stock Exchange price of £1/16/3d. UDT also offered an interim dividend in lieu of arrears from 1948 and 1949 and £313 for each Founders' share.

On 1 June 1950, LPCH reported that 90% of shareholders accepted UDT's offer, ending its existence as an independent, listed company. It was still uncertain whether, as a UDT subsidiary, it could or would resume its clearing house activities.

7
Complete Clearing in North America

7.1 THE MINNEAPOLIS CLEARING ASSOCIATION

Just three weeks after LPCH opened for business in 1888, it received an approach from the other side of the Atlantic. The board was told that 'leading flour millers of Minneapolis' had written to suggest US flour contracts could be passed through the newly established clearing house in London.[1]

Hermann Fortlage and Benjamin Tabor, both LPCH directors, opened negotiations with a Gunther de Ste Croix representing the millers from Minnesota. Although the talks came to nothing, the contact showed how information about clearing practices quickly spread from continent to continent in the globalised world of the late 19th century.

Despite such contacts, the European method of guaranteeing contracts pioneered in Le Havre and practised by LPCH did not take hold in the US. According to one 1896 account, the New York Coffee Exchange considered adopting the European method on several occasions but rejected it each time: 'It has been attempted more than once to introduce such a clearing-house into the New York Coffee Exchange, but the proposition has never got farther than the Board of Managers,' Henry Crosby Emery reported.[2]

Instead, in 1891, the Chamber of Commerce of Minneapolis, which was the city's grain exchange, launched its own clearing house with a novel method for mitigating the problem of counterparty risk for traders.

By 1890, Minneapolis had replaced Buffalo as the premier milling centre of the US. It was also an important regional banking centre and home to a confident business community that prided itself on being in the forefront of financial innovation. The local enthusiasm for new ideas in finance partly reflected an unwillingness to allow the region's economy to be dominated by Chicago, 350 miles to the southeast. It was also to counteract the disadvantage of the city's geographical separation from the deep water ports and cheap bulk transport opportunities of the Great Lakes and its consequent dependence on rail transport to move grain and flour to the east. Gripes about railway tariffs were a recurring feature of the annual reports of the city's Chamber of Commerce in the 1880s and 1890s.

The Chamber itself was incorporated in 1881 to provide a market for trading grains grown in the vicinity. It was primarily a cash market and, as such, gained greatly in importance after 1886 when the city's millers decided to use it instead of their own association for buying

[1] LPCH board minute 23 May 1888. The talks with de Ste Croix appeared to have finished by mid-June.

[2] Emery, Henry Crosby (1896), *Speculation on the Stock and Produce Exchanges of the United States*. In his classic work, Emery described the way the *Caisse de Liquidation* and *Liquidationskasse* took responsibility for fulfilling contracts and declared in a footnote: 'There is little reason to regret its absence in American Exchanges.' As described in Chapter 5, the clearing methods of the New York Coffee Exchange were inspected by M Le Normand of Le Havre during his 1882 fact finding mission to the US that preceded the foundation of the *Caisse*.

wheat.[3] The Chamber's first futures contract – for hard red spring wheat – was launched in January 1883.[4] Futures trading volumes were very low throughout the 1880s.[5] But the Chamber's board decided in the summer of 1891 to appoint a three-man committee to draw up a project for a clearing house for open trades.[6] Their aim seems to have been to improve hedging opportunities in Minneapolis for trading in the type of wheat grown in the region.

The committee came out in favour of a clearing house modelled on that of the Chicago Board of Trade (CBOT). In August the board duly approved a set of draft amendments to the exchange's by-laws, running to 23 paragraphs, to put to its members.[7] However, a specially convened meeting of the members on 2 September 1891 rejected the plan for the CBOT-style clearing house by 66 votes against to 62 votes for. The majority, the local press reported, wanted the clearing house to be separate from the Chamber of Commerce.[8]

The clearing house project passed out of the hands of the exchange and a few weeks later the majority had its way. On 28 September 1891, the Chamber of Commerce Clearing Association was incorporated with a capital stock of US$50 000, divided into 1000 shares of US$50 each, to be fully paid up when issued. The articles of incorporation described the company's business as 'the buying, selling, storing and handling of grain of all kinds including the handling of the same for commission and the buying, selling, leasing and mortgaging of estates in real property and personal property of every description.'[9]

The clearing association's foundation as a corporation under Minnesota law created a legal entity that could take the place of counterparties to trades on the exchange. The reference in the articles to the 'buying, selling, storing and handling' of grain is evidence that the association was what came to be known as a 'complete clearing house', acting as a seller to every buyer and a buyer to every seller and was therefore the ancestor of today's central counterparty clearers or CCPs.

On 6 October 1891, the Chamber of Commerce gave the clearing association exclusive rights to clear trades on the exchange. On 12 October, the exchange provided the clearing house with desk space for one year.[10]

Unfortunately, more detailed contemporary evidence about how the Minneapolis clearing house operated no longer appears to exist. Instead historians and writers – including this author – have relied on a voluminous report on the US grain trade, produced by the Federal Trade Commission (FTC) in 1920 – some 29 years later – for corroboration that the Minneapolis Chamber of Commerce Clearing Association was the first US clearing house to adopt complete clearing in 1891 as well as details of how it operated.[11]

---

[3] Kenney, Dave (2006), *The Grain Merchants: An illustrated history of the Minneapolis Grain Exchange.*

[4] According to www.mgex.com, the website of the Minneapolis Grain Exchange (accessed 6 December 2010). The Chamber changed its name to the Minneapolis Grain Exchange (MGEX) in 1947.

[5] Federal Trade Commission (1920), 'Report of the Federal Trade Commission on the Grain Trade'. See table 4.1.

[6] *Minneapolis Tribune* (24 July 1891), 'The grain clearing house'.

[7] Chamber of Commerce Board Minutes of 24 August 1891, a copy of which was kindly supplied to the author by MGEX.

[8] *St Paul Daily Globe* (3 September 1891), 'They voted it down'; and *Minneapolis Tribune* (3 September 1891), 'They don't want it: The Chamber of Commerce Clearing House Scheme dies a'bornin'.

[9] Photocopy of the original articles kindly supplied to the author by the Minnesota Historical Association of Minneapolis.

[10] Information from the minutes of the Board of Directors of the Chamber of Commerce, passed to the author by MGEX.

[11] The author has been unable to trace any copies of the early rules and by-laws of the Minneapolis clearing association to establish with certainty that it functioned as a 'complete clearing' house from the time of its foundation. According to WorldCat, the online library catalogue service, the US National Agricultural Library (NAL) in Beltsville, Maryland, possesses an early copy of 'Articles of incorporation and general rules of the Chamber of Commerce Clearing Association of the city of Minneapolis'. However, the document was missing when the author first contacted and later visited the NAL in 2009 with the hope of inspecting it.

Starting in 1920, the FTC produced what would become its seven-volume *Report of the Federal Trade Commission on the Grain Trade*, published by the Government Printing Office in Washington. In volume 2, on page 146, and volume 5, page 228, the FTC

According to the FTC, members of the clearing association had to be members of the exchange operated by the chamber of commerce. But not all exchange members needed to be members of the clearing house. The commission houses dealing in futures on the Minneapolis exchange became clearing association members by subscribing to its shares after being approved by the clearing house directors. Should a member run into difficulties and default on a payment, the clearing house could buy or sell the contracts involved to protect itself against loss.

The Minneapolis clearing house differed from that in Chicago in that it was not structurally part of the exchange. Its policy of margining was also different. Under the complete clearing system, the clearing house manager had the job of calling on the parties to the trades to pay the margins as necessary to protect the clearing house until the trades had been settled.

In Chicago, the counterparties to the trade called for margins from each other and deposited them in a mutually agreed place, which was usually with the treasurer of the exchange or with a bank approved by the CBOT. Margins in Chicago were not obligatory under the exchange's rules.[12] Writing about the CBOT in 1911, one commentator noted how: 'In many trades between members where each is perfectly confident of the other's financial stability, the calling of margins is unnecessary and is often disregarded. The contract is allowed to run with very little attention paid to this matter.'[13]

The Minneapolis method, in the words of the FTC, required 'bringing open trades to the market closing price each day'. It was the duty of the member firms of the Minneapolis clearing association to report details of all trades to the clearing house by a fixed point in the afternoon.[14] They would either pay to or receive from the clearing house cheques to reflect the paper losses or profits on their open trades.

Complete clearing made life easier for market participants. It was also safer than the Chicago method of clearing. Members of the Minneapolis clearing association had only to deal with the clearing house when it came to settling trades and putting up margins. The mandatory calling of margins won the support of smaller trading companies, which saw in the CBOT's discretionary approach a system that favoured the stronger firms.

The Minneapolis clearing house rules allowed members to settle trades bilaterally without clearing house intervention. But the FTC considered that the convenience of the complete clearing system meant practically all trades went through it.

That said, the clearing association appears to have grown more slowly than its founders anticipated. When the FTC produced its study in 1920, it reported that its 'membership includes

quoted section 1 of Rule VI of the Minneapolis clearing association's general rules to demonstrate how the new form of clearing worked.

The rule said: 'All transactions made in grain during the day shall be cleared through the clearing association, unless otherwise agreed to the parties of the transaction. Upon acceptance by the manager of such transactions, the clearing association assumes the position of the buyer to the seller and the seller to the buyer in respect to such transactions, and the last settling price shall be considered as the contract price.'

The second sentence was not in section 1 of the draft rules approved by the Minneapolis Chamber of Commerce board on 24 August 1891, which would have created a CBOT type clearing house, and which were rejected by the members of the exchange 10 days later. An implication of the FTC's report is that the complete clearing rule was devised very quickly between the 2 September 1891 vote that rejected the CBOT type solution, and 12 October 1891, when the clearing association was provided with desk space in the exchange building.

[12] 'Such margin *may* be demanded on or after the date of the contract, and from time to time, as *may* be deemed necessary to fully protect the party calling for same.' From CBOT rules adopted in 1865 and quoted in the FTC report of 1920, volume 5 page 28 (author's italics).

[13] Harris, Siebel (1911), 'The methods of marketing the grain crop', *The Annals of the American Academy of Political and Social Science*, **38**.

[14] 2:30 P.M. on weekdays and 1 P.M. on Saturdays.

slightly more than 100 members of the Chamber of Commerce and no others' and that its 'outstanding capital stock was about $25 000 in 1918', suggesting that only half the capital authorised in 1891 was issued after 27 years of operations.[15]

7.2 MINNEAPOLIS: A NEGLECTED INNOVATOR

The method of clearing adopted in Minneapolis was a significant innovation. But once set up, it commanded very little attention.

Whereas the *Caisse* in Le Havre was the subject of lively comment in newspapers inside and outside France,[16] was discussed in scholarly works and was copied in other leading European trading centres within a few years of its foundation, there appears to have been hardly any contemporary interest in complete clearing as practised by the Minneapolis clearing association.

One local newspaper – the *Minneapolis Tribune* – returned to the subject of the clearing house five weeks after its incorporation with a glowing account of how the clearing house was 'in advance of the world' and certainly superior to the Chicago model. Although the article detailed the system of margins, it failed to mention how the clearing association functioned as a central counterparty.[17]

The Chamber of Commerce made no mention whatsoever of the establishment of the clearing association in its annual report for 1891 and subsequent annual reports of the chamber simply listed it as one of 550 or so members of the exchange. US newspaper articles, books and academic journals over the next two decades commented on the novelty of Minneapolis having incorporated its clearing house in a separate 'clearing association'. But the role of the clearing house and its imitators as the buyer to all sellers and seller to all buyers went unremarked among commentators and academics for nearly 30 years.

In his otherwise detailed 1896 work, *Speculation on the Stock and Produce Exchanges of the United States*, Henry Crosby Emery made no mention of the Minneapolis clearing association being a complete clearing house. Instead, Crosby made a special note of how the clearing house, unlike others, directed physical deliveries of grain. When, in 1911, The American Academy of Political and Social Science devoted the 38th edition of its *Annals* to a series of articles on US commodities exchanges, it described the Minneapolis Chamber of Commerce Clearing House Association as 'the pioneer organisation of its kind in the country' without mentioning its complete clearing function as the buyer to every seller and seller to every buyer.[18]

If newspaper reports are any guide, Winnipeg's clearing house, which began operating in 1904 and is described below on page 100, was at least as well known in Chicago in the mid-1920s as the clearing association in Minneapolis. When the Chicago Board of Trade was agonising over whether to adopt complete clearing in 1925, the *Chicago Journal of Commerce*

[15] Federal Trade Commission (1920), 'Report of the Federal Trade Commission on the Grain Trade', Washington, DC: Government Printing Office. Volume 2, page 146.

[16] For example, the *Financial Times* and *Liverpool Mercury*.

[17] *Minneapolis Tribune* (2 November 1891), 'A Perfect Clearing House: The one established by the Chamber of Commerce works like a charm'.

[18] Various authors (1911) The Exchanges of Minneapolis, Duluth, Kansas City, Mo., Omaha, Buffalo, Philadelphia, Milwaukee and Toledo, *The Annals of the American Academy of Political and Social Science*.

described complete clearing as the system 'in vogue at Winnipeg and some of the smaller domestic "contract markets"'.[19]

The absence of comment might have reflected a disinclination on the part of the clearing association to court publicity. The account of the exchange and clearing house in the *Annals* of 1911 described the clearing association's manager as 'undoubtedly the closest mouthed individual in the community'. It might also have reflected the slow spread of complete clearing on the Minneapolis model in US regional grain markets, which for the most part were not centres of speculation or focused on futures trading.

When the FTC produced its 1920 report on the grain trade, 639 (64%) of Chicago's 1000 resident grain traders were primarily engaged in futures trading, marking out the city as the pre-eminent centre for futures trading in the US. By contrast, only 35 (7.5%) of 464 grain traders in Minneapolis were primarily futures traders, while in Kansas City, Missouri, which established its clearing house in 1899, just 17 (10.1%) of the exchange's 169 resident grain traders focused on futures.

It may also be no coincidence that the first detailed accounts of the Minneapolis Chamber of Commerce Clearing Association and its 'historic' role as the US's first complete clearing house appeared after the First World War.[20] By this time, the Federal Government was promoting complete clearing as a way of reforming Chicago's grain futures market in much the same way as its successor in 2008–9 identified CCPs as a way of reducing risk in OTC derivatives markets. The FTC report may have been part of Federal Government efforts to 'spin' the virtues of complete clearing.

In a society so quick to report business innovation as the US in the early 20th century, the absence of comment about the Minneapolis clearing system is curious. However, there appears to have been no challenge to the FTC's 1920 account of the development of complete clearing in the US at the time it was written, or since then. Despite trying, this author has found no evidence of a different series of events.

Instead, the lack of contemporary interest in the Minneapolis clearing association may simply show how complete clearing in the US spread more slowly than the system of registering and guaranteeing contracts among European countries in the years before the First World War.

7.3 THE GRADUAL SPREAD OF COMPLETE CLEARING

For a fuller idea of how the early American clearing houses operated and were governed it is necessary to look southwest to Kansas City, Missouri, and north of the US border to Winnipeg in Manitoba.

More than seven years passed before the Kansas City Board of Trade followed the Minneapolis clearing model and set up the Board of Trade Clearing Company in March 1899. Some details are known about clearing in Kansas City, thanks to a brief account in the American Academy's *Annals* of 1911. However, this made no mention of the clearing company being the seller to every buyer and buyer to every seller.

[19] *Chicago Journal of Commerce* (26 August 1925), 'Board of Trade to vote again on changing clearing methods'. In the paper of 30 July 1925, a *Journal of Commerce* article headlined 'Pit clearing house plans hit obstacle', told how CBOT reformers wanted a 'clearing house system as in operation at Winnipeg'.

[20] 1920 seems to have been the year when the Minneapolis clearing system and the details of complete clearing achieved wide recognition. See: Boyle, James Ernest (1920), *Speculation and the Chicago Board of Trade* as well as Federal Trade Commission (1920), 'Report of the Federal Trade Commission on the grain trade'.

As in Minneapolis, the aim of its founders was to develop futures trading and end the dependence of traders on Chicago for hedging the locally grown winter wheat, corn and oats.

They appear to have succeeded. The clearing house was capitalised initially at US$5000 through the issue of 100 shares valued at US$50 each to Board of Trade members. The stock issue was doubled through the sale of an additional 100 shares at US$175 each in 1902. According to the 1911 *Annals* article, clearing house membership by then stood at 110 and the shares were valued at US$350 each. The number of shares held by any one person was limited to 20. Annual dividends of US$20 a share had 'been regularly paid' and the clearing charge cut from 3 cents per 1000 bushels to 2 cents.

The work was done in a single room in the Board of Trade building between 8 A.M. and 4 P.M. with a rush of activity after the market closed at 1:15 P.M. on weekdays and noon on Saturday. The operating cost of the clearing house was just US$5000 a year. By 1911, according to the *Annals*, the Kansas City clearing model had been copied by the Merchants' Exchange in St Louis and was used in Nashville, Omaha, Wichita and New Orleans.

As in Kansas City, the clearing house in Winnipeg, Canada, was set up primarily to allow the city's traders and millers to hedge their grain purchases more efficiently than through the CBOT.

On 19 March 1901, 23 local grain merchants and millers agreed among themselves to set up the Winnipeg Grain and Produce Exchange Clearing Association 'for the purpose of buying, selling, storing, receiving and delivering all kinds of grain' as well as handling for a commission 'the settling, adjusting and clearing ... of all transactions in grain for future delivery' made by members of the association on the Winnipeg Grain and Produce Exchange.[21]

The clearing house was incorporated in July 1901 with a capital of C$25 000 Canadian dollars, divided into 500 shares of C$50 par value each. There were 22 founding shareholders. Each subscribed to five shares, paying initially just 10% of the C$250 due.[22]

The association took some time to organise. But the clearing house grew steadily after it began operating on 1 February 1904. It was user-owned and user-governed and organised on mutual lines. After acceptance by the board, new members subscribed to just five shares each – just like the founders.

The Winnipeg clearing association was a complete clearing house. As in Minneapolis, not all members of the exchange were members of the clearing association. But all members of the clearing association had to be members of the exchange. There was mandatory margining. The association's by-laws[23] specified that once a trade in grain had been accepted by its manager, the clearing house assumed the position as buyer to the seller and seller to the buyer. It also took responsibility for proper delivery in futures trades.

Business grew sufficiently so that by the end of 1907, the association decided to double its capital through the issue of 500 new C$50 shares. But rather than offer these at par, it priced the new shares at C$300 to help the association build up reserves and in part to keep its membership within limits.

[21] Winnipeg Grain and Produce Exchange Clearing Association (March 1901), 'Agreement and Subscription List'. The archives of the Winnipeg Grain and Produce Exchange Clearing Association are held in Winnipeg by the University of Manitoba. The university's Archives and Special Collections Department kindly provided photocopies at the request of the author.

[22] Winnipeg Grain and Produce Exchange (28 June 1901), 'Certificate of Incorporation'.

[23] Section 1 of By-law 13 of the General By-laws and Rules of the Association.

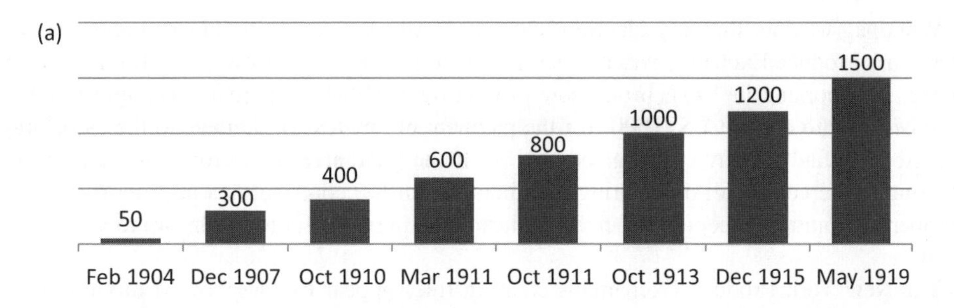

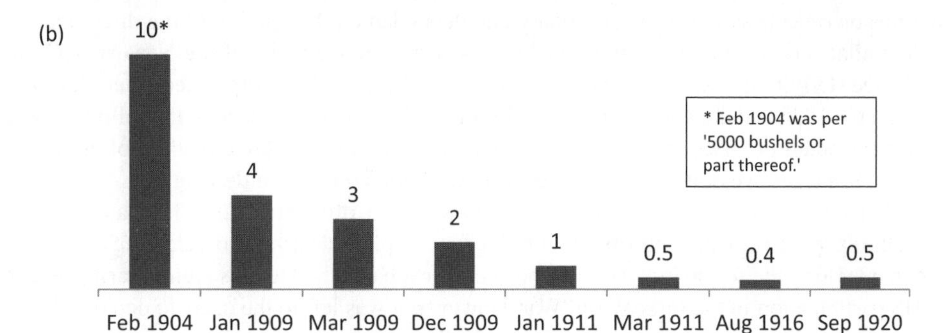

Figure 7.1 (a) Winnipeg clearing association shares 1904–1919 (subscription prices in Canadian dollars); (b) Clearing grain in Winnipeg (cost in Canadian cents per 1000 bushels)

Source: Winnipeg Grain and Produce Exchange Clearing Association.

As shown in Figures 7.1a and 7.1b, the issue price of Winnipeg clearing association shares was raised substantially in the years that followed, while its clearing fees were lowered at intervals until they bottomed out at 0.4 cents per 1000 bushels in 1916. The low 1916 fee level proved sustainable for four years only. It reflected a policy adopted in 1914 when the association's annual meeting decided to stop paying dividends and provide clearing services to members as close to 'at cost' as possible. This seems to be the first recorded case of a clearing house pursuing an at cost pricing policy. The association declared only two annual dividends before the First World War: 10% in February 1913 and 12% in March 1914.

By 1921, the Winnipeg clearing house had a nominal capital of C$30 750, divided among 123 members who held a total of 615 shares. In addition, the association had nearly C$293 000 in reserves. In that year, a management review of the clearing house's first 20 years concluded that the system was 'eminently satisfactory', although it admitted that the association had 'to accept one loss, which amounted to [C]$30 580.43'.[24]

[24] According to a description and history of the Association, entitled 'Nature of Organisation and Historical', dated 12 July 1921, and preserved among its archives. Unfortunately, the account gave no details or explanation of the loss. But it may have resulted from events in 1908, a turbulent year in the Winnipeg grain market. Under pressure from a hostile farming community, the for-profit Winnipeg Grain and Produce Exchange was forced to suspend trading for some months before reorganising under the name Winnipeg Grain Exchange as a voluntary, unincorporated not-for-profit organisation. In addition, minutes of the clearing association's board meetings in July 1908 refer to substantial losses incurred through an oats deal that went wrong. The loss appeared not to impede the civic career of Frank Fowler, the manager of the clearing association at the time, who was a Winnipeg alderman for 14 years and mayor of the City in 1922 (according to Levine, Allan (1987), *The Exchange: 100 Years of Trading Grain in Winnipeg*).

Winnipeg was not the only clearing house in North America to build extra reserves. The New York Produce Exchange was a venerable institution, dating back to 1861. But its clearing house, incorporated in 1904, broke new ground by establishing a guarantee fund in which members had to deposit US$1000 'for the payment of any loss or damage to the association caused by default of any clearing member'.[25] If the guarantee fund proved inadequate, the clearing house could call on clearing members for further contributions in proportion to the number of contracts accepted for clearing during the previous four months, up to a US$5000 limit.

The New York Produce Exchange's clearing rules appear to have been a mixture of the modern and the antiquated. While its guarantee fund was innovative, the calling of 'original margins on open trades' was discretionary and depended on the opinion of the directors.

A similar mix of old and new marked the clearing arrangements of the New York Coffee Exchange. Originally set up in 1882, the coffee exchange was incorporated by a New York State Act in 1885 and drew up its first set of by-laws – known as floor rules – the following year. As Emery noted in 1896, the exchange declined to adopt the Le Havre method of clearing.[26] Instead, as successive editions of its rules testify, it relied on ring settlement.[27]

In 1916, the coffee exchange became the New York Coffee and Sugar Exchange. At this point the exchange amended its rules to provide for complete clearing and a clearing association began operating the following year, just before the exchange had to close temporarily because of US participation in the First World War. However, it was left to the users to decide whether to use the clearing house as a buyer to every seller and a seller to every buyer.[28] As late as 1927, the rules allowed ring settlement as well as complete clearing as a means of clearing coffee and sugar contracts.

For nearly 30 years, the complete clearing houses set up in North America followed the Minneapolis lead of being incorporated entities distinct from, but still closely associated with, the exchanges that they served and to which their members belonged.

In 1919, however, a minor Chicago exchange devoted to the trading of butter and eggs brought complete clearing in-house. In October that year the Chicago Butter and Egg Board changed its name to the Chicago Mercantile Exchange (CME) and began trading butter and eggs futures on 1 December. The change of name was a sign that this mutually organised exchange harboured ambitions to trade other futures at a later date. Backing up those ambitions was a new complete clearing house 'to be maintained and operated under the rules of the Exchange for the purpose of clearing all future trading between members.'[29]

The first of the Clearing House Rules spelled out what this meant for the exchange and its members: 'Wherever these By-Laws create a right in favour of the Clearing House or impose a liability on the Clearing House, it shall be construed as the right or liability of the Exchange and shall be enforceable by or against the Chicago Mercantile Exchange.'

---

[25] Federal Trade Commission (1920), 'Report of the Federal Trade Commission on the grain trade', page 231.

[26] Emery (1896).

[27] There are references to Ring Settlement in the 1885 rules of the exchange and as subsequently amended in 1894, 1902 and 1914. The rules of the New York Coffee Exchange and the later Coffee and Sugar Exchange are preserved on microfilm in the New York Public Library.

[28] From 1916, section 88 of the New York Coffee and Sugar Exchange rules included the following wording: '... members *may* offer their contracts for clearance to the New York Coffee Clearance Association (all members of which Association are members of this exchange), which *may* become by substitution a party thereto in place of a member ...' (author's italics).

[29] Chicago Mercantile Exchange (15 June 1921), 'Constitution, by-laws and clearing house rules. Supplied to the author by Cornell University Library, Ithaca, New York.

At the CME, the clearing house was substituted as the buyer to the seller and the seller to the buyer of trades. But the buck stopped with the exchange when it came to guaranteeing their completion. The financial obligations on those exchange members who chose to be members of the clearing house were correspondingly rigorous.

All clearing members, whether individuals, partners in firms or directors of corporations, had to guarantee to take financial responsibility for any and all trades passing through the clearing house in their name. Each clearing member had to deposit and leave with the clearing house US$500 for its protection and the protection of its members. A clearing house committee of the exchange fixed initial margins that 'under no circumstances' were less than 5% of the value of the commodity margined. If market conditions required, the manager of the clearing house or chairman of the clearing committee could call for additional margin monies to be deposited 'during the next banking hour after demand'. In event of failure, the clearing house could close the trades of any delinquent and charge the loss to his account.

The clearing house rules also stipulated that exchange members acting as brokers 'must require their customers to deposit margins equal to ten per cent of the contract price of their trades'. In the event of market fluctuations, it was the job of the clearing member to call sufficient margin to maintain the 10% margin deposit 'at all times'. Any member failing to do so was to be 'considered guilty of uncommercial conduct and be subject to suspension or expulsion from the Clearing House'.

The CME clearing house rules specified a sequence for tapping resources to cover losses. The first line of defence would be the margins deposited by the insolvent clearing member, followed by the money in the clearing house guarantee fund. After this, a levy would be imposed on clearing members in proportion to the amount of charges paid to the clearing house for its services during the preceding three months. To ensure that the clearing members' US$500 deposits were not mixed up with users' margin payments or the clearing house fees or the exchange's income and outgoings, the rules obliged the CME to maintain at least five sets of accounts with three or more Chicago banks, each of which was required to have a representative holding a membership in the exchange.

At the time, the CME's clearing house attracted little attention. A bigger drama was playing out in Chicago, where the CBOT was under mounting pressure from some of its own members and the Federal Government in Washington to modernise its governance and its clearing arrangements. Six years after the CME opted for its in-house clearing solution, the CBOT chose an arm's length version of the Minneapolis model. The different clearing options chosen by the upstart CME in 1919 and the establishment CBOT in 1925 would play a crucial role in the destinies of the two exchanges some 80 years later when, as rivals, they battled for domination of US futures markets.

7.4 A CCP FOR THE CBOT

By the early 1920s, the grain futures market in Chicago was beginning to appear the odd man out in not clearing its trades through a CCP. Although 86% of US grain futures were traded on the CBOT, the exchange still used ring clearing. It took action by the US Federal Government to change the CBOT's mind.

In fact, the CBOT's members were divided. The Phillips bankruptcy of 1902 had prompted some exchange members to petition, without success, as early as 1903 for a complete clearing system in which the clearing house would be the seller to every buyer and the buyer to every seller.

Table 7.1 Votes of CBOT members to move to complete clearing: 1917–25

Date of vote	Members For	Members Against
20 September 1917	272	528
4 October 1920	228	502
27 January 1922	418	423
28 December 1923	136	551
3 September 1925	601	281

Source: Letter to James J. Fones, Secretary of CBOT, from P.W. MacMillan, the CBOT representative in Washington, 5 September 1925.

That petition was the first of many such efforts to bring a CCP to the CBOT. In 1911, CBOT members were balloted on rule changes that would have introduced some aspects of complete clearing but stopped short of providing guarantees of contract performance.[30] The proposals were defeated by a large margin.

A more substantial attempt to move the CBOT to adopt a CCP was made six years later. It was driven by a special CBOT Clearing House Committee, which argued that the Chicago market had fallen behind the rest of the world. In a letter of 17 July 1917, the committee claimed complete clearing was 'in successful and satisfactory operation in every important exchange in this country and abroad'.[31]

The reformers made progress. On 19 July 1917, CBOT members voted by 446 to 324 votes in favour of a committee proposal to draw up a detailed plan 'to change from the present antiquated system of clearing our trades to the most modern method'. But when the detailed plan for a 'Board of Trade Clearing House' – complete with rules and by-laws – was put to the vote two months later it was rejected by a two thirds majority (see Table 7.1).

There were two main reasons why members rejected the CCP. Some felt the existing system, which had been approved by the US Supreme Court, was more secure against potential adverse legislation. Others feared that clearing house employees could gain insights into confidential details of trading activity.

These arguments lost some of their force in the years following 1917. Several factors encouraged further efforts in the early 1920s to create a CCP for the CBOT:

- Court decisions relating to other markets upheld the complete clearing system proposed for the Chicago exchange.
- The Grain Futures Administration, established as part of the 1922 Grain Futures Act, subjected futures trading in Chicago to US government regulations, which included keeping trading records, reporting open positions to federal regulators and paying stamp taxes. Without a CCP, traders would have to keep their own records, make their own reports and pay taxes on their gross trades. The intervention of a CCP would enable them to carry out these duties on a multilateral net basis, saving back office costs and taxes.
- The CME was based in Chicago and operated a complete clearing house.

[30] Moser, James T. (1994), *Origins of the Modern Exchange Clearinghouse.*

[31] Letter dated 17 July 1917 of CBOT Clearing Committee to Members of the Board of Trade. The author is indebted to Dennis Dutterer, a senior executive of the Board of Trade Clearing Corporation between 1985 and 2005 and former CEO, who generously provided copies of this and other material relating to BOTCC from his archive.

However, it took pressure from US Secretary of Agriculture William M. Jardine to tip the balance in favour of the clearing house for the grain futures trade amid widespread hostility towards the CBOT in the farming community and among politicians in Washington.

The First World War had triggered a surge in prices for grains and other foodstuffs. In 1916, corn prices hit their highest level since the American Civil War. The following year, wheat hit an all time high. After the US entered the war in 1917, the government suspended futures trading in wheat, sugar, cottonseed and cottonseed oil and imposed price controls on commodities regarded as military essentials. Prices continued to rise until 1920 when the government discontinued wartime price guarantees. Prices then fell sharply. By May 1921, grain prices were one third the level of the previous June.

The sharp price fluctuations revived charges that the CBOT was a nest of gamblers and led to calls for it to be deprived of its designation as a 'contract market' – and thus able to trade futures – under the 1922 act.

Jardine wanted to end what he called the 'disastrous price changes', but he did not want to take away the CBOT's right to conduct business. He believed a CCP would help to solve the problem of excessive grain price fluctuations because, rightly or wrongly, he saw it as a means of curbing excessive speculation by a small group of professional speculators.

Jardine sought, through a series of high profile speeches during the summer of 1925, to bend the CBOT to his wishes while making clear he was prepared to use federal powers if necessary.

'As I see it, the grain exchanges of this country perform a useful function – at least we have perfected no better system of marketing,' Jardine told farmers on 4 July 1925.[32] But he warned bluntly that there was 'something wrong' when the price of wheat fluctuated 12 or 13 cents on the day. It was up to the grain exchanges to correct the situation:

> They must realise that they have to a large extent lost the confidence of the people and can reclaim this only by thoroughly putting their house in order. If they fail voluntarily to take appropriate action, it is my purpose to exercise to the fullest extent such power as the existing law gives me to require them to do so.

Jardine had strong support among many at the exchange. But there were problems along the way. At the end of July 1925, CBOT directors refused to allow a vote on a petition from exchange members for a complete clearing house on the grounds that 'the subject has been before the membership on a number of occasions and defeated in every instance – the last time by an overwhelming majority'. One journalist covering the decision described it 'as a bolt from a clear sky' given Washington's wish for a CCP and support for the project from Frank L. Clary, CBOT president.[33]

Supporters of a CCP promptly organised a new petition calling for a complete clearing house. Meanwhile the political temperature in Washington rose. In consternation, J.C. Murray and L.F. Gates, Chicago members the Grain Exchange Legislative Committee, a Washington lobby group, wrote a confidential letter to all present and former officers of the CBOT on 29 August. They did not pull their punches.

'Comparatively few realize the crisis with which we are faced. The situation is the most serious in the history of the exchange,' they began.

[32] In a speech to farmers in Mandan, North Dakota, 4 July 1925, quoted in Falloon, William D. (1998), *Market maker: A sesquicentennial look at the Chicago Board of Trade*.

[33] *The Chicago Journal of Commerce* (30 July 1925), 'Pit clearing house plans hit obstacle'.

The letter highlighted a 'growing feeling' among policy makers in Washington that the Secretary of Agriculture was 'entirely too lenient' with the CBOT 'particularly since refusal of the directors to follow his suggestion regarding adoption of a clearing house'. Warming to their theme and resorting to uppercase type to emphasise their points, the two officials told of demands 'THAT THE SECRETARY TAKE AWAY FROM THE CHICAGO BOARD OF TRADE ITS DESIGNATION AS A CONTRACT MARKET[34] under the Grain Futures Act' and the perception 'that affairs in Chicago are in the hands of the majority of the MEMBERSHIP WHICH DOES NOT SENSE THE PRESENT CONDITION, AND DOES NOT ADMIT THE NEED TO CHANGE'.

'It cannot be urged too strongly upon you the great need for changes in Chicago in order to avoid extreme action by the Secretary or Congress,' the two officials said. 'The warning is plain. Time is vital. Every hour lost is an added danger,' they stressed, as they called on 'every present and former officer' to lobby the members of the exchange to vote for reforms.

Their efforts and those of others reformers were rewarded on 3 September 1925 when a new CBOT rule, number XXXIV, was passed by 601 to 281 votes with 4 abstentions. The members had voted by a majority of 320 to set up 'a clearing corporation' that once in operation 'may be substituted as seller to each buyer, and as a buyer to each seller upon all trades in all commodities'.

Unlike the clearing house division of the CME, which was set up in 1919, the new body would not be integrated into the CBOT. The Board of Trade Clearing Corporation (BOTCC) was incorporated on 5 October 1925. But although a separate entity, BOTCC was very closely tied to the exchange.

According to rule XXXIV, the clearing corporation was 'organised under the supervision of the [CBOT] board of directors'. The CBOT board had to approve 'the charter, rules and clearing regulations of the clearing corporation, and all modifications thereto'. Rule XXXIV stipulated that once BOTCC took over the roles of seller to buyer and buyer to seller the contracts that it handled would be subject to CBOT rules and regulations as well as those of the clearing corporation itself.

And yet, despite this intertwining of the two organisations, the CBOT members made a less than firm commitment to the new clearing corporation. The rule change empowered CBOT directors 'by an affirmative vote of at least twelve' of them to opt for the old ring settlement form of clearing or another clearing method, should CCP clearing 'prove prejudicial to the best interests' of the exchange's members.

According to Dennis Dutterer, a former BOTCC CEO, there was never any formal contract to define the clearing arrangements between the CBOT and BOTCC. [35] Their relationship was determined instead by the rules and by-laws of the two organisations. The governance arrangements between the CBOT and BOTCC were to play a significant part in the reshaping of clearing arrangements and futures markets in Chicago 75 years later.

7.5 THE BOARD OF TRADE CLEARING CORPORATION

In early November 1925, it was announced that 141 companies had subscribed to 680 shares of Board of Trade Clearing Corporation stock, providing BOTCC with a paid-in capital of just under US$1.6 million. Three weeks later, a manager – one Howard S. Robb – was appointed

[34] Upper case as used in the original letter. Photocopy of the original document kindly supplied by Dennis Dutterer.

[35] Conversation with the author, 23 January 2009.

for the clearing corporation. BOTCC started operating on 4 January 1926 and the migration of trades to the new system began. This process was completed on Saturday, 30 January 1926, when BOTCC took over all trades in wheat, the CBOT's highest volume market.

BOTCC was incorporated in Delaware with a capital stock divided into 1000 shares of no par value.[36] Its by-laws specified that ownership of its stock was to be closely aligned with use of the clearing house.[37] That said, BOTCC's articles of incorporation enshrined voting arrangements at its annual meetings that ensured a disproportionate share of decision making rested with the small traders on the exchange who opted to be BOTCC clearing members.

The shares were subscribed by its users who were members of the CBOT. All but three or four of the clearing members of the former CBOT clearing house subscribed to the initial offering of BOTCC stock while 'about one dozen new names were added'.[38]

The amount of stock of each owner was to 'be approximately in proportion to the volume of clearances of such stockholder as compared with the total clearances of the clearing house'. If the board determined that any stockholder owned more shares than were justified by the volume of clearances over a preceding six month period, it could require him to surrender his excess shares, giving BOTCC the option of buying such shares at their book value. Conversely the board could deny clearing rights to stockholders whose stockholdings were inadequate compared with the volume of their clearing business.

One of the board's tasks was to fix the price of shares for new applicants from time to time. The first set of by-laws set a price of US$2500 per share. Subscriptions had to be in proportion to the estimated volume of clearing, but not for less than one share or more than 12.

The board was authorised to declare dividends from any surplus or net profit arising from BOTCC's clearing business. But the by-laws gave a strong hint that it should first determine whether to set aside money from BOTCC's accumulated profits for working capital or for contingency reserves.

The articles of incorporation enabled the company to pass by-laws that in turn gave the board the right to determine who should be a stockholder of BOTCC. This, combined with a provision that at stockholders' meetings each stockholder had 'one vote irrespective of the number of shares held by him', gave considerable power to the small CBOT traders who chose to become clearing members of BOTCC.

The power of the small CBOT traders over the affairs of BOTCC became evident in 1934–35 when the giant Cargill Grain Company of Minneapolis applied to become a clearing member of BOTCC. The BOTCC board referred the matter to the CBOT's directors because the exchange's own rule book also contained restrictions on corporate membership of BOTCC.

The upshot was a refusal by the CBOT directors to allow Cargill to become a clearing member of BOTCC even though the Minneapolis-based grain trader conducted an estimated 60% of its overall grain futures business in Chicago. The decision of the CBOT board contributed to a poisonous relationship between the exchange and Cargill that lasted for many years. It also highlighted the power of the small CBOT traders and clearing members of BOTCC, which remained a factor in the governance of the two institutions for the rest of the century.

---

[36] Certificate of Incorporation of the Board of Trade Clearing Corporation, made available to the author by the Daley Library of the University of Illinois at Chicago.

[37] By-Laws of the Board of Trade Clearing Corporation, made available to the author by the Daley Library of the University of Illinois at Chicago.

[38] Letter of 3 November 1925 from the special clearing house committee of the CBOT to the CBOT Board of Directors. Supplied by Dennis Dutterer.

7.6 PROSPERITY AND DEPRESSION

BOTCC was established in what turned out to be a brief sweet-spot in the interwar years. The US economy was growing at around 7% a year in the mid-1920s and in 1926 unemployment dropped below 2%.

According to James E. Boyle, a leading scholar of agricultural markets at the time, the comparative prosperity of the later 1920s prompted 'a great spurt in America and Europe in organising new commodity and stock exchanges' in the five years from 1924 to 1929.[39] In the US, new futures markets such as the Rubber Exchange of New York, established in 1926, furthered the spread of complete clearing.

Not that bilateral or ring clearing disappeared. Just as ring clearing continued alongside complete clearing for contracts on the New York Coffee and Sugar Exchange after 1916, so too the New Orleans Cotton Exchange provided a choice of clearing methods after introducing a cottonseed oil contract in 1925. As Boyle noted: 'Contracts may be settled through the Clearing House of the Cotton Exchange, or by offsets between members, or by ringing out and paying only the balance due.'[40]

Not even BOTCC acted as a central counterparty in all cases. From 1930, BOTCC cleared equities and bonds after the CBOT began trading a limited number of stocks, including American Cynamid, Armour & Co, Ford Motor Co., Standard Oil Co. of Indiana, Studebaker Corporation and William Wrigley.

BOTCC by-laws for clearing equities and bonds, adopted in 1930, underlined that: 'The clearing house will not be substituted as the other party to any transaction in securities, but merely acts as the common agent of the members for the purpose of facilitating deliveries.'[41] In this respect, BOTCC was no different from other clearing systems for US stock markets.

Clearing stocks in the US had a long pedigree, pre-dating the CBOT's clearing house. The first US stock clearing and settlement system was created at the Philadelphia Stock Exchange in 1870. But clearing stocks was a humdrum affair compared with clearing for futures exchanges and remained so for many years. The early US stock exchange clearing houses facilitated netting, much as did the CBOT's clearing house, and clarified the details of trades between parties prior to settlement. Unlike the CBOT clearing house, they also directed market participants to deliver stocks as necessary to other specified parties.[42] The New York Stock Exchange (NYSE) was the last major exchange to adopt clearing in 1892; however, it applied to only a few actively traded stocks.[43]

BOTCC's stock clearing business was launched at an unfortunate time and never became a significant part of its activities. The CBOT's securities business failed to prosper after the 1929 Wall Street Crash. Volumes peaked in 1931 when 1.67 million shares were traded on the exchange. From 1935 the number of securities listed on the CBOT shrank[44] and the market was finally closed in the 1950s.

---

[39] Boyle, James E. (1931b), 'The New York Burlap and Jute Exchange', *The Annals of the American Academy of Political and Social Science*. Boyle was Professor of Rural Economy at New York State College of Agriculture, Cornell University, Ithaca, New York.

[40] Boyle, James E. (1931a), 'Cottonseed Oil Exchanges', *The Annals of the American Academy of Political and Social Science*.

[41] By-Laws of the Board of Trade Clearing Corporation, Chapter 7, Section 200: By-Law for Clearing Securities through Board of Trade Clearing Corporation, made available to the author by the Daley Library of the University of Illinois at Chicago.

[42] Emery (1896).

[43] Forty three securities in August 1896, according to Emery (1896).

[44] Of the listed stocks that remained, there was a growing number each year that went untraded. In 1952, total stock sales on the CBOT's securities market amounted to just 35 shares of Atlantic Oil Corp with a market value of just US$73.75. There were no securities trades at all in 1954 and 1955 after which the market closed.

During its first 50 years, BOTCC's fortunes were tied to the CBOT's futures markets for farm products. The futures contracts cleared by BOTCC in its early years were invariably agricultural: wheat, rye, ribs, oats, lard, cotton, corn and pork bellies.

However, BOTCC came on the scene too late to clear the CBOT's record trading volume of 5.4 million contracts in 1925, which stood until 1963. Trading volumes at the CBOT fell sharply after 1929 during the Great Depression. By 1942 and 1943, CBOT trading volumes were less than 1 million contracts[45] as wartime rationing and price controls took their toll.

The clearing corporation survived the Depression and the Second World War. As it reported later, 'no customer lost money as a result of clearing member default' during these difficult years and BOTCC's 'financial obligations were always met on time'.[46]

7.7 GLOBAL POSTSCRIPT: SEPARATING THE WEAK FROM THE STRONG

The 1930s saw the last vestiges of the globalising world economy of the pre-First World War era swept away by economic depression, protectionism and the spread of dictatorships in much of Europe and Japan. War broke out in Europe in September 1939 – less than 21 years after the armistice that ended the First World War. On 7 December 1941, the Japanese attack on Pearl Harbor brought the US into the war, abruptly ending two decades of non-involvement in world affairs.

If trading conditions were difficult for futures markets and clearing houses in the US and Britain, they were harsher for the clearing houses of continental Europe. The years immediately after the First World War were overshadowed by revolutionary unrest and hyperinflation in Germany; the after effects of the collapse of the Austro-Hungarian, Russian and Turkish empires; Communism in the Soviet Union; and instability in many of the new nation states that emerged after the war.

A new problem was currency volatility. The ALK in Amsterdam omitted payment of a dividend for the first time in its history in 1922 after it was hit by the fall in value of the German Mark.

Nationalism and protectionism were especially problematic for clearing houses such as the *Caisse* in Le Havre and the two Dutch clearers, which had built up international businesses before 1914 and which were forced to rely more on their domestic markets.

Some fared better than others. Le Havre continued to have an important coffee futures market because of high coffee consumption in France[47] and close ties with the Brazilian government. In 1937, the *Caisse de Liquidation* reported having reserves of 11 million francs alongside capital of 6 million, indicating a fairly strong financial position.

Although the ALK in Amsterdam omitted its dividend for a second time in 1934 and profits were depressed during the 1930s compared with 1920s, it celebrated its 50th anniversary in 1938 as an independent, for-profit corporation. By contrast, the *Rotterdamsche Likwidatiekas* became part of the R Mees & Zoonen banking group in 1934, having encountered financial problems after the 1929 crash.

[45] Gidel, Susan Abbott (2000), '100 years of futures trading: From domestic agricultural to world financial', *Futures Industry Magazine*.

[46] According to *Trusting, Growing, Leading, Clearing: a History*, a brochure published by BOTCC around 2002–3.

[47] France overtook Germany during the First World War to become the world's second largest consumer of coffee after the US.

Trade and futures markets suffered as countries took control of commodity imports. Democracies were just as likely to act in this way as dictatorships. The ALK annual report for 1927 wrote of commodity imports coming under government control in Scandinavia and Czechoslovakia. From 1933, Hitler's Germany cut back imports of coffee through foreign ports so that none entered Germany via Le Havre or London in 1937, and only small amounts came through Amsterdam and Rotterdam.[48]

Looking back from September 1938 at 24 years of sugar trading since the start of the First World War, C Czarnikow of London noted that world sugar consumption in the period increased by 10 million tonnes. But 'much of this increase has been met by the extension of domestic industries and the establishment of new ones, and the trading in our article, which is governed by values obtaining in the world market, is of no greater volume than that in 1913'.[49]

The 1930s divided the weak from the strong. But very soon, it did not matter whether markets or clearing houses in continental Europe were strong or weak. All ceased activities after the outbreak of the Second World War and only resumed operations after long delays.

The war marked an end to all activity for some clearing houses. One such was the *Caisse de Liquidation* in Le Havre, which ceased operating in 1939 and, like the rest of the city centre, was reduced to rubble in September 1944.

In the US, government intervention during the Second World War had a dramatic effect on the country's grain markets, including those in Minneapolis. The city became home of the world's largest cash grain market, but futures activity slumped.[50]

The status of Minneapolis's pioneering CCP changed. The Chamber of Commerce's rules, by-laws and regulations of July 1943 for the grain futures market referred for the first time to the clearing association.[51] In the absence of evidence to the contrary, it seems reasonable to suppose that this was the moment when the CCP in Minneapolis assumed its present position as 'a department' of the grain exchange. Although the clearing house was still formally incorporated as a Minnesota corporation, the chamber became the CCP's owner with its clearing operations incorporated in the exchange's management.

In the context of a world war, the decision by North America's first complete clearer to adopt the clearing house structure introduced at the CME in Chicago in 1919 was a very small event. But it signalled a trend.

When, towards the end of the 20th century, financial markets embraced globalisation for the second time in 100 years, exchange-owned clearing houses on the CME model became the norm in futures markets around the world, rather than the separate clearing corporations as pioneered in Minneapolis and exemplified by BOTCC.

[48] Becker, Ursula (2002), *Kaffee-Konzentration*.

[49] C Czarnikow Ltd (15 September 1938), 'Weekly price current'. Although the company was named after its founder, the Czarnikow family ceased to have an interest in it shortly after Caesar Czarnikow's death.

[50] Kenney, Dave (2006), *The Grain Merchants: An illustrated history of the Minneapolis Grain Exchange*.

[51] By contrast, there was no reference to the clearing association in editions of the Chamber's rules and by-laws published in 1902, 1915, 1917, 1920, 1922, 1926 and 1934, which are held by the NAL in Beltsville, MD.

Part III

Formative Years

8

The Collapse of Bretton Woods and the Invention of Financial Futures

8.1 THE RETURN OF PEACETIME AND ECONOMIC GROWTH

The revival of futures markets and their clearing activities was a gradual process following the Second World War. Some US commodity markets closed during the war: for example, that for soya bean futures was shut from March 1943 until July 1947. On others, activity slowed to a trickle: potato futures, introduced on the New York Mercantile Exchange (Nymex) in the week before Pearl Harbor, traded only 80 contracts in 1945. Some markets were affected by war-time technical advances. Egg futures, a founding contract of the Chicago Mercantile Exchange when launched as the Chicago Butter and Egg Board in 1898, declined in importance after temperature control equipment in chicken houses enabled hens to lay eggs all year round instead of just in spring.[1]

By 1948 markets were recovering in the US and being reintroduced into parts of continental Europe. But progress was patchy and limited by controls on capital movements. In Britain, the government only began to relax its grip on commodity markets in 1951, whereas some food rationing continued for years after that. When, in November 1954, Le Havre's coffee futures market reopened in temporary accommodation amid ongoing reconstruction of the city, its focus and that of its new clearing house – the Caisse de Compensation des Affaires en Marchandises au Havre – were much diminished compared with pre-war days. The market was purely domestic, with its activities and those of the new Caisse de Compensation constrained by price controls, exchange controls and government limitations on speculation.[2]

In one respect, things had not changed. The transatlantic divide in clearing house structures remained. Where clearing houses reappeared in Europe, they guaranteed futures contracts much as they had in the 1880s, instead of substituting themselves for buyers and sellers as legal counterparties. US clearing houses, by contrast, were buyers to every seller and sellers to every buyer, irrespective of whether they were owned by exchanges and incorporated into the management of the exchange as at the CME, or were separate corporations like BOTCC.

Important for the longer term history of trading and clearing was the post-war political and economic framework. The world was divided by ideology. The Soviet Union was the dominant power east of the 'Iron Curtain' that ran through a divided Europe from the Arctic to the Mediterranean Sea. It imposed command and control economics over Eastern Europe and its own vast lands. Further east in China, a variant of communism was being introduced by Mao Zedong after the defeat of Chinese nationalist forces in 1948.

[1] Gidel, Susan Abbott (2000), '100 years of futures trading: From domestic agricultural to world financial', *Futures Industry Magazine*.

[2] Rufenacht, Charles (1955), *Le Café et les Principaux Marchés de Matieres Premiere*.

In the capitalist 'west' including Japan, democracies rebuilt their economies under the US nuclear umbrella on free market principles that included varying degrees of social protection.

Enlightened internationalism supported a gradual return of prosperity in the industrialised democracies. Growth was supported by commitments to freer trade and the international monetary system devised in the New Hampshire resort of Bretton Woods in 1944, which was centred on fixed exchange rates that could only be adjusted in exceptional circumstances. The Bretton Woods system together with the 1947 General Agreement on Tariffs and Trade[3] were designed to banish a repetition of the beggar my neighbour protectionist policies of the 1930s that accompanied and exacerbated the Great Depression and were held partly responsible for the world's drift to a total and devastating war in 1939.

The international monetary system invented at Bretton Woods was built around the dollar, which had a fixed value in terms of gold of US$35 an ounce. The values of all other currencies were expressed in terms of this dollar price of gold and only small fluctuations were allowed either side of the resulting parities. The system's credibility hinged on agreement that foreign monetary authorities could convert their US dollar holdings into gold at US$35 an ounce. This 'gold window' was devised when US gold reserves far exceeded the holdings of dollars of non-US central banks. Successful at first, the post-war economic and financial system began to run into trouble in the 1960s when large US current account deficits, other global payments imbalances and inflationary pressures undermined the dollar's pivotal role and the exchange controls that supported it.

The eventual collapse of Bretton Woods was accompanied and hastened by the rapid development of computing power, which greatly increased the scale and speed of financial market transactions. Together these developments would bring new opportunities in futures markets and new challenges for clearing houses.

8.2 LPCH RESUMES CLEARING

The Cocoa Terminal Market was the first UK commodity market to open after the war and J.P. Kimmins was on hand at LPCH to clear the trades. 'I took the first call when the markets reopened after the war,' he said some years later.[4] 'It was on cocoa in January 1951. We registered 51 lots that day in a small room in Mincing Lane borrowed from Czarnikow.'

The clearing routines that resumed after more than 10 years of enforced idleness were little changed from those encountered by Kimmins in 1923, in his first year as a registrations clerk at LPCH. They continued unchanged for some years, as Peter McLaren testifies.[5]

McLaren joined LPCH in 1954 after completing his national service and stayed with the company until he retired in 1992. He became an executive director of ICCH, the International Commodities Clearing House, as the clearing house was known after 1973. McLaren recalled that when he joined LPCH

> ...the only markets cleared were cocoa and wool and the calculation of margins was done literally on the back of an envelope without the aid of a calculator let alone a computer.
>
> The situation at LPCH when I started there was the same as experienced by Mr Kimmins in the 1920s. I worked with four men who had been employed by LPCH prior to 1939. They told

[3] GATT was the forerunner of the World Trade Organisation.

[4] As remembered in *100 Years of ICCH* (1988), published by the International Commodities Clearing House to mark the centenary of the founding of LPCH.

[5] As described to the author in emails of December 2008 and January and March 2009.

> me that when the company resumed business after the war it just took up the same system used before the war started.
>
> In a rather Dickensian manner, discipline was very strict. Smoking (which most people did then) was not permitted in the office until after 3 P.M., because it was considered un-businesslike to smoke before members of the Clearing House who attended the office to deliver contracts traded the previous working day. The working day was at times very long and often we worked until 9 or 10 in the evening without overtime. However, we were compensated by the payment of generous annual bonuses which was a common practice in the commodities trade with whom the Clearing House had to compete for staff. As in the 1920s no women were employed in the early 1950s.

The relationship of clearing members to clearing house was little changed from that in LPCH's early years. Full, associate and overseas members of the exchanges that it cleared were allowed to be members of the clearing house. The contracts of the associate and overseas members were submitted to LPCH by the full members – the successors of the authorised or privileged brokers – although registered directly in accounts of the associate and overseas members.

United Dominions Trust (UDT) promised continuity when it took over LPCH in 1950. It retained some of the clearing house's directors including Geoffrey Swann, LPCH's former chairman, who became a member of the clearing house's board. UDT also retained Antony Gibbs and Sons, a City firm that had made its fortune from the Guano boom of the early 19th century, and which provided the clearing house's secretarial and management services until the early 1970s.

But UDT was a dynamic enterprise under the restless chairmanship of John Gibson Jarvie, an outspoken advocate of free markets who had helped found the company in 1922 and chaired it until 1963. When Antony Gibbs proposed that the clearing house should explore new possibilities and, where necessary, should help create new futures markets, it found a willing backer in Jarvie, who also chaired the LPCH board.

The 1950s saw several commodity markets either open or reopen in London with active encouragement from LPCH, as a fully consolidated, wholly owned subsidiary of UDT. The wool terminal market opened on 29 April 1953. In 1956, LPCH was guaranteeing and clearing the newly established London Shellac Terminal Market. Trading in sugar resumed in 1957, after a gap of nearly 18 years, with LPCH guaranteeing and clearing the contracts. Coffee futures followed in 1958, after more than 30 years.

Some markets were more successful than others. The shellac futures market failed to prosper, partly because of Indian government intervention in the shellac trade, and partly because of a declining demand for top hats (which owed their shine to varnish made from this resinous material) and 78 rpm records.

Another LPCH initiative that fell foul of government interference was the London terminal market for fishmeal, a protein rich ingredient of chicken feed. The market opened in April 1967 to provide futures contracts in a commodity subject to wide price swings. But the government of Peru, the main source of fishmeal, immediately took steps to stabilise the price. The market closed in June 1970 after a period of inactivity.

The wool futures business was more successful. Reporting in August 1957 to UDT's annual meeting, Jarvie announced that LPCH had registered wool futures contracts worth £410 million in the previous four years, amounting to 31% of all contracts registered by the clearing house since its acquisition by UDT. By August 1960, the cumulative value of wool business was just over £1 billion. Two years later, it was £1.45 billion.

This growth encouraged LPCH to diversify and expand abroad. It created a subsidiary – Wool Testing Services – for testing wool quality. WTS, in turn, acquired the London Textile

Testing House, which tested 'the content and quality of all types of natural and man-made fibres' for 'manufacturers, government departments and members of the public'.[6]

By this time, UDT had set up offices throughout the UK and subsidiaries in some Commonwealth countries. LPCH's Wool Testing subsidiary also established overseas links as did LPCH itself. Following an approach from firms trading in Sydney, LPCH started guaranteeing and clearing contracts for the Sydney Greasy Wool Futures Exchange in 1969 and opened a Sydney branch office.

8.3 NEW ACTIVITIES AND THE COMING OF COMPUTERS

LPCH was not alone in seeking new activities. US exchanges were also developing new futures markets. But although there was a recovery in the volumes of contracts traded, growth was far from spectacular. According to Futures Industry Association figures, it was not until the 1960s that the number of US futures trades exceeded 10 million a year.[7] It was only in 1973 that the price of seats for trading at the CBOT passed US$62 500, a level last recorded in 1929. Activity was depressed in smaller futures exchanges where infrequent bouts of activity in the trading pits gave way to long hours in which traders could be found sitting on the pit steps reading newspapers for much of the day.

To boost turnover, the CME in Chicago broke new ground in the 1960s by developing contracts based on perishable products. It first traded futures in meats – beginning with frozen pork bellies in 1961 – and later live animals. Other US exchanges developed futures trading in other perishable products, such as frozen orange juice, or in metals, including platinum, silver and palladium.

But the real drivers of future change in clearing during this period were developing away from the trading floors. One agent of change was the growth of computer power, which transformed the perspectives of clearing houses and so many other businesses in the final quarter of the 20th century. The other was the gradual breakdown of the Bretton Woods system of mainly fixed and rarely adjustable exchange rates.

Computers made their debut in clearing houses on both sides of the Atlantic in 1963. Two years later, Gordon Moore, co-founder of chip maker Intel, promulgated the first version of Moore's Law, which has come to mean that computer power doubles every 18 months or so.

In 1963, BOTCC in Chicago bought its first computer to cope with rising volumes and to speed the process of trade checking. In consequence, the cost of clearing fell to 5 cents per contract in that year.[8]

In London in 1963, LPCH computerised a punch card system installed in 1960 to carry out clerical and accounting tasks linked to the registration and processing of contracts. Punch card technology followed a failed attempt at automation in 1956, breezily described 32 years later as a 'shambles' by Kimmins: 'We struggled with the new system for a while then we had to convert the whole thing back to manual to sort out the mess!' was how he described that episode.

When introduced, the punch card system was the first significant advance on the manual processes in existence at LPCH since 1888. The clearing house introduced a daily dealing

[6] According to UDT's 1965 annual report.

[7] Measured as buys plus sells or the number of contracts traded times two.

[8] 'Trusting, Growing, Leading, Clearing: a History', published by BOTCC around 2002–3, compared the 5 US cent cost of clearing a contract in 1963 with a per-contract clearing cost of 25 US cents in 1941.

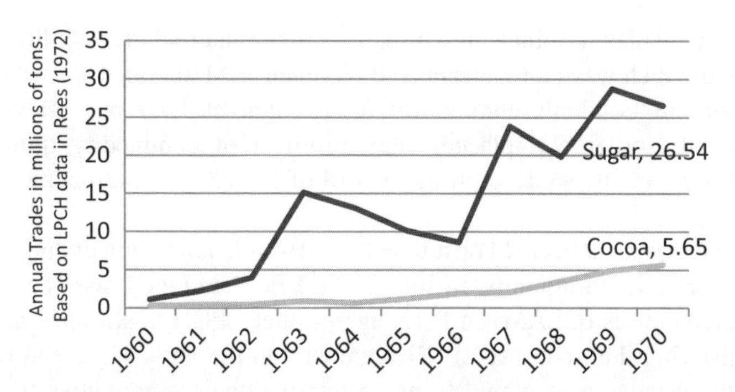

Figure 8.1 London sugar and cocoa futures in the 1960s. Computers at LPCH boost trading
Source: Author's illustration, based on LPCH figures as reproduced in Rees, Graham L. (1972), *Britain's Commodity Markets*, London: Paul Elek Books.

statement listing the trades carried out by each trading member, which became the official evidence of their transactions. It removed the need for members to prepare contracts for submission to LPCH for checking and matching and replaced the old distinctive certificates of guarantee that were produced on linen paper. The daily bought and sold totals were checked electronically by LPCH to ensure that the number and value of bought and sold contracts were equal.

These innovations dispensed with much copying and contract preparation, easing the pressure of work on LPCH and members' back offices. In 1965, LPCH upgraded its computer from a card system to one backed by magnetic tape storage and set up Assets Computer Services as a separate company to provide a 'round the clock service for the City of London'.[9] The ICT 1902 machine enabled it to carry out around 500 000 updates on the open interest and margin requirements of contracts each night. As a consequence, and as shown in Figure 8.1, transactions on the London sugar and cocoa terminal markets increased about 20 times during the 1960s.[10]

Computerisation enabled more than improvement in process. It brought the first significant reforms of clearing practice since the launch of LPCH. A mark-to-market system was introduced during the 1960s to determine margins. In the late 1960s the clearing house amalgamated positions on all markets on which a member traded so that it could offset profits on one market against losses on another. These advances were noted in the press. Under the headline 'One payment covers all', *The Times* reported in December 1969 that the continual upgrading of LPCH's computer system since 1963 meant brokers active on several markets needed only to make one cash payment to cover a net amount due in settlement on several markets. The investment in computers also lowered communications costs for out of town clients and clearing operations overseas.[11]

In November 1971, LPCH decided to hire an IBM 370/135 computer at an annual cost of £65 000 for delivery in January 1973.[12] LPCH then developed Intercom,[13] a computer system

[9] Report to the UDT annual meeting, August 1966.
[10] In Rees, Graham L. (1972), *Britain's Commodity Markets*.
[11] *The Times*, 4 December 1969.
[12] As reported in *The Times*, 3 November 1971.
[13] INTernational Enquiry Response system for COmmodity Markets.

that brought video display terminals into brokers' offices and real time confirmation of trades and positions and which was more advanced than much IBM-supplied software at the time.

Record activity in London's commodity futures markets was one reason for the new computer: when the order was placed, daily turnover of commodity futures in London exceeded 29 000 contracts, well up on the record of 21 000 contracts achieved on one day two years before.

Another reason was an expected boost to activity from Britain's impending membership of the European Economic Community. In June 1972, LPCH and the Caisse de Liquidation des Affaires en Marchandises (CLAM) in Paris agreed that LPCH could open an account with CLAM for registering the trades of LPCH members on the Paris sugar and cocoa markets. LPCH hoped the arrangement would bring to international commodities trading the same advantages of single payments and offsetting margins that it had produced for its members in London in the 1960s. There was even talk around Mincing Lane of 'an international clearing system under the auspices of LPCH', which *The Times* newspaper believed could be a 'UK contribution to furthering the commercial and industrial unification of western Europe'.[14]

LPCH's capital was raised to £2.5 million from £1 million during the summer of 1972, with UDT providing £1.25 million and the remaining £250 000 coming from LPCH's reserves. The new capital was to support the development of international clearing activities.

By this time, its name – the 'London Produce Clearing House' – fitted badly with the company's ambitions to expand abroad. Accordingly, the board organised an in-house competition to devise a name that better reflected the company's presence in Australia and Paris and its plans elsewhere. On 14 May 1973, LPCH changed its name to the International Commodities Clearing House (ICCH).

8.4 FLOATING CURRENCIES AND FINANCIAL FUTURES

Overall turnover on futures markets served by LPCH/ICCH in London and Sydney hit new records in 1972. Increasing speculative activity and volatile and active trading conditions were features of commodity futures markets between 1963 and 1982. As described later,[15] conditions on the sugar market in Paris in 1974 were so volatile as to precipitate a crisis that led to the closure of ICCH's partner CLAM, the central counterparty clearing house.

Although technical advance facilitated the jump in activity, the turmoil in commodities was symptomatic of a bigger upheaval caused by the gradual decay of the post-war Bretton Woods international monetary system.

The first serious strains in the Bretton Woods system appeared in 1963 when President John F. Kennedy introduced an Interest Equalisation Tax to stem an outflow of dollars from the US. A further blow was the 14.3% devaluation of the British pound against the dollar in November 1967. In August 1969, France devalued its franc, hammering a further nail into the coffin of Bretton Woods. Two years later, the US dealt fixed exchange rates a mortal blow, paving the way for a new era in futures markets that changed fundamentally the clearing houses that served them.

On 15 August 1971, President Richard Nixon abruptly suspended the dollar's convertibility into gold, effectively floating the US currency and all other exchange rates. Shortly afterwards, John Connally, a blunt Texan who was Nixon's Treasury Secretary, famously summed up the

[14] As reported in *The Times*, 16 May 1972. *The Times* was a strongly Europhile newspaper in the early 1970s.

[15] See Section 8.9.

new position of the dollar for distraught European finance ministers: 'It's our currency. But it's your problem.'

There were in Chicago men for whom the upheavals in the global currency system spelled opportunity. One was Leo Melamed, chairman of the Chicago Mercantile Exchange, a small man with great vision, energy and boundless zeal for publicising himself and his exchange. Melamed can fairly claim to be one of the founding fathers of financial futures.

By the 1960s, the CME depended heavily on trading meat futures. In a June 1987 interview,[16] Melamed recalled how in 1969 he was 'deathly afraid' that he would be chairman of a single product exchange.

He found the means of diversifying in currencies. There was a market in forward currencies in 1971 but it was limited to banks or their international clients. An individual could neither hedge a currency exposure nor speculate against a currency. When in 1971, Milton Friedman, the Chicago based monetarist and future Nobel laureate, tried to short the British pound, banks refused to take his business, saying he did not have the necessary commercial interest to deal in foreign exchange.

Following Nixon's closure of the gold window in August 1971, Melamed pushed ahead with plans for a futures market for foreign currency. On Monday, 20 December 1971, Chicago newspapers carried first reports of the scheme with quotes from Melamed. He had been bounced into disclosing his plans ahead of schedule by an agreement over the weekend of the finance ministers of the Group of 10 countries.[17]

The 'Smithsonian Agreements', named after the Smithsonian Institution in Washington where the meeting was held, tried to put Bretton Woods back together again in Humpty Dumpty-like fashion with a devaluation of the dollar against gold to US$38 an ounce and a realignment of currencies. Melamed's confidence that currency futures would still be needed was justified by spring 1973 when the Smithsonian accord collapsed following the adoption of floating exchange rates by most European countries and Japan. Years of turmoil on foreign exchange markets followed.

By this time the 'International Monetary Market' (IMM) had been operating for nearly a year. Officially incorporated as an independent financial exchange under the CME wing in December 1971 and active since 16 May 1972, the IMM ushered in a new era of financial derivatives and risk-management techniques with the launch of seven currency futures contracts.[18]

In its early days, the IMM faced the same sort of hostility that had met the foundation of LPCH in 1888. One New York based foreign exchange expert was widely quoted: 'I'm amazed that a bunch of crapshooters in pork bellies have the temerity to think that they can beat some of the world's most sophisticated traders at their own game.' But Chicago's traders did just that. In later years the 'crapshooters' remark would be turned against the early critics of the IMM and repeated time and time again in CME publicity material.

Before then, however, it took some time for financial futures to become established. The IMM traded 144 000 contracts in 1972 and volumes stayed low until around 1977. Activity started to pick up in that year. In 1979, six exchanges around the globe traded nearly 26 million financial futures contracts. In 1981, the IMM's volume was around 14.6 million contracts, 100 times the total of its debut year.

[16] Melamed, Leo (June 1987), 'The way it was – An oral history', *Institutional Investor magazine.*

[17] Comprising the financially most important countries at the time and confusingly including 11 members: Belgium, Canada, France, [West] Germany, Italy, Japan, the Netherlands, Sweden, Switzerland, UK and US.

[18] British pounds, Canadian dollars, Deutsche marks, French francs, Japanese yen, Mexican pesos and Swiss francs.

In 2009, the total volume of contracts for financial futures and options traded on organised exchanges and monitored by the Bank for International Settlements amounted to 9.45 billion, with a notional principal value of US$1659 trillion. A further two billion commodity contracts were traded that year.[19]

8.5 OPTIONS, INTEREST RATE FUTURES AND CASH SETTLEMENT

The IMM was set up to trade more than foreign exchange futures. 'We believe the IMM is larger in scope than currency futures alone,' the CME's annual report for 1972 declared, 'and, accordingly we hope to bring to our threshold many other contracts and commodities that relate directly to monetary matters and that would complement the economics of money futures.'

That role, however, was taken up by other US exchanges, which quickly embraced financial futures and related innovations including options.

The CBOT was exploring new trading possibilities well before first news broke of the CME's plans for the IMM. Having traded equities and bonds in the 1930s and 1940s, the CBOT wanted to trade futures on stocks, because these would be a counterweight to agricultural futures and reduce its traders' dependence on droughts, floods and other natural phenomena. But the idea was opposed by the SEC that regulated securities.

In 1969, Joseph Sullivan, a former Wall Street Journal reporter hired as assistant to CBOT president Henry Wilson, came up with the notion of a trading pit for options on stocks. The US was already home to limited trading in stock options. But it was a thin OTC market. Two years after putting forward the idea, the SEC gave Sullivan some encouragement and he began turning the idea into reality.

The Chicago Board Options Exchange (CBOE) opened on 26 April 1973 with Sullivan as its founding president. It traded a paltry 911 contracts spread among the 16 call options permitted by the SEC. The CBOE was separated from the Board of Trade because the CBOT's members, as traders of commodities futures, wanted no entanglement with the SEC's legalistic regulators.

Although the CBOE separated from the CBOT between conception and birth, it retained a good deal of the exchange's DNA. Its trading system harked back to its CBOT parentage by arranging for standardised option contracts to be traded like futures in a pit. The exchange was supported by a central counterparty clearing house to act as a buyer to every seller and a seller to every buyer of the options contracts. In this way, a secondary market was created that allowed hedging and speculation in options. As with futures, investors could close out contracts by taking opposite positions to those held.

Within weeks of the CBOE's launch, two economists – Fischer Black and Myron Scholes – backed by a third, Robert Merton, published a paper in the US *Journal of Political Economy* that contained a model for determining fair market value for call options.[20] The Black-Scholes model equipped traders with an easy-to-use pricing formula. It translated into greatly increased volumes on the new exchange. More than one million contracts were traded on the CBOE in 1973, with the volume rising to more than 35 million in 1979.

---

[19] Bank for International Settlements (March 2010), 'International banking and financial market developments, plus statistical annex', *BIS Quarterly Review*. Information on the notional value of commodity derivatives contracts traded is not available.

[20] Black, Fischer and Scholes, Myron (1973), 'The pricing of options and corporate liabilities', *The Journal of Political Economy*.

The other big area of innovation was interest rate futures. US interest rates became volatile in the late 1960s as America's economic problems mounted. By 1972 the CBOT's research department was engaged in detailed work on an interest rate futures contract under the leadership of Richard Sandor, the CBOT's chief economist, and another of the fathers of financial futures.

The researchers cast round for a suitable interest paying security on which to base the contract. They chose what were known as pass through certificates, issued by the Government National Mortgage Association (GNMA or Ginnie Mae), which were made up of collections of mortgages guaranteed by GNMA.

The SEC was not involved with interest rate futures so the CBOT's members had none of the reservations that coloured their attitude towards options. The CBOT introduced a futures contract based on the GNMA certificates in October 1975 and it proved a success. Other interest rate futures followed. The IMM began trading a three month Treasury Bill contract in January 1976 which also attracted strong investor interest. These developments encouraged the CBOT to introduce long-term US Treasury bond futures in 1977, which soon outperformed all other financial futures contracts in terms of growth of trading and investor participation.

The success of Treasury bond futures reflected, in part, a greater awareness among investors of Treasury bonds as the 'underlyings' for the contracts compared with the less familiar Ginnie Mae futures. But what really established the Treasury bond contract and interest rate futures in general was a revolution in domestic US monetary policy every bit as momentous as President Nixon's closure of the gold window was for international monetary relations.

The 1970s were difficult years for the capitalist world, with recurring bouts of currency turbulence, oil price shocks, soaring inflation and, at times, recession. In the autumn of 1979, the US was confronted with the toxic combination of a sharply declining dollar and double digit inflation.

The man charged with resolving this crisis was Paul Volcker, appointed chairman of the Federal Reserve Board in early August 1979. Determined to crush inflation, Volcker issued a statement on Saturday, 6 October 1979, which shifted the emphasis of the Fed's monetary policy from setting interest rates to targeting money supply.

Volcker's policy change caused interest rates to swing wildly. US prime rates rose to 15.75% in November 1979 to combat inflation running at 13%. The new policy triggered a revolution in the bond market as wild swings in interest rates prompted inverse movements in bond prices. Bonds were transformed from instruments favoured by the cautious investor into tools for speculation, rapid trading and the creation of vast profits and losses on Wall Street and beyond.

Volcker's policy shift also proved a watershed for interest rate futures. It created a hedging industry overnight. In October 1979, Salomon Brothers, one of the lead underwriters of a US$1 billion bond offering by IBM, hedged part of the issue with Treasury bond futures. The IBM bond flopped in the aftermath of Volcker's decision, but Salomon was able to offset heavy losses. There followed a decade of exponential growth for financial futures markets.

Further innovations fuelled that growth. While the CBOT laid claim to the market in long-term bond futures, the IMM scored in the short-term interest rate sector with the launch of a Eurodollar contract in 1981. This 90 day interest rate contract broke new ground in US markets in that it was the first in which cash settlement was allowed as a substitute for delivery.[21]

[21] A first for the US. But the Sydney Futures Exchange can claim to have introduced the world's first cash-settled futures: a US dollar contract in 1980, which was cleared by ICCH.

The approval of cash settlement in December 1981 by the US futures regulator, the Commodities Futures Trading Commission (CFTC), circumvented and superseded past decisions of the Illinois courts which had ruled that futures contracts that did not envisage the eventual delivery of a product were tantamount to gambling. It took the revolution in finance to a new level by aligning the interests of futures markets and banks.

As Alan Greenspan, then Federal Reserve Board Chairman, noted at the 30th anniversary celebrations of the IMM on 16 May 2002:

> Before the Eurodollar contract, many were unwilling to trade a contract that could not ultimately be settled through physical delivery of the underlying asset. And, before the Eurodollar contract, very few banks saw any use for financial futures. Twenty years after the launch of Eurodollar futures, most financial futures and the vast majority of swaps are cash settled and banks are the biggest users of Eurodollar futures and the dominant players in the swaps markets.

Cash settlement, in Melamed's words, 'became the gateway to the index markets'.[22] In February 1982, the CFTC approved the first futures contract based on a stock index, the Value Line Index Average traded on the Kansas City Board of Trade. Two months later, the CME launched a new trading division – the Index and Option Market (IOM) – with trading in a much more familiar Standard & Poors 500 futures contract. This stock index future became the CME's most popular traded contract.

Altogether, 89 new contracts were introduced on US futures markets in the 1980s – nearly matching the total number of products launched since the mid-19th century.[23] Looking back from 1986, Merton H. Miller, another Chicago-based Nobel laureate in economics, called financial futures 'the most significant financial innovation of the last 20 years'.[24] They propelled the futures industry from a little known backwater of market activity focused on agricultural products to the centre stage of global finance

According to Bill Brodsky, later Chairman and CEO of the CBOE:

> The people in Chicago had no fear. They had this belief you could take the futures structured product, which was basically the agricultural contract which could be used for hedging or speculating and which had this counterparty clearing, and you could apply it other concepts. And that is what really has endured.[25]

This revolution in finance was helped mightily by computerisation. Moore's Law – exemplified by the introduction of desktop personal computers in 1982 with power equivalent to the room-filling mainframe machines of the 1960s – had a continuing impact in raising the efficiency and reducing the labour intensity of clearing and other back office functions.

Trade entry, the process of feeding instructions into clearing systems, was a case in point. A growing problem in the 1970s, trade entry was traditionally the most labour-intensive part of a trading firm's operations. The strain on clearing members' back office staff grew as volumes surged. At BOTCC, for example, 'tens of thousands of punch cards were produced by members each day and fed manually into the Clearing Corporation's systems'.[26]

In 1981, BOTCC produced OTIS, its 'On-line Transaction Information System', to enter, edit and distribute trade information. OTIS was able to continuously match trade inputs,

[22] Melamed, Leo (1988), 'Evolution of the International Monetary Market', *Cato Journal*.

[23] Gidel (2000).

[24] Miller, Merton H. (May 1986) 'Financial innovation: The last twenty years and the next'.

[25] Conversation with the author at the 30th SFOA Bürgenstock Meeting, Interlaken, Switzerland, 10 September 2009.

[26] CCorp (2006).

helping both to detect and correct errors, and speed the collection and payment of variation margins. It also facilitated the handling of more complex financial instruments such as options on futures, which appeared on the US market in 1982.

But it would be some years before the clearing houses and the exchanges that either owned them or used their services began to perceive CCPs as strategic assets or as having critical functions. Clearing in the early 1980s was still seen as a 'just a back office, backwater operation,' says Phupinder Gill, President of the CME Group.[27] Clearing was a single batch process, carried out after trading had ceased at the end of the day. According to Gill, the prevailing attitude was: 'If it matches, it matches. If it doesn't, you fix it tomorrow.'

'Since those days, the time frames have contracted so much and technology has brought so much more efficiency,' adds Gill. 'But then, it was punch cards, card readers, single batch files and, if they didn't work, you just had to go back to the start of the day and try again.'

Such attitudes could not continue indefinitely. In the US at least, regulators started to take an interest in the clearing infrastructure serving the securities and futures exchanges. As market activity grew, so too did the number of mishaps involving clearing houses.

8.6 THE INFLUENCE OF REGULATORS

When Leo Melamed was planning the IMM, he was assured by the CME's legal counsel that there was no need for the exchange to obtain government approval for the venture. Melamed took the precaution of sounding out high government officials, including George Shultz, who became US Treasury Secretary shortly after the IMM's launch. But in 1972 there was no federal law or agency that had to approve the listing of currency futures contracts.[28]

Three years later, that was no longer the case. Regulators in the US had begun to exert increasing influence over financial markets. Their interventions in the case of clearing houses would result in two very different systems for CCPs handling securities and derivatives.

A new body, the Commodity Futures Trading Commission (CFTC) took over the task of policing US futures markets on 21 April 1975. The CFTC replaced the Commodity Exchange Authority (CEA), set up in 1947 to regulate agricultural commodities only and which traced its lineage back to the Grain Futures Administration of 1922.

The CEA was notoriously toothless. As Bill Brodsky recalled in conversation with the author: 'There was a modicum of regulation called the Commodity Exchange Authority, but we used to kid around that it was two guys in the basement of the Agriculture Department with a quill and eyeshade.'

Although the CFTC was born out of complaints about the CEA's deficiencies as a regulator, it was a notably more flexible body than the SEC, which had policed securities markets since 1934.

The CFTC developed into a principles-based regulator concerned with markets whose economic objectives are price discovery and risk mitigation. The SEC, created by the 1933 Securities Act that was passed during the Great Depression and in the aftermath of the 1929 Wall Street Crash, was and remains a rules-based body, staffed mainly by lawyers and primarily concerned with protecting the individual investor.

The two regulators came under different Congressional oversight regimes. Overseeing the futures industry and CFTC are the Agriculture Committees of House and Senate. The SEC is

[27] In a conversation with the author, Chicago, 26 September 2008.

[28] Melamed (1988).

scrutinised by the Senate Banking, Housing and Urban Affairs Committee and reports to the House Committee on Financial Services. In the 1980s, the SEC was accountable to the House Commerce Committee.

Congress gave the CFTC jurisdiction over all futures contracts, including contracts on groups of securities or indexes and over options on foreign currency futures, unless these were traded on a national securities exchange. These latter contracts were regulated by the SEC, in line with its responsibilities for regulating all US securities markets including options on stocks.

The Chicago-based futures industry – and the CME in particular – made a point of assiduously lobbying the CFTC. The regulator in turn had no difficulty supporting the futures industry practice of vertically integrating trading and clearing, whether by means of an in-house clearing division as in the case of the CME or a clearing house so closely identified with the exchange as to make no real difference, as was the case of BOTCC and CBOT at the time. The idea that trading and clearing of futures were really parts of a single product offering was firmly embedded in the CFTC's understanding of the futures business.

The SEC took a different view. When financial futures were taking off in vertically-structured exchange groups under CFTC regulation, the SEC was reacting to a paperwork crisis that had crippled Wall Street in the 1960s by creating a framework for US securities infrastructures that would separate trading, clearing and settlement.

By the 1960s, Wall Street's back office systems were unable to keep up with the growth of trading. Its manual systems were overwhelmed, causing processing blockages, paper mountains and gridlock. Bill Brodsky remembers how, on his first day on Wall Street in August 1968, 'I was most struck by the fact that the markets were closed on Wednesdays. And why? Because the back offices couldn't keep up with the paperwork.' The clearing and settlement of trades was carried out in a 'cage', in the airless bowels of the building, where the young Brodsky caught a glimpse of clerks behind a barred window, sifting certificates and clipping coupons.

In that year, the NYSE and leading New York banks took the first steps towards creating a paperless depository system with book entry procedures to hold and transfer US securities. An important technical advance for stocks clearing was the introduction in 1974 by the National Association of Securities Dealers (NASD) of Continuous Net Settlement (CNS), which enabled brokers to net a multitude of trades into one settlement obligation. In 1975, Congress – reacting after some delay to the crisis of the 1960s – passed the Securities Acts Amendments to promote a unified US market in trading, clearing and settlement and charged the SEC with securing these objectives.

The SEC decided that competition was highly desirable among brokers and to this end abolished fixed commissions in a manner later copied in the UK's 1986 'Big-Bang'. At the same time, the agency decided that an efficient, robust infrastructure that would encourage competition should take precedence in clearing and settlement and incorporated this goal into its plans for a 'National Market System' (NMS) to modernise the securities industry.

Responding to the Securities Acts Amendments, the SEC required stock market clearing houses and specialised securities settlement institutions, known as Central Securities Depositories (CSDs), to register with it as clearing agencies, so subjecting these organisations to regulation for the first time.

It prescribed what would become known as interoperability for post-trade infrastructures by ordering regulated free interfaces between regional infrastructures as the way towards NMS. The SEC encouraged a national system for post-trade services in other ways: for example, by publishing a report in the mid-1970s which highlighted the cost savings that consolidation of clearing houses would bring to the securities market.

The SEC created facts on the ground. The regulator intervened in Chicago's newly created market for trading options on stocks, giving an early insight into what it hoped to achieve.

When the CBOT sounded out the SEC about its plans for an options pit, the SEC ruled that options were securities. In consequence, the options market's clearing house – the CBOE Clearing Corporation – was regulated by the SEC under the 1933 Securities Act.

The SEC was given an early opportunity to apply the philosophy of the NMS after the American Stock Exchange (Amex) announced that it too planned to trade options from 1974. Although its legal authority was doubtful, the regulator refused to allow Amex to start trading the instruments and barred the CBOE from expanding its activities until the two exchanges agreed on a system for clearing options.

Wayne Luthringshausen, chairman and CEO of the Options Clearing Corporation, was head of the CBOE Clearing Corporation at the time. 'The SEC had a wedge. It made these developments conditional on clearing and gave two choices: either interoperability or a single clearing utility for the options market.'[29]

The exchanges opted for a single utility. In 1975, the CBOE agreed to sell Amex half of the CBOE Clearing Corp, which changed its name to the Options Clearing Corp. Later that year the Philadelphia Stock Exchange began trading options and was followed in 1976 by the Pacific Exchange. Both exchanges became shareholders of the OCC, thus establishing the system of a single central 'horizontal' clearing house for several options markets in the US.

8.7 HORIZONTAL INTEGRATION FOR US EQUITIES CLEARING

The 1975 Securities Acts Amendments, as implemented by the SEC, soon had an impact on the clearing infrastructures of US stock markets. The big exchanges – the NYSE and Amex, for example – had many members in common so that even before the amendments were enacted, market participants looked into the possibility of concentrating clearing. In 1976–7 the clearing houses of the NYSE, Amex and the NASD merged to form the National Securities Clearing Corp (NSCC).

At the same time, the CSDs attached to individual stock exchanges were linked by opening accounts with each other, to form a national system in which shares were transferred from one owner to another by book entry. At the centre of the network of CSDs was the Depository Trust Company (DTC), set up in 1973 by the NYSE, Amex and NASD in reaction to the paperwork crisis, to immobilise stock and bond certificates and transfer title.

NSCC adopted the continuous net settlement developed by NASD. CNS members were required to open customer accounts at DTC. It was through these accounts as well as NSCC's own account with DTC that the delivery and receipt of securities obligations cleared by NSCC took place and NSCC and DTC became intertwined.

Between 1977 and 1997, one after another of the US regional stock exchanges quit the business of clearing and settlement. Their clearing houses and CSDs were absorbed by NSCC and DTC respectively to create two single utilities serving the national securities industry.

By 1987 – the year of the Wall Street Crash – NSCC and DTC provided clearing and settlement for the Pacific, Cincinnati and Boston stock exchanges. In 1995, they absorbed Chicago's Midwest Clearing Corporation and Midwest Securities Trust Company. NSCC and

[29] Conversation with the author, Chicago, 20 October 2009.

DTC completed their respective national networks in 1997, when they integrated the Stock Clearing Corporation of Philadelphia and the Philadelphia Depository Trust.

The two horizontally-structured post-trade utilities gave the US the competitive advantage of a single securities market vis-a-vis Europe where post-trade infrastructures developed along national lines, leading to exorbitant costs in clearing and settling securities transactions across national frontiers.

It helped that the US had just one currency, one language and essentially one legal system where there was sufficient political will to overcome variations in state law. Three other factors combined to support the SEC in its pursuit of NMS, according to the Securities Industry Association of the US:[30]

- The SEC was a single regulator with strong powers to pursue its goal.
- NSCC and DTC were created when stock exchanges and infrastructure providers were typically not-for-profit entities owned by users, and therefore owned and governed as market utilities. DTC, for example, did not combine the infrastructure role of the CSD and commercial banking services.
- There was one predominant market centre: New York.

The New York post-trade infrastructure providers benefited from economies of scale that helped them absorb the regional CCPs and CSDs, making consolidation at a national level easier. They provided models of service and practice, promoting standardisation across the US. Because so many stocks from across the US were listed in New York, the legal changes needed to make NSCC and DTC work were replicated across the nation. The process of integration was aided by operations committees in which representatives from various parts of the securities industry were able to smooth out glitches.

The creation of the US system was not without controversy, however. The SEC's regulatory approach had to overcome a legal challenge in the courts. While banks and brokers supported consolidation, the exchanges resisted merging their CCPs because they provided a significant part of their income. The New York exchanges only agreed to the creation of NSCC after a deal which paid them a fee per trade to compensate for the loss of CCP revenues.[31]

By the later 1980s, however, the national market system had achieved sufficient critical mass for the eventual absorption of the remaining regional infrastructures to be regarded simply as a matter of time. Throughout the period of consolidation, NSCC and DTC took advantages of economies of scale, expanding and commoditising their services and cutting costs and fees.

8.8 FINANCIAL FUTURES IN THE UK

It took some time for financial futures to spread from the US around the world. One aspect of Bretton Woods that did not collapse with its exchange rate regime was the system's reliance on national controls over capital movements. In Britain's case, exchange controls introduced

[30] Explained in a Background Note on the Organisation in the US Market for Clearing and Settlement: prepared by the Cross-Border Subcommittee of the Securities Industry Association for the European Commission, May 2005.

[31] According to an SEC Staff Report to the SEC of 19 October 1976, the percentages of revenue generated by CCPs at exchanges in the first quarter of 1976 were: AMEX 11.49%; Boston Stock Exchange 41.32%; Midwest Stock Exchange 11.28%; NASD 42.01%; NYSE 15.81%; Pacific Stock Exchange 24.05%; Philadelphia Stock Exchange 52.66%. Details quoted in European Securities Forum (2 December 2000), 'EuroCCP: ESF's blueprint for a single pan-European central counterparty'.

in 1939 at the beginning of the Second World War were still in force in modified form more than 30 years after the war's end.

In the late 1970s, an embattled Labour government clung to power against a background of high inflation, austerity prescribed by the International Monetary Fund and serious labour unrest. But some City institutions – including ICCH – started to explore the perspectives for financial futures in London should a change of government lead to the removal of exchange controls. Since becoming part of the UDT group, the clearing house had a strong track record of investigating, developing and exploiting new markets. By the late 1970s, it was looking beyond commodities, its traditional area of expertise, and was well aware of futures and options in Chicago.

In 1978, ICCH began clearing contracts for the newly opened London Traded Options Market (LTOM), as managing agent for the London Options Clearing House.[32] In October the following year, the first financial futures market outside the US opened in Sydney with the contracts cleared and guaranteed by ICCH, which had cleared commodities contracts in Sydney since 1969.

During 1978, ICCH commissioned John Harding, a Chicago-based Englishman who worked for Conti Financial, a global commodity broker, to produce an 'American' view of how and why a financial futures market should develop in London. The clearing house also asked Robert Miller, an economist with the free-market Institute for Economic Affairs in London, to focus on why it would be good for the UK.

The two men worked on a report entitled 'Financial Futures in London?',[33] which was published late in November 1979. ICCH used it to suggest that London should have a futures market in short- and long-dated gilt edged government bonds and sterling certificates of deposit and possibly Eurodollar CDs, which were short-term interest bearing instruments.

The report focused on instruments that would mitigate interest rate risk. It would be the job of City professionals to get the market up and running. In those days pre-dating deregulation, that meant winning over potential market participants working in a variety of different institutions that included discount houses, money brokers, merchant banks, stockjobbers, stockbrokers, clearing banks and commodity brokers. The report predicted that once the City professionals demonstrated that the financial futures market had sufficient liquidity, corporate and institutional customers would use it to hedge risks.

The UK had an unhappy experience of forward trading in financial products that pre-dated these developments. In 1972, a market existed for trading sterling certificates of deposit for future delivery, in which the Scottish Cooperative Society, a mutual, suffered heavy losses and had to be bailed out. After this upset, the British forward CD market ceased to exist.

But, as ICCH pointed out, the forward sterling CD market had no clearing house, no margins and therefore none of the disciplines that create a framework in which speculators and hedgers could coexist. These defects boosted ICCH's case for a financial futures market in London supported by a clearing house.

'Financial Futures in London?' urged that the market's clearing membership 'should be widely spread to include all those who are acceptable to the clearing organisation'. It suggested

[32] LTOM was rather overshadowed by the European Options Exchange, Europe's first options exchange, which was launched by the Amsterdam Stock Exchange in 1978.

[33] Harding, John and Miller, Robert (21 November 1979), 'Financial futures in London?', a report commissioned by the International Commodities Clearing House Ltd, London.

an open outcry market on the Chicago model because it 'encourages high levels of liquidity, and provides transparent and widely distributed price information leading to very narrow buy/sell spreads'.

'It was really low budget,' Harding recalled much later. 'ICCH started hawking it around the City as a promotional thing. I went over once or twice [to the UK].' Harding remembers visiting ICCH in its then headquarters in Crutched Friars, a street in the City. 'It was a very small Victorian building. A bit of the Roman Wall was preserved in their basement – it actually formed one wall of their dining room.'[34]

Low budget or not, the report was well timed, coming just a few weeks after Volcker's dramatic change of US monetary policy and less than a month after the UK's recently elected Conservative government led by Margaret Thatcher abruptly abolished exchange controls on 23 October 1979.

The press gave the Harding–Miller report a rather cautious welcome. *The Times* pointed out that financial futures could mean changes for monetary control and regulation in the UK. There was also 'the issue of speculation' where ICCH would 'have to prove the positive benefits of speculation fairly convincingly'.[35]

But the Bank of England was already moving in favour of financial futures. Pen Kent, a Bank official seconded to the IMF, produced a report for the Bank on financial futures in September 1979 that was broadly favourable. Prominent City figures were also receptive, including John Barkshire, chairman of Mercantile House, a finance company, who later became a chairman of ICCH.

The idea of a financial futures market was taken forward in 1980 by a working group on which ICCH was represented and which liaised closely with the Bank. From the start, ICCH was seen as a contender for the job of guaranteeing and clearing contracts on the mooted exchange: it was in situ; it functioned; and it was known to the Bank. Around this time ICCH adapted its regulations formally to become a buyer to every seller and a seller to every buyer to bring it into line with CCPs internationally. There was one problem, however: its ownership.

UDT was a conscientious parent but had encountered difficulties. It was caught out in the secondary banking crisis of 1973–4 when a sudden credit squeeze resulted in losses for a number of so-called 'fringe banks' that had expanded rapidly by lending long term for unsound investments while refinancing that lending with short-term borrowing. UDT required support from the Bank of England's 'lifeboat' set up to rescue victims of the crisis.

In any case, there were doubts whether a financial futures market in London should be cleared by a clearing house owned by a single financial company. These concerns were compounded when UDT was taken over in 1981 by the Trustee Savings Bank, a once dozy mutual with big ambitions.

TSB, on securing UDT's support for its bid, pledged to sell ICCH as soon as practicable.[36] The Bank of England, meanwhile, backed ownership of ICCH by a consortium of the UK's clearing banks. This was the state of affairs when, at the beginning of March 1981, agreement was reached for a financial futures market to open in London in 1982.

In September 1981, the Bank authorised TSB to start negotiating the sale of ICCH to the clearing banks. Many observers expected the talks would be little more than a formality. But three weeks later, *The Times* reported that: 'Negotiations over the sale of the International

[34] Conversation with the author, Chicago, 23 September 2008.

[35] 'Interest Futures', *The Times*, 3 December 1979.

[36] 'UDT backs Savings Bank's bid', *The Times*, 31 January 1981.

Commodities Clearing House are becoming as tough and tricky as some of the deals in markets whose paperwork it handles.'[37] The newspaper reported that Tom Bryans, TSB's general manager, wanted £80 million for ICCH.

Only nine months earlier, the same newspaper had reported that TSB's agreed bid for the *whole* of UDT was worth £110 million. The banks objected. Stalemate ensued.

With 1982 approaching, the committee of City figures organising the new futures exchange threatened to set up their own clearing house unless there was agreement on transferring ICCH to the banking consortium by the end of January 1982. The exchange's promoters wanted to follow the example of the CME with its integrated CCP.

The Bank weighed into the fray, raising its eyebrows and twisting the clearing banks' arms. In the end, TSB obtained nearly £56 million for ICCH. The banks agreed to pay £51 million for the clearing house with Barclays, Lloyds, Midland and National Westminster each contributing 20% of the purchase price while Standard Chartered and Williams and Glyns[38] each bought 10%. TSB meanwhile took a special dividend of £4.9 million from ICCH's retained profit as part of the deal.

The banks were disgruntled. They felt they had been forced to pay too much. On the plus side, ICCH's profit before tax was £9.2 million in the year to June 1981. It was growing strongly under the leadership of Ian McGaw, its managing director since July 1978. In 1981 it began clearing for the new International Petroleum Exchange in London. It was helping to create a financial futures market in Hong Kong. It had re-established links with the Paris commodity markets that were broken after a crisis in the Paris sugar market in 1974. But all these ventures involved risk. ICCH's profits could be volatile: in 1978, for example, they dropped to £1.6 million. Since morphing in 1973 into ICCH from LPCH, the clearer had developed a considerable appetite for new capital: it raised capital in six steps from £500 000 to £15 million during the 1970s.

Looking back, David Hardy, who was seconded from Barclays Merchant Bank to ICCH in 1985 and became managing director of its clearing division two years later, says the amount the banks paid for ICCH was 'absolutely ridiculous'.[39] It was certainly counterproductive. 'It put the banks on the back foot from that point on,' he explains. 'They objected to how much they paid. They were a bunch of unhappy shareholders.'

When the London International Financial Futures Exchange (LIFFE) opened for business on 30 September 1982, ICCH's new shareholders saw this as an opportunity to recoup their investment by charging high fees. ICCH had put together what Hardy describes as 'an extraordinary deal', which established high costs for trading contracts on LIFFE, with only a fifth going to the exchange and the rest to the clearing house.

It was not long before LIFFE complained. The fee structure was changed in LIFFE's favour in 1984 and modified further after Hardy took responsibility for ICCH's relationship with LIFFE around the end of 1986. 'There was a very poor relationship with LIFFE,' Hardy admits:

> LIFFE didn't think the clearing house was terribly efficient or that they were getting value for money. In part they were right. The computer system, which was being used to manage members' positions and do margin and such like had been fabulous in the 1970s, when it was implemented. Called Intercom, it was ahead of its time, without any doubt. The problem was that ICCH did not renew it.

[37] 'Disposing of ICCH is tough and tricky', *The Times*, 12 October 1981.

[38] Part of the Royal Bank of Scotland from September 1985.

[39] Conversation with the author, 9 July 2008.

Phil Bruce, who joined LIFFE in 1983, remembers two companies that were on different wavelengths:

> ICCH was the incumbent and had been in the business of clearing the London commodity markets for a hundred years or so. And this upstart called LIFFE came along making demands. [...] We [at LIFFE] felt all the way through that we were dragging and pulling the clearing house with us. Moreover – and this was a thing we didn't realise at the time – the clearing house had other clients and we couldn't work out what else they were trying to do. In addition, ICCH didn't have much cash.[40]

LIFFE's executives had been much influenced by what they had seen in Chicago. 'The concept of the clearing house doing something against the wishes of the exchange that it served was just unthinkable,' Bruce explains.

LIFFE was an open outcry exchange whereas ICCH at the time was using its IT expertise to develop electronic infrastructure for financial markets. ICCH launched screen-based trading for soya bean meal contracts in London, using the British Post Office's Prestel 'viewdata' service.

In a development that would come back to haunt ICCH some years later, the group's Australian subsidiary set up a fully automated futures and options market in New Zealand in early 1985. Trading, clearing, margining and full client accounting were transacted on terminals in the offices of exchange members to circumvent the inability of New Zealand's leading cities to agree a single location for an open outcry trading floor. Wal Reisch, the brains behind the innovative systems of ICCH's Sydney operation, was appointed Group IT Strategist in 1986 and moved to London.

But when LIFFE wanted ICCH to join it in investing in new technology to improve its clearing capacity, ICCH stood aside. As a result, LIFFE went ahead with developing a system of its own to match trades conducted on its floor in close to real time.

LIFFE's Trade Registration System (TRS) was introduced for options trades in September 1987 and applied to all contracts a year later. According to Bruce, 'TRS got ever more sophisticated'. A trader could see whether there was a matched trade or not within half an hour. TRS also included a so-called 'give-up' function that would allow a trader to allocate trades to a third party, which would claim the trade and have it cleared through its own clearing member, thus saving capital. The give-up facility, which was superior to that on ICCH's Intercom, also met the needs of hedge funds and other institutions taking large positions that might otherwise become concerned about their credit exposure to a specific clearing member. These investors would use give-up mechanisms to distribute thousands of trades across clearing members, thus spreading credit risk and encouraging more liquidity in the market.

'So TRS became a real-time matching system, a real-time give-up system, and we kept pumping these trades into an ICCH system called Intercom, and it just seemed so clunky. It didn't suit our purposes at all,' Bruce recalled. 'So eventually we built something called the Clearing Processing System [CPS] to go with TRS'.

Developed in 1989, CPS provided position management and held the accounts of clearing members. By the time TRS/CPS was operational, ICCH had been restructured and a division known as the London Clearing House (LCH) cleared the futures and options markets in the City. 'LCH basically stopped the clearing processing of LIFFE business,' Bruce recalls. However, LCH continued to provide risk-management and banking services, including margin calculations, and the central counterparty guarantee for LIFFE.

---

[40] Conversation with the author, 14 August 2008. Bruce at the time of writing was the senior strategy adviser of LIFFE in NYSE Euronext, In his earlier career, he shuttled between exchanges and clearing houses, including the London Clearing House (LCH), the successor organisation to ICCH.

David Hardy can remember thinking there were 'pros and cons' to this unusual division of labour between ICCH/LCH and what had become its biggest customer:

> The pro was that LIFFE had very bright people and good computer expertise. This was 1986. I had no worries about the quality of their system, and it meant it cost us nothing. But it changed the relationship somewhat and there was always the risk that system-less, ICCH/LCH would be in a weaker position.

ICCH's involvement with financial futures in the UK began hopefully enough in the UDT era with the commissioning of the Harding–Miller report. When Bruce started his career in the futures business five years later, ICCH had parsimonious clearing bank owners and the ill feeling between LIFFE and its clearing house was palpable. That the two companies were able nonetheless to rub along together in the following years in a relationship that became very closely intertwined at times owed much to the temperament and leadership of Hardy who was chief executive of LCH until 2006.

8.9 CCP FAILURES

The volatile conditions in commodity and financial markets that accompanied the decline of Bretton Woods and the coming of floating exchange rates greatly increased the need for clearing house services. It also exposed them to risk.

The 1960s and 1970s were punctuated by investment and banking scandals. The June 1974 failure of Bankhaus I. D. Herstatt in Germany put the spotlight on risks lurking in the unglamorous world of cross-border settlement, when it emerged that the bank's counterparties were unable to recover funds owing to them from foreign exchange deals that were open at the time of the bank's closure by the German authorities.

The first post-Bretton Woods crisis to hit a clearing house occurred on the Paris white sugar market a few months after the Herstatt collapse and led to the insolvency of the Caisse de Liquidation des Affaires en Marchandises (CLAM), the sugar market's clearing house, in December 1974.

The crisis followed a year of rampant speculation on world sugar markets. White sugar prices more than quadrupled in the first 11 months of 1974. They doubled in Paris between September and November before succumbing to a violent downwards correction. The erratic movements hit speculative investors, including some CLAM clearing members who had traded on behalf of customers without advance authorisation. Many traders were unable to pay margin calls, in particular Maurice Nataf, a sugar broker and CLAM clearing member, who suffered big losses.

The crisis arose on 2 December 1974 when Nataf reported to CLAM that he could not meet a margin call. CLAM decided not to make good the contracts and requested the market be closed instead.[41] The sugar market's management committee complied and closure was supported by the French Ministry of Commerce. But instead of taking the sugar price of 2 December as the basis for settling outstanding contracts the authorities tried to apply a price equivalent to the average price of sugar over the 20 days before the closure, by invoking a rule devised for 'inter alia, general mobilisation, war, or causes of *force majeure*'. Because of tumbling sugar prices, this average price was much higher than prices on 2 December.

[41] According to *The Times* in: 'Dealers in Paris Sugar Market get Injunction to Stop Payments', a law report published on 18 December 1974, and various editions of the *Czarnikow Review* between 5 December 1974 and 29 January 1976.

This ruse to protect the loss-making market traders of Paris caused a furore. Moves to reopen the market were stymied by complex legal wrangles over the price that should apply to contracts caught in the chaos of the market's closure. The affair involved, among others, the Court of Appeal in the UK and, eventually, the *Conseil d'Etat*, France's highest administrative court, which on 20 June 1975 ruled that the Ministry of Commerce was wrong to have closed the market. With CLAM effectively insolvent, negotiations then focused on achieving a compromise that allowed creditors to retrieve some of what they were owed.

Many creditors of CLAM were London-based because of the June 1972 agreement allowing ICCH members to register their Paris sugar trades via an account at the Paris clearing house. It was on their behalf that ICCH finally agreed, under protest, to a settlement in November 1975 that was more generous than one based on the 20 day average price but less favourable than would have been the case if CLAM had not ceased to clear.

According to a later analysis by the Bank of England,[42] CLAM contributed to the crisis because

- It did not adjust margin requirements as prices rose rapidly, even after market participants asked for this in September.
- It was aware that Nataf held a sufficiently large share of sugar futures in the market to affect prices, but did not inform the exchange.
- The allocation of losses was not transparent.

Trading in sugar on the Paris terminal market resumed on 26 January 1976, under new clearing rules with Banque Centrale de Compensation (BCC) as the CCP.[43] BCC, established in 1969 to clear commodities, was owned by leading French banks and capitalised at 12 million francs. It later became Clearnet SA.

ICCH's experience with CLAM did not deter it from establishing closer ties with BCC and taking a 10% stake in it. In 1977, ICCH and BCC signed reciprocal agreements to provide clearing services for members of the partner CCP trading in the markets that they cleared.

Perhaps the first example of interoperability between CCPs,[44] the arrangement lasted until the 1990s, by which time commodity markets in the UK and France were operated by rival exchanges: LIFFE and MATIF respectively. MATIF called a halt to the cooperation after LIFFE, which traded white sugar futures electronically using technology developed by ICCH for New Zealand, used the clearing link to take business from Paris, where sugar futures were still traded by open outcry.

The Paris sugar market and CLAM, its clearer, had a long albeit chequered history going back to the late 19th century.[45] The next CCP failure involved a young institution: the Kuala Lumpur Commodity Clearing House (KLCCH), which had been operating for about three and a half years.

KLCCH was set up in 1980 with the help of ICCH, which held a minority stake and managed the clearing house under contract for its first three years. However, when the crisis broke in 1983, ICCH was no longer involved with KLCCH.

---

[42] Bank of England (1999), 'Central counterparty clearing houses and financial stability', *Financial Stability Review*. 'Dealers in Paris sugar market get injunction to stop payments', a law report in *The Times* of 18 December 1974, contains interesting details of the Paris sugar crisis.

[43] *Czarnikow Review*, 1268, 29 January1976.

[44] See Section 16.8.

[45] See Section 6.4 for details of a Paris sugar market scandal in 1905.

The CCP failed after defaults by six brokers totalling US$70 million on palm oil contracts traded on the Kuala Lumpur Commodity Exchange. The defaults followed a squeeze on prices and an accumulation of uncovered selling positions by a particular trader, who doubled as owner of the Kentucky Fried Chicken franchise for Malaysia.

A Malaysian government taskforce later criticised brokers but put much of the blame on management inaction at the clearing house, including a 12 day delay between the market squeeze and the broker default.[46] Officials at the clearing house were said to lack experience while the report highlighted a lack of coordination between the exchange, the clearing house and the Commodity Trading Council, the market regulator. Nonetheless, the taskforce recommended that the CCP be re-established.

Delay, insufficient rigour, lack of coordination with exchanges and other market participants, lack of transparency, and bad decisions by official bodies were some of the weaknesses exposed by these CCP failures. Two years after the Kuala Lumpur case, commodity markets had cause to reflect on problems that arose where a CCP was not in existence.

From 1956 onwards, the International Tin Council (ITC) sought to keep the price of tin stable for the benefit of producers in Malaysia, Cornwall and elsewhere. But by the middle of the 1980s, its endeavours were coming unstuck as a result of competition from aluminium for making cans, recycling and the emergence of new producers who stayed outside the ITC's International Tin Agreement. The council's mechanism of price support – a buffer stock – accumulated a surplus of 64 000 tons of tin and debts of US$1.2 billion by the time its manager ran out of funds in October 1985 causing consternation in metals markets.

The crisis focused attention on the London Metal Exchange (LME) where members were responsible for settling their positions as principals without a clearing system. Some years before, the Bank of England and the House of Lords Select Committee on Commodities voiced concern about the LME's arrangements. The collapse of a company in the LME's trading ring could, they feared, lead to heavy selling of contracts, causing prices to spiral downwards, and possibly spread financial instability to other companies in other markets.

LME members agreed a half way house solution in 1978 when the exchange, with ICCH, set up a system to monitor contracts. The tin crisis increased official pressure on the LME to install a central counterparty clearer. It was argued that an independent CCP for the exchange might have uncovered the ITC's weaknesses before it defaulted.

ICCH started clearing for the LME in May 1987: the exchange's 110th year. Five months later, the world was shaken by a market crash that put CCPs under scrutiny from politicians and regulators as never before and put risk management at the centre of their concerns.

[46] As reported by Bank of England (1999).

9

The 1987 Crash, Regulation and CCPs

9.1 THE 1987 CRASH

Like the financial market crisis of 2007–9, the 1987 crash started in the US. Unlike the 21st century cataclysm that had many of the qualities of a slow motion train crash, the market break of 1987 became international with the speed of light.

The crash was an early signal of how computerised communications and globalisation could spread trouble as well as prosperity in a world of freer flowing capital. It put the spotlight for the first time on the interaction between the by-now adolescent financial futures exchanges of Chicago and the traditional stock markets of Wall Street. In so doing, it opened the eyes of politicians, regulators and financiers to the infrastructure and financial plumbing that supported those markets.

'The catalyst for clearing to be considered as a strategic asset or as a critical function came on one date: October 19 1987,' Phupinder Gill, President of the CME Group, has commented.[1] 'That date brought the clearing function into extremely sharp focus for the entire world and especially the US derivatives industry.'

'Black Monday' came as a shock after several years of rising share prices. The strength of equities was fuelled by the liberalisation of financial markets in the US, UK and leading continental European countries during the 1980s and – since 1985 – greater cooperation between the US and its allies in dealing with global economic problems. The result was greater optimism, reflected in a burgeoning 'equity culture' among institutional and private investors in the industrialised democracies.

But the US and West Germany disagreed publicly over interest rate policy early in October 1987, prompting fears of a breakdown of efforts to stabilise currencies agreed eight months earlier.[2] On 14 October, the US announced an unexpectedly large trade deficit, causing the dollar to fall and bond yields to rise. That day, legislation was filed in Congress to terminate tax benefits for financing corporate takeovers.

Arbitrageurs started to sell takeover stocks in New York and share prices began to slide. In the seven days following 14 October, the Dow Jones Industrial Average fell by 31%. This included the Dow's largest one-day fall until then, when it tumbled 508 points (23%) on Monday, 19 October 1987 amid record trading volumes. The broader-based Standard & Poors 500 index slumped 22% that day. Chicago's derivatives markets also plummeted. The CME's S&P 500 futures contract – by now the most popular contract traded on the exchange – dropped

[1] Conversation with the author, Chicago, 26 September 2008.

[2] The Louvre Accord of 22 February 1987. Named after the palace in Paris, which at the time housed part of the French Finance ministry as well as the world famous museum, the Louvre Accord was an agreement of finance ministers from the Group of Seven leading industrial democracies to stabilise the dollar's value against other leading currencies. It modified the Plaza Accord of 22 September 1985, in which the US, Japan, Germany, France and the UK (the Group of Five) agreed to work together for an orderly decline in the dollar's value after half a decade of overvaluation.

28.6% while the CBOT's MMI index future, which was composed of 20 stocks including 17 DJIA stocks, fell by 24.4%.

The stock market weakness spread around the world. The Hang Seng Index in Hong Kong fell 420 points on 19 October before markets in Europe and the US opened. This drop of 11.3% would have dramatic consequences for the local clearing house. The London Stock Exchange fell 11% on Monday and 12% on Tuesday. Prices on the Sydney exchange fell nearly a quarter.

Disaster was averted after the Federal Reserve made clear early on 20 October that it would provide sufficient liquidity for the US financial system, and the authorities put pressure on large commercial banks to lend to firms heavily exposed to equities.

In the US, attention quickly focused on the way the equity futures contracts fell faster than the underlying indices. This phenomenon was blamed on program trading, the technique of using computer programs to trade shares and stock index futures in response to specified market events. Program-trading strategies relied on the flow of accurate information on share and index prices between the markets of New York and Chicago. In the event, this proved to be a big problem.

Immediately after the crash, Wall Street blamed stock index futures and the use of Chicago's 'shadow markets' by program traders for the market meltdown. Allegations flew thick and fast, prompting Leo Melamed, at this time chairman of the CME's executive committee, to launch an intensive lobbying campaign in defence of the CME and the futures industry in general.

The crash prompted a plethora of post-mortem reports.[3] One of the earliest and most influential was the 'Brady Report', delivered on 8 January 1988 by a Presidential Task Force on Market Mechanisms, set up by President Ronald Reagan under the chairmanship of future US Treasury Secretary Nicholas Brady.[4] Also published early in 1988 were reports from the two main US regulators: the Commodity Futures Trading Commission[5] and the Securities and Exchange Commission.[6]

Clearing and settlement systems for equities, options and futures markets were among the issues scrutinised by a Working Group on Financial Markets, set up by the President. Chaired by US Treasury Secretary James Baker, the group comprised the chairmen of the SEC, the CFTC and the Federal Reserve Board. It reported in May 1988 and its findings were the point of departure for an assessment of the risks attached to clearing and settlement by the US General Accounting Office (GAO), published two years later.[7]

Another study to focus on clearing and settlement during the crash was published in 1990 by Ben Bernanke, the future chairman of the US Federal Reserve Board and at that time a professor at the Woodrow Wilson School, Princeton University.[8]

Published less than three months after the crash, the Brady Report made no secret of the worries that were abroad on 19–20 October. 'While no default occurred, the possibility that a clearing house or major investment banking firm might default, or that the banking system would deny required liquidity to the market participants, resulted in certain market makers curtailing their activities and increased investor uncertainty,' it said.

The GAO's later analysis found that the unprecedented price falls and trading volumes in October 1987 caused trade processing problems at CCPs and exchanges. Some CCPs were

[3] Melamed eventually counted 77 different reports and studies about the crash and claimed that the most important of these exonerated the futures markets and the CME: Melamed, Leo with Tamarkin, Bob (1996), *Escape to the Futures*.

[4] Brady Commission (January 1988), 'Report of the Presidential Task Force on Market Mechanisms'.

[5] CFTC (1988), 'Final report on stock index futures and cash market activity during October 1987'.

[6] SEC (February 1988), 'The October 1987 market break'.

[7] GAO (April 1990), 'Report to congressional committees: Clearance and settlement reform'.

[8] Bernanke, Ben S. (1990), 'Clearing and settlement during the crash', *The Review of Financial Studies*, **3**(1), 133–151.

unable to determine their clearing members' financial risk and exposure in other markets. Some members of CCPs had insufficient funding to meet their obligations and had to increase their borrowings from banks. Some banks, CCPs and their members did not make necessary payments to each other within normal timeframes. The GAO identified the processing of information about trades, the risk-management procedures used by the CCPs, and payments to and from clearing organisations as three broad areas of concern.

According to a still later IMF study, the complexity and fragmentation of the clearing systems for US equities, futures and options 'created delay and confusion over payments of margin calls triggered by stock price falls, raising concern over the solvency of securities brokers and the ability of exchange clearing houses to make payments'.[9] Banks reacted swiftly by limiting lending to brokers. The resulting lack of liquidity and worries that investors would be forced to sell more investments to meet margin calls helped push prices lower and increased a flight of funds to quality in the form of cash and high quality bonds.

Not all the verdicts were so gloomy. Speaking up for the futures industry, the CFTC, in its final report on the crisis, pointed out that

> those safeguards already in place for the futures market worked effectively. No customer funds were lost as a result of a futures firm's failure or default; no Futures Commission Merchant (FCM) failed; exchange clearing organisations collected all margins due them from member firms, including daily and intra-day payments of unprecedented magnitudes; and the futures clearing mechanisms operated effectively despite record volumes, price swings and margin flows.[10]

BOTCC, which cleared the CBOT's financial futures contracts, came through the crisis without any loss or sense of perturbation and was, according to the April 1990 GOA report, 'only indirectly involved in the events of the October 1987 market crash'.

But for those caught up in the crash, the borderline between chaos and survival was often very fine. Gill of the CME Group remembers how 'rumours were flying around that the CME clearing house had defaulted, had failed and failed to meet its obligations'.[11]

The Monday of the market break was set to be challenging even if all had worked to plan. In the event, the CME suffered a technical glitch. Gill recalls that 19 October was the first day CME did intra-day margining on a large scale: 'We called for $1.2 billion – in those days the largest amount we ever called. And at the end of the day, we called for another $1.3 billion. The report that went out showed we were calling for another $2.5 billion. Our system didn't take into account what we had done earlier.'

Under the exchange's rules, the margin payments had to be collected from losing investors before the start of trading the next day, 20 October. Only then would margin payments be dispersed to investors making profits.

According to Gill, the recording glitch made banks fear that the margin calls exceeded lending limits. The unprecedented demands for money meant the CME's settlement banks that provided the exchange's credit lines became ultra cautious, threatening the capacity of the exchange's CCP to meet its margin obligations before the day's trading.[12] 'It was a shock event,' Gill recalled. 'Banks that were used to seeing in aggregate $200 million [of margin calls] being a high day, were seeing $2.5 billion.'

[9] IMF (September 2003), 'Global financial stability report'. Chapter III Appendix: Case studies.

[10] As cited in Bernanke (1990).

[11] Conversation with the author, Chicago, 26 September 2008.

[12] In its response to the GAO report, dated 29 January 1990, the CFTC said: 'The problem was largely caused by the fact that settlement banks did not receive accurate instruction sheets at the usual hour because certain non-cash intra-day variation payments made on October 19, 1987 were not accommodated by existing software and therefore were not reflected in the October 20 variation calculations.'

There are varying accounts of what happened at the CME in the early hours of Tuesday 20 October.[13] But there is agreement that the CME came close to having insufficient margin inflows to be able to start trading that day. Monday's trading activity left the CME owing US$670 million and US$917 million respectively to two of its 90 clearing members: Goldman Sachs and Kidder Peabody. Meanwhile, another large investment bank, identified in two accounts as Morgan Stanley, owed the CME a similarly large sum. It was only after emergency phone calls from CME executives to the investment bank and Continental Bank in Chicago in the early hours of Tuesday that the necessary funds arrived just before the start of trading.

The CME was not alone in experiencing problems. The Options Clearing Corporation (OCC) ran into trouble because of errors in the stock option prices it bought from information vendors. The GAO reported how, on the evenings of 19, 20 and 21 October, the OCC had to correct manually more than 5000 option reports received from its suppliers. According to the SEC's 'Market Break' report of February 1988, the automated price reporting systems dropped the first digit from three digit option prices.

The OCC suffered a loss of US$8.5 million closing out the open positions of H B Shaine, a clearing member that defaulted on 20 October. The deficit was covered by drawing on the contributions of other clearing members to the default fund on a pro rata basis.[14]

Notwithstanding these problems, the SEC report judged that 'OCC performed exceptionally well during this period of unprecedented volume and price volatility in a product which by its nature provides large exposure during volatile market conditions'. The CCP adopted a pragmatic approach to some difficult problems. In one case towards the end of the crisis week, the OCC's management waived a clearing member's margin payment, in consultation with the SEC, because the firm had options and futures positions that were intermarket hedges where losses in one market would be offset by gains in other markets so long as the hedge was maintained.

In this case, which was cited in the SEC report, the positions not cleared by the OCC were at the Intermarket Clearing Corporation (ICC), an OCC affiliate set up in 1984 to guarantee, clear and settle futures, options on futures and commodity options traded on contract markets formed by the OCC's participant exchanges.

According to Wayne Luthringshausen, who took the key decision at the OCC that day, the firm in question went on to be very successful:

> We had to assess what to do. We could liquidate them, but it would be nasty. So we actually forgave some calls by calling the SEC, talking with the SEC, explaining it, and saying we thought we would be better off giving the firm an extra day to get through this thing. We decided in a number of cases to forgo the margin calls.[15]

Among securities clearers, the NSCC experienced a US$400 000 loss when one member firm defaulted. However, this sum was small compared with the US$126 million of stock transactions that the NSCC had guaranteed for the company and the US$400 million default fund backing up the clearing house. The loss was covered from retained earnings.

The GAO report was critical of delays in payments by the CME and OCC during the morning of 20 October. Although both clearing houses met their legal obligation to pay

[13] As well as personal reminiscences, there are at least three published accounts that accord different roles to different protagonists and cite different figures for some of the payments involved. These are to be found in: Tamarkin, Bob (1993), *The Merc*; Melamed, Leo, with Tamarkin, Bob (1996); and Rodengen, Jeffrey L. (2008), *Past, Present and Futures: Chicago Mercantile Exchange*.

[14] At the time of writing (March 2010), this was the only occasion that the OCC drew on its default fund.

[15] Conversation with the author, 20 October 2009.

clearing members in same-day funds, there was a six hour delay in the payment of US$1.5 billion by the CME to Goldman Sachs and Kidder Peabody, while the OCC also delayed payments to all of its clearing members on that day by two to two and a half hours.

The glitches at the CCPs pointed to the need for technical improvements in the systems for trading and processing trades on US financial markets. But it also became clear that many deficiencies exposed by the large volume of trades during the crash reflected problems that were not the responsibility of the derivatives markets or their clearing houses.

The crash exposed disparities in technical capabilities between Wall Street and the Chicago exchanges, which tended to reflect badly on Wall Street. The New York Stock Exchange (NYSE) had an order processing system – known as DOT or 'designated order turnaround' – to aid program trades that proved to have insufficient capacity for trading during the crash. On 19 October, around one third of the shares in the S&P and DJIA indexes opened late.

Contrasting with the NYSE's patchy performance, the Chicago futures markets started trading on time on 19 October but amid heavy selling. The resulting gap between values on the two cities' exchanges triggered erratic computer-driven trading that added to the confusion on that day. The following day, when trading started on 20 October, the NYSE acted to prevent index arbitrage traders from using the DOT system to execute trades, contributing further to a decoupling of prices between the futures and cash equity markets.

Different settlement arrangements for different products and markets posed further difficulties. The disparity between same-day settlement for stock index futures and the practice of settling cash equity dealings on exchanges five days after a trade (the so-called T+5 settlement) meant investors who were hedged across the different markets could still face large cash demands.[16] Their need for cash added to the problem of near grid lock in payments systems caused by the very large margin calls of the US futures exchanges.

A serious problem affected the movement of money during the morning of Tuesday 20 October. Fedwire, the Federal Reserve's special communication system for transmitting funds among major US banks, shut down for two and a half hours because of computer faults. This disrupted the vital flow of funds between New York and Chicago.

Different settlement practices exposed an awareness gap between New York and Chicago. Wall Street bankers were insufficiently conscious of the need to make prompt payments on the Chicago futures markets. Press reports in the days after the market's slump told how large fund transfers were delayed for hours because the home phone numbers of important New York bankers could not be found.

Writing one year after the crash, Leo Melamed observed:

> October 19th taught us a crucial lesson, albeit an extremely expensive one. The disparity between market mechanics and those who make market decisions was dramatic. Most of our traditional markets were operating at a technological standard roughly equivalent to the steamboat. But market decision-makers were flying F-16s.[17]

Bernanke, in his 1990 review of the crisis, was rather more upbeat. Drawing comfort from the Federal Reserve's apparent commitment to respond when the financial system was threatened, he wrote 'it may be that changes in the clearing and settlement system can be safely restricted to improvements in the technology of clearing and settlement'.[18]

[16] Explained in Hendricks, Darryll, Kambhu, John and Mosser, Patricia (May 2006) 'Systemic risk and the financial system', Federal Reserve Bank of New York.

[17] Melamed, Leo (October 1988), 'Black Monday: What we know a year after the fact', *Chicago Enterprise*.

[18] Bernanke (1990).

9.2 US RESPONSES

By the time Bernanke's article was published, the US CCPs had already taken steps to rectify the most glaring deficiencies exposed by the 1987 crash. The OCC replaced its main outside price information supplier and strengthened its own option price calculation system. The CME modified its software to make payments and collection of intra-day margins routine and to allow payments to be made with securities as well as cash. The CFTC reported that routine intra-day margin arrangements were viewed by market participants as 'one of the single greatest improvements in clearance and settlement processes' since the crash.[19]

The events of October 1987 also produced an array of modifications that went deeper into the workings of the individual clearing houses. Many of these were announced sufficiently soon after the crash to be recorded among the responses of regulators and CCPs to the early drafts of the GOA report of 1990.[20]

The post-crash improvements were centred on risk management at CCPs, stronger relations between the CCPs and their banks, and even some steps towards cooperation among clearers where this would assist market integrity.

The CME, for example, instituted risk-management improvements in its audit department that allowed the exchange to monitor the concentration of risk among accounts of individual clearing members and track especially risky accounts across clearing members. Like many other CCPs, it adopted a twice daily mark-to-market revaluation of all positions to protect its capital.

After October 1987, the CME followed the example of BOTCC and introduced a 'parent guarantee rule' to prevent any company or individual holding more than 5% of a clearing member guarantee from setting up shell subsidiaries to evade payment of trading losses incurred on its behalf.

The CME and BOTCC worked together to conclude detailed settlement agreements with their Chicago settlement banks that clarified deadlines and when payments became irrevocable. In August 1989, the CME added two New York banks – Chemical and Bankers Trust – to its list of settlement banks to reduce the risk of a repeat of the 20 October Fedwire problem. It also obtained a US$250 million credit facility from a consortium of 14 international banks in July that year.

Among securities clearing houses, NSCC strengthened its financial support. Reacting to suggestions from supervisors, it acted in October 1989 to make its guarantee fund more liquid by reducing the amount that clearing members could post as collateral in the form of letters of credit. A few weeks later, it arranged a US$200 million line of credit with Bankers Trust. Together, NSCC reported, these measures lifted the proportion of liquid assets in its clearing fund to more than 75% from only 25% previously.

The unlocking of resources to invest in infrastructure after the crash reflected a structural change that had taken place in the US investment community. This was the rise of the professional investment manager that began with the Employment Retirement Securities Act (ERISA) of 1974, which triggered strong growth of defined-contribution pension funds.

On derivatives markets, the financial muscle of these market participants quickly overshadowed that of 'local' day traders who were traditionally reluctant to make investments that did

[19] In its response to the GAO (1990) report, dated 29 January 1990.

[20] The responses, which were published as appendices to the GAO (1990) report, were supplied by the SEC, CFTC, NSCC, OCC and CME. These organisations were noted more for their rivalries than their points in common. But in aggregate, their responses painted a more positive picture of progress than the GAO's own report.

not promise rapid returns. When the crash occurred, the investment managers – who controlled nearly US$2 trillion in assets, up from US$400 billion a decade earlier – were in control.

Professional investors operated on many exchanges. This created momentum for CCPs to cooperate and share information among themselves – a movement that gathered pace after the two exchanges that appeared most at odds in the immediate aftermath of the crash gave a powerful lead.

In April 1988, the CME and NYSE agreed to improve communications between the two exchanges and work out a system of circuit breakers, or trading halts, to be coordinated across equity and derivatives markets with the aim of slowing down price movements at times of extreme volatility.

Other less high-profile moves tackled concerns raised by the GAO and others about the problems faced by clearing houses when monitoring the financial position of firms trading in more than one market. While most US CCPs operated in just one market because of the futures industry's vertical structure, one fifth of member firms operated on more than one exchange.

One solution was information sharing. Even before October 1987, BOTCC began developing a scheme to share information among futures clearing houses. In May 1988, it unveiled SHAMIS, the Shared Market Information System, to provide risk and financial information on clearing firms to CCPs serving futures exchanges. The data included mark-to-market cash flows, options premium payments, information on whether margins were in surplus or deficit and historical trading information to establish whether a firm was straying from normal trading patterns.

Following the crash, the NSCC set up the Securities Clearing Group (SCG), which formalised arrangements to share information on margins, positions and settlement among CCPs and central securities depositories dealing with equities and options.[21] Its agenda included creating a central database to maintain information on clearing members; improving SEC financial reporting requirements to strengthen surveillance of clearing agencies; developing arrangements so that a defaulting clearing member's financial resources in one CCP could be used to meet obligations at other stock clearing organisations; and developing netting of clearing members' debits and credits across participating CCPs.

But information sharing met resistance inside the industry. It took arm-twisting by the CFTC before the OCC joined SHAMIS as a reluctant participant. The OCC was concerned that BOTCC could exploit its position as both participant in, and operator of, the system and complained that SHAMIS was a second best solution compared with arrangements to reduce risk by integrating collateral and credit facilities such as cross margining.[22]

9.3 CROSS MARGINING, TIMS AND SPAN

Cross margining involved calculating a single sum as margin in cases where each side of a hedged position was traded in a separate market. The idea was endorsed in the Brady Report and by the SEC and CFTC after the crash. It was, in fact, applied informally at the height of the crash thanks to a relationship of trust between the OCC's Wayne Luthringshausen and Bill Brodsky, who in 1987 was President and CEO of the CME.

[21] According to the NSCC's response to the GAO report, the SCG included the NSCC, OCC, Depository Trust Co (DTC), Midwest Clearing Corp, Midwest Securities Trust Co, the Stock Clearing Corporation of Philadelphia and the Philadelphia Depositor Trust Co.

[22] OCC response to the GAO draft, dated 8 December 1989.

Brodsky remembers that Luthringshausen called him after trading on 19 October about a clearing member firm that had long positions in S&P 500 futures that were traded and cleared at the CME and which were offset by a portfolio of options traded on the CBOE and cleared at the OCC.[23] The firm – a different one to that mentioned in the SEC report and cited above – was having problems meeting margin payments on both sets of positions. Yet the positions offset each other so that if they were viewed as a single portfolio, the company would not, in theory, have to pay margin to the respective clearing houses.

In this case, the offsetting positions were on two different exchanges and managed by two unaffiliated clearing houses with no mechanism that would allow the margin payments to be waived. However, the personal ties between Brodsky and Luthringshausen overcame these problems. The two men had known each other since 1974 when Brodsky joined the American Stock Exchange and developed options trading at the Amex. Brodsky was a member of the OCC board until moving to the CME in 1982.

As Brodsky recalled 22 years after the event, in conversation with the author:

> We trusted each other verbally for hundreds of millions of dollars – in those days a staggering amount of money. And it saved the system. There was no writing; no lawyers. It was in the middle of the night of the 19th to the 20th.

In Brodsky's view, this ad-hoc cross margining avoided the collapse of clearing members at the CBOE.

The OCC had pressed the CME to agree to cross margining before the 1987 crash because of the popularity of a hedging technique where market makers in the CBOE options market hedged their exposures with futures traded at the CME. Until the night of 19 October, the CME blocked the move because it was protective of its clearing house.

Afterwards, Brodsky made the case to the CME board that cross margining was needed to reduce systemic risk and would head off government intervention in its support. The board agreed to introduce it selectively. On 6 October 1989, the OCC and CME unveiled a cross margining partnership.

As Michael E. Cahill, OCC President and Chief Operating Officer, has explained: 'We had many firms that had very well positioned portfolios, especially in index options and equity index futures. But they got caught in a bind, because both of us were raising our margin requirements.' According to Cahill, cross margining provided these firms with an efficient way to offset their cash-flows 'and the savings on that over the years have been just huge'.[24]

'That was something that came out of the President's Working Group after the crash of 1987: that it would be beneficial to the system if there was netting of payment flows,' Kim Taylor, Managing Director and President of CME Clearing in Chicago, remembers:[25]

> Otherwise, you've got guys who overall have a flat position to the market, but it generates two different sets of margin requirements, and two different sets of cash flows, and those uncoordinated cash flows were thought to contribute to some of the systemic issues that came about during the Crash of 1987. By putting those two things together, you net down everybody's collateral requirements to be more reflective of their actual risk and then you also net off their payment flows.

[23] As told to the author in Chicago, 20 October 2009.
[24] Conversation with the author, Chicago, 26 September 2008.
[25] Meeting with the author, Chicago, 25 September 2008.

The OCC-CME agreement was preceded in June 1988 by a cross margining arrangement between the OCC and its ICC subsidiary. These pioneering programmes were followed by others in the 1990s, including agreements between the OCC and BOTCC, a trilateral cross margin arrangement for the CME, OCC and ICC, and in 1998 cross margining and common banking between the CME, BOTCC and CBOT. Early in 2002, the Government Securities Clearing Corp, a DTCC subsidiary, unveiled a clutch of cross margining agreements with BOTCC, CME and the short-lived BrokerTec Clearing Company.

The CME, LCH and LIFFE agreed an innovative cross-border cross margining arrangement to cut margin requirements for clearing member firms and their affiliates with positions in CME's Eurodollar contract and LIFFE's Euribor or Euro Libor contracts. This lasted until February 2010, when it was discontinued by the UK clearing house.[26]

The years just before and immediately after the crash saw a further development in risk-management techniques. The OCC and CME separately developed very similar computer algorithms for evaluating risk and calculating margins. The OCC introduced its Theoretical Intermarket Margin System (TIMS), a risk-based portfolio margin methodology, in 1986. The CME released its Standard Portfolio Analysis of Risk (SPAN) in December 1988.

TIMS works out the maximum possible loss in a portfolio of positions generated by a given percentage change in the value of its underlying assets. A risk-based system, TIMS is used for calculating margin requirements and haircuts for portfolios of options, futures and options on futures positions.

SPAN is a tool for determining margin requirements that leaves the exchanges and clearing houses to choose the parameters of risk that are then factored into its calculations. Its aim is to help CCPs set initial margins that are sufficient to cover the largest likely loss that a portfolio might suffer in reaction to a range of possible market events over a specified period of time, while making sure that clearing members do not have to tie up money unnecessarily in margin deposits. The algorithm was a response to the increased complexity of derivative instruments that followed the introduction of equity options in the 1970s and options on futures in the 1980s.

Updated four times in its first 20 years, SPAN proved to be an extremely flexible tool for the industry. The CME decided to license it to other exchanges and clearing organisations. It subsequently appeared in a number of different regional variations including London SPAN, the version used by LCH.Clearnet. By 2008, SPAN was used by more than 50 exchanges, clearing houses and regulators around the globe.

9.4 NEAR DISASTER IN HONG KONG

By the time SPAN was released, events in Hong Kong had brought home the importance of risk management to CCPs. While the financial infrastructures of Chicago, Wall Street and London emerged bruised from the shock of 1987, the Hong Kong futures market – and its clearing infrastructure – came close to disaster because of failures of structure and risk management.

The company that guaranteed the completion of futures trades in Hong Kong came close to insolvency, threatening a meltdown of financial markets. Disaster was only averted because

[26] LCH.Clearnet Ltd (12 February 2010), 'Cross margining agreement review'. LCH.Clearnet discontinued its arrangement with CME and NYSE Liffe because the cost of necessary changes 'would be disproportionate to the current usage and benefit derived from it'. The decision indicated that cross margining, although sometimes useful, was no panacea.

of an emergency support package from its shareholder banks and members of the futures exchange with government support.

On 20 October – after news reached the British crown colony of Wall Street's record percentage drop the day before – the Stock Exchange of Hong Kong (SEHK) decided to suspend trading for the rest of the week. The Hong Kong Futures Exchange (HKFE) followed suit, suspending trading in Hang Seng Index (HSI) stock futures contracts.

The stock exchange acted despite the misgivings of the colony's administration and for a number of reasons – none of which was confidence building. It feared panic selling and disorder in the market; had concerns about the liquidity of members; was worried about the possibility of bank runs; and was unsettled by a settlement backlog estimated at a quarter of a million deals – equivalent to a full week's trading.

The trading halt came after an 89% rise in the HSI to an all time high of 3950 in the year to 1 October. Stock market turnover during the first nine months of 1987 nearly trebled.

The HKFE's HSI index contract was a fairly recent innovation and trading in it had grown nearly 20-fold since its launch in May 1986. The futures exchange, as then constituted, was also a relatively young institution, having been re-licensed in 1984 after a previous crisis forced a reorganisation.

Later on 20 October, the HKFE chairman told the Secretary for Monetary Affairs that brokers were having difficulty margining contracts which had plunged in value the day before. Falling prices had hit limits imposed before trading on 19 October and caused ICCH (Hong Kong) Ltd, the clearing house, to make two intra-day margin calls on its members with long positions. The chairman also reported serious doubts about the ability of the Hong Kong Futures Guarantee Corporation (FGC) to meet its obligations: FGC was capitalised at only HK$15 million and had reserves of HK$7.5 million.[27]

HKFE's clearing arrangements were unusual. The exchange had contracted out the market's clearing function to ICCH (Hong Kong) Ltd, a wholly owned member of the ICCH group. Yet ICCH HK did not have any direct financial exposure arising from its clearing activities. Instead, it was a 20% shareholder in FGC, the limited company that guaranteed the contracts. The other FGC shareholders were Hong Kong Shanghai Banking Corp with 20%; Chase Manhattan Overseas Banking Corp and Chartered Capital Corp, each with 15%; and Crédit Lyonnais, Barclays Bank and Wing On Bank (an indirect subsidiary of Hong Kong Shanghai Banking), each with 10%.

On 20 October, the fragile state of the guarantee provider together with a large number of short positions among the estimated 40 000 outstanding HSI futures contracts raised fears of mass defaults that would produce a collapse of the futures market when it reopened – with potentially devastating consequences for the cash market and Hong Kong as a financial centre.

As a result, frantic efforts took place during the trading suspensions to create a support package for the Futures Guarantee Corp. These bore fruit in a HK$2 billion loan[28] at market-related rates to the FGC. The company's shareholders contributed one quarter; brokers and members of the HKFE a further quarter; and the Hong Kong Government's Exchange Fund a half.

The package, put together over the weekend of 24–25 October, also involved changes to the top management of the HKFE and undertakings from arbitrageurs not to engage in disruptive

[27] Worth respectively US$1.92 million and £1.03 million and US$961,538 and £517,241. One US dollar was worth HK$7.8 and one pound sterling worth HK$14.5 at the time.

[28] Equivalent to US$256 million at the then exchange rates.

sales of securities. When the markets opened on 26 October, the Hang Seng Index fell 33% to 2242 while the spot month for HSI futures dropped 44% to 1975 in after-hours trading.

The sharp falls triggered the feared defaults and prompted the FGC during trading to ask for more support. Another HK$2 billion facility – this time comprising HK$1 billion from the Government Exchange Fund and HK$1 billion shared equally by Hong Kong and Shanghai Bank, the Standard Chartered Bank and the Bank of China – was provided during the evening so that the FGC could withstand a fall in the index to 1000. Hong Kong banks also cut their prime lending rates on two successive days.

In the event, the second HK$2 billion package was not needed. But the FGC borrowed nearly HK$1.8 billion of the first support package to meet its obligations. This money was eventually paid back through recovering debts owed to the FGC by defaulted members of the clearing house as well as through levies placed on futures and stock market transactions.

On 16 November the colony's Governor appointed the Securities Review Committee, headed by Ian Hay Davison, a hard-nosed accountant and former chief executive of Lloyd's, the London insurance market, to investigate the constitution, management and operations of the two exchanges and their regulators.

When it reported six months later, Hay Davison's committee found serious defects in the running of the Hong Kong Stock Exchange, weak supervision of the colony's securities and futures industries and inadequate government surveillance of markets and brokers. It prescribed remedies in a large number of detailed recommendations.[29]

Hay Davison's report found that 'neither the market infrastructure nor the regulatory systems kept pace' with the HKFE's spectacular growth. 'In particular,' it said that

> the tripartite structure of Exchange, Clearing House and Guarantee Corporation confused lines of responsibility and effectively obstructed the development of an adequate risk-management system, which is essential to any futures market. All three agencies should have acted to contain the dangers in the expansion of business and the buildup of large positions by a few investors.

They failed. In the committee's view 'the fundamental cause of the HSI contract collapse lay in the inadequacy of the risk-management arrangements' of the HKFE with the tripartite structure displaying 'fatal flaws'.

In Hong Kong, control and accountability was lost because of the way the three bodies related to each other. Some years later, the Bank of England summed up the problem as 'an asymmetry of information and risk' among the three partners in the tripartite arrangement.[30]

In the Bank's view:

> The clearing house was responsible for monitoring positions, but was not exposed to losses in the event of default, whereas the guarantee fund was exposed to losses but dependent on the clearing house for its risk monitoring. This meant not only that the guarantee fund was exposed if information was not effectively shared, but that traders, who were not exposed to the losses of the guarantee fund, had little incentive either to monitor the clearing house's risk management or to follow prudent trading strategies.

In practice, margins on the HSI future had not been raised in line with the growth of the contract since its introduction.

[29] Hay Davison, Ian (May 1988), 'The operation and regulation of the Hong Kong securities industry: Report of the Securities Review Committee'.

[30] Bank of England (1999), 'Central counterparty clearing houses and Financial Stability', *Financial Stability Review*, June.

Although Hay Davison's report described a catalogue of defects in Hong Kong, he also wanted Hong Kong to keep its financial industry and indeed to aim 'to be the primary capital market for the South East Asian region'. His report therefore called for the continuation of the HKFE and its stock index contract. But his committee was equally convinced that the clearing and guarantee system needed to be restructured to strengthen risk management: 'in particular, the clearing house should become part of the exchange and the guarantee should be backed by a Clearing Member's Fund'.

The events in Hong Kong were bad news for ICCH in London and did nothing to increase the affection of the clearing banks for their joint subsidiary. David Hardy, recently seconded to ICCH, had to advise its clearing bank shareholders that they would have to contribute to the support fund for the guarantee corporation because of ICCH's holding in the company.

'I can well remember Sunday afternoon in my garden ringing round the bank directors and telling them they didn't have much choice other than to write a cheque,' Hardy says. 'These were the six banks.[31] It was probably the first time ever that the moral investment in a clearing house was called upon. The banks did not seek to get out at that stage, but they became even grumpier.'

The problems in Hong Kong showed how back office issues – including the role of CCPs – could no longer be neglected by top managers. The structure, governance and risk-management arrangements of the HKFE and its infrastructures were found wanting. But it would take the spectacular failure of one of Britain's oldest financial institutions before regulators around the world responded decisively to the risks present in exchange traded derivatives and their clearing systems.

9.5 THE COLLAPSE OF BARINGS

In 1986, the year before the crash, the US accounted for about 80% of trading of financial derivatives on organised exchanges around the globe.[32] In the immediate aftermath of October 1987, it still seemed to make sense that remedial action for any defects exposed by the market break should be a national matter.

But conditions were changing fast. Financial markets were becoming increasingly international in scope. The UK's deregulation of the London Stock Exchange also opened up the City to the big US investment banks. Although the old established City firms lost out to the newcomers, the City emerged as Europe's premier financial centre and its largest wholesale financial market. Another 1980s development was a proliferation of new futures exchanges in London, Paris, Hong Kong, Sydney, Montreal, Toronto, Singapore, Osaka, Zurich, Tokyo, Dublin and Frankfurt as well as in New Zealand and Brazil. Here too the US-owned investment banks became powerful players.

The CME played a part in internationalising financial futures. It entered a mutual offset arrangement with the Singapore International Monetary Exchange (SIMEX) in 1984 by which a trade executed in one exchange could be offset by a transaction on the other. In connection with applications by the CME to trade futures contracts based on Japanese, UK and world stock indices, the Chicago exchange entered into agreements to share information with the

[31] The owners of ICCH, as mentioned in Section 8.8.

[32] Both in terms of turnover and amounts outstanding: Bank for International Settlements (March 1997), 'Clearing arrangements for exchange traded derivatives'. The Committee on Payment and Settlement Systems of the central banks of the Group of Ten countries.

Tokyo Stock Exchange and The Securities Association in London, part of the self regulatory apparatus created after the UK's 'Big-Bang' deregulation of financial markets.

But as far as regulators and bankers were concerned, the main post-trade problems that needed addressing internationally after the crash were in securities markets. When the Group of 30, a high-powered think tank made up of eminent financiers and influential ex-policy makers from around the world, examined 'the state of clearance and settlement practices in the world's principal markets' and reported in March 1989, it gave no more than a passing nod to derivatives, admitting that they were 'considered only tangentially'.[33]

When, four years later in 1993, the G30 published a report of a global derivatives study group – with 24 recommendations on good management practice for dealers, end-users and supervisors – it focused solely on global OTC derivatives.[34]

By 1995 priorities had changed. By that year, as the Bank for International Settlements (BIS) reported later, turnover of financial derivatives contracts on non-US exchanges exceeded turnover on US exchanges and the value of outstanding contracts, in terms of notional principal amounts, was only slightly less.[35]

More immediately, Barings PLC, a venerable UK merchant bank and pillar of the City's financial establishment, had been ruined by the activities of Nick Leeson, a rogue trader in the bank's Singapore office, who had run up huge losses trading financial derivatives on SIMEX and the Osaka Securities Exchange. The Barings case put the potential for international contagion from exchange-traded derivatives and their clearing infrastructures on the agenda of policy makers.

Barings' fate was sealed during the evening of 26 February 1995 when the Bank of England acted to place it in administration after the failure of a weekend rescue attempt. As an official UK enquiry later made clear, Leeson's 'unauthorised and ultimately catastrophic activities' cost £927 million when finally totted up: more than twice the bank's total equity.[36]

The report of the Board of Banking Supervision told how the trader's activities went undetected because of 'a failure of management and other internal controls of the most basic kind'. This damning indictment of the bank's management did not let the markets or the clearing houses off the hook. Some 'warning signals' were either volunteered or visible as a result of the operations of the CCPs belonging to the exchanges on which Leeson traded. This raised the question as to why the trader's problems did not become clearer sooner, before he ran up losses that sank the bank.

Leeson traded for Barings' account mainly in Nikkei-225 stock index futures and 10-year Japanese government bond futures: contracts that were traded on both SIMEX and the Osaka Exchange. His bosses thought that he was engaged in arbitrage trading with positions that were hedged to exploit price differences between the contracts as they traded on the two exchanges. But starting in 1992, he engaged in unhedged trades on an increasing scale and concealed rising losses.

Leeson's attempts to recover his losses were thrown into disarray by the Kobe earthquake of January 1995, which triggered a sharp drop in Japanese share prices and extreme volatility in Japanese markets. His losses rose sharply from £208 million to £827 million in 57 days

[33] G30 (March 1989), 'Clearance and settlement systems in the world's securities markets, Foreword.

[34] G30 (July 1993), 'Derivatives: Practices and principles'.

[35] In Bank for International Settlements (March 1997).

[36] Board of Banking Supervision (18 July 1995), 'Report of the Board of Banking Supervision Inquiry into the circumstances of the collapse of Barings'.

between the end of 1994 and 27 February 1995. This rapid deterioration made the neglect of 'warning signals' a priority issue for investigators after Barings' collapse.

Leeson's activities generated rumours and queries and left traces in the infrastructures of the two exchanges. On 27 January 1995, for example, SIMEX wrote to Barings Futures (Singapore) for reassurance that it would meet its margin commitments and that letter was passed to London. On that day too, the BIS in Basel contacted Barings executives in London to report rumours in Asia that the bank had suffered massive losses on the Nikkei and could not meet its margin calls. Also on 27 January, a staffer of Bloomberg, the financial news service, told Barings in Japan that everyone was talking about Barings' very long positions in Japan.

By the time Barings collapsed, it had committed £742 million to finance margin calls for Barings Futures (Singapore) Pte Ltd of which £468 million – a large sum – was deposited with SIMEX. By 23 February, Leeson's activities accounted for 49% of the total open interest in the March 1995 Nikkei futures contract and 24% of the open interest in the June contract. His position in Japanese government bond futures represented 88% of the open interest in the June 1995 contract.[37] Some of Leeson's positions were in the public domain. Under rules applying in Osaka, his trading positions on that exchange were posted on a notice board. Had Barings or SIMEX contacted the Osaka exchange, they would have realised his positions in Singapore were not, as supposed, hedged in Osaka.

These signals went unheeded partly because of the sclerotic responses and ignorance of Barings' management but also because the exchanges and authorities in Singapore and Japan did not communicate with each other.

The collapse triggered a sharp fall in investor confidence in SIMEX and its CCP. Wall Street traders, who had used SIMEX in part because of its CME links, realised the exchange had failed to monitor Barings rigorously. When, after Barings' closure, SIMEX increased margins on the Nikkei stock index futures contract, some US clearing members objected for fear the money might be used to pay for Barings' losses. It took an assurance from the Singapore authorities that this would not happen to allay the market's doubts about the soundness of SIMEX's clearing house.

The collapse exposed other issues. One was the difference in legal treatment between jurisdictions of clients of clearing members of CCPs in case of bankruptcy. In the scramble to sort out who owned what after the collapse, it turned out that Japanese law – in contrast to that of the US – had no rules to segregate the accounts of Barings' customers from the bank's proprietary funds and therefore no simple means of protecting customer accounts from creditors of the failed bank. The non-segregation of accounts contributed to delays in closing out or transferring positions and margin funds.

9.6 THE REACTION OF REGULATORS

The reaction of regulators and the futures industry to the deficiencies exposed by Barings' fall was swift. In May 1995, officials from 16 countries responsible for supervising the world's leading futures and options markets met for two days in Windsor, west of London, to draw conclusions from the Barings debacle and the rapid growth of cross-border trading on futures and options exchanges. Co-chaired by the CFTC and the Securities and Investment Board, the relevant UK regulator at the time, the meeting focused on cooperation among market

[37] Kuprianov, Anatoli (1995), 'Derivatives Debacles: Case Studies of Large Losses in Derivatives Markets', *Economic Quarterly*, **81**(4), Fall.

authorities; the protection of clients' positions, money and assets; default procedures; and cooperation among regulators in emergencies.

The outcome was the 'Windsor Declaration', which set an agenda for improving the strength and safety of international derivatives markets when dealing with large exposures such as those created by Leeson's activities and for improving client asset protection. The agenda was followed up by IOSCO, the International Organisation of Securities Commissions, and a Global Task Force on Financial Integrity, organised by the Futures Industry Association (FIA) in March 1995.

The FIA taskforce also moved quickly, producing 60 recommendations in June 1995 aimed at exchanges and clearing houses, brokers and intermediaries, and customers. Drawing on the expertise of 60 participants from 17 jurisdictions, the task force underlined the importance of improved cross-border coordination and communication among exchanges, clearing houses and regulators. It also drew attention to the need for emergency mechanisms 'to facilitate the transfer or close out of positions and the return of clearing member or customer property . . . as promptly as feasible'[38] in the event of the failure of a clearing member or other intermediary.

In March 1996, futures regulators from 14 jurisdictions and representatives of 49 exchanges and clearing organisations from 18 countries converged on Boca Raton, Florida, to formalise mechanisms for sharing information in the first multilateral agreement of its kind. The 'Declaration on Cooperation and Supervision of International Futures Exchanges and Clearing Organisations' signed by the regulators[39] was backed up by a Memorandum of Understanding and Agreement (MOU) signed by the 49 exchanges and clearing organisations. Together, the Declaration and the MOU set out the mechanisms for bilateral sharing of information between regulators if certain 'triggering events' cause concern about the financial resources or positions of an exchange member.

The Declaration and MOU attracted further signatories. IOSCO took on the job of coordinating the addition of regulators wanting to sign up to Boca Raton Declaration. By March 1998 the number had increased to 25. IOSCO also directed its Technical Committee to produce a series of reports that fleshed out the Windsor Agenda.

The G10 Committee on Payment and Settlement Systems (CPSS) also became involved in the post-Barings agenda concerning the robustness of clearing systems for exchange traded derivatives. In its March 1997 report, dubbed the 'Parkinson Report' after Patrick Parkinson, the Federal Reserve Board official who chaired a CPSS study group on Exchange Traded Derivatives, the Basel central bankers' group switched the focus back to clearing house risk-management systems.[40]

They pinpointed the following sources of potential vulnerability:

- inadequate financial resources to meet losses and liquidity pressures from defaults of members caused by extreme price movements;
- a lack of mechanisms to control intraday risk;
- weakness in money settlement arrangements.

Parkinson's report recommended stress testing by CCPs to deal with the risks of extreme price movements; more timely trade matching for calculating margin requirements to reduce

[38] FIA Global Task Force on Financial Integrity (June 1995), 'Recommendations for regulators, exchanges and clearinghouses, forming part of Financial Integrity Recommendations for Futures and Options Markets and Market Participants'.

[39] Of the US, UK, Australia, Austria, France, Germany, Hong Kong, Ireland, Italy, the Netherlands, Quebec (*sic*), Singapore, South Africa and Spain.

[40] Bank for International Settlements (March 1997).

intraday risk; and clearer settlement agreements with clearing members as well as the use of real time gross settlement systems for payments – at that time a relatively recent innovation in payments infrastructures – to strengthen money settlement arrangements.

Taken individually, these initiatives to regulate the financial derivatives markets and their clearing organisations may not have appeared too dramatic. Viewed together, they bore witness to a futures industry that in less than two decades had grown dramatically in importance. The cooperation of regulators and industry showed how both sides were all too aware of the potential of futures and options exchanges and their clearing infrastructures to impact both positively and negatively on the global economy.

10 Continental Europe – CCPs in the Slipstream of Exchanges

10.1 ACRONYMS IN ABUNDANCE

As many as 49 exchanges and clearing organisations signed the March 1996 post-Barings memorandum of understanding in Boca Raton, Florida, which shows just how much the futures and options business had grown around the world since the 1987 crash.

Liberalisation, deregulation and the need of investors to obtain protection against market turbulence encouraged the spread of futures and options exchanges. As Figure 10.1 shows, the US share of financial derivatives trading on organised exchanges fell from more than three quarters in 1986 to less than half by 1995. LIFFE in London was an early example of this trend, having started operating in September 1982, nearly three years after the lifting of UK exchange controls.

An alphabet soup of acronyms followed, especially in continental Europe. Among the first countries to react was France, where political agreement to modernise financial markets and their infrastructure transcended the left–right political divide. The plans for a new futures exchange were hatched under a socialist government and promoted by finance minister Pierre Bérégovoy to improve the funding of a fast rising public debt.

MATIF[1] was launched to trade futures in France in February 1986. MONEP,[2] France's traded options market, followed in September 1987, by which time the administration had changed. Although France's socialist President François Mitterrand continued in office, the country was experiencing two years of political 'cohabitation' during which a right-of-centre government headed by prime minister Jacques Chirac actively promoted financial markets. In 1987, Chirac's government passed a law reforming futures markets to allow the merger of exchanges trading commodity and financial futures.

In 1988, it was the turn of Switzerland to launch SOFFEX[3], a futures and options exchange, owned 40% by the country's three leading bourses (Zurich, Geneva and Basel) and 60% by its five biggest banks and supported by the Swiss National Bank and government in Bern.

Germany acted at the end of the 1980s when new legislation greatly eased the restrictions on futures trading imposed by the 1896 *Börsengesetz*. The Deutsche Terminbörse (DTB) started trading financial derivatives in Germany in January 1990 and turnover grew rapidly after a modest first year. Owned by 17 banks, the new exchange had an active and ambitious chairman in Rolf-E. Breuer, a senior executive of Deutsche Bank. Breuer, known in Frankfurt as 'Mr Finanzplatz'[4] was a enthusiastic backer of efforts to boost financial services in Germany.

---

[1] Marché à Terme d'Instruments Financiers.

[2] Marché des Options Négociables de Paris.

[3] Swiss Options and Financial Futures Exchange.

[4] 'Mr Financial Centre'.

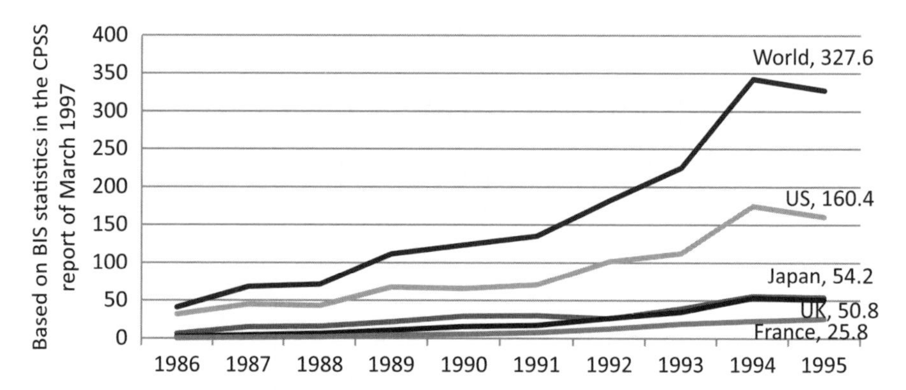

Figure 10.1 Financial derivatives traded on organised exchanges: annual turnover volumes in terms of notional amounts, in trillion dollars

Source: Bank for International Settlements (1997). *Clearing Arrangements for Exchange-Traded Derivatives*, Basel, Switzerland.

The exchanges adopted different methods of trading and developed differing approaches to clearing their financial derivatives contracts. MATIF followed the example of LIFFE and the big Chicago derivatives exchanges and opted for an open outcry system while SOFFEX and DTB adopted electronic screen technology from the start.

MATIF and MONEP developed their own clearing houses using technology bought from ICCH and developed by the London clearer's Australian operation.

MATIF's CCP was known as CCIFP, the Chambre de Compensation des Instruments Financiers de Paris. CCIFP was developed from the system used by the Sydney Futures Exchange and began operating with a staff of just 10. MONEP's transactions were cleared by Societé de Compensation des Marchés Conditionnels, which like MONEP was a unit of the Paris stock exchange SBF, Bourse de Paris.

LIFFE, as described earlier, used the central counterparty risk-management services of ICCH, which since 1982 was owned by the UK's main commercial banks and not linked by any shareholding to the exchange. On the other hand, LIFFE managed its own TRS/CPS clearing system that the exchange had developed and which differed in provenance and technical specifications from ICCH's Australian systems used by MATIF and MONEP.

By contrast, the planners behind SOFFEX commissioned Arthur Andersen, the consultancy, to develop a fully integrated trading and clearing system. In 1985, the committee of bankers and exchange officials creating the exchange had rejected the idea of using systems already on offer from Sweden's OM and ICCH of London.[5]

In 1987, even before SOFFEX was launched, the founders of DTB entered talks with the Swiss exchange about using its Arthur Andersen technology. Shortly after SOFFEX started trading, DTB acquired a licence to do so.

Although the Swiss and German exchanges were in separate jurisdictions either side of the European Community frontier, and although each added its own specifications to the systems developed by Arthur Andersen, they had integrated trading and clearing technology in common. Their shared technology was the basis for much closer links in the future.

[5] Meier, Richard T. and Sigrist, Tobias (2006), *Der helvetische Big Bang*.

Unlike ICCH, which was long-established and served a number of markets, continental Europe's CCPs operated in the slipstream of their exchanges. As they tried to build up their businesses, these exchanges were subject to complex and varied pressures not all of which were economic.

10.2 EUROPEAN UNION, EMU AND EUROPE'S SINGLE MARKET

The Berlin Wall fell on 9 November 1989. The 25 months that followed saw the elimination of communism as a political force, the collapse of the Soviet Union and the unification of Germany.

Having attracted growing support during the 1980s, market capitalism and policies of liberalisation and deregulation now appeared to reign supreme. The profit motive became the global norm, giving an enormous boost to privatisation and undermining such venerable concepts as mutual ownership. A parallel revolution in information and telecommunications technology made it easier and cheaper to communicate between nations and continents. Investors had more scope to move capital around the world in search of the best returns than at any time since 1914, and could do so much faster. A new era of globalisation had begun.

The events of the late 1980s gave new impetus to the ambitions of US investment banks to expand abroad. They had invested heavily in London following the October 1986 Big-Bang deregulation of UK financial markets, with the aim of using the City as a base for cross border dealings in Europe. They encountered a fragmented post-trade environment that was far more expensive than that at home. In consequence, they became increasingly determined in the course of the 1990s to obtain lower costs from financial infrastructure providers.

Politically, Europe reacted to the geo-political revolution of 1989–91 by pressing ahead with ambitious plans for greater integration. In December 1991, European Community leaders brought several months of difficult negotiation to a close in the southern Dutch town of Maastricht with agreement on far reaching revisions of the EC's founding Treaty of Rome. They agreed to turn the EC into a European Union with economic and monetary union (EMU) at its heart. Four years later, EU leaders at a summit in Madrid christened their planned single currency the 'euro' and named 1 January 1999 as the date when those EU members that decided to participate would irrevocably lock their currencies and adopt a single monetary policy. In 1999, 11 of by then 15 EU member states were founder members of the eurozone. Three years later, the euro became a fully fledged currency when 12 EU countries adopted euro notes and coins.

Its supporters saw EMU as the logical outcome of a process of integration that was already underway in the EU.

Several EU member states had pledged to keep their currencies within narrow margins of fluctuation in an Exchange Rate Mechanism. Launched in 1979 with the aim of boosting growth and employment, the ERM had weaknesses, however. It suffered from occasional, disruptive, speculative attacks, some of which forced weekend realignments of the 'central rates' that determined the relationships of the ERM's member currencies to one another. A huge wave of speculation in September 1992 forced sterling and the Italian lira out of the ERM. This crisis and continuing turbulence surrounding the French franc–D-mark relationship in the 11 months to August 1993 gave a major boost to financial futures markets in Europe.

When the Maastricht Treaty was agreed, the EU was already engaged in a programme to turn the economies of Europe's then 12 member states into a single market. But the single market programme was heavily focused on the trade in goods. Financial liberalisation was patchy and often obstructed by the protectionist behaviour of member states in the EU's Council of Ministers.

There was, it is true, a piece of EU legislation called the Investment Services Directive (ISD). Approved in 1993 for implementation in 1996, the ISD was supposed to create pan-European rules for financial markets in the EU. But it was a compromise that had emerged from negotiations in which many member states' governments appeared determined to defend national financial sectors and interests at all costs.

The ISD allowed regulated markets to offer remote access to investment firms from other EU member states for specified financial services. This 'single passport' greatly benefited screen-based traders and exchanges such as DTB. The directive also gave authorised investment firms remote access to clearing and settlement systems. But because post-trade infrastructures remained unregulated at the European level, member states were able to restrict access across national frontiers to them.

In fact, the directive contained many loopholes – omitting coverage of commodity derivatives, for example – and its implementation was slow. Underpinning the ISD was the principle of mutual recognition, which meant authorisation by an investment company's national or 'home' supervisor should enable the firm to trade or 'passport' its services throughout the EU. But mutual recognition was often undermined by thinly disguised protectionist provisions that allowed the foreign or 'host' country to impose its own local conduct of business rules.

Financial markets and infrastructure providers were given conflicting signals. EMU preparations gathered pace from 1996 and acted as a stimulus for integration and consolidation among exchanges and CCPs in Europe. But EU policies also lacked any sense that Europe's financial infrastructure should be guided towards continent-wide integration and consolidation like that in progress for securities markets in the US since the mid-1970s.

But while the EU policy framework was imperfect, the top managers of Europe's financial infrastructures faced big strategic questions in the 1990s. Industry-specific pressures pointed to a need for more integration and consolidation. Rapidly increasing turnover, increased competition and the stress placed on safety and risk management after the 1987 crash and the Barings collapse required increased expenditure on information technology. At the same time, the pressure from US investment banks on European infrastructure providers to cut costs kept growing. Caught between the twin pressures of user demands for lower costs and increased capital spending, Europe's exchanges and operators of CCPs looked for economies of scale.

Budgets were not limitless, despite strong growth of turnover. Should they therefore focus their technology spend on trading or back office activities? And once that choice was made, how best to invest? Computerisation was essential; but IT projects, unless skilfully managed, could easily go off the rails at costs that could be crippling.

The pressures from globalisation and European integration were undeniable. Should exchange and infrastructure managers look to solutions within their national boundaries, where the rules of the game were clear? Or should they anticipate the single market and single currency, even though these were work in progress where important issues such as taxation and national laws remained firmly under the control of national administrations?

And what did all these factors mean for company structures? Were efficiencies best achieved through integration? And if so, did the answer lie in the creation of vertical silos linking up the various stages of the transaction chain from placing the order through trading to its completion? Or was it better to integrate activities at the various stages of a trade in a horizontal manner according to function, first within European jurisdictions and afterwards beyond?

Finally, what were the implications of these financial and geopolitical pressures for corporate governance? The more competitive conditions that emerged after the 1987 crash contrasted with the herbivorous environment in which many European exchanges and infrastructures operated into the late 1980s. Demutualisation was one way for companies to acquire the wherewithal for increased investment. But how, if they took this route, could they simultaneously satisfy shareholders and users, not to mention the politicians and regulators who took an increasing interest in the workings of finance as the 20th century drew to a close?

The first and easiest option for exchange and financial infrastructure providers was to seek economies of scale from consolidation at home. This was the pattern in Germany and France. But as the 1990s progressed, there was a growing willingness among companies to explore the possibilities for improving services and lowering costs across frontiers. Cross-border contacts among companies became frequent and sometimes frantic, although an outsider assessing events in Europe's post-trade sector in the 1990s could easily conclude that the end result was much ado about relatively little.

And yet, the 1990s yielded two significant corporate restructurings affecting CCPs in continental Europe. The German and Swiss derivatives exchanges merged in 1998 to become Eurex, a cross-border, screen-based trading operation with vertically integrated central counter party clearing. Eurex became for some years the world's biggest derivatives exchange.

In France, the nation's exchanges were brought together under a single holding company with a horizontal twist at the end, when the clearing services of the country's cash and derivatives markets were put together in Banque Centrale de Compensation (BCC), the CCP, which was rebranded as Clearnet and endowed with ambitions for a wider European role.

The manoeuvrings that resulted in these very different outcomes took place amidst an increasingly frantic jockeying for position among European exchange groups as the odds on the euro's introduction on 1 January 1999 narrowed from possible through probable to inevitable.

The rest of this chapter looks at how Clearnet and Eurex emerged from the interaction of five companies in Europe: MATIF and SBF Paris Bourse in France, SOFFEX in Switzerland and DTB with its parent group Deutsche Börse in Germany, with the Chicago Mercantile Exchange playing an important supporting role offstage. The actions and attitudes of three powerful personalities – the chief executives of MATIF, SBF Paris Bourse and Deutsche Börse – greatly influenced developments.

10.3 THREE EXCHANGE LEADERS

Some people are instantly identified with the companies they lead. Others toil in the background long before being recognised for any special contribution that they make. Gérard Pfauwadel, the chairman and chief executive of MATIF, was one of the former.

In 1985, as a senior official in the French Treasury, Pfauwadel was one of those responsible for the legislation that brought MATIF into being. Three years later, he slipped effortlessly from being head of financial markets in the Treasury to become chairman and chief executive of France's futures exchange with ambitions to make it the most important derivatives market in Europe.

As an Énarque, or graduate of France's prestigious École Nationale d'Administration, Pfauwadel was automatically a member of France's financial and policy-making elite. With his American wife, this out-going executive was equally at home on either side of the Atlantic.

'Extremely bright and erudite' was how Leo Melamed described his French friend.[6] Pfauwadel set MATIF on a programme of expansion both at home and abroad.

In 1988, MATIF took advantage of France's 1987 futures market legislation and acquired the commodity exchanges of Paris, Lille and Le Havre, changing its full name in the process to Marché à Terme International de France. It acquired its first foreign members and expanded its product offering beyond the French bond future – the 'Notionnel' – which was the basis of its successful start. The following year, Pfauwadel announced plans for the exchange, which had an open outcry trading system, to join GLOBEX, the after-hours electronic trading platform developed by the CME and NYMEX. In January 1993, MATIF and DTB agreed to cooperate on marketing, operations and strategy and so link the French and German futures markets in preparation for EMU.

Nor did Pfauwadel neglect post-trade issues. He became chairman of Banque Centrale de Compensation (BCC) after MATIF acquired the commodity futures clearing house in 1990. Two years later, MATIF replaced its original clearing system adapted from ICCH's Australian technology with an in-house system based on Digital Equipment technology.

Turnover soared. In 1989, MATIF doubled its trading space. In June 1991, four months after its fifth birthday, the exchange traded its 100 millionth contract.

It was probably around that time that MATIF's fortunes peaked. Not that the exchange lost momentum: it continued to grow, expanding its trading floor area, adding new contracts and reaching out to other exchanges. For a while, MATIF could claim to be the world's fourth biggest derivatives exchange.

But LIFFE in London beat off MATIF's attempts to develop futures based on non-French financial instruments. Also, first in France and later in Germany, new leaders took charge of other exchanges who would constrain Pfauwadel's room for manoeuvre.

As described later, MATIF lost its independence at the end of 1997, becoming a subsidiary of SBF Paris Bourse, the operator of the Paris stock exchange and the MONEP options market. Four months after the takeover, Pfauwadel stood down as chairman and CEO of MATIF and was replaced by Jean-François Théodore, the chairman and CEO of SBF Paris Bourse who added the MATIF jobs to his existing portfolio.

Théodore was appointed chairman and chief executive of Société des Bourses Francaises (SBF) in 1990. A cursory glance at their CVs might have suggested that Pfauwadel and Théodore were twins. Both were Énarques. Both moved to their respective exchanges from the French finance ministry, the government department that helped bankroll the modernisation of France's financial markets in the late 1980s.

But the two men were rather different in character. Théodore was more of a background toiler, noted for the long hours he worked. A quiet man, who speaks English with a pronounced French accent, he could appear almost diffident. With his Mediterranean complexion and rumpled suits, he looked more like Columbo, the sartorially challenged Italian-American detective in the long-running TV crime fiction series, than 'a master of the universe'. But once ensconced at SBF, Théodore proved to be an able tactician, a visionary strategist and a brilliant financial engineer.

It was easy to underestimate Théodore, and many people did to their cost. A master of delay and calculated vagueness, when needed he could move boldly and rapidly to secure his objectives. He led his group through a succession of mergers, acquisitions and divestitures, first in France and later beyond, that culminated in the creation of NYSE Euronext, the

[6] Melamed, Leo, with Tamarkin, Bob (1996), *Escape to the Futures*.

first transatlantic exchange group in 2007. Théodore's financial manoeuvrings brought rich rewards to shareholders after demutualisation in 2001. Because of his achievements, Théodore would be the great survivor among the leaders of Europe's exchanges, retiring as deputy chief executive of NYSE Euronext at the end of 2009, aged 63.

The business that Théodore took over was in a different state than Pfauwadel's recent start-up. For Pfauwadel, post-trade structures and information technology were just two among several issues requiring attention. Partly because of circumstances, and partly through inclination, they were higher up Théodore's list of priorities. The operational side of the bourse needed repairing. Technical glitches, especially in the trading and settlement of registered securities, caused trades to be blocked and suspended at times. These difficulties escalated in the turbulent conditions of 1987.

'There were very big problems, especially in France after 1987,' Théodore recalled later.[7] 'There were lost securities; difficulties finding the accounts. They were not physically lost because France was in a paperless environment. But settlement was very late. Especially after the crash of 1987, the brokers' back offices were in a horrible mess. There was an accumulation of fails and we had to work a lot to correct this disorder.'

Luckily for Théodore, there were infrastructure improvements underway. SBF and Sicovam, France's central securities depository, were working together on a system called Relit[8] that would combine order confirmation, matching and settlement for equities and bonds traded on the Paris stock market. Unusually, this delivery versus payment system included a CCP. This was to cope with France's complex securities settlement practices, which at the time included settlement after intervals of a week, a fortnight and even a month depending on the type of security traded. The Relit CCP, known as Inter Sociétés de Bourse (ISB), was needed to guarantee against counterparty risk in the longer settlement schedules. As continental Europe's first CCP for equities, it was a well timed innovation. It fitted well with electronic trading platforms of the type used by Paris's screen-based stock exchange.

Relit was launched successfully in October 1990. ISB began operating in stages, drawing on technology developed by NSCC, the US equities CCP. It handled a small part of the market's equities business in November 1990 and the bulk of it a year later.

Thanks to ISB, the Paris stock exchange achieved a technical lead in Europe with its CCP for equities. This stood Théodore in good stead later in the 1990s and helped pave the way for a consolidation of the French securities and derivatives markets through a technology-led merger on his terms.

Events in Germany – where a programme of in-country consolidation of exchanges and post-trade infrastructures began in the early 1990s – also influenced Théodore's eventual reshaping of France's financial markets.

DTB was in a state of transition when Pfauwadel and Jörg Franke, DTB's chief executive, signed their January 1993 cooperation accord. Guided by Rolf-E. Breuer, Germany's banks had agreed in 1992 to form a single corporate entity by consolidating their holdings in the Frankfurt stock exchange – the country's largest – with their shares in DTB and the Deutscher Kassenverein (DKV), the German CSD. The resulting group – Deutsche Börse AG – was a closely held, unlisted, joint stock company owned mainly by the banks but with Germany's

[7] As told to the author, 25 July 2006; cited originally in Norman, Peter (2007), *Plumbers and Visionaries: Securities settlement and Europe's financial market*.

[8] REglement LIvraison de Titres.

small, independent regional stock markets having a minority stake of 10%. The merger took effect in January 1993.

Breuer's next move, in March 1993, was to engineer a coup at the top of the newly created Deutsche Börse. This coup brought in Werner Seifert, a 44-year-old main board director of the Swiss Re-insurance group, as chief executive of the Frankfurt-based exchange group from the end of July.

Seifert was the third of the strong personalities who shaped CCP clearing and exchanges in continental Europe in the 1990s. An alumnus of the McKinsey school of management consultants, Seifert had a quick, logical and powerful mind. He had studied game theory at university, was a jazz enthusiast and an accomplished performer on the electronic organ. He applied the combination of improvisation and teamwork that characterises playing jazz music to much of his working life. He fancied himself as both a lateral and strategic thinker and was much given to brainstorming with a team of enthusiastic, young and loyal managers, many of whom were McKinsey alumni.

There were downsides to Seifert's personality, however. He lacked diplomatic finesse and patience and had little awareness of the cultural and historical sensitivities of executives in Britain and France. He was also poor at handling the media.

He knew nothing about the business of exchanges when he got the Deutsche Börse job,[9] but he learned quickly. Seifert looked at exchanges unsentimentally 'from an industrial perspective' and set out to streamline their operations. He invested in the best available technology, on the grounds that an exchange was a fixed cost business where once the initial investment was made in a system that was 'scalable', every additional customer boosted returns.[10]

His other significant insight was that exchange operators could profit hugely from vertically integrating exchange trading with clearing and, in the case of cash markets, with settlement and custody to make a silo. He did not believe in user-run utilities, claiming instead that customers also benefited when 'for-profit' operators adopted vertical integration.

10.4 CORPORATE MANOEUVRING IN FRANCE

DTB and MATIF had agreed to implement their cooperation agreement by the end of 1993. The deadline was missed but discussions continued.

Such deadlines were often missed and so the news did not appear too ominous. MATIF pursued other opportunities. After much delay, MATIF's variation of CME's GLOBEX platform went live in 1993. According to François-Guy Hamonic, MATIF's deputy managing director, MONEP also approached MATIF to explore whether it should adopt its system to replace that used by Société de Compensation des Marchés Conditionnels, its CCP.[11]

Discussions followed in 1994–5. Although inconclusive, they prompted MATIF to look at its own CCP engine and conclude there was room for improvement. Further talks took place between MATIF and DTB during 1994–5 to see whether the French exchange could use DTB's trading system. Hamonic remembers that MATIF sent about 10 people to Frankfurt to find a way to unbundle DTB's integrated trading and CCP clearing system. Work stopped in April 1996 when DTB and MATIF called off their plans for closer cooperation.

---

[9] In Seifert, Werner, with Voth, Hans-Joachim (2006), *Invasion der Heuschrecken*.

[10] Conversation with the author, 12 October 2005, which is reported in greater detail in Norman (2007).

[11] Conversation with the author, 9 December 2008.

This was a serious blow for Pfauwadel. DTB found a new partner in SOFFEX, the Swiss derivatives market, later that year. MATIF was left looking exposed and Pfauwadel in a weak position to resist any approach from SBF.

Théodore moved in 1996. He proposed that MATIF, MONEP and SBF should merge to create a single company SBF Paris Bourse SA. Pfauwadel pleaded for the continuation of two French exchanges with MATIF maintaining entrepreneurial independence. But Théodore's leverage was considerable.

SBF had a stake in MATIF. In addition, MATIF's unbroken record of growth went into reverse in 1995 when the number of contracts traded fell by nearly a quarter from 93 million in 1994 to just over 71 million. MATIF, with a heavy reliance on French interest rate contracts, was deemed to be vulnerable to the introduction of the euro.

Théodore in the meantime had unified securities settlement in France as part of a longer-term strategy to consolidate the nation's financial infrastructure. SBF had a small stake in Sicovam, France's CSD. In 1993, Théodore became Sicovam's chairman and used his position to push through a 'technical consolidation' that involved the acquisition by Sicovam of the Banque de France's securities settlement business with the central bank taking a 40% stake in the enlarged CSD in return. As part of the deal, Sicovam initiated development of RGV,[12] a high speed Relit system for large value transactions with real time settlement that was linked to the central bank's real time gross settlement system for payments. RGV began operating in February 1998.

The changes at Sicovam brought into alignment the interests of Théodore and Jean-Claude Trichet, governor of the Banque de France. Théodore convinced Trichet of the merits of creating a single clearing and settlement provider for the benefit of the French financial sector.

Therefore SBF became the national champion of France's financial markets just as the failure of MATIF's talks with DTB left MATIF without an updated trading system. MATIF began to look at NSC, the Nouveau Système de Cotation, an electronic trading system developed by SBF for the Paris Bourse and in use since 1995.

Any plan for MATIF to adopt the NSC would involve untangling its agreement with CME to use GLOBEX. Hamonic went to Chicago to discuss the matter and there became aware that CME was developing a new clearing system, Clearing 21. CME also wanted to renew its trading system.

'We came up with the idea of a technology swap in December,' Hamonic explains. 'And the talks went very quickly.' On 24 January 1997, MATIF announced it would adopt SBF Paris Bourse's NSC trading system for after-hours dealings in place of GLOBEX and that it would cooperate with SBF Paris Bourse in developing futures contracts based on equity market indices. It was also announced that MATIF and CME together with SBF Paris Bourse were studying 'the possibility of future cooperative efforts in electronic and trading systems'.[13]

These studies were followed in February 1997 by a letter of intent between the French and US exchanges. In June 1997, SBF Paris Bourse, MATIF and MONEP agreed a technology swap with the CME. The three French markets adopted Clearing 21, the CME's CCP system, enabling a harmonisation of clearing principles and giving market participants common access to all three markets and clearing services. In return, CME was allowed to adopt the NSC trading system. The exchanges aimed to implement their new systems in the second half of 1998.

[12] Relit Grande Vitesse.

[13] BF Paris Bourse MATIF (24 January 1997), 'MATIF opts for NSC for off-hours trading. Joint SBF Paris Bourse–MATIF subsidiary to manage index futures', press release.

Experience would show that Clearing 21 was not the ideal system for clearing equities in Paris and would require a good deal of adaptation. But the technology swap played an important part in Théodore's strategy to merge France's exchanges and infrastructures.

10.5 EUREX AND CLEARNET

By this time, DTB's future was clear. Towards the end of 1996 a new company Eurex Exchange AG was founded in Zurich. Jointly owned by Deutsche Börse and SWX, the Swiss exchanges group, Eurex was the corporate structure in which DTB and SOFFEX came together as the first cross-border derivatives exchange.

SOFFEX and DTB always had a lot in common. They were screen-based exchanges, shared a common philosophy of integrated trading and clearing while their respective computer technologies had a common origin. They had maintained intermittent contact over the possibility of a link. Having set up Eurex Exchange, the two partners decided to base the exchange's trading and clearing systems on DTB's equipment and know-how. The new exchange started trading as one bourse in two jurisdictions on 28 September 1998, replacing DTB and SOFFEX.

The effectiveness of Eurex's screen-based offering quickly became apparent. In its first year, it became the world's second biggest derivatives exchange with 311 members from 14 countries.

The new exchange had momentum thanks to DTB, which in 1997 won the Bund futures business from LIFFE. In 1999, Eurex was the biggest derivatives exchange in the world. LIFFE had to modernise in response and scrapped its open outcry system in favour of screen trading in that year.

For a while it looked as if the planned launch of Eurex and the moves towards consolidating exchanges and their infrastructures in France were the first steps towards a much broader coalescence of exchanges and infrastructures across Europe. With the clock ticking towards 1 January 1999, the euro was rocketing up the agendas of companies throughout the EU.

In June 1997, Deutsche Börse disclosed discussions with the French stock exchange on an electronic link in anticipation of EMU. In July, there was a Franco–German agreement to cooperate on European equity indices. On 17 September 1997, a group comprising Deutsche Börse and SWX-Swiss Exchange, representing Eurex, and SBF Paris Bourse, MATIF and MONEP announced plans to develop a joint market for fixed income derivatives as a prelude to 'a fully fledged alliance also integrating the cash markets'.[14]

The so-called 'EURO-Alliance' sounded impressive. The partners proclaimed 'their understanding that the cooperation should eventually cover all products and services: equity and fixed income, cash and derivatives, trading and clearing'. It would 'entail linking trading and clearing systems by a planned common front-end technology, by cross-membership and mutual access, by harmonisation of rules and regulations as well as by mutual clearing arrangements'.

Ultimately, the EURO-Alliance proved a distraction. Although the partners continued to concoct plans, agree memoranda of understanding and issue press releases telling of progress, the 'common virtual market' never came to pass. The differences among the protagonists were too great. Of more immediate importance were developments at a national level in France.

[14] Deutsche Börse, MATIF, MONEP, SBF-Bourse de Paris and SWX-Swiss Exchange (17 September 1997), 'Frankfurt, Paris and Zurich Exchanges extend their alliance', joint press release.

On the same day that the EURO-Alliance was announced, SBF Paris Bourse made an offer for MATIF. It already held 26% of the equity and 33% of the voting rights in MATIF. Shortly before Christmas, SBF Paris Bourse's takeover of 100% of MATIF was complete. From 1 January 1998, the SBF Group included SBF, MATIF, MONEP and Société du Nouveau Marché, an exchange for small, entrepreneurial start-ups, and their various CCPs. Pfauwadel resigned as chairman and CEO of MATIF four months later.

Théodore was free to focus on synergies. He moved, perhaps surprisingly, on clearing first. The acquisition of MATIF brought BCC into the SBF Group. It was a CCP with 30 years experience and also had banking status.

While keeping Banque Centrale de Compensation as its official name, BCC began clearing as Clearnet. As such, on 6 November 1998, it started offering CCP services on cash and futures products for primary dealers in French government securities as well as on repurchase agreements or repos on these securities running from one day to 18 months. Among its selling points, Clearnet boasted that it could clear securities traded on exchanges and over the counter and that it was linked to the new real time RGV clearing and settlement system introduced in February by Sicovam.

On 1 June 1999, the various French clearing houses were merged under the Clearnet ^{SBF} SA banner as part of a broader consolidation of all regulated markets in the SBF Group, which was renamed ParisBourse ^{SBF} SA.

With capital of 800 million French francs, Clearnet became the legally recognised vehicle for clearing trades in regulated markets as designated by the EU's Investment Services Directive. It handled equities and bonds; interest rate and commodities futures and options; equity and index futures and options; OTC traded bonds and repos. Clearnet's offering included an ability to average out margins across different asset classes that promised to reduce costs for investors and boost efficiency. Clearnet's aim, according to ParisBourse was 'to become the core of a pan-European clearing body that will be the equivalent of the NSCC/GSCC in the United States'.[15]

The statement announcing the establishment of Clearnet as a specialised subsidiary of the ParisBourse group gave its capital in French francs even though the euro had been launched as a virtual currency at the beginning of the year. But – as the reference to the future pan-European clearing body revealed – Théodore's creation of a consolidated provider of CCP services for the French market was just the start of ambitions that reached across national boundaries.

During the 1990s, Théodore first pulled together all France's exchanges and their central counterparty clearing operations under one roof. He then set about structuring them in a horizontal manner. The reference to US clearing houses in the 1 June statement signalled his intention to opt for horizontal solutions in any bid to facilitate cross-border trading of securities and derivatives in Europe's new single currency area.

In contrast, Eurex would seek to exploit the success of its integrated screen-based trading and clearing platform in the US, the home of financial futures, where trading was still very largely conducted in pits.[16]

[15] SBF (1 June 1999), 'SBF Group restructures, specialising to meet international competition even more effectively', press release.
[16] See Chapter 13.

11

Users and Clearers

11.1 USER-GOVERNED CCPs IN THE UK AND US

In continental Europe the coming of the euro and the strategic ambitions of exchanges and their leaders were 'top down' factors behind the emergence of Clearnet and Eurex.

For the UK and the US, the users of CCPs constituted a 'bottom up' constituency that helped shape clearing developments in the final decade of the 20th century.

Despite differences in governance and ownership structures, the three clearing houses that served derivatives traders in Britain and the equities and options markets in the US had more in common with each other than with the new CCPs in continental Europe or with most CCPs clearing US derivatives markets. The member-owned Board of Trade Clearing Corporation (BOTCC) in Chicago was an exception to this rule and its story is covered in detail in Chapter 13.

The similarities grew more pronounced after Britain's ICCH temporarily abandoned its international ambitions and, as the London Clearing House (LCH), was restructured as a mainly user-owned company in 1996.

By the end of the 1990s, users influenced the governance of LCH in the UK and the National Securities Clearing Corporation (NSCC) and Options Clearing Corporation (OCC) in the US. All three CCPs were horizontal structures, clearing for more than one trading platform. And all three operated business models that were less than totally profit-oriented. Although LCH's policies on profit varied later, NSCC and OCC provided their clearing services 'at-cost' while managing to meet the expense of the rapidly evolving demands of the marketplace and the fast pace of technological change.

Regulation played an important role in setting the three clearing houses apart. The UK regulators in the 1990s had an anti-silo mentality while the Securities and Exchange Commission, which regulated NSCC and OCC, saw its job as ensuring an efficient and robust infrastructure for multiple markets on a continental scale.

None of the three clearing houses was wholly user-governed. Indeed, the OCC was owned by US options exchanges. But the role played in the governance of the CCPs by their users meant their approach to business was, for good and ill, more influenced by the 20th century ideals of mutuality and utility than came to be the case at other clearing houses that were put on the for-profit path as a result of the spread of demutualisation of exchanges that owned them in the 1990s and 2000s.

Despite NSCC's participation in a merger that was an industry-changing event in 1999 and the merger of LCH with Clearnet of France four years later, LCH, NSCC and OCC were positioned, in the early years of the 21st century, on a branch of the evolutionary tree that was distinct and separate from other CCPs covered in this history.

For this reason, the book turns now, before moving to Part IV, to the histories of LCH, NSCC and OCC in the years before and after the beginning of the 21st century.

11.2 THE UK: FROM ICCH TO LCH

February 1988 marked the centenary of the foundation the London Produce Clearing House, the forerunner of ICCH. In a special brochure, ICCH presented itself as a company diversifying at home and abroad and a pioneer in the automation of futures and options markets.

ICCH had been reorganised into several divisions the year before. The job of clearing markets in the City was entrusted to a separate division, which became known as the London Clearing House. The group's consultancy, technology and foreign clearing activities were managed separately. Writing in the centenary brochure, Ian McGaw, the group managing director, made clear that operations abroad were as much a part of ICCH's future as those in London.

'We believe we are well placed to continue our history of service to international commodity and financial markets,' he wrote. 'All ICCH staff in Auckland, Sydney, Melbourne, Hong Kong, Paris and London look forward with confidence and pleasure to the prospect of working closely with our many friends and customers in these growing markets.'[1]

His confidence was misplaced. Within five years ICCH was no more and McGaw had moved on. The non-clearing and foreign businesses were grouped together in ICCH Financial Markets Ltd (IFM), a separate entity. In 1991, the London Clearing House assumed a separate corporate identity, taking over the five digit Companies House number allocated to LPCH in 1888. IFM was wound down and the rump sold to Sungard Data Systems Inc. in January 1993.

David Hardy led the LCH through this difficult time. He was a manager at Barclays Merchant Bank when he was seconded to ICCH in 1985, aged 30. He had worked for Barclays for 12 years after completing a grammar school education in Essex. Hardy had no background in clearing. 'I was at the top of the list for something to be done and in line for rotation,' he explained later.[2] 'And they said: look, here's something different. How do you fancy a two-year secondment to this thing we own – ICCH. It needs a bit of a shake up. Go and see how you can help.'

Hardy had a two week crash course in commodities from the commodities director of Barclays and then started working with McGaw. 'We started looking at the structure of the organisation, and what we should potentially do with it.'

In September 1986, John Barkshire, one of LIFFE's founders, became the chairman of ICCH with the encouragement of the Bank of England. Barkshire, McGaw and Hardy worked together on the corporate restructuring that in 1987 separated ICCH's London clearing activities from divisions responsible for the group's other interests. The group's shareholder banks re-committed to ownership of ICCH and increased to £100 million (from £15 million) the guaranteed funds underpinning its clearing activities.

A big, unflappable man, Hardy had a 'good Crash' in October 1987. It was one of those occasions when the other managers of the clearing house were either abroad or away from the office, and he took charge. Afterwards, Barkshire suggested he should stay and run the London operation. 'I took about half a second [to decide],' he remembers. In December 1987, Hardy was appointed managing director of the London Clearing House division of ICCH.

It was in the non-LCH part of ICCH that more problems arose. ICCH's overseas ventures had grown haphazardly, often on the back of the sale of clearing systems developed by the

[1] International Commodities Clearing House (1988), *100 years of ICCH*.

[2] Conversation with the author, 9 July 2008.

group's operations in Australia. Two years after the events of the 1987 crash in Hong Kong, the group was hit by the default of a clearing member of the New Zealand Futures and Options Exchange (NZFOE).

ICCH cleared and guaranteed contracts traded on NZFOE through its office in Auckland, New Zealand. This was a sub-office of the group's Sydney-based clearing and guarantee activities. On 21 November 1989, Jordan Sandman Futures – a New Zealand broker – defaulted on a margin payment of NZ$7 759 443 that it owed to the NZFOE's clearing house. Its difficulties were linked to fraudulent trades in a New Zealand government bond futures contract.

The margin held by the clearing house was insufficient to meet the loss. Because of a decision by the board of the exchange, the New Zealand clearing house was unable to follow a standard procedure and invoice back the loss to the market at a price sufficient to cover its deficit.[3] As a result, it sustained a loss that turned out to be around £1 million.

After the problems in Hong Kong, this additional setback in part of ICCH's overseas activities – now grouped in IFM – proved to be one foreign entanglement too many for the group's clearing bank owners. Although the loss was relatively small, it prompted the closure of the foreign branch clearing network and the sale of its IT interests.

The retrenchment was fortuitously timed. Focusing on the London markets for CCP services was an attractive option in its own right at the start of the 1990s. The 1986 'Big-Bang' deregulation of the London Stock Exchange (LSE) had injected new life into the City across its many markets and LCH was well placed to exploit this situation.

ICCH had expanded its clearing activities in London beyond the traditional soft commodities during the 1980s. It began clearing for London's International Petroleum Exchange in 1981, LIFFE in 1982 and the 110-year-old London Metal Exchange in May 1987 (see Box 11.1). The London Clearing House division acquitted itself well when Drexel Burnham Lambert Ltd, its fourth largest member, defaulted in 1990. Open positions were closed out with the return of around US$18 million of surplus margin to Drexel's liquidator and without any disruption in the market.

Box 11.1: Futures and options contracts on London exchanges cleared by LCH in 1990

- LIFFE (London International Financial Futures Exchange) – UK Gilt, US T-Bond, German Bund, Japanese Bond, three month Sterling, Eurodollar, Euro D-mark and ECU interest rate, and UK Stock Index contracts.
- The International Petroleum Exchange (IPE) – gas oil, crude oil, heavy fuel oil.
- The London Metal Exchange (LME) – aluminium, copper, lead, nickel, tin, zinc.
- The Baltic Futures Exchange (BIFFEX) – cattle, pigs, soya bean meal, potatoes and Baltic Freight Index.
- The London Futures and Options Exchange (London FOX) (renamed the London Commodity Exchange in 1991 after merging with BIFFEX) – coffee, cocoa, raw sugar, white sugar, rubber.

Source: London Clearing House division of ICCH, 1990.

[3] Securities Commission (1 November 1990), 'Report of the Securities Commission on its enquiry into the trading in the five-year government stock No 2 futures contract on the New Zealand Futures and Options Exchange'.

The geo-political upheavals that followed the fall of the Berlin Wall and extreme currency turbulence in Europe in the early 1990s provided abundant opportunities for hedging and speculation and for the LCH to grow.

The week beginning 14 September 1992 was one of national humiliation for Italy and the UK as they were forced out of the European ERM. But it was a week of records for LCH. Nearly 876 000 lots were traded on LIFFE on 'Black Wednesday' before sterling left the ERM. On that day, 16 September, LCH cleared more than 1 million lots for the first time. By the end of the week, LCH was holding more than £1.75 billion in margin cover.[4]

The volume of lots cleared by LCH increased by a third in its next accounting year to 31 October 1993 which included a period of intense speculative pressure against the French franc. Yet despite the growth, it became clear during 1992–3 that the six owner banks wanted to give up their ownership of the clearing house.

The banks wanted out because they were no longer happy financing LCH's financial safety net. The £100 million of guaranteed support for LCH's operations that the banks pledged in 1987 was backed by insurance. During 1992, the company writing the policy withdrew from the market and LCH was unable to arrange an alternative when the cover expired in January 1993. In response, the owner banks provided a facility totalling £150 million on which LCH could draw, but in return for fees that Hardy considered outrageous.

'This highlighted a conflict of interest,' Hardy recalled to this author later. 'The bankers were sitting round the [LCH] board table and approving the fees for themselves. They were insisting on better returns from the business. I told them that I couldn't deliver that in markets where we operated as a monopoly supplier.'

Hardy feared the sack. But Tom Frost, newly appointed as chairman of LCH,[5] stood by him. Meanwhile, the banks made clear there would have to be a parting of the ways. Daniel Hodson, chief executive of LIFFE, formed a committee with the heads of the IPE, LME and London Commodities Exchange, with the aim of arranging a LIFFE-led takeover of LCH. Hardy resisted this solution and instead persuaded Michael Jenkins, the founding chief executive of LIFFE, to chair a group representing the exchanges and LCH's leading users to work out its future.

The outcome, announced in the summer of 1996, was an agreement to turn LCH into a user-owned, user-governed clearing house. The company planned to raise £50 million of new share capital with clearing members subscribing £37.5 million in equal amounts per member and the four exchanges – IPE, LCE, LIFFE and LME – subscribing £12.5 million in proportion to the volumes of business channelled to LCH. The clearing house would have several layers of protection in the event of a member's default.

Members were to contribute to a £150 million default fund on the basis of their daily average clearing activity, weighted at 75% initial margin collected and 25% volume transacted. The fund replaced the £150 million stand-by facility provided by the banks.

In the event of a member of the clearing house defaulting, the first call to staunch losses would be the defaulting member's margin deposited with the clearing house. The next call would be on the defaulting member's contribution to the default fund. After that, up to £10 million could be taken from LCH's pre-tax, pre-rebate earnings for the year. Only then would other members' contributions to the default fund be called. LCH also arranged an extra US$100 million of insurance cover on a rolling three years basis that could be drawn if the default fund were ever exhausted.

---

[4] Figures from *Open House*, the journal of the London Clearing House, October 1992.

[5] Frost was a former chief executive of National Westminster Bank who became LCH's chairman on 1 September 1993.

LCH had managed three defaults in London since 1982 and on each occasion the clearer's margins covered the closing out of positions. In the most recent case – the collapse of Barings in February 1995 – LCH used only £6000 of £11 million of margin cover and so returned just under £11 million to Barings' administrators and to a bank that had provided guarantees.

The transfer of ownership was completed on 10 October 1996. Jenkins took over from Tom Frost as chairman at the head of a new board representing the industry. The banks were paid £19.61 million made up of the previous capital of £15 million plus distributable reserves.

Of the 174 firms that were clearing members before the restructuring, 148 supported the change. The actual number that became clearing members in the restructured LCH was lower, at 126. All were required to hold one share, valued initially at £297 619. The membership fell after about a year to 119. Some firms decided to amalgamate their membership with affiliated companies. Other – mainly small – companies opted to be non-clearing members in the markets where they traded. Altogether, the firms approving the new structure at LCH accounted for more than 99% of the volume of business conducted by the clearing house.

Among the exchanges, LIFFE was the biggest shareholder with 17.7% of the capital, followed by the LME with 5.45% and the IPE with 1.85%.[6]

The clearing operations of LCH were very different in scale compared with 14 years earlier when the banks acquired the clearing house. In 1996 LCH cleared 226 million contracts traded on IPE, LIFFE, LME and Tradepoint, a small electronic, for-profit exchange in London that was trying to break into the market for cash equities trading dominated by the London Stock Exchange. In 1982, it cleared roughly 3 million commodity futures contracts in London.

LCH employed just over 100 members of staff who moved in September 1996 from the office in Crutched Friars, which had been the home of the clearing house for 25 years, to larger, refurbished premises in Aldgate.

Hardy recalled:

> I regarded the clearing members as customers and the exchanges as partners. In the end, everybody was happy with the exchanges as minority shareholders. Many of the members had thought they should own the whole thing. But given its very close relationship with the exchanges, I thought LCH would be stronger with their part ownership as well.
>
> Clearing houses elsewhere were either wholly member owned – as was the case with the BOTCC in the US – or exchange-owned like CME's clearing division or Deutsche Börse's internal clearing department. Ours was a hybrid. And I revelled in that. To me it made an immense amount of sense.
>
> My job was to make sure we would deliver everything that the clearing members wanted to the best of our ability, not on a not-for-profit basis, but on a controlled profit basis.

11.3 NEW PRODUCTS: REPOCLEAR AND SWAPCLEAR

The change of ownership brought a change of pace and style at LCH. The board approved a three year strategic plan – a new departure for the company – to explore how best to meet the needs of members. LCH also established new risk and operations committees, reflecting a clutch of growing challenges as the end of the century approached. As described in previous chapters, risk and risk management were becoming higher priorities for regulators and policy makers. In addition, clearing houses had to prepare for the euro's introduction and take precautions against the much hyped Millennium Bug threat to computer systems.

LCH came up with two innovative clearing products for important 'over the counter' markets in 1999. In August, it launched RepoClear, a central counterparty service for the

[6] By this time LCH had three exchanges as shareholders after the LCE merged with LIFFE in September 1996.

market in repurchase agreements (repos) in European government bonds, starting with German government bond repos.

RepoClear was inspired by the US Government Securities Clearing Corporation (GSCC) and for a brief period was part of a joint venture with GSCC and Euroclear of Brussels, called the European Securities Clearing Corporation.[7] The latter was intended to provide multinational netting services with cross margining in European bond markets but it turned out to be one of many joint financial infrastructure projects of the time that came to nothing. LCH went on to develop RepoClear on its own and quickly extended the service to other fixed income products. By early 2002 daily volumes cleared averaged €100 billion, up from €5 billion on good days in the early months of the service.

Following 18 months of study and design that involved LCH managers making fact-finding visits to more than 30 leading international banks, the LCH board approved funding for an even bolder project for clearing the global interbank swaps market in June 1998. SwapClear was a response to the rapid growth in the value of the interest rate swaps market to more than US$22 trillion by the end of 1997.[8]

SwapClear represented a revolutionary step forward in clearing OTC derivatives. Unlike other OTC clearing solutions, which processed contracts that were standardised in order to be cleared in an 'exchange look-alike' manner, SwapClear allowed clearing of fully customised interest rate swap contracts. These were typically arranged between corporate clients and dealers and would involve swapping the cash flows from debt onto a different basis while respecting precisely the bespoke aspects of the original transaction such as its start and end dates.

The secret of SwapClear was that the process of clearing rather than the instrument cleared was standardised. For a product to be standardised, its economic terms such as start date, coupon and maturity would have to be harmonised. In the case of SwapClear the clearing infrastructure surrounding the product was standardised instead.

As Roger Liddell later explained:

> Swap Clear is completely different to exchange look-alike OTC clearing. With SwapClear you take a transaction with a start date, an end date and interest rates and it just become part of a massive stream of cash flows and interest rates, and that one transaction can be different to any other that you get.
>
> Unlike all other clearing, where it is a matter of X number of Y contracts, and you have a price for a contract and a quantity of it, SwapClear takes transactions occupying different points on a yield curve so the system values the cash flows based on the curve. The US$9 trillion notional of swaps cleared after Lehman fell in this category. It's not that complex. It's just that it is not standardised. It is vanilla but non-standard.[9]

Progressing with SwapClear required some courage in the conditions of the late 1990s. LCH built SwapClear without having any users committed to it. Indeed, some leading participants in the swaps market, led by Chase Manhattan, were openly hostile towards the venture. But there were pressing reasons for LCH to add to and diversify its portfolio of activities. In particular, it needed to reduce its dependence on LIFFE, its main customer, which was suffering a drastic loss of market share to Eurex, its German-Swiss screen-based rival.

---

[7] SEC (28 December 1999), 'Government Securities Clearing Corporation; Notice of filing of proposed rule change relating to the formation and involvement in the European Securities Clearing Corporation', *Federal Register*. The failure of ESCC provided a foretaste of the difficulties that surrounded the failure in 2007–8 of merger plans for DTCC, Euroclear and LCH.Clearnet. See Sections 17.5 and 19.3–19.5.

[8] The notional amount of interest rate swaps outstanding at the end of 1997 was US$22 115 billion, according to the 68th annual report of the Bank for International Settlements.

[9] Conversation with the author, 18 June 2009.

The necessary investments of around £16 million were funded ultimately by clearing members who experienced a sharp fall in rebates and a multi-year suspension of LCH dividend payments from 1998 onwards. They were also required to strengthen LCH's default protection by boosting the ceiling of the default fund to £300 million in order to cover SwapClear and RepoClear.

SwapClear got off to a slow start despite the best efforts of David Hardy who remembers visiting New York with Simon Grensted, LCH's business development manager, and 'pounding pavements and cajoling people into wanting to use the service'.

LCH promoted SwapClear as offering a wide range of benefits for banks. These included: reduced regulatory capital requirements; the freeing up of OTC credit lines for higher margin business; margin offsets with LIFFE; more efficient use of collateral; and significant back office operational savings. Yet SwapClear launched in September 1999 with only five members. It was only after eight of the main dealing banks created OTCDerivNet in September 2000 and were given a stake in SwapClear's governance that the service began to gain acceptance. At the time, the mitigation of counterparty risk provided by the CCP was probably the least of SwapClear's attractions. But, as already described in Chapter 3, it proved its worth in September 2008 during the bankruptcy of Lehman Brothers.

EquityClear was the third business stream launched by LCH after it threw off the dead hand of UK clearing bank ownership and became a mainly user-owned, user-governed enterprise. LCH launched a CCP service with CRESTCo, the British CSD, and the London Stock Exchange for the exchange's electronic SETS market in February 2001. The average daily volume of trades on SETS increased from 50 000 to around 80 000 by mid-2002, when LCH, LSE and CREST developed the service further by introducing optional settlement netting for trades executed through SETS. Hardy sought and obtained members' support for a further increase in the default fund to cover EquityClear: this time to a maximum of £400 million.

That LCH's service for the London Stock Exchange was part of a horizontal post-trade solution for the LSE reflected the preferences of UK regulators and the City following the costly failure in March 1993 of Taurus, an LSE-owned securities settlement project that would have led to a vertical silo in the UK, if successful. CREST provided most of the processing capacity and LCH focused on the risk-management aspects of the CCP. The division of labour between LCH and CREST was similar to that between LCH and LIFFE after LIFFE's adoption of TRS/CPS. But the relationship between LCH and CREST started as an uneasy compromise and remained difficult.

During the 1990s, LCH focused on the UK market. It was only in 1999 that it joined the carousel of cooperation talks that preoccupied CCPs in continental Europe. Its UK focus was partly a reaction to the succession of foreign misadventures experienced by ICCH, its one time parent. It also reflected the needs of London's financial markets and the UK's decision not to join the euro.

But, as will be described in Part IV, LCH did not stand aside from international developments for long. Having built a strong position in the UK, it ventured once again beyond the British Isles.

11.4 THE CREATION OF DTCC

At the end of the 1990s, an event took place in the US that concentrated the minds of European CCPs, including LCH. America's National Securities Clearing Corporation (NSCC) and the Depository Trust Company (DTC) – the post-trade infrastructure providers for US securities markets – merged in November 1999 under the umbrella of a holding company, The Depository Trust & Clearing Corporation (DTCC), to create a clearing and settlement giant.

The two New York-based companies had been closely linked since they were set up in the 1970s following Wall Street's paperwork crisis.[10] Gradually, over 20 years, both NSCC – which provided CCP and netting services for the securities markets – and DTC (the securities depository) absorbed the clearing and settlement infrastructures of America's regional exchanges.

Consolidation of America's regional clearing services made a great deal of sense for companies trading on more than one US stock market. Stocks were fungible instruments. It was therefore far more economical not to post margin in the different places where they traded but have all the positions offset and netted down in one CCP. The benefits of scale were already apparent by 1983 when the cost of NSCC clearing a trade was 35 cents a side – less than half the 82 cents charged in 1977, its first year of operation.

While absorbing their regional brethren, NSCC and DTC improved their post-trade infrastructure and began providing services for markets other than stock exchanges. Not all of NSCC's new businesses involved the creation of CCPs to guarantee trades against counterparty risk. In 1984, NSCC automated trade comparison and netting for the municipal bond market. Two years later, it introduced Fund-SERV to automate and standardise the processing of transactions in the fast growing mutual funds market.

Also in 1986, NSCC launched an affiliate, the Government Securities Clearing Corporation (GSCC), to provide automatic clearing and netting for US Treasury bonds and government securities. Three years after that, GSCC became a central counterparty clearing house that guaranteed trades in US government bonds (see Box 11.2).

Box 11.2: Turning GSCC into a CCP

The challenges that GSCC had to overcome during the period between its launch and the introduction of its CCP for US government securities throw an interesting sidelight on the post-Lehman drive by governments and regulators to subject OTC derivative contracts to central counterparty clearing.

The US government bond market was an OTC market, where traders made their living from the spreads between bid and offered prices. The existing settlement system, operated by the Federal Reserve, was unable to keep pace with the growth of activity in the 1980s. For this reason, NSCC was encouraged to provide a clearing solution.

According to Tom Costa, one of the architects of GSCC, setting up clearing for an OTC market is inherently more difficult than establishing a CCP for an exchange, where operations are relatively straightforward once agreement exists for the exchange to supply the CCP with a feed of trading data.[11]

The most certain way of introducing clearing for an OTC market is for it to be mandated by a regulator. A crisis or the failure of existing post-trade mechanisms can also trigger rapid adoption of a CCP. Otherwise, progress depends on powers of persuasion and appealing to the different interests of separate groups of market participants.

Market participants approach the prospect of a CCP from different angles depending on whether they are strong or weak. By taking over counterparty risk, a CCP helps create a

[10] See Sections 8.6 and 8.7.

[11] Conversation with the author, 14 October 2009.

more level playing field, which benefits weaker participants rather than the strong. But by narrowing spreads, clearing should over time boost market activity and liquidity, creating conditions from which stronger players should profit.

To succeed, GSCC needed to win a critical mass of support from three main groups engaged in the US government bond market – market makers, interdealer brokers who facilitated anonymous trading between them and clearing banks – all of which had different vested interests.

It took around 18 months before support for the CCP outweighed resistance. During this period, the big losers were the inter-dealer brokers, which fell in number from 18 to 6. There was also resistance from operations staff in the settlement banks for whom the CCP meant the loss of work and power.

However, after about 18 months a tipping point was reached when the CCP provided obvious economies of scale, attracting new entrants to the market and winning acceptance from initially reluctant market participants.

GSCC expanded throughout the 1990s. By 1994 it was processing around 85% of all new US Treasury debt issues. It developed increasingly sophisticated netting services for the securities repurchase (repo) market and provided the inspiration for LCH's RepoClear service.

By the end of the 1980s, NSCC was guaranteeing matched trades from midnight after the trade – so-called 'T+1' compared with 'T+4' previously. In cooperation with the securities industry, trade groups and regulators, NSCC and DTC acted in 1995 to shorten the securities settlement cycle to T+3 from T+5 previously.

The 1990s saw further broadening of the activities of NSCC and DTC, including the addition of processing services for the insurance sector to NSCC's portfolio. Post-trade services for the mortgage backed securities market were located in NSCC's offices after the operations of the Mortgage-Backed Securities Clearing Corporation (MBSCC) – a netting system rather than a CCP – were bought by its members from the Chicago Stock Exchange and moved to New York in 1994. In 1998, NSCC helped launch the Emerging Markets Clearing Corporation (EMCC) to clear and settle emerging market debt instruments.

The 1990s were not all plain sailing, however. In 1995, Adler Coleman Clearing Corporation (ACCC), an NSCC clearing member, became insolvent after one of its clients, a market maker in penny stocks, collapsed and ACCC did not have the financial resources to complete its trades.

ACCC's failure attracted media attention after it became a subject of complex litigation between short sellers of stocks promoted by Adler Coleman's client and the trustee of the Securities Investor Protection Corp, the industry financed agency that insured customer accounts with US brokers. The failure also had important lessons for NSCC. It demonstrated the need to monitor more effectively the market-making correspondent brokers that dealt with the CCP's clearing members and to require additional collateral for the CCP's clearing fund when such market makers had built up dominating positions in illiquid securities.

As NSCC and DTC developed, many of their activities began to overlap. The demarcation line between the activities of the two companies was always fuzzy, partly because they were formed in the 1970s when the functions of the clearing house and securities settlement system were blurred. A pointer to eventual integration was the formation in 1996 of a joint venture, the International Depository & Clearing Corporation, to focus on cross-border settlement issues.

Merger talks began in the summer of 1998. Nine months later, the two boards gave their approval. On 4 November 1999, The Depository Trust & Clearing Corporation (DTCC) was created to vertically integrate US clearing and settlement infrastructures for securities. The resulting organisation was no exclusive silo, however. DTCC was an at-cost, user-governed, regulated monopoly that provided services to a growing number of markets, many of which were in competition with each other.

At the time of the merger, NSCC processed almost all equity and bond trades in the US, guaranteeing settlement of all transactions that entered and were confirmed in its system. It provided services to more than 2000 brokers, dealers, banks, mutual funds, insurance companies and other intermediaries. It processed nearly 950 million equity, bond, investment trust and mutual fund transactions valued at US$45 trillion. NSCC's Continuous Net Settlement system (CNS), netted 94% of this total, reducing the value of securities that required settlement by US$42.6 trillion.

DTC meanwhile processed more than 164 million book-entry changes of securities ownership, had custody of securities worth more than US$20 trillion and handled more than US$1 trillion annually in dividend, interest and other payments.

As well as charging what were thought to be the lowest fees in the world, DTCC promised to speed the introduction of new products, services and technologies for its users. Integration, it declared, would facilitate the harmonising of clearing and settlement processes and help the industry move to what was, at the time, a cherished goal of clearing and settling trades in T+1. The combined group promised also to flex its muscles internationally, becoming 'a true global competitor' in its own right.[12]

Many users in Europe looked with envy at the creation of DTCC. US trading platforms at the time were generally inferior to the screen-based systems adopted in Europe in the 1990s. Hence, the conviction grew that America's low cost, integrated post-trade infrastructure gave the US securities industry a comparative advantage against its fragmented European competitors.

DTCC was a clearing and settlement behemoth compared with other infrastructure providers around the world. For this reason alone, its creation gave an impetus to thoughts among Europe's industry practitioners and regulators of CCPs clearing across national frontiers. These thoughts hardened with the bedding down of Europe's single currency and as DTCC began to make its presence felt outside the US.

But although the DTCC model, combining a CCP and CSD under a single holding company, had its attractions, it was not obvious that it could be transposed easily to the EU where cultural, legal and fiscal barriers between member states – as well as vested interests – would have to be overcome before the single market could become reality.

DTCC was the product of market forces reacting to decisive legislative action by Congress, which in the 1970s directed the SEC to promote a unified market for trading, clearing and settling US stocks. Even though the SEC pushed hard for integration, it took 20 years for NSCC and DTC to turn into nationwide infrastructure providers in their own right before finally merging.

Nor were the two US companies without critics. European infrastructure providers muttered that monopoly status made DTCC's constituent parts slow to innovate and that they were technologically behind the curve. CNS, the engine that netted down the total number of obligations requiring settlement, was based on 1970s technology.

[12] DTCC (1999), 'How we serve the financial industry': a DTCC brochure explaining the new group and the reasons for integrating NSCC and DTC.

It was with such mutterings in the air that Jill Considine took over as CEO and chairman of DTCC in 1999. Previously President of the New York Clearing House, a bank clearing house and operator of the Clearing House Interbank Payments System (CHIPS), Considine brought to her twin roles at DTCC scientific training (having conducted DNA research in an early career as a biochemist) and 30 years experience of banking, including, since 1985, senior positions administering and regulating the financial sector.[13]

Approachable but tough when necessary, Considine was determined that DTCC should keep up with the pace of new technology in financial markets. That meant 'dealing with accelerating trends, including changes in demographics, industry consolidation, technology innovation and the influence of globalisation'.[14] She waged war on complacency, instituting structures and disciplines to spread high standards of quality and improve efficiency throughout the organisation. In 2001, she added the title Chief Quality Officer to those of CEO and chairman to show where that particular buck stopped.

The merger of DTC and NSCC was the prelude to further consolidation and expansion. Under Considine's leadership, DTCC developed into a surprisingly nimble giant.

During 2001, GSCC, MBSCC and EMCC – the affiliated clearing houses for bonds, mortgage-backed securities and emerging market sovereign debt – became wholly owned subsidiaries of DTCC. The consolidation, which brought the three subsidiaries under an integrated management structure from 1 January 2002, produced greater efficiencies and savings for users. The following year GSCC and MBSCC merged to become the Fixed Income Clearing Corp (FICC) with the aim of further boosting synergies for the fixed income market under the DTCC umbrella. As described later in Part IV of this book, DTCC entered new markets, providing services for the fast growing OTC derivatives market and establishing a CCP in Europe.

DTCC's at-cost business model returned to users a substantial part of each year's revenues as rebates, discounts and interest.[15] NSCC boasted the lowest fees for equities clearing in the world.[16]

In March 2006, the group took steps to become more clearly user-owned and user-governed. DTCC's common shares were reallocated among users in proportion to the amount they used its services. This meant a 'significant reduction in ownership' by the three exchanges that founded DTC and NSCC and which until then held about 35% of DTCC's common stock.[17]

Although DTCC's governance and business model had a distinctly 20th century feel at a time when many clearing houses in other markets were demutualising and pursuing for-profit policies, the group's transformation under Considine was profound. Managers, according to Richard Beales in the *Financial Times*, likened the process to 'teaching the 800lb gorilla to tap dance'.[18]

---

[13] Before her spell as president of the New York Clearing House Association between 1993 and 1998, Considine was a managing director, chief administrative officer and member of the board of American Express Bank from 1991 to 1993 and the New York State Superintendent of Banks from 1985 to 1991.

[14] Remarks in Las Vegas, 29 June 2006, on being named Six Sigma CEO of the year.

[15] DTCC generated revenues of just over US$1.3 billion in 2006 and gave back US$580 million in rebates, discounts and interest.

[16] According to DTCC's 2008 annual report, the average cost of NSCC clearing one side of an equities trade was the lowest in the world, averaging one third of a US cent per transaction.

[17] DTCC's annual report for 2006 disclosed that the NYSE owned 27% and NASD and AMEX 4% each of DTCC at the end of 2005. At the same time, NSCC was taking feeds from a growing number of exchanges and trading platforms: 'more than 50', according to DTCC's annual report for 2008.

[18] *Financial Times* (5 July 2006), 'Teaching a gorilla to tap-dance'.

This influence was acknowledged by Donald Donahue when he was named to succeed Considine as president and CEO of DTCC from 1 August 2006. Donahue, a 20-year veteran of DTCC who joined DTC in 1986, noted how under Considine's leadership, management 'successfully transformed the culture of DTCC to operate more like a for-profit company with a competitive drive and bottom-line accountability for results, even while we operate on an "at-cost" basis'.[19]

11.5 THE OPTIONS CLEARING CORPORATION

For the Options Clearing Corporation in Chicago, 1999 turned out to be every bit as transformational as it proved to be for DTC and NSCC. However, in OCC's case the impetus for change came from America's antitrust watchdog and the regulator of the US options market.

In November 1998, the US Department of Justice (DoJ) launched an investigation into allegations that four options exchanges – the AMEX, the CBOE, the Pacific Exchange and the Philadelphia Stock Exchange – had colluded in limiting competition among themselves by not listing equity options that were previously listed on another exchange.[20] Around the same time, the SEC opened an investigation of its own into the US options market.

At issue was the question of fungibility of options contracts in the US. Although the OCC was founded in the early 1970s as the single CCP for several options exchanges, investors in the US options market were unable to benefit from fungibility of contracts for many years because SEC rules prohibited most equity options from being traded on more than one exchange.

The regulator then had a change of heart. It decided that equity options should be opened to multiple listing in stages between January 1990 and late 1994 when all equity options should be listed and traded on any US options exchange. Some options trading was liberalised, as foreseen by the SEC. But according to the DoJ, the exchanges started to obstruct multiple listings from the early 1990s so that the most actively traded options continued to be restricted to one exchange only.

The obstruction continued until the summer of 1999 when, as a result of the DoJ probe, the exchanges began to allow multiple listing of the most popular options. In September 2000, the case was brought to a close when the DoJ filed a civil antitrust action against the four exchanges at the same time as a consent decree that resolved the lawsuit. The decree, together with an order from the SEC, prohibited the anti-competitive conduct and ordered reforms to ensure multiple listing and fungibility of contracts in the future.[21]

The impact on the options market and the OCC's business was dramatic. In 1999 the volume of cleared options contracts exceeded 500 million for the first time as multiple listings soared on the four exchanges. May 2000 saw the launch of the International Securities Exchange (ISE), which joined the OCC as a participating exchange. ISE was the first new options exchange in the US since 1985 and the first to be all electronic. Spreads narrowed by 30–40% within six months of ISE's entry into the market. In January 2003, ISE overtook AMEX to

[19] DTCC (1 June 2006), 'Donald F Donahue elected President and CEO of DTCC', press release.

[20] US Department of Justice (November 1998), 'Antitrust Division versus American Stock Exchange, CBOE, Pacific Exchange and Philadelphia Exchange: Civil Action No. 00-CV-02174(EGS)'. Documents include: Final Judgment; Complaint and Competitive Impact Statement.

[21] US Department of Justice (11 September 2000), 'Justice Department files suit Challenging Anticompetitive Agreement among Options Exchanges', press release.

become the second largest US options exchange by volume and a year later was battling for supremacy against the CBOE.[22]

That the ISE was able to grow so quickly was due largely to the openness of the US options market following the intervention of the DoJ and the SEC. Also crucial, however, was the OCC's ability to deal with the associated upsurge of volumes that continued through the first decade of the 21st century. And here, the clearing house's system of governance appears to have contributed to its effectiveness.

The OCC is owned by the five leading exchanges that it serves but governed by its users. Its board structure has been designed to neutralise tensions among and between its owners[23] and the 140 or so clearing member firms that support and depend on the clearing house's operations.

According to Michael Cahill, OCC's President and Chief Operating Officer, the multiple marketplaces create a healthy tension among the US options exchanges, which trade a fungible common pool of assets constituting the deepest options market in the world. Clearing these assets is the OCC. Thanks to the commonality of the assets cleared, the OCC has, Cahill says, 'no incentive to overprice, underprice, queue or be biased with regard to risk-management policies'.

The OCC's statutes stipulate that there must always be a majority of clearing member representatives on the board. Says Cahill:

> The idea of the board structure is to ensure that OCC stays the low cost utility that is efficient for both exchanges and clearing members. It is the clearing members' money that is coming in. They are most interested in efficiencies and savings. So they drive us constantly. Cost containment is one of our major focuses. But at same time they routinely are looking for ways of making the process more efficient.[24]

It is here that the interests of the exchanges and users coincide.

This balance of interests between exchanges and users paid dividends in the 1990s. According to Wayne Luthringshausen, the OCC's CEO since its foundation, the clearing house invested heavily in new systems in that decade. The result was ENCORE, a proprietary clearing system, which provided fast, flexible and scalable clearing capabilities in time for the surge of activity after 2000.[25]

In line with its at-cost business model, the new systems allowed the OCC to cut fees and increase rebates as volumes soared. OCC refunded nearly US$220 million of excess revenues in respect of the four years to the end of December 2008, while lowering its effective net charge per contract to 1.55 cents in 2008 – the lowest in its history.

The volume of options contracts cleared by OCC exceeded 1 billion for the first time in 2004, 2 billion in 2006 and 3.5 billion in 2008. In consequence, this modest, relatively little known company was able to claim to be the world's largest derivatives clearing organisation.

For all their differences, LCH, NSCC and OCC constituted a group of user-governed clearing infrastructures that presented an alternative business model to the vertically integrated CCPs that came to predominate in the early years of the 21st century.

---

[22] Binder, Jim (2008), 'Seven exchanges, one clearing house, intense competition', *Swiss Derivatives Review*.

[23] The AMEX, the CBOE, the ISE, the Pacific Exchange and the Philadelphia Stock Exchange.

[24] Conversation with the author, 26 September 2008.

[25] Conversation with the author, Chicago, 20 October 2009.

There were others, notably the Board of Trade Clearing Corp, the user-owned CCP set up to clear futures contracts for the CBOT in 1925. The venerable BOTCC played a central role in a major reshaping of futures exchanges and clearing houses in Chicago in the early years of this century.

BOTCC's fate is described in Part IV of this book, which looks first, in Chapter 12, at the broad factors that shaped the development of central counterparty clearing and clearing houses from around the year 2000 onwards, before examining in more detail the activities and interaction of leading CCPs on both sides of the Atlantic in the years before the bankruptcy of Lehman Brothers.

Part IV

CCPs in a Decade of Boom and Bust

12
Shapers of Change

12.1 CHALLENGES OF THE NEW MILLENNIUM

The 2000s got off to a confident start, helped greatly by a nonevent. Fears that a computer bug (dubbed 'Y2K') would cause financial systems to crash and aeroplanes to drop out of the sky, because early software still in use would not cope with the shift in the year from 1999 to 2000, proved wrong. The first of January 2000 passed into history without mishap.

Instead a prosperous future appeared to beckon thanks in good part to financial innovation and benign regulation.

Governments were competing to improve the competitiveness of their economies and make it easier for companies and individuals to make money.

The US set the tone, repealing the 1933 Glass Steagall Act that separated investment and commercial banking in November 1999 and passing legislation a year later that kept OTC derivatives trading unregulated.

The UK's Labour government, elected in 1997, professed to be 'intensely relaxed about people becoming filthy rich, as long as they pay their taxes'.[1] It placed financial regulation in the hands of a new Financial Services Authority that implemented a 'light touch' regulatory regime to boost the nation's financial sector.

The EU followed up the launch of the single currency on 1 January 1999 with a 42 point 'Financial Services Action Plan' (FSAP) to free up financial activity across national frontiers and create a single market for financial services. One of the FSAP's main goals was to lower the cost of trading across borders.

Markets got bigger and traded faster, boosted by the continuing exponential growth of computer power. Nominal values expressed in billions were no longer remarkable. Whether preceded by dollars, yen or the new European currency, the euro, trillions – each one amounting to a million-million – became commonplace as a measure of economic activity and wealth.

A new priesthood of money makers – the hedge fund managers and the proprietary traders at investment banks – came forward as providers of liquidity to the financial markets. New trading techniques, deploying powerful computers and ingenious algorithms, relied on speed of execution to make money from high volume trades. Taking huge positions for ever shorter periods of time, the new liquidity providers turned miniscule trading margins into bumper profits and bonuses.

Financial activity moved away at a quickening pace from regulated marketplaces. Business developed 'over the counter' in direct dealings between banks and other market participants. Conventional loans formed a diminishing percentage of the balance sheets of international banks as they were bundled together into securities and sold on to other financial institutions. This combination of 'securitisation' and the 'originate and distribute' model of transferring

[1] According to the senior Labour government politician Peter, later Lord Mandelson.

risk was applied to an increasing variety of asset classes reflecting the innovative capacity of 'sell-side' investment banks in leading financial centres. The strategy, invented partly in reaction to the capital adequacy rules introduced by the BIS in 1988 and partly to maximise profits through harvesting fees in less transparent areas of activity, was viewed by regulators as a way of distributing and therefore diluting risk in the financial system. That faith would prove to be horribly misplaced in the global financial crisis of the late 2000s.

Looking back from the start of the century, it appeared as if financial markets and the global financial system had easily weathered the 1990s emergencies such as Barings' collapse, the Asian and Russian debt crises and the implosion of the Long Term Capital Management hedge fund. These incidents may not have been forgotten. But they did little to dent faith in liberal free market economics as financial markets had bounced back after each upset to business as usual.

Instead, innovations in finance appeared to offer the best of all worlds for policy makers, regulators, financial companies and individuals alike. Investment bankers grew rich from promoting new products and services, not all of which were of obvious utility. Policy makers were only too happy to be told that financial innovation was the way to macro-economic efficiency.[2] Some administrations, such as Britain's Labour government, were lucky enough to rule in jurisdictions where financial markets were based. For them, the increasing pace of financial activity meant sharply rising tax revenues which could be used to boost government spending at home – and fight wars abroad.

But the celebrations that surrounded the millennium quickly gave way to more troubling times. Just as EU leaders were embracing the 'new economy' in March 2000 at a special summit meeting in Lisbon, a speculative bubble in technology stocks burst. The 'dot.com boom' turned into a 'dot.com bust', which was in full swing 18 months later when the 9/11 terrorist attacks on New York and Washington gave the global economy a further downward push. Adding to the mood of crisis, the energy trading group Enron, the seventh largest US company, filed for Chapter 11 bankruptcy protection in December 2001 in consequence of fraud on a massive scale.

Central bankers, led by Alan Greenspan, Chairman of the US Federal Reserve Board, responded by lowering interest rates and keeping them low. The switchback ride of 2000–3 came to be viewed as a blip as easy money policies in the industrialised countries and imports of low-cost manufactures from China produced a mix of strong economic growth with low inflation, which was hailed by some as the continuation of a 'Great Moderation' that began in the early 1980s.

The recession and the dot.com excesses of the early 21st century turned out to be modest by the standards of the global financial and economic crisis of 2007–8. But the swings from boom to gloom and back to boom between 2000 and 2003 highlighted an unhealthy appetite for risk which grew stronger in financial markets as the decade progressed. Beneath a seemingly calm surface, markets and some big banks were becoming increasingly complex and difficult to manage. They harboured long-tail risks that were unrecognised or ignored.

[2] Especially influential was research by US academics who argued that the source of America's prosperity in the 1990s lay in the US securities–based financial system. In February 2001, an EU panel of 'wise men', chaired by Baron Lamfalussy, one of the architects of the single currency, drew up a plan for accelerating financial innovation through new streamlined forms of EU legislation. Their report cited 'Financial dependence and growth' by Raghuram G. Rajan and Luigi Zingales, and 'Stock markets, banks and economic growth' by Ross Levine and Sara Zervos, both published in the *American Economic Review*, 88, of June 1988; and 'Finance and the sources of growth' by Thorsten Beck, Ross Levine and Norman Loayza in the *Journal of Financial Economics*, 58, of 2000.

Among exchanges and their clearing and settlement providers, the millennium celebrations ushered in years of corporate manoeuvrings that bewildered observers and yielded a rich harvest of unintended consequences for the company executives who initiated them.

As with other areas of business activity, two overarching forces shaped the fortunes of central counterparty clearers: globalisation and technological change in the form of fast growing computer power. People and businesses became ever more networked as these forces combined in the rapid development of the Internet. On both sides of the Atlantic, the more ambitious exchange and post-trade companies began to consider expanding activities beyond their own national frontiers.

Globalisation meant the spread of ideas, technologies and notions of governance. It caused the many diverse trends that had transformed CCP activities in individual markets and nation states during the previous three decades to collide and interact, releasing new energies and exacerbating old tensions.

Equally strong at times were countervailing forces, which often reflected the disappointments and uncertainties that globalisation also brought in its wake. Protectionism among business leaders, policy makers and regulators; personal whims, preferences and failings of individuals; and historic legacy issues in terms of corporate governance played their part in upsetting the best laid plans of clearing house managers.

Until September 2008, the main focus of policy makers and market practitioners lay in promoting competition among financial infrastructure providers. Among their aims were lower fees for clearing and settlement to help cut the costs of trading.

Despite dramatic changes in the global macro-economic, political and financial market environment after 2000, it was only after Lehman Brothers defaulted that the emphasis of public policy shifted to curbing systemic risks in the financial system.

A number of forces influenced the business of clearing during the years preceding the bankruptcy of Lehman Brothers:

- pressure from users for lower costs of trading and post-trade services;
- the stock market listing of exchanges;
- partial consolidation of financial infrastructure companies across borders and within national frontiers;
- the non-appearance of transatlantic clearing solutions;
- the use of regulation to promote the competitiveness of national and regional financial service sectors;
- financial innovation;
- the concentration of financial business – both cleared and uncleared – among a diminishing number of increasingly powerful financial companies.

This chapter looks in turn at each of these shapers of change to set the scene for Part IV of the book, which covers the story of CCPs between 2000 and the Lehman bankruptcy.

12.2 USERS DEMAND LOWER COSTS

Not all was rosy for the big investment banks as the new century dawned. To support the expansion of their activities, they invested heavily in computer-driven trading capacities as the 1990s progressed. Trading volumes soared but margins shrank, in some cases close to zero.

The banks looked for opportunities to cut costs and turned to their financial infrastructure providers to share the pain. The enthusiasm of exchanges in Frankfurt and Paris for new technology during the 1990s was in part a reaction to pressure from their users for lower costs. In the US, pressure to lower the cost of trading equities gave impetus to the absorption into NSCC and DTC of the remaining regional clearing and settlement infrastructures and the eventual consolidation of the two national infrastructure providers under the DTCC holding company.

But such changes did not halt the pressure from the banks for lower post-trade fees, least of all in Europe where barriers to cross-border trading meant there was no pool of liquidity comparable to that in the US to generate economies of scale.

In May 1999, two of the most senior figures in European investment banking founded the European Securities Industry Users' Group (Esiug), as a high level forum to interact with service providers and lobby for lower financial infrastructure costs. The initiative of Sir David Walker, the influential London-based chairman of Morgan Stanley Dean Witter Europe, and Marcel Ospel, the chief executive officer of UBS, was triggered by plans for a radical change in Europe's securities settlement infrastructure.

A few days before, Werner Seifert, the CEO of Deutsche Börse, André Lussi, chief executive of Cedel, a Luxembourg-based, bank-owned International Central Securities Depository (ICSD) that provided settlement services to the international bond market, and Jean-François Théodore, the Chairman and Chief Executive of Paris Bourse, announced the merger of their securities settlement activities.

At first sight, such a consolidation would seem to be just what users wanted. The plan to create the rather confusingly named 'European Clearing House' was the first cross-border initiative to consolidate post-trade infrastructure in Europe.

But Walker and Ospel suspected that Seifert's aim was less to reduce costs as to extend his for-profit, vertical silo business model at the expense of users. Walker therefore directed Esiug's fire against Seifert's plans.

Walker's opposition to the vertical silo was significant. Walker was a City grandee whose career had included stints as an executive director of the Bank of England and as the UK's top securities markets regulator. Unusually for such a patrician figure, he was interested in post-trade infrastructures. His office in London's Canary Wharf was a 'must-visit' destination for those wanting to modernise Europe's financial infrastructure and lower its costs to users, as Walker himself became an *éminence grise* at the centre of multiple networks of investment bankers, central bankers, commercial bankers, policy makers, regulators and post-trade professionals. Théodore was among those who made a point of getting in touch with Walker when in London.

Under Walker's guidance, Esiug became one of the main promoters of the 'horizontal' approach to clearing and settlement where post-trade activities were owned and controlled separately from trading with the possibility of being integrated with the activities of other service providers according to function.

Among Esiug's members was Chris Tupker who represented ABN AMRO, the Dutch bank. Tupker and others formed a working group in Esiug to develop a strategy for the securities industry that rallied user support behind horizontal post-trade structures. 'We came up with this idea of horizontal integration of the trading, the clearing and settlement layers as opposed to vertical integration,' Tupker explains. 'And we started to articulate the benefits of that compared with what Seifert was doing.'[3]

[3] Conversation with the author, 27 March 2006.

In 2000, Esiug was relaunched as the European Securities Forum (ESF), a more formal and structured organisation, based in London with an initial membership of 24 investment banks. It gradually lost momentum. But in their heyday, Esiug and the ESF were emblematic of the polarisation of interests between Europe's exchanges and their users that first surfaced in the 1990s and which gathered force in the 2000s. The parting of the ways grew deep seated because of the demutualisation and transformation of exchange groups into listed companies.

12.3 IPOs FOR FINANCIAL INFRASTRUCTURES

Demutualisation of financial infrastructures began on a modest scale in Europe in the 1990s. It became a worldwide phenomenon after the turn of the century.

OM,[4] a Swedish derivatives exchange and later one of the constituents of the Nasdaq OMX Group, became the world's first publicly listed exchange in 1987.

OM's listing created few waves, possibly because it had grown out of an IT-based company rather than a traditional exchange. Instead, what caught the world's attention was the demutualisation in 1992 of Deutsche Börse, the Frankfurt-based exchange group. It became a joint stock company – an Aktiengesellschaft – although demutualisation at that stage did not mean a stock market listing.

The demutualisation of Deutsche Börse was intended to pep up the modernisation of Germany's financial sector that began in the late 1980s. The change of status still left the Deutsche Börse group mainly owned by German banks, although now as shareholders of a for-profit company rather than members of a club. But crucially it gave Werner Seifert, Deutsche Börse's ambitious chief executive, a freer hand to expand derivatives capacity and vertically integrate trading and post-trade activities into a silo.

On the eve of the millennium, Seifert was ready to go further. In December 1999 he announced that the group would seek a stock exchange listing. After some delay, Deutsche Börse completed its initial public offering early in 2001.

Advocates of the 'for-profit' business model argued that it encouraged greater efficiency and innovation than was possible in the often dozy mutual institutions that ran other stock exchanges. But IPOs were also driven and shaped by a coincidence of executive ambitions among the managers of the companies involved and the greed and need of former owners, who remained users. They sometimes backfired on their backers, as at Deutsche Börse, where the IPO led eventually to Seifert's departure as CEO in 2005 following a shareholders' revolt.

Deutsche Börse's IPO encouraged ambitious imitators. Euronext, a multinational exchange formed under Théodore's leadership from the merger of the Paris, Brussels and Amsterdam stock exchanges in September 2000, completed an IPO in July 2001 and listed its shares on Euronext's Paris market.[5] In that month too, the London Stock Exchange, which demutualised in 2000, was listed on the LSE.

Demutualisation and public listing of exchanges spread to other continents. In the Asia-Pacific region, Hong Kong's stock and futures exchanges demutualised and merged in the course of 1999 and 2000, setting a trend that was followed quickly in Singapore and after a few years in South Korea and Australia. The Chicago Mercantile Exchange became the first listed exchange company in the US after it demutualised and launched an offering of its shares in the autumn of 2002. Other US exchanges followed.

[4] OM stood for Optionsmarknaden.

[5] See Section 15.2.

By becoming public companies, exchange groups gained in financial fire power and were better able to upgrade their trading and post-trade services. But as listed, for-profit businesses, they also became subject to the disciplines and uncertainties of a stock exchange quotation and prey to conflicts of interest. They were soon at odds with their former owners, who continued to use their services.

As mutual institutions, the exchanges and their post-trade infrastructures had been monopolies, but as such were acceptable to user firms because these were also their owners and could therefore profit from rebates and other types of payment if not from dividends.

Listing, however, meant exchanges acquired outside owners who demanded shareholder-friendly, for-profit policies. This shift in governance crystallised tensions between exchanges and investment banks, their biggest and most assertive users, after the banks took advantage of listings to sell their shareholdings and realise long-dormant capital gains. Disputes that were confined to board rooms when exchanges and post-trade utilities were mutual operations with the banks among their owners, came into the open with a vengeance.

Again, to take the example of Deutsche Börse: the exchange group's owners before its 2001 IPO were essentially the same institutions that owned and used the Frankfurt stock exchange before and after it demutualised in 1992. By the end of 2003, however, these so-called 'strategic shareholders' held just 3% of the company's equity. They had been replaced by hedge funds and other investors with no local allegiance. The banks that had been shareholders in the exchange had sold out to raise funds for new profit opportunities or, as was the case for many after the dot.com bust and 9/11, to cover losses.

Memories are short in financial markets and gratitude is seldom in evidence. The banks that sold their shareholdings after the exchanges' IPOs quickly forgot the windfall profits they had made. Instead, they were all too aware that clearing and other post-trade costs tended to hold steady while their own margins were under pressure.

While users saw post-trade infrastructures in terms of cost, the demutualised and publicly quoted exchange groups learned to appreciate CCPs as a way of adding more value in the chain of transactions from trading to clearing and settlement.

CCPs were caught up in the tension between exchanges and investment banks. Before stock exchange listings became the norm, CCPs operated as utilities. They were mutually owned, or part of mutually owned exchange groups, or at least imbued with a mutual ethos. They served national financial markets and were not exposed to forces of international competition. Theirs was an environment in which it mattered little whether a CCP was integrated with an exchange in a vertical structure – like the CME in Chicago – or was separate from exchanges – like LCH in London – or somewhere in between – like BOTCC, the user-owned CCP long affiliated with the Chicago Board of Trade.

That changed after demutualisation and the exchange groups' IPOs. The structure and governance of CCPs became a subject of furious debate as they became involved in efforts to consolidate capacities in the trading and post-trading sectors.

12.4 EUROPE'S DIVISIVE CONSOLIDATION OF POST-TRADE SERVICE PROVIDERS

The divergence between exchanges and infrastructure providers on the one hand and their investment bank users changed the rules of the game about consolidating financial infrastructures in Europe.

At a national level, infrastructure consolidation had proved a successful means of lowering costs and increasing efficiency in financial markets. This was the logic, after all, behind the creation of DTCC late in 1999, which marked a giant step towards consolidating the post-trade infrastructure of the US securities markets.

In Europe, the launch of the euro appeared to augur well for wider cross-border consolidation. The freezing of the exchange rates of the participating eurozone states from 1 January 1999 meant there was no longer any exchange rate risk among 11 of the then 15 members of the EU. It seemed reasonable to consider consolidation of infrastructures, including CCP clearing, across national boundaries for the first time, even though Europe's action plan for creating a single, barrier-free European market for financial services had little to say about post-trade services when published in May 1999.[6]

But at the corporate level, every step forward towards consolidation seemed to be offset by another step back. In the US, as described in the next chapter, a March 1998 agreement by the CME and CBOT in Chicago to pool their clearing facilities survived less than six months. In Europe, the tripartite plan to create a multinational European settlement group from the merger of Cedel, the Luxembourg-based ICSD, and the French and German central securities depositories (CSDs) was equally short lived, lasting just over six months before the French pulled out in November 1999.

The tripartite initiative narrowed down into a cross-border merger of Cedel and Deutsche Börse Clearing (DBC), the securities settlement arm of the German exchange group. This led to the creation of Clearstream, Europe's first multinational financial infrastructure provider, in January 2000 which was owned 50% by Deutsche Börse and 50% by Cedel International, a holding company set up by the 92 banks that previously owned all of Cedel, the ICSD.

But instead of Clearstream forming the basis for a wider cross-border consolidation of Europe's securities settlement companies, as many hoped, there followed a strengthening of the vertical–horizontal divide among Europe's financial infrastructure providers amidst a bewildering succession of corporate manoeuvres over a four-year period.

Problems at Clearstream gave Werner Seifert the opportunity to expand Deutsche Börse's vertically structured silo by buying out Cedel International's 50% stake in the company. By July 2002, Clearstream was a wholly owned, fully consolidated subsidiary of the publicly listed, for-profit Deutsche Börse exchange group.

By this time Jean-François Théodore had become Europe's leading promoter of horizontal consolidation. He oversaw the merger of the Paris, Brussels and Amsterdam stock exchanges to form Euronext in 2000, in which Clearnet, the CCP of the Paris bourse, took over the Belgian and Dutch CCPs. Clearnet was established as a Euronext group subsidiary with a certain degree of independence and plans to offer shares to users.

Théodore also backed the acquisitions by Euroclear, the Brussels-based ICSD, of Sicovam, the French CSD, in 2001, and CREST, the UK securities settlement provider, in 2002, to create a user-owned, user-governed, horizontally-structured securities settlement group that was separate from the Euronext exchange group. By the end of the decade, the Euroclear group provided securities settlement services in France, Belgium, the Netherlands, Britain, Sweden and Finland as well as for the greater part of the international bond market.[7]

[6] EU Commission (May 1999), 'Financial services: Implementing the framework for financial markets – Action plan'.

[7] For a fuller account of these manoeuvrings in the European securities settlement industry at the time and their consequences, see the author's description and analysis in: Norman, Peter (2007), *Plumbers and Visionaries: Securities settlement and Europe's financial market*.

After a false start in 2000, these years of flux also produced LCH.Clearnet, a horizontally structured, multi-asset, multinational CCP group from the merger of LCH of London with Paris-based Clearnet at the end of 2003.[8]

However, developments between 1999 and 2003 failed to consolidate Europe's financial infrastructures to a degree that satisfied users or policy makers and hardened the divide between Europe's vertical and horizontal structures. Nor did globalisation provide an adequate catalyst for further consolidation.

12.5 THE NON-APPEARANCE OF TRANSATLANTIC CLEARING SOLUTIONS

At the beginning of the 21st century, there seemed good reason to expect that pressures for consolidation would cross the Atlantic from the US. American investment banks were playing an ever bigger role in the European user community. Advances in technology and electronic communications had the potential to stimulate 24-hour trading. The development of common risk-management models such as SPAN and the computer software to apply such systems to cash and derivatives markets had already given cross-border trading a boost.

The June 1997 technology exchange between the Paris markets and the CME in Chicago, which brought the CME's Clearing 21 to Europe, was being implemented by both sides. There was a regular exchange of ideas among CCPs in the US and Europe. Many of the users agitating for reform in Europe were the big US investment banks that had greatly increased their global reach during the 1990s.

Conferences and exhibitions – often held in plush resorts – provided occasions in which views were exchanged and corporate manoeuvres plotted among executives from both sides of the Atlantic. The US Futures Industry Association conferences in Boca Raton each spring and in Chicago each autumn provided an opportunity for derivatives industry leaders and their clearing providers to meet on US soil. The Bürgenstock conferences hosted by the Swiss Futures and Options Association and attended by brokers, exchanges, clearing houses and regulators from around the globe early each September enabled similar high level networking in a relaxed environment on European soil.

There had been talk of CCPs linking up across the Atlantic in previous decades. The OCC and ICCH discussed merging in the early 1980s. To take advantage of the far greater opportunities that were expected from a globalised world economy, DTCC created a toehold in Europe in 2001. It launched a wholly owned subsidiary, EuroCCP, to provide cross-border CCP services for Nasdaq Europe, a new venture of the US exchange, and let it be known that it was ready to clear for other partners.

But when push came to shove, the heady rhetoric of globalisation tended to remain just that. By September 2002, DTCC was winding down its EuroCCP venture following a disappointing take-up of Nasdaq's European offering.

The setback for DTCC partly reflected the onset of more difficult economic conditions after the collapse of the dot.com boom in 2000 and the 9/11 terrorist attacks of September 2001. It was also a sign that talk of globalisation had done little to change systems of regulation, taxation and law that were anchored in nation states around the globe. Any CCP seeking to expand its activities across national boundaries posed a threat to incumbent service providers.

[8] See Sections 15.3 and 15.5.

And when cross-border consolidation moved into the realm of public policy, there were legions of lobbyists at the disposal of incumbents to defend the status quo.

The offices of regulators and legislators were where proxy wars were fought between the proponents of vertical and horizontal structures, stock-exchange-listed and mutually-owned utilities, and at-cost and for-profit business models. When faced with a choice, it was often easiest for regulators in national capitals to ally with their 'own' local champions. This was standard practice since time immemorial in Washington. In Europe, there was plenty of resistance to cross-border consolidation and integration at the level of the member states.

12.6 REGULATORS TORN BETWEEN SAFETY AND COMPETITIVENESS OF FINANCIAL MARKETS

Regulators of CCPs were pulled two ways. At the beginning of the 21st century, the policy makers who defined the activities of regulators in the US and Europe were still actively pursuing the deregulation agenda begun in the 1980s. At the same time, CCPs merited special attention. The central counterparty function of clearing houses mitigated risk in financial markets but concentrated risk in CCPs, making them a potential danger point in the financial system as a whole.

The libertarian approach to regulation was championed by Alan Greenspan, chairman of the Federal Reserve Board since 1987. A hugely influential figure in the US and around the globe, Greenspan believed that market participants were generally better able than regulators to monitor and control the risks involved in trading with their particular counterparties. In speeches, Greenspan worried that 'such private prudential regulation' could be impaired or even displaced by government regulation. 'Except where market discipline is undermined by moral hazard, for example, because of federal government guarantees of private debt, private regulation generally has proved far better at constraining excessive risk-taking than has government regulation,' he once said.[9]

By the late 1990s, the US Commodity Exchange Act (CEA) needed to be revised to take account of the rapid growth of volume and scope of derivatives trading both on and off exchange during the years since it became law in 1974. In particular, there was a demand for legal certainty for trading OTC derivatives in place of the less formal framework that had emerged in the 1980s and 1990s through a series of policy statements from the Commodity Futures Trading Commission (CFTC) and which exempted OTC activity from regulation.

Legal certainty in the context of the late 1990s meant either no regulation or self regulation by the industry. Despite a number of headline grabbing incidents in the 1990s in which unwary investors – including corporations such as Procter & Gamble and public bodies such as Orange County in California – sustained heavy losses, Congress did not consider the ballooning trade in OTC derivatives to be a threat to financial stability. Financial lobbyists and trade organisations, such as the International Swaps and Derivatives Association (ISDA), reassured law makers that the financial sophistication of OTC market participants would safeguard against excessive risk-taking.

In 1999, the President's Working Group on Financial Markets nudged Congress in the direction of industry self regulation. It warned Congress that transactions could move offshore, discouraging innovation and growth and damaging US leadership in financial markets, unless

[9] Greenspan, Alan (5 May 2005), 'Risk transfer and financial stability', remarks delivered via satellite to the Federal Reserve Bank of Chicago's forty-first Annual Conference on Bank Structure, Chicago.

it removed legal uncertainty surrounding privately negotiated swaps and OTC energy contracts concluded off exchange between commercial counterparties.

Following many months of debate, the Commodity Futures Modernization Act (CFMA) was signed into law in December 2000 in the dying days of the Clinton administration. It promised, inter alia, 'to promote innovation for futures and derivatives and to reduce systemic risk' by enhancing legal certainty and also 'to enhance the competitive position of United States financial institutions and financial markets'.[10]

To provide legal certainty for OTC traders, the CFMA excluded from CEA coverage and regulation by the CFTC a broad range of swap agreements and other derivatives trades that were not executed on trading platforms, provided these trades were between sophisticated and financially robust professionals known as 'eligible contract participants'.

Also excluded from most CEA coverage and CFTC regulation were OTC transactions in 'exempt commodities' among 'eligible contract participants'. Mainly energy products, chemicals and metals traded off exchange, the exempt commodities remained subject to CFTC jurisdiction as far as anti-fraud and anti-market manipulation matters were concerned, reflecting Congressional fears that such products could be subject to price rigging.

The CFMA repealed an 18-year-old ban on the trading of single stock futures.

In addition to traditional derivatives exchanges, the act allowed the creation of new 'exempt commercial markets' on which sophisticated professionals could trade a wide variety of excluded and exempt contracts without submitting to the regulation of the CFTC. It retained CFTC regulation of agricultural derivatives and financial futures and options, traded on exchanges.

The CFMA was one factor boosting OTC derivatives trades. Another was the rift between investment banks and exchanges that encouraged the banks to channel more of their trading activities into commission-rich, opaque OTC markets. Having expanded at a compound rate of about 30% a year in the later 1990s, the OTC markets for trading derivatives grew at an even giddier pace. By mid-2008, when the global derivatives market peaked in size at US$684 trillion as measured by the notional amount of contracts outstanding, 88% were traded OTC, dwarfing the US$82 trillion notional value of exchange traded contracts outstanding at the time.[11]

The libertarian approach of the CFMA towards trading derivatives was tempered somewhat when it came to clearing. One aim of the act was 'to reduce systemic risk and provide greater stability to markets during times of market disorder by *allowing* the clearing of transactions in over-the-counter derivatives through appropriately regulated clearing organisations.'[12] The act therefore expanded the scope for companies to clear derivatives contracts that were traded on a bilateral basis OTC rather than on exchange, but – unlike the US post-crisis legislation of 2010 – stopped well short of mandating OTC clearing.

The CFMA gave exchanges the option of unbundling their clearing houses from the trading platforms. Clearing houses in the US had to register with the regulator responsible for the financial instrument that they cleared in order to be regulated independently of the trading facilities they served. Therefore derivatives clearing organisations (DCOs) registered with the CFTC.

In July 2001, the CFTC registered the first DCO that was not affiliated with a trading facility to clear energy derivatives traded OTC.[13] Three months later, LCH – which had developed

---

[10] Commodity Futures Modernization Act, HR 5660, Section 2, paragraphs 6 and 8.

[11] Figures from Bank for International Settlements (November 2009), 'OTC derivatives market activity in the first half of 2009'.

[12] Commodity Futures Modernization Act, HR 5660, Section 2, paragraph 7, author's italics.

[13] EnergyClear, a Houston-based DCO created to provide clearing and settlement of OTC energy derivatives contracts.

SwapClear for clearing the OTC global interbank swaps market – was recognised by the CFTC as the first offshore DCO under the CFMA and only the second clearing house not linked to an exchange.

CCPs also had to sign up to core principles so that they conformed to common standards regarding sufficient financial resources, adequate risk-management skills, suitable capacity for settling trades and such like.

With its twin objectives of reducing systemic risk and removing barriers to financial innovation, the CFMA became a much praised part of the US financial system until that system's near collapse in 2008. America's CCPs survived the 9/11 terrorist attacks and their regulatory framework proved adequate during the 2007–8 financial crisis. The deficiencies of the CFMA that the crisis exposed lay in areas of business that were unregulated and uncleared.

Until the Lehman bankruptcy, financial legislation in Europe also focused on deregulation but with the important additional requirement of promoting integration across national boundaries.

Once clearing and settlement grabbed the attention of EU policy makers, they looked at the US experience and focused on solutions for equity markets, leaving derivatives to one side irrespective of whether they were traded on exchange or OTC.

Inspired by the creation of DTCC to serve a continent-wide market for equities, the EU emphasised the need to break down national barriers to lower costs and promote competition among financial infrastructure providers. But until 2006 the EU Commission was unable to decide whether to mandate a single market in post-trade services for equities or to engineer an industry solution. When the Commission eventually acted, it was by brokering an industry Code of Conduct. Voluntary in name, the code was made possible only by the threat of EU legislation in the background.

The EU also moved cautiously when faced with the differing types of governance and ownership that existed among national clearing and settlement infrastructures. The Commission adopted a neutral stance between vertical and horizontal, for-profit and at-cost, and publicly-listed and user-owned, user-governed.

Some issues could not be left undisturbed, however. The moves to update regulation in Europe and the US, together with the changes wrought by globalisation, necessitated some rethinking about risk management at clearing houses.

The ability of CCPs to reduce the counterparty risk of participants meant a concentration of risk in the CCPs themselves. Practices that had grown up behind national frontiers were sometimes no longer suitable for a globalising world or for a European single market in which investment banks, such as the backers of the ESF, were pondering the merits of a single cross-border CCP.

The answer lay in minimum standards for safety and risk management across national frontiers. Policy makers entrusted this work to multinational committees of officials that were known to the cognoscenti by an alphabet soup of hyphenated-acronyms but which, as far as the general public and the mainstream media were concerned, toiled away in obscurity.

At the global level, the job fell to a CPSS-IOSCO task force, set up by the Basel-based Committee on Payments and Settlements Systems (CPSS) of the leading central banks and the Technical Committee of the International Organisation of Securities Commissions (IOSCO). In the EU, many of the same officials belonged to an ESCB-CESR working group. Formed of officials from the European Central Bank and national central banks of the EU[14] as well

[14] The ECB and the national central banks of the EU form the European System of Central Banks or ESCB.

as from the securities commissions belonging to the Committee of European Securities Regulators (CESR), the ESCB-CESR group worked on adapting the CPSS-IOSCO conclusions to conditions in Europe.

12.7 FINANCIAL INNOVATION

Those officials in Basel who worried about safety standards for CCPs were in a small minority in the early years of the 21st century. Financial markets were having a ball, spurred on by loose monetary policies and benign regulatory regimes. Trading volumes soared, both on and off exchange.

Financial innovation continued on its merry way, unimpeded by the CFMA and the EU's efforts to create a single market for financial services. For CCPs, there were two innovations of significance in the years leading up to the start of the financial crisis in 2007.

First, there was especially strong growth in algorithmic trading in equity markets. Developed first in the US, computerised algorithmic trading harnessed huge amounts of data and put trades on automatic pilot through increasingly complex market environments. A bull market in PhDs in mathematics and applied physics emerged as securities firms hired 'quants' to devise complex algorithm-driven 'black box' techniques to enable traders to beat benchmarks and conceal the scale of their activities from other market players.

Equity trading volumes grew rapidly. Studies in the US estimated that algorithmic trading accounted for 14–25% of total US equity trading by the spring of 2005, starting a trend that would see high frequency, algorithmic trades account for about 60% of all US equity trades by 2010. In London, the centre for quantitative black box trading strategies in Europe, market estimates suggested that algorithm-driven transactions accounted for 28% of trades by the end of 2006 and were behind an average year-on-year growth of nearly 60% in trading volumes on the London Stock Exchange's SETS electronic order book.

The effects could be seen in the value and volume of trades processed by NSCC, the clearing division of DTCC, which rose strongly in the years before the crisis from 4.8 billion, worth US$82 trillion, in 2003 to 13.5 billion, valued at US$283 trillion, in 2007.

The new trading techniques relied on the netting capacity of CCPs to keep the flow of instructions to settlement infrastructures within manageable bounds. Much higher trading volumes demanded investment, however. NSCC, for example, tripled its daily processing capacity from 160 million transactions in 2006 to 500 million two years later.

The surge in trading volumes went hand in hand with a fall in the size of orders as trading algorithms broke up large orders to reduce the chances of provoking adverse market movements. The high volumes and smaller ticket sizes were, at first sight, great news for exchanges and post-trade service providers. They meant more invoices and much higher revenues from fees. But especially in Europe, such business growth added to the pressure from users for lower charges and cost-cutting measures and encouraged them to develop strategies to disintermediate exchanges and other infrastructure providers when costs did not fall to their satisfaction (see Figure 12.1).

Adding to the urgency of the users' demands was the highly competitive environment in which they operated: there were no prizes for investing heavily in high speed computer technology only to be second best in the world of 'black box' computer trading where instructions were executed far faster than the blinking of an eye.

The computer whiz-kids who brought algorithmic trading to world equity markets also brought a quantum leap in the number and complexity of derivatives traded over the counter.

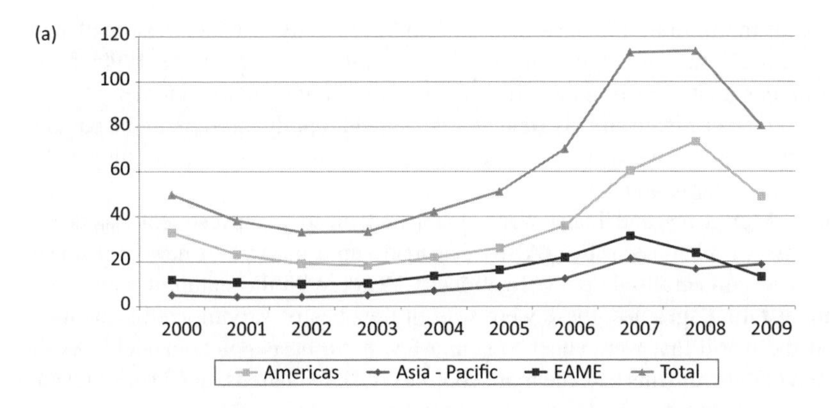

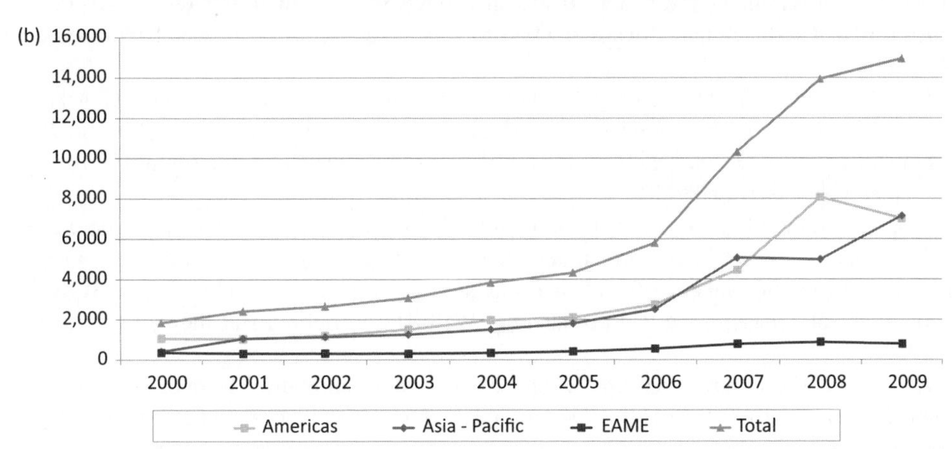

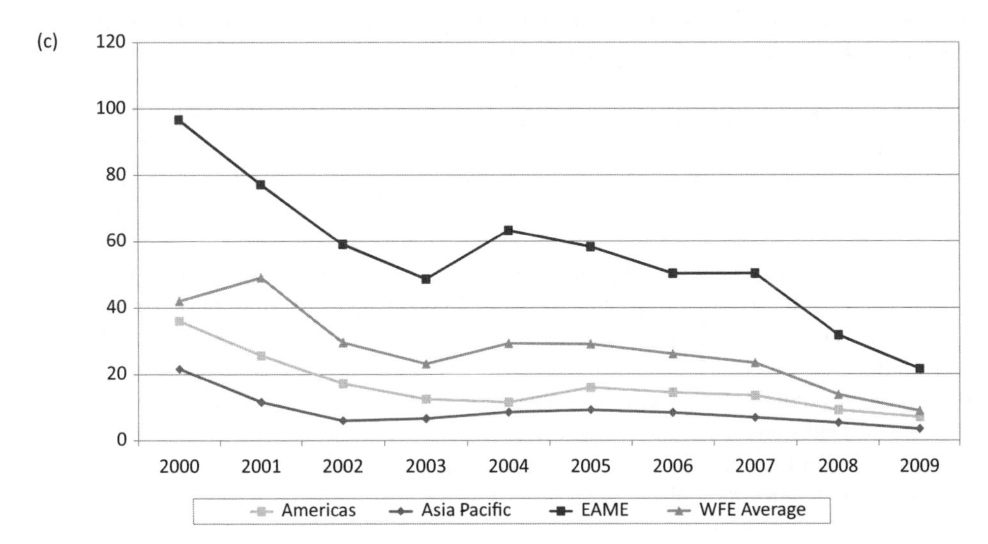

Figure 12.1 Global Equity Markets 2000–9: (a) Total value of share trading (in US$ trillions); (b) Total number of trades in equity shares (in millions); (c) Average value of trade (in US$ thousands, weighted by share value trading)

Source: World Federation of Exchanges. Reproduced by permission of the World Federation of Exchanges.

The second major innovation in finance, which would eventually provide great challenges and opportunities for clearers, was the explosion from small beginnings in the 1990s in the issuance of instruments that transferred credit risk from one counterparty to another.

Securitisation and the originate and distribute model spread rapidly throughout the banking world as managers sought ways to boost yields in the low interest rate environment that followed the dot.com collapse and 9/11.

Credit boomed. Mortgages and loans were sliced and diced by investment banks and transformed into asset backed securities (ABS) that made up a mixture of new instruments known generically as collateralised debt obligations (CDOs). With the stamp of approval of the world's leading rating agencies, these were sold in tranches of varying credit quality to investors around the world that were eager to gain a few extra basis points of yield. As the decade progressed the instruments became more complex. CDO-squareds, or CDOs of CDOs, made their appearance. Investment banks also developed synthetic CDOs by assembling portfolios of Credit Default Swaps (CDSs) to imitate the features of a collateralised debt obligation.

Credit default swaps were embryonic and unknown to policy makers when the CFMA was approved. Gary Gensler, appointed by President Barack Obama to head the CFTC in 2009, later recalled how CDSs never crossed his computer screen when he was a senior US Treasury official between 1997 and 2001.[15]

'I served in the Clinton administration, and I do not remember one meeting where credit default swaps came up. I don't remember one briefing paper on credit default swaps,' Gensler told an audience of bankers, officials and media in Brussels in September 2009. 'At the US Department of Treasury, we had no meeting. We had no briefing. But they already existed in 1999.'[16]

A bilateral OTC contract, a Credit Default Swap is, at its simplest, a form of insurance. The CDS allows an investor to lay off the risk of a default or a specified 'credit event' affecting an asset or 'reference entity' to a third party for a fee. The purchaser of protection pays a premium at agreed intervals to the protection seller who enjoys an income (the premiums) in return for accepting the risk of having to pay the protection buyer should the reference entity default on its obligations. As most CDSs were issued with favourable credit ratings, the chances of mishap or credit event appeared remote during the years of the 'Great Moderation'.

CDSs were tradable. The premium paid to protection sellers fluctuated in price and could provide a useful guide to the riskiness of the reference entity. But CDSs had two special characteristics:

- Neither the purchaser nor the seller of protection need have any connection to the underlying asset or 'reference entity' covered by the swap. In this respect, there were some similarities between CDSs and the trades conducted through 'bucket shops' in the early years of futures trading.
- CDSs had a unique payoff profile. When a credit event took place, the protection buyer expected a substantial payment in return for the premiums paid. This 'jump to default risk' made the CDS market inherently unpredictable and potentially very volatile, particularly if a cluster of defaults took place.

[15] As Assistant Secretary of Financial Markets between 1997 and 1999 and Under Secretary of Domestic Finance from 1999 to 2001.

[16] Unscripted comments made during his keynote speech to a European Commission conference on *OTC Derivatives Regulation* in Brussels on 25 September 2009.

Three main types of CDS developed: single name CDSs where the reference entity is an individual company or government; index CDSs where the contract consists of a pool of liquid single name CDSs; and basket CDSs which comprise between three and 100 single name CDSs and are less standardised, more opaque and therefore less liquid than other CDSs.

Trading in credit derivatives was conducted over the counter, was unregulated and passed the CCPs by. Although concerns grew about the quality of back office processing and steps were taken from 2005 with the encouragement of the Federal Reserve Bank of New York to address these problems, the transfer of risk was generally perceived as one of the strengths of the global financial system in the early years of the 21st century.

In remarks beamed by satellite, Alan Greenspan caught the spirit of the age when he told a May 2005 conference organised by the Federal Reserve Bank of Chicago that: 'The use of a growing array of derivatives and the related application of more sophisticated approaches to measuring and managing risk are key factors underpinning the greater resilience of our largest financial institutions.'[17]

Exempt from regulation, the markets for credit derivatives grew rapidly before they began to impinge on the consciousness of policy makers. The Bank for International Settlements, for example, only started regular half yearly reporting of CDS statistics in December 2004.

Figures since published by the BIS show that the annual issuance of US and European 'structured credit products' jumped from just over US$500 billion in 2000 to around US$3 trillion in 2006.[18] The notional amount outstanding of credit default swaps soared from US$700 billion at the end of June 2001 to US$4.5 trillion three years later and US$57.4 trillion by the end of June 2008.[19]

A dangerous mix of leverage, interconnection and complexity lay behind the statistics and underpinned the rapid growth of credit derivatives. But this went largely unnoticed until exposed in the crisis of 2007–8. It was only after the near collapse of the investment bank Bear Stearns in March 2008 that momentum began to build behind providing CCP clearing for the new generation of credit derivatives.

The more exotic instruments were so complex that the most assiduous 'eligible contract participant' authorised under the CFMA would have difficulties understanding the risks involved. An investor conducting due diligence on a residential mortgage backed security (RBMS) would need to read about 200 pages of documentation – a 'just about feasible' task for a busy person, according to Andrew Haldane, executive director for financial stability at the Bank of England. But, with a typical CDO comprising 150 RMBSs and perhaps 125 tranches of ABS CDOs making up a CDO squared, 'an investor in a CDO^2 would need to read in excess of 1 billion pages to understand fully the ingredients'.[20]

12.8 CONCENTRATION AMONG CLEARING MEMBERS

Lehman Brothers' default removed at a stroke one of the leading clearing member firms of CCPs around the world. But well in advance of its bankruptcy, a process of concentration was

[17] Greenspan, Alan (5 May 2005).

[18] Bank for International Settlements (September 2009), 'The Joint Forum Report of Special Purpose Entities', Basel Committee on Banking Supervision. The total, summarised in a table on page 7 of the report, includes asset backed securities (ABS), mortgage backed securities (MBS) and collateralised debt obligations (CDO).

[19] Bank for International Settlements (December 2004, November 2007, November 2008): 'Triennial and semiannual surveys on positions in global over-the-counter (OTC) derivatives markets' at end June 2004 and end June 2007, and 'OTC derivatives market activity in the first half of 2008'.

[20] Bank of England (April 2009a), 'Rethinking the financial network', speech to the Financial Student Association, Amsterdam.

underway among banks and financial conglomerates that changed the relationship between clearing houses and their clearing members.

For most of their history, CCPs existed to clear and net trades and take responsibility for counterparty risk of a multitude of firms, which, as clearing members, would act as the channels between the clearing house and a far greater number of intermediaries and end-investors.

By the beginning of the 21st century, fewer companies were willing or able to be clearing members. The two dozen founder members of the European Securities Forum in 2000 included most of the large globally active clearing members at the time.

Concentration among clearing members advanced further in subsequent years despite the arrival in their midst of new participants such as Getco, a high frequency trader, and ICAP, an inter-dealer money broker that decided to create a new business stream in post-trade activities.

The fall in numbers reflected a concentration of financial power around the world among a few, mainly US-owned, investment and commercial banks from around 1990 onwards. In Europe, the US banks led the way in developing cross-border business, in the process becoming more important as clearing members. Some leading European clearing members at the end of the 1990s dropped down the international league tables. Others merged or created joint ventures, as in January 2008 when Calyon and Société Générale of France merged their global futures brokerage businesses to form Newedge.

In the US, concentration among banks was boosted by legislation. The Gramm-Leach-Bliley Act of 1999, which repealed the 1933 Glass Steagall law, was introduced to permit the previous year's merger of Citicorp, a commercial bank, and Travellers Insurance, a financial group that included the investment bank Smith Barney.

The creation of Citigroup was followed by other mergers that resulted in 'large and complex financial institutions'. These included the merger in 2000 of JP Morgan and Chase Manhattan Bank, which in turn was followed in 2004 by the merger of JP Morgan Chase and Bank One, and the 2004 acquisition by Bank of America of FleetBoston Financial, itself the product of a significant merger in 1999.

In some cases, the concentration reflected business failures. When Refco, a US commodity and financial futures broker, filed for bankruptcy after the discovery of fraud in October 2005, it was the biggest broker operating on the CME. In March 2008, as the financial crisis escalated, the US investment bank Bear Stearns abruptly dropped out of the ranks of top clearing members when it was taken over by JP Morgan Chase in a rescue orchestrated by the New York Federal Reserve Bank. By the time of Lehman's collapse, there were perhaps only a dozen large clearing member firms for any given asset class that could claim to be globally active.

As the number of globally active clearing members shrank, so their potential to influence the financial infrastructure providers grew. This was a trend that Chris Tupker noted shortly after taking over the Chairmanship of LCH.Clearnet in 2006: 'One of the changes of the past six to seven years is that market power has been concentrated in fewer hands: fewer users playing a much more important role,' he said.[21] Estimating that 'perhaps 50 or 60% of the business' of LCH was done by 10 firms, he added:

> Viewed from the perspective of LCH, which clears commodities, derivatives, debt, and equity, I look at the top 10 players in each of the asset classes that we clear, and it is always the same firms. The biggest gold traders and biggest oil traders are now Goldman Sachs and Morgan Stanley. So a huge concentration has taken place, and that gives these firms market power.

[21] Conversation with the author, 4 December 2006.

As the decade progressed, the big players increasingly deployed their concentrated market power in different areas of trading to compete with and disintermediate the exchanges. They then became far more assertive as clearing members in wanting to shape the destinies of CCPs.

The next chapter will describe what happened to CCPs in Chicago and the business of clearing in general when investment banks and other assertive financial institutions tried to shake up the city's long established futures exchanges.

13 The Chicago Roller Coaster

13.1 COMMON CLEARING FOR SCREEN-BASED TRADERS

By the late 1990s, Chicago's futures exchanges were under pressure.

They were no longer the most modern in the world. Although both the CBOT and CME had introduced screen-based trading systems for after-hours activity, the influence of the local traders on each exchange ensured that most trading was still conducted by open outcry in the pits.

Efficient, cost effective screen-based trading technology enabled exchanges in continental Europe, led by Deutsche Terminbörse (DTB), to increase turnover and market share. LIFFE, chastened by the loss of its benchmark 10-year Bund futures business to DTB during 1997, announced in March 1998 that it would switch most contracts to screen-based trading in 1999.

Away from the exchanges, more and more derivatives were being created and traded OTC in a global market place. The 1993 G30 report, which focused exclusively on OTC derivatives, had caught the trend. Whereas turnover of exchange-traded derivatives and OTC products grew in parallel between 1987 and 1992, OTC activity expanded significantly faster after 1993.

The US$4.45 trillion notional amount of OTC derivatives outstanding at the end of 1991 was about a quarter higher than the equivalent US$3.52 trillion total for exchange-traded derivatives. By the end of 1998, the notional amount of OTC derivatives outstanding was US$51 trillion – nearly four times the $13.55 trillion notional amount of exchange-traded instruments outstanding at the end of that year.[1]

Chicago had to respond and respond it did. Two announcements in March 1998 suggested a future based on consolidation at home and the import of best practice from abroad:

- On 18 March 1998, the CBOT and the Eurex partners, Germany's DTB and SOFFEX of Switzerland, revealed plans for an alliance aimed at creating a common trading platform by June 1999.
- Two days later – on 20 March – two arch rivals, the CBOT and CME, reached a tentative agreement to pool their clearing facilities.

The idea of common clearing had been advanced and rejected on various occasions during the previous two decades as relations between the two exchanges blew hot and cold. This latest initiative appeared promising. It owed much to Merton H. Miller, a Nobel prize winning economist and Emeritus Professor of Finance at the University of Chicago's graduate school of business, who had worked closely at different times with the boards of both the CBOT and CME.

[1] Figures from the 67th and 69th annual reports of the Bank for International Settlements.

Since the end of January 1996, Miller had chaired a joint strategic committee set up by the two exchanges, which focused on seven major areas: clearing; technology; marketing; regulatory issues; market data information; electronic trading; and 'members' opportunities'.

But instead of launching an orderly process of modernisation, the two announcements of March 1998 were followed by a messy roller-coaster ride of alliances and ruptures. Although Chicago's exchange and clearing landscape was eventually transformed, the full process took nine years.

Eurex came to Chicago, first to cooperate with the CBOT, then to challenge it and ultimately to fail. The venerable CBOT lost its position as America's leading futures exchange and was eventually taken over, becoming part of a greatly expanded, vertically-structured, for-profit and publicly quoted CME Group. The Board of Trade Clearing Corporation (BOTCC) sought an independent role as a central counterparty clearer serving more than one market. But instead of finding a new future as a horizontally-structured CCP for Eurex and others, BOTCC lost its main business and shrank dramatically under a new ownership structure, dominated by investment banks, before aspiring to clear OTC derivatives in even more turbulent times.

Many factors contributed to the outcome, some of which are discussed in the previous chapter. But many were specific to the parties involved and the political circumstances of the time.

Eurex and BOTCC proved to have limited room for manoeuvre because of past decisions. Some of these – such as those relating to the governance of BOTCC – were taken generations earlier.

Much of the turmoil reflected conditions at the CBOT. The membership of the exchange was split between the 'locals', independent floor traders steeped in the customs of pit trading, and representatives of the large mainly New York-based investment banks, that had been attracted to the exchange to trade financial futures. Tensions focused on the technological changes needed to modernise futures trading and were reflected in the rapid acceptance and fierce rejection by CBOT members of business partners and of chairmen. The divisions at the exchange were accentuated by an allocation of voting power among the members that privileged the locals and the old grain-trading elite.

As befitted a mutual organisation, the governance of the CBOT was traditionally based on the principle of one vote per member. But the introduction of financial futures in the 1970s had been followed by the creation of a separate category of associate member with only a fraction of the voting power of a full member.

For many years the different categories of membership rubbed along together. The associate members, represented largely by employees of Wall Street firms, formed a minority of the CBOT board and were content to leave governance issues to the exchange's old grain trading elite and the locals. The newcomers preferred to get on with making money. When the modernisation agenda came to the fore in 1998, the full membership votes of the pit-based grain and local traders were six times weightier than those of the associate members trading financial contracts.

Despite having a similar system of weighted votes, the CME was able to make more of its opportunities. It demutualised in November 2000 and greatly increased its financial fire power through an initial public offering in December 2002 when it became the first publicly quoted US exchange group.

By this time, Eurex's presence in the Chicago market was being additionally handicapped by local Chicago patriotism which was mobilised by Chicago's powerful futures lobby and found a receptive ear in Congress. Eurex's failure to establish a futures exchange in Chicago also hinged on a controversial procedural decision by the CFTC, the industry regulator.

The economics and politics of clearing played an important role in the unfolding saga. CCP clearing moved centre stage in the reshaping of Chicago's futures industry, mirroring its transformation from a back-room, utility activity to a strategic asset prized by the exchanges and their often disgruntled customers among the investment banks.

13.2 MARRY IN HASTE; REPENT AT LEISURE

Both the common clearing initiative between the CME and the CBOT and the CBOT's alliance with Eurex fell foul of internal divisions at the CBOT within months of the March 1998 announcements.

First to falter was the common clearing project. Common clearing of trades at the CME and CBOT was strongly supported by the Futures Industry Association (FIA), the lobby group representing the big financial futures traders. FIA members were impressed by the performance of LCH in clearing several futures markets in London and saw it as a cost-saving measure. But the CBOT board voted to withdraw its support on 2 September 1998 following a mass protest by local traders.

The same board had approved the Eurex alliance just two weeks earlier in August 1998. Indicative of the turmoil at the CBOT, the exchange members voted in December 1998 to oust as chairman Pat Arbor, an advocate of change, in favour of David Brennan, a conservative. In January 1999, the CBOT board rejected the Eurex alliance.

As so often in the previous two decades, the plans for common clearing went into hibernation. But the projected alliance between the CBOT and Eurex was quickly revived. In March 1999 the news broke that Eurex had displaced the CBOT as the world's biggest derivatives exchange. A few weeks later, CBOT members voted in June 1999 to approve an alliance with the Swiss-German exchange on terms similar to those rejected at the start of the year.

Just over a year later, in August 2000, Eurex and the CBOT launched their cooperative venture in derivatives trading. Their platform, dubbed a/c/e,[2] was based on Eurex technology.

The launch did not mean harmony between the CBOT and Eurex, however. The CBOT's traders complained that a/c/e was expensive. According to people familiar with the matter, the US operation was handicapped by having to pay high costs for technical services provided by Deutsche Börse Systems, another member of the Deutsche Börse group.

Eurex had gripes of its own. In May 2001, it emerged that Eurex was in formal dispute resolution procedures with its partner in Chicago.

The strains in the relationship as perceived by Eurex had been aired in the prospectus for Deutsche Börse's Initial Public Offering in Germany, published in February 2001. In the section detailing risk factors for potential shareholders, the document described how the CBOT had delayed one planned computer upgrade and was refusing to participate in another. These developments, the prospectus warned, could 'have considerable negative effects on the business, financial and earnings position of Deutsche Börse'.[3]

The IPO prospectus also acknowledged that competition clauses agreed between Eurex and the CBOT as part of the alliance could pose a competitive handicap for the Deutsche Börse group. The clauses barred Eurex from offering to trade or clear financial futures contracts

[2] alliance/cbot/eurex.

[3] Deutsche Börse (2 February 2001), 'Verkaufsprospekt/Börsenzulassungsprospekt'. Author's translation from the German.

denominated in US or Canadian dollars or Mexican pesos for four years after the eventual termination of the deal and also banned the Swiss-German group from offering trading facilities for a number of agricultural futures contracts.

The CBOT and Eurex drifted apart. Shortly after the news that the two exchanges were in formal dispute resolution procedures, the CBOT joined its Chicago rivals, the CME and the Chicago Board Options Exchange, in a plan to launch an electronic single stock futures exchange that would be cleared through the Options Clearing Corp. Eurex was not informed in advance about the move, which was viewed by the local Chicago media as a calculated affront by the CBOT towards its partner.

It became a priority of Rudolf Ferscha, the head of Eurex, to undo the a/c/e alliance. Ferscha had joined the Deutsche Börse board in November 2000 from Goldman Sachs and was not involved in negotiating the original agreement with the CBOT. In July 2002, the CBOT and Eurex agreed to end their alliance with effect from 2004, four years ahead of the original planned date of 2008. The revised agreement eliminated the product and cooperation restrictions on Eurex's activities, enabling Eurex to compete in the US and establish new partnerships – at least in theory.

The allies became competitors. In January 2003, the CBOT's board decided to replace the a/c/e platform at the end of that year. As a replacement it chose LIFFE Connect, at the time Eurex's strongest competitor technically among other platforms.

Hours before the CBOT announced this decision on 10 January, Eurex unveiled plans to launch its own US exchange. Ferscha's plan was nothing if not audacious.

He sought to capture the CBOT's business in US Treasury derivatives by offering Eurex services to traders by way of their familiar a/c/e screens. Their trades would be cleared, as before, by BOTCC, which had cleared CBOT trades since 1926. Traders using the Eurex platform would be able to compete directly with their rivals at the CBOT because they would gain access for offsets to the open interest in the CBOT contracts cleared by BOTCC.

The CBOT and Eurex contracts would be interchangeable, or as US market parlance put it 'fungible', giving the newcomer exchange the opportunity to draw off liquidity from its incumbent rival so long as it offered better financial terms and service levels and provided there were no additional impediments to competition.

13.3 CBOT AND BOTCC ON DIFFERENT TRAJECTORIES

Ferscha's plan was a very real threat to the CBOT and turned an already difficult relationship between the CBOT and Eurex into an all out war. The clearing arrangements of the two exchanges became the battlefield between the two combatants.

The Eurex chief was an international lawyer by training and had studied the law on open interest in the US. He thought he could buy into BOTCC and make its members accept Eurex as a trading platform next to the CBOT. Traders using Eurex could then clear through the same clearer and benefit from the open interest that the CBOT had built in BOTCC.

Ferscha did not have BOTCC's support for his plan when he launched it. But the relationship between the Chicago exchange and its clearing house had changed sufficiently in the years before the break-up of the alliance between the CBOT and Eurex to give him some hope of success.

If the relationship between Eurex and CBOT was a case of 'marry in haste, repent at leisure', that between CBOT and BOTCC was more like a parting of the ways of an aging couple that turned very unpleasant towards the end.

As noted earlier, BOTCC was set up under the supervision of the CBOT board of directors but with a corporate identity separate from the exchange.[4] The arm's length relationship reflected concerns among the exchange's directors in 1925 that clearing with responsibility for completing trades could be risky and costly if things went wrong. These worries were underlined at BOTCC's birth by the provision in the CBOT's rules that its board could vote for a 'modified or other method' of clearing if BOTCC's methods should ever 'prove prejudicial to the best interest' of the CBOT.

There was no written contract to define the relations between the CBOT and BOTCC. Contractual relationships were between individual CBOT members and the minority of their peers who were clearing members and therefore shareholders of BOTCC. By contrast, the CME's clearing house was integrated as a division of the exchange.

For half a century, the CBOT's board exercised considerable control over BOTCC's by-laws and its management. The relationship worked well enough as long as the two organisations thought and behaved like mutuals and were jointly focused on providing an infrastructure for trading and clearing farm commodities futures. But, according to Dennis Dutterer, a senior BOTCC executive for many years,[5] the relationship began to fray as the rapid growth of the financial futures business from the 1970s onwards put the governance models of the two organisations under varying degrees of strain.

BOTCC's governance differed somewhat from that of CBOT. As at the CBOT, individuals could be BOTCC members and hence shareholders with a vote. But as noted earlier,[6] the rules also limited the number of shares that BOTCC's big clearing members could hold.

This cap enabled the clearing house to preserve a voting system based on one vote per one clearing member firm, and so uphold the influence in BOTCC of the CBOT's grain trading companies. But it meant BOTCC's capital failed to reflect the risks generated by the large futures commission merchants (FCMs) who dominated financial futures trading and accounted for most of the risk on the books of the CCP.

By the mid-1980s, the balance between voting rights and share ownership established in the early BOTCC by-laws was no longer sustainable. It was being undermined by risk-management issues which were climbing up the BOTCC agenda.

The 1987 Crash was an important catalyst. BOTCC, unlike many CCPs, had no guarantee fund at the time. For its financial cushion against default, the clearing house relied on the margins collected from its clearing members, accumulated reserves of around US$40 million, and its share capital.

Under the leadership of Neal Kottke, BOTCC's chairman between 1986 and 1988, the clearer decided to strengthen its financial cushion. But the method chosen fuelled the divergence of interests between the clearing house's traditional and financial futures users.

Instead of creating a guarantee fund to guard against losses, BOTCC instituted a three year programme for clearing members to buy new shares. The formula chosen related subscriptions to the volume of trades conducted on the CBOT and the riskiness of these trades as reflected by the margin required from the clearing firm.

---

[4] See Section 7.4.

[5] As told to the author, 23 January 2009. Dutterer was with BOTCC, later The Clearing Corporation, from 1985 to 2005. He was President and CEO between 1999 and 2005, when he was also interim President and CEO of the CBOT in 2000 to 2001. Dutterer was BOTCC's Executive Vice President and Chief Administrative Officer from 1992 to 1998 after serving as General Counsel and Corporate Secretary between 1985 and 1991.

[6] See Section 7.5.

The formula resulted in a sharp increase in the percentage of BOTCC shares held by the big traders in financial futures and a proportionately smaller increase in shares held by the CBOT's grain traders and 'locals', who were often day traders who squared their positions at the end of each trading day. But it made no provision for a commensurate increase in the voting power of the big financial futures traders.

At the same time, BOTCC built up its reserves from retained earnings to more than US$150 million rather than share its profits with its users. It took out US$200 million in default insurance in addition to cover risks. Such prudence was rewarded in 1997 when BOTCC became the first clearing house in the world to be awarded a 'triple A' rating from Standard and Poor's.

But the financial futures traders complained about being outvoted. According to Dutterer, small clearing members owning just 8% of BOTCC's capital in total, held shares with 51% of the votes. Firms putting up 92% of BOTCC's risk capital could be outvoted over the clearer's policies.

Pressure mounted on the smaller clearing members among BOTCC shareholders to accept rule changes that increased the influence of the big financial institutions which put up most of the capital of the clearing house and had most of the risk. In 1999, a three-tier board was created in place of the nine member BOTCC board previously elected by the votes of all shareholders on a one vote per one clearing member firm basis.

Using a complex formula to determine each clearing member firm's ranking as a shareholder, the top third of BOTCC clearing members comprising the big institutions elected three board members; the bottom third consisting of the smallest clearing members elected another three; the remaining three were elected by all the clearing house shareholders. These changes enabled the 12 to 14 biggest users, which represented more than 50% of the capital of the clearing house, to have some influence in the BOTCC board whereas before they had none.

BOTCC began to explore other business opportunities. It began clearing contracts traded on smaller exchanges that did not compete with the CBOT, such as barge freight futures contracts traded on the Merchants' Exchange of St Louis.

When, in 1999, BrokerTec, an Internet-based bond trading platform set up by leading international fixed income dealers, announced plans to create an electronic platform for futures and options trading, it asked BOTCC to provide post-trade services. In the BrokerTec consortium were some of BOTCC's biggest shareholders. Much to the chagrin of the CBOT, and its smaller members in particular, BOTCC agreed to clear for the new venture from November 2001, although it did not guarantee the contracts.

The BrokerTec deal marked a fork in the road for BOTCC and the rank and file members of CBOT. It was because the CBOT's 'locals' supported BOTCC that the exchange's board withdrew its backing for common clearing with the CME in September 1998. The BOTCC decision to provide clearing services for the electronic upstart BrokerTec Futures Exchange was seen as a betrayal by the CBOT's smaller and more vulnerable pit-based members.

Led by Dennis Dutterer, its president and CEO, BOTCC became an advocate of the horizontal clearing model where a number of exchanges could use one or several clearing houses, according to choice. The model – similar to that used for the US equity and equity options markets from the mid-1970s – embraced interoperability among CCPs and was the antithesis of the vertical approach found at the CME and most US derivatives exchanges. As Dutterer explained in 2002: 'A key element of such an arrangement would be the absence of any kind of mandated clearing – the choice would be that of a clearing firm to choose the marketplace and the clearinghouse that was best.'[7]

Towards the end of 2002, the CBOT attempted to restructure its relations with the clearing house. It offered BOTCC a contract which included the provision that BOTCC should clear exclusively for the exchange. The plan had the support of BOTCC's smaller clearing members. But the clearing corporation's board – by now dominated by New York-based financial interests and chaired by Mike Dawley, global co-head of futures services at Goldman Sachs in New York – dragged its feet, prompting the CBOT's management to reopen contacts in secret with the CME.

The CME and CBOT dropped their bombshell on 16 April 2003 just as the BOTCC board was starting a long arranged meeting to vote on the CBOT contract offer. The CME and CBOT announced they would implement a clearing link and common clearing of contracts traded on the two exchanges from 2 January 2004. This was the date the CBOT was due to adopt the LIFFE Connect platform and when Eurex hoped to launch its electronic futures market in direct competition with its former partner. Procedurally, the CBOT would become a derivatives clearing organisation (DCO) under US law and contract out the business to the CME's clearing division.

13.4 THE ASCENT OF THE CME

In the five years since the March 1998 announcement of the previous, failed attempt to introduce common clearing, the CBOT had succumbed to internecine strife. The underlying struggle between modernisers and conservatives had been punctuated by abrupt changes of chairmen, alliance partners and electronic trading platforms. Successive chairmen failed to make progress on the big strategic question, discussed extensively in 1998–99, of whether to demutualise and convert the exchange to a for-profit business model.

The CME, by contrast, had transformed itself. After a considerable struggle and following the 1997 technology swap with the French exchanges, it had made a success of its GLOBEX II trading platform and Clearing 21 real time matching and clearing technologies. It demutualised and launched an offering of its shares, becoming the first listed exchange company in the US in the autumn of 2002.

It also upgraded the importance of clearing in its overall operations. Phupinder Gill, CME Group President, recalls how around the turn of the century the company carried out a strategic review of its future role in world markets. At a time when there were suggestions that the CME should outsource its clearing to LCH in London, Fred Arditti, the CME's chief economist, convinced the board that the clearing house should not be considered a back-office, backwater operation.

Benefiting from a US$97.65 million cash injection through its share offering and boosted by a rapidly rising share price, the CME selected its priorities.

As Gill said:[8]

> We decided a few things. [...] We were going to grow our business on a global basis as an exchange. We were going to get good electronically: we were still then pretty much floor based. And we would grow the infrastructure that we had.

---

[7] Before a CFTC roundtable on clearing issues 1 August 2002.

[8] Conversation with the author, Chicago, 26 September 2008.

> And we said: why not leverage the infrastructure, provide services to folks, become the 'Intel Chip' for all these exchanges that might need our help? And on the clearing side that was the whole motivation. The profit margin of this business, based on marginal cost, was exceptionally high for us. We had the scale. We had excess capacity. We could clear the Board of Trade stuff. We had so much commonality in terms of the Merrill Lynchs and big broker dealers in our memberships, that it brought enormous savings. And the integration was done as perfectly as you could do it.

It helped that in March 2003 the CBOT members elected a new chairman, Charles P. Carey, who had a strong rapport with CME executive chairman Terrence Duffy. The two first met when trading hog futures at the CME in 1983 and remained friends after Carey left the CME to trade corn futures at the CBOT.

The importance of personal relationships in the Chicago financial milieu should never be underestimated. In his memoir,[9] Leo Melamed recalled how the two exchanges agreed around 1990 to begin discussions on a unified clearing system only for the plan to be scrapped three years later: 'a victim of the deteriorating climate between the leadership of the Chicago exchanges' at that time.

The common clearing link threatened to deprive BOTCC of 85% of its business. The clearing house began casting around for other clients. Its board ignored a US$207 million offer from the CBOT to buy BOTCC, on the grounds that it would be a preliminary to closing down the clearer and that the money offered was only a few million dollars more than the US$187 million cash and other assets on BOTCC's books. Towards the end of May 2003, BOTCC agreed a clearing partnership with Eurex.

From a geopolitical standpoint, it was a difficult time for BOTCC to throw in its lot with a German-dominated exchange. The US-led invasion of Iraq began on 20 March 2003, and the German government of Chancellor Gerhardt Schröder was one of the most vocal critics of the US.

Within three weeks of the Eurex-BOTCC agreement, the CME and CBOT chairmen launched a fierce lobbying campaign in Congress against foreign competition in US futures markets. Carey called for 'special regulatory rules' to apply to foreign-owned futures exchanges offering US futures products while Duffy warned of the risk of hidden subsidies and 'abusive practices' in the battle for market share.[10]

But the real blow toFerscha's ambitions came when the CBOT changed its rules to implement the clearing link with the CME. The proposed rule 701.01 was sweeping in its implications. Under the headline 'Transfer of Open Positions to Clearing Services Provider' it stated that: 'Each clearing member shall comply in all respects with any statement of policy or other notice issued by the Exchange relating to the procedures and processes that must be followed to effectuate the transfer of open positions to any Clearing Service Provider.'

The rule gave the CBOT the power to move the open interest arising from contracts traded on the exchange from BOTCC to another CCP. Another proposed amendment – to rule 911.00 – made clear that the clearing provider would be the CME.

The proposed rule changes would make it economically impossible for CBOT members to switch to Eurex's a/c/e platform and continue to clear their trades through BOTCC as envisaged in Ferscha's scheme. The cost of building up sufficient open interest in The Clearing

[9] Melamed, Leo, with Tamarkin, Bob (1996), *Escape to the Futures.*

[10] *Financial Times* (FT.Com) (19 June 2003), 'CME and CBOT fight foreign rivals'.

Corporation (as BOTCC was to be known) to compete on margin conditions with the CBOT and CME would be prohibitive at a time when the CBOT and CME would be pooling their open interest in one clearing house.

Ominously for Ferscha and BOTCC, the CBOT rule changes were passed overwhelmingly with 564 and 3/6th votes in favour against nine dissenters when put to the CBOT membership on 24 June 2003.[11] But they still had to be approved by the CFTC, the futures industry regulator.

On Tuesday 8 July 2003, the CFTC announced it would vote on the CBOT and CME rule changes. It set a remarkably short deadline of noon, Monday 14 July, for comments on such a weighty issue. Because of the 4 July holiday weekend, the consultation period lasted just four business days compared with a normal 45-day review period. Nevertheless, the notice attracted a number of comments, of which some were hostile to the CBOT's plans.

BOTCC and its lawyers argued that CBOT had no right to order the transfer of open interest. Regulation 701.01 would, if implemented, force clearing members to breach contracts with BOTCC to which the CBOT was not a party. Some of the big FCMs including Morgan Stanley and Deutsche Bank voiced fears that the provision, by its sweeping nature, had adverse implications for risk management. The FIA, although long a supporter of common clearing, warned that approval by the CFTC 'would effectively mean that the Commission has concluded that an exchange has the unfettered right to determine where contracts traded on that exchange are cleared.'

Dutterer complained in vain that the rule changes 'would constitute an unlawful interference with the Clearing Corporation's contracts with its members'.[12] On 15 July 2003, the CFTC voted 4–0 to approve the new rules, deeming them necessary for an orderly implementation of the common clearing link and continuity of financial integrity and customer protection in the futures markets. The CFTC opined that the link would support innovation in the futures industry.

The sole hint of criticism came from Commissioner Sharon Brown-Hruska. She took the unusual step of issuing a statement which voiced concern that the rapid approval process 'may have foreclosed comment by, among others, agricultural interests who are affected by the transfer from BOTCC to the CME'.[13] But while intimating that there should be 'a more open process for future rule submissions that seek Commission approval', Ms Brown-Hruska concurred with the proposal and noted with approval how opportunities for cross margining and netting would lower the cost of hedging complex financial positions.

13.5 AFTER THE CFTC's DECISION

The CFTC's support for the clearing link and CBOT's transfer of open interest to the CME was hugely damaging to Eurex's attempt to break into the Chicago market. It also signalled the eclipse of BOTCC as a leading US CCP.

To compete, Ferscha and Dutterer drew up innovative plans for the customers of Eurex's US operations to access both US-dollar and euro-denominated products using a single transatlantic margin pool. The plan, which also involved Eurex US taking a 15% stake in The Clearing

[11] According to Bernie Dan, president and CEO of the Chicago Board of Trade, in a letter to the CFTC dated 14 June 2003.

[12] BOTCC (14 July 2003) in an email to the CFTC dated 14 July 2003.

[13] *Concurring Statement of Commissioner Sharon Brown-Hruska.* The author's copy was provided by a market participant. The statement appears not to be on the CFTC website.

Corporation or CCorp[14] (as BOTCC became known) would, Ferscha calculated, compensate investors using Eurex's Chicago operation for nearly all the loss of the open interest linked to the CBOT's contracts.

Eurex set 1 February 2004 as the launch date for its US challenge to the CBOT in the market for US Treasury futures and applied to the CFTC for a licence to open its electronic futures exchange.

The German-Swiss exchange had many hurdles to overcome. It needed majority approval of CCorp's 87 shareholders, voting on the basis of one vote per one clearing member firm, for the corporate restructuring that would bring in Eurex US as a 15% shareholder of CCorp. Other far reaching governance changes at the US clearing house included a revision of the voting method to one share one vote; provisions to de-restrict the transfer of shares in CCorp; and the scrapping of rules that required clearing members to own shares in the clearer and shareholders to be clearing members.

The fight for shareholders' votes was bitter. Eurex took legal action in a Washington district court against CBOT and CME alleging that they offered 'financial inducements valued at over US$100 million' to CCorp shareholders to reject the proposals to restructure CCorp's ownership.[15] The CBOT retaliated with aggressive fee reductions which strengthened support among its members for the clearing link with the CME.

Nonetheless, on 23 October 2003, CCorp's restructuring was approved by 50 votes to 34 using the one vote per one clearing member formula which had been retained for 'big' issues such as changes to the clearing house's articles of incorporation. The outcome was a sign that some of the smaller clearing members firms voted with the large, mainly Wall Street-based FCMs. One explanation is that they backed the restructuring as a hedge in case Eurex's US venture should prove a success. The dominance of Wall Street firms in the future governance of CCorp became more obvious when 39 clearing members, most of them smaller 'locals' or commodity traders, cashed out after changes were approved.

Over the 2004 New Year holiday, the CBOT successfully shifted its US Treasury derivatives contracts to the CME clearing division. The move completed a process begun in late November. The migration was a significant technical achievement that required CCorp to cooperate closely with the CME and CBOT. That it went without a hitch showed how the underlying ethics of the clearing business were intact despite the infighting in Chicago. CCorp put the integrity of the market before considerations about its own uncertain future.

In January 2004, Eurex US took over BrokerTec Futures Exchange, which had suspended trading operations in November 2003. By the time it closed, BrokerTec Futures Exchange had lost what little share it had grabbed of the CBOT's Treasury futures franchise, having split from the BrokerTec Global bond broking business, which was acquired by ICAP, the inter-dealer broking firm.

Eurex's acquisition of BrokerTec Futures Exchange resulted in 17 US financial institutions, including a heavy representation of Wall Street investment banks, taking a 20% minority stake in Eurex US. CFTC approval for Eurex US's electronic futures exchange followed shortly afterwards, early in February.

[14] The Clearing Corp was initially known as TCC after it ceased to be the CBOT's CCP. It adopted CCorp as its abbreviated name later and the two abbreviations have coexisted since. To avoid confusion, however, the text uses CCorp as the short form of The Clearing Corp.

[15] *Financial Times* (15 October 2003), 'Eurex sues its rivals in Chicago: Open warfare breaks out over plans of world's largest derivatives exchange to enter the US market'.

Based in Chicago's iconic Sears Tower, Eurex opened its US operation on 8 February 2004, a month after the successful migration of CBOT contracts from CCorp to the CME's clearing division. But the promised 'global clearing link' between Eurex and CCorp ran into regulatory delays. An end of March 2004 target date for its launch came and went.

The CFTC approved a first phase in October 2004 that permitted the partners to offer clearing services at CCorp for US and foreign customers of certain futures and option contracts traded in Frankfurt. Obtaining regulatory approval for the all important second phase, however, proved difficult. In March 2005, Eurex was still submitting papers to the CFTC for approval of its plans to open up the US Treasury derivatives market to transatlantic clearing with use of a common collateral pool and contracts fungible on both sides of the Atlantic Ocean.

In June 2005, five weeks after a management upheaval in Frankfurt that forced the resignation of Werner Seifert, Deutsche Börse's chief executive, Eurex announced it would no longer market US Treasury products – the business that it had sought to take from CBOT. By the end of 2005, Ferscha had quit the Deutsche Börse group. On 27 July 2006, Deutsche Börse sold a 70% stake in Eurex US (by now renamed US Futures Exchange) to the Man Group PLC, a UK-based financial group.

In the meantime, the CBOT trumpeted the success of its common clearing link with the CME with CBOT chairman Charles Carey putting the savings it had achieved at US$1.8 billion in March 2005.[16]

Although Eurex's challenge to the CBOT failed, it exposed the uncompetitive nature of the US futures business. In October 2003, while Eurex US's application for CFTC approval of its electronic exchange was still pending, the CBOT announced cuts of 54% in transaction fees for members and 20% for non-members. A few months later, it reduced its fees for the electronic trading of US Treasuries still further, giving members a six-month fee waiver and cutting non-member fees for options on futures by about 65%. It also liberalised membership requirements so that more firms could qualify as members to benefit from the lower fees.

Shortly after Eurex abandoned the US Treasury market in 2005, the CBOT raised its fees for non-member trades by 50% and its fees for electronic trades from 3 to 5 cents a contract, highlighting the downside of the withdrawal of competition. In July 2006, the CBOT increased its clearing fees for its financial futures contracts. Further increases in exchange fees for non-member trading of Treasuries followed in October 2006.[17]

The CBOT followed the example of the CME and demutualised, floating its shares in the autumn of 2005. The two exchanges moved closer together, building on the experience of common clearing and their battles against Eurex. In October 2006, they agreed to merge. The CME was the dominant partner, offering US$8 billion for its older and previously more prestigious rival.

The all-Chicago deal was completed in July 2007, paid for by CME shares and helped along by the cosy relationship between Duffy, the CME chairman, and Carey, his CBOT colleague.

However, the deal was sealed only after the CME had been obliged to raise the value of its offer to around US$11.5 billion to fend off a counterbid from the Atlanta-based Intercontinental Exchange (ICE) energy exchange and clearing group. The intrusion of this ambitious and fast-growing company in the otherwise amicable nuptials of the two Chicago exchanges did the

[16] *Financial Times* (15 March 2005), 'Interview: Charles Carey, Chicago Board of Trade'.

[17] This summary of fee changes draws on US Department of Justice (31 January 2008), 'Comments of the US Department of Justice in response to the Department of Treasury's request for comments on the Regulatory Structure Associated with Financial Institutions', which obtained its information from press reports published between October 2003 and August 2006.

CBOT's members a favour by extracting extra value from the CME takeover that otherwise would have gone unrealised. It also signalled in dramatic fashion the arrival of a new force in CCP clearing, both nationally and internationally.

The CME Group was on the acquisition trail again about six months after taking over the CBOT. In January 2008, it bid for New York Mercantile Exchange Holdings (Nymex), a New York-based energy and commodities exchange that had demutualised in 2006 after 135 years as a private, member-owned body.

The Clearing Corporation which emerged from the October 2003 restructuring looked strong on paper: it was capitalised at US$107 million and had a guarantee fund of some US$165.5 million. The company did not lack ambition; instead, it lacked customers. It signed contracts to clear for some small trading platforms in the course of 2004. Dutterer also initiated a shift into technology and consultancy services by buying OnExchange, a provider of software to clearing houses.

But its new business could not prevent a plunge into loss. CCorp staff was cut by a third to 100 in the first quarter of 2004 and further reductions followed. Restructuring charges meant that CCorp made losses of US$29.3 million on turnover of just US$6.7 million in 2004, its first year of operating without clearing CBOT contracts.

Dutterer retired from CCorp in March 2005. He was succeeded by Richard Jaycobs, the former CEO of OnExchange. Jaycobs also focused on technology and consulting services, reflecting his own background as former CEO of a trade processing software vendor. In June 2005, CCorp announced a plan to develop clearing and central-counterparty services for the fast growing OTC market in credit derivatives.

The proposed area of activity was well chosen. Regulators and investment banks were becoming increasingly worried about the chaotic state of back office processing in the lucrative market for credit default swaps (CDS). Recommendations for dealing with these problems were published in July 2005 by the Counterparty Risk Management Policy Group, comprising senior risk managers of leading private sector financial institutions, chaired by Gerald Corrigan, a former president of the New York Federal Reserve Bank and now a managing director of Goldman Sachs & Co.

CCorp's efforts to tackle back office processing problems in the OTC derivatives sector moved up a gear around the start of 2007. But in its shrunken state, it lacked the capacity to develop a CCP solution for the CDS market on its own.

On 20 December 2007 its ownership structure was changed once more to leave CCorp with 17 stock holders who appeared ready to support its drive to clear OTC derivatives, including CDSs.

The shareholders included 12 leading global broker-dealers;[18] three inter-dealer brokers – GFI Group, ICAP and Creditex; as well as Eurex and Markit, the financial information service provider. The tally of 12 broker dealers on CCorp's share register gave an indication of how far the numbers of internationally significant clearing members had shrunk since the start of the decade.

When in 2008, demands for CDS clearing intensified, CCorp required the financial and technical support of ICE to meet the challenge. Until that time, however, the investment banks that backed BrokerTec Futures Exchange, Eurex US and BOTCC in the clearing battles against the CME and CBOT were net beneficiaries from the years of conflict, despite the rise

[18] Bank of America, Bear Stearns, Citigroup, Credit Suisse, Deutsche Bank, Goldman Sachs, JP Morgan, Lehman Brothers, Merrill Lynch, MF Global, Morgan Stanley, UBS.

in exchange and clearing fees from the summer of 2005. What they lost from supporting the challengers to the Chicago exchanges, they gained from the fee cuts adopted previously by the CBOT and CME to see off the competition.

13.6 VERTICAL INTEGRATION AND OPEN INTEREST

Eurex's failure in the US was a sobering experience for the German-Swiss exchange and its clearing partner. Even at its peak, Eurex US was unable to gain more than 5% of the US Treasury futures market. The Clearing Corporation lost 90% of its business, and was loss making from the first quarter of 2004.

There were clearly some Chicago-specific factors behind the debacle. The friendship between the chairmen of the CME and CBOT counted for a lot when faced with a challenge from out of town. It contrasted with the often poisonous relations that existed between top management of the two exchanges in previous periods when cooperation was on the agenda.

The speed with which the CFTC dealt with regulatory filings from the CBOT and CME contrasted starkly with the many delays that affected applications from Eurex. At the very least, the disparity suggested that years of assiduous lobbying of lawmakers and regulators in Washington by the Chicago exchanges had not been wasted.

The relationship forged between the CBOT and BOTCC in the mid-1920s was unable to cope with the gradual divergence of interests between the local CBOT members and the investment banks that dominated financial futures trading, often at arm's length from Wall Street rather than as active members of the Chicago futures trading fraternity.

By contrast, the move to common clearing helped build trust between the CBOT and CME, as CBOT chairman Carey later acknowledged.[19]

But there were also wider lessons for those in the business of clearing. In the 1970s, the CCP was regarded as a back office operational burden. Thirty years later, it was an important part of the business chain from trading to completion of trades.

Scale was important. The common clearing link between the CME and CBOT produced tangible financial benefits for CBOT and CME members without compromising the security of their investments.

Common clearing and the subsequent merger of CME and CBOT gave a substantial boost to the vertical integration of exchanges in the US and around the world and an extra fillip to the ambitious expansion of the CME Group.

The value embedded in CCPs was seen to accrue very obviously to exchange groups that operated vertical silos. That value could be realised through demutualisation. The CME was the dominant partner in the eventual merger with CBOT partly because it demutualised first. Its share price soared 10-fold in the three years that followed the initial public offering of its shares at US$35 in 2002. Using its own shares as currency, CME Group was able to add even more to its competitive advantage with its 2008 acquisition of Nymex, which brought its share of US futures markets to about 98%. As Figure 13.1 shows, the CME and Eurex groups became rivals for global leadership among futures exchanges.

The completion of the CME-CBOT and CME-Nymex deals, and the fact that they were nodded through by the US Justice Department which was responsible for competition policy in the US, had an impact beyond US territory.

[19] *Financial Times* (FT.Com) (17 October 2006), 'Merger bolsters Chicago's business profile'.

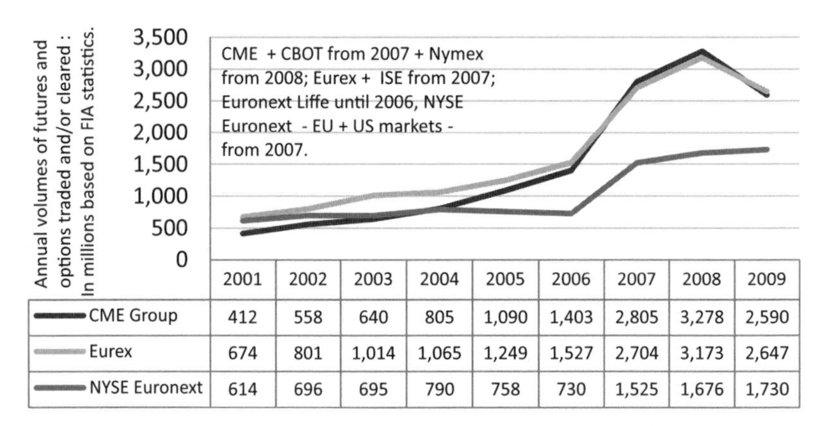

	2001	2002	2003	2004	2005	2006	2007	2008	2009
CME Group	412	558	640	805	1,090	1,403	2,805	3,278	2,590
Eurex	674	801	1,014	1,065	1,249	1,527	2,704	3,173	2,647
NYSE Euronext	614	696	695	790	758	730	1,525	1,676	1,730

Figure 13.1 CME Group versus Eurex: Annual volume in exchange-traded derivatives

In an increasingly globalised market place, the for-profit, publicly-quoted CME Group was seen to enjoy a competitive advantage vis-a-vis other quoted exchange groups that did not control their CCP clearing facilities. The CME could leverage the value of its clearing division through its share price. In Europe, ICE and Euronext.liffe – unlike Eurex – were unable to do this because they had no proprietary control over the CCP that cleared their contracts traded in Europe.

The benefits that were perceived to accrue to exchanges from the concentration of open interest registered in captive or allied clearing houses was one factor behind a race towards vertical integration among other exchange groups that gathered pace from the middle of the decade.

The transfer of the CBOT's open interest to the CME was an industry-changing event. Although it required a supportive regulator, prepared – some would argue – to play fast and loose with the legal niceties of the case, the transfer set a precedent.

It doomed Eurex's bid to grab the US Treasuries business of the CBOT, its venerable Chicago rival, and the hopes of CCorp that it might shrug off the loss of its biggest client of the previous 78 years. As we shall see in Chapter 17, it inspired ICE and Euronext.liffe in Europe to claim for themselves the benefits of the open interest of the derivatives contracts registered in the books of LCH.Clearnet, their CCP.

14
Risks and Opportunities

14.1 THE NEED TO MITIGATE RISK

The first decade of the 21st century began by delivering continuing prosperity, but it was soon punctuated by violent disruptions.

The dot.com boom and bust showed how stresses could spread quickly throughout the increasingly complex and intertwined global economy.

The 9/11 terrorist attacks on New York and Washington brought to the fore issues of operational risk, business continuity and the resilience of established infrastructures for CCPs and their users.

The bankruptcy of Enron, coming soon after the passing of the Commodity Futures Modernization Act, gave an impetus to clearing for OTC energy markets in the US, with ICE, the electronic market place, offering cleared contracts in partnership with LCH.Clearnet's London CCP before going on to acquire and develop its own clearing houses.

The economic benefits of CCP clearing continued to promote change in Chicago, helping supercharge the CME Group to its control of 98% of exchange traded futures in the US, for example. At the same time, the risk mitigating capabilities of clearing houses was increasingly prized.

Responding to globalisation, regulators from central banks and securities commissions drew up minimum international standards for CCPs that set benchmarks for operators and highlighted the different categories of risk that they faced.

The rapid growth of OTC trading, especially in the credit derivatives area, created post-trade processing problems that prompted action by policy makers and responses from financial infrastructure providers, including DTCC.

But it was only after the start of the financial crisis in June 2007 that specific plans emerged for CCPs to clear credit derivatives. Although these efforts were dogged by delays – motivated in part by the profitability of OTC derivatives trading for investment banks and other market participants – moves underway by the time of Lehman Brothers' collapse helped to provide the foundations for future progress.

This chapter touches on each of these developments, after which the remaining three chapters in Part IV of this book shall focus on the development of central counterparty clearing in Europe following the introduction of the euro.

14.2 OPERATIONAL RISK AND 9/11

Shortly after the fall of Berlin Wall in 1989, Francis Fukuyama, a US academic, proclaimed the 'end of history' by which he meant 'the end point of mankind's ideological evolution and the universalisation of Western liberal democracy'.[1] Less than 12 years later, history came back with a vengeance out of a clear blue sky on a crisp September morning.

The terrorist attacks that destroyed the World Trade Center on 11 September 2001 took place 10 blocks away from DTCC headquarters and wiped out communications links for many financial firms in Lower Manhattan. 9/11 underlined the need for financial infrastructures to have robust protection against operational risks ranging from extreme terrorist attacks through cyber attacks to systems failures and human error.

Equity markets were closed on 9/11 but DTCC had to continue operating. 'We still had the obligation in a T+3 environment to complete the settlement of trading that occurred on the prior Friday and Monday,' notes Stuart Goldstein, head of DTCC's Corporate Communications and Public Affairs. Failure to complete settlement could have resulted in a liquidity crisis. So although the streets in Lower Manhattan were sealed off by the police, '500 people stayed in this building for three days. On 9/11 we settled US$280 billion in trading obligations. In the remainder of that week, we settled US$1.8 trillion. That's what allowed the markets to reopen the following week.'[2]

DTCC's ability to cope with massive unexpected events was further in evidence two years later when the company continued operating through the 'Northeast Blackout', which cut power supplies to an estimated 45 million people in eight US states, including New York, and 10 million in Ontario, Canada, during the afternoon of 14 August 2003. As a sign of the importance now accorded to operational risk, DTCC decided after 9/11 to build a new operations centre in Tampa, Florida, to diversify capabilities away from New York. It also operates a remote data centre in a secret location to safeguard the continuity of US capital market operations.

The CFTC, whose New York regional office was destroyed in the attack on 1 World Trade Center, was the first US federal regulator to publish a reaction to 9/11. Reporting in March 2002, it urged CCPs to take account of all operational needs when planning for emergencies and providing back up facilities and to be prepared for floods, earthquakes, communication failures and prolonged power outages as well as terrorist attacks.[3]

Presciently, the CFTC alerted CCPs to problems that surfaced during the financial crisis of 2007–9. Foreshadowing the Lehman default and the Madoff investment scandal, it warned of

> the bankruptcy or other collapse of a key institution, particularly one that creates a ripple or 'domino' effect on other market participants; and fraud and other malfeasance on a sufficiently large scale to undermine the credibility of one or more key markets or market participants.

It also urged the industry to bear in mind the continuing globalisation of markets and 'the critically important but not always obvious interconnections among entities that present the threat of network failures in mission-critical functions'.

In June 2002, US private sector firms set up the Financial Services Sector Coordinating Council (FSSCC) for Critical Infrastructure Protection and Homeland Security. Recognised by the US Treasury and including banks, insurance companies, exchanges, financial infrastructure providers and trade associations, the FSSCC's task was to coordinate and share best practice for dealing with external events that might disrupt the business of finance. Ten months later,

---

[1] Fukuyama, Francis (1992), *The End of History and the Last Man*. Fukuyama first outlined his thesis in a 1989 essay and expanded on it in his 1992 book.

[2] Conversation with the author, 1 February 2008.

[3] CFTC (11 March 2002), 'Summary report of the Commodity Futures Trading Commission on the Futures Industry Response to September 11th'.

the leading US financial regulators issued a joint paper spelling out the key business continuity objectives for all financial firms.[4] Regulators around the globe followed suit, issuing their own business continuity advice and encouraging financial infrastructure providers to boost their operational capabilities.

On 7 July 2005, terrorist attacks in London underlined the importance of CCPs having effective business continuity plans in place. One of four terrorist bombs detonated in London that day exploded in the underground railway station adjoining LCH.Clearnet's head office. With the surrounding area designated a crime scene, the CCP implemented a disaster recovery plan that entailed evacuating its building and transferring key staff to a fully equipped back-up site in another part of London. Despite disruption in large parts of the City, the clearing house continued its operations as normal.

14.3 INTERNATIONAL STANDARDS FOR CCPs

9/11 focused regulators' attention on operational risks in critical financial infrastructures just as concerns about the concentration of risk in post-trade organisations such as CSDs and CCPs were beginning to grow internationally among central banks and supervisors.

In November 2001, the CPSS-IOSCO group of experts from the central banks of the Group of 10 countries and IOSCO member states published 19 recommendations for minimum standards for securities settlement systems.[5] They followed up this work by agreeing 15 recommendations for CCPs in November 2004, summarised in Box 14.1. These amounted to international standards for CCP risk management aimed at preventing failures that could disrupt payments and securities settlement systems and the overall safety of financial markets.[6]

Box 14.1: CPSS-IOSCO recommendations for CCPs

1. *Legal risk:* A CCP should have a well founded, transparent and enforceable legal framework for each aspect of its activities in all relevant jurisdictions.
2. *Participation requirements:* A CCP should require participants to have sufficient financial resources and robust operational capacity to meet obligations arising from participation in the CCP. A CCP should have procedures in place to monitor that participation requirements are met on an ongoing basis. A CCP's participation requirements should be objective, publicly disclosed and permit fair and open access.
3. *Measurement and management of credit exposures:* A CCP should measure its credit exposures to its participants at least once a day. Through margin requirements, other risk control mechanisms or a combination of both, a CCP should limit its exposures to potential losses from defaults by its participants in normal market conditions so that the operations of the CCP would not be disrupted and non-defaulting participants would not be exposed to losses that they cannot anticipate or control.
4. *Margin requirements:* If a CCP relies on margin requirements to limit its credit exposures to participants, those requirements should be sufficient to cover potential exposures in normal market conditions. The models and parameters used in setting margin requirements should be risk-based and reviewed regularly.

[4] Federal Reserve Board (7 April 2003), 'Interagency paper on sound practices to strengthen the resilience of the US financial system', Office of Comptroller of the Currency, SEC.

[5] Bank for International Settlements (November 2001), 'Recommendations for securities settlement systems', CPSS-IOSCO.

[6] Bank for International Settlements (November 2004), 'Recommendations for central counterparties', CPSS-IOSCO.

5. *Financial resources:* A CCP should maintain sufficient financial resources to withstand, at a minimum, a default by the participant to which it has the largest exposure in extreme but plausible market conditions.
6. *Default procedures:* A CCP's default procedures should be clearly stated, and they should ensure that the CCP can take timely action to contain losses and liquidity pressures and to continue meeting its obligations. Key aspects of the default procedures should be publicly available.
7. *Custody and investment risks:* A CCP should hold assets in a manner whereby risk of loss or of delay in its access to them is minimised. Assets invested by a CCP should be held in instruments with minimal credit, market and liquidity risks.
8. *Operational risk:* A CCP should identify sources of operational risk and minimise them through the development of appropriate systems, controls and procedures. Systems should be reliable and secure, and have adequate, scalable capacity. Business continuity plans should allow for timely recovery of operations in fulfilment of a CCP's obligations.
9. *Money settlements:* A CCP should employ money settlement arrangements that eliminate or strictly limit its settlement bank risks, that is, its credit and liquidity risks from the use of banks to effect money settlements with its participants. Fund transfers to a CCP should be final when effected.
10. *Physical deliveries:* A CCP should clearly state its obligations with respect to physical deliveries. The risks from these obligations should be identified and managed.
11. *Risks in links between CCPs:* CCPs that establish links either cross-border or domestically to clear trades should evaluate the potential sources of risks that can arise, and ensure that the risks are managed prudently on an ongoing basis. There should be a framework for cooperation and coordination between the relevant regulators and overseers.
12. *Efficiency:* While maintaining safe and secure operations, CCPs should be cost-effective in meeting the requirements of participants.
13. *Governance:* Governance arrangements for a CCP should be clear and transparent to fulfil public interest requirements and to support the objectives of owners and participants. In particular, they should promote the effectiveness of a CCP's risk-management procedures.
14. *Transparency:* A CCP should provide market participants with sufficient information for them to identify and evaluate accurately the risks and costs associated with using its services.
15. *Regulation and oversight:* A CCP should be subject to transparent and effective regulation and oversight. In both a domestic and international context, central banks and securities regulators should cooperate with each other and with other relevant authorities.

Source: Committee on Payments and Settlement Systems (CPSS) and Technical Committee of the International Organisation of Securities Commissions (IOSCO) (2004), 'Recommendations for Central Counterparties', Basel, Bank for International Settlements, November. Reproduced by permission of the Bank for International Settlements.

In its report, the CPSS-IOSCO group also gave an overview of the different types of risk a CCP would encounter. These were far more wide-ranging than the counterparty credit risk that CCPs were created to mitigate or the operational risk that leapt to prominence after 9/11.

A CCP could, for example, face:

- liquidity risks if a participant was late in settling obligations;
- settlement bank risk should there be a failure of the bank used for money settlements between the CCP and its members;
- custody risk should the custodian holding the collateral posted as margin fail;
- legal risk should the laws or regulations where the CCP operated not support its rules and contracts or the property rights associated with the CCP.

Legal risk could occur if bankruptcy administrators failed to recognise a CCP's rights, as seemed possible at times in the experience of LCH.Clearnet immediately after the default of Lehman Brothers. Legal risk could also pose some especially tricky problems in a cross-border context where links existed between CCPs.

In summary form, the 15 CPSS-IOSCO recommendations for CCPs covered less than two pages of A4 paper and appeared in some cases to be statements of the obvious. But they were emblematic of a ratcheting up of supervisory interest in CCPs, notably by central banks.

The recommendations set benchmarks that national supervisors could use when assessing the risk-management standards of their CCPs. They formed the basis of later recommendations for CCPs in the European Union from the European System of Central Banks and the Committee of European Securities Regulators (ESCB-CESR).

The recommendations were elaborated in considerable detail in the body of the 69-page CPSS-IOSCO report. For example, the detailed notes for recommendation 5 concerning 'financial resources' gave CCP operators a handy guide on stress testing and also made clear that clearing house operators should be prepared for much worse circumstances than the minimum outlined in the headline recommendation. Hence: 'Planning by a CCP should consider the potential for two or more participants to default in a short time frame, resulting in a combined exposure greater than the single largest exposure.'

On the potentially thorny issue of governance, recommendation 13 put particular stress on the role of the board and the objectives it set for management. Boards, the report underlined, 'should contain suitable expertise and take account of all relevant interests'.

The report also highlighted the dangers for risk management of conflicts of interest between a CCP's owners, managers, clearing members and the exchanges and clearing platforms that it served. Its answer was to insist that a CCP's risk managers were sufficiently independent with a clear demarcation of reporting lines for risk management and other CCP operations. 'In many cases, this may involve the creation of an independent risk committee,' it suggested.

14.4 CONFLICT AND INNOVATION IN ASIA

The importance of vigilance and good corporate governance is highlighted in a cautionary tale from Japan. In April 2005 an investment fund controlled by Yoshiaki Murakami, one of Japan's few activist investors, acquired a 10% stake in the recently listed Osaka Securities Exchange (OSE). As the exchange's biggest shareholder, the fund put pressure on the board to raise its dividend sharply.

The Osaka exchange had an in-house CCP that enabled it to function as Japan's leading derivatives market. The policies of the investment fund would have meant the exchange 'cashing out' some of the financial resources set aside for use by the CCP in the event of clearing member's default.

The case brought to the fore in an acute form some of the conflicts of interest to beset CCPs following demutualisation. It was resolved indirectly and in stages. In August 2005, Japan's Financial Services Agency put a cap on Murakami's ambitions by refusing to allow his funds to acquire more than 20% in the OSE. Late in December, no doubt after behind the scenes manoeuvring, it was announced that Murakami's fund had sold all its holdings in the OSE. The following year, Murakami was prosecuted on an unrelated insider trading charge that resulted in a fine and a jail sentence in July 2007.

The moral of this case, according to Tomoyuki Shimoda, director of the Institute for Monetary and Economic Studies of the Bank of Japan, was that there should be an 'optimal degree of intimacy' between CCPs and demutualised exchanges when designing governance structures.[7] This would include a separate reporting line for CCP risk managers, the explicit earmarking of financial resources for risk-management purposes and clear policies covering the contribution of shareholders in loss sharing arrangements.

The Osaka incident also brought into focus the changes affecting financial infrastructures including CCPs in the Asia-Pacific region in the early years of this century.

Asia's financial and economic crisis of 1997–8 resulted in a temporary slowdown to infrastructure developments in the region.

CCPs were well established in the Asia-Pacific region before the crisis, and in some cases were leading innovators. The Sydney Futures Exchange (SFE) achieved some notable 'firsts' in the early years of financial futures including the world's first cash settled futures contract in 1980, which was cleared by ICCH. Thanks largely to the work of Wal Reisch, the Sydney office of ICCH was a pioneer in the technical development of clearing systems in the 1980s.

Another achievement in the region was the mutual offset agreement of 1984 between the CME and its protégé SIMEX, the Singapore International Monetary Exchange, which enabled selected contracts to be offset at either exchange. India's stock exchanges – the Mumbai-based Bombay Stock Exchange and National Stock Exchange of India – had CCPs to clear and guarantee trades some years before most leading European equity markets.[8]

But it was in the US and Europe that the big developments in clearing took place around the close of the 20th century. The merger of NSCC and DTC to form DTCC in 1999 created a continent-wide giant for clearing and settling securities with global aspirations. In Europe, clearing houses such as LCH, Clearnet and Eurex were beginning to explore business opportunities beyond their national frontiers. In Asia, still recovering from the crisis of 1997–8, CCPs were nationally focused in a region that was more fragmented economically than the US or Europe.

Even so, when the CCP12 group of leading clearing organisations was founded in 2001, four of its 13 members came from the Asia-Pacific region and Reisch, by now the executive vice president of Hong Kong Exchanges and Clearing, became vice chairman of the group and was designated to take over as chairman after a year.[9] Catch-up had begun and a rapid consolidation at the national level of trading and clearing capabilities in the Asia-Pacific region was underway.

During 1999 and 2000, the Hong Kong stock and futures exchanges demutualised and merged with the Hong Kong Securities Clearing Co. (HKSCC) under a holding company,

[7] Shimoda, Tomoyuki (2006), 'Exchanges and CCPs: Communication, governance and risk management'.

[8] Respectively, Bank of India Shareholding Ltd, founded in 1989, and the National Securities Clearing Corp Ltd (not to be confused with the US NSCC), which began clearing in April 1996.

[9] The other three Asia-Pacific members were the Australian Stock Exchange Ltd (ASX), the Singapore Exchange Ltd (SGX)/the Central Depository (PTE) Ltd and the Tokyo Stock Exchange.

Hong Kong Exchanges and Clearing Ltd, known by its acronym HKEx. In Singapore, SIMEX and the Stock Exchange of Singapore combined to form Singapore Exchange Ltd (SGX), which became a public company in November 2000.

The merger of four domestic stock and derivatives markets created the Korea Exchange (KRX) in January 2005, with a unified CCP bringing economies of scale. The huge popularity of options and futures trading among retail customers in South Korea placed the Korea Exchange among the busiest derivatives exchanges in the world in terms of numbers of contracts traded and cleared.

In Australia, the completion in July 2006 of a merger between the Australian Stock Exchange (ASX) and SFE Corporation brought the country's CCPs together in the Australian Securities Exchange, which continued to operate under the ASX brand.

The same period also saw some significant moves solely at the clearing level. They included:

- The founding of the Clearing Corporation of India (CCIL) in April 2001 to provide clearing and settlement of trades in government securities, money market instruments and foreign exchange products.
- The consolidation in 2002 of the clearing houses of Japan's five stock exchanges in Japan Securities Clearing Corp. following the model of NSCC in the US. Owned 86.3% by the Tokyo Stock Exchange and 12.9% by the Osaka Securities Exchange, JSCC began providing cross-market clearing for stocks and fixed interest securities from January 2003 and CCP services for derivatives traded on the Tokyo Stock Exchange from February 2004.
- The launching in May 2006 of SGX AsiaClear, the first platform in Asia to provide CCP clearing for OTC derivatives, starting with oil and freight.

The rising importance of Asian CCPs in the globalised world was marked in April 2008, when JSCC hosted CCP12's second 'global dialogue' meeting since 2001 in Tokyo. By this time, CCP12's membership had expanded to 20. With seven Asian members[10] plus ASX, CCP12 included more CCP organisations from the Asia-Pacific area than from any other region in the world.

In the case of CCIL of India, catering for the specific needs of a fast growing emerging country yielded a notable innovation: the provision of a CCP to clear virtually all foreign exchange trades between banks in US dollars and Indian rupees.

The need for clearing arose because the time difference between market hours for currency trading in India and the US precluded settlement of trades on a payment-versus-payment (PvP) basis and therefore exposed traders to settlement and counterparty risk. This combination of risk was not covered by CLS Bank, the specialised institution set up to manage settlement of foreign exchange trades. One of the first goals of the newly established CCIL was the development of a CCP for interbank trades in rupees and dollars to protect traders over two working days to settlement.

The system began operating in November 2002 after approval by the Reserve Bank of India and the Federal Reserve Bank of New York and was refined in 2004. It resulted in a dramatic fall in counterparty risk, a big drop in payments transactions and sharply reduced back-office costs for market participants. According to CCIL, the system of novating foreign exchange contracts reduced principal risk for participants by 95% to 98% and had the added

[10] The seven Asian members attending the Tokyo meeting of CCP12 were the Clearing Corporation of India, HKEx, JSCC, Korea Exchange, National Securities Clearing Corp Ltd (of India), SGX/the Central Depository (PTE) Ltd and TSE.

benefit – important in a huge emerging economy such as India – of allowing smaller or less capitalised entities 'to deal with all in the market on near normal terms'.[11]

Following the Lehman Brothers bankruptcy, US law made provision for the mandatory clearing of certain foreign exchange contracts, albeit subject to US Treasury discretion.

14.5 ENRON, ICE AND CLEARING OTC ENERGY DERIVATIVES

It's an ill wind that blows nobody any good. The bankruptcy of Enron in December 2001 provided the perfect opportunity for a former power plant developer based far from the financial centres of New York and Chicago to build a multinational business providing electronic energy-trading platforms and clearing services from next to nothing.

Jeffrey Sprecher formed IntercontinentalExchange (ICE) in May 2000. In less than a decade ICE was running electronic markets for contracts in energy, farm products, equity indices, foreign exchange and credit derivatives with three futures exchanges, two OTC markets and five central counterparty clearing houses providing integrated execution and clearing.

As befits a former racing car driver, Sprecher is a dynamic and forceful character given to taking calculated risks. While some competitors have found him abrasive, employees speak warmly of how he encourages and inspires team effort. There is a thoughtful and reflective side to Sprecher which is evident when he speaks about the challenges facing ICE and the business environment in which it operates. He has displayed a talent for superimposing strategic vision on ventures that were sometimes opportunist.

In 1999, Sprecher was the owner and CEO of Continental Power Exchange (CPEX), a small Atlanta-based technology company that he acquired in 1997 and which linked about 40 electric utilities by means of a hard-wired network. Previously, as a power plant operator, he had been unable to buy and sell natural gas and electricity at market prices because of a lack of transparent trading opportunities in the US OTC market. Using the Internet, he determined to plug that gap and turned CPEX into an online electronic power exchange. He attracted 13 of the biggest energy traders – names such as Goldman Sachs, Deutsche Bank, Morgan Stanley and BP Amoco – as users and shareholders and launched ICE in August 2000 as a neutral platform for OTC energy contracts in the North American market outside California.

The launch of ICE bore witness to Sprecher's vision, entrepreneurial flair, energy and skills as a leader and salesman. He was also fortunate in his timing.

The Internet was going mainstream. In 1999, Enron had launched an online trading platform that got people used to the idea of trading electronically but fell short of being a proper exchange because Enron was the sole counterparty to other traders. President Clinton signed the Commodity Futures Modernization Act (CFMA) in December 2000 which allowed 'exempt commercial markets' for energy products and other contracts traded off exchange and expanded the scope for companies to clear OTC derivatives contracts that were traded bilaterally.

And then Enron went bust, creating a widespread demand for clearing in a market previously dominated by large merchant energy companies such as Enron and a few big investment banks that were happy to trade OTC. Replacing Enron were new entrants including hedge funds, other investment banks and their proprietary trading desks. They entered the market at a time of volatile price movements, heightened international tension and doubts about the financial solidity of some counterparties. They needed risk-management services and were used to clearing.

[11] Roy, Siddhartha (2006), 'India's experiment with a new settlement system for its domestic foreign exchange market', http://www.ccilindia.com/RSCH_ATCL.html (accessed 9 December 2010). Roy is the chief risk officer of CCIL.

Clearing gave new entrants access to the US energy market without their having to reach bilateral agreements with other market participants. They could also benefit from the anonymity that clearing confers on market participants.

Sprecher responded to these needs in two ways. He added a regulated, international futures market to ICE's portfolio of businesses by buying London's International Petroleum Exchange (IPE) for US$130 million in July 2001. This was the first step of a strategy to make ICE an international brand. In 2002, ICE also started offering to clear OTC energy contracts.

In each case, ICE's clearing partner was LCH. It had been the CCP for the IPE since its establishment in 1981. It also had experience clearing OTC contracts through its SwapClear and RepoClear businesses and in October 2001 was recognised by the CFTC as America's first offshore Derivatives Clearing Organisation under the CFMA.

Relations between ICE and LCH turned sour some six years later when ICE terminated its contract with LCH.Clearnet and created ICE Clear Europe in London to clear its own contracts and credit derivatives. But early in the decade, LCH played a key role in supporting ICE and helping the young marketplace develop.

ICE was not alone in developing clearing for US OTC energy markets. In May 2002, Nymex, the New York Mercantile Exchange, launched ClearPort to offer clearing for OTC oil, gas and electricity contracts. As with ICE's clearing initiative for OTC energy contracts, ClearPort was well-timed to benefit from the Enron collapse.

Both offerings took time to gain traction. It was only in 2004 that clearing began to develop strongly as a business for both companies.

Although both Nymex and ICE brought clearing to the US OTC energy market, their products differed in design and attracted different types of client. ICE integrated clearing and trading processes on the same screen while at Nymex, which operated a trading floor as well as offering clearing services for OTC contracts, trading and clearing were not integrated.

The Nymex system appealed to voice brokers operating in the OTC energy market who feared that they would be disintermediated by ICE's electronic offering, which was strongly backed by the big investment banks that had helped Sprecher launch ICE.

The two clearing solutions also differed in their treatment of the contracts once they were novated. The ICE contracts remained OTC instruments after they were cleared by LCH. With ClearPort, the OTC contracts were 'futurised' and converted into exchange-traded futures contracts. Although this distinction had little practical effect for clearing house clients on a day-to-day basis, it provided investors using Nymex's ClearPort with some additional protections in the event of bankruptcy of a clearing member.

In one important respect, ICE came to feel that it was at a disadvantage vis-a-vis Nymex and ClearPort. Nymex had its own clearing house and was able to increase the number of OTC contracts qualifying for clearing at a much faster rate than ICE, which depended on LCH. This caused tensions between LCH and ICE that culminated in ICE terminating its relationship with LCH.Clearnet in 2008. ClearPort, meanwhile, became a jewel in the crown of Nymex and was adopted for OTC clearing by the CME Group after its acquisition of Nymex, also in 2008.

14.6 OTC PROBLEMS

While clearing made significant inroads into North America's OTC energy markets after the Enron bankruptcy, there was no equivalent impetus to bring CCPs to other OTC derivatives markets.

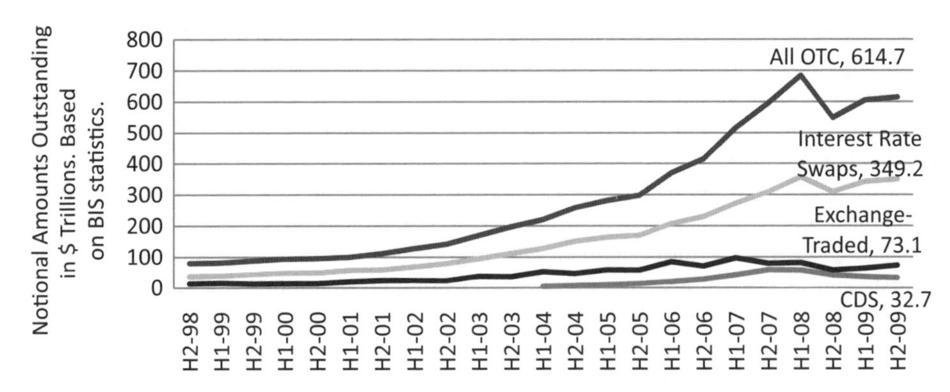

Figure 14.1 Global OTC and exchange-traded derivatives markets 1998–2009

Certainly, the CFTC saw no reason to alter the CFMA's exclusion of OTC transactions from regulation following Enron. Speaking in July 2003, James E. Newsome, CFTC chairman, warned against 'the imposition of additional, prescriptive or burdensome regulations that could adversely affect legitimate activity'.[12]

The hands off approach was similarly in evidence when Refco, a US major commodities and derivatives broker, filed for Chapter 11 bankruptcy in October 2005, a week after disclosing that its former chief executive had hidden US$430 million of debt; and when Aramanth Advisors, a large hedge fund, reported in September 2006 that it lost US$6 billion of capital from trading futures and other natural gas derivatives.

But although the overall thrust of policy was not to interfere in OTC markets, there were areas where the authorities felt obliged to intervene and involve users while, in some cases, financial infrastructure providers were ahead of the regulators in devising solutions to pressing problems.

The OTC derivatives markets were still growing very rapidly after 2000 as shown in Figure 14.1. Credit derivatives – a relatively recent innovation – were growing especially strongly from a low base. According to the International Swaps and Derivatives Association (ISDA), outstanding credit derivatives contracts jumped by 48% to US$12.43 trillion in the six months to the end of June 2005 when the total was 128% higher than a year earlier.

Also hedge funds were much bigger players in the OTC markets and had introduced new practices. In particular, they tended to exit positions by novating contracts through trade assignments. This meant that instead of negotiating the termination of a contract or entering into an offsetting deal, funds would step out of the contract and substitute a new counterparty in place of the original, sometimes without informing the original partner to the trade.[13]

As the OTC markets still relied on manual operations and fax machines for much of their back-office work, clearing and settlement problems accumulated. A processing backlog built up that was reminiscent of Wall Street's paperwork crisis in the 1960s. Measured in day's worth of business, the backlog of confirmations of OTC derivatives deals at large firms ranged

[12] Speaking to the Global Energy Management Institute, University of Houston, 9 July 2003.

[13] Bank for International Settlements (March 2007).

on average between 7.9 days for currency options in 2005 to 30.5 days for non-vanilla equity derivatives.

The OTC derivatives markets were becoming riskier. During the winter of 2004–5 supervisors, led by the New York Federal Reserve Bank and Britain's FSA, and some in the industry began to take note.

In February 2005, the FSA wrote to the CEOs of leading dealers in London to voice its concern over the backlogs. Around the same time, the US Federal Reserve became aware of the problem of assigning trades. Encouraged by Timothy Geithner, president of the New York Federal Reserve Bank, Gerald Corrigan, a managing director of Goldman Sachs and former head of the New York Fed, convened a group of senior risk managers from banks and broker-dealers with some hedge fund participation to investigate potential systemic risks arising from OTC markets in the increasingly complex and interconnected global financial world.

Corrigan's Counterparty Risk Management Policy Group (CRMPG) II reported in July 2005 and put forward a set of recommendations and 'guiding principles' to improve transparency and risk management. Presciently, CRMPG II urged that 'financial intermediaries and end-users of credit derivatives redouble their efforts to ensure that they fully understand the nature of their credit derivative transactions'. It highlighted the need for proper management and funding of 'all elements of financial infrastructure' including payments, settlement, netting and close-out systems. The CRMPG II report singled out 'as a matter of urgency' the need for additional resources to cope with a backlog of unsigned confirmations in the OTC market and urged that trade assignments be subject to 'the same rigorous controls and discipline as new transactions'.[14]

Geithner followed up the report by summoning 14 leading US and European investment banks and international regulators to the New York Fed in September 2005. The rapid growth of credit default swaps and their use in complex synthetic collateralised debt obligations was a matter of particular concern. The bankers pledged to cut the backlogs and improve back-office automation. Within a year, confirmations outstanding for credit derivatives fell by 70% and the percentage of trades confirmed electronically doubled to more than 80% of total trade volume.[15]

The rapid take-up partly reflected advances already underway in the product offering of infrastructure providers. In late 2003, DTCC launched Deriv/SERV to match electronically and confirm OTC derivatives contracts. Based on DTCC clearing technology, Deriv/SERV went live within nine months. Initially focused on credit default swaps (CDSs), it was later expanded to process other OTC contracts and then leveraged to provide other services.

Of these, the most notable was the Trade Information Warehouse, launched in November 2006 after eight months in development. The warehouse provided a global central registry of OTC CDS derivatives contracts. It was linked to the Deriv/SERV matching engine so that its database could be updated with new credit transactions and, during 2007, back-loaded with information on more than 2.2 million outstanding CDS contracts. The warehouse was further developed during 2007 in cooperation with CLS Bank to net and execute automatically the quarterly payments generated by CDSs and due to counterparties.

Although some time elapsed before Deriv/SERV and the warehouse gained broad acceptance in the market, they were felicitously timed developments. But, as one industry participant

[14] Counterparty Risk Management Policy Group II (25 July 2005), 'Toward greater financial stability: A private sector perspective'.
[15] According to Bank for International Settlements (March 2007).

commented, DTCC's product line-up on credit derivatives 'looked like the egg without the yolk'. Missing was a CCP.

This was not for want of trying. Late in 2007, LCH.Clearnet and DTCC made a joint proposal to the leading banks in the CDS market to build a CCP for OTC credit derivatives within nine months. The plan would have leveraged LCH.Clearnet's experience of clearing OTC interest rate swaps through SwapClear and DTCC's Trade Information Warehouse.

They were turned down. Word came back that the dealers wanted to use CCorp, the former BOTCC, which in June 2005 had announced a plan to develop clearing and central counterparty services for the OTC credit market.

Looking back, Don Donahue, chairman and CEO of DTCC, says he can understand 'why the industry tilted to others'. There was a qualitative difference in the risk-management tasks of the warehouse compared with those of a CCP for credit derivatives.[16]

In dealing with the matching, confirmation and reconciliation of positions, DTCC's Deriv/SERV subsidiary was engaged in mitigating operational risk. A CCP would be providing a trade guarantee and have to mitigate counterparty credit risk. Although DTCC had broad CCP experience in managing exposures related to stocks and various kinds of debt securities, these risks could be measured in days. The exposures related to credit derivatives are to be measured in years, which dramatically changes the risk profile.

Another consideration, reportedly stressed by US regulators, lay in the nature of the warehouse itself. It was argued that the warehouse needed to operate as a utility, with all market participants pledged to support it. If DTCC entered into competition with other infrastructure providers to supply CCP services in the credit derivatives sector, the neutrality of the warehouse could be compromised.

Others took a less charitable view. There was a strong suspicion among some clearing professionals that the CDS dealers wanted control over any proposed CCP and the criteria for its use. This was thought to be the reason why a 17-strong consortium of CDS market participants had acquired CCorp in December 2007.

CCorp was a shadow of its former self. Although it boasted that it was 'the oldest independent derivatives clearing house in the world' and claimed to be 'in a unique position to provide more innovative and customer-focused OTC and exchange traded derivatives clearing services', the former BOTCC cleared only for a few small exchanges such as the Chicago Climate Futures Exchange. Staff numbers in its downtown Chicago office had dwindled to about 40.

14.7 A CCP FOR CREDIT DERIVATIVES?

CCorp's announcement of its ownership changes spoke also of an expanded product line 'to include a centralised clearing facility for a number of OTC derivatives products'. Its first new clearing product would be in the CDS market 'beginning in early 2008'.[17] It would come not a moment too soon.

The years of the 'Great Moderation' ended during the summer of 2007. In June, two hedge funds managed by Bear Stearns and which had invested in mortgage-backed securities announced that they were having problems meeting margin calls. In July, IKB, a specialised German lender, warned of huge losses from risky property loans and had to be rescued. In

[16] Conversation with the author, 12 January 2009.

[17] CCorp (20 December 2007), 'The Clearing Corporation announces restructuring and investment by global financial institutions focused on OTC derivatives clearing', press release.

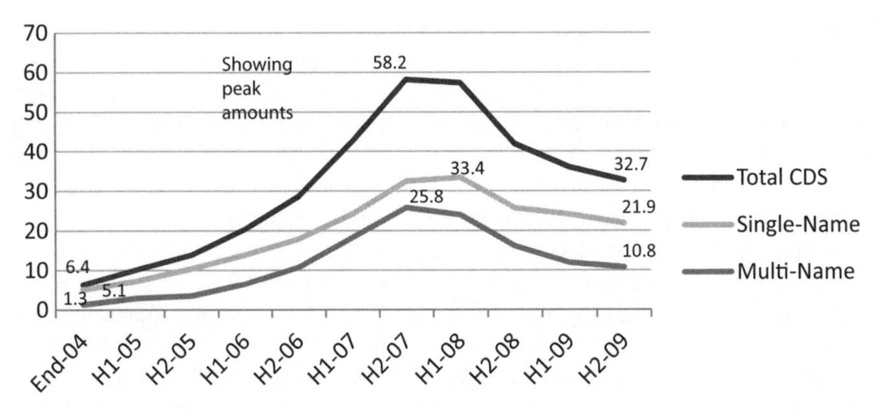

Figure 14.2 The market for Credit Default Swaps (notional amounts outstanding in $ trillions)
Source: BIS half-yearly OTC derivatives statistics.

August, BNP Paribas, the French bank, froze redemptions on three of its funds, prompting the European Central Bank to inject massive dollops of liquidity into overnight lending markets. It was the first of many such emergency central bank liquidity measures as central bankers sought to combat the tightening of credit conditions throughout the industrialised world. In September, the UK experienced its first bank run since the 1860s after an emergency cash lifeline from the Bank of England failed to reassure depositors in Northern Rock, a mortgage lender that was no longer able to finance its business through wholesale markets.

The financial turmoil of the summer of 2007 undid much of the progress achieved earlier in clearing up the backlog of credit derivatives transactions. Patrick Parkinson, a senior Federal Reserve Board official, later reported to Congress that 'CDS backlogs grew almost fivefold from June to August 2007'.[18] As Figure 14.2 shows, the notional amount of CDSs outstanding peaked around this time.

The credit crunch also put the question of counterparty risk on the agenda of bankers, regulators and policy makers. Regulators started fretting about the linkages in the OTC derivatives markets where low yields and computer-driven financial innovation during the years of the Great Moderation had produced a huge increase in the issuance of complex contracts, which found their way into the portfolios of institutional investors around the world. Sticking out like a sore thumb was the vast intertwined web of CDS positions amongst a host of bilateral counterparties, which had been fuelled by the tendency of market participants to open new offsetting positions with different counterparties rather than engage in the more complex task of unwinding existing trades.

The promised early 2008 launch of CCorp's CDS clearing product failed to materialise. The delay did nothing to quell suspicions that the investment bank dominated consortium of owners had a vested interest in holding up the launch of CCorp's credit derivatives CCP to protect the lucrative bid-offer spreads on OTC credit derivative contracts. Unclear at this stage was whether the rebooted CCorp would provide CCP services for CDSs beyond the small club of its owners for a broader marketplace.

[18] Patrick M. Parkinson, deputy director, division of research and statistics, Board of Governors of the Federal Reserve System before the US Senate subcommittee on securities, insurance and investment; committee on banking, housing and urban affairs, Washington, 9 July 2008.

That marketplace – and the club of CCorp owners – was shrinking, however. During the weekend of 15–16 March 2008, the New York Fed had to orchestrate the emergency sale of the investment bank Bear Stearns to JPMorgan Chase for a knock down price. As a counterparty to hundreds if not thousands of firms, Bear Stearns, was too interconnected to fail. It posed a threat to the financial system once it hit trouble. The problem was not just Bear Stearns' exposures but the exposures of other firms to Bear, raising the spectre of multiple defaults across financial markets had Bear Stearns been allowed to collapse.

Before the Bear Stearns weekend, there was no sign that US regulators backed CCPs as a solution for the credit derivatives problem.[19] Nor did a CCP for CDSs form any part of commitments submitted to the New York Fed by leading OTC market participants on 27 March 2008.

But when, a few weeks later, the New York Fed summoned leading OTC dealers, buy side firms and US and international supervisors to a review of the industry's strategy for dealing with the weaknesses of the operational infrastructure of the OTC market, a CCP for CDS appeared on the agenda. The measures agreed at the meeting on 9 June 2008 included 'developing a central counterparty for credit default swaps that, with a robust risk-management regime, can help reduce systemic risk'.[20]

The 9 June promise of a CCP was inspired by Timothy Geithner, president and CEO of the New York Fed. The same day, he told the Economic Club of New York that the planned new infrastructure would 'help improve the system's ability to manage the consequences of failure by a major institution'.[21]

Seven weeks later, on 31 July, the Operations Management Group (OMG) of OTC dealers and buy side institutions represented at the 9 June meeting pledged 'the formation and use of a central counterparty for index CDS trades by December 31, 2008'. The CCP would comply with CPSS-IOSCO risk-management standards. Expansion of the CCP's activities to other products would begin in 2009, according to their written promise.[22]

By this time, CCorp appeared to be making progress in creating its CCP for CDSs. In May, CCorp and DTCC announced an agreement to link CCorp's netting and risk-management processes to DTCC's Trade Information Warehouse, initially to allow CCorp and DTCC warehouse members to replace bilateral CDS agreements with guaranteed trades backed by CCorp's CCP.[23]

In July 2008, when updating a US Senate committee on its preparations for clearing credit derivatives, CCorp disclosed it was in talks about incorporating its planned CCP for CDSs as a limited purpose trust company that would be supervised by the New York Fed. The written testimony said CCorp's CCP for CDSs would be open to other participants as well as its shareholders, provided they met certain conditions. These included having: a minimum net capital of US$5 billion; a minimum long-term debt rating of 'A' from Standard & Poors; operational competence in CDSs, including an outstanding notional contract value of at least

---

[19] For example, there is no specific reference to clearing among the recommendations in the 'Policy Statement on Financial Market Developments' published by the President's Working Group on 13 March 2008. The Working Group, created in March 1988, is chaired by the US Secretary of the Treasury and includes the Chairmen of the Federal Reserve Board, the Securities and Exchange Commission, and the Commodity Futures Trading Commission.

[20] Federal Reserve Bank of New York (9 June 2008), 'Statement regarding June 9 meeting on over-the-counter derivatives'.

[21] Geithner, Timothy (9 June 2008), 'Reducing systemic risk in a dynamic financial system', Remarks at the Economic Club of New York.

[22] Operations Management Group (31 July 2008), 'Summary of OTC derivatives commitments'.

[23] CCorp and DTCC (29 May 2008), 'The Clearing Corporation and The Depository Trust & Clearing Corporation announce Credit Default Swap (CDS) Clearing Facility linked to DTCC's Trade Information Warehouse', press release.

US$500 billion; demonstrated risk-management capabilities; and membership in CDS industry bodies such as ISDA and DTCC's Deriv/SERV.[24]

Many still doubted whether CCorp could meet its commitments. As the summer of 2008 advanced, rival companies made their opening moves in the battle to clear CDS.

In June, ICE announced a deal worth US$625 million to buy Creditex, an interdealer credit derivatives broker that was developing a platform with Markit, a London-based data vendor, to compress portfolios of CDSs. Because of its ability to reduce the huge notional amount of such swaps outstanding in the market before novation, the platform, launched in August 2008, was seen as a first step towards creating a central counterparty for CDSs.

A month later, LIFFE, the London-based futures and options exchange owned by NYSE Euronext, announced plans to use Bclear, its service for clearing OTC equity derivatives, to process and clear CDSs in cooperation with LCH.Clearnet, starting with contracts based on the iTraxx European indices from the final quarter of 2008.

With the New York Fed apparently determined to support CCorp in the US, Eurex Clearing put itself forward as a eurozone champion with plans to start clearing CDSs in the first half of 2009 and so 'complement current US initiatives with a European solution'.[25]

Also in July, the Chicago-based CME Group announced a clearing service for interest rate swaps from September, fuelling speculation that it was also planning to clear credit derivatives.

Amidst the excitement, it was easy to forget that CDS clearing posed some serious challenges. In August, Gerald Corrigan surfaced once more to deliver some unpalatable truths.

Corrigan revived the Counterparty Risk Management Policy Group as CRMPG III in April 2008 to examine steps the private sector could take to reduce the chances of a re-run of the credit crisis that began the previous summer. Among the policy group's many recommendations was 'the prompt creation of a clearing corporation that would begin clearing credit default swaps in the fourth quarter of 2008'.[26]

This goal, as Corrigan acknowledged, was 'extremely ambitious' and the CRMPG III report made clear why. After briefly outlining the benefits of a 'robust CCP' for CDSs, the report stressed the 'many challenges in ensuring that a CCP is in fact robust and actually reduces risk, rather than providing merely the appearance of risk reduction'.

To be effective

- The CCP must deal only with sound and reliable counterparties, which would mean establishing 'rigorous financial requirements for participation'.
- To clear CDSs, it would have to ensure 'sufficiently transparent end-of-day pricing across the entire cleared portfolio' to set acceptable margin and guarantee fund requirements.
- The establishment of an appropriate margin and guarantee fund structure presented 'perhaps one of the greatest challenges a CCP for credit derivatives may face'. Participants might have to contribute more to the CCP should the margin and guarantee fund be insufficient to deal with clearing member defaults.
- Any CCP for CDSs should have the support of regulators and conform with the CPSS-IOSCO recommendations. That would 'require interaction with the various regulatory bodies that regulate not only the CCP itself but also clearing participants'.

[24] CCorp (9 July 2008), 'Testimony of the Clearing Corporation to the US Senate subcommittee on securities, insurance and investment; committee on banking, housing and urban affairs'.

[25] Eurex Clearing (22 July 2008), 'Eurex clearing plans to build European CCP platform for clearing services in OTC derivatives'.

[26] Counterparty Risk Management Policy Group III (6 August 2008), 'Containing systemic risk: The road to reform'.

Although CRMPG III 'strongly' recommended that the industry set up a CCP for CDSs, it left little doubt that the hurdles were formidable. A CCP for CDSs would be a step into the unknown.

On the other hand, the world financial system was thrust into a far greater unknown within a matter of weeks when the US authorities allowed the bankruptcy of Lehman Brothers. Before this book turns to the wider consequences of the Lehman bankruptcy for CCPs in Part V, the next three chapters catch up on clearing developments in Europe in the first decade of the 21st century.

15
Cross-border Clearing in Europe

15.1 CCPs FOR EQUITIES

Just as America's futures markets and CCPs were ripe for reshaping at the turn of the century, so the spread of central counterparty clearing to Europe's equity markets was overdue.

There was nothing to match NSCC in the US which cleared virtually all equity and bond trades on a continental scale. The realignment of clearing and settlement infrastructures at a national level in Europe in the 1990s hardly advanced the spread of equities clearing and left untouched the problems of high cost and complexity for clearing cross-border trades. Central counterparty clearing of equities in Europe remained a minority sport.

As a result of Jean-François Théodore's reshaping of French financial markets in the 1990s, the Paris stock exchange was home to the continent's leading CCP for equities. Two smaller stock exchanges – Amsterdam and Brussels – also provided central counterparty clearing for equities by the end of the 1990s whereas LCH began clearing for Tradepoint, a small London-based electronic stock market, in September 1995.

Belgium put a CCP between its trading and settlement infrastructures when it adopted the vertical silo model late in the 1990s. Some years earlier, the Amsterdam Stock Exchange set up a wholly-owned subsidiary – Effectenclearing BV – that became the counterparty for buyers and sellers trading government securities, corporate bonds and shares on the exchange. Effectenclearing netted the positions on a daily basis for settlement by Necigef, the Dutch central securities depository. If a counterparty was unable to meet its obligations, the stock exchange had a guarantee fund to ensure completion of payments and deliveries.[1]

In other European trading centres, where banks owned securities settlement systems, there was little support for clearing equities. This was because CCPs, through settlement netting, cut the flow of transactions to CSDs and reduced the fee income of custodian banks.

Banks owned Deutscher Kassenverein, the German CSD, before it became part of the Deutsche Börse group in 1992, and continued to be the CSD's indirect owners after it restructured and changed its name to Deutsche Börse Clearing in 1997, because they held 90% of Deutsche Börse until the exchange group's IPO in 2001. Tellingly, there was no move in Germany during the 1990s to introduce a CCP to clear equities. Similarly, bank ownership of settlement infrastructures in Scandinavia kept CCPs at bay.

Towards the end of the 20th century, however, several factors combined to make clearing of equities in Europe a more attractive proposition:

- CCPs were well suited to electronic trading. Linked to screen-based systems, they facilitated post-trade anonymity and so helped protect the prices and positions of individual traders using exchanges and other regulated platforms.

[1] European Monetary Institute (1996), 'Payment systems in the European Union' [The Blue Book].

- Although netting damaged banks' fee income, the reduced flow of transactions to central securities depositaries allowed more trades for a given settlement capacity. Netting reduced expenditure on fees and back-office costs for users and helped deepen the liquidity of the trading platforms using CCPs.
- CCPs also reduced the amount of regulatory capital that traders needed to support their activities. The reduced counterparty risk could also encourage more trading across borders on a continent-wide scale.

Europe's CCPs had developed efficient clearing and netting services for their domestic markets within national frontiers but a fragmented and costly infrastructure for cross-border trading. The introduction of the euro as a virtual, wholesale currency on 1 January 1999 forced exchange operators and their infrastructure providers to think in cross-border, continent-wide terms.

When they did so, they looked inevitably to the US experience where the fees charged by NSCC, the clearing subsidiary of DTCC, were estimated to be about one tenth of those charged for cross-border trades in Europe.[2]

15.2 CLEARNET: EUROPE'S FIRST CROSS-BORDER CCP

The advent of the euro triggered intense discussions among operators and users of exchanges and market infrastructures on all manner of future possibilities including cross-border cooperation, links, mergers and even the creation of a single European CCP.

The announcement in May 1999 of the project to merge the French and German CSDs with Luxembourg-based, user-owned Cedel emerged out of a welter of contacts, discussions and negotiations conducted among exchanges, CSDs and CCPs in Europe before and after the launch of the euro on 1 January 1999. The three-way 'European Clearing House' project encouraged other infrastructure providers to come up with equally ambitious plans.

During the summer of 1999, the Brussels and Amsterdam stock exchanges were working with the London Clearing House and Brussels-based Euroclear, Europe's other ICSD and a long-term rival of Cedel, on a possible alliance to bring the Belgian and Dutch exchanges' equity netting technology to LCH and link the resulting CCP to Euroclear's settlement capacity. That plan got nowhere but the contacts forged between the two exchanges and with Euroclear proved valuable when the tripartite agreement to link the German, French and Luxembourg-based settlement providers began to unravel during the summer of 1999.

The French participants had become increasingly disenchanted with the negotiations to create the proposed European Clearing House. At the heart of the problem was Deutsche Börse's attitude towards Clearnet, the netting and CCP subsidiary of the Paris bourse group.

The French negotiators regarded Clearnet as a valuable part of the French contribution to the merger alongside Sicovam, the French CSD. In their view, Clearnet justified France having a one-third stake in the planned venture as an equal partner to Cedel and Deutsche Börse Clearing.

[2] The European Securities Forum, covered later in this chapter, reported in its 2 December 2000 publication, 'EuroCCP: ESF's blueprint for a single pan-European central counterparty', that NSCC's fees were as low as US$0.032 for clearing trades of equities, warrants or rights. The figure applied to 'locked-in' trades that were already compared and verified before being reported for clearing by NSCC.

Werner Seifert, Deutsche Börse's CEO, considered that the French CCP was not needed. At the time, Seifert believed that the future for securities settlement lay in real-time processing that would render redundant a CCP, which netted down positions at the end of the day. Another factor may have been the banks' ownership of 90% of Deutsche Börse: the German exchange group's announcement of an IPO and stock exchange listing that enabled the banks to unload their Deutsche Börse shares was still in the future.

Seifert therefore insisted that the French contribution was worth less than 30% of the proposed combined group. While the negotiations between Deutsche Börse Clearing and Cedel progressed well, the talks with Sicovam began to drag. The French settlement provider started discussing an alliance with Euroclear instead. In November 1999, the French were ready to jump ship.

In Belgium, Olivier Lefebvre, the head of the Brussels Bourse, became aware of Sicovam's disenchantment with the tripartite plan. He contacted George Möller, his Amsterdam counterpart, and persuaded him that the two should go to Paris on 18 November 1999 to talk to Théodore, the chairman and CEO of Paris Bourse ^{SBF} SA, chairman of Sicovam, and chairman of Clearnet.

Over dinner in the Hotel Crillon, the three exchange chiefs agreed in principle to put their equity netting expertise together in Clearnet and link the resulting CCP to Euroclear for settlement services.

The Belgian and Amsterdam exchanges suspended working with LCH on the CCP project. Four days after Hotel Crillon pact, Sicovam pulled out of the tripartite negotiations with Cedel and Deutsche Börse. Within 24 hours, Sicovam and Clearnet announced an agreement to ally with Euroclear.

The French defection left Deutsche Börse Clearing and Cedel with the merger of their settlement activities, minus Sicovam and Clearnet. In January 2000, Deutsche Börse and the banks and brokerages that owned Cedel placed their securities settlement activities in an equally owned subsidiary that was named Clearstream International.

Meanwhile, the French, Belgian and Dutch exchanges worked on their project for a cross-border CCP and concluded, early in February 2000, that they should also link their trading operations. 'When we found out we were able to solve the clearing issues by putting our clearing businesses together on Clearnet, the idea came that we could go to a merger, because the trading issues were less difficult than those to do with clearing', Théodore said later.[3]

Lefebvre, Möller and Théodore took advantage of new opportunities provided by the euro's introduction to bring about a 'horizontal' integration across three EU member states of their market infrastructures.

As Olivier Lefebvre later explained:

> If you look at the mid-90s, you see in most countries – except the UK and France, where there was a hybrid situation – a general trend towards national vertical silos: exchanges combining not only with derivative exchanges, but also with clearing house and settlement system. That's what I did in Belgium in 97–98. As long as you look at markets from a national viewpoint, what you want to achieve is efficient straight-through processing and perfect cooperation between the trading and the settlement layer.

[3] Conversation with the author, Paris, 25 July 2006.

> Then when you look at it from a cross-border viewpoint, you realise the efficiency gains you can create by creating economies of scale, by merging layer for layer on a cross-border basis, are much more important than the gains from making a vertical silo. Just take the IT component, when you create a vertical silo, you can have some benefits by rationalising your data centres, but basically your main applications remain very specific for each kind of function. Once you can create a horizontal combination, then you have full economies of scale.[4]

On 20 March 2000, the three exchange leaders announced their agreement to merge the Paris, Amsterdam and Brussels stock exchanges and create a new multinational exchange called Euronext. Four days later, a separate stream of negotiations reached a provisional conclusion when Euroclear announced it would take over Sicovam, making the French CSD part of a more diversified settlement group with the Brussels-based ICSD. The agreement also gave Euroclear an option to buy up to 20% of Clearnet.

These separate but related negotiations produced more results in September 2000 when the trading, clearing and settlement arrangements in France, Belgium, the Netherlands, Germany and Luxembourg were transformed.

Euroclear agreed memoranda of understanding for the eventual takeover of the Belgian and Dutch CSDs and signed an agreement to merge with Sicovam. The creation of Euronext was officially announced on 22 September after the owners of all three participating exchanges placed their shares in a single Dutch holding company, Euronext NV.

Clearnet, the cross-border CCP fashioned from French, Belgian and Dutch components, was incorporated as a subsidiary rather than a division of the Euronext exchange group to give it more operational freedom and with a long-term objective of offering some of its capital to users as well as to Euroclear.[5] The clearing house already enjoyed a certain degree of independence: it supplied netting and CCP services for companies outside the Euronext group, including bond and repo clearing for interdealer brokers and electronic trading platforms whose trades were channelled into the CCP through 'designated Clearnet gateways'.[6]

The Euroclear group, undergoing a radical transformation through the addition of national CSDs to its core ICSD business, was designated Euronext's preferred settlement partner – a status that was aimed at promoting the straight through processing of trades without specifying an exclusive relationship between Euronext and its settlement providers.

Although much remained to be done fully to implement the Euronext project, the creation of a multinational, integrated, single currency stock, derivatives and commodities exchange group with horizontally-structured clearing and settlement arrangements marked a radical departure from previous practice. It established Théodore's reputation as a visionary innovator in the European exchange business.

With its 50–50 ownership, Clearstream International might also have formed the core of a horizontally-structured settlement group. But Seifert, as outlined earlier, had other ideas. In July 2002, after 30 months of internal upheaval at Clearstream, the Deutsche Börse group acquired full control of the company, which became the settlement division of a vertical silo with integrated trading, clearing and settlement activities.

[4] Conversation with the author, 21 October 2005.

[5] According to Patrice Renault, CEO of Clearnet, quoted in *Clear News*, Issue 1, April 2000.

[6] Around the end of 2000, IDBs and trading platforms linked to Clearnet included: Euro-MTS, E-Speed, BrokerTec, SLAB, MTS France, Prominnofi and ETCMS.

15.3 LCH AND CLEARNET CONSIDER MARRIAGE

The division of Europe's clearing and settlement providers into horizontal and vertical structures was one of the lasting consequences of the corporate realignments that created Euronext and Clearstream in 1999–2000. It would help stymie future consolidation of Europe's financial infrastructures.

But in the short term Werner Seifert of Deutsche Börse and Jean-François Théodore of Euronext could be content with their achievements.

The Deutsche Börse group had run into problems developing new platform technology towards the end of 1998, so for Seifert the deal with Cedel promised the acquisition of new technology and possible scale benefits. The creation of Euronext rescued Théodore's reputation as a master strategist after the failure to include Sicovam in the tripartite deal with Deutsche Börse Clearing and Cedel. It left him well placed to take the initiative in further consolidating market infrastructures in Europe.

The smaller Brussels and Amsterdam stock exchanges also reaped benefits. By pooling CCP technology and linking to a big partner in trading, they gained scale advantages. The Amsterdam exchange also stood to make big savings because it could adopt the technology used in Paris to replace its ageing IT platforms.

As far as Clearnet was concerned, the process of consolidation had a further, giant step to go. On 4 April 2000, just over a fortnight after the Euronext announcement, Clearnet and LCH announced a 'strategic initiative' to create a consolidated European clearing house that would be 'the largest central counterparty in Europe for capital, energy and commodity markets, cash and derivatives, traded on regular exchanges and/or on the OTC market'.[7]

According to David Hardy, LCH's chief executive at the time, discussions with Euronext had been 'going on for a bit' after an initial contact with Théodore at the Bürgenstock meeting the previous autumn.[8] The initiative – approved unanimously by both boards – would start with a joint venture by early 2001 and envisaged a full merger between the two companies 'as soon as possible thereafter'. The two sides aimed to reach a legal agreement by July 2000 on the joint venture and talked of turning that into a merger in the third quarter of 2001.

The consolidated clearing house would be 'user-governed, market and settlement independent and open to all markets, systems and/or users requiring clearing services'. It would use a single set of clearing and netting systems, based on the Clearing 21 technology adopted by Clearnet as a result of the transatlantic technology exchange of 1997.

Arrangements for netting and position management would take place under English or French law, 'giving the market jurisdictional choice irrespective of trading location'. The plan's architects hoped other jurisdictions could be included in due course.

The consolidated clearing house would be open to collaboration with other European clearing houses. The venture was portrayed as complementing the consolidation taking place among Europe's exchanges and between securities settlement systems.

According to Théodore, the alliance of LCH and Clearnet would cover 70% of the European market and so set 'a European standard for clearing'.[9]

These high hopes and lofty ambitions were very quickly put on ice, however. It was all very well for Euronext and LCH to come together and forge ambitious plans. But the leaders of the

[7] LCH and Clearnet SA (4 April 2000), 'Clearnet and LCH to create consolidated European clearing house', joint press release.

[8] Conversation with the author, 14 December 2009.

[9] As quoted in Clearnet SA's *Clear News* (April 2000).

Frankfurt and London stock exchanges had other ideas. On 3 May 2000, the London Stock Exchange (LSE) and Deutsche Börse announced a merger of equals with the aim of creating a 'mega-bourse' to be known as iX.

Euronext had boasted it would be continental Europe's largest exchange with more than 1300 domestic listed companies having a market capitalisation of €2380 billion and the largest equity and index options market in Europe.

The iX mega-bourse would trump this. It would be the world's third biggest stock market by turnover, with 53% of all share trading in Europe by volume. Headquartered in London, with Seifert as its chief executive, the new exchange planned to forge an alliance with Nasdaq of New York. It aimed to trade more than 80% of high tech growth stocks in Europe, making it the 'largest pan-European growth market' alongside the biggest cash equity market in Europe and the largest derivatives market worldwide. These claims took no account of the collapse of the dot.com boom that was gathering momentum at an alarming pace.

The plans for iX envisaged a central counterparty but left open which company should supply it. LCH already had an agreement with the LSE to supply CCP services from 2001. The German side wanted Eurex Clearing but Eurex, at that point, was a derivatives clearing house only.

The infrastructure providers of the two exchanges had to react to these changed circumstances. Clearstream and CREST, the British CSD, promised immediately to work together 'on delivering products for the benefit for the European securities markets'. During the early summer of 2000, LCH and Eurex Clearing entered into talks on a joint CCP that would clear derivatives, swaps and cash market products.

The iX venture proved shortlived. It collapsed early in September 2000 after the LSE pulled out of the deal. The immediate cause was a hostile counter bid from the Scandinavian OM group. In truth, iX was no longer tenable because of widespread opposition in the City of London.

But the demise of iX came too late to reverse a loss of momentum behind the joint venture between Clearnet and LCH. Hardy recalls Théodore telling him in autumn 2000 that he wished to give priority to the Euronext project, thus putting the merger discussions between Clearnet and LCH on hold.[10] By this time Hardy was committed to consolidation in Europe. Despite the failure of iX, the talks between LCH and Eurex continued until December when they were suspended ahead of the somewhat delayed IPO of Deutsche Börse that was now scheduled for completion in February 2001.

Clearnet refocused its efforts on integrating the Belgian and Dutch CCPs into the larger French clearing house. On 1 February 2001, the activities of the Brussels and Amsterdam equity CCPs and Amsterdam's options clearing house[11] were transferred to Clearnet, which became the sole clearing house and CCP for almost all the Euronext markets in Amsterdam, Brussels and Paris.[12]

Clearnet's clearing activities generated nearly 24% of Euronext's revenues, with more than two thirds coming from the cash equities business.[13] It portrayed itself as a for-profit,

[10] As told to the author by David Hardy on 14 December 2009.

[11] Respectively BXS-Clearing, AEX-Effectenclearing and AEX-Optieclearing.

[12] Exceptionally, commodity-based derivatives trading in Amsterdam was cleared by a separate company, Euronext Amsterdam Commodity Clearing NV, which became a wholly owned subsidiary of Clearnet on 1 February 2001.

[13] According to a Euronext circular of 5 July 2001 to explain an offering of 24 533 772 shares to institutional investors, Clearnet generated revenues of €164.5 million in 2000, of which €113.1 million came from clearing cash trades and €51.4 million from derivatives.

commercially independent company, ready to forge partnerships outside the Euronext group. It pushed ahead with plans to phase in Clearing 21 as a common clearing platform for all the markets that it served, and meld the different clearing membership rules of its three constituent CCPs into one.

But turning the plans for a cross-border clearing house into reality was a complex and difficult task, as Olivier Lefebvre later recalled:

> I was involved in the harmonisation of the French, Dutch and Belgian markets: it is much more difficult to harmonise infrastructures than the markets themselves, because they go much deeper into the workings of the banks, and so the resistance of the banks to changing their systems is enormous.[14]

15.4 THE QUEST FOR A SINGLE CENTRAL COUNTERPARTY

The initiative to merge LCH and Clearnet and provide consolidated CCP services in four countries won strong support from big investment banks operating in Europe. The European Securities Forum (ESF), representing 24 leading users of financial infrastructure, applauded the move primarily as a step towards cutting costs.[15]

The ESF had grown out of Esiug, the users' group founded in 1999. Re-launched and rebranded in April 2000, the lobby group now had an executive chairman in the person of Pen Kent, a former senior official of the Bank of England.

Kent had worked at the Bank from 1961 to 1997. He was an authoritative figure in a rather understated Threadneedle Street way. He knew about financial infrastructure having helped set up the UK's CREST securities settlement system within a tight budget as a user-owned, horizontally-structured utility. He was CREST's first chairman after it began operating in the summer of 1996.

Kent decided to focus on the lack of low-cost CCP facilities for Europe's investment community, pointing out that it was 10 times more costly to trade in Europe than in the US largely because of the duplication of function and investment in clearing and settlement.

Kent wanted 'to restructure the vertical silos into independent, separate horizontal layers' of trading, clearing and netting, and settlement and 'create a single pan-European CCP for all securities' that would yield 'massive economy of administration and management of risk' and eliminate 80% of the difference in transaction costs between Europe and the US.[16]

Kent set out first to persuade existing providers of CCP services to come together and produce this 'hourglass' model that would enable every firm in the wholesale market to concentrate all its clearing and netting into one entity. The users would have a majority voice in the service's ownership and governance. Tariffs would reflect its costs – ideally on a not-for-profit basis.

This was an ambitious programme that would be difficult to negotiate at the best of times. But Kent felt it was well timed. Securitisation was blurring the edges between trading different assets such as equities and bonds. Big innovating investment banks wanted to improve the efficiency of their post-trade activities, including collateral management and IT. 'They wanted to be able to pool everything, to get economies of real scale,' Kent recalled later.[17] 'Here was

---

[14] Conversation with the author, 9 September 2008.

[15] European Securities Forum (15 June 2000), press release.

[16] Kent, Pen, Speech to the International Bar Association 2000 Conference in Amsterdam, 19 September 2000.

[17] Conversation with the author, 1 August 2005.

a moment when investments in clearing would have to be made. It was a question of seizing the right time. There would be massive economies for the industry as a whole.'

Kent started in 2000 by trying to encourage the merger of LCH and Clearnet. He held informal talks with LCH and, as he reported later, had 'interesting and tough talks with Euronext' which controlled Clearnet. But although Théodore supported a merger with LCH, he set conditions. 'Théodore wanted a return on his asset,' Kent explained.

Some of ESF's members grew impatient. In October, an inner group of the biggest users met to discuss options. Including Citibank, Deutsche Bank, Goldman Sachs, Morgan Stanley Dean Witter and UBS Warburg, the 'CCP-Action Group' produced a plan for the ESF to build its own CCP.

In December 2000, the ESF's CCP-Action Group produced a blueprint for a single pan-European counterparty to overcome the fragmentation of cross-border clearing and settlement and avoid duplication in investment spending of at least US$500 million over the following two to three years.[18] The blueprint drew heavily on the US historical experience that led to the creation of DTCC. The proposed CCP was called EuroCCP, a name later appropriated by DTCC.

Not all ESF members were enthusiastic. The initiative also raised suspicions among Europe's financial infrastructure providers, which were already in a state of alert because of rumours that the CCP-Action Group banks were talking informally with DTCC of the US. Kent felt that the blueprint was a victory for the idea of the single CCP, but that implementing the project would require substantial capital outlays and a commitment to replace existing service providers.

Among the CCPs, LCH seemed positive, with David Hardy suggesting that the ESF blueprint would provide a catalyst to help maintain the momentum for a single CCP. But neither Euronext nor Deutsche Börse were willing to press ahead. The German exchange group was focusing on its IPO while Euronext pleaded that it needed to concentrate on integrating its existing components. It also had plans to list its own shares later in 2001.

Moreover, the competitive environment in Europe was changing in ways that were damaging to the idea of a single European CCP:

- The ESF was manoeuvring into an increasingly crowded market where there were several other projects to develop CCPs for the securities industry. In February 2001, the LSE, together with CRESTCo and LCH, launched a CCP for the LSE's electronic order book (SETS). At Deutsche Börse, preliminary work started on what would become a CCP for cash equities, operating under the Eurex brand. Around mid-2001 Borsa Italiana, the Italian stock exchange company, announced that it was in talks with Italian banks and broker-dealers to use a CCP for equities clearing, operated by Cassa di Compensazione e Garanzia (CC&G), in which it had a 59% stake.
- Europe's banks were no longer so willing to invest in new financial infrastructures because of losses following the dot.com bust of 2000 and the economic downturn in the US and elsewhere.
- The stock exchange listing of Deutsche Börse in February 2001 and Euronext's IPO of July 2001 raised the barriers against a user-controlled, not-for-profit European CCP. The two exchanges now had shareholders whose dividends were partly dependent on income from settlement and clearing respectively.

[18] European Securities Forum (2 December 2000).

A broader CCP agenda was also emerging that helped to nudge ESF's EuroCCP to one side. DTCC followed up ESF's October 2000 announcement of plans for a single European CCP by issuing a 'white paper' calling for a global debate on clearing.

The notion of cross-border clearing on a global scale gained support among CCPs in Europe, Asia and the Americas during the winter of 2000–1. In early February, a conference in London organised by 10 CCPs produced a 'compact' with the ambitious, if rather nebulous, goal of setting the stage for seamless global cross-border clearing. Following this, an international group of CCPs, that included DTCC, LCH, Clearnet and Eurex, set up an association called CCP12[19] aimed at improving global clearing, netting and CCP services.

The launch of CCP12 in July 2001 took the wind out of the ESF's sails. A few days later, Kent admitted that his member banks – now about 30 in number – were not ready to invest in the single CCP. There were, he said, 'profound obstacles of law, regulation, technology, national and commercial interest, and frankly cost, which make immediate progress towards a single EuroCCP unlikely'.[20]

But although the ESF abandoned its plan, the hourglass model did not disappear. The single CCP was proposed several times in future years as a solution to the fragmentation of Europe's post-trade infrastructures. The ESF's failed project also left behind a constituency of CCP users among the big investment banks who were quick to register dissatisfaction with the services provided by Europe's incumbent clearing houses.

15.5 LCH AND CLEARNET FINALLY MERGE

At the end of October 2001, Jean-François Théodore pulled off a notable coup. Using funds raised through Euronext's IPO, he acquired LIFFE, snatching the London derivatives market from under the nose of the LSE with a £555 million all cash offer.

The deal, which took effect from the beginning of 2002, put new life into the idea of merging LCH and Clearnet. By buying LIFFE, Euronext acquired a 17.7% stake in LCH, the CCP for the London derivatives market. It held 80% of Clearnet after Euroclear exercised its option and bought 20% of the Paris-based clearing house at the end of January 2002.

Talks resumed between the two clearing houses. But they took a long time to come to a result. LCH and Clearnet announced on 25 June 2003 that they intended to merge, more than three years after their 'strategic initiative' to create a consolidated CCP.

The combined LCH.Clearnet group was to be structured horizontally as a separate entity from trading and settlement platforms. Its goal was to be a neutral partner for each of the trading platforms that it served and become 'the partner of choice for CCPs and international markets around the world'.[21]

It would clear cash equities, derivatives and commodities traded on exchanges as well as interest rate swaps, bonds and repos traded on international OTC markets. In some cases, LCH.Clearnet would be the CCP for rival exchanges, as with cash equities clearing for the

[19] CCP12 followed a curious tradition of international financial organisations by including an erroneous number in its title. The press release announcing CCP12 in July 2001 listed 13 members, reflecting the late addition of the CME to the founding group. By December 2009, its membership had increased to 25 member organisations operating more than 30 CCPs in the Americas, Europe and Asia.

[20] As quoted by Reuters News (17 July 2001), 'Banks see no pan-European share trade counterparty'.

[21] David Hardy, Chief Executive of LCH, and Patrice Renault, Chief Executive of Clearnet, in the foreword to LCH and Clearnet (2003), 'Creating the Central Counterparty of Choice', a guide for users of the two systems.

LSE and virt-x, the London-based electronic exchange created in June 2001 after Tradepoint was merged with Switzerland's SWX Group.

LCH and Clearnet promised to integrate their operations in phases, eventually giving users a single clearing interface into multiple markets. Outlining the merger plans, the chief executives of LCH and Clearnet declared: 'No longer will users require myriad systems and interfaces, thereby helping to control costs.'

The ownership structure and valuation of the combined group were among the tricky issues to solve in the merger discussions. Clearnet was a for-profit company and Théodore, as he made clear in the discussions with the ESF on a single CCP, wanted a proper return on his asset. LCH had since the mid-1990s operated as a user-owned clearing house, with exchanges as minority shareholders, although in the two to three years before the merger David Hardy shifted the company towards a more profit-oriented approach. That said, LCH's clearing members were accustomed to rebates and its user shareholders were interested in low-cost services.

Reconciling these different vested interests required a complex set of compromises. It was a situation that played to Théodore's strengths. Once the complexities were unpicked, it turned out that he had engineered an extremely favourable deal for Euronext shareholders.

The merger valued LCH and Clearnet each at €600 million giving LCH.Clearnet a substantial total value of €1.2 billion. When the 2003 annual report and consolidated financial statements of the LCH.Clearnet Group were published a few months later they revealed a remarkably generous valuation for Clearnet SA. Included in the group's fixed assets of €569.5 million at the end of December were €503.8 million of goodwill reflecting the excess cost of the acquisition of LCH.Clearnet SA over the fair value of the net assets that the French subsidiary contributed to the combined group.

The LCH.Clearnet Group was owned 45.1% by exchanges (including Euronext with a 41.5% stake) and 45.1% by users. The remaining 9.8% belonged to Euroclear. This structure – with its balance of users and exchanges as owners – required Euronext to sell down 7.6% of LCH.Clearnet to user shareholders. The price, reflecting the high fixed asset valuation, was set at €10 per share. Without this step, which took six months to complete, Euronext would have completely dominated the merged company with a 49.1% stake.

The Euronext holding was split into ordinary shares, which accounted for 24.9% of LCH.Clearnet ownership, and redeemable convertible preference shares, which made up the remaining 16.6% of Euronext's stake. The idea was that Euronext would, if the opportunity arose, sell its preference shares to bring new shareholders into the group, with the caveat that for at least five years shareholders (apart from Euroclear) would have to be users. Euronext's voting rights were capped at 24.9% and further provisions ensured no single shareholder or group of shareholders could control the company.

The €10 selling price for the shares had unforeseen consequences for LCH.Clearnet in subsequent years. It created a body of user shareholders for whom it was effectively a minimum selling price. That meant Euronext would also expect to receive at least €10 per share when it eventually decided to dispose of more of its stake.

The balance of ownership was reflected in the structure of LCH.Clearnet's 19-member board, which included six directors appointed by the exchanges four of whom were Euronext nominees. The user shareholders appointed another six directors, Euroclear two, while there were three independents. Also appointed to the board were David Hardy, formerly of LCH, who was appointed LCH.Clearnet's CEO, and Patrice Renault, his deputy, who was formerly chief executive of Clearnet. As chairman, LCH.Clearnet appointed Gérard de la Martinière, a prominent businessman in the French insurance sector who was on the board of several other companies. De la Martinière had some experience of clearing, acquired in the 1980s when he was responsible for the merger of Matif and the French commodity markets.

The board's structure was intended to allay concerns that Euronext would have too much influence over the combined group. In addition, the group's articles of association were intended to ensure the board's neutrality and prevent Euronext having access to confidential information. Directors were bound by confidentiality rules and obliged to take into account the interests of all clearing members and exchanges. When conflicted, directors were excluded from receiving information and voting on the issue concerned.

These concessions by Euronext on ownership and governance made possible the marriage of the for-profit and user-owned CCPs. But in return, LCH.Clearnet's profits were apportioned in such a way as to give Euronext a continuing income stream.

LCH.Clearnet was to operate on a for-profit basis and aim for annual earnings before interest and tax (EBIT) of at least €150 million from the 2006 financial year onwards. This threshold – estimated to be roughly equivalent to a 15% after-tax return on equity in 2006 – compared with EBIT of €40.9 million at Clearnet on turnover of €183 million in 2002 and EBIT of €33.6 million on turnover of €299 million at LCH in the year ended 31 October 2002.

Once EBIT exceeded €150 million, 70% of the excess would be for the benefit of users and 30% available for distribution to LCH.Clearnet shareholders. In the ordinary course of events, at least 50% of the group's annual distributable profits would be paid to shareholders, provided regulators approved and after the preference shares held by Euronext had first been serviced. The preference shares would pay a dividend at least level with that paid on the ordinary shares or one set at 125 basis points over the six-month Euro-Libor rate, if this were higher.

Euronext continued to benefit from certain arrangements dating from its ownership of Clearnet. These included 'retrocession' fees paid by LCH.Clearnet SA, which represented a share of the fees collected from the clearing members for clearing trades on the markets operated by Euronext. Booked as revenues from cash and derivatives trading in Euronext's accounts, retrocession fees greatly increased the cost of clearing equity transactions in Paris. In 2005, Euronext received retrocession fees totalling €46.9 million.[22]

Euronext also profited from information technology deals agreed with Clearnet. The maintenance and development of LCH.Clearnet SA's Clearing 21 software was outsourced to Atos Euronext, a 50–50 joint venture of Euronext and Atos Origin, a French IT company. Although David Hardy negotiated fee reductions a few months after the merger, LCH.Clearnet Group paid €11 million to the Euronext group to cover IT costs in 2004 and €8.6 million in 2005.[23]

Before the merger went through, Clearnet paid a special dividend of €150 million to its shareholders (Euronext and Euroclear). LCH announced a special rebate of £23.6 million to its users.

The deal testified to Théodore's skills as a negotiator and financier. It did not please everybody. The LSE was concerned that Euronext would have too much influence over the combined group. It responded to the June merger announcement with the frosty observation that it left 'a number of questions unanswered' and that it was 'seeking specific assurances through a new clearing services agreement with LCH'. It reinforced its objections by sending 'requests for information' to four potential clearing providers.[24]

[22] Euronext NV (2006), 'Notes to the consolidated financial statements: Registration document and Annual Report 2005'.

[23] LCH.Clearnet Group, Annual reports and notes to the consolidated financial statements, Annual report 2005.

[24] According to the UK Office of Fair Trading, 11 August 2003, in its decision not to refer the proposed merger to the UK Competition Commission.

Relations between LCH and the LSE were never easy. The LSE held no shares in LCH. It was a fairly recent addition to the list of exchanges and platforms cleared by LCH, which launched a CCP in cooperation with CREST for the LSE's electronic SETS market in February 2001. That venture was criticised on cost grounds by many of the smaller, domestic stock exchange members. It was only in July 2002 that the three companies introduced optional settlement netting for trades executed through SETS.

Relations went from bad to worse a few weeks after the June 2003 announcement of the merger between LCH and Clearnet.

The cause of the trouble was a decision by LCH to raise the fees it proposed to charge for clearing Dutch shares traded on the London exchange. The service was part of a planned venture, hatched before the LCH.Clearnet merger announcement, to divert business from Euronext's Amsterdam exchange to London. The LSE saw the LCH decision as a sign that a continental for-profit mentality was taking hold even before the merger with Clearnet was completed. The bust up prompted the LSE to enter into talks with other potential CCPs, including Eurex, before settling its dispute with LCH late in November.

The merger of LCH and Clearnet was completed on 22 December 2003. David Hardy hailed the marriage of the two CCPs as 'a major step forward in the integration of European capital markets infrastructure'. In fact, it marked a high point rather than a step forward. The horizontal merger of LCH and Clearnet would disappoint all concerned.

Even before this became clear, vertical integration was emerging as the strategy of choice elsewhere in Europe, ensuring the continued fragmentation of Europe's post-trade infrastructures.

In March 2003, the Deutsche Börse group launched Eurex Clearing AG as the central counterparty for Xetra equity trades and floor trading on the Frankfurt Stock Exchange. In May, the Borsa Italiana launched its CCP for cash equities, run by CC&G.

Europe's single market was not supposed to be like this. In consequence, legislators and regulators took notice and joined forces with the disgruntled users of Europe's post-trade services in pressing for lower fees and change.

16

Post-trade Policy in Europe

16.1 FRAGMENTED REGULATION: THE EXAMPLE OF LCH.CLEARNET

When LCH and Clearnet sealed their merger at the end of 2003, the regulators' arrangements for the LCH.Clearnet Group put in stark relief the absence of a single market in Europe for post-trade services.

Despite the launch of the euro in January 1999 and the Financial Services Action Plan (FSAP) later that year, a dozen or so regulators had a say in the regulation and oversight of the newly formed group.

Although the group was a UK-registered limited company, its lead regulator was the Commission bancaire (Cb) of France. The Cb held this role because the LCH.Clearnet Group was a financial holding company (a *compagnie financière*) whose subsidiaries included LCH.Clearnet SA, a limited purpose bank incorporated in France, and the one and only credit institution in the group.

SA's banking status also meant involvement in its supervision by France's Comité des Établissements de Crédit et des Entreprises d'Investissement (CECEI), the body responsible for authorising banks in France, and the Banque de France, the French central bank. As a clearing house, SA was regulated by the Autorité des Marchés Financiers (AMF), the French financial markets regulator.

In the UK, the FSA, the AMF's counterpart, authorised and regulated LCH.Clearnet Ltd, the Group's London-based CCP, as a Recognised Clearing House (RCH), meaning that it was not restricted in terms of what products it could clear or how those products were traded. The UK regulator took the view that clearing houses and exchanges were operated by experts and should be able to operate with 'a wide degree of freedom to set and police their own market rules'.[1]

LCH.Clearnet was also regulated outside the EU because Ltd registered with the CFTC in Washington as an offshore Designated Clearing Organisation (DCO) in October 2001.

Also involved in the supervision of SA were regulators from France, Belgium and the Netherlands who formed a 'college'.[2] These were originally representatives of organisations that signed a January 2001 Memorandum of Understanding (MoU) which followed the takeover by Clearnet of the CCPs in Brussels and Amsterdam. The college grew in 2003 to include two Portuguese authorities after SA became the CCP for Euronext's Portuguese markets.

[1] HM Treasury (February 1999), 'Financial Services and Markets Bill: Draft recognition requirements for investment exchanges and clearing houses'.

[2] The original college comprised the Banque de France, the Cb, the French Financial Markets Council (*Conseil des Marchés Financiers* that became part of AMF as a result of legislation in August 2003), the National Bank of Belgium, the Belgian Banking and Finance Commission, the Netherlands Financial Markets Authority (AFM) and the Netherlands Central Bank. The Bank of Portugal and Portuguese Securities Market Commission (CMVM) joined the college in 2003.

Membership of the college expanded and contracted somewhat in subsequent years, reflecting changes in the supervisory arrangements of the participating states. As of March 2010, SA's CCP services to markets in France, Belgium, the Netherlands and Portugal were subject to the regulation, supervision and oversight of nine competent authorities after the Commission bancaire and CECEI were subsumed into a larger regulatory body, the ACP – Autorité de contrôle prudentiel, charged with supervising the French banking and insurance sectors. In May 2010, SA was granted Recognised Overseas Clearing House (ROCH) status by the UK FSA and so became subject to UK regulation.

This collection of national regulators in Europe – each with its own preoccupations and including authorities from both the eurozone and the UK – had a significant impact on the way the LCH.Clearnet Group was structured.

In April 2000, LCH and Clearnet announced plans to create a consolidated European clearing house. But the idea of a single CCP with a single legal status was subsequently vetoed by French and British regulators. Instead, the group had to set up French and British subsidiaries, governed by separate legal and regulatory systems and with independent boards.

Although in 2005 the French, Dutch, Belgian and Portuguese central banks and financial markets regulators signed another MoU with their UK counterparts to manage cooperation when regulating LCH.Clearnet Group,[3] only the European Central Bank (ECB) had produced any guidance for the regulation of CCPs in a cross-border context at the time of the merger of LCH and Clearnet.

Published in September 2001 on behalf of the Eurosystem, which comprised the ECB and the national central banks of the single currency area, the ECB's 'policy line' on CCP consolidation probably hardened rather than eased national divisions for any company trying to provide clearing services inside and outside the eurozone.

As a central bank, the ECB was understandably worried that the possible consolidation of central counterparties in its region 'could have implications for the smooth execution of monetary policy operations, the smooth operation of payment and settlement systems and the stability of the financial markets in general'.[4]

It took note of a growing demand for central counterparty clearing following the euro's introduction and the European Securities Forum's (ESF) support for a single, multi-currency, multi-product CCP. The ECB's policy line reflected one long established central bank concern: that CCPs should have effective risk-management standards.

Consolidation, the ECB said, should be driven by the private sector unless there were 'clear signs of market failure'. It called for open and fair access to facilities for trading, clearing and settlement to 'guarantee a level playing field and avoid excessive fragmentation of market liquidity' irrespective of whether they were vertically or horizontally-structured.

So far, so good. But the ECB's statement also put on record an important principle:

> The natural geographical scope for any 'domestic' market infrastructure (including central counterparty clearing) for securities and derivatives denominated in euro is the euro area. Given the potential systemic importance of securities clearing and settlement systems, this infrastructure should be located within the euro area.

With this in the background, it was unsurprising that the French authorities insisted that LCH.Clearnet Group keep SA as a separate subsidiary in Paris rather than accede to a

[3] They were known as the Joint Regulatory Authorities.

[4] ECB (27 September 2001), 'The Eurosystem's policy line with regard to consolidation in central counterparty clearing'.

consolidated structure that might have resulted in the clearing of euro-denominated instruments moving to London.

When the ECB produced its 'policy line' there was only a faint glimmer of an emerging EU policy for creating a single market in post-trade services. International standards for risk management at CCPs were still in the future at both the global and European levels. The priority among EU policy makers was to encourage the international competitiveness of Europe's financial markets to help the European economy catch up with the United States. And in the US, the spirit of the age favoured deregulation even after the dot.com boom and bust, as policy makers remained confident that a combination of strong growth, low inflation and financial innovation was producing stable economic conditions.

16.2 THE FIRST DRAFTS OF EU POST-TRADE POLICY

The convoluted nature of LCH.Clearnet's supervisory arrangements shed a unflattering light on the lack of EU policy to promote the integration of post-trade services. Policy formulation in the European Union is a long and complex process at the best of times. It often relies in the early stages on reports by experts commissioned by one or another of the EU's institutions.

Clearing and settlement were simply neglected by the European Commission in 1999 when it drew up the 42 measures of the FSAP to create a single market for financial services.

That began to change in the summer of 2000 when the EU appointed a committee of 'wise men' to explore ways of making EU laws planned as part of the FSAP easier to introduce and more adaptable to the fast-changing conditions of financial markets. Chaired by Alexandre Lamfalussy, a retired Belgian central banker and one of the fathers of the euro, the committee produced two reports for EU finance ministers which outlined how the EU could speed up and improve the passage and regulation of financial legislation.[5]

The advisors' second report, published in February 2001, was the first EU document to give more than the briefest consideration to Europe's fragmented post-trade infrastructure and the path Europe should take to bring the costs of cross-border trading securities down to US levels.

Even though it devoted just one of its 109 pages to the need for Europe to improve its cross-border clearing and settlement arrangements, the report set out a road map for EU public policy on the issue in the years that followed.

The Lamfalussy committee argued that the private sector should be mainly responsible for restructuring clearing and settlement in Europe. But public policy was also important and should focus on the following:

- the excessive costs of cross-border clearing and settlement compared with the US;
- competition issues such as open and non-discriminatory access to systems;
- the soundness of technical links between central securities depositories (CSDs);
- the prudential implications of a single CCP (should one be created);
- whether clearing and settlement systems should be authorised and supervised according to common European standards.

[5] Lamfalussy Group (November 2000), 'Initial report of the committee of wise men on the regulation of European securities markets'; http://ec.europa.eu/internal_market/securities/docs/lamfalussy/wisemen/initial-report-wise-men_en.pdf (accessed 10 December 2010). Lamfalussy Group (February 2001), 'Final report of the committee of wise men on the regulation of European securities markets': European Commission; http://ec.europa.eu/internal_market/securities/docs/lamfalussy/wisemen/final-report-wise-men_en.pdf (accessed 10 December 2010).

The wise men urged policy makers to show a clear lead 'if in due course it emerged that the private sector was unable to deliver an efficient pan-European clearing and settlement system for the EU'. The committee also strongly suggested that the European Commission's competition directorate should examine whether EU competition rules were being properly respected in the sector.

The group advised 'serious consideration' of an EU regulatory framework for clearing and settlement activities. It floated the idea of involving the ECB because of the importance of clearing and settlement for the operation of monetary policy and the payments system. The wise men mooted the idea of separating issues relating to clearing systems from those concerning settlement, because (they added in parentheses) an efficient clearing system was 'a public good'.

These ideas took up about 1% of the report. But Baron Lamfalussy and his colleagues had put clearing and settlement firmly on the EU's financial services agenda and others, including the European Commission, took up the cause.

Another experts' report marked the next step towards an EU policy on clearing and settlement.[6] This pinpointed the barriers to cross-border equities trading that pushed up costs and hindered the creation of a single European post-trade market.

In charge of this group was Alberto Giovannini, an Italian financial expert, who advised the European Commission as chairman of a 'consultative group on the impact of the Euro on European capital markets'. A graduate of the University of Bologna with a PhD in economics from the Massachusetts Institute of Technology, Giovannini had worked in academic research, investment management and banking. He was senior advisor and strategist at the ill-fated Long-Term Capital Management fund from 1995 to 1999. He had also advised the Italian government, the IMF and the World Bank.

Giovannini made big claims for the importance of Europe's post-trade sector. In November 2001, in the first of two reports, his group declared: 'It is perhaps no exaggeration to conclude that inefficiencies in clearing and settlement represent the most primitive and thus the most important barrier to integrated financial markets in Europe.'

The Giovannini group's work focused largely on the settlement side of the business. The report identified 15 barriers, divided among three categories: divergent technical requirements and/or market practices; differences in national tax procedures; and differences relating to legal certainty. It won the support of Frits Bolkestein, the EU's internal market commissioner, and his senior officials in the Commission's internal market directorate.

A second Giovannini report in April 2003 produced a strategy for removing the barriers and replacing them with technical standards, market conventions, rules, regulations and laws designed to overcome the fragmentation of the EU's post-trade services.[7] The report set out a sequence of actions to remove the barriers within 'aggressive but realistic deadlines' of between 27 months and three years. The private sector was given responsibility for removing six barriers, leaving the public sector to deal with nine. Giovannini stressed that success would depend on good cooperation between the two sides.

Giovannini called for a regulatory and supervisory structure with powers 'to make clearing and settlement providers deliver fair and low-cost access, respond quickly and flexibly to changes in their operating environment, and charge prices that are close to a minimised level of costs'.

[6] Giovannini Group (November 2001), 'Cross-border clearing and settlement arrangements in the European Union'.

[7] Giovannini Group (April 2003), 'Second report on EU clearing and settlement arrangements'.

His committee's reports marked out a clear strategy for transforming Europe's financial market into an 'integrated entity' from 'a juxtaposition of domestic markets'.[8] They put pressure on the private sector to work towards a market-led convergence of market practices and technical specifications. Progress in these areas would allow interoperability between national systems and give users a choice of clearing and settlement locations.

Giovannini made clear that his recommendations were not intended to solve all problems. He left the choice of system for delivering pan-European clearing and settlement to the companies involved. Meanwhile, two EU bodies, the European System of Central Banks (ESCB) and the Committee of European Securities Regulators (CESR), the second of which had been set up as a result of the Lamfalussy recommendations, took on the task of drawing up 'standards and/or recommendations' for CCPs and securities settlement systems in the EU.

16.3 THE ESCB-CESR STANDARDS

The EU initiative to create its own standards and/or recommendations for CCPs and CSDs was launched in October 2001.

At first sight, it seemed quixotic that the EU felt the need to have its own standards for clearing and settlement organisations. As outlined in Chapter 14, the CPSS-IOSCO group was in the throes of producing recommendations for minimum standards for post-trade services to be applied internationally. EU officials engaged fully in that work. The CPSS-IOSCO recommendations for CCPs were duly published in November 2004, becoming the internationally accepted minimum standards for risk management around the world.

However, the ESCB-CESR group's goals went beyond providing risk-management benchmarks. Its job was to help build the single market for post-trade services through having a level playing field on which firms could operate and overcome problems – such as regulatory arbitrage – caused by legal and legislative differences between European countries.

So far, so good. But the ESCB-CESR initiative soon ran into difficulties and provided an object lesson on how a seemingly innocuous project could be stymied by missteps in the arcane world of EU policy making.

After obtaining input from the industry, a working group of officials from the ESCB and CESR published a first draft consultative report in July 2003, which floated the idea that the EU standards should be more binding than the CPSS-IOSCO recommendations that were then in preparation.

The report caused uproar. The European Parliament was upset because it considered that the ESCB-CESR standards encroached on its legislative prerogatives. Although the standards would not have the status of EU law, 'regulators, supervisors and overseers' were expected to adopt them and ensure their implementation by the industry. Opposition came from many banks active in securities settlement which feared an additional burden of regulation.

In September 2004 – after two consultations and two public hearings – the ESCB-CESR working group published a new draft that dealt with the banks' problems. A month later, in October 2004, the ECB governing council and CESR approved the group's report. But the standards could not be implemented because BaFin, the German securities regulator, unexpectedly raised concerns about the legal basis for their adoption in Germany.

[8] From the Foreword of Giovannini Group (April 2003).

Among EU regulators, there were some who thought BaFin's objections amounted to disguised protectionism. Their effect was to put the activities of the ESCB-CESR working group on hold and the standards in limbo until the financial crisis in 2007.

The crisis focused the attention of policy makers on the importance of sound financial infrastructures. As a result, the ESCB and CESR decided in June 2008 to complete the job. A compromise was reached by which the standards would be downgraded to recommendations and addressed to public authorities only. In addition, the work would apply only to CSDs and CCPs, leaving banks to be regulated by other measures.

When the ESCB-CESR recommendations were at last published in May 2009, they were similar to the CPSS-IOSCO recommendations that had become the industry benchmark since 2004. The ESCB-CESR recommendations paid a bit more attention to interoperability among CCPs, emphasised rather more the importance of stress testing for multiple defaults of participants and advocated independent audits of business continuity plans.[9]

The ESCB-CESR recommendations were, however, given a different spin than the CPSS-IOSCO work. Their main aim was 'to promote competitive, efficient, safe and sound pan-European post-trading arrangements' which should lead ultimately to greater confidence in securities markets, better investor protection and less systemic risk. The recommendations were expected to promote and sustain the integration and competitiveness of European markets by improving the efficiency of market infrastructure across borders.

These were worthwhile aims, tainted only by the nature of their production. For all the talk of Europe's single market, the saga of the ESCB-CESR standards showed how national securities regulators in the EU were still some way from giving priority to continent-wide concerns about safety, level playing fields and competitiveness over national advantage.

16.4 THE EU COMMISSION MOVES TOWARDS LEGISLATION

Both the Lamfalussy and Giovannini reports had complained about the excessive costs of cross-border clearing and settlement in Europe. Although precise figures were lacking at this stage, it was evident to market participants and policy makers that the cost of cross-border trading in Europe was significantly higher than in the continent-wide US market. Nationally based post-trade structures were held partly responsible for this situation.

It was in this context, and between publication of the first and second Giovannini reports, that the European Commission released its first thoughts on the clearing and settlement market.

Its 'communication'[10] or consultative document, published in June 2002, marked the first step in a process that in the normal course of events would end in EU legislation. It took the removal of Giovannini's 15 barriers as a starting point for increasing the efficiency of cross-border clearing and settlement in the EU and spelled out a programme to sharply lower costs.

Like Giovannini, the Commission did not define any form of market infrastructure for the EU. However, it laid great stress on creating a level playing field among institutions involved in clearing and settlement with a view to encouraging open access to all systems.

[9] ECB and CESR (May 2009), 'Recommendations for securities settlement systems and recommendations for central counterparties in the European Union'.

[10] European Commission (2002), 'Clearing and settlement in the European Union. Main policy issues and future challenges'.

'All markets, infrastructure providers and market participants should be able to access all necessary systems, regardless of their location,' it said. 'Fully integrated markets require that rights of access to systems be comprehensive, transparent and non-discriminatory and, above all, effective.' It proposed the 'parallel application of competition policy' to reinforce such measures.

The Commission posed questions which implied that EU bodies should be heavily engaged in helping market forces create an integrated clearing and settlement industry. It asked whether EU legislation should 'provide comprehensive rights of access and choice across and between all levels of the trading and settlement chain'. Noting the lack of a common system of regulation for CCPs, settlement systems and custodians, it mulled the possibility of an EU law containing 'some high level principles' to cover issues such as 'the authorisation, supervision, risk-management techniques, default arrangements or capital treatment of such institutions'. It also wondered whether common functional definitions of clearing and settlement activities at the EU level would help achieve a level playing field. As with Giovannini's work, the Commission's paper was more relevant to settlement than clearing.

The Commission's 2002 paper initiated a lengthy consultation that revealed splits among post-trade service providers about the industry's future and how to lower the costs and increase the efficiency of cross-border transactions.

The period of consultation overlapped with negotiations on a new law to replace the Investment Services Directive (ISD), which became known as the Markets in Financial Instruments Directive (MiFID). At the end of April 2004, after months of intensive lobbying and often bitter infighting among EU member states, the EU's Council of Ministers adopted MiFID to open up the trading of securities in Europe to greater competition.

MiFID was one of the most important components of the FSAP. A replacement for the 1993 ISD, it enabled investment firms, banks and exchanges to provide their services across EU borders on the basis of their home country authorisation. It opened up stock market trading in countries such as Italy where the exchange previously had a monopoly over retail investor orders. Among its liberalising measures, MiFID enabled investment banks to set up alternative platforms known as 'multilateral trading facilities' (MTFs) as rivals to established exchanges. But MiFID was a so-called framework directive,[11] which left many details to be sorted out after its adoption by EU ministers. It did not take effect until 1 November 2007.

MiFID had some relevance to clearing. Articles 34 and 46 obliged EU member states to make sure investment firms from other member states had access to clearing, CCP and CSD services in their territory on the same conditions as local firms. Market participants had the right to choose the settlement location (but not the CCP clearing location) for their trades so long as links were in place between the regulated market and the organisation in question. Regulated markets were also given the right to choose a particular CCP and/or CSD to clear and settle their transactions.

In a similar vein, MiFID's Article 35 told member states with an MTF in their jurisdiction that they could 'not oppose the use of central counterparty clearing houses and/or settlement systems in another member state except where this is demonstrably necessary in order to maintain the orderly functioning of that MTF'.

However, the precise wording of MiFID left a lot of scope for maintaining fragmentation along national lines. The directive did not regulate relations among post-trade infrastructures and so left open how the goals outlined in Articles 34, 35 and 46 should be implemented.

[11] A legislative innovation proposed by Baron Lamfalussy's committee of wise men.

MiFID therefore lobbed the ball back into the court of the Commission, which responded in April 2004 with the second of two promised communications on clearing and settlement.[12]

The Commission put forward a carefully calibrated strategy. It endorsed the elimination of the Giovannini barriers and decided not to intervene in the structure of the industry. It therefore kept aloof from several ongoing and heated debates among infrastructure providers and their users over whether to consolidate existing settlement systems, on the merits of user-owned against for-profit governance structures and whether to separate the intermediary and banking functions of CSDs.

The Commission wanted investors and the intermediaries acting on investors' behalf to have all possible options for clearing and settling cross-border securities transactions in the EU. Its goal was for the users of clearing and settlement services to have free access to the system of their choice. It wanted a common regulatory framework covering the functions performed by the various actors in the market. This would allow mutual recognition of clearing and settlement systems across the EU, thus enhancing integration, protecting investors and lowering costs.

To help implement these goals, the Commission proposed EU legislation in the form of a framework directive. The proposed legislation would be subject in advance to a regulatory impact assessment (RIA) to make sure EU intervention would benefit the sector. EU competition law would be applied effectively to clearing and settlement activities to support the initiative. The Commission asked for responses by the end of July.

The Commission also set up three groups of experts from the public and private sectors to provide new impetus to efforts to remove the Giovannini barriers. The most high profile of the three groups was Cesame, the Clearing and Settlement Advisory and Monitoring Expert Group, which was charged with helping to remove those barriers for which the industry was wholly or partly responsible.[13]

Cesame met for the first time in July 2004. All seemed set, after appropriate consultation and study, for new EU legislation to remove the log-jam on clearing and settlement. However, this glide path was upset by the appointment, with effect from November 2004, of a new Commission and the arrival in Brussels of Charlie McCreevy, who gave up the post of Irish finance minister to succeed Frits Bolkestein as Internal Market Commissioner.

16.5 McCREEVY PUSHES FOR AN INDUSTRY SOLUTION

In just over three years, the Commission had moved from being a bystander in the debate over clearing and settlement in Europe to having set out a framework for EU laws to nudge Europe's fractious post-trade sector towards greater integration. Charlie McCreevy put this process on hold.

McCreevy arrived in Brussels after seven years running Ireland's finances with a strong reputation as a free marketeer who had delivered prosperity unprecedented in his country's history as an independent state.

In 2004, the deep recession that hit the Irish economy in the global financial crisis of 2007–8 was some years in the future. Instead, Ireland was the 'Celtic Tiger' and routinely hailed as the

[12] European Commission (28 April 2004), 'Clearing and settlement in the European Union – The way forward'.

[13] A Legal Certainty Group (LCG) and a Fiscal Compliance Experts Group (Fisco) were set up some months later. While Cesame aimed to bring together the sector's key decision makers to experience peer group pressure in favour of action, the LCG and Fisco groups also included experts from academia and the legal and accountancy professions to look at how to remove the legal and tax barriers that were the responsibility of the public sector.

EU's best performing economy. Open markets and McCreevy's tax cutting and pro-business policies were given the credit for a booming economy. Hopes rose in Brussels that some of that magic would rub off on the EU as a whole with McCreevy installed as Internal Market Commissioner.

McCreevy took over the single market portfolio to a chorus of complaints about the burden of regulation imposed by the FSAP. Bolkestein's time at the Commission saw the adoption of nearly all the 42 FSAP measures proposed in 1999, although most were still waiting to be implemented in the EU member states when his term expired in late 2004.

Bolkestein's achievement was built on the complex and time-consuming processes of proposal, consultation, compromise, legislation and adoption that characterised the passing of all EU legislation. The passage of MiFID from its origins as a Commission proposal through the European Parliament and the Council of Ministers was a bruising experience for all concerned. There was widespread 'regulatory fatigue' in financial markets and especially in the City of London.

McCreevy matched this mood perfectly. In June 2004 – seven weeks before his nomination as Internal Market Commissioner at the age of 54 – McCreevy told a conference in Brussels organised by DG Markt, the internal market directorate that he later headed, that new legislative measures to promote financial integration should be 'a last resort'. They should only be proposed if they passed a strict cost-benefit test and where non-legislative measures were deemed ineffective or where there was a clear case of market failure.

Not everyone agreed with McCreevy when it came to clearing and settlement. Some permanent officials in DG Markt made no secret of their wish to start drafting legislation.

Views in the European Parliament were mixed. In the EU Council of Ministers – which would have joint responsibility with the Parliament for turning a Commission proposal into law – there appeared little enthusiasm for new legislation. When the EU's economics and finance ministers reviewed the FSAP in November 2004, they agreed that its future focus should be convergence of supervision and implementation of measures already approved.

McCreevy made clear that he would not be rushed. In his first speech on financial services, he swore off bringing forward EU legislation aimed at securities markets during 2005. Clearing and settlement might require action 'from 2006 onwards,' he said early in December 2004.[14] But 2005 would be 'a year of preparation, analysis, economic impact assessment and building consensus'.

Although temperamentally opposed to new laws, McCreevy kept the threat of legislation hanging over the infrastructure providers. On 13 September 2005, he called on 'all interested actors to take their responsibilities and collectively to put their foot on the gas'.[15] Condemning the high costs of cross-border clearing and settlement, he warned that the Commission was taking a close look at the economic case for action. 'We will decide whether any European legislation, or other intervention, is necessary. [. . .] The next six months are crucial. As far as I am concerned the clock is ticking.'

Days before the six-month deadline, McCreevy and Neelie Kroes, the competition commissioner, gave the industry an ultimatum. In a joint statement on 7 March 2006, they told market players to come forward with effective and realistic changes to improve clearing and settlement before the EU institutions broke for the summer at the end of July.

[14] At a CESR conference in Paris on 6 December 2004.

[15] European Commission (13 September 2005) at the 14th annual *ALFI-NICSA Europe-USA Investment Funds Forum.*

If there was no substantive move by the industry towards self regulation, the two would take action on the basis of EU internal market and competition rules. The industry had four months in which to agree to draw up a viable plan for an EU-wide market for clearing and settlement.

16.6 COMPETITION AUTHORITIES AGAINST VERTICAL SILOS

The signature of Neelie Kroes alongside that of McCreevy on the March 2006 ultimatum to the industry was a sign that the EU's efforts to build a policy for the post-trade sector had moved up a gear. And not before time: much was still needed to improve the competitiveness of cross-border clearing and settlement in the EU, as a July 2005 ECB study of post-trade infrastructures in the 12 nation eurozone underlined:[16]

> Despite the single currency, the trading, clearing and settlement industry still shows a relatively high degree of fragmentation and insufficient harmonisation, with around 22 stock and derivatives exchanges, 8 CCPs, 18 local CSDs and 2 ICSDs active in the euro area, all operating on the basis of different technical procedures, prices, market practices and legal frameworks.

CCPs came under the scrutiny of competition authorities after a new wave of corporate manoeuvring and speculation about further consolidation in Europe's exchange and post-trade sectors began just days after McCreevy's December 2004 announcement that 2005 would be a year for reflection and consensus building on the future of clearing and settlement in the EU.

On Monday 13 December 2004, the news broke that Werner Seifert, Deutsche Börse's chief executive, planned to bid for the London Stock Exchange. Seifert's indicative offer of £1.35 billion (or just under €2 billion) valued LSE shares at 530 pence each, about 50% up on the average of the preceding three months.

The LSE's management – unlike its predecessors at the start of the iX project in 2000 – was in no mood to accommodate him. Clara Furse, the LSE's chief executive, rebuffed the approach as too low and too vague. Although willing to talk, the LSE prepared its defences and waited for other approaches from Deutsche Börse's rivals, including – it was confidently expected – one from Euronext.

The reappearance of Deutsche Börse – a for-profit, vertically-integrated group – as a bidder for the LSE caused concern in London's investment community and among Deutsche Börse's competitors in the post-trade sector. It injected new urgency into the 'vertical versus horizontal' debate.

In a letter to the *Financial Times*, Chris Tupker, Euroclear's chairman, warned that the proposed takeover of the LSE was 'the beginning of the end game of the consolidation of all the infrastructure of financial markets in Europe – not just the equity trading platforms'.[17]

Tupker feared that a successful takeover of the LSE by the Frankfurt exchange could lead to trades in London being cleared and settled through Deutsche Börse's own post-trade operations to the disadvantage of users – and to the disadvantage of Euroclear, which had taken over CREST, the UK CSD, in the autumn of 2002.

He asked whether it was right that trading, clearing and settlement at the LSE should become a monopoly in the hands of a company 'driven by the goal of maximising shareholder profits'. This, he added, 'could well be the outcome' if the winner of a battle for the LSE also owned clearing and settlement functions.

---

[16] ECB (2005) 'Integration of securities market infrastructures in the Euro Area', Schmiedel, Heiko and Schönenberger, Andreas, ECB Occasional Paper No. 33, Frankfurt; http://www.ecb.int/pub/pdf/scpops/ecbocp33.pdf (accessed 10 December 2010).

[17] 7 January 2005.

This message evidently resonated with the UK competition authorities. On 27 January 2005, Deutsche Börse published details of its offer for the LSE while Euronext, its multinational rival, indicated that it might also make a cash offer for the London exchange. Both companies notified the UK's Office of Fair Trading about their plans. The OFT referred the possible acquisition of the LSE by the rival continental exchanges to the UK Competition Commission at the end of March.

Deutsche Börse soon shelved its offer because of a shareholders' revolt that eventually cost Seifert his job in May 2005. At Euronext, which agreed a handshake deal to merge with the LSE on the very night that the UK competition authorities took up the case, Théodore also came under pressure from some hedge funds not to bid for the London exchange. But the UK Competition Commission carried on with its probe regardless. It published its provisional findings on 29 July 2005.

The Competition Commission concluded that the involvement of both Deutsche Börse and Euronext in CCP clearing might result in a 'substantial lessening of competition'[18] in the market for the provision of on-book equity trading services in the UK should the London exchange be acquired by either suitor. This was because 'the ownership or influence over clearing services' that Deutsche Börse or Euronext would have through Deutsche Börse's control of Eurex Clearing or Euronext's stake in LCH.Clearnet would make it more difficult for other exchanges to compete with the LSE in UK equities trading.

In its provisional report, the Competition Commission said a takeover of the LSE by either of the two continental rivals could only go ahead with measures in place to safeguard competition. In the case of Deutsche Börse, it suggested the possible sale of Eurex Clearing, a ban on its use as a provider of clearing services for the LSE and behavioural commitments such as an obligation to provide access to vital clearing services for other exchanges on fair and reasonable terms. Similarly, Euronext was presented with a menu of options ranging from divesting its stake in LCH.Clearnet to the provision of access to its clearing services.

In its final report of 1 November 2005, the Competition Commission stipulated that neither Deutsche Börse nor Euronext should hold more than 14.9% of the equity and voting rights of the LSE's clearing provider in the event of either taking over the London exchange.

Although the hostility of the shareholders of Deutsche Börse and Euronext to any acquisition of the LSE made the ruling somewhat academic, this first official investigation by a competition authority into the structure of post-trade services in Europe was still a setback for the vertical silo business model.

It was in line with thinking in Brussels. During 2003, DG Comp, the European Commission's competition department, sent a questionnaire to the EU's national competition authorities seeking details 'regarding exclusive arrangements relating to the trading, clearing, settlement and depository of securities'.[19] The responses, together with replies from the industry and some EU central banks to a further consultation launched in August 2004, fed into a 'factual snapshot' of conditions in March 2005 that was written by the consultancy London Economics for DG Comp.

---

[18] Competition Commission (29 July 2005a), 'Notice of provisional findings made under rule 10.3 of the Competition Commission Rules of Procedure in respect of i) The anticipated acquisition of London Stock Exchange PLC by Deutsche Börse AG and ii) The anticipated acquisition of London Stock Exchange PLC by Euronext NV'. Also: Competition Commission (29 July 2005b), 'CC considers LSE mergers would harm competition', news release.

[19] European Commission (30 June 2005), 'Securities trading, clearing, central counterparties and settlement in EU 25 – An overview of current arrangements'.

The London Economics report was published on 30 June 2005 and was a trenchant piece of work. After reviewing the securities trading, clearing and settlement infrastructures of the cash equities and bond markets in the 25 EU member states, it concluded that 'at the present time, in the vast majority of securities cash markets in Europe, users have no choice with respect to the providers of clearing and settlement services that are to be used to clear and settle a trade in a specific security on a specific market'.

The report drew a link between restrictive practices and vertical silos. It noted that in some cases, trading or clearing membership rules prescribed just one clearing and settlement provider. In others, users were offered some choice, but this was theoretical because in practice only one service provider existed in the country concerned. These arrangements accounted for 'the vast majority of vertical arrangements between trading, clearing and settlement infrastructures in the European Union'.

DG Comp followed up the London Economics report by launching a deeper probe into vertical silos in July 2005. The swift reaction suggested that Kroes was prepared to live up to her nickname of 'Nickel Neelie' and take a hard line on clearing and settlement. A new batch of questionnaires went to exchanges, operators of alternative trading systems, selected broker-dealers, banks, banking associations and clearing and settlement providers. The questions focused on trading and post-trade infrastructures for cash equities.

But around this time DG Comp also had to admit that its powers to act were limited. EU competition rules had a narrow scope and were aimed at specific abuses between companies or the abuse of dominant positions. They were unlikely to deal with all barriers to competition. The Commission required a very high level of proof to implement competition law and this virtually precluded *ex-ante* actions against suspected offenders.

Nevertheless, the EU Commission's competition directorate still caused a stir when it published the results of its investigation on 24 May 2006.[20] DG Comp's verdict on vertical silos in equities markets was damning. 'Vertical integration may result in foreclosure at all levels of the value chain and therefore lead to welfare losses,' it wrote 'While there may also be efficiencies, so far the Commission has seen no convincing evidence to substantiate this.'

The report took a dim view of monopoly CCPs and CSDs even when these were user-owned. More competition, it declared, would lower the cost of capital for Europe's businesses and 'translate ultimately into additional growth and jobs'. The report cited studies that estimated the efficiency gains from integrating EU securities markets at around €100 billion. Adding grist to the mill, DG Markt reported that cross-border equity trades in Europe cost investors on average between two and six times more than domestic transactions. At the same time, domestic trades in EU post-trade infrastructures were up to eight times more expensive than DTCC in the US.[21]

Less than a fortnight after publication of the DG Comp report, and still to make up his mind on whether or not to legislate on clearing and settlement, Commissioner McCreevy received word from Germany, the EU's biggest member state, that it would not support any directive that hurt Deutsche Börse or its silo structure.

Addressing the annual convention of the Federation of European Securities Exchanges (FESE) in Zurich on 8 June 2006, Jörg Asmussen, the director general of Germany's federal finance ministry, warned against regulatory intervention that favoured or discriminated against 'certain efficient structures'.

[20] European Commission, Competition DG (May 2006), 'Competition in EU securities trading and post-trading: Issues paper'.

[21] European Commission, Internal Market DG (May 2006), 'Draft working document on post-trading', plus Annex I, 'Analysis of studies examining European post-trading costs'.

'We cannot have integration at any price,' Asmussen warned. Asmussen, whose partner coincidentally headed Deutsche Börse's public affairs office in Berlin, added: 'Well functioning and efficient national structures which have evolved over many years may not be just simply left by the wayside. Against this background, Germany would not be able to accept a clearing and settlement directive.'

Little was heard against vertical silos from the Commission's competition directorate following this warning. For McCreevy and his officials in DG Markt, Germany's intervention was a signal that a proposal for legislation from the Commission, which would require the backing of EU member states and the European Parliament to become law, might not be the easiest way of advancing the single market for post-trade services.

16.7 THE ECLIPSE OF THE SINGLE CCP

With hindsight, the May 2006 report from DG Comp marked the high point of the EU Commission's opposition to vertical silos. The report also provided one signal among many that the idea of a single CCP for Europe was past its sell-by date as it declared the following:

> While there exist economies of scale in securities clearing, and a number of market participants have actively called for the creation of a single European CCP, no study, at least to our knowledge, has empirically investigated the minimum efficient scale or whether the costs of monopoly provision (such as in terms of higher prices) would outweigh the scale effects.[22]

The single CCP idea had resurfaced several times after being abandoned by the ESF in 2001. In December 2003, the European Financial Services Round Table, an elite financial ginger group consisting of 17 chairmen and chief executives of European banks and insurance companies, called for a European CCP that would be 'a single entry point across securities (equities and bonds) and across markets (cash and derivatives, regulated markets, ECNs, OTC, etc.)'.[23] For good measure, it should also operate across currencies, which would include the euro and 'at least the British pound, Swedish krona and Swiss franc'.

The idea appeared to catch the attention of McCreevy in September 2005, when he commented that it was 'At face value . . . an interesting prospect' where 'there could indeed be cost savings and improved efficiencies'.[24]

It gathered momentum thereafter amid reports that Deutsche Börse and Euronext were discussing a merger. In February 2006, three private sector initiatives were put forward during a meeting of the Cesame group and in high level discussions between McCreevy and CEOs and senior executives of users of clearing and settlement systems in Brussels:

- Four trade associations from the UK, Italy and France[25] urged more horizontal consolidation for post-trade activities. They suggested that LCH.Clearnet and Eurex Clearing among CCPs and Euroclear and Clearstream on the settlement side of the business should form 'the first two building blocks towards pan-European infrastructures'.

[22] European Commission, Competition DG (May 2006).

[23] European Financial Services Round Table (December 2003), 'Securities clearing and settlement in Europe'.

[24] European Commission (13 September 2005) at 14th annual *ALFI-NICSA Europe-USA Investment Funds Forum*.

[25] The French Association of Investment Firms (AFEI), the Italian Association of Financial Intermediaries (ASSOSIM), the French Banking Federation (FBF) and the London Investment Banking Association (LIBA): AFEI, ASSOSIM, FBF, LIBA (20 February 2006), 'European Trade Associations' Call for EU Action on European Exchanges and Market Infrastructure', joint statement issued through AFEI and LIBA.

- Bob Wigley, chairman for Europe, the Middle East and Africa of Merrill Lynch International, called for a cross-border, user-owned single CCP featuring cross-product clearing facilities and a choice of settlement providers.
- David Hardy, chief executive of the LCH.Clearnet Group, put forward a discussion paper advocating the full consolidation of CCPs in the EU with the aim of delivering economies of scale and scope, lower fees, better risk management and greater competition at the trading level.

These plans yielded nothing, however. Users were divided, with some warning that a single CCP could stifle innovation. A practical problem, arising from the renewal of corporate manoeuvrings in the listed exchange sector and high trading volumes at the time, was that the valuations put on CCPs belonging to exchange groups were so high that there was no financially feasible way of engineering a single CCP.

In April, DG Markt, the EU Commission's internal market directorate, concluded that establishing a single CCP was beyond the Commission's powers.[26] In May, Euronext put an end to any hopes of a transformational cross-border European merger with Deutsche Börse by agreeing to merge with the New York Stock Exchange instead. In July, Hardy lost his job as CEO of LCH.Clearnet. The fact that his forced resignation was partly the result of a failed IT programme designed to integrate the French and UK parts of LCH.Clearnet did nothing for the credibility of the single CCP idea.

16.8 INTEROPERABILITY ON THE MENU

In its May 2006 paper, DG Comp floated a different idea: that of greater interoperability among clearing houses in Europe.

Access to clearing arrangements was 'one prerequisite for competition to be effective and therefore must be assured on a non-discriminatory basis,' it said. 'CCP services could – and probably should – operate in a competitive environment provided issues of interoperability are overcome.'[27]

Interoperability, or 'open architecture' as it was known in the US, had quietly emerged as a policy option over the preceding three years. In the US, it had driven the process of consolidation of CCPs into NSCC and CSDs into DTC in the 1980s and 1990s that culminated in the creation of DTCC.

Interoperability was a central theme in a January 2003 report on improving cross-border clearing and settlement from the eminent G30 think tank. This suggested its benefits could be as great as those gained from the national standardisation of railway track gauges in the US in the 19th century, or internationally from the automation of air traffic control services through the standards and protocols of the International Civil Aviation Organisation.[28]

Reaping such rewards would need far reaching changes. To work, the G30 vision of interoperability would require 'like or compatible processes, business practices, controls, technologies, products, access arrangements and fee structures' – conditions that existed in the US market for equities but were far from being realised in the EU.

---

[26] Mario Nava, the official responsible for financial market infrastructure in DG Markt, at an ECB Seminar *Issues related to Central Counterparty Clearing* on 4 April 2006.

[27] European Commission, Competition DG (May 2006).

[28] G30 (January 2003), 'Global clearing and settlement: A plan of action'.

DG Comp's report admitted there were barriers to interoperability in Europe. But it suggested that CCPs – as a relatively recent innovation in European equity markets – should be in the forefront of removing these.

Interoperability might be one way to overcome the differences between horizontal and vertical models of integration – provided the owners of vertical structures allowed open access and fair tariffs for users of other exchanges and trading platforms and, in turn, allowed their own users to clear and settle trades elsewhere. It was an alternative to the single CCP as a way of facilitating cross-border securities trading.

As if on cue, the Commission's suggestion was followed almost immediately by news that the LSE would offer its customers the choice of central counterparty clearing through Switzerland's SIS x-clear as well as LCH.Clearnet. Although virt-x, the London trading platform for Swiss and European blue chips, already offered SIS x-clear and LCH.Clearnet services as well as a choice of settlement location, the LSE was the first big European exchange to promise users a choice of CCP. The service, slated to start from late 2007, aimed at cutting users' costs. The announcement undermined claims that CCP services were not amenable to competition.

The interoperability idea gained support. When Commission officials met industry representatives on 12 June in Brussels for another Cesame meeting, Monte Titoli, the settlement arm of the Borsa Italiana group, proposed interoperability as a way forward for the industry, claiming it could provide short-term solutions at minimum cost.

Also in June, Massimo Capuano, CEO of Borsa Italiana and FESE president, had argued that 'interoperability could lead to a higher degree of competition, ultimately reducing costs for market users'.[29] Under Capuano's guidance, FESE proposed an industry-wide interoperability agreement with CCPs, CSDs and users. It was a suggestion that the Commission was happy to follow up.

16.9 THE CODE OF CONDUCT

On 11 July 2006, after months of saying little amid furious lobbying from backers and opponents of EU legislation, McCreevy outlined an industry 'Code of Conduct' to lower the costs and enhance the efficiency of cross-border clearing and settlement of equities in the EU.[30]

The Commissioner gave infrastructure providers until 31 October to produce an industry-led solution, with a timetable until the end of 2007 for behavioural changes to overcome the barriers to cross-border clearing and settlement of equities.

The proposed code contrasted with a radical plan, launched just days earlier by the ECB, for a harmonised securities settlement service, dubbed Target2-Securities (T2S), to be owned and operated by the ESCB for the eurozone.

Whereas the ECB adopted a top-down approach, the Commissioner's plan was all about creating the conditions for the industry to change itself. Drawing lessons from consultations in the Cesame group and the May 2006 report from DG Comp, McCreevy set out a road map to achieve greater efficiency in EU capital markets through price transparency and increased competition.

---

[29] Remarks during FESE's 10th *European Financial Markets Convention*, Zurich.

[30] European Commission (11 July 2006), 'Clearing and settlement: the way forward', McCreevy's speech of 11 July 2006 announcing the code to the Economic and Monetary Affairs Committee of the European Parliament.

McCreevy's preference for an industry-led solution rather than EU legislation mirrored his own deeply held free-market beliefs as well as his fears that the European Parliament would radically amend any Commission proposal. It also reflected a widespread concern that, despite the Lamfalussy wise men's reforms, EU law-making still took far too long for fast-changing markets and could lead – as with MiFID – to rules that many regarded as excessively complex.

The code outlined by McCreevy in July 2006 comprised three elements, to be introduced in stages:

1. Price transparency in post-trade services by the end of 2006. Companies would make public the prices, specific content and conditions of each service offered, and fully disclose rebate and reduction schemes to eliminate price discrimination.
2. Effective rights of access on a fair, transparent and non-discriminatory basis to service providers along the chain from exchanges to CCPs, from CCPs to CCPs, from CCPs to CSDs and from CSDs to CSDs, by the end of June 2007. The code would also set conditions for interoperability, entailing more advanced relationships between providers aimed at producing customised services.
3. Separate accounting for providers' main activities and unbundling of their services by 1 January 2008.

The three elements were intended to be mutually reinforcing and dovetail with other initiatives including the removal of the Giovannini barriers, where progress was slow, and the much delayed ESCB-CESR recommendations for CCPs.

Intellectually, the code owed much to Giovannini who had advocated general remote access to, and open architecture for, post-trade services to foster competition, and had pushed for a clean separation of services. The hope was that unbundling, fair access and price transparency would lead to simplified and reduced tariffs, especially for basic and standard services. These would compress earnings among Europe's profit-oriented infrastructure providers, cut costs for users and perhaps speed up consolidation in the post-trade sector.

Where Giovannini differed from McCreevy was in believing that such developments would best be directed through EU legislation.

Underlying McCreevy's preference for the code was a deep scepticism about the potential benefits of EU legislation when financial markets were changing rapidly. However, McCreevy kept the threat of new regulations in the background to encourage the industry to comply with his wishes: 'Regulators always have the range of measures at their disposal to force changes through,' he said.

The Commissioner wanted bankable promises by the end of October 2006. The code would initially apply to cash equities and include a verification and auditing procedure to ensure the industry met its commitments. In parallel, the Commission pledged to keep pressing the industry and governments to remove the 15 Giovannini barriers.

McCreevy insisted that the Commission's role was 'not to pick winners, nor dictate a particular outcome. Nor determine the final architecture' of clearing and settlement in Europe. Instead, its job was to work with the grain of the market, ensure that unnecessary barriers were removed and that 'EU Treaty provisions, particularly competition policy, are applied to the full'.

The planned code was a novelty in EU regulation, a hybrid of industry self regulation and 'soft law' where the Commission steered the process and promised to enforce compliance. It was, McCreevy admitted, 'not without risks'.

Successful cases of commercial rivals cooperating to solve an industry problem through Commission encouragement were rare: one of few examples cited by officials was an agreement some years before among auto manufacturers to harmonise the height, off the ground, of car bumpers.

One striking feature of the code was its emphasis on interoperability. Although interoperability had gained traction among policy makers, worries remained about linking different infrastructure providers supplying similar services to facilitate cross-border trading. Some argued that interoperability was difficult to organise because of legal and tax barriers and could require often expensive duplication of IT equipment. In the case of CCPs it raised concerns that risk-management standards could become compromised.

The code had to overcome other doubts. There were many – among European Parliamentarians, in member states, among Commission officials and in parts of the industry – who wanted post-trade legislation and would shed no tears if the code failed.

But it passed its first hurdle on 7 November, when McCreevy appeared with senior executives of Europe's securities trading and post-trade sectors before the Brussels press corps to announce that the industry's leaders had signed the code.[31]

It was, he stressed, 'a first step', covering cash equities initially. McCreevy made clear he wanted the industry to consider extending it to other asset classes, 'specifically bonds and derivatives' and to other service providers.

The code was signed by the chief executives of the EU's exchanges, CCPs, CSDs and the two ICSDs rather than their trade associations in order to give it credibility. The one significant sanction for the Commission to enforce compliance was the naming and shaming of backsliders. Also signing the code were non-EU financial infrastructures, including the CCPs of Switzerland and Norway as well as the CCP/CSD of Serbia.

The signing ceremony came after only four months of negotiations – a remarkably short period compared with more than five years of debate on clearing and settlement preceding McCreevy's July 2006 announcement. The rapid progress reflected intensive work by Martin Power, the *chef de cabinet* or head of McCreevy's office, David Wright, director of financial markets in the EU Commission's DG Markt, and Mario Nava, head of DG Markt's financial market infrastructure unit, who were backed by officials from DG Markt and DG Comp, and by EACH, ECSDA and FESE,[32] the lobby groups for Europe's financial infrastructure providers.

The code's 'ultimate aim' was

> to offer market participants the freedom to choose their preferred provider of services separately at each layer of the transaction chain (trading, clearing and settlement) and to make the concept of 'cross-border' redundant for transactions between EU member states.

However, the code was a compromise with limited reach. It could not erase legal barriers between member states or deliver a harmonised regulatory framework. The code did not apply to bonds. Nor did it cover agent banks. The exclusion of exchange-traded derivatives was testimony to the lobbying skills of the Brussels office of FESE on behalf of those of its members, such as the Deutsche Börse group, with lucrative derivatives businesses. Some difficult negotiations were left for later, notably over the details of access and interoperability where participating companies might have to adapt their business models, incurring costs in the process.

The code cleared a second hurdle on 1 January 2007 when the signatories published details of prices, discounts and rebates in line with their price transparency commitments.

---

[31] EACH, ECSDA, FESE (7 November, 2006), 'European Code of Conduct for Clearing and Settlement'; and European Commission, 'McCreevy speech at press conference'.

[32] Respectively, the European Association of Central Counterparty Clearing Houses (EACH), the European Central Securities Depositories Association (ECSDA) and the Federation of European Securities Exchanges (FESE).

On 28 June 2007, EACH, ECSDA and FESE agreed an 'Access and Interoperability Guideline' as part of the code.[33] Consisting of a 128 densely written paragraphs, the guideline was the most difficult part of the code to implement especially as far as interoperability was concerned. By comparison, the access clauses of the guideline were relatively straightforward. The code envisaged various degrees of access among market infrastructures and defined relations that were standardised or customised as well as the handling of transaction feeds from a trading platform or a CCP to a CSD and from a trading platform to a CCP.

The precedents for interoperability among market infrastructures were mixed. In the securities settlement business, a successful electronic 'bridge' between Euroclear and Clearstream had existed since 1980 to carry out securities transactions between the two rival ICSDs. But for much of its existence it had been the cause of acrimonious disputes between the two companies and of niggling discontent among users.

Among CCPs, there had been several successful instances of interoperability. As noted earlier,[34] the first was probably the 1977 reciprocal clearing services agreement between ICCH and BCC. Another early example was the 1984 Mutual Offset System (MOS) between the CME of Chicago and SIMEX in Singapore, which allowed certain futures contracts to be traded in one jurisdiction and closed in another with traders able to choose where to clear their trades. London's virt-x equity trading platform enabled LCH and SIS x-clear to provide competing clearing services from 2003. In the bond market, MTS Italy, a bond trading platform, enabled both CC&G (the Italian CCP) and LCH.Clearnet to clear corporate and government bonds traded on MTS from 2005.

The secret of these and other successes lay in their being commercially beneficial to the sponsoring exchanges, often by expanding trading opportunities that attracted more users. There had to be a suitable level of trust or contractually-agreed safety arrangements between the participating CCPs. Prescribing interoperability was more difficult, as the jargon of the code's guideline indicated.

For the lay reader, the interoperability guideline was almost impenetrable. Interoperability meant 'advanced forms of relationships' between organisations that agreed to 'establish mutual solutions' going beyond standardised or customised services. It could apply between CCPs or between CSDs but not between different categories of market infrastructure. Interoperability was not an automatic right for a CCP that requested to enter an advanced relationship with another. It depended on agreement based on the business cases of the CCPs involved.

CCP to CCP interoperability was commercially difficult to set up. Without proper reciprocity, CCPs asked to provide interoperability were effectively being invited to share their business with a rival or rivals. The nightmare scenario for a CCP would be to find itself in an interoperable relationship with a weaker CCP in which it could be obliged to share its partner's losses and, *in extremis*, to bail it out.

16.10 PROBLEMS WITH THE CODE OF CONDUCT

In box ticking terms, the provisions on access and interoperability got off to a rollicking start. By January 2008, EACH, ECSDA and FESE had counted no fewer than 82 requests for links between trading, clearing and settlement infrastructures with 29 involving CCPs. Of the

[33] EACH, ECSDA, FESE (28 June 2007), 'Access and interoperability guideline'.

[34] See Section 8.9. The list of agreements in this chapter is not exhaustive.

latter, 17 requests were for CCP to CCP links and 12 for links between CCPs and settlement providers.

LCH.Clearnet was among companies filing requests. In August 2007, it asked Deutsche Börse and Borsa Italiana for full interoperability with their CCPs: Eurex Clearing and Cassa di Compensazione e Garanzia. It requested peer-to-peer clearing links so that users of the German and Italian stock markets and the LSE and virt-x could consolidate clearing of cash equities at LCH.Clearnet Ltd in London.

Choosing not to betray the deep scepticism with which LCH.Clearnet had signed the code, Roger Liddell, by this time LCH.Clearnet's chief executive, expressed confidence that access would 'be swiftly granted'. The hoped-for extension of LCH.Clearnet's CCP services to include Germany and Italy would help lower unit costs and so pave the way for lower fees across all markets.[35]

Liddell's privately held doubts were well founded. Nine months later, LCH.Clearnet was no nearer to achieving interoperability with its continental competitors. It had even run into difficulties implementing the guideline between LCH.Clearnet Ltd and LCH.Clearnet SA for clearing trades executed on the LSE, virt-x, NYSE Euronext cash markets and the LSE's Dutch Trading Service. As Liddell explained to a June 2008 conference in London, the code cut no ice with national regulators who had not signed it:

> The biggest frustration that we have is that there are certain parties who are key to making it work in certain countries, particularly Frankfurt, that were not signatories to the code. So those that did sign up to it signed, knowing that it was not entirely in their gift to make it work. And the cynic may even say that they may have been comforted by the fact that it was unlikely those other authorities would be quick to fall in line.[36]

In France, LCH.Clearnet's London subsidiary fell foul of *Banque de France* regulations for the Euronext markets that effectively required a CCP to be a bank in the eurozone to interoperate in the French market. When in response, LCH.Clearnet set out to frame its interoperability strategy in the eurozone around LCH.Clearnet SA, which was a Paris-based bank, it hit problems with German regulations that required trades in Frankfurt to be cleared by a German bank.

The large number of requested links added to the difficulties, generating, in Liddell's view, 'massive activity with the potential for fog, inertia and a good excuse for lack of progress'. Compounding that problem, link requests were processed on a first-come, first-served basis with little regard to the importance of the markets or infrastructures concerned.

These rules and draft rules provided many opportunities for bureaucratic delay. As Liddell observed: 'We are not receiving any stop signs; we have received no red lights. We haven't quite received any green lights. Instead, we have received a whole lot of amber lights and some of them are quite bright amber lights.'

'We are frustrated,' Chris Tupker, LCH.Clearnet's chairman complained in September 2008. 'We haven't had a contact from the German regulator to our questions to them since late August 2007.'[37] Noting that 'time goes on. These are very fast moving markets and you just can't wait,' Tupker appealed to the Commission to apply 'some authority, some power, or at least

[35] LCH.Clearnet Group (9 August 2007), 'LCH.Clearnet requests interoperability links under Code of Conduct with Deutsche Börse and Borsa Italiana', press release.

[36] At the *Mondo Visione Exchange Forum*, London, 4 June 2008.

[37] Speaking at the 2008 Eurofi Conference, *EU Priorities and Proposals from the Financial Services Industry for the ECOFIN Council*, Nice, 12 September 2008.

moral suasion to get some of these blockages addressed'. He told his audience of top European bankers and policymakers:

> The Commission, quite rightly, says that the Code of Conduct is an industry initiative and they should look after themselves. But we have said from the beginning that we would likely need some help: Whether it's from the father and mother or midwife, we don't really care. But we can't do it on our own.

LCH.Clearnet's cry for help highlighted the weakness of the code. At the trading level, MiFID shook up competition by allowing MTFs to enter the market unencumbered by existing infrastructure and regulation. By extension, the clearing houses that provided CCP services for the MTFs enjoyed the same benefits.

But MiFID and the code provided little help for incumbent CCPs. And of the incumbents, and as Europe's sole horizontally-structured, multinational clearing house, LCH.Clearnet suffered most from inadequacies of the framework put in place on McCreevy's watch. Adding to the urgency of LCH.Clearnet's lament were the group's own problems, which escalated in 2007 to a point where its very survival was threatened.

17

LCH.Clearnet Under Threat

17.1 DAVID HARDY DEPARTS

On 5 July 2006, David Hardy resigned as chief executive of LCH.Clearnet at the insistence of the group's board. His departure after 19 years with LCH followed the failure of a big IT project, the Generic Clearing System (GCS), and reflected the group's inability to integrate the London Clearing House and Clearnet businesses two and a half years after their merger.

Hardy's resignation was the most dramatic event thus far in a worsening crisis at LCH.Clearnet. That day was also the last day for the chairman Gérard de la Martinière whose decision to step down had been announced some seven weeks earlier.

Chris Tupker, chairman of Euroclear, was drafted in to take de la Martinière's place with effect from 10 July. Two weeks after taking the LCH.Clearnet chair, Tupker appointed Roger Liddell, a former Goldman Sachs managing director, as chief executive of the LCH.Clearnet Group. One of the first acts of the new team was to write off the full €121.3 million cost of GCS.[1]

The costly IT failure had much in common with other failed computer projects that had punctuated the development of financial infrastructures since the marriage of computers and markets in the 1960s. Hardy commissioned GCS to integrate the many different clearing platforms and risk-management systems inside the LCH.Clearnet Group. Overburdened with consultants and lacking adequate management controls, the GCS project ran into difficulties some time before Hardy's forced exit. GCS incurred an impairment charge of €20.1 million in the group's 2005 consolidated income statement. The write off in the 2006 accounts was more than double that at €47.8 million.

The technology failure was symptomatic of deeper problems at LCH.Clearnet. The group's management failed to deliver the synergies and efficiency gains promised with the 2003 merger, putting LCH.Clearnet at odds with users, regulators and the exchanges for which it cleared.

A climate of suspicion that existed between London and Paris as financial centres infected relations between the British and French parts of the group and helped to fuel a breakdown of trust at several levels. By the time Hardy resigned, he had lost more than the support of his board. His relations with the *Commission bancaire*, the lead regulator in France, were dire. The chief executives of the LCH.Clearnet Group's two operating subsidiaries in Paris and London had also expressed concerns about Hardy in writing to their respective chairmen.

The group board was dysfunctional. It was riven by conflicts of interest between users and exchanges and also among the exchanges represented on it. The board was beyond the control of de la Martinière, who was a part-time chairman with many other commitments.

Tensions surfaced between LCH and Clearnet soon after the merger. When LCH and Clearnet first put forward their plan for a consolidated European clearing house in 2000, they

[1] LCH.Clearnet Group (29 August 2006), 'Interim report for the half year to June 2006'.

announced that they would use a single set of clearing and netting systems, based on the Clearing 21 technology that ParisBourse had acquired and adapted as a result of the 1997 technology exchange with the CME.

When LCH and Clearnet merged, Clearnet believed Clearing 21 was still to be the system for the merged group. Hardy, however, thought it was unreliable and unsuitable and wanted GCS instead. It was only after the merger was agreed and approved by the regulators that Clearnet managers (now working for SA) found LCH had started the GCS project a few months before.

These differences created resistance to change in France. Among the staff of Clearnet, who had experience of integrating the French, Belgian and Dutch CCPs, the view took hold that Hardy was set on swallowing their company and replacing their technology and jobs with a clearing system made in London. Having invested in Clearing 21, the last thing that many LCH.Clearnet customers on the continent wanted was more IT upheaval, especially as the supposed benefits of new systems were often difficult to pin down. Among French regulators, there was a suspicion – in no way alleviated by Hardy's suggestion that the clearing of French government debt should move to London – that LCH.Clearnet group policy was to concentrate all business in London. In consequence, the group found that it was increasingly difficult to push ahead with the integration of LCH and Clearnet.

The structure of the group was hardly conducive to integration. The CCPs in Paris and London were run by subsidiaries of the group, each of which had its own board. Both the French and UK subsidiaries had to achieve a *modus vivendi* with their own national regulator. Each regulator saw its job as upholding the operations of the group within its area of jurisdiction. Relations between the UK's FSA and France's *Commission bancaire* were hallmarked by rivalry rather than cooperation. In these circumstances, the day-to-day priorities of management in the London and Paris subsidiaries could diverge from those of the LCH.Clearnet Group.

The group's board provided little help in these circumstances. The representatives of the exchanges had different interests to those of the users. Among the exchanges, Euronext, with its big business in equities and substantial income from retrocession fees and preference shares, had different priorities to the International Petroleum Exchange and London Metal Exchange where energy and metals futures were traded.

The chairman's message in the group's 2005 annual report made no secret of problems of governance at group level: 'The board is organised to reflect the peculiar nature of the company,' de la Martinière commented, 'its size and composition may have undermined the efficiency of its work, despite the capacity and good willingness of the individuals'. LCH.Clearnet commissioned Zygos Partnership, a consultancy, to review the board's governance in a bid to improve its performance. 'Their conclusion was they had never in their experience seen a board that was functioning so badly,'[2] de la Martinière later recalled.

With his many other commitments, de la Martinière was not the man to bring matters under control. He held Hardy in high esteem and protected the CEO when problems surfaced. Nor was Hardy challenged by Jean-François Théodore, CEO and Chairman of Euronext who, with Hardy, had been the architect of the merger of LCH and Clearnet.

Théodore's aims in merging LCH and Clearnet, however, differed from those of Hardy.

For Hardy, the merger of LCH and Clearnet was primarily a response to the market's wishes for consolidation, lower costs and improved capital efficiencies in an increasingly integrated

[2] Conversation with the author, 11 September 2008.

European capital market. Over time, with the help of new IT capacity, he wanted to give users the opportunity to choose either London or Paris to book all their trades and so enhance the efficiency of their netting, use of collateral and capital when trading in Europe.[3] Given his background, it was inevitable that this European vision was refracted through a London prism.

Théodore's immediate goal followed from Euronext's acquisition of LIFFE and the subsequent combination of Euronext's derivatives markets in Euronext.liffe. He wanted to bring together the clearing services for these markets which were divided between LCH and Clearnet.

His second aim was strategic. Théodore wanted to burnish Euronext's credentials as suitor for the LSE as part of a wider plan for consolidation along horizontal lines of major European trading, clearing and settlement infrastructures, which would leave Euronext as the dominant player.

Consolidation was already happening at the settlement level, because the Euroclear Group, which operated the central securities depositories that served the Euronext markets in France, Belgium and the Netherlands, also owned CREST, the UK CSD. As Olivier Lefebvre, one of Euronext's representatives on the LCH.Clearnet board from 2004 to 2007, later observed: 'Because Euroclear was combining with Crest, it seemed logical to tie up LCH with Clearnet in an approach to the LSE.'[4]

Théodore's attitude towards and actions regarding LCH.Clearnet were strongly influenced by his ambition to do a deal with the LSE. He wooed Clara Furse, the LSE's chief executive, who was hostile towards Euronext following its acquisition of LIFFE and as part of a charm offensive gave her one of Euronext's seats on LCH.Clearnet group board.

But from the moment Werner Seifert launched the Deutsche Börse bid for the LSE in December 2004, Théodore had other pressing issues on his plate as Euronext was caught up in a blizzard of bids and counterbids among exchange groups based on both sides of the Atlantic.

Having come within an ace of reaching agreement with the LSE in March 2005, Théodore kept alive his hopes of a deal despite the restrictions imposed by the UK Competition Commission later that year. During the winter of 2005–6 he had to fend off political pressure from the governments in Berlin and Paris to merge Euronext with Deutsche Börse. In April 2006, Euronext again came close to sealing a deal with the LSE only to be blown off course by news that Nasdaq of the US had acquired 14.99% of the London exchange. In May 2006, as the problems at LCH.Clearnet were coming to a head, Euronext was once again fending off an approach from Deutsche Börse. At this point, the recently demutualised New York Stock Exchange came riding to Théodore's rescue. On 22 May 2006, the NYSE offered nearly €8 billion in cash and shares for Euronext. The two exchanges signed an agreement on 1 June for a 'merger of equals' creating 'the first global exchange'.[5]

The intense corporate manoeuvring among the exchanges in 2005–6 distracted Théodore from the worsening state of LCH.Clearnet. When he did act, his decisions were influenced by tactical considerations.

Thus, in May 2005, the GCS problems came before the LCH.Clearnet group board and prompted some board members to call for Hardy's dismissal. Théodore, whose success in creating Euronext was based to a large extent on the successful integration of IT, was under no illusions as to the gravity of the situation. But he gave his support to Hardy and in the process ensured the survival of the embattled CEO for another year. According to people familiar with

[3] LCH.Clearnet Group (25 June 2003), 'An interview with David Hardy'.
[4] Meeting with the author, 9 September 2008.
[5] NYSE Group and Euronext NV (1 June 2006), 'NYSE Group and Euronext NV agree to a merger of equals', joint news release.

developments at the time, Théodore was still hoping to fulfil his dream of merging with the LSE. Therefore, he wanted neither a clash with the City nor to be seen by the UK Competition Commission as exercising too much control over LCH.Clearnet.

A year later, the problems with GCS had worsened. Hardy had also angered some UK board members by failing to send them a letter from the FSA that had criticised LCH.Clearnet's corporate governance. Moreover, he had decided to give a big IT support contract to IBM that would mean a decline in the work carried out by Atos Euronext for LCH.Clearnet, provoking hostility among the French regulators. By this time, some members of the group board were again mobilising against Hardy. Adverse perceptions about LCH.Clearnet were filtering through to its regulators, prompting the Banque de France in particular to put its considerable prestige behind pressure for change.

In Paris, Christophe Hémon, the chief executive of LCH.Clearnet SA, was disturbed by some of Hardy's decisions and what he perceived as a lack of transparency in decision making in London. Hémon was also under pressure from SA's regulators who were telling him that he had an obligation under French law to share any concerns about the company with the authorities.

During the weekend before the July 2006 board meeting in Paris, Hémon sent a letter to the chairman of Paris-based LCH.Clearnet SA voicing his doubts about Hardy's plans and the management of the group. Patrick Birley, the chief executive of LCH.Clearnet Ltd, the London subsidiary, also put his concerns in writing to Ltd's chairman.

On the night before the board meeting, Hémon, Hardy and several members of the LCH.Clearnet group board attended a dinner organised for Paris Europlace, the lobby group for France's biggest financial companies. It was at the dinner that Hardy began to realise that his position was untenable. The following day, Hardy arrived for the group board meeting with a strategic plan to take LCH.Clearnet forward in the years ahead. It was not discussed.

17.2 TUPKER AND LIDDELL TAKE COMMAND

The task facing Chris Tupker and Roger Liddell at LCH.Clearnet was to transform the battered group's prospects for the better. Both were post-trade professionals who also brought fresh perspectives to their respective jobs of chairman and chief executive.

A Canadian national of Dutch origin, Tupker had overseen a dramatic change during his six years as Chairman of Euroclear. As Sir Nigel Wicks, his successor at Euroclear, noted in a valedictory tribute, Euroclear developed on Tupker's watch 'from what was in 2000 a mainly fixed-income securities settlement service provider, operated under contract by Morgan Guaranty Trust Company of New York' into 'the world's largest fully integrated, user-owned and user-governed provider of domestic and cross-border settlement and related services for bond, equity and fund transactions'.[6] In the process, Tupker coaxed Euroclear from being an introspective, technology-oriented subsidiary of a US bank into a company able to pull its weight among the many decision makers, lobbyists and regulators who made financial policy in Europe.

Tupker knew how users reacted. Before 2000, he was senior executive vice president of ABN Amro Bank responsible for securities processing, IT, finance, custody, risk and compliance within its investment banking division. Having been Brussels-based, there was little chance of him succumbing to City parochialism. Because Euroclear had a substantial

[6] Quoted in a media release from Euroclear (20 July 2006), 'Sir Nigel Wicks to become Euroclear Chairman as of 1 August 2006'.

stake in LCH.Clearnet, Tupker could also bring a shareholder's perspective to the job of revitalising the ailing clearer.

He was recruited to be a far more hands-on chairman than de la Martinière. Although he still tried to take long summer vacations in Canada, he was constantly in touch and ready to fly back to London if necessary. Tupker's greater responsibilities were reflected in his pay cheque. His total emoluments as chairman in 2007, his first full year in post, were €513,000 compared with €76,000 paid to de la Martinière in 2005.

Roger Liddell brought to LCH.Clearnet the discipline and work ethic of a Goldman Sachs executive. He had prospered in unglamorous professions. After leaving university with a degree in mining engineering, he worked for state-owned British Coal for 10 years before obtaining an MBA in 1989 and joining Goldman Sachs in 1993. Fast talking, quick witted and down to earth, Liddell rose to be head of global operations at Goldman Sachs where he was responsible for the operational support of the investment bank's businesses worldwide. He knew Tupker well because he was a member of the Euroclear board until 2005. Liddell was also no stranger to LCH.Clearnet, having been appointed by Tupker in January 2005 to represent Euroclear's interests on the LCH.Clearnet Group board. He brought to the chief executive's job up-to-date experience as a user of the clearing house's services.

The new top team at LCH.Clearnet faced serious problems and only limited time in which to repair the damage. The failures at LCH.Clearnet had alienated users, exchanges and regulators at a time of rapid change in the market for post-trade services, which rivals were eager to exploit.

Integration between LCH.Clearnet Ltd and LCH.Clearnet SA was so limited that the group only decided to develop interoperability between the London and Paris CCPs after publication of the Access and Interoperability Guideline of the European Code of Conduct.[7]

LCH.Clearnet's users complained about paltry fee reductions and an absence of rebates. Those who were also shareholders had seen dividend payments suspended. Clearing members using LCH.Clearnet SA to clear equity deals in Paris were especially hard hit by fees that far exceeded those of CCPs serving exchanges in London, Frankfurt, Milan and Zurich and even the other Euronext markets of Amsterdam, Brussels and Lisbon.[8]

There was discontent among the exchanges that LCH.Clearnet served. The derivatives exchanges felt LCH had focused too much on equity clearing since the merger with Clearnet and complained that their vertically-structured rivals could innovate more easily than horizontally-structured LCH.Clearnet, which appeared slow to respond to their needs.

Euronext, although profiting as a 'returns-focused' shareholder from retrocession fees and the dividends on its preference shares, griped that the scrapping of the GCS system left Euronext-Liffe's TRS-CPS clearing system in need of updating.

The LSE's Clara Furse was among the board members who had actively sought to remove Hardy. It was at her initiative that SIS x-clear of Switzerland was invited to compete against LCH in clearing UK equities. The plan, announced six weeks before Hardy's resignation, was intended to push down clearing fees at LCH.Clearnet, so lowering costs for investors trading on the London exchange.

Amid the manoeuvrings among leading exchanges on both sides of the Atlantic, there were other changes afoot with serious implications for LCH.Clearnet's future business.

One was the transformation of London's International Petroleum Exchange into an ambitious and restless electronic trading concern under US ownership. When LCH and Clearnet

[7] LCH.Clearnet Group (20 September 2007), 'LCH.Clearnet to implement Code of Conduct internally', press release.
[8] According to European Commission, Competition DG (May 2006).

first started talking to each other in 2000, the IPE was a dozy mutual with a small shareholding in LCH. In 2001, it was acquired by IntercontinentalExchange (ICE), the US Internet-based electronic marketplace founded the year before to trade energy and OTC contracts. In 2005, ICE closed the IPE's traditional trading floor, moved the exchange's energy contracts onto an electronic platform and rebranded its London operation ICE Futures.

In 2006, clearing for ICE Futures and ICE OTC contracts traded in the US was one of LCH.Clearnet's fastest growing areas of business. But in September, ICE, the parent company in Atlanta, agreed a US$1 billion takeover of the New York Board of Trade (NYBOT), a soft commodity exchange with a clearing house – the New York Clearing Corp – attached. ICE put clearing synergies at the top of strategic and financial benefits to be expected from the acquisition, which took effect in January 2007.

The continuing expansion of the CME Group was the underlying reason Jeffrey Sprecher, the CEO of ICE, wanted to strengthen his company's clearing capabilities. The CME's share price had risen exponentially since its clearing division began clearing for the CBOT back in 2004. Listed exchanges groups without clearing saw their stock prices languish in comparison.

The statement announcing the NYBOT deal pointed out that ICE customers paid US$36 million in fees to LCH.Clearnet over the previous 12 months.[9] This indicated that ICE would be looking to change its contractual arrangements with LCH.Clearnet and might choose to disintermediate the UK-based clearer.

Another development, announced in November 2006, was Project Turquoise. Conceived in anticipation of the implementation of the EU's MiFID directive, Turquoise would be a London-based 'multilateral trading facility' owned by investment banks. The seven large investment banks[10] that launched the project accounted for about 50% of European equities trades.

There was much debate late in 2006 about whether Turquoise was really intended to disintermediate Europe's exchanges in general and the LSE in particular, or just to put pressure on them to lower fees. What was indisputable was that the announcement signalled widespread disenchantment among users with all financial infrastructure providers.

The users' main complaints were directed at the exchanges and their rising profits but post-trade service providers did not escape criticism. The big investment banks felt they had not benefited sufficiently from the recovery in stock markets since 2003 that followed the dot-com bust. While the profits and share prices of listed exchange groups soared, banks' trading margins were under pressure because of heavy investment in algorithm-driven capacities and fierce competition among trading desks.

As Sir David Walker, by now a senior adviser to Morgan Stanley, complained:

> The margins at the front-end have been greatly compressed, and we do some of this business for practically nothing. In circumstances where clearing and settlement costs are either the same or rising slightly, the significance of clearing and settlement costs is greatly increased.[11]

Tupker and Liddell were aware of these concerns. Walker was one of those who had persuaded Tupker to take on the challenge of LCH.Clearnet rather than retire as planned at the end of 2006 after nearly seven years chairing Euroclear. Liddell, as a Goldman Sachs alumnus, was only too conscious of the investment banks' complaints. Turquoise was one

[9] ICE (14 September 2006), 'IntercontinentalExchange enters into agreement to acquire New York Board of Trade', press release.
[10] Citigroup, Credit Suisse, Deutsche Bank, Goldman Sachs, Merrill Lynch, Morgan Stanley and UBS.
[11] Conversation with the author, London, 16 January 2006.

facet of a bigger user-driven agenda to reduce the frictional costs of trading. It was not long before ripples were felt in the post-trade sector.

In Tupker's view, market power was moving to users, a group in which power had become more concentrated in the hands of fewer, bigger companies. Projects such as Turquoise, aimed at disintermediating trading on established exchanges, could be followed by plans to disintermediate clearing and settlement activities. In any event, there would be downward pressure on fees.

Tupker and Liddell acted quickly in response to this new, much tougher competitive environment, as Tupker explained:

> We decided we had to march the company down a completely different road, which was to make the company's ambition to clear as many products as possible, for as many customers as possible, as safely as possible, and as cheaply as possible.[12]

The company took steps to 'minimise or remove the incentive for disintermediation, whatever its source'. Its method, as it later explained,[13] entailed 'adjusting its operating model to focus more clearly on delivering benefits to users, in particular by providing an immediate financial benefit to users in the form of substantially lower fees rather than future rebates, or dividends to shareholders'. In October 2006, LCH.Clearnet announced clearing fee cuts of up to 26% for trades on LSE and the smaller virt-x exchange and cuts averaging 15% on Euronext cash markets.

The new management was confident the group had the financial resources to cut fees. Trading volumes were rising across the board generating huge amounts of money. But there was only a limited amount of time before users would demand a greater share of the bonanza. And during this period, LCH.Clearnet had to make the new strategy palatable to Euronext, its biggest shareholder and customer which had engineered the merger between LCH and Clearnet in such a way as to maximise its profits.

To some extent, LCH.Clearnet was pushing at an open door. Euronext had signalled that it was willing to cut its stake and board representation in LCH.Clearnet during the previous year's probe by the UK Competition Commission. But Théodore was not prepared to sell at a loss.

Negotiations between LCH.Clearnet and Euronext began in autumn 2006. In February 2007, the two companies reached agreement for LCH.Clearnet to buy back most of Euronext's 41.5% holding in its capital.

Euronext's LCH.Clearnet convertible preference shares were redeemed ahead of the due date of December 2008 at their redemption value of around €199 million. Euronext also sold back 26.2 million ordinary LCH.Clearnet shares at €10 each, unchanged from the issue price in December 2003 when LCH merged with Clearnet. In a profitable deal for Euronext, Théodore monetised gains that had been booked several years earlier.

The deal was approved unanimously by LCH.Clearnet shareholders in June 2007. Euronext's share of LCH.Clearnet capital fell to just 5% by the end of 2008 and its representation on the board dropped to one. The users ended up with 73.3% of the company's ordinary shares, turning LCH.Clearnet into more of a user-owned, user-governed entity. Of the remaining shares, 4.4% were held by the London Metal Exchange, 1.5% by ICE and 15.8% by Euroclear, which therefore became the clearer's biggest shareholder. The €461 million cost of the

[12] Conversation with the author, 4 December 2006.

[13] Joint announcement of LCH.Clearnet and Euronext (12 March 2007).

buy-back was paid in part from retained earnings and partly through a €200 million bond issued in 2007.

To sweeten users, Liddell promised 'aggressive clearing fee cuts' and 'significant member rebates in due course'. LCH.Clearnet followed through with plans for tariff reductions starting in 2007 that would aggregate 'to an average of 30% of annual net revenues by 2009'.

But any relief at the success of the negotiations with Euronext was short lived. In April 2007, LCH.Clearnet suffered a devastating blow to its pride and its pocket. The seven banks behind the Turquoise project appointed EuroCCP, a wholly owned London-based subsidiary of the Depository Trust & Clearing Corporation of New York, to handle the new platform's central counterparty clearing and netting. The seven banks were also LCH.Clearnet's biggest customers. Their decision marked the start of an *annus horribilis* for the group.

17.3 TURQUOISE AND EUROCCP

The selection of DTCC by the Turquoise consortium marked the return of a potent competitor to Europe, able to offer economies of scale, 30 years experience of equities netting and risk-management at its NSCC subsidiary and 10 years experience of serving alternative trading systems in the US. EU post-trade services for equities across national frontiers were estimated at the time to be anywhere up to eight times more expensive than those in the US.

A post-trade behemoth, DTCC boasted that it settled more than US$1.5 quadrillion[14] worth of securities transactions in 2006. It won the Turquoise contract in competition against seven rival European clearers, including LCH.Clearnet, by promising low fees. EuroCCP would be operated on an 'at cost' basis, meaning that revenues exceeding the costs of supporting the operation would be returned to clearing members.

The deal with Turquoise was not DTCC's first attempt to enter the European market. EuroCCP was established some six years earlier but was mothballed without having cleared a single trade after a planned expansion of Nasdaq in the EU folded amid the general retrenchment of exchanges during the bear market of 2000–2.

DTCC, however, kept an office in London and its New York-based executives were frequent speakers at industry conferences in Europe, using these opportunities to schmooze regulators and potential users. According to Don Donahue, DTCC's CEO, plans for EuroCCP were revitalised after the NYSE and Euronext embarked on the road to their merger and before the announcement of Project Turquoise.[15]

The agreement between Turquoise and EuroCCP showed how the MiFID reforms could overcome the barriers to cross-border trading in equities in Europe. EuroCCP would initially clear equity trades in 14 countries and in seven different currencies.

'The clearing solution we created with EuroCCP was developed in concert with participants in the European market and has the ability to operate on a pan-European basis,' Michael Bodson, the senior DTCC executive appointed as EuroCCP's Chairman, explained.[16] Behind EuroCCP were the technology infrastructure and business continuity backup capabilities used by NSCC in the US. 'Leveraging our processing scale from the US domestic market gave us the advantage of very low unit costs. These were passed on to EuroCCP users.'

[14] DTCC (2007), 'Putting customers first; Annual report 2006'. A quadrillion is a million billion, making DTCC's annual turnover in 2006 more than US$1500 000 000 000 000.

[15] Speaking on 24 May 2007 at the *Mondo Visione Exchange Forum* in London. Donahue was promoted from CEO to be DTCC's Chairman and CEO in August 2007.

[16] Conversation with the author, New York, 1 February 2008, and subsequent email exchange.

DTCC could easily absorb any extra business generated by Turquoise. 'We've created a clearance and settlement solution that is tailored for Europe, but we're leveraging our mainframe processing capacity which is extendable,' Bodson added. 'When we look at some estimates that total shares traded across Europe is about 1.5 billion shares, we have more than enough capacity to support Turquoise and other trading platforms.'

The global transaction services business of Citi, the US bank, was contracted to act as settlement agent for EuroCCP. Although the deal with Citi inserted an extra layer into the clearing and settlement infrastructure of Turquoise, the decision to buy rather than build spared costly investment in new securities settlement capacity. By harnessing Citi's branches and direct connectivity to numerous CSDs, EuroCCP was able to benefit from Citi's scale economies. Otherwise, the lead time and costs of developing settlement capacity for Turquoise's 14 markets 'would be very high'. Diana Chan, who was appointed CEO of EuroCCP in November 2007, went on to say:[17]

> A CCP could open its own account for settlement in every local market CSD, but that could be a long process and would certainly involve higher operational risks. You would need someone who knew how to set up and operate in the CSDs of these 14 markets; knew the reporting, the instructions, the processing timing, corporate actions, everything. It is very unlikely that any CCP could service a multi-market MTF such as Turquoise without using a third-party provider, and outsourcing this work to someone else who has the local market expertise.

EuroCCP's reliance on New York meant that its London staff was small, at between 15 and 20. These were strongly focused on risk management. As Chan explained:

> Risk management has to be local because we are in this time zone and we have to be able to react. We need to be able to monitor the collection of margin and take action swiftly if we need to close out a defaulted participant's positions. Also important is to ensure that our regulators have ready access to our risk manager whenever needed.

At the end of March 2008, EuroCCP was approved by the UK FSA as a Recognised Clearing House (RCH) – a status under UK law that would allow it to clear contracts for multiple trading platforms. The following month it signed the European Code of Conduct for clearing and settlement.

EuroCCPs ambitions stretched well beyond the Turquoise deal. Chan declared that her goal was to make EuroCCP 'the CCP of choice for the MTFs to begin with, and for national markets eventually'. Clearing for other MTFs alongside Turquoise would enable EuroCCP to net down the same stock across several platforms, producing economies for its clearing participants.

Such were the hopes. In reality, EuroCCP turned out not to be all conquering in the market for clearing MTFs. The Turquoise launch was subject to delays – so much so that jokers in the City dubbed the project 'Tortoise'. When Turquoise, with the support of EuroCCP, began operating in August 2008, it had sacrificed first mover advantage.

In 2007, Fortis, the Dutch-Belgian bank with a long history in the clearing business, set up a company, European Multilateral Clearing Facility (EMCF), to act as a CCP for MTFs and other securities exchanges. On 30 March 2007, EMCF began clearing for five Dutch and five German equities traded on Chi-X, a new MTF specialising in low-cost, high speed services for algorithmic traders.

[17] Conversation with the author, London, 21 February 2008.

From these small beginnings, Chi-X, which was largely owned at the time by Instinet Europe Ltd and backed by investment banks and hedge funds, grew rapidly. Within six months, it was providing a trading platform for UK and French blue chips and after a year could claim market shares of 10% or more in Europe's more liquid stocks. EMCF's clearing business also grew rapidly in line with Chi-X's turnover and as new MTFs signed up for its CCP services.

17.4 ICE, LIFFE, RAINBOW AND THE LSE

Twelve days after the April 2007 announcement that EuroCCP had won the Turquoise contract, the Atlanta-based IntercontinentalExchange (ICE) unveiled its plans for a new London-based subsidiary – ICE Clear Europe – to clear its OTC derivatives business and energy futures traded on ICE's London exchange.

It applied for ICE Clear Europe to have RCH status. This was a signal to the market that ICE was serious in wanting to build up its clearing activities as part of its corporate strategy in the years ahead.

The plan for ICE Clear Europe involved moving the open interest for ICE's contracts from the books of LCH.Clearnet Ltd and a loss of clearing fees for the London CCP that ICE estimated at about US$50 million in 2006. It was a severe blow to LCH.Clearnet's business of providing risk management for several exchanges, with economies of scale in margining and the default fund.

There was little by way of precedent to say how ICE's plan should be implemented. There were, to be sure, some lessons from the migration of the CBOT's open interest from BOTCC to the CME's clearing division in 2003–4, although the CFTC as regulator played a role in that case that was almost certainly unique to the US.

In London, the success or failure of ICE's move depended crucially on whether the users of ICE Futures, the former IPE, would agree to migrate their contracts to a new and untested clearing house. ICE Clear Europe also had to be approved by the UK's FSA and also, because it was to be an RCH, by the Office of Fair Trading.

There followed 15 months of fraught relations between ICE and LCH.Clearnet. The IPE had renegotiated its clearing contract in the course of the 2003 merger that created the LCH.Clearnet Group and the resulting agreement protected ICE's open interest. ICE gave notice that it would cease using LCH.Clearnet as its CCP from 18 July 2008 when it would cut the trade data feed from ICE to the clearing house.

Early indications suggested that the users opposed ICE's move, partly because it threatened them with higher costs and in part because ICE offered them no choice of clearing venue. But, with staffers from the US drafted in to support its local team, ICE began an intensive campaign to win support from regulators and users and reassure them that it would have the technical capability and human resources to clear in London.

It decided to make a contribution of US$100 million to the default fund, on the grounds that having 'skin in the game' would sharpen the focus of its risk-management staff and win over users faced with making higher contributions to capitalise a new fund. It provided sweeteners for users who committed early to ICE Clear Europe, including a 'founder member programme' under which users would have a 10% share of the clearing house's revenues until the end of 2010.

LCH.Clearnet fought back. In March 2008, it announced an agreement with Nymex, the New York-based energy exchange and rival to ICE Futures, under which Nymex would offer a new range of OTC and exchange-traded futures for clearing through LCH.Clearnet with the aim of winning users away from ICE Futures.[18]

LCH.Clearnet also raised objections on systemic risk grounds to the proposals put forward by ICE Futures for migrating the contracts and open interest in July 2008. A particular concern for LCH.Clearnet was that ICE's plan for migration during the weekend starting Friday 18 July envisaged the transfer of the version of the TRS/CPS software used by LCH.Clearnet for clearing ICE contracts without any provision to 'roll back' the operation or retain LCH.Clearnet's capability for clearing ICE contracts should problems arise.

But by early July 2008, Paul Swann, a former LCH.Clearnet executive who had been appointed chief executive of ICE Clear Europe the year before, secured backing for the migration from all 44 firms that traded ICE Futures contracts and cleared them through LCH.Clearnet. ICE and LCH.Clearnet began talks on ways of bridging their differences over the migration. The 18–20 July weekend was no longer a realistic option. But a new date was set – for the weekend of 13–14 September.

Several factors contributed to the success of ICE. The application to set up ICE Clear Europe was approved by the Office of Fair Trading in April 2008, which ruled that the new clearing house would not have a significantly adverse effect on competition. Indeed, when judging the possible impact of ICE Clear Europe on competition among exchanges, the OFT suggested that such competition 'may even be enhanced'.[19]

FSA approval followed in May. Despite repeated representations from LCH.Clearnet's management in the months after ICE gave notice, the FSA did not take up LCH.Clearnet's concerns about the systemic risks of ICE's migration plan.

A year later, systemic risk would be high on the agenda of policy makers around the globe. ICE's application was made in the twilight of the era in which regulators were just as concerned to promote competition.

In dealing with ICE, Tupker and Liddell were disadvantaged by the failures of the previous management. ICE made a strong case to users that it would be able to offer more contracts, more quickly with its own CCP. It pointed out that Nymex – because it had its own CCP – had launched four times as many contracts as had ICE in the four years since the New York exchange had introduced comparable products.

LCH.Clearnet's alliance with Nymex may also have proven counterproductive among ICE Futures' users. Although Richard Schaeffer, Nymex's chairman, foretold significant benefits, 'including margin and other capital efficiencies, access to established global markets, an increased product slate and the ability to transact business virtually 24 hours a day',[20] ICE played on fears that the venture, if successful, could worsen the competitive environment for traders.

The market benefited from competition between ICE and Nymex. If users kept LCH.Clearnet as their clearing house they would have to abandon ICE as their trading venue and Nymex could be left with a monopoly of exchange-traded energy contracts at a time when it was likely to be taken over by the CME, the world's dominant futures exchange group. In the event, the CME acquired Nymex and the venture with LCH.Clearnet never went live.

---

[18] Quoted in LCH.Clearnet and Nymex (6 March 2008), 'Nymex and LCH.Clearnet announce historic clearing alliance', press release.

[19] Office of Fair Trading (30 June 2008), 'ICE Clear Europe Ltd: Application to become a recognised clearing house'.

[20] LCH.Clearnet and Nymex (6 March 2008).

Another factor undermining LCH.Clearnet's position was the fact that earlier in 2008 it was obliged to concede the principle of transferring its open interest to another of its customers.

Troubles, they say, often come in threes. This was certainly the case for LCH.Clearnet in the six months following the allocation of the Turquoise contract to EuroCCP and the incorporation of ICE Clear Europe in April 2007. In the summer of that year, John Thain, the chief executive of NYSE Euronext, contacted Roger Liddell and told him that NYSE Euronext wanted to open negotiations to change the commercial relationship between LCH.Clearnet and Liffe, the international derivatives business of the NYSE Euronext group and LCH.Clearnet's biggest customer.

'At that particular point in this company's life, it looked as if it might actually die,' Chris Tupker recalled later. 'We were at our wit's end. We had been here for a year. We had solved the initial problem of the IT, when all of a sudden the tectonic plates on which we were dwelling started to move in ways we had not expected.'[21]

To a large extent the new management was suffering from a backlash among users and exchanges for the problems that surfaced during the first three years after the merger of LCH and Clearnet.

But the actions of ICE and Liffe also reflected new market realities. The merger of the CME and CBOT was completed in July 2007. The creation of the hugely profitable, vertically-integrated CME Group went without challenge from the US competition authorities. As Tupker observed, the seemingly unstoppable rise of the CME 'put pressure on other publicly quoted derivatives exchanges to own their clearing so as to benefit from the enhanced earnings and price/earnings multiples this affords'.[22]

Thain, the former NYSE CEO and Goldman Sachs alumnus who had taken the top job at NYSE Euronext on the creation of the transatlantic exchange group in April 2007, faced additional pressure. During the summer of 2007 a group of investment banks – most of which were in the Turquoise consortium – began working on a new venture, dubbed Project Rainbow, to launch a new trading platform for financial futures to compete with Europe's established derivatives exchanges.

The consortium's manoeuvrings became public after some delay in press reports towards the end of January 2008.[23] Among the Rainbow group were prominent users of LCH.Clearnet, including, it was said, Barclays, Credit Suisse, Deutsche Bank, Goldman Sachs, JP Morgan, Lehman Brothers, MF Global, UBS and the Citadel Investment hedge fund group. One of their major objectives was to compete with Liffe in the market for euro and sterling interest rate futures, its most actively traded contracts. David Hardy was one of the Rainbow consortium's advisors.

While the ICE decision was a direct threat to LCH.Clearnet and not unexpected after the ICE's acquisition of NYBOT and its integrated New York Clearing Corp CCP, the threat of the investment banks to disintermediate established derivatives exchanges in Europe created difficulties of a different kind.

The Rainbow banks approached LCH.Clearnet to clear contracts that would be fungible with those on Liffe and which could therefore be offset using the open interest in similar Liffe contracts already being cleared by LCH.Clearnet. If allowed to happen, this would siphon off liquidity from Liffe's trading activities.

---

[21] As told to the author, 22 December 2009.

[22] LCH.Clearnet Group (2007), 'Chairman's statement from the report and consolidated financial statements'.

[23] *Financial News* (28 January 2008), 'Banks mull European derivatives exchange'.

Project Rainbow came before the LCH.Clearnet board on 6 February 2008. It was a poisoned chalice for the clearer. Without waiting to see whether Rainbow would be launched, Liffe warned LCH.Clearnet off any idea of cooperating with the consortium and looked for ways to reduce its own vulnerability to attack. It sought negotiations to revise its contract with LCH.Clearnet, which unlike that between ICE and the clearer was not rewritten at the time of the LCH and Clearnet merger to provide Liffe with explicit intellectual property rights over the open interest in its contracts.

The issue was discussed by the LCH.Clearnet board in February and March 2008. After a difficult meeting it was agreed that negotiations would start between Liffe and the clearing house for the exchange to take control of its own clearing, reducing substantially the services provided by LCH.Clearnet.[24] The exchange would set up an in-house CCP – LiffeClear – to protect the open interest of its contracts while outsourcing to LCH.Clearnet the tasks of managing the risk and guaranteeing the trades.

When announced seven months later,[25] the arrangement between Liffe and LCH.Clearnet presented Liffe's users with a halfway house between the vertical and horizontal. LiffeClear became the counterparty to the open interest in Liffe's contracts instead of LCH.Clearnet, so giving the exchange group the clearing revenues and other advantages of 'verticality'. But Liffe's users did not have to capitalise a new default fund and continued to benefit from the diversified portfolio of positions in LCH.Clearnet's default fund. LCH.Clearnet would continue to run the day-to-day clearing functions for Liffe, such as collecting margin. In case of a default, LCH.Clearnet would become the counterparty and fully responsible for managing it.

The arrangement gave Liffe greater control over its TRS/CPS platform, which it previously rented out to LCH.Clearnet and which suffered from lack of investment during LCH.Clearnet's failed attempt to build the Generic Clearing System. On the other hand, the exchange at this stage had no ambitions to compete with LCH.Clearnet in the wider market for CCP services. It opted to set up LiffeClear as a clearing service for Liffe, which as a recognised investment exchange (RIE) could also act as a central counterparty for its own business. Unlike ICE Clear Europe, LiffeClear would not have RCH status and so could not clear trades for others.

The revised relationship with Liffe meant a further cut in income for LCH.Clearnet although the reduced fees paid by Liffe – estimated at €30 million a year – still enabled the clearer to cover its overheads. As a sweetener to compensate for a three year notice period, NYSE Euronext made a one off payment to LCH.Clearnet of €260 million, which was roughly equivalent to three year's revenue from the Euronext contract.

In pursuing its policy, Liffe aimed to avoid acrimony with its users and any political controversy that could arise if it was perceived to provoke LCH.Clearnet's demise. This was considered a possibility when the rearrangement of the relationship between Liffe and LCH.Clearnet was first mooted in 2007. By the time negotiations got underway in 2008, however, the clearer's fortunes had improved somewhat.

Group operating profit in 2007 rose 45% to €257 million. Despite tariff reductions, net revenue after payment of interest to clearing members and similar charges rose nearly 13% to €501million. A record 1.72 billion trades were cleared, up 36% on 2006, and with a record cleared value of €616 trillion.[26]

---

[24] NYSE Euronext (15 March 2008), 'Liffe to create LiffeClear', news release.

[25] LCH.Clearnet Group (31 October 2008), 'LCH.Clearnet and LIFFE agree new clearing arrangement', press release.

[26] LCH.Clearnet Group (29 April 2008), 'Results and announcements', press release.

The group was expanding its business in novel areas such as freight. It was also finding a new customer base among trading platforms in the energy field and in the European market for equities, where MTFs were sprouting up to take advantage of market liberalisation under MiFID and the EU Code of Conduct (see Section 16.9).

At the end of November 2007, LCH.Clearnet signed its first new exchange customer after many months of drought when it announced it would provide CCP services for Nodal Exchange, a market for forward power trading in regions of North America. In March 2008, it reached a preliminary agreement to clear for Börse Berlin Equiduct Trading, an MTF, while Paris-based LCH.Clearnet SA launched the first CCP services for the Luxembourg Stock Exchange, the listing venue for 30 000 international bonds. As 2008 progressed, the group, previously known for sluggish innovation, produced a steady flow of announcements of new services and customers.

Although these new deals were not large, they partly offset the prospective loss of business with ICE Futures and Liffe. But there was still the risk of further disintermediation by the clearer's customers.

The London Stock Exchange was a case in point. Relations between the LSE and LCH had rarely been easy, but since the failure of its own attempt to set up Taurus, its own post-trade infrastructure in 1993, the exchange had supported the horizontal model of clearing and settlement in Europe.

In June 2007, however, the LSE agreed a merger with Borsa Italiana, Italy's vertically-integrated exchange group that owned 86.36% of Cassa di Compensazione e Garanzia (CC&G), manager of the CCP for Borsa's equities and derivatives markets.

When seeking the approval of its shareholders for the merger, which finally took effect on 1 October 2007, the LSE signalled a policy shift. The merged group, it suggested, would be strongly positioned to take advantage of greater customer choice in clearing and settlement under the European Code of Conduct.[27] It was not long before it tested the waters.

Having pressed LCH.Clearnet to allow a choice of clearing provider for member firms' equity trades in 2006, the LSE surprised the London market, Europe's CCPs and the European Commission late in March 2008 by announcing a strategic review of its clearing arrangements. It blocked competitive clearing for LSE trades between LCH.Clearnet and SIS x-clear which, after nearly two years in the making, was now ready for implementation.

Several months of stalemate followed until the LSE backed down after coming under pressure from users in the City and the European Commission. But the exchange's allegiance to the horizontal model of clearing and settlement was no longer a given. This provided a further incentive for LCH.Clearnet to find a safety net to help it survive. It chose to look for a stronger partner with a view to merging.

17.5 LCH.CLEARNET SEEKS SAFETY WITH OTHERS

The LCH.Clearnet Group board was told in July 2007 about the likely need to change the relationship with Liffe so that the exchange could have economic control of its open interest.

At the same meeting, the board looked at choices for the future, including merging LCH.Clearnet with a stronger partner. One option was to merge with Euroclear, which was on the way to becoming the clearer's biggest shareholder; another was to merge with DTCC, which had impressed LCH.Clearnet's main users sufficiently for them to award the Turquoise

[27] London Stock Exchange (23 July 2007), 'Proposed merger of London Stock Exchange Group plc and Borsa Italiana SpA'.

contract to the US clearer; a third was to link or merge with both of them; the fourth was to tough it out at considerable risk in terms of LCH.Clearnet's long-term survival prospects.

Of the four options, the company chose first to follow up the three-way solution with Euroclear and DTCC.

The merger agreement between NYSE and Euronext in 2006 had already led to some consideration of a link between LCH.Clearnet and NSCC to exploit synergies between the US and European parts of the merged NYSE Euronext group. There was some talk of an electronic bridge across the Atlantic that would also involve Euroclear and DTCC's DTC subsidiary to clear and settle stocks that were dual-listed and fungible in New York and Paris.

During 2007, preliminary talks began between DTCC, LCH.Clearnet and Euroclear on a more elaborate venture. On the face of it, the three companies had much in common. They were all user-owned and user-governed with many of the same firms among their shareholders. Each of the three had something to contribute. LCH.Clearnet had clearing and risk-management capabilities in derivative and OTC markets that DTCC lacked. When up and running, DTCC's EuroCCP subsidiary would provide equities clearing capabilities that could replace the high cost system used by LCH.Clearnet's Paris subsidiary. Euroclear, with its International Central Securities Depository and CSDs in Euronext markets, brought European settlement capabilities and know-how, notably in the fields of corporate actions and collateral management. It also provided the netting capability for LCH.Clearnet's London equities CCP service.

According to people familiar with the discussions, the original idea was for Euroclear and DTCC to join forces to control LCH.Clearnet, leading to a merger that would create an at-cost utility CCP. But there were difficulties with the trilateral approach.

The issue of who would hold the top jobs in the merged entity proved a problem. Also important was the fact that the two financially robust partners – Euroclear and DTCC – were differently structured. DTCC's at-cost operating model meant that it had relatively little ordinary capital and its shares were valued at a correspondingly low level. Euroclear, while describing itself as user-owned and user-governed, was profit-oriented so that its shares were valued at a much higher level than those of DTCC or LCH.Clearnet.

As a result of years of expansion in which it used its shares as acquisition currency to buy CSDs, Euroclear had large shareholders, especially among French financial institutions, which were not major users and regarded their holdings as financial investments. Any move by Euroclear to shift to an at-cost model to fit in better with DTCC and LCH.Clearnet, which was also in the process of turning into an at-cost business, would take time and be difficult to reconcile with the interests of these shareholders. Although Euroclear was prepared to sacrifice some revenue in an attempt to resolve these dilemmas, a solution proved elusive.

After some months, LCH.Clearnet and DTCC decided that the three cornered approach was too complex and that Euroclear should first reduce the value of its business. The decision left some bruised feelings in Euroclear's Brussels headquarters. The talks narrowed down to bilateral discussions on a merger of DTCC and LCH.Clearnet that would really be a takeover of the European clearer by the larger US utility. On 22 April 2008, the LCH.Clearnet Group board authorised the management to open negotiations with DTCC. The codeword for the talks – 'bicycle' – underlined Euroclear's non-participation.

There was strong industrial logic to commend a merger. Concern about OTC derivatives was climbing the policy makers' agenda, especially in the US. Viewed from LCH.Clearnet's angle, users would benefit greatly from a combination of LCH.Clearnet's clearing expertise, especially in SwapClear, with DTCC's DerivServ and OTC trade information warehouse which provided services that stopped short of clearing for the OTC market. Chris Tupker also hoped that the combined DTCC–LCH.Clearnet group could then take over the Clearing Corporation (CCorp) and, in the process, get a grip on its faltering efforts to create a CCP for credit derivatives.[28]

17.6 VERTICAL ASCENT

The courtship between LCH.Clearnet and DTCC took place during a period of growing turmoil in global finance.

The cracks that first appeared in 2007 widened as 2008 progressed. The US investment bank Bear Stearns collapsed in March 2008 and disappeared into the arms of JPMorgan Chase for a knock-down price at the behest of the US federal government. The crisis that began in the market for subprime mortgages in the US spread to financial institutions around the world as bad debts in one bank quickly infected others. The banks' practice of packaging and securitising duff loans for resale to other banks spread contagion throughout the financial world. Unnoticed by regulators, a high degree of interconnectedness had developed among banks and financial institutions outside the traditional banking system. The era of the 'Great Moderation' was coming to a grisly end.

Central counterparty clearers were as yet untested by the crisis. But CCPs faced plenty of uncertainties. The future of clearing was in flux.

There was rapid change at the level of trading platforms. Demutualisation among exchanges, the clearers' customers, had continued, especially in North America, where ICE in 2005 and the NYSE and Nymex in 2006 followed the example of the CME and became listed companies.

At the same time, established equities exchanges faced growing competition from alternative trading venues which tended to focus on high volume, low margin algorithmic trading. These were backed usually by investment banks and other large exchange users that had sold their shares in the exchanges after demutualisation and re-invested the proceeds in new platforms to reduce costs.

Known in the US as Electronic Communications Networks (ECNs), alternative trading venues had blossomed during the dot.com boom and retrenched during the subsequent bust. They multiplied once more.

In Europe, the multilateral trading facilities allowed by the MiFID directive proliferated. MTFs turned first to new providers such as EuroCCP and EMCF for clearing services rather than to incumbent clearing providers. Whereas a few years before, pundits and policy makers assumed there would be falling numbers of CCPs in Europe, there was instead an increase.

Demutualisation and increased competition for established exchanges encouraged some consolidation and diversification through mergers and acquisitions. The CME's acquisition of the recently demutualised CBOT in 2007 was followed by its takeover of Nymex in 2008.

Having acquired the IPE in London and NYBOT in New York, ICE cheekily challenged the CME in its bid to take over the CBOT. After failing to secure that target, ICE acquired the venerable Winnipeg Commodity Exchange in 2007. It bought Creditex Group Inc., an innovative brokerage that executed and processed CDSs, during the summer of 2008. On the equities side, NYSE merged with Archipelago, the most successful of the new US cash equity trading venues, as part of the NYSE Group's transformation into a publicly listed, for-profit concern.

[28] Conversation between Chris Tupker and the author, 8 September 2008. See Chapter 13 for the launch of CCorp's programme to create a CCP for credit derivatives and Chapter 18 and 19 for subsequent events.

In Europe, the failure of Euronext and Deutsche Börse to overcome their differences and merge opened the way for the creation of NYSE Euronext, the first transatlantic exchange, in 2007. This development spawned some equally unexpected pairings within Europe, such as the merger between the LSE and Borsa Italiana, and opened the way for more transatlantic takeovers and the talks between LCH.Clearnet and DTCC.

Clearing-driven mergers played a growing part in the process of demutualisation and consolidation. The rise in the CME share price to peak at nearly US$715 in January 2008 from US$35 at the time of the IPO in December 2002 partly reflected the financial fruits of clearing. ICE's 2006 bid for NYBOT was motivated to a large extent by its wish to acquire a clearing infrastructure. Clearing capacity was one of the attractions for the LSE of Borsa Italiana. In October 2007, Nasdaq's acquisition of the Boston Stock Exchange was motivated by its desire to own the Boston Stock Exchange Clearing Corporation.

Ownership of CCP clearing made financial sense for for-profit exchange groups. During the early years of the 21st century, demutualisation and the adoption of for-profit governance among financial infrastructure providers went hand in hand with the ascendancy of vertical integration among exchanges, clearing houses and, sometimes, settlement infrastructures.

As well as Liffe, other long-term supporters deserted the horizontal model. In Switzerland, the banks that owned three separate companies providing exchange platforms, clearing and settlement services and payments services initiated their merger under the aegis of a single strategic holding company in the same year that the LSE merged with Borsa Italiana. The merger of Switzerland's SWX Group, SIS Group and Telekurs to form the SIX Group with effect from the beginning of 2008 was aimed at strengthening Switzerland's financial centre by bringing financial infrastructure providers into one group.[29]

Although the SIX Group companies said they were not intent on creating a vertical silo, there was no denying the growing attraction of vertical integration of CCPs for Europe's market infrastructures. To some extent, this outcome was a paradoxical consequence of the EU Code of Conduct, to which the Swiss adhered. The code's provision of rights of access and interoperability among exchanges, CCPs and CSDs, combined with the EU authorities' decision not to mandate any specific structure for post-trade service providers, conferred respectability on CCPs in vertically-structured groups.

The code implied that it was possible to have vertical integration without exclusive silos. Europe appeared to have stumbled on a middle way between the extremes of the vertical and the horizontal. A similar spirit of synthesis was apparent in the acceptance by the UK competition authorities of ICE Clear Europe and in the compromise between LCH.Clearnet and Liffe that resulted in the 'diagonally' structured LiffeClear. Horizontally-structured and mutually-owned post-trade infrastructures in Europe were on the back foot – not least because of the imperfect delivery of interoperability under the code.

In the US, acts of Congress continued to define the dividing lines between vertical and horizontal. But there was some skirmishing in between. Following the vertical integration of NSCC and DTC to form DTCC in 1998, there was further consolidation of clearing and settlement providers under the DTCC umbrella. But the dangers of a monopoly in clearing and settlement for securities markets were tempered somewhat by DTCC's at-cost, user-owned,

[29] The group adopted the SIX Group brand in August 2008 in place of Swiss Financial Market Services, which was the name given to the holding company when it started operating at the start of 2008. As a result of the rebranding, SIS x-clear, the CCP, became known as SIX x-clear.

user-governed model. Serving all US options exchanges, the Options Clearing Corp similarly provided common clearing along horizontal lines.

Until 2008, the vertical silo model appeared all-conquering on US derivatives exchanges. In 2003 the CFTC encouraged the CME to take over CCP clearing for the CBOT and in the process dealt a mortal blow to the plans of the BOTCC to become a horizontal clearing provider to a number of exchanges. The subsequent merger of the CME and CBOT in 2007 was unopposed by the US Department of Justice. So too was the merged CME Group's acquisition of Nymex in 2008.

In February 2008, stock markets gave an indication of the importance of the CME's vertical structure to its business model. On 6 February, the shares of CME Group and Nymex Holdings fell by a record 18% in New York. The tumbling stock market prices came just a week after CME launched a bid for Nymex to be paid partly with CME stock. They wiped US$1.7 billion off the US$11 billion value of the deal.

The cause of the kerfuffle was a report from the US Justice Department which concluded that 'current rules and policies related to clearing futures contracts may be unnecessarily inhibiting competition among futures exchanges in the development and trading of financial futures contracts, to the detriment of the economy and consumers'.[30] Responding to a US Treasury call for comments for a study on regulation, the DoJ's paper advocated fostering competition among exchanges 'by, *inter alia*, ending exchange control of clearing'. It commended the regulatory framework and clearing structure of the US equities and options markets, suggesting that under such a model 'futures clearinghouses would likely clear for multiple exchanges and treat identical contracts as fungible'.

This was incendiary stuff. It elicited predictable howls of protest from the CME Group, its lobbyists and supporters. CFTC Commissioner Bart Chilton found the Justice Department's opinion 'troubling on several counts'. Illinois Senator Dick Durbin and congressman Rahm Emanuel wrote to Treasury Secretary Henry Paulson and US Attorney General Michael Mukasey to register their 'strong objections' to the DoJ's opinion.

On 8 February, the Justice Department pinned responsibility for the comments on its Antitrust Division and downplayed the opinion as one of several contributions to a study by the Treasury Department.

Washington insiders suggested the opinion reflected the opposition of dissident officials inside the Justice Department to the earlier approval of the merger between CME Group and CBOT. But those predicting difficulties for the CME Group's Nymex bid were confounded later in 2008 when the DoJ nodded through the acquisition.

The victory of Chicago-based, Illinois senator Barack Obama in the 2008 presidential election tipped the scales further against any federal initiative against vertical structures. A year after the Justice Department's letter was made public, Rahm Emanuel was installed in the White House as President Obama's chief of staff.

Years of assiduous lobbying by the CME Group in Washington helped uphold the vertical integration of trading and CCP clearing on US futures exchanges. In the 2000s, first the CBOT as an independent exchange and subsequently the CME Group successfully brushed aside challenges from BrokerTec, Eurex and Euronext-Liffe for chunks of their financial futures business. As will be discussed in Chapter 20, this catalogue of setbacks did not deter new challengers prepared to take on the Chicago-based leviathan.

---

[30] Comments of the US Department of Justice (31 January 2008) in response to the Department of Treasury's request for comments on the Regulatory Structure Associated with Financial Institutions.

17.7 TRANSATLANTIC PERSPECTIVES

As the financial crisis gathered strength in 2008, there was one trend amid the many uncertainties in the markets for CCP services that appeared firmly rooted.

The launch of NYSE Euronext in 2007 was followed by other transatlantic mergers and acquisitions among exchanges. After giving up its attempts to take over the LSE, Nasdaq acquired the Nordic exchange operator OMX, resulting in the creation of the Nasdaq OMX Group in December 2007. Also in that month, Eurex completed a US$2.8 billion acquisition of the International Securities Exchange (ISE), the fast growing New York-based pioneer of electronic options trading in the US.

In the view of Don Donahue, DTCC's CEO and chairman, the NYSE Euronext merger and the arrival of DTCC in Europe marked a new paradigm, a 'stitching together of markets around the globe'. Speaking in May 2007 to an exchange conference in London, he concluded that the market for post-trade activities in Europe was no longer confined by national boundaries or to continental areas such as the eurozone.[31]

The coincidence of US-owned ICE Clear Europe and EuroCCP starting their operations in London in 2008 – the 120th anniversary year of the founding of the London Produce Clearing House – added to the impression that American clearing houses were set to become dominant in a global market for CCP services.

The absorption of LCH.Clearnet by DTCC seemed only a matter of time. As LCH.Clearnet's chairman Chris Tupker noted: 'We are dealing these days in the transatlantic market. So logically, if the front end of the market is recognising this transatlantic environment, it really is time that the plumbing sector recognises it too'.[32]

But hopes of an agreement between LCH.Clearnet and DTCC by June 2008 proved optimistic. The US authorities allowed Lehman Brothers to go bankrupt over the weekend of 13–14 September. When, five weeks later, DTCC and LCH.Clearnet finally announced their plans to merge,[33] the tectonic plates on which their activities were based had shifted once again.

Clearing, as Roger Liddell exclaimed, 'came of age' in the year of Lehman's default.[34] But the bankruptcy of the US investment bank caused a paradigm shift in global financial markets on a far greater scale than the merger of NYSE and Euronext.

The following chapters will describe how central counterparty clearing moved centre stage as a vitally important part of the response to the worst financial crisis since the Great Depression of the 1930s. But, as Part V of this book will also explain, part of the fallout from the step change upwards in the status of CCPs was the end of the ambitious project to create a transatlantic clearing giant from the merger of DTCC and LCH.Clearnet.

---

[31] Speaking on 24 May 2007 to the *Mondo Visione Exchange Forum* in London.

[32] Conversation with the author, 8 September 2008.

[33] DTCC and LCH.Clearnet (22 October 2008), 'DTCC and LCH.Clearnet announce plans to merge and create world's leading clearing house', joint press release.

[34] LCH.Clearnet Group (2008), 'Chief Executive's Review, annual report and consolidated financial statements'.

Part V

New Paradigms: Clearing After the Crisis

18 Mitigating Risk in OTC Markets

18.1 TOO BIG AND TOO INTERCONNECTED TO FAIL

In an odd way, the bankruptcy of Lehman Brothers Holdings was a last hurrah for market liberalism. The refusal of the US authorities to bail-out the stricken investment bank reflected a belief that the market could cope with the consequences of its collapse. Financial markets had, so it was argued, six months since the rescue of Bear Stearns to prepare for the failure and orderly wind down of a similarly large institution.

Within 24 hours the idea that more large interconnected financial institutions could be allowed to fail was dead. On 16 September 2008, the US government was forced to provide American International Group (AIG) with a US$85 billion loan in exchange for a 79.9% share in AIG to stave off the bankruptcy of the US insurance group. Its bail-out ultimately cost the taxpayer US$180 billion.

While Lehman Brothers was heading for collapse, the giant US insurer was haemorrhaging capital. Its problems came to light in February when AIG's auditors found a 'material weakness' in its internal controls over the valuation of a 'super senior' credit default swap portfolio built up by its subsidiary, AIG Financial Products.

By the time Wall Street's finest were converging on the New York Fed building for the fruitless attempts to save Lehman Brothers during the 13–14 September weekend, it was public knowledge that AIG had racked up losses of US$18.5 billion in the previous three quarters. Its shares fell 30% on Friday 12 September and slumped a further 60% on Monday 15 September as the three leading US ratings agencies first prepared and then announced downgrades for its long-term debt. The agencies' action triggered demands for US$20 billion of collateral and other payments that AIG did not have.

AIG was huge. It was the largest industrial and commercial insurer in the US with US$1 trillion of assets and US$110 billion in revenue in 2007. It employed more than 100 000 people worldwide and was active in more than 100 countries, with a particularly strong position in Asia. It was one of the US's biggest life insurers and an important provider of retirement incomes through its large fixed annuities business. But, through a little known subsidiary operating largely out of London's fashionable Mayfair, it had written credit default swaps, derivatives and futures contracts with a notional value of around US$2.7 trillion, including around US$440 billion of CDSs.

The CDSs that contributed to AIG's downfall were written on 'super senior' triple A rated tranches of collateralised debt obligations for which AIG had received a steady income during the quiet times of the Great Moderation. Many of these exposures were not collateralised, but instead were guaranteed by AIG's own triple A rating. AIG had also invested heavily in highly rated mortgage backed securities, funding the investments with money generated through securities lending.

Problems arose after the subprime crisis started. AIG was caught in a vicious downwards spiral as its mortgage backed and super senior investments turned sour and illiquid and inflicted large mark-to-market losses on the group. As the financial crisis gathered pace in September – with the US government deciding to put the mortgage lenders Fannie Mae and Freddie Mac into conservatorship[1] – AIG's partners in the stock lending schemes returned their securities and demanded cash back to the tune of US$24 billion. AIG ran out of funds when the ratings agencies further downgraded its debt at the time of Lehman's collapse.[2]

The company's management prepared for Chapter 11 bankruptcy. But that was a step too far for the US Treasury.

AIG was not the last important financial institution to be rescued. Within a week, the British bank Lloyds TSB was encouraged to take over its ailing rival HBOS and the US investment banks Goldman Sachs and Morgan Stanley became bank holding companies in order to access funding from the Federal Reserve. Within a month of Lehman's bankruptcy

- the US devised and obtained House approval for a US$700 billion Troubled Asset Relief Program (TARP) to rescue the US financial system;
- the UK government recapitalised and part-nationalised the UK's banks;
- the Belgo-Dutch Fortis Bank was bailed out and split, with the Dutch part nationalised;
- Icelandic banks collapsed.

Governments were obliged to guarantee money market funds in the US and bank deposits in Ireland, the UK and other EU member states. Amid fears of a new Great Depression caused by a massive contraction of liquidity and widespread bankruptcies, the US, eurozone and US central banks cut interest rates in a coordinated move to support their economies. Other measures to loosen monetary policy followed in later months including the radical step in the UK of injecting money directly into the economy by 'quantitative easing'.

Dramatic though all these developments were, the crucial event for the future of central counterparty clearing was the near collapse and rescue of AIG. Unlike Lehman Brothers, AIG was simply too big, too interconnected and too important a part of the US economy to fail. Credit default swaps written mainly in happier times between 2003 and 2005 were later judged to be 'at the core' of AIG's woes.[3] Ironically, AIG was not in the top flight of CDS market participants. It was ranked 20th according to the 2006 derivative survey of Fitch, the ratings agency.[4]

But AIG's position as a 'one way' seller turned it into a systemic risk. The huge cost of the bail-out and the fact that about two thirds of the initial bail-out funds flowed through AIG to

[1] A legal process in the US by which control of an entity is transferred to another entity – the conservator – by court order or statutory or regulatory authority. Conservatorship is generally perceived as avoiding the stigma of nationalisation. In the case of Fannie and Freddie, the Federal Housing Finance Agency took control on 7 September 2008 after which they were given access to capital and funding from the US Treasury.

[2] This summary of AIG's crisis has drawn on the author's discussions with market participants; the US House of Representatives Committee on Oversight and Government Reform (7 October 2008), 'Hearing on the AIG bailout' testimony of Eric Dinallo, Superintendent, New York State Insurance Department; Robert B. Willumstad, former Chairman and CEO of AIG at the time of the crisis; Martin Sullivan, former President and CEO of AIG; and ECB (August 2009), 'Credit default swaps and counterparty risk'.

[3] For example, Gary Gensler, CFTC chairman (CFTC (9 March 2010), Keynote address to Markit's *Outlook for OTC Derivatives Markets* conference) said CDSs 'played a lead role throughout the story' of the financial crisis and 'were at the core of the $180 billion bailout of AIG'.

[4] As cited in ECB (August 2009).

counterparties outside the US[5] placed its rescue and the regulation of OTC derivatives at the centre of an ongoing political storm.

Had AIG Financial Products' activities been subject to the discipline of a CCP, they might not have been dragged by the insurance group down so far. The subsidiary would have been obliged to post margin and mark-to-market the CDSs that it wrote. Instead, AIG's investment in CDSs concentrated risk on such a scale that it threatened the stability of the global financial system.[6]

Clearing rocketed up the agenda of policy makers, both in the US and internationally. CCP clearing promised benefits in the short as well as the long term. The short-term benefits were highlighted by Walter Lukken, acting chairman of the CFTC, in October 2008 in written testimony to a Congressional committee. Pointing out that no US futures clearing house had defaulted on a guarantee, Lukken explained that twice daily mark-to-market practices lessened the risk of contagion effects: 'While comprehensive financial reform might take time, encouraging centralised clearing is one immediate step that can reduce risk in the markets and benefit the US economy.'[7]

Longer term, central counterparty clearing promised greater transparency for regulators and market operators and a sharp reduction in complexity, by replacing a host of bilateral contractual relationships forming an extremely complex web with a multitude of simple bilateral links between buyers, sellers and CCPs.

Clearing became a subject for summit communiqués as governments, trying to act in coordination through a number of international fora, announced steps to subject OTC derivatives trading to greater control. In the EU, the Commission, the ECB and CESR shifted their policy focus from promoting cross-border clearing as a way of increasing competition in equity markets to encouraging CCPs in order to mitigate risks in OTC derivatives markets. In the US, Congressional hearings were quickly followed by legislative initiatives that included proposals to mandate central counterparty clearing for standardised OTC derivatives.

Work already in progress was stepped up. The New York Fed increased pressure on US derivatives dealers and clearing providers to speed up the development of CCPs for CDSs. CCP operators on both sides of the Atlantic rose to the challenge with competing projects for CDS clearing. Meanwhile, as described in the next chapter, incumbent providers and new contenders rushed out new services that extended clearing to financial instruments and markets previously neglected. These included the provision of CCP services for big 'buy-side' investors such as mutual funds and hedge funds.

Progress on none of these fronts was linear. The extreme events of September 2008 initiated a secular shift of mood among politicians, regulators and voters in the world's leading economies away from support for free markets towards backing government intervention. If anything, public hostility in the US and EU towards banking and finance increased as the crisis spread to the real economy. Such powerful shifts in attitudes meant efforts to reregulate global finance took place in a radically changed environment. There was much greater risk that politics,

[5] According to Gensler in his prepared remarks to a conference on *OTC Derivatives Regulation* in Brussels: CFTC (25 September 2009).

[6] As the IMF noted: 'If these contracts had been novated to central counterparties, collateral calls would still have been problematic for AIG, but they would have come sooner and more frequently. Hence, uncollateralised exposures would not have been given the chance to build to levels that became systemically critical.' IMF (April 2010), 'Global financial stability report. Chapter 3: Making over-the-counter derivatives safer: the role of central counterparties'.

[7] Written testimony before the House Committee on Agriculture: CFTC (15 October 2008).

partisanship and protectionism could be harnessed either to further the ambitions or upset the best laid plans of law makers and clearing house managers.

18.2 CLEARING AS HIGH POLITICS

Two months after the Lehman Brothers collapse and AIG bailout, central counterparty clearing was on the agenda of world leaders.

The summit meeting in Washington of the Group of 20 nations on 15 November 2008 was not just a sign of the scale and gravity of the global economic crisis. It was also symptomatic of the relative diminution of power inflicted by the crisis on the G7 industrialised countries of North America, Western Europe and Japan which had assumed responsibility for the global economy after the collapse in the 1970s of the Bretton Woods system. Although President George W. Bush was in the chair, international economic cooperation in future would be shared with the 'Brics' – Brazil, Russia, India and China – and other fast growing economies which had managed to avoid the excesses that led to the near collapse of the world financial system.[8]

That said, because they played host to most OTC market activity, the US and European G20 members were the ones mainly concerned with clearing and derivatives. President Bush himself reportedly intervened at one point in the summit to stress the importance of strengthening the underlying infrastructure of OTC credit derivatives markets to reduce risk in the system.[9] OTC issues were reflected in an 'Action Plan' published alongside the final communiqué that included a reference to CCPs.

Among the Action Plan's 47 bullet points was a call on 'supervisors and regulators, building on the imminent launch of central counterparty services for credit default swaps in some countries' to speed efforts to reduce the systemic risks of CDS and OTC derivatives trades. They were urged to pressure market participants to support exchange traded or electronic trading platforms for CDS contracts; expand the transparency of OTC derivatives markets; and ensure that the infrastructure for OTC derivatives could support growing volumes.[10]

It is easy to be cynical about summits. The mixture of grandstanding, politicking and bickering that lies behind their serious intent all too often results in communiqués that are remarkable for their banality.

But the G20 Action Plan was well timed to build on work in progress. It was prepared largely by the Financial Stability Forum (FSF), comprising top officials responsible for financial stability in the G7 countries, the IMF and other international financial institutions as well as representatives of international committees of central bankers and supervisors.[11] Responding to the gathering storm, the FSF had already published a first report on ways of strengthening financial markets and institutions in April 2008.

[8] The G20 is made up of the finance ministers and central bank governors of: Argentina, Australia, Brazil, Canada, China, France, Germany, India, Indonesia, Italy, Japan, Mexico, Russia, Saudi Arabia, South Africa, Republic of Korea, Turkey, UK and US plus the EU, which is represented by the Council Presidency and the ECB. The managing director of the IMF and the President of the World Bank also attend G20 meetings.

[9] According to a 'senior administration official' briefing the press in the White House after the meeting.

[10] The White House (15 November 2008), *Declaration of the Summit on Financial Markets and the World Economy*.

[11] Financial Stability Forum (10 October 2008), 'Report of the Financial Stability Forum on enhancing market and institutional resilience: Follow up on implementation'.

The European Commission in Brussels was pushing for central clearing of derivatives. In October, Charlie McCreevy, the European Union's internal market commissioner, described a CCP for CDSs as a 'pressing need' and convened a working group of industry experts and regulators to produce by year-end 'concrete proposals as to how the risks from credit derivatives can be mitigated'.[12]

The main US regulators acted to reduce the risk of any initiative being hampered by turf wars among themselves. Just before the November G20 summit, the Federal Reserve Board, the SEC and the CFTC signed a memorandum of understanding on a framework for consulting and sharing information 'on issues related to CDS central counterparties'.[13]

Hearings in Congress during October and an informal summit of EU leaders on 7 November 2008 demonstrated an appetite for action on both sides of the Atlantic. When the G20 leaders stipulated that the bullet point on OTC trading and clearing should result in 'immediate action' by their finance ministers and be subject to monitoring at subsequent G20 summits, there appeared to be a good chance that deeds would follow words.

A road map was at hand. On 14 November, the President's Working Group produced tougher and more specific policy objectives for the OTC derivatives market 'with a primary focus on credit default swaps'.[14] The objectives, although leaving much detail undefined, set the tone for the subsequent debate on regulating CDSs in the US and elsewhere. They included the idea that CCPs should be used to clear all 'eligible' OTC contracts. The notion that 'standardised' CDS contracts should be traded on an exchange was also set down in black and white.

18.3 ACTIVISM AT THE NEW YORK FED

The inclusion of CCP clearing in summit communiqués gave extra support to initiatives already underway at the New York Fed before the events of mid-September.

Three weeks after the AIG bail-out, Timothy Geithner, the bank's president, was an angry man. He had lost patience with the failure of CCorp and its investment bank backers to make good on their promises to produce a CDS clearing house. Instead of making CDS clearing a priority, the OTC dealers that owned CCorp appeared to be stalling progress. Having inspected CCorp's plans and found them wanting, Geithner engaged with other aspiring providers – Eurex, NYSE Euronext, CME Group/Citadel and IntercontinentalExchange (ICE).

On 10 October 2008, the New York Fed called in the companies to review progress towards creating a CCP for CDSs. After making plain that it wanted 'to accelerate market adoption of central counterparty services',[15] the Fed pushed CCorp into bed with ICE. The two companies announced that ICE had 'joined forces to support a joint global clearing solution' for CDS with market participants including CCorp.[16] The shotgun marriage was regularised at the end

[12] European Commission (17 October 2008), 'Statement of Commissioner McCreevy on reviewing derivatives markets before the end of the year'. The statement marked a significant change of direction by the Commission. Until the Lehman collapse, officials were working on plans to bring listed derivatives under the Code of Conduct, which with its interoperability provisions is aimed at promoting competition among CCPs.

[13] US Department of the Treasury (14 November 2008), 'PWG announces initiative to strengthen OTC derivatives oversight and infrastructure'.

[14] President's Working Group on Financial Markets (14 November 2008), 'Policy objectives for the OTC derivatives market'.

[15] Federal Reserve Bank of New York (10 October 2008), 'New York Fed to host meeting regarding Central Counterparty for CDS', press release.

[16] ICE, The Clearing Corp (10 October 2008), 'Industry Group signs letter of intent to establish global central counterparty clearing for credit default swaps', joint press release.

of the month with agreement that ICE would take over CCorp and push ahead with plans for the CDS CCP with the support of nine major CDS dealers.[17]

At the same time, the work of the Operations Management Group of dealers and buy-side institutions was beefed up under the New York Fed's watchful eye. Measures agreed with the industry in June 2008 were turned into commitments and high level goals that were made public at the end of October.

The commitments and goals published on 31 October amounted to a wide ranging programme to strengthen the credit derivatives market. The industry held out the hope that one or more CCPs for CDSs would be operational by the year's end. It promised to reduce the number of outstanding CDS trades through portfolio compression or 'tear-ups'. One measure that helped to demystify and calm the market was a decision by the DTCC to publish aggregate CDS trade data from its Trade Information Warehouse (TIW).[18]

Tear up programmes, by which specialised companies such as TriOptima eliminated offsetting trades, caused a rapid reduction in the reported size of the market. According to ISDA, the OTC derivatives trade association, the total notional amount outstanding of CDS fell to US$38.6 trillion by the end of 2008 from US$54 trillion six months earlier and US$62.2 trillion at the end of 2007.[19]

Data released from DTCC's warehouse had already helped calm nerves at the height of the crisis following the Lehman Brothers Holdings' bankruptcy. During October 2008, rumours in New York put market participants' exposure to CDS contracts written on Lehman bonds at around US$400 billion. Responding to regulators' concerns, DTCC rushed out a press release on a Saturday that estimated the overall net notional value of the market's exposure to Lehman at US$6 billion or so. DTCC later disclosed that US$72 billion of CDSs were written on Lehman and registered in the warehouse at the time of the bankruptcy and that a comparatively low US$5.2 billion was eventually transferred from net sellers of protection to net buyers.[20]

Publication of the industry's commitments on the New York Fed's website was part of a strategy of keeping the industry's feet to the fire. Further meetings followed and the process was extended to include buy-side firms and cover other OTC markets including commodities, equity and interest rate derivatives. The meetings and commitments continued after Geithner's move to Washington in 2009 to become Treasury Secretary in the Obama administration and the appointment of William Dudley as Geithner's successor in New York.[21]

The commitment letters sent by the leading OTC dealers to the New York Fed grew in precision to include targets to be achieved and monitored in partnership with supervisors,

[17] ICE, The Clearing Corp (30 October 2008), 'IntercontinentalExchange, The Clearing Corporation and nine major dealers announced new developments in global CDS clearing solution. ICE to acquire The Clearing Corporation as clearing initiative advances', joint press release; and discussions between the author and market participants. The nine CPS dealers were Bank of America, Citi, Credit Suisse, Deutsche Bank, Goldman Sachs, JP Morgan, Merrill Lynch, Morgan Stanley and UBS. Barclays Capital joined the group later.

[18] Federal Reserve Bank of New York (31 October 2008), 'New York Fed welcomes further industry commitments on over-the-counter derivatives'. Issued with a NY Fed press release were copies of the commitment letter and 23 pages of annexes providing details. Also: DTCC (31 October 2008), 'DTCC to provide CDS data from Trade Information Warehouse', press release, New York.

[19] The ISDA figures are provided here as an illustration. There are other sources of data, including the BIS and the DTCC's Trade Information Warehouse, which provide different figures. However, the overall picture is of a sharp downwards trend.

[20] DTCC (11 October 2008), 'DTCC addresses misconceptions about the Credit Default Swap Market' and DTCC (22 October 2008), 'DTCC Trade Information Warehouse completes Credit Event Processing for Lehman Brothers'.

[21] Further announcements and commitment letters followed on 2 June 2009, 8 September 2009 and 1 March 2010.

government departments, trade associations and infrastructure providers. The process entered a new stage in September 2009 when 15 leading OTC dealer banks set percentage targets with dates for clearing in CCPs the vast majority of new eligible trades in CDSs and interest rate derivatives conducted among themselves. They also targeted a significant proportion of their historical trades for CCP clearing.[22]

The process was far from perfect, however. The Fed's demands met push-back from the industry. The commitments reflected compromises that followed sometimes difficult discussions, so that 'as appropriate' and other qualifications cropped up in the texts. Distrust between the dealer and buy-side participants was an abiding problem.

That the process was liable to setback was evident early in 2010 when the Fed tried to obtain the support of buy-side investors for targets. It ran up against concerns that the possible added costs of clearing would be incompatible with asset managers' and hedge funds' fiduciary duties to obtain the best possible returns for their clients.

The result was a fudge. A commitment letter of 1 March 2010 promised that the signatories, comprising 14 dealers as well as leading buy-side firms, would 'continue to work collaboratively to deliver structural improvements' to the global OTC derivative markets only for a footnote to make the undertakings 'subject to the applicable fiduciary responsibilities of signatory firms, including any and all client-specific duties, obligations and instructions'.[23]

18.4 MISTRUST ACROSS THE ATLANTIC AND INSIDE THE EU

Cajoling market players to improve the post-trade processing of credit default swaps was one aspect of the post-Lehman/AIG agenda. So too was calming financial markets. But for the G20 initiative to work it was also vital to overcome mistrust between governments and reconcile differences about the strategy for clearing credit derivatives within and between jurisdictions.

As the global financial system teetered on the edge of collapse in late 2008, there was serious tension between US and European regulators and among EU regulators about the number and location of future CCPs to clear CDSs. Encouraged by the US OTC dealer community, authorities in New York and Washington pressed for one CCP only to clear for a global market and demanded it be based in the US.

This was unacceptable in Europe. Anger at the US authorities for letting Lehman Brothers collapse ruled out any possibility that the Europeans would allow vital market infrastructures to be subject solely to US regulation.[24] US regulators had, after all, manifestly failed to head off the crises at Lehman Brothers and AIG or discover the massive fraud against investors perpetrated by Bernie Madoff.

[22] Federal Reserve Bank of New York (8 September 2009), 'Market participants commit to expand central clearing for OTC derivatives'. The 15 committed to individually submit for CCP clearing 95% of new eligible CDS trades and collectively submit for clearing 80% of all such eligible trades, beginning October 2009. As regards interest rate derivatives, the OTC 15 agreed by December 2009 to submit individually for clearing 90% and submit collectively 70% of new eligible trades, as well as collectively submit 60% of trades that were historically eligible for clearing. The percentages of trades submitted individually were based on notional amounts while the percentages of trades submitted for clearing collectively were calculated on an average notional basis, weighted according to the historical eligible activity of each OTC 15 counterparty. Eligible trades were those between two reporting OTC 15 counterparties, each with a clearing relationship with one or more eligible CCPs, which meant the targets applied only to dealer-to-dealer transactions. However, the dealers promised to work on expanding the set of eligible counterparties, as well as the set of derivative products for clearing, and increase target levels as they improved their clearing capabilities.

[23] Federal Reserve Bank of New York (1 March 2010), 'New York Fed welcomes further industry commitments on over-the-counter derivatives'. Published with the announcement were copies of the participants 1 March letter and a summary of their commitments.

[24] The anger surfaced at a meeting of G7 finance ministers in Washington on 10 October 2008 and was later vividly described by Hank Paulson, then US Treasury Secretary, in his 2010 book *On the Brink*.

It was also open to dispute how far the CDS market was a single global market. About half of credit derivatives were traded out of Europe. According to Eurex Clearing, the European share of credit derivatives outstanding was an estimated 48% against 41% for America with most of the remainder divided about equally between Asia/Australia and Japan. CDS index products accounted for about 42% of the total, of which half were iTraxx products covering non-US regions.[25]

With such facts in mind, Commissioner McCreevy corralled industry groups and leading dealer banks in the EU to commit in December 2008 to support 'the establishment of one or more central counterparties in the European Union'. The goal was to facilitate the clearing of CCP-eligible credit default swaps on European reference entities and indices based on these entities, and promote back-loading of outstanding eligible contracts.[26]

McCreevy's deal unravelled almost as soon as the bank signatories reported back to their principals. The suspicion was rife among European regulators that the US Treasury played a part in the decision of the banks to renege on their agreement with the Commission.

The Commissioner's plan was put back on track in February 2009 with the help of the European Parliament. With McCreevy's encouragement, its influential economic and monetary affairs committee (ECON) backed an amendment to the EU's revised Capital Requirements Directive (CRD) which would have meant only CCP-cleared CDSs would benefit from favourable capital requirements. With the threat of legislative action in hand, McCreevy was able to extract a reaffirmation of the December commitments from the OTC dealer banks and trade associations as well as an engagement to use EU-based central clearing by 31 July 2009.[27]

In pushing for clearing in the EU, the Commission had the backing of member states[28] and was supported by the ECB. The central bank's governing council in fact went further. It issued an updated policy statement on CCP clearing in the eurozone in December 2008 that 'confirmed that there was a need for at least one European CCP for credit derivatives and that, given the potential systemic importance of securities clearing and settlement systems, this infrastructure should be located within the euro area'.[29]

The ECB's statement added strength to Europe's position vis-a-vis the US and supported the Commission in its tussle with the dealer banks. But it did nothing to ease tension within the EU where strains had appeared between Britain and its eurozone partners, notably France.

Instead, the discussion over the location of CDS clearing capacity fed into concerns in France about the future of Paris as a financial market and the perception that in LCH.Clearnet SA, the French clearing house of the LCH.Clearnet group, France had a major asset that was under threat. At the time – as described in Chapter 19 – the LCH.Clearnet Group was negotiating the terms of a takeover by DTCC and had recently become the object of bid interest from a consortium of banks in the OTC derivatives trading community.

In reaction, the Banque de France drew up confidential plans for an integrated CDS clearing system for the eurozone as the first stage of a broader integration of clearing services for

[25] In a Powerpoint presentation to a 14 November 2008 meeting of COGESI, the European Central Bank's 'Contact Group on Euro Securities Infrastructures'. Eurex gave sources as BIS, November 2008 and BBA Credit Derivatives Report 2006.

[26] Released by the EU Commission (18 December 2008), 'Industry commitment to the European Commission regarding central counterparty clearing of credit default swaps in Europe'. Signed by Citigroup, Credit Suisse, Deutsche Bank, Goldman Sachs, HSBC, JP Morgan Chase, Morgan Stanley, UBS.

[27] Letter to Commissioner McCreevy of 17 February 2009 concerning the foregoing *Industry commitment to the European Commission regarding central counterparty clearing of credit default swaps in Europe*: with Barclays Capital and later Nomura International as additional signatories. Also reflects author's discussions with officials and market participants.

[28] EU Council of Ministers (2 December 2008), 'Ecofin Council conclusions on clearing and settlement'.

[29] ECB (18 December 2008), 'Decisions taken by the governing council of the ECB (in addition to decisions setting interest rates)'.

equities, derivatives and fixed income trades. Advocating a 'building blocks approach', the French central bank suggested pooling Eurex's system for clearing derivatives and the equity clearing system of LCH.Clearnet SA 'as part of a common platform for multi-product and multi-polar clearing'.[30]

The authors of the French plan admitted that this scenario, which implied the dismemberment of the LCH.Clearnet Group, was almost impossible to realise without public intervention – and neither the UK Treasury nor Britain's FSA was ever likely to support the idea. An unpalatable truth for those seeking to locate CCPs for CDSs in the eurozone was that trading in OTC derivatives was concentrated in London. A paper published by the City of London pointed out that the UK accounted for 43% of derivatives turnover in 2007, followed by the US with 24% of trading: 'The amount of OTC business undertaken in France, Germany and Japan combined amounted to less than 15% in 2007.'[31]

But the Banque de France plan, which was circulated in January 2009, showed how far control of clearing infrastructure had become an important political issue inside Europe as well as across the Atlantic. Shortly afterwards, Christine Lagarde, France's finance minister, wrote to Jean Claude Trichet with a call for the ECB to design, supervise and implement a clearing system for the eurozone. One reason she gave was that France and other EU states did not want a US monopoly outside European regulators' control.[32]

18.5 WORKING TOGETHER

The main differences between the US and Europe and within the EU were resolved by the time G20 leaders descended on London for their second post-Lehman summit on 2 April 2009. With an all important reference to CCPs in the plural, their final communiqué pledged to 'promote the standardisation and resilience of credit derivatives markets, in particular through the establishment of central clearing counterparties subject to effective regulation and supervision'.[33]

The London accord reflected an understanding between authorities and industry in the US and EU that EU-referenced index and single name CDSs should be cleared by one or more EU-based CCPs while CDSs written on US entities should be cleared by one or more US CCPs. In the meantime, LCH.Clearnet met French sensitivities by promising to launch a service for clearing CDSs in the eurozone by the end of the year that would be managed by LCH.Clearnet SA, its Paris-based, eurozone-regulated clearing house.[34]

The transatlantic settlement grew out of a realisation that, although the CDS market was global, there were regional differences in the legal treatment of credit events between the US and EU which needed to be accommodated. This insight emerged during work at the industry level on standardising CDS contracts which made good progress.

Within a week of the London summit, ISDA, the industry body, implemented a protocol for CDS documentation known as the 'Big-Bang'. Marking an important step towards standardising contracts, more than 2000 banks, hedge funds and asset managers signed up to the process known as 'hardwiring', which incorporated auction settlement terms into standard CDS documentation. This provided investors with clearer procedures for settlement in cash in

[30] Confidential Banque de France progress report entitled, 'On clearing in France and the European approaches to clearing OTC derivatives', dated 16 January 2009.

[31] Jones, Lynton, April 2009, 'Issues affecting the OTC derivatives market and its importance to London'.

[32] *Financial Times* (30 January 2009), 'Paris toughens regulation line with call for clearing system'.

[33] G20 (2 April 2009), 'Declaration on strengthening the financial system'.

[34] LCH.Clearnet (13 February 2009), 'LCH.Clearnet to launch Eurozone clearing of Credit Default Swaps', press release.

the case of default of a US-referenced CDS contract.[35] Three months later, ISDA unveiled a 'Small-Bang' protocol that adapted the approach to conditions in Europe.

Combined with market conventions that established standard fixed coupons for CDS contracts, the Big- and Small-Bang protocols helped concentrate liquidity respectively in the US and non-US standardised CDS markets. This made credit derivatives more suited to central clearing.

The resolution of transatlantic and intra-EU differences about the location of CCPs for OTC derivatives encouraged an intensification of international cooperation at the level of officials.

The meetings with OTC market participants at the New York Fed were expanded to include foreign supervisors and central bankers ahead of the London summit.[36] Cooperation among international regulators moved up a gear afterwards with William Dudley, by then President of the New York Fed and Chairman of the central banks' Committee on Payment and Settlement Systems (CPSS), well positioned to play a pivotal role.

In July 2009, the CPSS-IOSCO committee of experts set up a working group to fast-track a review of its 2004 risk-management recommendations for central counterparties and adapt these, where necessary, for CCPs handling OTC derivatives.[37] With an eye to ensuring consistent implementation of existing and new recommendations, the New York Fed announced a few weeks later the creation of the OTC Derivatives Regulators' Forum to improve cooperation and information exchange among international regulators on CCPs and trade repositories handling OTC derivatives.[38] Early in 2010, CPSS-IOSCO launched a comprehensive review of existing standards for financial infrastructures, including CCPs, with the aim of issuing draft revised standards for public consultation all by early 2011.[39]

Although these moves lacked the force of legislation, they marked progress towards having consistent regulation across jurisdictions for CCPs serving global OTC derivatives markets.

18.6 TWIN TRACKS TOWARDS LEGISLATION

After the worst financial crisis in 80 years, it was evident to politicians on both sides of the Atlantic that new laws were needed to correct failures and restore trust, and that strengthened regulation of OTC derivatives markets must be part of this renewal.

In the US, Congressional hearings into the crisis led quickly to legislative initiatives. Collin Peterson, the House Agriculture Committee Chairman, signalled early in January 2009 that he would introduce a bill to mandate clearing for OTC derivatives. Two days after the inauguration of President Barack Obama on 20 January 2009, Tom Harkin, Peterson's counterpart in the Senate, introduced legislation to eliminate the statutory exclusion of swaps from regulation and push OTC derivatives trading onto regulated exchanges.

---

[35] ISDA (8 April 2009), 'ISDA announces successful implementation of "Big Bang" CDS protocol'.

[36] The fifth such meeting on 1 April 2009 included representatives of 10 foreign supervisors and central banks, 12 US regulators (including the host, the New York Fed), 4 US industry groups, 8 US buy-side firms and the 15 main OTC dealers.

[37] Bank for International Settlements (20 July 2009), 'CPSS-IOSCO working group on the review of the "Recommendations for Central Counterparties"', press release.

[38] Federal Reserve Bank of New York (24 September 2009), 'A global framework for regulatory cooperation on OTC derivative CCPs and trade repositories', press release. Represented in the forum were 35 international financial regulators from 13 countries and the EU, plus the international standard setting groups CPSS and IOSCO.

[39] Bank for International Settlements (2 February 2010), 'Standards for payment, clearing and settlement systems: review by CPSS-IOSCO'.

In May, Timothy Geithner, by now Treasury Secretary in the Obama administration, wrote to Peterson, Harkin and other Congressional leaders to outline the government's plans to regulate OTC derivatives trading. To contain systemic risks, he proposed amending the Commodities Exchange Act and other laws 'to require clearing of all standardised OTC derivatives through regulated central counterparties (CCPs)'; prudential supervision and regulation of all OTC derivatives dealers; and 'moving the standardised part of these [derivatives] markets onto regulated exchanges and regulated transparent electronic trade execution systems for OTC derivatives'.[40] The risks involved in a customised, bilateral OTC derivatives trade that could not be handled by a CCP were to be dealt with through a 'robust regulatory regime' for dealers that included conservative capital requirements.

More formal steps followed. On 17 June, President Obama unveiled a package of regulatory reforms for the financial system. The Treasury White Paper included the promise of comprehensive regulation of all OTC derivatives, including CDSs, to prevent their posing excessive risks. The US plan also aimed at improving the OTC markets' efficiency and transparency; preventing manipulation, fraud and other abuses; and ensuring that OTC instruments were not sold to unsophisticated investors.[41] In August, the administration sent its proposals in the form of a detailed legislative text to Capitol Hill.[42]

The Administration's draft legislation required the following:

- Standardised OTC derivatives to be centrally cleared by a derivatives clearing organisation regulated by the CFTC or a securities clearing agency regulated by the SEC to reduce risks to financial stability from the web of bilateral connections among major financial institutions.
- Standardised OTC derivatives to be traded on a CFTC- or SEC-regulated exchange or regulated swap execution facility to improve transparency and price discovery.
- Higher capital and higher margin requirements for non-standardised derivatives to encourage greater use of their standardised brethren and the migration of OTC derivatives onto central clearing houses and exchanges as a consequence.
- Federal supervision and regulation for the first time of any firm dealing in OTC derivatives and or taking large positions in OTC derivatives.

The draft presumed an OTC derivative accepted for clearing by any regulated central clearing house would be standardised and promised the CFTC and SEC clear authority to stop market participants using 'spurious customisation' to avoid central clearing and exchange trading.

It gave all relevant federal financial regulatory agencies access on a confidential basis to the OTC derivative transactions and related open positions of market players and the public access to aggregated data on open positions and trading volumes.

The administration's draft built on the plans outlined by the President's Working Group in November 2008. Mandatory CCP clearing and exchange trading of standardised OTC derivatives were now firmly part of US policy. But when Geithner appeared at a Congressional hearing in July 2009, what constituted standardisation remained obscure.

[40] US Department of the Treasury (13 May 2009), 'Letter of Timothy Geithner to Senate Majority Leader Harry Reid and others'.

[41] US Department of the Treasury (17 June 2009), 'Financial regulatory reform: A new foundation'.

[42] US Department of the Treasury (11 August 2009), 'Administration's regulatory reform agenda reaches new milestone: Final piece of legislative language delivered to Capitol Hill'.

'We will propose a broad definition of standardised OTC derivatives that will be capable of evolving with the markets and will be designed to be difficult to evade,' he promised, going on to say:

> We will employ a presumption that a derivative contract that is accepted for clearing by any central counterparty is standardised. Further attributes of a standardised contract will include a high volume of transactions in the contract and the absence of economically important differences between the terms of the contract and the terms of other contracts that are centrally cleared.[43]

Despite the lack of precision on standardisation, the US plans set a new benchmark for efforts elsewhere, including the EU, where the European Commission had just launched procedures likely to lead to EU legislation on OTC derivatives and clearing.

Early in July 2009, the Commission started a public consultation on ways to increase the safety of the derivatives market which would be rounded off at a public hearing on 25 September. Its initial position paper came out in favour of CCP clearing, central data repositories and the standardisation of eligible OTC derivatives, which it considered a prerequisite for the deployment of the other measures.[44] Predictably, it argued there were strong reasons for CCP clearing to be located in Europe and so subject to European rules and supervision. The Commission was less certain, however, about the merits of pushing standardised OTC contracts onto exchanges.

The Commission promised to draw 'operational conclusions' before the end of its mandate – scheduled for 31 October – and 'present appropriate initiatives, including legislative proposals as justified' before the end of 2009. It promised to work with the US authorities to ensure global consistency in policy making and avoid regulatory arbitrage.

18.7 THE PITTSBURGH CONSENSUS

Over the summer of 2009 there emerged what McCreevy described as a 'transatlantic consensus' on OTC derivatives policy. Speaking on the eve of the EU Commission's September hearing, he listed three elements:

- Clearing as far as possible of standardised OTC products by central clearing houses.
- Central data repositories to give supervisors an overview of risks in the system.
- Tighter and more secure bilateral clearing of those segments of the market that might not fit into CCP clearing because they were too customised.[45]

A day later, this consensus was formalised – with the addition of a deadline – as one of many targets in the final declaration of the third G20 leaders' summit, held in Pittsburgh, USA.

'All standardised OTC derivatives contracts should be traded on exchanges or electronic trading platforms, where appropriate, and cleared through central counterparties by end-2012 at the latest,' the G20 declared. 'OTC derivative contracts should be reported to trade repositories. Non-centrally cleared contracts should be subject to higher capital requirements.'[46]

[43] US Department of the Treasury (10 July 2009), Timothy Geithner, US Treasury Secretary, before the House Financial Services and Agriculture Committees joint hearing on regulation of OTC derivatives.

[44] EU Commission Communication (3 July 2009), 'Ensuring efficient, safe and sound derivatives markets'.

[45] EU Commission (24 September 2009), 'Derivatives and risk allocation', Remarks by Charlie McCreevy at the Derivatives Conference Speakers' Dinner.

[46] G20 (25 September 2009), 'Leaders' statement: The Pittsburgh Summit'.

The next step in EU policy making came less than four weeks after the Pittsburgh meeting when the Commission set out its future actions for the OTC derivatives market and clearing. Although the plans still took the form of a communication or policy statement rather than specific legislative proposals, McCreevy described them as marking a 'paradigm shift away from the traditional view that derivatives are financial instruments for professional use and thus require only light-handed regulation'.[47]

Couched in terms of the G20 consensus, the Commission's policy statement was rather more nuanced in tone than the draft of the US administration. It set as goals: increasing the transparency of the OTC derivatives market; reducing counterparty and operational risk; and strengthening market integrity and oversight.

It identified CCP clearing as 'the main tool to manage counterparty risks'. Because of their systemic importance, the Commission signalled EU legislation to govern the activities of CCPs and eliminate discrepancies among national laws to ensure their 'safety, soundness and proper governance'.

There would be rules to make sure CCPs did not employ low risk-management standards; legal protection for collateral and the positions of clearing members' customers to encourage greater use of CCPs; and a system of authorisation to allow CCPs to provide services in all member states.

The planned legislative proposal would mandate trading of standardised derivatives on organised trading venues as defined by MiFID[48] and central clearing of such derivatives, in line with the G20 declaration. To this end the Commission promised to work with the industry and US to define which contracts could be defined as standardised. This process would entail setting 'ambitious European targets, with strict deadlines, for legal- and process-standardisation' while taking 'due account of European specificities'.

The Commission recognised that not all derivatives were suitable for clearing. But where bilateral clearing remained, firms would have to hold more collateral and post initial and variation margin. Bilateral clearing would also involve higher capital charges in line with the G20's Pittsburgh statement. To achieve this, the Commission would widen the difference in capital charges between centrally cleared and bilaterally cleared contracts in the EU's Capital Requirements Directive.

In the interests of greater transparency, the Commission envisaged mandatory reporting of all transactions to trade repositories, such as DTCC's Trade Information Warehouse for credit derivatives and others being set up for other OTC derivatives sectors. It underlined that repositories should be subject to European regulation and supervision. But the Commission left open whether Europe should have its own repositories. A key determinant would be whether European regulators were denied 'unfettered access to complete global information' of non-EU repositories such as the TIW. In that case, the Commission would encourage the building and operation of repositories in Europe.

The Commission's ideas came shortly before the end of its mandate. But the impending lame duck status of McCreevy and the other Commissioners did not bring work to a halt. While waiting for a new Commission to take office, officials took the first steps towards preparing draft laws. The aim was 'to come forward with ambitious legislation to regulate derivatives in 2010'.

[47] EU Commission (20 October 2009), 'Ensuring efficient, safe and sound derivatives markets: future policy actions'. Also: EU Commission (20 October 2009), 'Financial services: Commission sets out future actions to strengthen the safety of derivatives markets', press release.

[48] Regulated Markets (i.e., exchanges), Multilateral Trading Facilities and Systematic Internalisers.

18.8 SETTING BOUNDARIES

The formulation of legislation did not take place in a vacuum. The US and EU proposals on clearing formed part of bigger agendas on financial reform that mobilised legions of lobbyists in Washington and Brussels.

In the US, public anger towards the banks spilled over into the Congressional deliberations on derivatives and clearing. In December 2009, the House of Representatives backed Stephen Lynch, a Massachusetts congressman, who proposed that 'large swap participants' (in other words, dealer banks) should own no more than 20% 'in the aggregate' of any swaps clearing house. The amendment followed heavy lobbying by Nasdaq OMX, which held a majority stake in International Derivatives Clearinghouse (IDCH), a recently formed US CCP that was seeking to break into the market for clearing interest rate swaps. If eventually accepted without qualification, the Lynch amendment would exclude LCH.Clearnet's successful SwapClear service from the US market.

In view of the public mood, the goal of industry representatives and users on both sides of the Atlantic was not to block legislation on derivatives and clearing but to shape it.

Perhaps surprisingly, senior exchange executives were among the first to point out the risks of over-ambition when mandating exchange trading or clearing for OTC derivatives. Mark Ibbotson, chief operating officer of NYSE Liffe, the global derivatives business of NYSE Euronext, was one of many speaking out at industry conferences during the summer and autumn of 2009.

Pleading that mandates be 'kept to a minimum', Ibbotson stressed that

> Certain products don't lend themselves to going into the security of a clearing house. They are difficult to price and difficult to margin. It could actually damage the security of a clearing house to force things in there that shouldn't really be there.[49]

Next to raise objections were corporate users of OTC derivatives. Catching financial policy makers rather by surprise, companies including Caterpillar and Boeing in the US and Lufthansa and EADS in the EU, launched intensive lobbying campaigns in the autumn of 2009 which warned that mandatory clearing of OTC derivatives would saddle their commercial hedging activities with huge, uneconomic margin requirements. Such hedging, the companies insisted, posed no systemic risk.

Academic economists voiced reservations about the emerging regulatory landscape. One influential paper by Darrel Duffie and Haoxiang Zhu of Stanford University demonstrated that multiple CCPs for one asset class – as exemplified by US and European plans for multiple CCPs to clear CDSs – reduced netting efficiency and could increase average exposures to counterparty default.[50]

The message that CCPs, although valuable, were no panacea for managing risk in OTC derivatives markets was underlined some months later in a staff paper published by the Federal Reserve Bank of New York. Written by Duffie and two New York Fed staff members, the paper argued that current international standards for safeguarding CCPs against 'extreme but plausible' market conditions were insufficient. It also acknowledged there would 'remain

[49] To the 2009 *Mondo Visione Exchange Forum*, London, 3 June 2009.

[50] Duffie, Darrell and Zhu, Haoxiang (9 March 2009), 'Does a central clearing counterparty reduce counterparty risk?'.

a population of customised derivatives that are more suitably negotiated or risk-managed bilaterally'.[51]

Uncertainty persisted over how to define standardisation when considering which OTC derivatives should be centrally cleared. The UK authorities, for example, put the case that standardisation was an insufficient criterion to determine whether a product was eligible for CCP clearing and would leave CCPs exposed to risks. For an OTC product to be 'clearing eligible' it was also necessary to take into account whether there was: regular availability of prices; sufficient depth of market liquidity; and whether the product contained 'inherent risk attributes that cannot be mitigated by the CCP'.[52]

A number of practitioners developed the idea of basing eligibility for clearing on standardised process rather than product. Paul Christensen, co-head of the European Principal Strategic Investment Team of Goldman Sachs International, urged standard setters to concentrate on issues such as trade processing, confirmation and collateral management rather than the economic terms of a contract, which in the case of a plain vanilla interest rate swap would be its start date, coupon and maturity. 'There is often confusion between the requirements to standardise a contract in order to be able to clear it or trade it on an exchange,' Christensen said. 'Clearing requires a standard process. It doesn't require standard products. Exchange trading requires standard products.'[53]

In earlier years, the views of practitioners and lobbyist aired in airless committee rooms in Washington and Brussels would have played an important and perhaps decisive role in shaping legislation. Mixed into the brew this time was the raw anger of voters, hurt by the financial crisis and recession and facing higher taxes and reduced state services following the state bail-outs of the financial sector. In the US, where mid-term elections loomed in November 2010, no member of Congress could afford to ignore the hostility of Main Street towards the bankers of Wall Street.

When debate turned to regulating and clearing OTC derivatives, Main Street found an articulate and persuasive champion in Gary Gensler, who took over as CFTC chairman on 26 May 2009. Gensler was a persistent advocate of comprehensive regulation. He kept the issue alive while the Obama administration was preoccupied with pushing health care reform through Congress and US legislative initiatives on derivatives and central clearing were lost to view in Congressional committees. In his thought leadership role, Gensler lifted the profile of the CFTC from an also ran among US regulators to an international player.

As a member of the Clinton administration's Treasury team, the former Goldman Sachs partner had failed to spot the then nascent credit derivatives market. He now called for a radical overhaul of the entire swaps sector, with robustly regulated CCPs playing a greatly enhanced role:

> A comprehensive regulatory framework governing over-the-counter derivatives should apply to all dealers and all derivatives, including interest rate swaps, currency swaps, foreign exchange swaps, commodity swaps, equity swaps, credit default swaps and any new products that might be developed in the future.[54]

[51] Duffie, Darrell, Li, Ada, Lubke, Theo (January 2010), 'Policy perspectives on OTC derivatives market infrastructure'. As with all NY Fed staff reports the views expressed are those of the authors and not necessarily those of the bank or the Federal Reserve System.

[52] Financial Services Authority and HM Treasury (December 2009), 'Reforming OTC derivative markets, A UK perspective'; www.fsa.gov.uk/pubs/other/reform_otc_derivatives.pdf (accessed 13 December 2010).

[53] Comments during a panel discussion at the *Eurofi Financial Forum* in Gothenburg, Sweden, 1 October 2009.

[54] Gensler, Gary (18 March 2010), 'OTC Derivatives Reform' to a meeting at Chatham House.

Gensler was prepared to challenge sacred cows. Not only should centralised clearing be mandated for all standardised products, but 'clearing houses should be required to take on OTC derivatives trades from any regulated exchange or trading platform on a non-discriminatory basis' and 'accept as clearing members any firm that meets objective, prudent standards to participate, regardless of whether it is a dealer or another type of trading entity'.[55]

His vision embraced what he called fungibility, an 'F-word' for vertically-structured US futures exchanges. Outlining an industry in which CCPs for swaps would be structured like the Options Clearing Corporation (OCC), he told *Futures Industry Magazine* that a clearing house for swaps should 'have open access, that a contract that is brought onto that clearing house from one trading platform is fungible and can be taken off through another trading platform'.[56]

After commercial companies fought back against clearing for their OTC hedging contracts, Gensler urged Congress to decide 'explicit and narrow' exceptions from clearing for end-users.[57]

He noted how BIS data suggested only 9% of the interest rate swap market was made up of trades between dealers and commercial customers, while 57% were trades between dealers and financial customers. Exemptions for customer trades should therefore be limited 'to the 9% of the market involving commercial customer transactions,' he told bankers in London. 'It is critical that we directly address with mandatory clearing the 57% of the market that so interconnects the dealers with the rest of the financial system.' Because of the unique nature of CDSs and the fact that more than 95% were traded between financial institutions, 'there should be no end-user exceptions for those contracts'.[58]

Congress resumed working on legislation to bring more clearing to OTC markets in March 2010, after approving healthcare reform.

In the EU, the cast of characters had changed after European Parliament elections in June 2009 and the selection and confirmation of a new Commission. Michel Barnier, the former French foreign minister who followed McCreevy as single market commissioner, set June 2010 as the target date for publishing the Commission's draft legislation on OTC derivatives and their clearing.

Some 18 months on from the bankruptcy of Lehman Brothers and the bail-out of AIG, many details of future regulation were still unresolved in the US and the EU. But clearing houses on both sides of the Atlantic had read the runes sufficiently to provide CCP clearing for credit derivatives and to plan solutions for other OTC markets.

---

[55] CFTC (25 September 2009), 'Prepared remarks of Gary Gensler', CFTC Chairman, to an EU Commission conference on *OTC Derivatives Regulation* organised by the EU Commission in Brussels.

[56] *Futures Industry Magazine* (September 2009), 'The Gensler Agenda, an interview with Will Acworth'.

[57] Gensler, Gary (18 November 2009), 'Testimony before the Senate Committee on Agriculture'.

[58] Gensler, Gary (18 March 2010), 'OTC Derivatives Reform' to a meeting at Chatham House.

19
Clearing Swaps

19.1 NEW PRODUCTS, NEW CONTENDERS, NEW HORIZONS

The events of September and October 2008 inspired a rapid expansion of products and financial instruments considered suitable for clearing. New and established CCPs came forward with a host of novel projects to serve a wide range of markets in response to concerns about counterparty defaults and in anticipation of legislation to regulate OTC derivatives.

Four forces helped to determine which assets were either introduced or considered for clearing: the ambition of regulators; the needs – sometimes newly discovered – of users; competition among clearing providers; and the disruption of established market patterns, often through wild price swings.

The attrition rate was high, however. Some projects, announced with great fanfare, failed to progress beyond the development phase because of technical problems. Others wilted under the scrutiny of regulators. One of the steepest hurdles was gaining acceptance in financial markets marked by tribal divisions of which the most pronounced was that between the OTC community and exchanges. As with gold rushes down the centuries, the feverish activity, innovation and jockeying for position that gripped the business of clearing after Lehman's bankruptcy and the bail-out of AIG generated a huge amount of turmoil. It will be some years before all the winners and losers from the 'clearing Klondike' of 2008–10 are known.

Pressure from regulators such as the New York Fed was the main spur for CCPs to enter the market for clearing OTC credit derivatives. In other OTC markets, a combination of regulatory pressure, the profit motive and user demand encouraged initiatives.

Contrary to some expectations, the crisis produced no rapid growth of derivatives exchanges.[1] However, it spurred those US exchange operators, which before the crisis acquired clearing capabilities through investment or acquisition, to exploit their new assets.

ICE had shown a lead when it built up its own clearing houses from 2007 onwards. Nasdaq and the NYSE followed, drawing on the clearing expertise of OMX and Euronext, their respective European acquisitions, to develop new opportunities and challenge incumbent clearers.

Strategies varied. Nasdaq OMX, for example, adopted a pick and mix approach to clearing. In Europe, it continued to use OMX infrastructure for clearing its derivatives markets while contracting out equity clearing to EMCF, in which it took a minority stake. While harnessing

[1] While the notional amount outstanding of all OTC derivatives contracts fell in value by about 20% in the second half of 2008 to US$547.4 trillion, the rate of decline of the much smaller total of exchange-traded contracts was a steeper 29% to US$57.9 trillion, according to the BIS. Both the exchange-traded and OTC markets rebounded by 10% in the first half of 2009. But the much lower base for exchange-traded activity meant that by the end of June 2009 the notional amount of exchange-traded contracts outstanding was well below the level recorded at the end of 2007, while the amount of contracts outstanding in the global OTC derivatives market was back above the end-2007 level. Bank for International Settlements (November 2009), 'OTC derivatives market activity in the first half of 2009'.

OMX technology, Nasdaq used acquisitions in the US to build capacity to clear interest rate swaps and OTC power and gas contracts.

To the frustration of CME Group, the powerful OTC dealer banks proved hostile to clearing solutions based on the practices of derivatives exchanges. In response, CME had to adapt its OTC clearing products to the dealers' requirements. But it also set up CME Clearing Europe in London in early 2011 to extend the geographic reach of its OTC clearing services.

Other companies decided to pool their expertise to exploit new opportunities. In 2009, Wall Street heavyweights, NYSE Euronext and DTCC, teamed up to develop New York Portfolio Clearing to provide cross margining between cash bonds and derivatives and in the process challenge CME Group's dominance of trading and clearing interest rate futures.

A new phenomenon was a strong interest in central counterparty clearing from buy-side institutions following Lehman Brothers' collapse. The discovery by hedge funds and large asset managers that many of their swap holdings were not protected by CCPs generated strong buy-side pressure for central counterparty clearing – to the gratification of clearing houses and the alarm of some dealers.

Although safety first became the mantra of regulators around the globe, the change of emphasis did not stifle competition. In EU markets for trading equities, the pre-crisis policy of breaking down barriers to cross-border clearing and settlement had resulted in the creation of new equity CCPs.

These engaged in a fiercely competitive price war in 2009 long after the Lehman Brothers' bankruptcy prompted what the Commission called a 'paradigm shift' in EU financial services policy towards risk reduction. As CCPs reported losses from clearing equities, regulators subjected plans to introduce interoperability among CCPs to extra scrutiny amid fears of a possible race to the bottom in risk-management standards.

At the company level, the changed environment for clearing undermined some ambitious projects conceived before the crisis peaked. Among these was the plan for DTCC to takeover LCH.Clearnet, which lost momentum after a London-based consortium of interest rate swap dealers plotted a counter offer.

New contenders emerged for clearing the US$342 trillion global interest rate swap market. Among those hoping to challenge the 10 year dominance of LCH.Clearnet's SwapClear service were the CME Group and the International Derivatives Clearinghouse (IDCH), the operating arm of a recent start-up, the International Derivatives Clearing Group (IDCG), in which Nasdaq OMX took an 80% stake towards the close of 2008.

CCPs, including LCH.Clearnet, drew up plans to clear the US$48.8 trillion market for OTC foreign exchange contracts. The OCC entered negotiations with dealers to provide a clearing service for the US$6.6 trillion market for OTC equity-linked swaps and options that could harness the OCC's systems and expertise. The scope of cleared financial instruments widened to include securities lending and contracts for difference.

Although the notional value of OTC commodity contracts, at US$3.7 trillion, amounted to less than 1% of the US$600 trillion global market for OTC derivatives in the first half of 2009,[2] sharp movements in prices for commodity and energy products opened up many new niche opportunities for CCPs.

Booming demand for steel in China caused the 40-year-old system of setting iron ore prices through annual contracts between mining companies and steelmakers to crumble in 2009 and

[2] The notional amounts mentioned in this and the preceding paragraph are for the end of June 2009 and drawn from Bank for International Settlements (November, 2009).

collapse in 2010. The resulting extreme price volatility spurred on the emergence of a new global market for hedging iron ore contracts, which were cleared by CCPs.

That a CCP in Singapore was the first to clear iron ore contracts pointed to another facet of change – the geographic spread of CCPs and a growing interest in central counterparty clearing to the 'new' emerging economies of the G20 with a particular focus on Asia.

The rest of this chapter focuses on the clearing of OTC derivatives, turning first to the CDS clearing before reviewing the battles for dominance of the market for clearing interest rate swaps. The next chapter will examine how clearing developments impacted on stock markets and derivatives exchanges after the crisis month of September 2008.

19.2 CLEARING CREDIT DERIVATIVES

The active intervention of politicians and regulators in the market for credit derivatives created a hot-house atmosphere, which forced the pace for those infrastructure companies in the US and EU that were in the race to provide CCP clearing for CDSs.

The October 2008 agreement for ICE to acquire CCorp and help build its credit derivatives clearing house provided some much needed backbone for a project that was drifting. It also killed off LCH.Clearnet's hopes that CCorp might become part of a merged DTCC-LCH.Clearnet group.

In January 2009, an important piece of infrastructure for clearing CDSs slotted into place when DTCC announced that its Trade Information Warehouse (TIW) would support all companies offering CCP solutions without discrimination.[3]

ICE was not the first company to offer CCP clearing for credit derivatives. That prize went to Liffe, the derivatives business of NYSE Euronext, which teamed up with LCH.Clearnet Ltd, the London clearing house of the LCH.Clearnet Group, to offer clearing of CDS contracts just before Christmas 2008. The offering employed Liffe's Bclear service, originally launched in 2005 for processing OTC equity derivatives, to register and process trades in CDS index contracts based on Markit iTraxx indices. Once turned into exchange look-alike contracts, the trades were to be cleared by LCH.Clearnet.[4]

The only problem was that there were no takers. The Liffe Bclear service failed to attract the all important dealer community because, as Chris Tupker said later, it did 'not involve the dealers in the resolution of risk-management problems'.[5] The service was unused for six months and dropped after Liffe disclosed it was 'under review' in early July 2009. ICE, which had dealer support for its service, became the first company to clear credit derivatives in March 2009.

ICE US Trust, a New York registered company, was approved to clear CDSs by the Federal Reserve System on 4 March 2009. Two days later, ICE's takeover of CCorp was completed with a cash payment of US$39 million.

Regulated by the Fed, ICE Trust began operating within a week and quickly became established. By mid-June 2009 it had cleared CDSs totalling US$1 trillion in notional value. In its first year up to 22 March 2010, ICE Trust cleared more than 60 000 trades made up of US$4.4 trillion in gross notional value covering 31 CDS index contracts and US$71 billion

[3] DTCC (12 January 2009), 'DTCC to support all central counterparties for OTC credit derivatives', press release.

[4] LCH.Clearnet, Liffe NYSE Euronext (22 December 2008), 'Liffe and LCH.Clearnet lead the way with the launch of Credit Default Swaps on Bclear', joint announcement.

[5] In comments to the *Eurofi Financial Forum* 2009, Göteborg, Sweden, 1 October 2009.

notional of CDSs referencing 33 single names. Open interest amounted to around US$300 billion, reflecting a compression rate of more than 90% of the total volume cleared.[6]

Unlike Liffe's Bclear offering, ICE Trust was very evidently supported by the market players that had been arm-twisted by the New York Fed into agreeing to sell CCorp to ICE in October 2008. This was in part because ICE's business plan for CDS clearing contained sweeteners for the dealer community. More important, ICE Trust's CDS clearing model drew on lessons from LCH.Clearnet's experience with SwapClear and complemented existing OTC market structures.

The companies that sold CCorp to ICE were encouraged to continue their links with the clearer and its new owner. Together with Barclays Capital, which joined the group after its acquisition of the US operations of Lehman Brothers, they became ICE Trust's founder clearing members. They were rewarded with a favourable pricing structure and participation in a 50% profit sharing arrangement with ICE Trust that kicked in fully from April 2010 after an initial period in which a substantial share of revenues were absorbed by operating expenses.

The 11 strong ICE Trust board had a majority of independent members of which four were nominated by clearing members. Dirk Pruis, ICE Trust's first president, was drawn from the clearing member community. As managing director responsible for global bank relations and market infrastructure at Goldman Sachs, he had been involved in the planning and design of the clearing house.

While the former CCorp provided ICE Trust with infrastructure for clearing operations and risk management, ICE contributed know-how drawn from its recent acquisitions – Creditex, its CDS execution and processing brokerage, with T Zero, a CDS affirmation and novation service.[7] DTCC's TIW provided a 'golden record' of the credit derivatives ICE Trust cleared while CLS handled its payment flows. ICE Trust agreed with Markit, the data company, to produce the daily settlement prices needed for mark-to-market pricing, margining and clearing.

ICE Trust's CDS margin pool was ring-fenced from other clearing operations of the ICE group. Copying LCH.Clearnet's SwapClear, the company imposed tough eligibility requirements on its clearing members. Only firms with a net worth of US$5 billion or more and a credit rating of 'A' or better could become members. Each prospective participant also had to demonstrate it had systems, management and risk-management expertise relating to CDS transactions.

ICE Trust's clearing operations were backed up by the familiar 'waterfall' of safeguards, which included initial and mark-to-market margins and stress testing. In addition, ICE Trust required each clearing member to contribute a minimum of US$20 million to the guarantee fund plus additional amounts based on the clearing members' expected levels of exposure which would be assessed at least quarterly. If, in the event of a default, the guarantee fund was insufficient to cover the losses, ICE Trust would be able to tap non-defaulting clearing members for additional guarantee fund contributions. By the end of 2009, ICE Trust's guarantee fund amounted to US$2.4 billion.

ICE Trust demanded a lot of its clearing members. But its parent company also put some 'skin in the game' to emphasise its commitment to the new venture. In addition to funding

[6] ICE News releases of 4 March, 5 March, 6 March, 10 March 2009 and 9 March 2010, plus: 2 July 2009, June and second quarter results. Also: Federal Reserve System (Effective 4 March 2009), 'Ice US Trust LLC, New York, Order Approving Application for Membership'.

[7] Later called ICE Link.

ICE Trust to the tune of US$35 million before it was launched, ICE contributed an initial US$10 million to the guarantee fund from cash in hand and announced that it planned eventually to contribute US$100 million to this safety net.

ICE steadily expanded the product range and geographical range of the CDSs that it cleared. Its European subsidiary, ICE Clear Europe, started clearing European referenced iTraxx indexed CDSs from 27 July 2009, a couple of days ahead of Eurex Clearing. The German-Swiss clearing group launched Eurex Credit Clear for European CDS products referencing iTraxx benchmark indices and 17 single name iTraxx index constituents from the energy sector, just before the end-July deadline agreed earlier in the year with the EU Commission.

In mid-December 2009, ICE Trust began clearing buy-side CDS trades while ICE Clear Europe started clearing single-name CDSs. Just before Christmas, ICE Trust added single names to its portfolio.

Like its US cousin, ICE Clear Europe quickly emerged as the market leader in its region of operations. It cleared €1.48 trillion of index contracts and €133 billion of single names by late March 2010.

While ICE's business was soon measured in trillions and billions of dollars and euros, that of its competitors languished. The contrast with Eurex Credit Clear was particularly striking, because Eurex had launched what appeared to be a very competitive offering at about the same time as ICE Clear Europe.

Eurex Credit Clear was linked to DTCC's TIW, enabling it to offer straight through processing and claim 'seamless integration into the existing OTC market infrastructure'.[8] Making an exception to the Deutsche Börse Group's traditional insistence on wholly owned silo structures, Eurex Clearing offered up to 90% of the equity of its CDS clearing house to clearing members. In some respects, Eurex was ahead of all other competitors: it offered to clear single name CDSs from day one and was also accessible to buy-side companies – provided these were proposed by clearing members.

Eurex Credit Clear successfully cleared its first CDS contract on 30 July and followed this with the first ever clearing of a single name CDS less than a month later. But the single name CDS based on energy giant RWE was for a notional value of €5 million only. Despite meeting the EU deadline and winning awards,[9] Eurex Credit Clear did a fraction of the business of ICE Trust or ICE Clear Europe.

At mid-March 2010, the Eurex website listed transactions in two CDS indices with a total open interest of just €85 million plus €10 million worth of open interest relating to single name CDSs referenced to RWE. These totals were unchanged since early October 2009, suggesting that no trades had been cleared in the meantime and that Eurex had been unable to achieve the economies of scale implied by the open interest of ICE Clear Europe. Towards the end of March 2010,[10] ICE Clear Europe's website valued the open interest of ICE Clear Europe's cleared CDS index contracts at €89 billion and that of its single name contracts at €105 billion.

Although ICE Clear Europe was able to leverage expertise from ICE Trust in the US, it had no obvious first mover advantage over Eurex Credit Clear in Europe. The latter's poor

[8] Eurex Clearing Press (24 July 2009), 'Eurex Credit Clear – the European OTC clearing solution for credit default swaps – to start on 30 July 2009'.

[9] Eurex Credit Clear won the Technology Innovation Award from *Credit* magazine, a specialist publication for fixed income markets, in November 2009.

[10] The Eurex figures date from 18 March 2010 and ICE Clear Europe from 22 March 2010.

performance suggested that other – more tribal – factors were at work in supporting the continued rise of ICE.

Despite ICE having been parachuted in to rescue CCorp's CDS clearing house, the dealer community evidently felt ICE Trust was more 'its' CCP for CDSs and relatively untainted by the exchanges that ICE owned. By contrast, the Eurex offering was shunned by the OTC dealer community. An explanation frequently heard was that it was perceived as representing the thin end of a wedge that would end with contracts being put on exchanges for trading.

Similar attitudes played a key part in the failure of Liffe's Bclear offering, which was seen to be based on exchange-related techniques. They also clouded the prospects for CME Group, which was another contender for CDS clearing.

CME Group did not launch its CDS initiative until mid-December 2009. With Citadel, the hedge fund, it had earlier tried but failed to attract the large Wall Street dealer banks to support a trading platform as well as clearing for credit derivatives. After that setback in September 2009, the group focused on creating a clearing service for CDS contracts based on the ClearPort system.

When launched, CME's CDS initiative claimed the support of many leading OTC dealer banks[11] as well as big buy-side firms such as AllianceBearnstein, BlackRock, BlueMountain Capital Management, Citadel, D E Shaw Group and Pimco.

But opposition formed over CME Group's plans to commingle customer funds used to margin, secure or guarantee cleared CDSs with other funds held in the customer-segregated account. By late March, CME Group had cleared CDS index contracts with an open interest of only US$47.5 million.[12]

Also somewhat delayed was LCH.Clearnet SA's Paris-based CDS clearing house for the eurozone supported by French dealer banks.[13] After a 'technical' launch in December 2009, the largely user-owned clearing house put off clearing CDS index contracts until March 2010, to allow its clients time to adjust their systems.

Mitigating risk in new markets has always been a gamble for infrastructure providers and the success of ICE in the market for CDS clearing illustrated the 'winner take all' quality of the CCP business. But the mixed fortunes of the CCPs that set out to clear credit derivatives also reflected the peculiarities of a market where the impetus for clearing came from politicians and regulators and where a small cohort of powerful dealer companies trading CDSs gave the market a notably tribal quality that appeared to militate against any offering with exchange trading in its DNA.

For all its notoriety after the Lehman bankruptcy and bail-out of AIG, the market for CDSs – with a notional value of US$36 trillion at the end of June 2009[14] – was one of the smaller OTC derivatives markets in terms of notional value outstanding, especially after the successful tear up or compression of offsetting obligations. A much bigger prize was clearing for the ten-times larger interest rate swaps market, which in 2009 was central in a battle for the control of LCH.Clearnet.

[11] Barclays Capital, Citi, Credit Suisse, Deutsche Bank, Goldman Sachs, JP Morgan, Morgan Stanley, UBS plus Bank of America Merrill Lynch, Nomura Group and Royal Bank of Scotland were named among initial members or expected members of the CME initiative early in December 2009. See: CME Group (3 December 2009), 'CME Group announces dealer founding members for CDS initiative', http://cmegroup.mediaroom.com/index.php?s=43&item=2968&pagetemplate=article (accessed 20 December 2010).

[12] CME Group website data of 24 March 2010; www.cmegroup.com (accessed December 2010).

[13] Initially BNP Paribas, Société Générale, Natixis and Crédit Agricole.

[14] According to the BIS: Bank for International Settlements (November 2009).

19.3 DTCC AND LCH.CLEARNET UNVEIL THEIR MERGER PLAN

It took six months for the merger negotiations between the LCH.Clearnet Group and DTCC to result in provisional agreement on a deal.

The 'non-binding heads of terms' disclosed by the two companies on 22 October 2008 would see LCH.Clearnet adopt an at-cost, user-owned, user-governed structure comparable to that of DTCC over a period of three years as part of a much enlarged transatlantic clearing group.

Presented as a merger, DTCC's planned takeover of LCH.Clearnet promised significant benefits to users. The at-cost model would return excess revenues in the form of rebates or discounts or lower fees. With operations in Europe and the US supported by a common infrastructure, there would also be savings of 7–8% of the combined group's operating costs thanks to economies of scale, savings on IT and integrated collateral management.

The two groups had complementary strengths. LCH.Clearnet was strong in derivatives while DTCC's main business was cash securities. A big attraction of the deal for Donald Donahue, DTCC's chief executive and chairman, was the possibility of combining SwapClear's expertise in clearing interest rate swaps with his company's capabilities in the market for credit derivatives. In Europe, DTCC's EuroCCP subsidiary would provide a replacement for the important but costly equities clearing service of LCH.Clearnet SA in Paris and would be developed further to provide a 'seamless cross-border infrastructure' for equities clearing in Europe.[15] EuroCCP charged about 5 euro cents a side to clear a trade against an average of about 14 cents at LCH.Clearnet SA which was still using Clearing 21 technology.

DTCC had experience of successfully acquiring and integrating financial utilities, albeit in a single jurisdiction: the US. The several thousand clients of DTCC and LCH.Clearnet around the globe could also take comfort from the fact that the two companies performed well during 2008's chaotic conditions on financial markets without losing a cent, centime or penny of the trades they guaranteed.

But the financial details of the agreement were horribly complex. In moving from a for-profit to an at-cost structure, LCH.Clearnet needed the support of those shareholders who were financial investors interested in income and share values as well as the user shareholders for whom promises of cheaper or improved services were more important.

Despite the huge scale of its business – settling more than US$1.86 quadrillion worth of securities trades in 2007 – DTCC operated with a slender capital base. Like all CCPs, it relied on the margin and default fund contributions provided by its members for protection against the risks of clearing. DTCC's at-cost model meant that its shares provided no return to their holders and so their price was low, based only on the tangible net asset value of the company. LCH.Clearnet would have to align the value of its shares with those of DTCC as a preliminary to the merger of the two groups. That implied cutting its capitalisation – and hence the value of its shares – to around one tenth of their pre-merger level.

LCH.Clearnet made a start in reducing the proportion of financial investors among its shareholders in 2007 when it bought back most of Euronext's holding in a deal that lowered the clearer's value to around €770 million from €1.2 billion. But the buyback established €10 per share as a benchmark that other shareholders would expect from a takeover by DTCC.

[15] DTCC (29 October 2008), 'Delivering certainty, creating possibilities, managing risk', Donald Donahue presentation to the DTCC Executive Forum 2008.

The proposed solution was for LCH.Clearnet's shareholders to receive up to, but no more than, €10 a share, or €739 million, in the course of three years. Most of the €739 million would be paid from LCH.Clearnet Group revenues. Some would be paid through the issue of 12 186 new DTCC voting shares to LCH.Clearnet shareholders, giving them 34% of the combined group's enlarged capital. The far greater part of the payment of up to €10 per share would come in the form of a special financial instrument to be redeemed for a portion of LCH.Clearnet profits over three years, plus a pre-closing special dividend from LCH.Clearnet.

Between 12 and 18 months after completion of the merger, the shareholder base of the combined group would be rebalanced in line with DTCC policy to bring shareholdings in line with usage. Special provisions were made for Euroclear, which supported the deal 'in principle'. It would sell its 15.8% stake in LCH.Clearnet and then buy a similar proportion of the capital of LCH.Clearnet Holdco. This new DTCC subsidiary would contain the businesses of LCH.Clearnet plus EuroCCP. It would have Roger Liddell as CEO, a 'substantial representation' of former LCH.Clearnet shareholders on its board, and be chaired by Don Donahue.

The negotiations with Euroclear took longer than expected. Time was needed to reconcile Euroclear's wish to 'cement a strong partnership in European post-trade solutions'[16] with a financial solution compatible with Euroclear's for-profit business model.

There were other hurdles to clear if LCH.Clearnet and DTCC were to sign a definitive agreement on 15 March 2009 as planned. As well as needing the support of LCH.Clearnet's shareholders, the deal was conditional on the approval of regulators, the backing of the works council of LCH.Clearnet SA and the completion of mutual due diligence.

The approval of regulators and shareholders was no longer a foregone conclusion, however. The world had changed dramatically since April 2008 when DTCC and LCH.Clearnet began their bilateral negotiations.

Relations between US and European financial authorities and regulators were dire in the weeks after Lehman Brothers bankruptcy. The French authorities, who were the lead regulators for the LCH.Clearnet group, were particularly incensed at the way the US had allowed the investment bank to fail and precipitate a global crisis. They regarded LCH.Clearnet SA as an important asset for the Paris financial market and all the more worthy of protection because it was perceived as having been put at risk through the past failings of the LCH.Clearnet Group in London. Following the takeover of Euronext by the NYSE and OMX by Nasdaq, the takeover of LCH.Clearnet Group by DTCC appeared to many as a deal too far. This was especially true in Paris, where NYSE was seen to be calling the shots in the merged NYSE-Euronext group.

The crisis following Lehman Brothers' collapse had demonstrated just how important clearing and CCPs were. With LCH.Clearnet clearing such a wide variety of products, it was not difficult to find differing user groups with very mixed views on the planned takeover by DTCC. In particular, derivatives dealers, who felt they had been short-changed by LCH since its merger with Clearnet, feared an even greater tilt in the direction of equities clearing at LCH.Clearnet as a subsidiary of DTCC.

Nonetheless, it was a surprise that landed on the desks of Roger Liddell, Chris Tupker and other LCH.Clearnet Group directors on 20 November 2008. A consortium, mainly consisting of banks active in the OTC swaps market, notified the board of its intention to launch a counterbid. The battle for LCH.Clearnet had begun.

[16] Mentioned in DTCC and LCH.Clearnet (22 October 2008), 'DTCC and LCH.Clearnet announce plans to merge and create world's leading clearing house', joint press release.

19.4 THE LILY APPROACH

Dubbed 'Lily', the consortium's approach was an attempt by part of the OTC derivatives trading community to increase its control over the governance of LCH.Clearnet. It was inspired by the importance of its SwapClear service to the OTC derivatives business and led by dealers in Deutsche Bank's London operation with strong support from dealers in part of JP Morgan. Underlying the initiative was a belief that the takeover of LCH.Clearnet by DTCC would create a clearing house with too many objectives and stakeholders and, with an at-cost business model, the wrong system of governance to enable consortium members to maintain their influence over SwapClear.

After successfully managing Lehman Brothers' US$9 trillion interest rate swap portfolio in September 2008, LCH.Clearnet's SwapClear service was a proven asset that was rising in value. Since the early 2000s, SwapClear had been developed in partnership with main dealer banks in OTCDerivNet, which provided strategic direction and shared in its governance and funding for investments. However, there was a widespread view in the market that SwapClear had been somewhat neglected by LCH.Clearnet's management.

Although also made up of interest rate swap dealers, the Lily consortium came from a rather different background than the OTCDerivNet banks. It was more European than OTCDerivNet, which had been co-founded by big Wall Street investment banks and which in February 2009 was reinforced by the addition of HSBC and JP Morgan.[17]

The Lily consortium originally comprised eight members – Deutsche Bank, the swap trading activities of JP Morgan, BNP Paribas, HSBC, RBS, UBS, the London Stock Exchange and ICAP – and grew in January 2009 to include Société Générale and Citibank. Deutsche Bank and JP Morgan dealers, the leaders of the Lily initiative, were riding the crest of a wave, having come through the crisis months of September and October 2008 in better fettle than such OTCDerivNet stalwarts as Morgan Stanley and Merrill Lynch.[18]

The consortium's approach was anything but transparent. News of Lily's existence did not surface in the press until February 2009 whereupon it hired a public relations agency primarily to spin news of its activities to a selected few. Only one participating company – the inter-dealer broker ICAP – ever admitted in public to being a part of the group. Rather like the Cheshire Cat in Lewis Carroll's *Alice in Wonderland*, the Lily consortium waxed and waned before eventually fading away. Yet it thoroughly undermined the DTCC bid for LCH.Clearnet.

The main aim of the Lily banks was to gain control of LCH.Clearnet in order to develop SwapClear in such a way as to preserve the very high margins of the consortium banks' interest rate swap business. For this reason, they proposed a for-profit business model for the group rather than the at-cost approach of DTCC.

But although they were large scale users of one of the clearer's services, the Lily banks were nowhere near being LCH.Clearnet's biggest shareholders. The 10 institutions that made up the consortium in January 2009 owned just 13.34% of LCH.Clearnet and included two members – the LSE and ICAP – which held no shares in the target company.

Altogether, LCH.Clearnet had about 120 shareholders, whose holdings were only rarely in line with their use of its CCP services. LCH.Clearnet's two biggest shareholders were

[17] LCH.Clearnet (3 February 2009), 'HSBC and JP Morgan become OTCDerivNet shareholders, further consolidating support for LCH.Clearnet's SwapClear service', press release.

[18] After the upheavals of 2008 and the inclusion of JP Morgan and HSBC, OTCDerivNet had 13 members: Bank of America Merrill Lynch, Barclays Capital, BNP Paribas, Citigroup, Credit Suisse, Deutsche Bank, Goldman Sachs, HSBC, JP Morgan, Morgan Stanley, Royal Bank of Scotland, Société Générale and UBS. Source: www.otcderivnet.com.

institutions at other points along the trading and post-trading value chain rather than users. Euroclear, the securities settlement group and LCH.Clearnet's biggest shareholder, had a 15.84% stake which was bigger than the combined holding of the Lily 10. The next biggest shareholder, the transatlantic exchange group NYSE Euronext, held 5%.

The line-up of firms behind Lily was intriguing for several reasons. As the French authorities were quick to note, there was a majority of non-eurozone participants in Lily, which suggested that a successful bid would benefit London rather than Paris.

The presence in the Lily group of the LSE – itself the owner of a clearing house in Italy – had possible negative implications for LCH.Clearnet's business relationship with the LSE's rival NYSE Euronext. Ominously, in February 2009, NYSE Euronext warned that it would look to other suppliers to clear its European cash equity business unless costs came down. NYSE Euronext made good on that threat 15 months later when it announced it would begin clearing its European securities and derivatives business in late 2012 through two new, purpose-built clearing houses in London and Paris.[19]

Like many other consortium initiatives, Lily was unstable. The LSE dropped out of the consortium in mid-March. Towards the end of April, Credit Suisse, Barclays and Nomura became members. A month later, the LME (London Metal Exchange) joined and Goldman Sachs was reported to be a member. By this time, the big French banks – BNP Paribas and Société Générale – had dropped out.

Not all members were as determined to gain control of SwapClear as Deutsche Bank. By mid-summer 2009, Lily watchers spoke of a core group that included Deutsche, part of JP Morgan, RBS, Barclays and Nomura. As with all such consortia, some members were in the group to keep an eye on rivals. The adherence of the LME seemed to be motivated primarily by fears that it might otherwise be perceived as a second-tier shareholder at a time when clearing was being introduced or planned for products such as iron ore and bullion futures.

To stand a chance of success, the consortium needed to overcome the concerns of regulators – especially in Paris – as well as win the support of a broad spectrum of LCH.Clearnet's shareholders, including the two big nonuser investors. This meant that any bid Lily devised would have to appeal to a far wider community than OTC swaps traders.

19.5 THE BATTLE FOR LCH.CLEARNET

The appearance of Lily was an unwelcome development for Roger Liddell and Chris Tupker. The eminence of the institutions involved in the consortium was tempered by the realisation that Lily's main promoters were not the top decision makers in the consortium's member firms. It also became clear that the dealers had launched the initiative without having first defined a business plan or offer.

For Tupker, the dealers' initiative was reminiscent of Rainbow, the earlier disruptive assault by a consortium of derivatives traders on LCH.Clearnet's business relationship with Liffe. Backing Rainbow were many of the firms that now supported Lily. LCH.Clearnet saw off Rainbow but in the process was forced to renegotiate its clearing arrangement with Liffe, reducing the services it provided for the exchange. Although LCH.Clearnet terminated its 'exclusivity agreement' with DTCC in December to be able to enter a dialogue with Lily, Tupker and Liddell interacted only grudgingly with the consortium while seeking other options for the company.

[19] NYSE Euronext (12 May 2010), 'NYSE Euronext announces European clearing strategy'. See also Section 20.5.

By March 2009, with still no offer from the consortium, LCH.Clearnet was working on a plan of its own to buy out those of its shareholders that were large investors but not actively involved as users. Codenamed Valkyrie, the plan was aimed at rationalising the LCH.Clearnet shareholder base to give the Lily members a better representation in the group while ensuring that the clearing house's governance did not end up just in the hands of a sub-group of members with no real interest in services other than SwapClear.

LCH.Clearnet also engaged heavily with the clearing house's regulators on both sides of the Channel, finding a more sympathetic ear in Paris than at the FSA in London.

Valkyrie showed how LCH.Clearnet's fortunes had improved for the better. Despite the preoccupation of its top management with the Lily initiatives, the clearer was introducing new products and had experienced a boost in earnings that were swollen by a post-crisis surge in treasury earnings and clearing activity. Meanwhile, DTCC's bid looked less and less likely to succeed. The 15 March deadline for concluding the DTCC deal passed without a result.

The Lily group in the meantime was trying to address two problems: winning the support of Euroclear and finding a clearing solution for the continental equities market in place of DTCC's EuroCCP platform. Their task was complicated after it emerged that BNP Paribas and Société Générale made keeping equities clearing at LCH.Clearnet in Paris a condition of their continuing membership of Lily.

The issue of equities in Paris moved centre stage for several weeks. The consortium tried to win the support of Euroclear with a plan to outsource some equity clearing functions in Paris to Euroclear France, its French CSD. This proved a false move, however, because in reaction BNP Paribas – a historic foe of Euroclear – pulled out of the consortium with Société Générale following suit.

With no French banks left in the consortium, the French regulators ruled that none of the equities clearing business of LCH.Clearnet SA in Paris should be outsourced to Euroclear. Mounting its own counter-attack, LCH.Clearnet announced at the end of April that it would cut its cash equity clearing fees for the NYSE Euronext market and the smaller eurozone cash equity markets that it cleared by 30% from 1 July 2009.

News of the cut in fees came one day after DTCC announced that it was bowing out of the negotiations to takeover LCH.Clearnet. DTCC's brief statement of 29 April reflected six months of mounting frustration at what Don Donahue once described as 'soap opera stories' emanating from London.[20] It was heavy with regret, tinged with irritation, contained a thinly veiled threat and yet held the door ajar for possible future cooperation with LCH.Clearnet. DTCC laid the blame for not consummating the merger at the door of LCH.Clearnet's management and board. But although declaring that it saw 'no choice but to pursue other strategic alternatives to develop seamless transatlantic clearing services to support the needs' of its customers and the industry in general, DTCC held out hope of opportunities for future collaboration.[21]

In early May, the Lily consortium – by now including Credit Suisse, Barclays and Nomura – made its long awaited bid for LCH.Clearnet. It underwhelmed. The offer of €11 per share was only marginally more generous than the now defunct offering from DTCC. Comprised of €3 in cash, €5 in the form of a special dividend to be taken from LCH.Clearnet's own reserves and €3 to be paid after 30 months from LCH.Clearnet's revenues from equities clearing, the bid was too low for the LCH.Clearnet board. The consortium was offering only €1.50 per share above the asset value of the business, which it planned to buy largely with LCH.Clearnet's

[20] DTCC (23 March 2009) Remarks at the ISITC15th annual industry forum in Boston.

[21] DTCC (29 April 2009), 'Proposed merger between LCH.Clearnet and DTCC not proceeding', press release.

own money. The Lily consortium's plan to operate LCH.Clearnet on a limited for-profit basis should have meant a higher valuation.

Never good, relations between the Lily group and LCH.Clearnet were by this time fraught. The animosity was noticed in the higher echelons of some of the Lily participants. Richard Berliand, chairman of JP Morgan Futures & Options, put himself forward as a mediator. Berliand was formerly a member of the LCH board before the merger with Clearnet. Historically he had a very close relationship with the management of LCH. Berliand was no narrow OTC specialist. He knew about clearing and could voice opinions on a relatively broad cross section of asset classes.

19.6 HOSTILITIES SUBSIDE

Berliand failed to broker a settlement. The Lily bid was rejected by LCH.Clearnet's independent directors, who had been charged with deciding whether or not to recommend it to shareholders. But the worst of the hostilities was over.

Although relations between Lily and LCH.Clearnet remained difficult, the positions of the two sides began to converge. By the summer of 2009, the LCH.Clearnet management was working on incorporating some of the Lily group's goals in the clearer's business plan and structure, with the aim of removing nonusers from the share register and accommodating the wishes of the consortium with those of the clearer's other main users.

The code word chosen to disguise the new initiative spoke volumes. 'Marigold' took the place of 'Valkyrie' as Tupker and Liddell put together a new proposal to deploy the LCH.Clearnet group's reserves to finance a realignment of its shareholder base.

Towards the end of September 2009 and after much delay, the company announced its results for 2008 together with a plan to put ownership in the hands of LCH.Clearnet's main users. NYSE Euronext and the LME, two long-standing exchange shareholders that had a clearing relationship with the company, would remain significant minority shareholders.

Marigold involved paying up to €444 million to LCH.Clearnet's owners, through a voluntary redemption of up to 33.3 million shares at a price of €10 a share plus payment of a dividend of €1.50 from bumper 2008 profits at a cost of €110.9 million. The one-off payment of €260.4 million from NYSE-Liffe following the restructuring of the exchange's clearing relationship with LCH.Clearnet went a good way towards meeting the cost of the buy-back. As part of the arrangement, Euroclear redeemed its 15.8% stake in LCH.Clearnet, thus exiting the company, while committing to a 'collaborative initiative' aimed at providing cost savings and operational efficiencies for customers of the two companies.[22]

The plan was approved by 97% of shareholders at LCH.Clearnet's annual general meeting on 15 October, effectively signalling the end of the Lily challenge. Once the buy-back was completed early in November, the group was owned 83% by users and 17% by NYSE Euronext and the LME. Large users – defined as contributing more than 1% to group clearing fees and which together accounted for more than 80% of LCH.Clearnet clearing revenues – increased their total shareholding to 63% from 37%.

The buy-back was, in the end, too successful to produce a neat realignment of the LCH.Clearnet share register. It was oversubscribed by 2.4 million shares so that individual

[22] LCH.Clearnet (29 September 2009), 'LCH.Clearnet to return up to €444 million to shareholders', LCH.Clearnet group results and announcements; LCH.Clearnet with Euroclear (29 September 2009), 'LCH.Clearnet and Euroclear to jointly improve post-trade processing'; LCH.Clearnet Group, '2008 annual report and consolidated financial statements'.

redemptions were scaled back, leaving some small shareholders on the group's register and a relatively high total of 105 shareholders.[23] LCH.Clearnet introduced a matched bargain facility from January 2010 to enable small shareholders to sell their unwanted shares and allow clearing members that held no shares and yet wished to become shareholders, to acquire stakes in the clearing house group.[24]

The retreat of the Lily consortium came not a moment too soon for LCH.Clearnet's top management. After a difficult and distracting year, Roger Liddell, LCH.Clearnet's CEO, could once again focus on running LCH.Clearnet. The battle for LCH.Clearnet had caused Chris Tupker, the chairman, to postpone his plans to leave the group during 2009. With the announcement of a solution in sight, the clearer's board announced on 21 September that he would step down in 2010 after the appointment of a successor.

On the plus side, the opportunities for clearing houses had grown dramatically during the stand-off between the clearer and the bidding group. A programme of system upgrades, initiated after the failure of the GCS project, enabled capacity to more than keep pace with demand. In addition, LCH.Clearnet was developing a new generation multi-asset clearing platform – called Syn*α*pse– for derivatives.

Offsetting the migration of energy contracts to ICE Clear Europe in November 2008 and the end-July 2009 transfer of CCP functions for the NYSE Liffe derivatives business to NYSE Liffe Clearing,[25] the group's CCPs in London and Paris churned out new products at an unprecedented rate.

LCH.Clearnet was particularly active in the volatile commodity, freight and energy markets, demonstrating that if a product is tradable, sufficiently standardised and deliverable in the future, it could be cleared. As well as expanding its existing dry freight clearing business, the group launched new clearing services for OTC container freight swap agreements and iron ore, fertiliser swaps and coal swaps. Concerns about systemic risk and demands for greater transparency prompted a second look at OTC markets, such as wholesale bullion trading in London, which previously were considered for clearing but where, for a variety of reasons, things had never taken off.

On the exchange-traded side, LCH.Clearnet expanded clearing services for Nodal Exchange, the US regional energy market. Of far greater significance in 2010 were the decision of NYSE Euronext to cease using LCH.Clearnet as its CCP from late 2012 and the growing possibility that the LSE would also develop its own clearing capacity. These challenges, to which must be added the escalation of a price war in the market for clearing equities in Europe, are described in the next chapter.

SwapClear, the service at the centre of the Lily bid, prospered during the turmoil and was strengthened afterwards. More dealer banks joined the service, bringing the total number of members to 32 by August 2010. It expanded its product offering to include 50-year interest rate swaps for trades denominated in dollars, euros and pounds sterling and overnight index swap (OIS) contracts.

The service's management was beefed up with the appointment in August 2010 of Michael Davie as SwapClear CEO. Previously with JP Morgan, Davie had 20 years experience in financial services, including trading, marketing and operational positions. His brief in the newly created post included a focus on the delivery of services to the buy-side, where opportunities

[23] LCH.Clearnet (6 November 2009), 'LCH.Clearnet successfully realigns shareholder base'.

[24] LCH.Clearnet (16 February 2010), '2009 annual report and consolidated financial statements'.

[25] The CCP service was previously known as LiffeClear

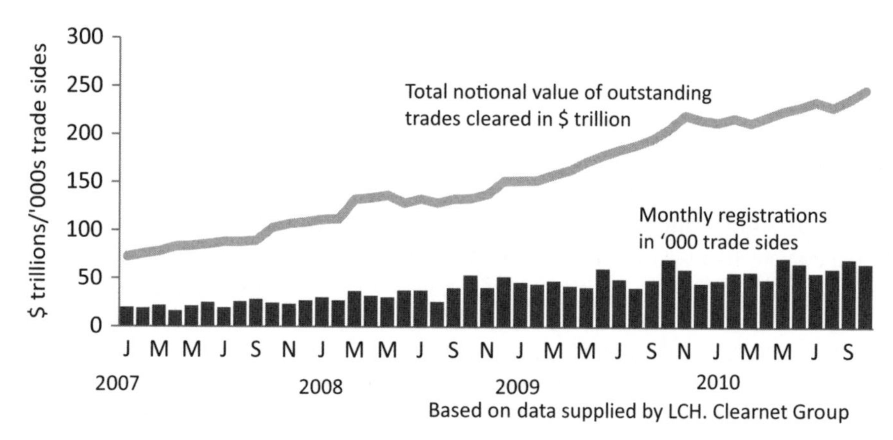

Figure 19.1 SwapClear: growing through the crisis

opened up because of the regulatory changes following the Lehman bankruptcy and AIG bail-out.

In December 2009, LCH.Clearnet became the first CCP to provide clearing services for interest rate swaps to buy-side clients. By March 2010, following the necessary regulatory approvals, the service could be accessed by buy-side firms through clearing members in the US, UK, France, Germany, Ireland and Switzerland.

As Figure 19.1 shows, the total notional value of trades cleared by SwapClear increased by 62% to US$247 trillion between January 2009 and October 2010 with the service clearing more than 40% of the global interest rate swap market in the course of 2010.[26] Around the end of 2009, SwapClear was clearing around 90% of all new inter-dealer swap activity[27] in line with the commitments of the OTC dealer banks to the New York Fed.[28]

Symptomatic of more finely honed commercial savvy in the group, in 2010 LCH.Clearnet developed a Spanish government bonds and repos service as part of Ltd's RepoClear offering. Launched in August and therefore well placed to attract business after the eurozone sovereign debt crisis of the spring, the service offered banks trading Spanish debt anonymous bond and repo trading, so reducing counterparty risk and increasing potential for balance sheet netting. Within a month, the market had used it to clear more than €130 billion in notional volumes, helping confirm the LCH.Clearnet group as the largest clearer of bonds and repos in Europe. The group claimed that it cleared around 85% of the cleared European government bond repo market, with second quarter 2010 volumes up 37% on 2009 to a record €35 trillion.[29]

The Lily episode was not devoid of ironies. In challenging Chris Tupker, Lily picked a fight with a man who from the start of his term as LCH.Clearnet chairman had recognised the need to bring the clearer's shareholder base into line with its users and took action to achieve this end. The outcome was a compromise. According to some estimates, the Lily consortium stood to gain as much as 80% of its original aims.

[26] Data drawn from various LCH.Clearnet Group news releases about SwapClear issued in 2009 and 2010.
[27] Reported by LCH.Clearnet (17 December 2009), 'LCH.Clearnet launches buy-side clearing for global OTC interest rate swaps'.
[28] As detailed in Section 18.3.
[29] LCH.Clearnet (9 September 2010), 'Notification: €130 bn of Spanish debt cleared in the first month'.

At the same time, Lily's failure demonstrated that there were constraints on dealers acquiring power over clearing houses. The course of events was influenced at crucial moments by the actions of the French regulators, which were far more engaged with LCH.Clearnet and the Lily bid than their UK counterparts. The Banque de France and the French Finance Ministry applied pressure to ensure that equities clearing capacity was maintained in Paris. Their appreciation of the strategic importance of clearing was in some respects similar to that of the New York Fed, which in October 2008 made clear its distaste for dealer ownership of important CCPs when it forced the leading credit derivatives dealers in the US to accept ICE's rescue of CCorp in order to complete its clearing house for CDSs.

With hindsight, the aspirations of the Lily consortium appeared quixotic and its actions politically inept. The consortium members were trying to corner the market for clearing interest rate swaps when big dealer banks were close to being political pariahs on both sides of the Atlantic. Not only was the New York Fed orchestrating more transparency and setting targets for OTC credit and interest rate derivatives, but the mood in Congress grew increasingly hostile to dealer banks as the details of the AIG bail-out emerged. Had the Lily consortium succeeded, the resulting concentration of the banks' ownership of LCH.Clearnet would have given extra momentum to the Lynch amendment, which appeared very soon after the failure of the Lily bid.

19.7 RIVALS TO SWAPCLEAR

By the time the Lily consortium withdrew, LCH.Clearnet was no longer the sole contender for clearing the global interbank interest rate swaps market.

Two US providers came forward with plans to serve this market in anticipation of US legislation that would mandate central clearing of standardised OTC contracts. First to produce an offering was Nasdaq OMX through its International Derivatives Clearing Group (IDCG) subsidiary.

A year or so after Nasdaq took over OMX at the end of 2007, Nasdaq OMX defined clearing as a prime area for growth. The group built a diverse portfolio of clearing assets during 2008. Nasdaq obtained a US clearing licence when it acquired the Boston Stock Exchange in August 2008. OMX came into the merged group with a rich experience of clearing and clearing technology. The plan was for the newly established Nasdaq Clearing Corp to undercut DTCC in the market for clearing equity trades.

In October 2008, Nasdaq OMX agreed to buy a 22% minority stake in EMCF, the clearer for several European MTFs, from Fortis Bank Global Clearing. Towards the end of that year, it spent US$20 million acquiring 80% of International Derivatives Clearing Group (IDCG), a newly founded clearing company for the OTC interest rate swaps market. IDCG's International Derivatives Clearinghouse (IDCH) was approved by the CFTC in December 2008.

Nasdaq OMX's threat to undercut DTCC turned out to be short lived. The plan was abandoned in October 2009. DTCC saw off the challenge with lower fees and a fierce lobbying campaign against Nasdaq Clearing Corp based on the argument that 'bifurcating clearing and settlement in the US' would add to systemic risk when the global financial system was still weak after the Lehman Brothers bankruptcy.

Nasdaq OMX got further, however, with its plans to clear interest rate swaps.

Although SwapClear had the advantage of incumbency and the kudos of successfully managing the Lehman default, the newcomer notched up some early gains.

IDCH gained CFTC approval at a promising moment. As described in the previous chapter, the US made CCP clearing of interest rate swaps a priority of post-trade policy during 2009 with the New York Fed setting percentage targets for central clearing of interest rate swap trades among OTC dealer banks with effect from December that year.

In June 2009, Bank of New York Mellon, one of the top global custodians, took a minority stake in IDCG and announced that it would provide margin and collateral management services for IDCH. Nine months later Newedge, a large futures brokerage, became a clearing member of IDCH in order to offer its clients CCP services in the interest rate swaps market.

The Lynch amendment favoured IDCH as a clearing house largely owned by a publicly quoted exchange group.[30] Although eventually dropped from the US legislation on OTC derivatives, its inclusion in the House version of the financial reform bill in December 2009 spoke volumes for the lobbying prowess of Nasdaq OMX on Capitol Hill, where many commentators called it the 'Nasdaq amendment'.

But it was the emergence in March 2010 of IDCH as a potential clearer for the very large swaps portfolios of Fannie Mae and Freddie Mac, the US housing finance groups, that defined the company as challenger to LCH.Clearnet.[31] Fannie and Freddie used interest rate swaps to hedge the interest rate differentials between their mortgage portfolios – estimated at a combined US$2.5 trillion to US$3 trillion – and their cost of borrowing. Clearing the agencies' swaps was a business that LCH.Clearnet had been pursuing for some months.

In April 2010, LCH.Clearnet launched a strongly worded attack on IDCH's risk-management standards, suggesting that the CCP was competing on risk and so breaking one of the great taboos of the clearing business. Liddell alleged that the margins charged by LCH.Clearnet's US rival were 'bordering on the reckless'.[32]

Liddell complained that IDCH used the standards of the futures markets as the basis for its margins for clearing swaps. One particularly damaging charge was that LCH.Clearnet's rival only looked back at 125 days of swap trading data when setting its margins. This meant it ignored price movements at the time of the Lehman default. LCH.Clearnet, by contrast, looked back at swap price movements over five years.

Liddell's charges were strongly rebutted by IDCH. But his remarks were unusually frank and open and brought to public attention a long rumbling debate about the risk of a 'race to the bottom' in clearing house standards.

The risk-management controversy underlined the different approaches towards clearing swaps adopted by the two providers. IDCH's model was based on converting interest rate swaps into interest rate swap futures, a feature which, the company argued, justified its margins policy. LCH.Clearnet, however, took the view that look-alike swap futures carried the same risk as swaps cleared by SwapClear.

The market targeted by IDCH also differentiated the newcomer from SwapClear.

SwapClear was a partnership with the dealer community. This was reflected in the dealers' commitment to help – by providing assets if necessary – in the resolution of a clearing member's default.

---

[30] See Section 18.8.

[31] The news emerged at the Boca Raton conference of the US Futures Industry Association on 11 March 2010 when Martha Tirinnanzi, head of a clearing working group at the Federal Housing Finance Agency, disclosed that Fannie and Freddie had tested clearing a shadow portfolio of swaps with IDCH, LCH.Clearnet and a clearing platform still in a development phase owned by CME Group.

[32] Wood, Duncan (15 April 2010), 'LCH.Clearnet CEO calls rival "reckless" as Fannie, Freddie clearing battle heats up', *Risk Magazine*.

IDCH, as shown by the support of Newedge, aimed to develop a market serving futures commission merchants (FCMs), which act as brokers in many asset classes. According to John Ruskin, Newedge's global head of financial futures and options execution, the push by the US to have OTC products in a listed format opened opportunities for FCMs. For Newedge, clearing membership of IDCH was part of a policy of developing execution as well as clearing for clients.[33]

IDCH was not alone in attempting new approaches to interest rate swap clearing. The CME Group launched a multi-asset class clearing service for OTC interest rate swaps in October 2010 that was developed with swap dealers, clearing member firms and buy-side companies.[34] The service promised a novel system of cross-margining OTC products with benchmark Treasury and Eurodollar futures that, once given approval by the CFTC, would deliver capital efficiencies for users and shake up the market.

19.8 SECURITY FOR THE BUY-SIDE

The emergence of Fannie Mae and Freddie Mac as possible clients of CCPs pointed to a huge potential market for clearing services among end-users of swaps. Known collectively as the 'buy-side', the hedge funds, fund administrators and commercial enterprises that used interest rate swaps accounted for a bigger share of the total amount outstanding than banks that dealt in them.

In June 2009, the BIS estimated that the buy-side accounted for interest rate swaps with a total notional value of US$208 trillion out of a total market of US$341 trillion. When in December 2009, LCH.Clearnet launched its SwapClear Client Clearing Services for the buy-side, it estimated that interest rate swaps with a notional value of US$146 trillion were potentially eligible for clearing by SwapClear.

Until the Lehman default, buy-side firms showed little interest in central counterparty clearing. That changed overnight, as hedge funds and asset managers learned the hard way to value the security that clearing could provide.

Speaking four months after the Lehman default, DTCC's Don Donahue recalled how the crisis affected buy-side institutions that had not taken up the clearing services for mortgage backed securities (MBS) provided by FICC, the Fixed Income Clearing Corp subsidiary of DTCC.

'There were many buy-side firms that were not members in the MBS division of FICC and therefore did not have the risk protection that FICC provided,' he recalled. 'They were aghast when they realised the position they were in. Their trades were unknown to DTCC and not margined, so FICC could not make them whole. Soon after the crisis, buy-side firms began pushing to become members of the clearing corp.'[35]

There were solid reasons why the buy-side had held back from becoming clearing members of CCPs. Buy-side firms generally had smaller financial resources than sell-side broker-dealers. They lacked the funds and expertise to contribute to clearing house default funds and clear-up measures. It was unlikely that any buy-side company would have been able to help LCH.Clearnet in the way that SwapClear dealers helped manage Lehman Brothers'

---

[33] Ruskin was speaking on 8 June 2010 in a panel discussion on 'The New FCM Landscape' at IDX, the *International Derivatives Expo* 2010 in London.

[34] According to CME Group (18 October 2010) 'CME Group begins clearing OTC interest rate swaps', news release; http://cmegroup.mediaroom.com/index.php?s=43&item=3073&pagetemplate=article (accessed 20 December 2010).

[35] Conversation with the author, London, 12 January 2009.

US$9 trillion interest rate swaps portfolio after the default of Lehman Brothers Special Financing, the SwapClear clearing member.

This suggested that the way to involve buy-side companies with CCPs was as clients of clearing members. And this indeed was the route chosen by ICE Trust US when it launched a buy-side solution for clearing credit default swaps in the US in December 2009 in partnership with 12 clearing members and 10 buy-side firms.

But accessing CCPs through clearing members was a far from obvious solution for buy-side institutions in Europe. Although, as described in Chapter 3, CCPs successfully transferred client accounts from Lehman Brothers International Europe (LBIE) to other clearing members after LBIE defaulted, there were cases where clients' margin funds were returned to PwC, the administrator, and frozen for many months.

This, warned Thomas Book, the Eurex executive board member responsible for clearing, was an important issue for the industry. The administrator's action following the Lehman default called into 'question the value proposition of clearing houses for their individual customers'.[36]

'For the first time,' Book said

> we had a big intermediary failing and indirect customers of that intermediary who were locked in. In the end, if I use a clearing house as an end customer what I want to know is that I am safe with my counterparty risk. We as an industry have to address the issue so that it does not come up again that collateral or assets or positions are locked in such a default scenario.

One cause of the problem at LBIE was the UK system of personal liability for bankruptcy administrators. Therefore, before LCH.Clearnet and other clearing houses could promote buy-side clearing, they had to find ways of keeping client monies out of administrators' hands. The solutions relied on buy-side institutions channelling their trades through clearing members, but with segregation of customer funds and enhanced portability of positions and margins in the event of default.

When LCH.Clearnet launched its SwapClear Client Clearing Service in December 2009, it was structured to enable client positions and collateral to be transferred to, or replaced by new trades with, a substitute clearing member should the client's clearing member default. Clients were offered the option of individual segregated client accounts. In addition LCH.Clearnet devised a 'deed of assignment' to be agreed between client and clearing member that would prevent monies being trapped by the administrator.

Eurex too came up with 'an individual segregation solution' for implementation at the end of 2010 to provide legal certainty for the immediate transfer of clients' positions and collateral in case of a clearing member default. This solution, according to Book, would also apply to the listed side of Eurex Clearing's business.

In the US, where discussion over clearing for Freddie Mac and Fannie Mae exposed continuing uncertainty over UK bankruptcy law, LCH.Clearnet adapted SwapClear to enable buy-side clients to access the service by way of FCMs, a model that protected the portability of client collateral and positions and was governed by New York law.

Enthusiasm for clearing fluctuated among buy-side institutions in the early months. The case for participation in CCPs appeared less compelling as memories of the Lehman crisis

[36] Comments made on 8 June 2010 in a panel discussion on 'The Evolving Clearing Model' at IDX, the *International Derivatives Expo* 2010 in London.

faded. The margins required by CCPs posed problems for some asset managers because they added extra and unfamiliar costs.

However, in September 2010, it was announced that MPS Capital Services, a subsidiary of Banca Monte dei Paschi di Siena, had agreed to clear interest rate swaps on SwapClear through Barclays Capital. The significance of the deal lay in the volume – more than US$200 billion in notional value – of trades being backloaded.

It remained to be seen how far other clearing models, based on turning OTC products into exchange-based or exchange look-alike products, could gain traction. This approach, which appeared well suited to the buy-side, was initially backed by CME Group which launched a short-lived service of this type in 2008. CME's 2010 cleared interest rate swap offering was pitched also at the dealer community and featured the trade execution processes and other features of bilateral OTC contracts as well as a US$1 billion net capital requirement for clearing members.[37]

Whatever the future, clearing houses no longer ignored the buy-side. As Kim Taylor, President of the CME Group's CME Clearing Division, observed in June 2010: 'Every offering we are working on in OTC clearing will also have a buy-side solution. It is a very important part [of our business] going forward.'[38]

[37] The CME Group's cleared IRS service was announced just as this book was being completed and so too late for detailed consideration in these pages.

[38] Comments made on 8 June 2010 in a panel discussion on 'The Evolving Clearing Model' at IDX, the *International Derivatives Expo* 2010 in London.

20
Exchanging Places

20.1 COMPETITION, PROLIFERATION AND EXPANSION

The drive to clear OTC derivatives trades told only half the story of clearing in the years after the Lehman bankruptcy. Clearing also became a vital part of the strategies of exchanges to strengthen their businesses in much tougher competitive conditions.

The years of deregulation that preceded the crisis culminated in measures to boost competition at the trading level which undermined the traditional structures of many exchanges on both sides of the Atlantic.

Stock and derivatives exchanges were affected differently, however. Also, as far as stock markets were concerned, regulatory changes that were similar in scope on both sides of the Atlantic had very different consequences for clearing because of the different ways exchanges and their clearing services were structured and regulated.

In the US, the biggest change to stock market regulation in 30 years took effect in March 2007. The Regulation National Market System, known as Reg NMS, aimed at stimulating competition in US equity markets. One of its most potent provisions required all brokers to ensure that investors got the best price, no matter where it was published, when they bought or sold stock.

Its effect on the long-established stock exchanges of America was dramatic. Market share, fees and profits tumbled. Incumbents invested massively in electronic trading technology to speed trades and attract the increasingly important algorithmic traders. Their efforts went largely unrewarded. In the early months of 2010, for example, the NYSE's share of trading in its listed stocks was below 30% compared with about 75% four years before. Benefiting from falling market shares at the NYSE, Nasdaq and other stock exchanges were alternative trading venues such as BATS Exchange, based in Kansas City, Missouri, which was backed by JP Morgan, Morgan Stanley and other investment banks.

This upheaval in US stocks trading had little direct impact on clearing. DTCC acted as the CCP for hard pressed incumbents and upstart trading venues alike. Its challenge was to cope with the rising trading volumes, triggered partly by Reg NMS and partly by heightened volatility.[1]

The new US rules had an indirect impact on clearing, however. Stock exchanges in the US, as elsewhere, concluded that their future growth lay in developing markets for derivatives trading. In consequence and as noted earlier, NYSE and Nasdaq acquired derivatives trading

[1] In 2007, the year Reg NMS took effect, DTCC's NSCC subsidiary processed an average of 54 million transactions a day, up from 34 million in 2006, according to DTCC's Annual report for 2007. The 13.5 billion transactions cleared in 2007 were 59% more than the 8.5 billion cleared the previous year. Before netting, the trades were worth US$283 trillion, up from US$175 trillion. In 2007, netting reduced the value of trades to be settled by 98% to US$5.2 trillion.

capacities and CCPs in a rush of mergers and acquisitions, bringing increased competition to the exchange-traded derivatives business.

These developments set in train a tentative and still incomplete blurring of long-established demarcation lines between the US markets for options, futures and cash securities and their clearing houses, which encouraged new contenders to compete in the markets for listed derivatives and deploy innovative clearing solutions to achieve their aims.

The EU's MiFID directive was similar to Reg NMS. It too insisted on best execution and gave the green light for Multilateral Trading Facilities (MTFs) and other alternative platforms. As with Reg NMS in the US, MiFID unleashed a savage price war among equity trading platforms in Europe which in turn encouraged stock exchanges, such as the LSE, to diversify their activities into derivatives and clearing.

But, in contrast to the US, the price war spilled over directly into the business of clearing cash equities, because in Europe there was no monopoly CCP such as DTCC's NSCC providing clearing services for all the different equity trading venues. Moreover, because MiFID and the Code of Conduct for clearing and settlement were focused primarily on equity markets, there was also nothing to stop the further verticalisation of derivatives exchanges in Europe.

Indeed, once it became apparent that neither regulators nor competition authorities would intervene to hinder the trend, vertical structures for trading and clearing derivatives became as much the norm in Europe as in the US.

The intense competition squeezed incumbent clearers, notably LCH.Clearnet in Europe and the CME Group in the US. LCH.Clearnet faced some particularly stiff challenges as profits from equity clearing slumped and its main exchange customer – NYSE Euronext – announced plans to take full control of clearing in Europe.

20.2 FALLING FEES FOR CLEARING EUROPEAN EQUITIES

While fending off the Lily consortium (see Section 19.4), LCH.Clearnet's management also had to contend with acute challenges in the European market for equities clearing.

The fee cuts initiated in 2006 were just the first shots in a price war that escalated following MiFID's coming into force in November 2007. MTFs such as Chi-X, Turquoise and BATS Trading Europe took market share from established exchanges and forced trading fees lower. The proliferation of the MTFs[2] and their tendency to choose new clearers such as EMCF and EuroCCP spread competition to the clearing level, hitting the profitability of incumbent and newly founded CCPs alike.

Clearing costs per equity trade in Europe tumbled from 2007 onwards with fee cuts accelerating in 2009. In April that year, EuroCCP cut its clearing fees from six to five euro cents a side after Turquoise, its main customer, had suffered a dreadful few months of falling trading volumes and share prices. EMCF reacted with a 40% fee cut for clearing UK equities. When LCH.Clearnet responded in May with new EquityClear fees of just one UK penny per trade for large scale users trading on the LSE and client MTFs, it claimed its cash equity clearing fees in London were more than 60% lower than in January 2007.

[2] Others to start operating in 2009 included the Hungarian-based QUOTE MTF, Burgundy (the rather oddly named regional MTF for Nordic securities) and Nasdaq OMX Europe, also known as NEURO. Nasdaq closed NEURO, which was a separate enterprise from Nasdaq OMX Nordic, in May 2010 because of lack of market support.

More reductions followed, as CCPs competed to attract the trading platforms used by algorithmic traders and in readiness for the expected spread of interoperability under the Code of Conduct. EuroCCP, for example, set fees of between 3 and 0.2 euro cents a side from 1 October 2009, depending on volumes traded.

The MTFs lost money. In 2009 the investment banks that launched Turquoise as a challenger to the LSE agreed to its acquisition by the London exchange. They become minority shareholders in the MTF which was then merged with the LSE's 'Baikal' dark pool business.

The turmoil left its mark on the revenues and profits of equity CCPs. Lower tariffs at LCH.Clearnet contributed to a drop in equity clearing revenues for the group to €60.6 million in 2009 from €114.6 million in 2008. Because of the impact of the tariff reductions on future revenues, the group recognised an impairment charge on its investment in Clearnet SA of €393.4 million. This lowered goodwill in the balance sheet to €110.4 million from €503.8 million and resulted in a net loss for the year of €91 million.[3]

'At current rates of revenues and costs, I suspect that nobody is making money,' observed Chris Tupker, LCH.Clearnet's chairman, in September 2009. For LCH.Clearnet, clearing cash equities in Europe had become 'pretty much a break-even proposition'.[4]

Some months later, EuroCCP reported an operating loss of €11 million in 2009, its first full year of operations, compared with a €14 million loss in 2008, its start-up year. Warning that its losses could persist until 2015, the equities CCP disclosed that DTCC, its parent, injected €29.6 million of capital into EuroCCP during the first seven months of 2010, to ensure it complied with the capital requirements of the FSA, its regulator.[5]

By contrast, EMCF reported profits for 2009. Clearing an average 1.6 million trades a day, or 35% of the market, EMCF increased its 2009 net profit by 120% to €6.63 million from €3 million the previous year on revenues up 42% to €17.2 million. However, it paid no dividend for 2009 (in contrast to the previous year when it distributed €1.42 million from retained earnings), choosing instead to boost shareholders' equity to €14.63 million from €8 million.[6]

Rivals sniped that EMCF's net earnings were a result of the benefits accruing from the infrastructure of its Dutch parent company and it not having to remunerate a large capital base rather than the roar-away success of Chi-X, its main client.

Undeterred, EMCF took the price war into a new phase in 2010 amid lacklustre equity trading volumes, with an aggressive price schedule to attract high volume clearing members.

At the end of August, LCH.Clearnet trumped this – at least for clearing members trading very high volumes in London – with a sliding scale of fees culminating in free equity clearing for average daily volumes of more than 150 000 trades.

A week or so later SIX x-clear, the Swiss clearer, announced a new tariff schedule, effective in January 2011, with fee cuts averaging 15% and reductions of 30% for the biggest clients.

Looking back from September 2010, Mike Bodson, Chairman of EuroCCP, put the fall in European equity clearing costs at nearly 80% over the two years since the DTCC subsidiary entered the European market with its at-cost business model.[7]

[3] LCH.Clearnet Group (2010, 2009) 'Annual report and consolidated financial statements'. For background about the goodwill in the LCH.Clearnet Group balance sheet, see Section 15.5.

[4] At the Eurofi Financial Forum, Göteborg, Sweden, 30 September 2009.

[5] EuroCCP (2010), 'Report and financial statement for the year ended 31 December 2009'.

[6] EMCF (2010), 'Clearing solutions for all to see, Annual report 2009'.

[7] Comment in an email to the author, 7 September 2010.

Box 20.1 charts the effects of MiFID and the financial crisis on clearing in Europe in more detail. It shows how falling equity turnover after 2007 and competition from MTFs put downward pressure on equity clearing revenues and led to low clearing fees for high volume users.

Box 20.1: European equity trading and clearing: The effects of MiFID and the financial crisis

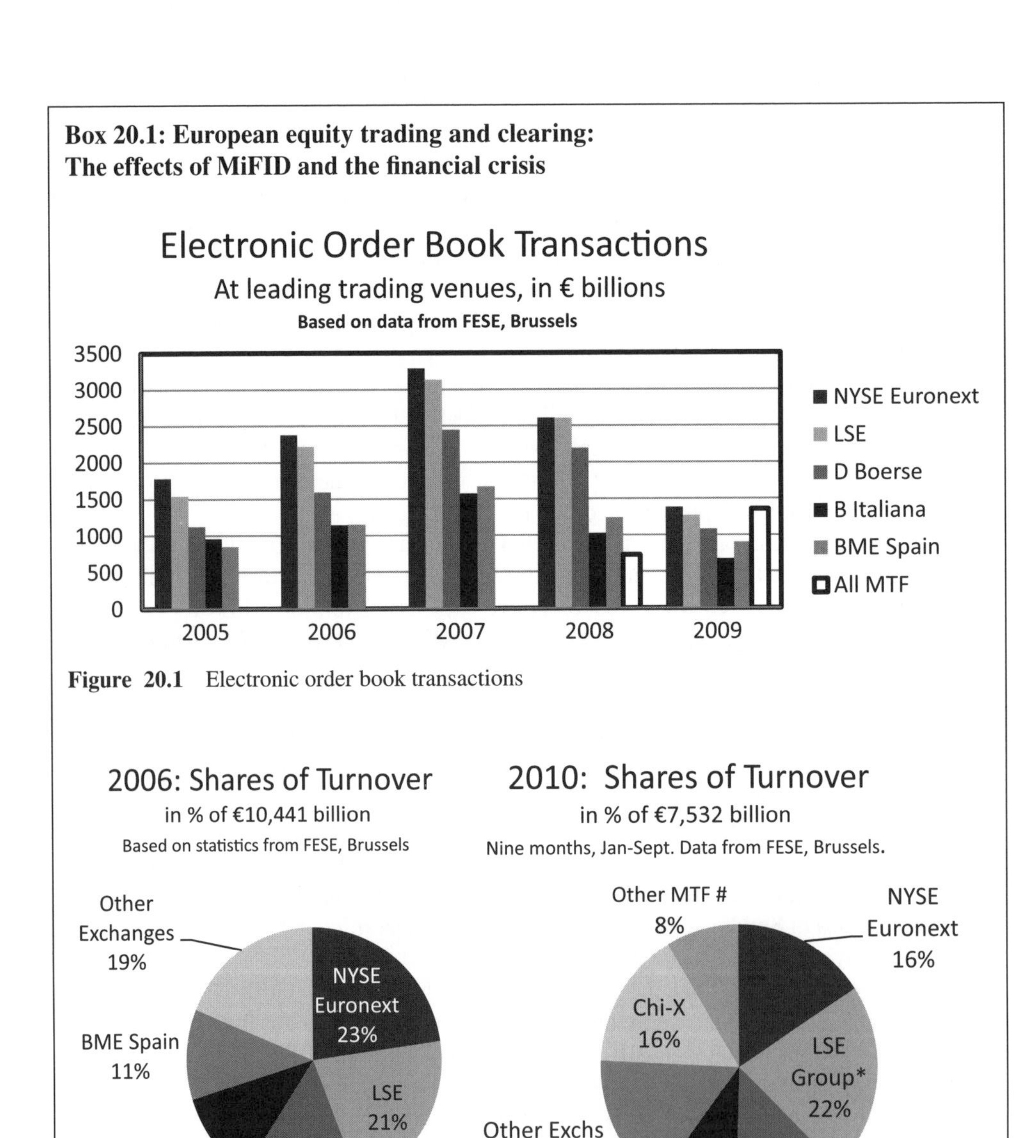

Figure 20.1 Electronic order book transactions

Figure 20.2 2006 shares of turnover

Figure 20.3 2010 shares of turnover
Includes BATS 4.7% and Turquoise 2.9%.
*Includes Borsa Italiana

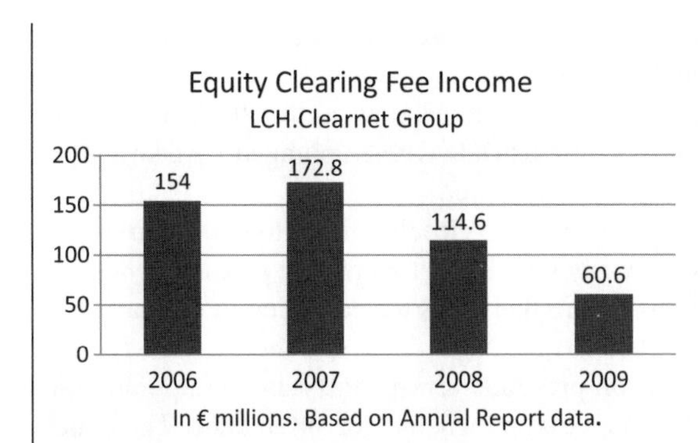

Figure 20.4 Equity clearing fee income

Equity Clearing Fee Structure:
The Example of LCH.Clearnet Ltd
Tariffs per trade, in pence, from 1 Oct 2010
For average daily volumes of:

Above 150 000	0p
75 001 - 150 000	0.5p
50 001 - 75 000	1p
40 001 - 50 000	4p
20 001 - 40 000	5p
10 001 - 20 000	7p
Up to 10 000	10p

Figure 20.5 Equity clearing fee structure

20.3 CLEARING ALGORITHMIC AND HIGH-SPEED TRADING

The structure of the clearing fee cuts in the summer of 2010 testified to the rapidly growing importance of algorithmic and high-frequency trading for equity markets. Often mentioned in the same breath, 'algo' and 'HFT' trading were distinct, albeit closely related, species of the same genus.

By the end of the decade, virtually all trading involved algorithms at some stage. But high-frequency trading was a different kettle of fish. The execution of trading strategies using computers to capture trading opportunities in very small periods of time, HFT had resulted in soaring volumes of equities trades that were held for extremely short periods and very rarely open overnight.

The onward march of HFT resulted in an arms race among trading platforms as established exchanges and MTFs competed with expensive systems' upgrades to attract order flow from traders who demanded execution, first in milliseconds (one-thousandths of a second) and later in microseconds (millionths of a second). That meant literally thousands of trades could be executed in the blink of an eye.

HFT traders were prized by the platforms above all as providers of liquidity and therefore as important contributors to the process of narrowing the bid/offer spreads that helped determine the platforms' competitive positions. This gave the traders leverage that they exploited to drive down fees, pushing the trading platforms, both old and new, into twin spirals of falling fees and rising investment costs. Inevitably, this process also put downward pressure on equity clearing fees.

Quite how HFT affected volumes was a matter of debate. But by 2010, it was generally thought that around 60% of US trades were HFT while in Europe, where volumes were lower, the proportion was estimated at about 40%.

But although HFT contributed to lowering trading costs for investors, there were downsides. Some argued that the algo and HFT techniques were used to manipulate markets by using speed to replicate the advantages of 'front running', the illegal practice by which traders execute orders for their own account while taking advantage of advance knowledge of pending orders from investors. HFT, with holding periods in some cases measured in seconds, clearly had little value in terms of providing capital to businesses.

Bigger worries crystallised on 6 May 2010 in what became known as the 'flash crash' when in the space of 20 minutes or so the Dow Jones Industrial Average plunged by nearly 1000 points before suddenly reversing to close 347.8 points lower.

In a country where individual retirement incomes were closely related to stock market performance, the 'flash crash' had a devastatingly negative impact on private investor sentiment. It did not help that it took nearly five months before there was a clear official explanation for the extraordinary events.[8]

The 'flash crash' triggered a lively debate on pre-trade transparency and an upgrading of circuit breakers to 'put sand in the works' of HTF trading when it got out of hand. The impact of HTF on clearing was less immediate. The preponderance of 'day flat' trades meant that at the end of each trading day, HFT trading was neutral as regards the overnight risk carried by CCPs and clearing members. CCPs in any case had reacted to the increased volatility of equity markets since the Lehman default by raising their initial margin for equities clearing and stepping up intraday margin calls when necessary.[9]

Although most of the lessons to be learned appeared to be in the pre-trade area, the sheer scale and speed of the 'flash crash' raised some uncomfortable questions about the intraday risk carried by clearing houses, which could be enormous.

This in turn breathed new life into thoughts of real-time clearing of equity trades – a process which, if feasible, could dispense with all the paraphernalia and margining that helped underpin the business model of the equity CCP. Werner Seifert, when CEO of Deutsche Börse, had pursued the grail of real-time clearing for a time and this was held to be one of the reasons he vetoed the project for a trilateral merger of the French, German and Luxembourg securities settlement infrastructures in 1999.[10]

Real-time clearing was a dream too far at the start of the century. But by 2010, at least one company – Sweden-based Cinnober, a relatively small but successful maker of trading and reporting platforms – had developed a clearing system geared to the high-frequency world. Ardently promoted by Nils-Robert Persson, Cinnober's chairman, at successive clearing and settlement conferences, TRADExpress RealTime Clearing offered a multiple asset class clearing system that calculated risk in real time. According to Persson, the system's capacity to perform risk calculations in milliseconds made it the fastest in the world and minimised the risk of defaults. Applicable to cash equity, derivative or OTC clearing, he claimed the system would provide users with a competitive edge in a world in which risk-management capabilities were of prime importance.

The history of clearing is littered with much trumpeted technical breakthroughs that failed to live up to expectations. In Cinnober's case there may be an opportunity to compare reality against promise, because the company announced its first order for the system from an (at that time) unnamed customer in February 2010.

[8] The flash crash was triggered when a mutual fund decided to sell 75 000 E-Mini S&P 500 Futures Contracts, valued at US$4.1 billion, in a very volatile and thinning market, using a sell algorithm. The algorithm executed the sell program in just 20 minutes, precipitating falls in the E-Mini, other futures contracts and individual stocks. CFTC and SEC (30 September 2010), 'Findings regarding the market events of May 6, 2010'.

[9] For example, LCH.Clearnet raised the number of margin calls when clearing equities in London to between five and eight per day following the Lehman bankruptcy.

[10] See Sections 12.4 and 15.2.

20.4 INTEROPERABILITY IN EUROPE: PROGRESS AND SETBACK

The downward spiral of clearing fees was helped on its way towards the end of 2008 when LCH.Clearnet and SIX x-clear established competitive clearing for the LSE.

Their interoperable link was the outcome of the May 2006 agreement between the two CCPs that pre-dated the signing of the EU Code of Conduct. Moving quickly to take advantage of user choice, the investment banking arm of UBS shifted the clearing of its equity trades in London from LCH.Clearnet to SIX x-clear in December 2008. Deutsche Bank followed suit a few months later.

Taking interoperability from the stage of agreement to action had been a slow and wearisome process, marked by delay, backsliding and obfuscation over two and a half years. While Marco Strimer, SIX x-clear's CEO, was consistent in his enthusiastic support for interoperability, first LCH.Clearnet and later the LSE raised objections that caused delays.

But in 2009, interest in interoperability suddenly took off. The dam broke late in January when the Nasdaq OMX Group completed the acquisition of a 22% stake in EMCF, becoming a minority shareholder alongside Fortis Bank Nederland, which by this time was Dutch government-owned. Nasdaq OMX chose EMCF to provide CCP services for Nasdaq's Nordic markets, which until then had no central counterparty clearing for equities. Coupled with the announcement was a pledge to support interoperability across Europe. A plethora of agreements for interoperable links between trading platforms and CCPs and among CCPs followed (see Box 20.2).

Box 20.2: Agreements to interoperate: February–May 2009

- *3 February 2009:* EMCF signs a memorandum of understanding (MoU) with SIX x-clear to allow choice of the two CCPs for Chi-X users.
- *5 February 2009:* SmartPool, a dark pool operated by NYSE Euronext, begins operating with LCH.Clearnet clearing Belgian, French, Dutch and Portuguese stocks and EuroCCP clearing ten other markets.[11]
- *5 May 2009:* BATS Europe, which used EMCF for clearing, appoints LCH.Clearnet as its second CCP for UK and Swiss Stocks.
- *6 May 2009:* LCH.Clearnet announces an MoU to provide CCP services for Chi-X and later that it has been selected to clear for NYSE Arca Europe, an MTF of NYSE Euronext.
- *7 May 2009:* EuroCCP and SIX x-clear sign an MoU on interoperability to allow Turquoise – and any other platform that chooses – to offer competitive clearing between the two CCPs.
- *Mid-May 2009:* Deutsche Börse agrees to open its equities clearing silo for the first time with a deal for a reciprocal clearing link for equities trades with SIX x-clear.
- *19 May 2009:* EMCF signs an interoperability MoU with LCH.Clearnet opening the way for three-way competitive clearing with SIX x-clear that would allow traders to choose a single CCP for trades common to platforms served by the three clearing houses.

[11] This agreement fell short of interoperability as defined by the code. It nonetheless marked a further step towards freeing up the European market for clearing cash equities.

In the case of LCH.Clearnet, scale benefits for users combined with a flight to quality following the crisis of 2008 prompted several MTFs to appoint the group to clear their trades alongside the newer CCPs. Interoperability promised to reduce the need for traders to fund margin arrangements across different CCPs, thus enabling costs of trading to fall and risk to be managed more efficiently. In the case of BATS Europe, for example, the inclusion of LCH.Clearnet as a clearing house alongside EMCF would enable some traders to benefit from collateral efficiencies and cost reductions by adding trades on BATS Europe to their existing LCH.Clearnet volume traded on other platforms.

In October 2009, clearing for equities in Europe entered a new geographical area. Nasdaq OMX Nordic introduced mandatory central counterparty clearing for nine Nordic securities traded on the company's exchanges in Copenhagen, Helsinki and Stockholm.[12] But the next stage of the strategy – to have EMCF, SIX x-clear and EuroCCP providing competitive clearing from January 2010 – was blocked.

The various agreements and MoUs signed during 2009 were subject to regulators' approval. In October, regulators held up implementation of the pending agreements between LCH.Clearnet, SIX x-clear, EMCF and EuroCCP for fear that their proposed inter-CCP margin arrangements could pose systemic risks in extreme circumstances. The Deutsche Börse agreement with SIX x-clear was also put on hold.

The action by regulators from the Netherlands, the UK and Switzerland followed their discovery that a CCP in an interoperability arrangement might not have the collateral to cover positions with other participating CCPs when volumes spiked. The existing interoperability arrangements between LCH.Clearnet and SIX x-clear for clearing equities traded on the LSE continued to function.

The regulators' decision illustrated a new awareness in the post-Lehman world of the risks of contagion among interoperating CCPs. Before the Lehman crisis, the European Commission considered extending the Code of Conduct to derivatives. Now, regulators shared doubts previously expressed by some clearing house managers.

In June 2008, for example, the European Central Bank was told at a meeting of COGESI, its contact group on euro securities infrastructures, that 'market participants were extremely concerned about the implications that interoperability would have as regards the soundness of CCPs'. When discussion turned to the danger of CCPs competing on risk, one unnamed participant reportedly warned that links between CCPs could create a 'hole in the boat'.[13]

To help allay such worries, EACH, the European CCP association, had published standards in July 2008, providing a framework to help CCPs assess requests for interoperability under the code from a risk-management viewpoint.[14]

But doubts had lingered. Following the May 2009 flurry of MoUs, Diana Chan, the chief executive of EuroCCP, proposed a 'European Convention on Interoperability' which would require all CCPs to agree transparent risk-management standards in order to avoid systemic contagion that could result 'if risks are offloaded by one CCP onto another'.[15]

[12] The late arrival of CCPs in Scandinavia was a quirk of history. As important regional custodians with stakes in Scandinavia's central securities depositories, the big banks in the region stoutly resisted the introduction of equity CCPs for many years, apparently for fear that netting by CCPs would have meant less business and lower revenues for Scandinavian CSDs. In 2008, Euroclear, the Brussels-based operator of CSDs, acquired the Nordic Central Securities Depository, which owned and ran the Finnish and Swedish CSDs. Almost immediately, the resistance to the introduction of CCPs in Scandinavia melted away.

[13] ECB (19 June 2008), 'Summary of the 18th meeting of the Contact Group on Euro Securities Infrastructures (COGESI)'.

[14] EACH (July 2008), 'Inter-CCP risk management standards'.

[15] Conversation with the author, 3 June 2009. Also: EuroCCP (17 June 2009), 'EuroCCP proposes European Convention on Interoperability'. Such a convention could, in theory, be used instead of a proliferation of confidential bilateral agreements in cases

At the same time, however, European cash equity market users still wanted interoperability to exert downward pressure on costs and to attack the entrenched position of vertical silos. The affected CCPs did not, therefore, abandon their plans. Instead, they produced proposals to overcome the regulatory blockage.

EuroCCP suggested that interoperating CCPs should increase their own default funds to include exposure to CCP counterparties 'in extreme but plausible conditions'.[16] EMCF urged a change in EU law to harmonise CCP legislation.[17] As their contribution to the debate, LCH.Clearnet and SIX x-clear published details of their 'Global Master Link Agreement' which had withstood the Lehman default.[18] Published later in full,[19] the agreement gave each clearing house the authority to determine the eligibility of trades for clearing and incorporated a margining process that preserved the integrity and safeguards of each CCP. The pact also included protections to minimise contagion in case of a CCP default.

LCH.Clearnet was by this time chafing at the regulatory delay. Ironically, given its initial reservations about interoperability, the CCP was keen to begin serving the MTFs with which it had signed MoUs in 2009. It now felt it had a competitive advantage against the other CCPs because of fee reductions, its adoption of 'at-cost' policies and its multi-asset class business model.

A joint letter in February 2010 from the Dutch, Swiss and UK regulatory authorities gave LCH.Clearnet and the others some grounds for hope.[20] The regulators did not reject interoperability from a conceptual standpoint so long as the risks could be adequately mitigated by the CCPs involved.

However, inter-CCP credit exposures arising from interoperability had to be 'priced in' and matched by appropriate collateral over and above the normal collateral and default protections each CCP held to mitigate counterparty risk. So long as the additional protection was transparent and liquid and held in a 'pre-funded' manner, an interoperating CCP could mitigate added risk by increasing its default fund or taking supplementary margin from participants to allow it to meet its margin liabilities.

Before approving the interoperability arrangements, the regulators required reassurance that CCP arrangements to manage the extra risks would be scalable and that operational, technical, legal, settlement and liquidity risks, including the failure of one or more CCPs in an interoperable arrangement, were appropriately mitigated. From a systemic viewpoint, another important requirement was that the surviving CCP's assets were not trapped in the estate of a defaulted CCP.

The affected CCPs submitted new evidence in support of their plans and by the summer of 2010, CCP executives appeared quietly confident that interoperability would be approved. At the time of writing, however, the regulators appeared in no hurry to let the interoperability arrangements go ahead.

---

where several CCPs agreed to interoperate. As Ms Chan pointed out, the more interoperating CCPs, the more bilateral contracts required: therefore four interoperating CCPs require six bilateral contracts, while six interoperating CCPs require 15 contracts and so on, creating potential conflicts on rights and obligations that could be invisible to the affected parties.

[16] EuroCCP (January 2010), 'Recommendations for reducing risks among interoperating CCPs: A discussion document'.

[17] EMCF (29 December 2009), 'Interoperability for CCPs: A way forward'.

[18] According to a Link agreement summary between LCH.Clearnet Ltd and SIX x-clear AG', published 8 February 2010, the 'Global Master Link Agreement' stipulated that the net position of each CCP with the other should be subject to margin calls and collateralisation requirements broadly equivalent to the requirements that the calling CCP would apply to its own members.

[19] On 6 September 2010.

[20] FSA, AFM, DNB, FINMA and SNB (12 February 2010), 'Communication of regulatory position on interoperability'.

20.5 NYSE EURONEXT PLANS ITS OWN EUROPEAN CLEARING HOUSES

While CCPs were wrestling with falling equity fees and the enforced halt to implementing interoperability agreements, NYSE Euronext startled the clearing community and financial markets by planning to take complete control of clearing for its markets in Europe. In May 2010, the transatlantic exchange group announced plans to sever its remaining ties with LCH.Clearnet, signalling its abandonment of the horizontal system of clearing that the Euronext exchanges had pioneered and championed a decade earlier.

NYSE Euronext said it would build two new purpose-built clearing houses based in London and Paris to begin clearing its European derivatives and securities business in late 2012.[21] At that point, the group's contractual arrangements with LCH.Clearnet Ltd and LCH.Clearnet SA would cease without any payment of termination fees or penalties to LCH.Clearnet.

The strategy involved a realignment of NYSE Euronext's clearing along asset class lines. The new clearing house in London would clear listed interest rate, commodities and foreign exchange products while that in Paris would clear equities and equities derivatives.

The NYSE Euronext decision showed how vertical clearing structures were now considered essential to the survival and prosperity of exchanges. By taking full control over its clearing business, NYSE Euronext would be able 'to compete better with the other vertical clearing houses that are around,' according to Declan Ward, executive director of NYSE Liffe Clearing.[22]

The group promised benefits for customers and shareholders alike from what would be a transformational project. Although the London and Paris clearing houses would operate respectively under UK and French law, the NYSE Euronext plan aimed for cross-border synergies from common technologies much as LCH and Clearnet had in 2003 before their merger and the failure of the GCS project.

'We need to put all our derivatives markets onto a single clearing technology,' Paul Mac Gregor, Director of Fixed Income Securities at NYSE Liffe, told an exchange forum in London.[23] He went on to say:

> It is very, very important for clients that we don't have one clearing technology in London and one clearing technology in Paris which is the current situation. If you run with dual technology any clearing member will tell you it's very expensive and you have to make expensive choices between which markets you are going to offer access to for your clients. A common technology will drive down the costs for our customers.

Ward described similar benefits on the equities side. A single technology solution across both clearing houses would offer clearing members 'efficiencies in their operations with a single set of processes and procedures around it'.

As well as taking control of the clearing for its cash and derivatives businesses in Europe, NYSE Euronext planned to compete in other markets. Its statement spoke of plans 'to extend clearing services to OTC markets and certain other trading platforms on attractive and competitive commercial terms'.

---

[21] NYSE Euronext (12 May 2010), 'NYSE Euronext announces European clearing strategy'.

[22] Declan Ward was speaking in a panel discussion on 'The Evolving Clearing Model' at IDX, the *International Derivatives Expo* 2010, in London on 8 June 2010.

[23] Paul MacGregor was responding to a question from the author during the *Mondo Visione Exchange Forum*, London, 2 June 2010.

For shareholders, the change in strategy to vertical clearing would involve investments of up to US$60 million until the end of 2012. But from 2013, there would be an estimated additional revenues of at least US$100 million a year from insourcing the group's European securities and derivatives clearing business as well as 'significant' annual cost savings through dispensing with clearing services provided by LCH.Clearnet Ltd in London.

NYSE Euronext presented the strategy as a logical extension of the creation in 2009 of NYSE Liffe Clearing as the CCP for the London listed derivatives business of its NYSE Liffe subsidiary. NYSE Euronext would 'move wholly away from all its outsourced contractual arrangements' with LCH.Clearnet Group's subsidiaries.

NYSE Euronext's change of strategy sounded the death knell for horizontal clearing of exchange-traded derivatives in Europe. The horizontal structure could only survive where interoperability existed and that required policy support either through a Code of Conduct, such as the EU Code for cash equities markets, or legislation.

The move was a serious blow to LCH.Clearnet after the sharp cutback in the services it provided to NYSE Liffe during 2009. It provided a baptism of fire for Jacques Aigrain, a former investment banker and Swiss Re chief executive, who had succeeded Chris Tupker as LCH.Clearnet Group chairman in April 2010.

The planned NYSE Euronext clearing house for equities in Paris was especially worrying for Paris-based LCH.Clearnet SA whose main business was clearing NYSE Euronext's cash and derivatives markets in France, Belgium, the Netherlands and Portugal. LCH.Clearnet SA had sharply reduced cash equity fees charged to NYSE Euronext in 2009 and accepted a nearly 9% drop in revenues over the year, all to no avail.[24]

Roger Liddell, LCH.Clearnet's chief executive, put a brave face on developments. Stressing that LCH.Clearnet was well placed to benefit from the efforts of regulators and policy makers to reduce systemic risk, Liddell said the group would seek continued diversification of its revenues through the development of new exchange and OTC initiatives.[25]

NYSE Euronext's announcement held open the possibility of a rethink in the event of 'discussions on any potential restructuring' of the LCH.Clearnet Group and/or its subsidiaries. Although both sides began talking in the summer of 2010, NYSE Euronext officials left enquirers in little doubt about the exchange group's determination to implement its plans. The talks seemed to be one set among many separate contacts among companies on scenarios for reshaping the industry after the NYSE Euronext move.

Following the decision, Standard & Poor's, the rating agency, put LCH.Clearnet's counterparty credit rating on 'creditwatch with negative implications'. At the same time, however, the agency lowered NYSE Euronext's ratings by one notch on the grounds that its plans for clearing changed 'the company's risk profile, introducing a degree of credit and financial risk' not hitherto reflected in its ratings.[26]

20.6 CHALLENGES TO THE CME

NYSE Euronext's new clearing strategy in Europe came as the group was already pushing ahead with an equally transformational joint clearing venture in the US. In June 2009, NYSE

[24] LCH.Clearnet SA reported revenues of €179.5 million in 2009, of which €89 million were derived from clearing fees.

[25] LCH.Clearnet Group (12 May 2010), 'NYSE Euronext Clearing Services'.

[26] AFP (13 May 2010), 'S&P cuts credit ratings on NYSE Euronext'. Also, Finextra (14 May 2010), 'S&P cuts NYSE Euronext rating on clearing plans; puts LCH.Clearnet on "creditwatch"'.

Euronext teamed up with DTCC to create New York Portfolio Clearing (NYPC), an equally-owned, joint clearing venture that was scheduled to start operating in 2010.

For those with long memories, the project had the feel of a family reunion: until 2006, NYSE – as it was before its merger with Euronext – was by far the biggest shareholder in DTCC with a 27% stake. But NYPC had a deadly serious purpose for NYSE Euronext: it aimed at breaking the CME Group's near monopoly over trading and clearing fixed income derivatives on exchanges in the US.

NYPC's unique selling point would be 'single pot' margining of derivatives traded on NYSE Liffe US, the US futures exchange of the NYSE Euronext group, and of cash fixed income securities cleared by FICC, DTCC's Fixed Income Clearing Corporation subsidiary.[27] The idea was to provide traders with greater operational and capital efficiency in risk managing and clearing a 'natural hedge' between the futures and cash markets for US Treasuries.

After its merger with Euronext, NYSE had moved quickly to bring the European exchange's derivatives expertise to the US, setting up NYSE Liffe US in 2008. The new derivatives exchange initially provided a platform for trading some precious metals futures and equity index products, which were cleared by the Options Clearing Corporation (OCC).

NYPC was designed to propel NYSE Liffe US into a different league so that it could compete with CME Group in its core markets for Eurodollar and US Treasury futures and, in the process, break the Chicago exchange's near monopoly of trading in Treasury futures on the CBOT.

FICC was not a trading platform. It provided trade matching, risk management, netting and other services for trades in US Government debt issues and for the mortgage-backed securities market. It processed about US$4.5 trillion worth of trades each day in the fixed income market in 2008 – about four times the value of equities cleared by NSCC. Among its activities, it cleared cash US government securities traded among dealers for delivery the following day, taking a small amount of margin in the process.

The plan for NYPC envisaged that NYSE Liffe US would provide a platform for trading US Treasury futures, much as the CME Group did. But those traders with open positions in cash Treasuries and futures would be able to net their margin payments to NYPC against each other, reducing their need to provide capital to cover the risks of clearing.

'People have huge cash Treasury positions against Treasury derivatives positions, which in the US are kept in completely separate clearing houses,' NYSE Liffe's Paul MacGregor explained in June 2010.[28] 'By working with FICC to create NYPC we hope to release a large amount of capital that was locked up in the large clearing houses that have to separately margin derivatives positions against their cash positions in the US.'

This 'single pot' or cross margining approach distinguished this latest challenge to the CME Group from an earlier attempt in 2004 by Euronext Liffe to go 'head to head' in competition in the market for Eurodollar futures. The launch then of Euronext's Eurodollar futures contracts in the US on its Liffe.Connect electronic platform with clearing by LCH.Clearnet happened before the merger with the NYSE and failed because the CME prevented access to its open interest.

NYPC would have the advantage of being located in the US. It would draw on FICC's risk-management, settlement, banking and reference data systems and NYSE Euronext's TRS/CPS

[27] NYSE Euronext and DTCC (18 June 2009), 'NYSE Euronext and DTCC to create Joint Venture for more efficient clearing of US Fixed Income Securities and Derivatives', joint press release.

[28] MacGregor was speaking during the *Mondo Visione Exchange Forum*, London, 2 June 2010.

technology. Dennis Dutterer, the former BOTCC CEO, was appointed interim chief executive. On 1 May 2010, Walter Lukken, the former acting CFTC Chairman, took over as CEO and, with that, responsibility of securing CTFC approval for NYPC as a derivatives clearing organisation.

Early estimates suggested that NYPC could, in its first phase of operation, unlock US$3–4 billion of capital that would otherwise be tied up in participants' margin accounts.[29] To increase further the allure of the new clearing concept for traders, NYSE Euronext committed a US$50 million financial guarantee to the default fund.

NYSE Euronext also sold a minority stake in its NYSE Liffe US futures platform to six of its biggest users in an attempt to break down the tribal barrier between the exchange and its users. This partial 'remutualisation' saw Goldman Sachs, Morgan Stanley, UBS, Getco, Citadel Securities and DRW Ventures (a subsidiary of the Chicago-based proprietary trader DRW Trading Group) join the NYSE Liffe US share register. It followed a similar sale by NYSE Euronext of a minority stake in its NYSE Amex options market to a group of leading banks and liquidity providers.

The NYPC project proved controversial with the investment banking community, nonetheless. The announcement that the 50–50 venture was 'an exclusive arrangement' between NYSE Euronext and DTCC provoked a hostile reaction from ELX Futures, a small recently-founded exchange which also nurtured ambitions to challenge the mighty CME Group.

The DTCC response that NYPC would 'accept and clear trades from any trading platform, including ELX Futures, after an initial pre-open access period' was scant consolation.[30] Although DTCC explained that the delay would be necessary to ensure that NYPC's 'systems and risk management are working optimally and consistent with the requirements of regulators', NYSE Liffe US would have crucial early months of exclusive use of NYPC in which to establish its futures contracts as serious competition for the CME Group.

New York-based ELX Futures was the latest in a succession of electronic platforms backed by investment banks that attempted from 2000 onwards to break the Chicago exchanges' grip on the markets for US Treasury and Eurodollar future.

Its foundations were laid in December 2007 when a group of investors, which included some of the new generation of high-frequency traders among the potential liquidity providers, circulated plans for a futures exchange, provisionally dubbed Four Seasons. When the venture was unveiled as ELX Electronic Liquidity Exchange in March 2008, the list of backers contained some familiar names.[31]

They included investment banks and other trading entities that had tried to create Rainbow in Europe and had backed previous efforts to break the CME Group's domination of futures trading on exchange in the US. As with earlier ventures, an experienced and energetic CEO was hired – in this case Neil Wolkoff, a combative former chairman and CEO of the American Stock Exchange and before that Chief Operating Officer of Nymex.

ELX began operating in July 2009. Whereas NYSE Euronext's challenge to the CME Group was based on NYPC's novel single pot clearing approach, the ELX business plan was based

[29] According to Walter Lukken, speaking at a NYSE Euronext function on 9 September 2009 during that year's Bürgenstock meeting in Interlaken. Lukken joined NYSE Euronext as senior vice president responsible for global market structure issues in the Office of the General Counsel on 13 July 2009.

[30] Pozmanter, Murray (10 September 2009), 'Why competition really is the future'. Letter to the *Financial Times*. Pozmanter was Managing Director of DTCC's Fixed Income Clearance and Settlement Group.

[31] Citigroup, Citadel Investment Group, Deutsche Bank, Merrill Lynch, Bank of America, Barclays Capital, Credit Suisse, eSpeed, Getco, JPMorgan Chase, Peak6 and Royal Bank of Scotland according to press reports at the time.

on low-trading fees and gaining regulatory acceptance for portability of contracts that would allow futures traders to move positions between clearing houses in order to consolidate them in a single CCP.

The key to obtaining what was also known in the US as 'fungibility' of futures contracts lay in ELX obtaining CFTC approval for an 'Exchange of Futures for Futures' (EFF) rule. According to ELX, this off-exchange rule would permit market participants to trade positions in two different designated contract markets offering the same product: in other words, ELX and the CME Group's CBOT. If approved by the CFTC, the EFF rule would enable traders to open a position at one exchange and close it at another, undermining the CME's protection of its open interest.

The CFTC appeared sympathetic to ELX's case[32] and, after some months of deliberation amid furious lobbying from both sides, wrote to the CME Group in August 2010 supporting ELX's EFFs, which had been prohibited by the CBOT. However, it had still to produce a final judgement at the time of going to press. ELX meanwhile carved out a modest 3% share of the market for US Treasury futures products and, apparently undeterred by slow progress on the EFF front, extended its product offering in July 2010 to Eurodollar futures contracts.

That ELX was able to challenge the CME Group at all, was due to the fact that OCC, the CCP for the horizontally-structured US options market, was on hand to provide clearing services for US futures exchanges that did not have their own CCPs.

ELX selected OCC as its clearer in December 2008, two months after NYSE Liffe US also chose OCC to clear its gold and silver futures contracts and options on gold and silver futures. In a business dominated by vertical structures, OCC considered the promotion of competition among exchanges as part of its mission. By 2009, it cleared for five US futures exchanges as well as US equity options markets.[33]

Sustaining a rivalry with the CME Group and its clearing division across the road on the other side of Chicago's North and South Wacker Drives was part of OCC's DNA. But OCC's willingness to act as a clearer for futures exchanges challenging the CME Group showed how the old demarcation lines were fading between clearing houses handling securities, options and futures trades in the US.

The involvement of FICC in the NYPC project marked potentially an even more radical rupture of the traditional demarcation lines that separated US clearing structures according to the asset class served.

When DTCC and NYSE Euronext finalised their formal agreement to create NYPC in October 2009, DTCC announced it would 'support competition in the US futures markets' through its open access model and would extend the NYPC risk methodology 'to multiple markets and products'.[34] This suggested DTCC would back further challenges to the CME Group's hegemony in futures markets. Slowly but surely, the tectonic plates underneath the differing US clearing house structures were on the move.

---

[32] ELX Futures (14 October 2009), 'CFTC approves ELX "EFF" Rule', press release.

[33] According to The Options Clearing Corp (2010), 'Good news and new opportunities', OCC's annual report for 2009, the five exchanges were: CBOE Futures Exchange, Chicago; ELX Futures, New York; NASDAQ OMX Futures Exchange, Philadelphia; NYSE Liffe US, New York; and OneChicago, Chicago.

[34] NYSE Euronext and DTCC (13 October 2009), 'NYSE Euronext & DTCC finalize Joint Venture Agreement to create New York Portfolio Clearing', joint press release.

20.7 CLEARING AT THE LSE: SYMPTOMATIC FOR AN INDUSTRY IN FLUX

While the CFTC's deliberate step-by-step approach to the controversy between ELX and the CME group helped slow the pace of change in the US, there was no such brake in Europe, where the announcement that the NYSE Euronext group would set up its own clearing houses unleashed a frantic round of contacts and negotiations among all clearing service providers.

Although there were some who doubted whether NYSE Euronext would be able to translate its plans into action, no rival could afford to ignore the exchange group's decisions in case they turned out to signal the long awaited corporate realignment of the sector. As in 1999–2004, projects for mergers and consolidation were devised, discussed and discarded. Only a few initiatives became known to a wider public. If the past was any guide, fewer of these ventures – and the other plots that went unreported – would ever get off the drawing board.

EMCF was at the centre of many rumours, having been put up for sale after the rescue of Fortis, its parent, in 2008.

DTCC, having been rebuffed by LCH.Clearnet in 2009, cast around for opportunities to boost the activities of its EuroCCP subsidiary. To this end, it called a meeting with Europe's exchanges and MTFs to discuss possibilities in the late spring of 2010. That this gathering became known to the cognoscenti as the 'Heathrow Group' suggested that the contact was meant to be more than a one-off event.

Another focal point of speculation was the LSE, where Xavier Rolet, a former investment banker, faced a baptism of fire after being appointed to the LSE board in March 2009 and taking over as chief executive from Clara Furse in May that year.

The heightened competition and the fall in fees for trading and clearing unleashed by MiFID had a marked impact on London, the most open of the European financial centres. Having spent 25 years working for big investment banks, with the last eight at Lehman Brothers, Rolet came to the LSE with a keen awareness of what the exchange's big clients wanted. He was anxious to bridge the divide that had emerged between the exchange and its sell-side clients since demutualisation.

His CV was rich in equity market experience, a market sector on which his new employer was over-dependent compared with international rivals. He faced other problems, including trade execution technology that was slower than that of Chi-X and other MTFs and vulnerable to outages.

His predecessor had spent much of her time fending off unwanted takeover bids from other exchanges before merging the LSE with the Borsa Italiana Group in October 2007. Borsa Italiana brought to the LSE derivatives trading and post-trade capacities, including the clearing house CC&G. But the jury was out over whether Borsa was a truly valuable asset or a poison pill for the LSE.

Following the implementation of MiFID, the LSE's trading fees and equity market share in London came under pressure as competition from the MTFs and investment bank-owned 'dark pool' trading venues grew. Rolet set out to make the exchange bigger, faster and cheaper for clients. He cut the workforce in London. In October 2009, the exchange acquired MilleniumIT, a Sri Lanka-based systems maker, for US$30 million to replace its trading platform and develop other technologies. As already noted, it acquired Turquoise, giving the LSE pan-European reach in equities trading.

The LSE also identified post-trade costs and especially clearing as a drag on growth and profits. In November 2009, Rolet took aim at the fees charged by Euroclear UK and Ireland

(EUI) for netting trades before they were sent to the CCPs that cleared for the exchange. Following a difficult and sometimes acrimonious negotiation, the two sides agreed a restructuring of EUI's tariff in February 2010, which according to Euroclear amounted to a reduction in the cost of trade netting to clients of 90% compared with 2006.

Rolet kept up a barrage of complaint about post-trade costs in London throughout 2009 and 2010.[35] But during his first year, development of the LSE's clearing business was incremental rather than radical.

In July 2009, the LSE obtained FSA approval for CC&G to operate in the UK and started using the CCP to clear the exchange's UK derivatives business. In January 2010, Rolet appointed Kevin Milne, formerly chief executive of Xtrakter, a trade-matching and risk-management company acquired by Euroclear in 2009, as Director of Post Trade Services. Milne was given responsibility for 'driving the growth and diversification' of the exchange group's post-trade services, which the LSE now described as one of its 'three main business divisions'.[36]

In June 2010, Rolet gave an indication of where the LSE's ambitions lay.[37] Pitching the company as a 'David' against such 'Goliaths' of the derivatives industry as NYSE Liffe, Eurex and the CME Group, Rolet announced the LSE's intention to become a pan-European equity derivatives exchange within nine months. He divined a competitive advantage from cross-margining across risk-correlated assets, claiming that no exchange or clearing house in Europe offered such a service.

This was a project in which clearing would have a key role to play. At this stage, however, the LSE's future clearing arrangements were shrouded in mystery.

Various options were mooted. There were reports during the early months of 2010 that the LSE was in negotiations to acquire the 78% stake in EMCF owned by Fortis Bank Nederland: these apparently came to nothing. Since acquiring MilleniumIT, the LSE had the capacity to produce its own CCP software.

There were recurring rumours – nurtured by hints from Rolet himself – that the exchange was planning to sever its links with LCH.Clearnet. Despite the evident difficulties of making money from clearing equities in Europe, these rumours gained credibility in August 2010 when news leaked out that Rolet had resigned in July from the CCP's group board.

In February 2011, the LSE announced that LCH. Clearnet would act as CCP for its new derivatives market. Its other clearing plans remained obscure, however, symbolising the state of flux in the European clearing sector following NYSE Euronext's decisions.

20.8 A DIFFERENT FUTURE FOR LCH.CLEARNET

The rapid and sometimes unpredictable changes that swept the business of clearing between the Lehman default and the NYSE Euronext decisions posed special challenges for the LCH.Clearnet Group.

After initial surprise, its managers quickly became reconciled to the loss of the Liffe clearing business in London, recognising that the shift towards verticalisation on futures exchanges was unstoppable. Also, although Xavier Rolet seemed in no hurry to reveal his hand, his decision

[35] The 'drag' of post-trade costs on the LSE's performance was a recurring theme of LSE chief executive Xavier Rolet. A typical example was Rolet's keynote speech to the *Mondo Visione Exchange Forum* in London on 1 June 2010.

[36] LSE Group (18 January 2010), 'London Stock Exchange Group appoints new Director of Post Trade Services', press release.

[37] In a keynote address to IDX, the *International Derivatives Expo* 2010 in London on 8 June 2010.

over the summer of 2010 to resign from the CCP's group board was taken as a fairly solid indication that the LSE too would probably part company from its clearing house.

But whereas such events would have spelled catastrophe before the Lehman default, LCH.Clearnet presented a confident face to the world. The upheavals on the exchange clearing front were unsettling. But at the same time, a bright future beckoned as a clearer of OTC derivatives – in the plural.

SwapClear, as described in the previous chapter, was developing well and stood to profit mightily from the global wave of regulation for OTC derivatives, which got underway with the passage of the Dodd-Frank act in the US in July 2010. Ambitious plans were developed in concert with LCH.Clearnet's leading bank shareholders to launch a clearing service for foreign exchange derivatives that were traded overwhelmingly over the counter.

Managers remained optimistic that the group's CCP for CDSs in the Eurozone would gain traction, despite ICE's first mover advantage in the US and Europe. With its Paris base, LCH.Clearnet SA was viewed favourably by French regulators and leading French banks. After nearly six months in operation, SA's CDS clearing service had cleared 622 contracts with a notional value of €22 billion and open interest of €1.6 billion.[38] However, this compared with totals of US$7.4 trillion gross notional value of CDSs cleared by ICE Trust US and €3.5 trillion by ICE Clear Europe, resulting in open interest of US$497 billion and €441 billion respectively.[39]

Although the clearing business was notorious for generating hopes and expectations that far outstripped reality, the group could even tell itself that there might be some silver lining to its separating from NYSE Euronext. Thanks to 'Syn*α*pse', its own clearing system developed originally for the London Metal Exchange business, LCH.Clearnet had the wherewithal to compete in clearing derivatives for any plucky upstart attempting to challenge the European trading duopoly of Liffe and Eurex.

On the equities front, there was the consolation of knowing that the business in Europe was unprofitable. Meanwhile, NYSE Euronext's decisions and uncertainty over the LSE's intentions had generated so much speculation and rumour that anything appeared possible – even a grandiose realignment of European capacities that could fulfil the long-held dream of European integrationists of merging clearing houses in Paris and Frankfurt.

In its day-to-day operations, the group's CCPs were performing well, with very few fails. Alongside Syn*α*pse, the group had invested heavily in systems upgrades and these were paying off.

So when, in July 2010, Roger Liddell decided to retire the following year, there was none of the *angst* that accompanied David Hardy's departure in 2006. Ian Axe, global head of operations at Barclays Capital, was later appointed CEO from early April 2011. Liddell's well signalled exit followed one of Chris Tupker's corporate governance principles: that companies like LCH.Clearnet needed regular change at the top to be fit to master change itself.

And the clearing agenda in 2010 was all about change. For while the industry, especially in Europe, was in a state of self-induced flux, a tsunami of new regulation flooded into the in-boxes of clearing executives, as first the US and then the EU produced their responses to the crisis that had so nearly destroyed the world's advanced economies.

[38] LCH.Clearnet (5 October 2010), 'LCH.Clearnet enhances CDS Clearing Service: Totals for the period from 31 March to 24 September 2010', press release.

[39] ICE (4 October 2010), 'ICE reports record futures volume; $12.1 trillion cleared in CDS: Totals from respective launches of ICE Trust and ICE Clear Europe to 30 September 2010', news release.

21

The Way Forward

21.1 THE DODD-FRANK ACT

On 21 July 2010, President Obama signed into law the biggest and most sweeping overhaul of US financial regulation since the Great Depression.

As its title suggested, the 'Dodd-Frank Wall Street Reform and Consumer Protection Act' was a wide ranging piece of legislation.[1] Named after Senator Christopher Dodd and Congressman Barney Frank, the two legislators who piloted the law through Congress, the 2319 page act aimed to kill off the doctrine of 'too big to fail'.

Congressional approval followed frantic negotiations, lobbying and compromise right up to the final vote, as legislators sought to reconcile the House and Senate versions of the bill and win over Republicans from northeastern states to enable the Democrat-sponsored legislation to circumvent a filibuster. It passed the Senate by 60 to 39 votes.

Despite determined lobbying by the financial sector and last-minute haggling, the act was tougher than had seemed probable a year before when the Treasury published its draft. This reflected a groundswell of resentment against Wall Street, its profits and bonuses, at a time of high unemployment on 'Main Street' throughout the rest of the USA.

Reversing three decades of financial deregulation, Dodd-Frank's goal was to make sure that big banks in the US could never again bring the world to the brink of economic and financial collapse, that US consumers had greater financial protection and that gaps in the regulation of capital markets, exposed in the crisis, were plugged.

Although Dodd-Frank was not the first legislative initiative in the G20 following the crisis – in March 2010, for example, the Japanese Financial Services Agency presented a draft bill to the Diet to mandate CCP clearing, data storage of trade information and reporting requirements – the new US law had a global resonance and set a benchmark for re-regulation of the financial sector in the G20 and beyond.

Title VII of the act subjected OTC derivative trades to regulation for the first time. The legislation to establish a new regulatory infrastructure for swaps, swap markets and their participants was complex, consisting of 73 sections accounting for nearly a fifth of the act's overall word-count.

To prevent the recurrence of another AIG or the risk of a chain reaction of clearing member failures, the law prescribed that, as a general rule, swaps must be cleared, with margin posted, if the relevant commission – the CFTC or SEC – so decided. To bring transparency to OTC derivatives pricing and assist in the risk-management of OTC derivatives markets, it laid down that, as a general rule, cleared swaps must be executed electronically on an exchange or a swap execution facility, a new type of regulated platform created by the act, and reported to a trade repository.

[1] Dodd-Frank Wall Street Reform and Consumer Protection Act, 111th Congress (2009–2010).

Dodd-Frank divided the world of swaps into two, reflecting the division of regulatory responsibilities between the CFTC and SEC, depending on the nature of the swaps and markets concerned. This division meant different rules and different names for markets, financial instruments and market participants' jobs depending on whether the legislation related to 'swaps', regulated by the CFTC, or 'security-based swaps', regulated by the SEC.

Thus, the CFTC was given jurisdiction for 22 categories of swap including those written on interest rates, currencies, commodities, government securities, weather, energy, metal, emissions and CDSs on broad-based securities indices. The SEC took responsibility for swaps on single securities or loans, narrow-based securities indices and single name CDSs. Mixed swaps, where contracts combined elements of the two categories of swap, would be the responsibility of both bodies.

Players in the market were to be registered. They were divided between 'swap dealers' and 'major swap participants', regulated by the CFTC, and 'security-based swap dealers' and 'major security-based swap participants', regulated by the SEC. For simplicity's sake and except where necessary, this book will henceforth refer simply to swaps, swap dealers and major swap participants irrespective of whether regulated by the CFTC or SEC.

By regulating major swap participants, the act reached out to cover companies that

- had substantial positions in the swaps markets;
- whose exposure could have a serious adverse effect on the US economy or banking and financial systems; or
- were highly leveraged, and not covered by bank capital requirements.

Like dealers, these organisations would have to subject their swaps trades to clearing.

One major exception to the clearing requirement applied to commercial end-users using swaps to hedge or reduce commercial risk. By definition, an end-user could not be a financial company unless it was a so-called captive finance affiliate: financial subsidiaries of manufacturing companies that used swaps for hedging but whose activities were at least 90% related to the commercial or manufacturing activities of the parent or other group companies.

As Dodd-Frank shuffled through Congress, a significant amount of debate – both on and beyond Capitol Hill – was devoted to a few headline-grabbing amendments. Attracting perhaps the most attention was the Volcker Rule, named for Paul Volcker, the former head of the Federal Reserve, which prohibited banks from proprietary trading activities and restricted their ability to invest in hedge funds and private equity.

A close second, and of great importance for the swaps market and clearing, was the Lincoln provision, named for Arkansas Senator Blanche Lincoln, Chairman of the Senate Agriculture Committee. Her goal was to force banks to divest themselves of their hitherto lucrative swap trading activities by prohibiting federal assistance in the form of emergency financial support to any swaps entity.

Senator Lincoln's 'push out' proposals were modified in the course of Congressional horse trading. But as a general principle, Dodd-Frank prohibited absolutely the provision of federal financial assistance to swap dealers and major swap participants. Although exceptions were made for banks engaged in legitimate hedging activities or trading in swaps that referenced assets in which a national bank could invest, the Lincoln provision was expected to force banks that wished to continue as active swap trading entities to create separately capitalised affiliates to carry on the business.

As attention focused on these provisions, the Lynch Amendment that would have limited dealer banks and major swap participants from owning more than 20% in the aggregate of any swaps clearing house was dropped from the legislation. Instead, the issue of ownership restrictions was left to the CFTC and SEC. It surfaced very early in the CFTC's drafting of detailed rules for implementing the act.

Although Dodd-Frank marked the way ahead for clearing, an enormous amount of detail remained to be filled in. It was left to the CFTC and SEC and other federal bodies to write hundreds of precise rules and definitions, generally within 360 days.

In some cases CFTC and SEC were to work together, such as when deciding exactly what constituted a swap, a swap dealer or a major market participant. Mixed swaps was another aspect where joint action was essential. In other areas, the two agencies would consult and coordinate and engage with other bodies, including the Federal Reserve Board, the New York Fed, the US Treasury and the Federal Deposit Insurance Corporation, all of which would be involved in putting flesh on Dodd-Frank's bones.

The legislation shied away from defining 'standardised' OTC derivatives for clearing. Deciding which swaps had to be cleared would be a joint effort of clearing houses and regulators.

Clearing houses would submit to the agencies the swaps that they planned to accept for clearing whereupon the CFTC and SEC would decide which swaps had to be cleared. In reaching their decisions, CFTC and SEC would take into account issues such as outstanding notional exposures, trading liquidity and pricing data; the framework of rules, operational expertise and credit support infrastructure to clear the contract; the effects on systemic risk and competition; and whether there was legal certainty concerning the treatment of customer and swap counterparty positions in the event of insolvency of a clearing house or one or more clearing members.

The act prescribed that clearing houses should provide open non-discriminatory access for swap contracts mandated for clearing and so appeared to allow offsetting of contracts having the same terms. However, among the many ambiguities in the act was a provision that in order to minimise systemic risk, under no circumstances should a DCO 'be compelled to accept the counterparty credit risk of another clearing organisation'.

Regulators – including prudential regulators in the case of banks – would have the job of setting minimum capital requirements and minimum initial and variation margin requirements for swap dealers and major swap participants trading uncleared swaps. The legislation indicated that these requirements would be tougher than for cleared swaps to reflect the greater risks involved. This issue was simultaneously a matter of negotiation among international bank regulators, working together on the so-called 'Basel III' proposals to update bank capital adequacy rules in the Basel Committee on Banking Supervision at the Bank for International Settlements in Basel.

Dodd-Frank required the CFTC and SEC to make rules for real-time public data reporting of swap trades and prices to enhance price discovery. It required the registration of swap data repositories and permitted clearing houses to register as repositories.

The two agencies were also to set new business conduct standards for swap dealers and major swap participants that would cover issues such as record keeping and deal with fraud, manipulation and other abuses.

In addition to CFTC and SEC-regulated clearing houses, the act made provision for a third category. The Financial Security Oversight Council (FSOC), a new super forum of regulators created by the act, was empowered to designate some derivatives clearing houses as 'systemically important'.

The Council, which held its first meeting on 1 October 2010, comprises leading US financial regulators, including the Federal Reserve, the CFTC and the SEC, and is chaired by the US

Treasury Secretary. It can single out clearing houses and other financial infrastructures as 'designated financial market utilities' which have to meet higher standards in terms of financial resources, risk management and prudential rules.

The FSOC's main purpose is to identify risks and prevent large interconnected banks and other financial institutions ever again threatening the US economy with Armageddon. One of its goals is to promote market discipline among systemically important organisations by eliminating any expectations among their shareholders, creditors or counterparties that the government will shield them from losses.

An exception was made, however, for designated financial market utilities. To mitigate systemic risk and promote financial stability, these utilities could *in extremis* seek discount and borrowing privileges at the Fed. Such support would be provided 'only in unusual or exigent circumstances', after a positive, majority vote of the Federal Reserve Board governors and consultation with the Treasury Secretary, and when the designated utility in question showed it was 'unable to secure adequate credit accommodations from other banking institutions'.

This section of the act appeared to mark the acceptance, for the sake of the US and world economies, of a category of utilities that could be 'too important to fail'. Another section of the act entrusted the Federal Deposit Insurance Corporation (FDIC) with a 'resolution authority' for the orderly liquidation of systemically important financial institutions to make sure none would be 'too big to fail'.

Although vast, Dodd-Frank did not cover all the issues requiring attention in the US financial system. Missing from its pages were any new rules for Fannie Mae and Freddie Mac. It would not be the last word on financial law making in the US.

Immediately after President Obama signed the act, the CFTC identified 30 'topic areas' of rule making required to implement the legislation. Giving an indication of the task involved, CFTC Chairman Gary Gensler explained how 'teams of staff within the agency have been assigned to each rule-writing area and will see the process through, from analysing the statute's requirements, to broad consultation, to recommending proposed rulemakings to publishing final rules'.[2] Six of the teams focused on rules related to clearing.

According to Gensler, initial estimates suggested that more than 200 entities would register as swap dealers. He estimated that Dodd-Frank could result in between 20 and 30 firms registering as swap execution facilities or 'designated contract markets', in addition to the 16 futures exchanges already regulated by the CFTC. Moreover, the number of US-registered DCOs or clearing houses was expected to rise from 14 to around 20.[3]

Observers in Washington were presented with the unusual sight of the CFTC and SEC – two agencies that for much of their existence cordially loathed each other – apparently working in harmony. Within 24 hours of the President signing the act, more than 20 of the CFTC's rule-writing team leads were at the SEC meeting their counterparts.

The detailed implementation of Dodd-Frank would be no rubber-stamping exercise, however. The proposed rule changes were subject to public consultation. Within agencies, there were differences of approach, as illustrated by the CFTC's first rule-making session on 1 October 2010.

At this, Gensler supported proposing rules of governance for DCOs that would enable the CFTC to impose limits on the voting power of clearing house members. These included an aggregate limit of 40% in certain cases and, where voting ownership was more diverse, a limit

[2] CFTC (21 July 2010), 'CFTC releases list of areas of rule-making for over-the-counter derivatives', press release.

[3] CFTC (16 September 2010), Chairman Gary Gensler, 'Remarks before the ISDA Regional Conference'.

of 5% per clearing member or named entity.[4] But Jill Summers, one of the Republican members of the Commission, dissented on the grounds that voting limits would restrict competition. To support her case, she drew attention to the rejection of such measures by the EU Commission on 15 September 2010. A third commissioner, Scott O'Malia, called for a more flexible approach.[5]

For lobbyists in Washington, the act's passage fired the starting gun for another year of frenetic activity to shape its final terms.

For lawmakers around the world, Dodd-Frank – despite all its uncertainties – became the benchmark to take into account as they drew up their own legislation for regulating OTC markets.

21.2 'EMIR' – THE DRAFT EUROPEAN MARKETS INFRASTRUCTURE REGULATION

Less than two months after President Obama signed Dodd-Frank into law, the European Commission agreed wide ranging and detailed proposals for legislation to regulate the OTC derivatives market and CCPs.

The proposals,[6] presented by Michel Barnier, the Internal Market Commissioner, on 15 September 2010, took the form of a draft Regulation, the type of EU law that, once passed, applies without any discretionary features in the 27 member states.

The unveiling – two years to the day after Lehman's default – marked the first step of a procedure in which the European Parliament and the EU member states would negotiate the Regulation's final shape in a process known as co-decision. Known by its working title of EMIR – the European Markets Infrastructure Regulation – the draft was launched following an exhaustive and in many ways exemplary consultation with the post-trade sector, member states and key parliamentarians.

The Commission had engaged in intensive preparatory discussions with US agencies in order to limit the risk of regulatory arbitrage. It looked into clearing practices and legislation further afield: in Japan and Brazil, for example. It also took into account the Dodd-Frank act and steps elsewhere to meet the G20 target of clearing all 'standardised' OTC derivatives through central counterparties by the end of 2012.

The draft Regulation was the first legislative proposal to be produced on Barnier's watch and reflected nine months' unstinting effort by Patrick Pearson, who took over the Commission's financial infrastructure brief at the end of 2009. Because it would apply in 27 sovereign member states, it was far more detailed than the equivalent parts of the Dodd-Frank act.

To fulfil the end-2012 pledge made by G20 leaders at their 2009 summit in Pittsburgh, the Commission's proposals

- required CCP clearing for OTC derivatives that met predefined eligibility criteria;
- set specific targets for their standardisation in legal and processing terms;

[4] For LCH.Clearnet the proposed limits were less of a threat than the Lynch amendment, because the clearing house already applied a voting cap of 5% to its owners.

[5] CFTC (1 October 2010b): the Statements of Gensler, Sommers and O'Malia on DCO governance are published on the CFTC website (www.CFTC.gov) under Press Room, Speeches & Testimony (accessed 20 December 2010).

[6] EU Commission (15 September 2010), 'Proposal for a Regulation on OTC Derivatives, Central Counterparties and Trade Repositories'.

- set conditions – some still to be clarified under the Basel III process – for bilateral clearing of OTC derivative trades; and
- required market participants to report 'all necessary information' on their OTC derivatives portfolios to a trade repository, so bringing transparency to a hitherto opaque business.

In several important respects, the proposed legislation addressed wider issues than the Pittsburgh pledge on clearing OTC trades. It brought CCPs and trade repositories under EU regulation for the first time, with the draft rules for authorising and supervising CCPs to apply to all clearing houses and not just those clearing OTC derivatives. The proposals outlined rules to ensure the sound operation of trade repositories and the reliability and security of the information they held.

However, the part of the G20 agreement that called for OTC derivatives contracts 'to be traded on exchanges or electronic trading platforms, as appropriate' was not covered by the draft. This would be tackled later when the Commission published proposals for revising the MiFID directive.

The draft Regulation laid down uniform requirements for financial counterparties in OTC derivatives trades, for non-financial (or corporate) counterparties that exceeded certain thresholds and for all categories of OTC derivatives contracts.

It detailed the procedures required to define standardised OTC contracts and so meet the G20's Pittsburgh obligation to clear all 'standardised' OTC derivatives by end-2012 while steering clear of subjecting the industry to a definitional straitjacket.

Standardised contracts were construed as those eligible for clearing by CCPs. They would be defined through a two-pronged approach aimed at ensuring as many OTC contracts as possible would be cleared, while taking care not to force CCPs to clear contracts that they were unable to risk-manage and which could therefore upset the stability of the financial system. Thus, there would be:

- A 'bottom-up' approach, in which a CCP would decide to clear certain contracts and would then be authorised to do so by its national regulator. The regulator (the CCP's 'competent authority' in Commission jargon) would then be obliged to inform the European Securities and Markets Authority (ESMA), a new EU body set up in January 2011.[7] ESMA would then have the powers to decide whether all these contracts should be cleared across the EU.
- A 'top-down' approach, according to which ESMA, together with another new body – the European Systemic Risk Board (ESRB) – would determine which contracts should potentially be subject to clearing. This provision was to identify and capture contracts in the market that were not yet being cleared by CCPs.

In deciding whether an OTC contract was eligible for clearing, ESMA – rather like the US regulators – would take into account the potential reduction of systemic risk, its liquidity, the availability of pricing information, the ability of the CCP to handle the volume of contracts and the level of client protection provided by the clearing house.

The Commission argued that both approaches were necessary because meeting the G20 clearing commitment could not be left to the industry. The procedure would also provide a

[7] ESMA is one of three European supervisory authorities, which with the ESRB form the European System of Financial Supervision (ESFS). Created in response to the crisis, the ESFS provides a much tougher regime for financial supervision in the EU and follows the recommendations of a report drawn up by Jacques de Larosière, former IMF managing director and governor of the Banque de France. ESMA has replaced CESR, the Committee of European Securities Regulators. Two other authorities have replaced committees of regulators for the banking and insurance sectors.

regulatory check in advance at European level of the suitability of planned clearing arrangements.

Counterparties subject to the obligation to clear OTC derivatives would not be able to duck the requirement by opting out of participation in a CCP. Those uninterested or unable to become CCP clearing members would have to access CCPs as clients of clearing members.

In order to preserve the global nature of the OTC derivatives market and maintain a competitive level playing field, CCPs clearing eligible derivative contracts would have to clear such contracts on a non-discriminatory basis regardless of where they were executed. There would be no exclusive vertical silos in OTC derivatives clearing in Europe: CCPs would be barred from only accepting transactions concluded on execution venues with which they had privileged relationships or which were part of the same group.

The draft legislation determined that in principle non-financial or corporate counterparties would not be subject to the clearing obligation unless their OTC derivatives positions reached thresholds that were systemically important. The Regulation assumed that such firms' derivatives activities were generally linked to commercial activity rather than speculation. This distinction marked a significant achievement by corporate lobbyists such as the European Association of Corporate Treasurers which campaigned vigorously for their clients' legitimate hedging activities to be exempted from this aspect of the G20 clearing obligation.

However, the Commission draft did not exempt non-financial firms completely from clearing their OTC derivatives contracts. Corporates that were particularly active in OTC derivative markets would have to clear their trades. This, the Commission argued, was necessary to reduce risk in the financial system, avoid regulatory arbitrage and keep the proposed EU law in line with the Dodd-Frank act. Another reason was to remove the possibility of financial firms circumventing their clearing obligations by establishing new non-financial entities through which to channel their OTC derivatives business.

The Commission proposed to define two distinct thresholds – after input from ESMA and other authorities – to bring non-financial counterparties with really systemically significant positions in OTC derivatives contracts under the clearing obligation:

- an 'information threshold', which would require non-financial corporate firms meeting the threshold to notify positions to a competent authority, that would be designated by their member state; and
- a 'clearing threshold' after which they would be required to clear all their derivatives contracts.

When defining these thresholds, the relevant contracts would have to net out to a systemically relevant sum and, importantly, should not be taken into account if 'entered into to cover the risks arising from an objectively measurable commercial activity'.

This would mean in practice that the clearing obligation would only apply to those OTC contracts of non-financial firms that engaged in speculation. It was thought that some of Europe's large energy suppliers might fall into this category.

As not all OTC derivatives would be eligible for clearing, there remained a need to improve the arrangements and safety of those contracts that continued to be managed bilaterally.

In these cases, the Regulation would require electronic confirmation of the contract terms where possible, and the existence of risk-management procedures with daily marking to market of the contracts, and 'timely, accurate and appropriately segregated exchange of collateral' and an 'appropriate proportionate' holding of capital. The Commission would adopt technical standards specifying collateral and capital levels nearer the time of the Regulation entering into force.

To ensure greater transparency of the OTC market for regulators, policy makers and the marketplace, financial counterparties would have to report the details of any derivative contracts they had entered into, plus any subsequent modifications such as novation or termination, to a registered trade repository. It would be the Commission's job to determine the details, type, format and frequency of the reports for the different classes of derivatives in line with technical standards to be developed by ESMA.

An important part of the draft laid down detailed rules for authorising and supervising CCPs. Responsibility would rest with the national regulators (the so-called competent authorities). But because of the systemic importance of clearing houses and the cross-border nature of their activities, it was judged that ESMA should also play a central role in the process. This would be achieved by:

- drafting the legislation in the form of a Regulation to make clear ESMA's central role and responsibility for its common application;
- requiring ESMA to develop a large number of draft technical standards to ensure the Regulation's correct application;
- making ESMA a party with the national regulators to the authorisation, withdrawal of authorisation and changes to the authorisation of a CCP.

During 2009, the Commission suggested giving ESMA full supervisory authority over CCPs in the EU. It backed down after the UK and others insisted responsibility should reside with the CCP's home state whose taxpayers might have to bail out an insolvent clearing house.

Because CCPs would be considered systemically important institutions, their national regulators – together with ESMA and other regulators involved with the CCPs' clearing members and the markets that CCPs served – would have to form 'colleges' to define contingency plans for emergencies. The Commission, which at the time was in the throes of preparing a separate initiative on crisis management and resolution, was charged with defining the specific policy and measures to deal with a crisis in 'a systemically relevant institution' such as a CCP.

ESMA would have direct responsibility for recognising clearing houses from third countries, provided the Commission had recognised that country's legal and supervisory framework as being equivalent to that of the EU, and so long as ESMA had established arrangements for cooperating with the third country's regulators and was satisfied with the risk-management standards of the CCP.

The draft laid down that CCPs must have access to adequate liquidity, either from a central bank or 'creditworthy and reliable commercial bank liquidity'. In earlier versions, the Commission had sought to nudge CCPs in the direction of becoming banks with access to central bank liquidity, but this was toned down after vigorous intervention by the UK, backed by the US, which feared it would be interpreted as a demand for CCPs to be based in the euro-zone.

The final version then upset the ECB which felt that the proposals underplayed the prerogatives of central banks in general and itself in particular, especially in a crisis. Gertrude Tumpel-Gugerell, the ECB executive board member responsible for financial infrastructure, underlined that any provision of central bank liquidity was entirely at the ECB's discretion, should in no way influence monetary policy and, in the case of the ECB and the eurozone, would only be offered to CCPs that were banks.[8]

[8] In remarks to the *Eurofi Financial Forum* 2010, Brussels, 28 September 2010.

The draft regulation paid close attention to the robustness and regulation of CCPs. It insisted on strong governance arrangements for CCPs to cope with any potential conflicts of interest between owners, management, clearing members and indirect participants, especially in the clearing of OTC derivatives. The draft placed particular emphasis on the role of independent board members and defined clearly the roles and responsibilities of risk committees. It stipulated that a CCP's risk management should report directly to its board and not be influenced by other business lines. It also required that governance arrangements be publicly disclosed and that CCPs should have adequate internal systems and operational and administrative procedures that were subject to independent audits.

Because CCPs bore the risk of counterparty failure and counterparties themselves carried the risk that clearing houses might fail, the draft law paid special attention to the need for CCPs to mitigate their counterparty credit risk. To do this, it stipulated that CCPs should have stringent but non-discriminatory participation requirements for members, adequate financial resources and other guarantees.

Because of their new G20 mandated responsibilities, the Commission judged that in almost all cases the failure of a CCP would become a potential threat to the financial system. Therefore it stressed the need for strict prudential regulation of CCPs at the EU level, arguing that existing national laws regulating CCPs, which differed between member states, produced an unlevel playing field, made cross-border provision of CCP services potentially less safe and more costly, and were a barrier to the integration of the European financial market. Basel III and work in progress by regulators in the CPSS-IOSCO group on revised international risk-management standards for CCPs would also serve to plug this gap.

Each CCP would be required to have a mutualised default fund made up of contributions from members. The draft provisions drilled down in considerable detail into how CCPs should to deal with risk, specifying, for example, that margins should be sufficient to cover losses resulting 'from at least 99% of the exposures movements over an appropriate time horizon' and specifying that a CCP's default fund and other backup resources should enable it to withstand the default of the two clearing members to which it had the largest exposures.

Building on CPSS-IOSCO and ESCB-CESR risk-management recommendations, the draft gave the Commission powers – to be defined later – 'to adopt regulatory technical standards specifying the appropriate percentage and time horizon' for margins on different classes of financial instrument. Similarly, it would have powers to set regulatory technical standards specifying the types of collateral acceptable from clearing members and the 'haircuts' applying to these assets, and the nature of the 'highly liquid financial instruments' CCPs would be allowed to invest in.

The draft Regulation introduced important rules on segregation and portability of positions and corresponding collateral, reflecting the need for a level playing field in this area as well as some lessons from the Lehman bankruptcy. The Commission proposals were strongly pro-client, giving CCPs considerable powers to transfer assets and positions of clients without the consent of clearing members, for example. Having apparently absorbed lessons from PwC's handling of the LBIE default, the draft proposed that the segregation and portability requirements 'shall prevail over any conflicting laws, regulations and administrative provisions of the member states that prevent the parties from fulfilling them'.

As before, the Commission refrained from interfering with market structures, arguing that the measures it proposed would be more effective for dealing with potential conflicts of interest than any form of regulation that limited the ownership of CCPs.

The proposals, therefore, did not tackle the issue of vertical silos where CCPs were owned by exchanges. Nor did they seek to limit ownership of CCPs by dealer banks. However, regulators would have to be informed in advance of changes in a CCP's ownership, giving the 'competent authorities' an opportunity to oppose acquisitions or disposals that reached or exceeded 10%, 20%, 30% or 50% of the voting rights or capital of the clearing house.

The proposals laid down strict rules for outsourcing CCP functions, saying this should only be allowed if it did not impact on the proper operation of the clearing house and its ability to manage risks. The Commission also stressed that a CCP must have a minimum amount of capital (in practice €5 million) in order to be authorised, because a CCP's own capital was the last line of defence in the event of the default of one or more clearing members. When preparing the Commission's proposal, Pearson had been disturbed to find that the capital of CCPs varied widely from €98,000 at one extreme to more than €100 million at the other.

The draft also proposed regulatory approval of interoperability arrangements, reflecting the imperfections in this area of the industry's Code of Conduct. While declaring interoperability to be an essential tool for achieving effective integration of the post-trade market in Europe, the Commission acknowledged that it could expose CCPs to additional risks.

Because of the complexity of derivatives markets and the early stage of development of CCP clearing for OTC derivatives, the Commission decided against mandating interoperability for asset classes other than cash securities. However, the draft targeted 30 September 2014 as the deadline for ESMA to report on whether to extend interoperability. Meanwhile, derivatives clearing houses would be able to enter into interoperable arrangements if they wanted, provided these were safe and complied with the conditions of the Regulation.

Turning to trade repositories, the draft gave ESMA the powers to register, withdraw registration and exercise surveillance over trade repositories. It chose ESMA for this key role rather than the member states to ensure a level playing field.

To be registered by ESMA, trade repositories 'must be established' in the EU. At the time of Barnier's announcement, TriOptima in Stockholm had been operating a global Interest Rate Trade Reporting Repository for nearly five months while DTCC had recently launched its Equity Derivatives Reporting Repository in London, where the US group's FSA-approved DTCC Derivatives Repository subsidiary also maintained global CDS data identical to that held in the DTCC's New York-based Trade Information Warehouse (TIW).

Under the Commission proposals, a third country repository such as TIW could also be recognised by ESMA provided it was subject to equivalent rules and appropriate surveillance. That said, there would have to be unfettered access to the data maintained in the third country repository with such access underpinned by international agreements. Without any such agreement, ESMA would be unable to recognise the third country repository in question.

The Commission's proposals were far more detailed than the Dodd-Frank provisions. But hurdles remained before Europe's market infrastructure providers could have a complete view of future regulation.

The draft regulation was only a proposal and so subject to revision by EU member states and the European Parliament in the course of the co-decision process. This would give business lobbies a chance to influence the final outcome.

Much was being left to ESMA, a new and untested body that would have to pick its way between conflicting pressures from member states, with the UK, in particular, inclined to limit its powers. There were also differences among the member states about the rules governing the location of CCPs.

Clearing and CCPs would be affected by policy actions still to be formulated. It would be early 2011, for example, before Barnier and his officials produced proposals for having eligible derivatives contracts traded on organised venues under a revised MiFID directive, giving time for Europe's exchanges and MTFs to lobby for the EU to follow the lead provided by Dodd Frank.

Having laid out the stall for CCP clearing of OTC derivatives, the Commission could not propose how the 'carrot' and 'stick' of differentiated capital charges for CCP-cleared and non-CCP cleared contracts would work until early 2011, when it was due to put forward its draft to revise the EU's Capital Requirements Directive in line with new 'Basel III' bank capital rules.

21.3 BASEL III AND CCPs

The Dodd-Frank act and the Commission draft proposals marked important steps towards the G20 goal of a largely consistent post-crisis global regulatory architecture. Another element, specified in the Pittsburgh G20 commitment to shift OTC derivatives contracts to CCPs, was the requirement that 'non-centrally cleared contracts should be subject to higher capital requirements'. Defining these fell to the Basel Committee on Banking Supervision which was charged with strengthening existing bank capital standards, known as 'Basel II', and replacing them with 'Basel III'.

Basel II had proved inadequate during the crisis. It tackled the issue of bank exposures to uncleared OTC derivatives, prescribing a 20% risk weighting to account for counterparty credit risk in the event of a default. But this had failed to ensure banks were adequately capitalised for certain OTC derivatives risks that surfaced before and after the Lehman bankruptcy. The deficiencies in the Basel II approach to uncleared OTC derivatives trades were documented after the crisis by the European Commission which found that[9]

- The Basel II framework dealt with counterparty credit risk (CCR) as a default and credit migration risk, but did not fully account for market value losses short of default. It did not directly require capital for mark-to-market losses caused by credit valuation adjustments (CVA) even though roughly two-thirds of counterparty credit losses were caused by CVA losses and only one-third by actual defaults.
- Basel II did not adequately capture the problem of 'wrong-way risk', where the probability of default of counterparties was adversely correlated with general market risk factors. Wrong-way risk arose because defaults and deteriorations in the creditworthiness of trading counterparties in the crisis occurred exactly when market volatilities and counterparty exposures were higher than usual.
- Large financial institutions were more interconnected than recognised by Basel II. When financial markets entered the downturn, banks' counterparty exposures to other financial firms also increased. Banks turned out to be relatively more sensitive to systemic risk than non-financial firms and their credit quality deteriorated simultaneously with the downturn.
- The close-out period for replacing OTC trades with counterparties with large netting sets or netting sets consisting of complex illiquid trades lasted longer than allowed for the

[9] European Commission Services (January 2010), 'Staff Working Document on possible further changes to the Capital Requirements Directive'.

calculation of capital adequacy under Basel II, so that the regulatory capital charge significantly underestimated losses incurred.

- Securitisation bonds when used as collateral were often ascribed the same risk exposure as similarly rated corporate debt instruments. After the crisis, securitisations continued to exhibit much higher price volatility than similarly rated corporate debt.
- Basel II lacked sufficient incentives for posting adequate initial margins at all points of the cycle. In consequence, initial margining was typically very low when the crisis started and ballooned as the turmoil grew. Higher initial margin protected some banks but may also have caused counterparties to fail or reduce positions, thereby exacerbating the crisis.

The crisis also revealed significant shortcomings in banks' risk management of counterparty credit exposures, including back-testing and stress testing, and these contributed to an underestimation of potential losses. The EU Commission identified concerns about the operation of collateral management processes, including systems and data integrity, levels of staffing, risk reporting and the legal terms of collateral agreements, which resulted in more large and lengthy collateral disputes across the industry. Some banks suffered losses or liquidity strains due to the reuse (for example, through re-hypothecation or reinvestment) of collateral assets received from counterparties and which had to be returned at short notice.

By providing an insufficiently rigorous capital adequacy regime, Basel II did not create sufficient incentives to move bilateral OTC derivative contracts to multilateral clearing through CCPs. Consequently, CCPs were not widely used to clear trades.

Agreement on the Basel III reforms to raise global minimum capital standards for banks was announced by leading central bank governors on 12 September 2010. Presenting the package, Jean-Claude Trichet, the President of the European Central Bank and chairman of the 'Group of Governors and Heads of Supervision' – the Basel Committee's oversight body – praised the agreements as a 'fundamental strengthening of global capital standards'. Basel III would be phased in over many years. Trichet forecast that the reforms would make a 'substantial' contribution to long-term financial stability and growth.[10]

Only the 'main design elements' of the Basel III capital requirements were published. Whereas both the Dodd-Frank act and the Commission's EMIR proposals were comprehensive and drafted in language that was fairly accessible to a wider public, many of the components of the Basel III capital requirements were obscure. Most of the proposals relating to counterparty credit risk, CCPs and OTC derivatives were couched in the professional jargon of bank supervisors and OTC derivatives specialists.[11]

---

[10] Bank for International Settlements (12 September 2010), 'Group of Governors and Heads of Supervision announces higher global minimum capital standards', Basel Committee on Banking Supervision, press release plus Annex.

[11] The Bank for International Settlements Basel Committee published annexes and press releases on 26 July 2010 and 12 September 2010 to summarise the 'main design elements' of the Basel III agreement at each of those dates. Each annex contained a section headlined 'Counterparty Credit Risk' giving four bullet points with measures to incentivise banks with uncleared OTC derivatives exposures to use CCPs. The fourth bullet point in each case referred to the proposal for a modest risk weight for banks' mark-to-market and collateral exposures to a CCP, mentioned in the main text. The other three bullet points, summarising measures to place extra capital requirements on banks with uncleared OTC derivative exposures, read as follows:

'– Modify the bond equivalent approach to address hedging, risk capture, effective maturity and double counting;

– To address the excessive calibration of the CVA (credit valuation adjustment), eliminate the 5× multiplier that was proposed in December 2009;

– Keep the asset value correlation adjustment at 25% to reflect the inherent higher risk of exposures to other financial entities and to help address the interconnectedness issue, but raise the threshold from $25 billion to $100 billion.'

Despite requests, no further explanation was forthcoming from the BIS as this book was being written.

Basel III broke new ground by subjecting banks' mark-to-market and collateral exposures to a CCP to a modest risk weight (it suggested in the 1–3% range rather than zero) so that banks would realise that their CCP exposures were not risk free.

The committee's other decisions on uncleared OTC derivatives trades addressed risks resulting from the volatility of the credit valuation adjustment and banks' interconnectedness. Basel III also required that estimates of counterparty credit risk must include data from times of market stress, so making these more conservative than hitherto.

In consequence, the Basel III rules set out to increase the capital that banks with uncleared and unclearable OTC derivatives exposures would have to set aside. Fortunately, for those confused by its decisions, the committee was expected to issue somewhat clearer guidance at a later date – possibly a range of capital risk weights for uncleared OTC derivative exposures. This would follow agreement on a coordinated approach with the CPSS-IOSCO group of central bank officials and securities regulators who were engaged in a separate exercise to upgrade the CPSS-IOSCO recommendation for risk-managing CCPs to take account of the lessons of the crisis and the plans to mandate clearing for standardised and eligible OTC derivatives contracts.[12]

Behind the scenes, meanwhile, bank supervisors and the CPSS-IOSCO group were looking more closely at the risks that might be lurking behind CCPs, especially at the level of clearing members.

The 'waterfall', which prioritised the financial resources a CCP should access in the event of a default, came in for much closer inspection. Banks' default fund contributions were a particular area of discussion. Automatically given a zero risk weighting under Basel II, it dawned on regulators after the crisis that such contributions were not completely risk free because a CCP's default fund could be used in the event of the collapse of another clearing member.

Another area for discussion was CCP capital and its relationship to initial margin and risk. The more capital a CCP might have, the less initial margin or default fund contributions it might require from clearing members. Issues such as these had implications for competition as well as risk, and raised questions about how far internationally-agreed rules could be applied in different jurisdictions with different traditions.

Basel III continued to raise as many questions as answers in the weeks following the 12 September announcement. One certainty was that it would keep regulators, supervisors and the legal and compliance departments of banks and CCPs fully employed for years to come.

21.4 CONTEMPLATING CCP FAILURE

The Dodd-Frank act, the EU's draft EMIR Regulation and Basel III explicitly recognised the risks embedded in CCPs and borne by clearing members. From thinking about the conditions that necessitated tougher rules, it was but a short step to thinking about the unthinkable: the failure of a CCP.

By 2010, clearing houses had developed into institutions placed at the centre of such huge and systemically-important markets as those for government bonds and CDSs, and this raised important questions. If the failure of an international investment bank such as Lehman Brothers could bring the world to the brink of financial collapse, how much greater would be the impact of several banks going down? And in a world where countries would be hard pressed to bail

[12] See Section 18.5.

out banking systems as they did in 2007–9, how long could a CCP cope with the multiple failure of several international banks among its clearing members?

These questions were made all the more acute by the leap into the unknown that CCPs were asked to make after the Lehman and AIG debacles. As one senior executive with responsibilities for the clearing activities of a big investment bank commented:

> I am totally supportive of the move to put standardised OTC derivatives onto a CCP. But people who sit and say this is as safe as houses are wrong. We are piling the most monumental amount of risk onto a relatively small number of institutions which have got – by and large – very good rules. But we have relatively little experience of default in the credit derivatives market whose risk is extremely complicated. We have very few people who can handle liquidation: in other words bid for a portfolio.[13]

The elevation of CCPs to a front-line role in absorbing systemic risk raised questions of what would happen, and what role the authorities should play, if a CCP itself failed.

Although CCPs performed well during and after the Lehman default, this book has shown how luck also played a part in their successful handling of Lehman's bankruptcy. Moreover, CCPs had failed in the past. The crises in the Paris sugar market in 1974 and the Malaysian palm oil futures market in 1983 affected small institutions in markets of no systemic importance. The Hong Kong crisis of 1987 was different, in that it involved the clearing of financial futures but the emergency rescue worked and at comparatively little cost.

Circumstances were very different after 2008. There would be no such easy restoration of calm if a CCP clearing government debt instruments or CDSs failed in a leading financial centre.

On the rare occasions that official documents addressed the possibility of CCP failure, they used language designed to de-dramatise the fall-out. The implications of CCP failure were still scary, however, as the CPSS-IOSCO group made clear, when explaining why regulators and central banks had a strong interest in CCP risk management:

> A risk management failure by a CCP has the potential to disrupt the markets its serves and also other components of the settlement systems for instruments traded in those markets. The disruptions may spill over to payment systems and other settlement systems.[14]

With experience of the crisis fresh in their minds, staff members of the New York Federal Reserve were a little more outspoken when they addressed the issue in 2010:

> The failure of a CCP could suddenly expose many major market participants to losses. Any such failure, moreover, is likely to have been triggered by the failure of one or more large clearing members, and therefore to occur during the period of extreme market fragility.[15]

Patrick Pearson, head of the financial market infrastructure unit at the EU Commission and the official responsible for EMIR, put it more bluntly. He warned that a clearing house failure could unleash 'financial Armageddon'.[16]

The question of having some sort of safety net for CCPs had been a subject of muttered conversation among clearing house managers for some time. Many believed the problem

[13] Background conversation with the author, March 2010.

[14] Bank for International Settlements (November 2004), 'Recommendations for central counterparties'.

[15] Duffie, Darrell, Li, Ada, Lubke, Theo (January 2010), 'Policy perspectives on OTC derivatives market infrastructure'.

[16] The expression used by Pearson at a conference in London on 11 May 2010: *Financial Times* (12 May 2010), 'Brussels warns on 'widely' varying clearing house rules'.

would be solved if central banks stepped in as lenders of last resort should a CCP run into difficulties.

The issue became a matter of open discussion after Xavier Rolet, the chief executive of the LSE, suggested in December 2009 that central banks 'should have at least a funding relationship with a clearing house' in case clearing members were unable to cover margin calls in the case of a default.[17]

Rolet's proposal breached the long-established principle of 'creative ambiguity', which allowed central bankers discretion over whether to lend to individual institutions. Rules and practices varied from country to country, adding to the complexity of the issue.

In countries where CCPs were obliged to be banks – as in France and Germany – they already had access to central bank accounts and intraday liquidity. In Sweden and Switzerland, the national central banks offered intraday liquidity to regulated nonbank financial institutions, including CCPs. In the UK and the US, the picture was deliberately unclear, reflecting the authorities' studied caginess in order not to encourage moral hazard.

But after 2008, regulators and legislators had to accept that the battle against moral hazard had been lost – at least temporarily – with the rescue of AIG and the subsequent shoring up of the global financial system.

The UK FSA and Treasury raised the spectre of CCP failure in a joint paper of December 2009, and in so doing acknowledged the possibility of taxpayers having to bail out clearing houses. After pointing to the danger 'that in the most extreme circumstances, default of several of a CCP's members could result in the failure of the CCP itself,' they observed:

> As CCPs will be increasing in systemic importance, failure brings with it the possibility that public authorities would need to step in to provide support, for example acting as lenders of last resort in order to support CCPs during a temporary liquidity problem. An insolvent CCP could impose a direct cost to taxpayers of the home state.[18]

The International Monetary Fund proffered some thoughts about support for CCPs in its Global Financial Stability Report of April 2010:

> At a minimum, CCPs should have access to liquidity backup commitments from banks and other financial institutions that are preferably not CMs [clearing members], in order to cover temporary shortfalls in payments from otherwise solvent CMs, and as an additional source of support to fulfil contract performance. Such liquidity lines should be denominated in the same currency as the contracts cleared.

The report recognised central bank help might be justified in cases where there was extra risk:

> Hence, those [CCPs] deemed to be systemically important should have access to emergency central bank liquidity. However, any such emergency lending should be collateralised by the same high-quality liquid securities as those typically posted against monetary policy operations. Also it should not be done in any way that might compromise the central bank's monetary policy or foreign exchange policy operations.[19]

[17] *Financial Times* (FT.Com) (29 December 2009), 'Rolet urges safeguards on clearing houses'.

[18] Financial Services Authority and HM Treasury (December 2009), 'Reforming OTC derivatives markets, a UK perspective'. The UK authorities made the point while putting forward arguments against the idea of giving EU institutions – in this case the future ESMA – supervisory authority over CCPs operating in Britain.

[19] IMF (April 2010), 'Global financial stability report, Chapter 3: Making over-the-counter derivatives safer: the role of central counterparties'.

The problem was that any greater emergency support, especially from taxpayers, had become politically difficult to contemplate, especially in the US.

Both the CFTC's Gensler and Mary Schapiro, SEC chair,[20] cast doubt on the merits of providing emergency Fed liquidity for clearing houses.[21] Speaking to a conference of bank operations staff in May 2010, DTCC Chairman and CEO Don Donahue warned the Fed would never allow DTCC access to liquidity from its discount window in the extreme event of a multiple failure of clearing members despite the Bear Stearns and AIG precedents:

> Quite aside from the Fed's long-standing policy position on this very question – which has always been quite clear – we all know of the vehement public opposition to anything that smacks of another bailout of private sector financial institutions. We must find a solution on our own, without looking to the Federal government.[22]

Like many clearing professionals, Roger Liddell, the CEO of LCH.Clearnet, disliked the idea of emergency central bank support because it would represent professional failure. When asked by the chairman of the UK House of Lords EU Committee whether 'a CCP should have access to central bank liquidity *in extremis*,' Liddell replied:

> I think there are two possible reasons why a CCP may wish to have central bank money. One is to improve potentially the certainty of its day-to-day operations, certainly as it pertains to immediate intraday finality of payments which is best achieved by a direct account at central banks. The other reason why it may need access to central bank money could be as a means of providing some backstop liquidity in the event of a real crisis. The two are really quite different. So the answer to the first would be definitely yes, because it makes the system more robust; the answer to the second is there are some situations where temporary liquidity could be beneficial. Again, each of the clearing houses really is designing their business model to prevent the need for that, but in the event that it was necessary then it would be a sensible measure to take. I am very nervous, however, about the sort of moral hazard associated with explicit guarantees to organisations like ours. I really believe that in principle we should not feel we have any guarantee from anybody at all, and should be operating on that basis.
>
> We should be designing business on the assumption we have no access to anything at all other than what we have under our control, and if that does not work we have failed.[23]

Attitudes shifted somewhat during 2010 as the Senate resumed its deliberations on what became the Dodd-Frank act.

In testimony to a Senate subcommittee in May, both Gensler and Schapiro spoke in support of emergency access for clearing houses to the Fed's discount window. Between May and September, they were echoed by US exchange and clearing house leaders. The CME's Terry Duffy, Wayne Luthringshausen of the OCC and Jeffrey Sprecher of ICE called on separate occasions for access to Federal Reserve funding, albeit with different emphasis on the degree of emergency needed to trigger such support.

But, as Jean-Claude Trichet reminded bankers, infrastructure executives and regulators in September 2010, they would be ill-advised to count on taxpayer support should there be a repeat of the crisis. Taxpayers had provided 'gigantic support' and saved the day at the cost of

[20] Like Gensler, Schapiro was appointed by the Obama administration and was sworn in as the SEC's first woman chairman on 27 January 2009.

[21] Reuters (28 April 2010), 'CFTC, SEC frown on bigger safety net for clearers'.

[22] At the Sifma annual operations conference, 5 May 2010, Palm Desert, CA.

[23] Evidence given to the House of Lords European Union Committee, 9 February 2010 in: House of Lords (2010), 'The future regulation of derivatives markets: Is the EU on the right track?'.

assuming risk amounting to a staggering 27% of GDP on both sides of the Atlantic. 'If we had again, by misfortune, to cope with the same acute challenge, I am convinced that this time we would not obtain from our political democracies the same gigantic effort. Then a depression would be unavoidable.'[24]

The Dodd-Frank act – with its provision for emergency financing of 'designated financial market utilities' alongside an ambitious agenda for a 'resolution regime' to allow the US authorities to manage the winding down of systemically important financial companies without recourse to taxpayer support – appeared to provide a way of overcoming this conundrum. However, it remained open to question whether any unforeseen problems would surface during implementation in the US and how far the Dodd-Frank construction was transferrable to other members of the G20 and elsewhere.

There were mixed signals on the international front. On the one hand, officials from the G20 and the Financial Stability Board[25] worked during 2010 on policy recommendations for the 11–12 November G20 summit in Seoul about how best to wind down systemically-important financial institutions (SIFIs) without recourse to taxpayers.

On the other hand, prospects for harmony in the G20 darkened after the summer as macroeconomic policy tensions mounted between the US and China. With the US accusing China of keeping its currency artificially low and China accusing the US of destabilising the world's emerging economies through its ultra-loose monetary policy, prospects dimmed for early agreement on important but politically second-line issues such as whether or not to include CCPs in the ranks of SIFIs, with the attendant responsibilities that would entail.

21.5 CCPs SPREAD AROUND THE WORLD

The strains among the leading G20 nations in 2010 did nothing to slow a rapid growth of central counterparty clearing beyond the main industrialised countries.

Strong economic growth, rapid development of financial markets and greater awareness of risk management stimulated a burgeoning demand for clearing services in those fast growing areas of the world which had avoided the worst of the financial crisis.

The G20's general encouragement of clearing and the group's Pittsburgh summit commitment to have CCPs clear standardised OTC derivatives contracts by the end of 2012 encouraged countries as varied as South Africa and Russia to propose or at least consider laws to regulate CCPs. The upshot was rapid development of CCPs outside the main industrialised countries and tempestuous growth in Asia.

For national governments and international organisations alike, the setting up of a CCP came to symbolise the modernisation of a country's financial sector. One reason Chile set up a securities clearing house in 2010 was to qualify for membership of the Organisation for Economic Co-operation and Development, the Paris-based club of advanced countries.[26]

For Russia's National Clearing Centre (NCC), membership of EACH, the European Association of CCP Clearing Houses, was both a badge of international recognition and a way of

[24] ECB (29 September 2010), 'Keeping the momentum for financial reform'. Keynote address by Jean-Claude Trichet, the ECB President, at the *Eurofi Financial Forum* 2010, Brussels.

[25] The Financial Stability Board was created after the April 2009 G20 summit to coordinate and promote effective regulatory and supervisory financial policies among national financial policy makers and international standard setters. The Financial Stability Forum (see Section 18.2) was upgraded and expanded to include officials from: the G20 members; Hong Kong, the Netherlands, Singapore, Spain and Switzerland; the leading international financial institutions; and the major international committees of regulators.

[26] *Financial Times* (31 May 2010), 'Clearing reforms for Chile's Exchange'.

acquiring know-how on risk management and clearing methods from established EU CCPs. Wholly owned by MICEX, the Moscow Interbank Currency Exchange, NCC began clearing currency trades in 2007 and had ambitions to clear securities, forward trades, commodities and government securities markets. It joined EACH in November 2009.

The flow of know-how was not always one way, however. When preparing its draft regulation for OTC derivatives and CCPs, the European Commission scrutinised Brazil's clearing practices in recognition of the robust financial infrastructure it established following a serious banking crisis in 1999.

The geographical diversity and fast growing membership of the increasingly inappositely named CCP12 group of clearing houses was an indicator of the rapid spread of clearing around the globe.

By mid-2010, the CCP12 website named 28 member organisations operating 35 CCPs in North and South America, Europe and the Asia-Pacific region as well as in Israel and South Africa. Of its 28 members, 13 were based in non-G7 countries. It almost appeared that in the 21st century, setting up a clearing house was as much a rite of passage for a country climbing the international economic league-table as setting up a national airline was in the 1950s or 1960s.

The big US and European exchange groups and clearing houses had a long tradition of forging business links outside their home regions. In the post-Lehman world, the likes of NYSE-Euronext, the CME Group, Eurex, Nasdaq OMX and LCH.Clearnet reached out to forge strategic partnerships with infrastructure providers in the BRIC countries (Brazil, Russia, India and China) and in other, smaller but dynamic economies in Latin America, the Middle East and Asia.

21.6 AN ASIAN CENTURY FOR CLEARING HOUSES?

It was in Asia that clearing really took off after 2008. A sign of its rapid adoption in the region came in April 2009 when SGX Singapore Exchange launched the world's first cleared OTC iron ore swaps contract. This was some weeks before LCH.Clearnet started clearing similar contracts from 1 June 2009.

That the first derivatives market to respond to the revolution in iron ore pricing was located in Asia highlighted not only the massive demand for raw materials of China's steel industry but also the region's post-crisis rise up the global economic rankings. It was just one of many examples of a shift of economic power from west to east in the exchange and financial infrastructure areas:

- The value of share trading on the 16 Asia-Pacific member bourses of the World Federation of Exchanges overtook that of the 26 WFE members in Europe, Africa and the Middle East in 2009. Over 10 years from 2000 to 2009, the value of shares traded on the Asia-Pacific bourses increased to about US$18.6 trillion from US$5 trillion against a decline from US$17.4 trillion to US$13.1 trillion in the value of trading on EMEA markets.[27]
- Financial infrastructure providers, notably in Europe, stepped up their efforts to do business with fast growing Asian markets. Among them, Eurex opened offices in Hong Kong, Singapore and Tokyo in 2009.

[27] World Federation of Exchanges (2010), *WFE 2009 Market Highlights*; www.world-exchanges.org (accessed 20 December 2010).

- At the same time, Western CCPs and stock exchanges turned to Asia for new technology. In 2008 LCH.Clearnet, for example, commissioned TCS Financial Solutions, a unit of India's Tata Consultancy Services, to help develop Synαpse, which it trumpeted as the world's first multi-asset derivatives platform capable of handling all exchange-traded and most OTC contracts. In October 2009, the London Stock Exchange acquired MilleniumIT of Sri Lanka.

Developments in Asia after the Lehman bankruptcy appeared to replicate past trends in Europe, although at a much faster speed. New trading platforms and exchanges appeared, bringing competition, fragmentation and, often, outside clearing providers in their wake.

For example, the Hong Kong Mercantile Exchange (HKMEx), founded in 2008 to be a 'bridge' between China and international commodities markets, turned in 2009 to LCH.Clearnet to be its CCP. A few months later, Chi-East, a joint venture of Chi-X Global and SGX, also appointed LCH.Clearnet to clear the Australian, Hong Kong and Japanese listed securities to be traded on its non-displayed trading platform – a so-called dark pool.

Highlighting the giddy pace of change in the Asia-Pacific region, SGX and ASX of Australia disclosed plans for an ambitious cross-border merger of the two exchange groups towards the end of October 2010. Although the move to create the region's second largest exchange group by market capitalisation faced formidable regulatory hurdles in Australia, it raised expectations of change and consolidation of financial infrastructures in Asia and elsewhere.

Following the G20 summits of 2009, it became evident that Asian countries would also participate in clearing OTC derivatives contracts. Of six Asia-Pacific countries among the G20 members,[28] China, India, Japan and South Korea set up task forces to study the pros and cons of clearing houses for OTC products. Outside the G20, Singapore and Taiwan took similar action.

The fastest mover was SGX, operator of the SGX AsiaClear OTC derivatives CCP for oil, freight and iron ore contracts in Singapore, which announced plans to begin clearing interest rate swaps denominated in US and Singapore dollars in October 2010.[29]

The Reserve Bank of India encouraged Clearing Corporation of India (CCIL) to extend its activities to interest rate and forward foreign exchange derivatives traded OTC 'initially for reporting and gradually for novated settlement'.[30] In turn, CCIL finalised a business model that included risk-management processes for settling rupee-denominated interest rate swaps and forward rate agreements.[31]

Japan's JSCC made 'further expansion of clearing services' the priority of its business plan to March 2012[32] and, with the Tokyo Stock Exchange, set up a working group to develop clearing for interest rate and credit default swaps.

Building on a March 2009 study of OTC post-trade processing in Japan conducted by JSCC, TSE and the Japan Securities Depository Center with leading trading firms, Japan's Financial Services Agency suggested mandatory CCP clearing for plain vanilla interest rate swaps and

[28] Australia, China, India, Indonesia, Japan and South Korea.

[29] SGX (20 September 2010), 'Singapore Exchange – First in Asia to clear OTC traded financial derivatives', announcement on www.sgx.com (accessed 20 December 2010). When announced, the service was still subject to regulatory approval.

[30] Reserve Bank of India (March 2010), 'Financial stability report'.

[31] According to www.ccilindia.com, 'Future Plans' section (accessed 20 December 2010).

[32] JSCC (24 March 2010), 'Three year business plan' available at http://www.jscc.co.jp/en/news/2010/3/Three-year%20Business%20Plan(FY2010~FY2012).pdf (accessed 20 December 2010).

CDS contracts.[33] Japan's FSA even dangled a cautiously worded invitation to foreign clearing houses, such as LCH.Clearnet, to consider working with the Japanese. Although the regulator said clearing of swaps should ideally be carried out by domestic Japanese CCPs, it recognised that foreign CCPs could be used because they were already up and running.

However, it was unclear how welcoming the authorities were in practice. The invitation was subject to conditions. Foreign CCPs would have to be covered by regulations equivalent to those in Japan and should draw on the expertise of Japanese CCPs when clearing derivatives such as CDSs which were affected by Japan's bankruptcy laws. Domestic CCPs should be responsible for clearing where there were sufficient contracts to have systemic implications while contracts written on the iTraxx Japan CDS index should be subject to mandatory clearing by Japanese CCPs.

China too joined the drive towards clearing OTC derivatives. The Shanghai Clearing House was formally inaugurated in November 2009 by Zhou Xiaochuan, governor of the People's Bank of China (PBC), as a 'professional and independent inter-bank clearing house'.[34]

Although vague about exactly which products would be cleared by the new CCP (it existed, Zhou Xiaochuan said, 'to better meet the demand for ever increasing and diverse services'), the governor's speech at the opening ceremony referred to the need for centralised clearing 'to ensure secure and orderly development of the OTC derivatives market'. He set the provision of an 'efficient and cost effective clearing service' in the context of the G20's agenda and the PBC's effort 'to address the global financial crisis' as well as domestic financial market reform and the promotion of Shanghai as an international financial centre.

The development of clearing in Asia was supported by global players. Six of the 14 companies that assisted in the study group on post-trade processing of OTC derivatives trades in Japan in 2008–9 were subsidiaries of foreign investment banks. The group held a meeting to exchange views with DTCC while its report suggested that cooperation with LCH.Clearnet would be required when Japan set up its own clearing house for interest rate swaps.[35]

The Shanghai Clearing House ceremony was a magnet for representatives of Western financial infrastructure providers, including LCH.Clearnet, Euroclear Bank, CLS Group and Deutsche Börse. It provided the occasion for the signing of a cooperation agreement between the clearing house and Deutsche Börse.[36]

The turnout for the Shanghai ceremony showed how Western clearers and other financial infrastructure providers were focusing their attention on Asia. For clearing houses and clearing professionals in the post-Lehman world, Asia was the continent of opportunity in the second decade of the 21st century.

[33] Financial Services Agency (21 January 2010), 'Development of institutional frameworks pertaining to financial and capital markets'.

[34] People's Bank of China (28 November 2009a), 'Speech of Governor Zhou Xiaochuan at the Opening Ceremony of the Shanghai Clearing House', http://www.pbc.gov.cn/publish/english/956/2010/20100524152218896622313/20100524152218896622313_.html (accessed 20 December 2010).

[35] JSCC, TSE, Japan Securities Depository Center study group (27 March 2009), 'Report on improvements of post-trade processing of OTC derivatives trades in Japan'. Reference purpose translation issued by The Study Group on Post-Trade Processing of OTC Derivatives Trades.

[36] People's Bank of China (28 November 2009b), 'Interbank Market Clearing House Co Ltd set up in Shanghai', 'News' at www.pbc.gov.cn/english (accessed 20 December 2010).

22
Reflections and Conclusions

This book has followed the development of central counterparty clearing through a great arc of history, concluding in Asia, the region where the harbingers of today's CCPs emerged 280 years ago to clear rice futures contracts.

When the clearing houses of Osaka took responsibility for completing futures trades in the Dojima Rice Market in the decades following 1730, Asia was where most of the world's economic activity took place.

In 1750, before the industrial revolution, China accounted for nearly a third of world manufacturing output – some 40% more than the share of all Europe at the time and around twice China's share of about 16% today – while the Indian sub-continent accounted for a further quarter. Japan's share of global manufacturing output in 1750 was an estimated 3.9%, twice that of Britain in pre-industrial times and nearly 40 times the share of a string of colonies in North America that went on to found the United States.[1]

So with Asia growing strongly and reclaiming some of the economic power that it ceded to the west during the industrial revolution, it seems only logical to expect that growth and, with that, innovation in clearing will gravitate eastward.

Such a shift in today's globalised world would fit the patterns outlined in this book. It was as Europe and the US grew in economic power during the late 19th century that enterprising brokers and merchants set up futures markets, supported by clearing houses, to maximise the benefits from trade in their globalising world. It was from those roots, in the ports of western Europe and the trading centres of the US Midwest, that today's CCPs have sprung rather than from the clearing houses of Dojima.

But while demand for clearing services is rising in the emerging world, and growing strongly in Asia, it would be wrong to regard Europe and the US as in any way sidelined.

Although the mature economies of the US and Europe have struggled to recover from the worst financial crisis for 80 years, today's clearing house executives stand to profit from something that would have been completely alien to their predecessors in the 18 and 19th centuries: a tsunami of regulation that will boost their business rather than constrain it.

Because CCPs were among the few components of the financial markets to perform well during and after the Lehman bankruptcy, they are an important part of the policy makers' tool kit to prevent a repetition of the financial upheavals of recent years.

Thanks to Messrs Dodd and Frank and the European Commission, CCPs have a central part to play in strategies to ensure there will never again be a financial meltdown like that which started in 2007. For this reason alone, clearing will be a growth industry in Europe and the US for the foreseeable future.

---

[1] Historic figures taken from Kennedy, Paul (1988), *The Rise and Fall of the Great Powers*. In 2009, China's share of the global total of manufacturing value (MVA) was 15.6%, making it the world's second largest industrial manufacturer, according to The United Nations Industrial Development Organisation (UNIDO).

It is true that much detail of the new regulation in the US, Europe and elsewhere remains to be filled in. Moreover its impact – not least on the economics of clearing – is unclear.

One view, expressed by Scott O'Malia, a CFTC Commissioner, is that: 'Market participants should have no illusions that the cost of clearing will increase dramatically.'[2] He has argued that the more stringent capital requirements of Dodd-Frank and Basel III will be passed on to the clearing members and customers of US derivatives clearing organisations (DCOs). If true, that will presumably apply in other G20 jurisdictions as they also regulate clearing and OTC derivatives.

But while the financial sector as a whole faces a sharp rise in costs from the wave of new regulation, there are pressures bearing down on the cost of clearing. Continued technological progress, allowing benefits of scale, combined with a rise in units to be cleared should enable costs per unit to fall and encourage continued fee competition.

Although uncertainties persist, politicians and regulators have at least defined their frameworks for the future of clearing. The industry, by contrast, is in various states of flux.

This is not obvious at the big picture level. The current differentiated models for clearing futures and cash securities look set to persist, while in the new area of clearing for OTC derivatives, action by the industry in anticipation of regulation has already created what seems likely to be an enduring structure.

Well before President Obama signed the Dodd-Frank act and the EU Commission produced its proposed regulation for CCPs, clearing companies had moved to establish or consolidate their positions in key OTC derivatives markets. While LCH.Clearnet's SwapClear service has built on a commanding position in the market for interest rate swaps, other contenders have thrown their hats into the ring. Similarly, in the market for clearing CDSs the early lead established by ICE in the US and Europe is impressive. But that has not prevented other clearers, such as LCH.Clearnet's Paris CCP or the CME Group from launching competing offerings.

Importantly, the structure of having more than one CCP clearing each different class of OTC derivative has been accepted by lawmakers and regulators in the US and the EU. Providing the number of offerings remain limited, competition among CCPs also fits the needs of users who fear the operational risk of having all their clearing depend on one provider but have no wish to incur the costs and complexities of dealing with several. So long as there is scope for companies to emerge and challenge incumbents, there is hope that the resulting structures will be efficient and economic.

In the case of clearing futures contracts, the trend towards verticalisation appears unstoppable and global. Long standard in the US, the CME Group model has become the norm for futures markets in Asia and Latin America. In Europe, the decision of the NYSE Euronext group in 2010 to build its own clearing houses for its derivatives and securities trades marked the death knell of the horizontal approach to clearing futures in Europe.

In the case of equities clearing, it is necessary to differentiate between the US and Europe. Having successfully seen off a challenge from Nasdaq in 2009, DTCC has remained the monopoly provider of clearing services for a multiplicity of fiercely competing equity trading platforms in the US, its near at-cost service protected by a regulatory framework for trading and clearing stocks and bonds in place since the mid-1970s.

In Europe, where the MiFID deregulation of financial markets freed competition at the level of clearing as well as trading, the clearing business is in ferment. There has been a

[2] CFTC (1 October 2010), Commissioner Scott O'Malia's 'Opening statement on Public Meeting Governance, Financial Resources, Interim Final Rule: Pre-Enactment Swaps'.

proliferation of equity CCPs in Europe serving a market where the barriers to trading equities across national borders have been circumvented by the multilateral trading facilities authorised under MiFID. Europe's equity CCPs have been forced by competition to slash fees and struggle to be profitable.

NYSE Euronext's May 2010 decision to set up its own clearing houses in London and Paris was a catalyst. Paradoxically, it revived ideas for consolidating Europe's fragmented market infrastructures. All CCPs were suddenly talking to one another to make sure none missed out on a game-changing opportunity. Soon afterwards, some of the world's leading exchange companies entered secret negotiations that have resulted in dramatic merger plans. If realised, these could transform clearing in Europe.

As this book was undergoing final revision in February 2011, the London Stock Exchange Group and TMX Group of Canada announced an agreement to merge. They were upstaged within 24 hours by news that Deutsche Börse and NYSE Euronext also planned a merger of equals that would create the world's biggest exchange group by revenues, backed by powerful clearing and settlement capabilities. If completed as announced, the marriage of Deutsche Börse and NYSE Euronext will mean the scrapping of NYSE Euronext's planned CCPs in Europe and the use of Deutsche Börse's clearing and risk management assets instead. Meanwhile, the LSE and TMX have mooted developing their clearing capabilities to create interoperability across the Atlantic.

A similar rash of mergers between 1999 and 2004 left a still fragmented European post-trade sector. This time – post crisis, with different business leaders and new EU regulations in the pipeline – things could be different. Even so, barriers to CCP consolidation remain in Europe, 12 years after the EU launched its action plan for a single market in financial services.

Unlike the US, which has a single market with demarcation lines in clearing defined by the different financial products cleared, the barriers in Europe have continued to be defined by national boundaries, behind which differences were accentuated by different national legal systems, bankruptcy laws, regulatory traditions and – sometimes – protectionism and parochialism.

Such barriers are extremely difficult to remove. But the imperfections in the markets for clearing services in both the US and Europe also reflect the non-engagement of competition policy with the sector.

It looked at one point as if the European Commission's competition directorate would take on vertical silos, but its resolve evaporated in 2006 when Germany made clear that it would block any move towards regulating clearing and settlement that threatened to disrupt the established silo structure of the Deutsche Börse group. The refreshing and radically critical review of vertical structures for clearing in the US futures market by US Justice Department officials in 2008 was immediately disowned at higher levels.

In general, the competition authorities on both sides of the Atlantic have been notably absent from this history of clearing. It remains to be seen whether they will have any incentive or inclination to become involved in the much changed conditions created by the financial crisis.

The signals are mixed. To encourage competition, the EU Commission has made provision for interoperability in the European cash equities market in its legislative proposals for the clearing sector. At the time of writing, the CFTC has indicated some willingness to enable ELX, as a competitor to the CME Group, to have access to the CME's open interest through ELX's 'Exchange of Futures for Futures' rule.

But in Europe, interoperability can always be blocked by regulators, as shown by the extended impasse after October 2009 over the implementation of the interoperability agreements agreed that year by LCH.Clearnet, SIX x-clear, EMCF and EuroCCP. The EU's proposed regulation will not change this.

In the US, the odds must remain stacked against a successful attempt by ELX or any other challenger to undermine the vertical silo structure of the CME Group unless and until Congress or one of the regulators accountable to it decides to force change.

Achieving an optimal level of competition has never been easy. In clearing, the problem has grown since the demutualisation of exchanges with (where they have them) their integrated CCPs. Since demutualisation in the 1990s and early 2000s there has been an unfortunate coincidence of regulators adopting a neutral stance towards the structure of clearing houses and competition authorities being reluctant to enforce a level playing field for clearing house operators. Reshaping the business of clearing will be nigh impossible so long as the authorities deny themselves the opportunity to intervene in corporate structures.

And yet, with the crisis still fresh in the memory and the eurozone's sovereign debt crisis creating new challenges, it is difficult not to sympathise with politicians, regulators and clearing house professionals if they err on the side of safety when trying to find an appropriate balance between safety and competition in the clearing sector.

It was rather anomalous – if not disturbingly asynchronous – that the 'paradigm shift' away from market liberalisation to putting safety first, that was signalled by regulators after the Lehman bankruptcy and described in Part V of this book, came at a time of huge countervailing momentum. For Europe's equity CCPs in particular, the new wave of regulation for clearing houses was drawn up while they were having to absorb the impact of the drive for greater competition and competitiveness in financial markets that characterised more than 20 years of deregulation from the 1980s until the onset of the financial crisis in 2007.

There are risks in the present situation. To date, the consensus against competition on risk management among CCPs seems to be holding and this is a healthy sign. But despite all the protestations that it could never happen, the temptation for clearing houses to be sucked into a 'race to the bottom' on risk-management standards has not been banished.

Although CCPs acquitted themselves well during and after the Lehman default, a certain amount of luck was involved.

CCPs have since entered unknown territory in clearing CDSs, raising important questions for clearing house managers, clearing members and regulators. Can CCPs clearing instruments such as CDSs, with their unusual 'jump to default' risk profile, be left to experience the discipline of the market if they run into trouble?

That question opens the complex issues of whether CCPs, which are pursuing a public policy goal (while expecting to profit from it), should expect access to lender of last resort facilities or even be bailed out by the state in case of crisis. Or should their owners and/or the mutualised contributors to the default fund be expected to take the financial hit in the new regulatory environment designed to ensure that taxpayers are never again liable for a company that otherwise would be too interconnected or too big to fail?

Although CFTC Chairman Gary Gensler invariably reminds US audiences that no US clearing house serving the futures markets has ever failed, this is not true of CCPs in other jurisdictions.

The fact that CCPs concentrate risk has been a recurring theme in this book. Central counterparty clearing does not eliminate risk. Clearing controls risk, which is then concentrated at the CCP and mutualised among the members of the clearing house.

In these circumstances, there is little wonder that systemic risk managers in some of the world's leading financial institutions have been combing through the default fund rules of the

CCPs that clear for them to determine the scope of their institution's liability in times of crisis. Similarly, regulators drawing up the new laws for CCPs have paid particular attention to the default 'waterfall' of who pays what and when in the case of trouble.

If these are the risks that face CCPs, how can they be mitigated?

The first defence is humility. Clearing is not a panacea for dealing with the aftermath of the crisis. Not all bilaterally traded instruments are suited to clearing. The safety of CCPs can be threatened if they are required to clear products that are complex, illiquid and difficult to price. CCPs can only be one component in the overhaul of global finance. Other infrastructures and processes, including trade information warehouses and portfolio compression, have important roles to play in controlling risk.

The Dodd-Frank act and the EU Commission's proposals recognise that clearing is not a silver bullet. The next step is to ensure that this principle applies when the laws governing OTC derivatives and CCPs are implemented and choices made about which derivatives are to be cleared.

A further line of defence hinges on the relationship between CCP managers and their regulators. There has been a revolution in the level of involvement of regulators with clearing houses and clearing houses with regulators in recent years. The lives of CCP managers, regulators and supervisors are intertwined as never before.

The contrast with conditions a century ago when clearing houses such as the London Produce Clearing House were becoming established in Europe's nascent commodity futures markets is striking. If the LPCH board minutes are any guide,[3] the clearing house's directors had no need to think about regulators during the quarter of a century between LPCH's foundation and the First World War, when the British government imposed controls on trade in commodities.

Today's CCP managers and board members have to be in constant touch with regulators and supervisors in their home countries and abroad in what amounts to a symbiotic relationship.

Jeffrey Sprecher, Chairman and CEO of ICE, has described how regulators flocked to learn about clearing credit default swaps at the group's ICE Trust clearing house, obliging the exchange and clearing house operator to rearrange its premises:

> We had literally to move to new offices just to create space for regulators to have a place to work. [...] I think that is a glimpse of what we are all going to be looking at for every listed asset class that goes through clearing houses. This means that the compliance function that many of us have now at the exchange level is going to be moved down to the clearing house level, or at least reproduce itself, and there will be a level of compliance and oversight at the clearing house level.[4]

Today's CCP leaders must not only weigh the interests of users, exchanges and other bodies that create the products to be cleared. They need close and constant contact, based on trust and understanding, with regulators and supervisors. Moreover – as lobbying can play such an important part in influencing legislation and regulation – that applies increasingly to relations with the politicians who make the laws.

There are other challenges ahead. Finding sufficient talented and experienced leaders with the breadth of vision needed to steer what has become a growth industry through the complexities of the modern age will be one.

Another will be putting to rest the divisions that have plagued relations between some clearing houses, their owners and users. Managers must navigate the cultural divide between

[3] See Chapter 6.

[4] Remarks during a panel discussion with other exchange leaders at IDX, the International Derivatives Expo 2010, in London, 8 June 2010.

exchanges and investment banks that has upset, and in some cases poisoned, the delicate three-way relationship between clearers, users and trading platforms since exchanges demutualised towards the end of last century and the beginning of this.

Here there are some hopeful signs. The CFTC's proposed limits on the voting power of clearing sent a signal that should resonate worldwide and put a shot across the bows of any future Lily-type adventure, with all the disruption that entailed. Although they appear to have had only a limited success, the attempts by exchanges to find common ground with the dealer community through 'remutualisation' or putting 'skin in the game' show good intentions.

Perhaps more important has been the exchange of personalities between exchanges, clearing houses and investment banks with former employees of Goldman Sachs, in particular, forming a network that crops up in many institutions. Duncan Niederauer moved to be CEO of NYSE Euronext in 2007 after 22 years at Goldman Sachs. Before taking over as chief executive of the London Stock Exchange in 2009, Xavier Rolet spent eight years at Lehman Brothers, having earlier worked at Goldman Sachs where he and Niederauer got to know each other well. Roger Liddell, chief executive of LCH.Clearnet from 2006 to 2011, is another alumnus of Goldman Sachs.

But in a crisis, the CCP is thrown back on its own resources. No amount of shared corporate DNA with exchanges and users or past schmoozing of regulators and politicians will count if the risk-management and governance of the CCP is not up to scratch.

Here there have been steady improvements since the stock market crash of October 1987. 'That was when we realised we were in the risk management and not the transaction processing business,' recalls Rory Cunningham, Chairman of EACH, the European Association of CCP Clearing Houses, and Director, Public Affairs, of LCH.Clearnet.[5]

For two decades from 1987, CCPs learned from a succession of scares and crises on financial markets. Standard-setting committees such as CPSS-IOSCO and ESCB-CESR groups of regulators provided recommendations against which practices could be compared. Issues of governance have featured strongly in the regulations either passed or proposed for CCPs during 2010. 'Requirements for CCPs' account for no fewer than 27 of the 72 articles comprising the EU Commission's September 2010 proposal to regulate CCPs, OTC derivatives and trade repositories.

As the world economy headed towards the abyss in September 2008, the past preparation of CCPs stood them in good stead. Clearing houses successfully survived the bankruptcy of Lehman Brothers. As the world moves forward into an uncertain future, the hope must be that this record stays intact.

[5] From an email exchange with the author, 14 October 2010.

Appendix A
References and Bibliography

REFERENCES

AFEI (France), ASSOSIM (Italy), FBF (France), LIBA (UK) (20 February 2006), 'European Trade Associations' call for EU action on European Exchanges and Market Infrastructure', joint statement issued through AFEI and LIBA, London and Paris.

AFP (13 May 2010), 'S&P cuts credit ratings on NYSE Euronext', Paris.

Baehring, Berndt (1985), *Börsen-Zeiten*, Frankfurt: Frankfurter Wertpapierbörse.

Bank for International Settlements (March 1997), 'Clearing arrangements for exchange traded derivatives', Committee on Payment and Settlement Systems of the central banks of the Group of Ten Countries, Basel.

Bank for International Settlements (June 1997), '67th annual report', Basel, www.bis.org.

Bank for International Settlements (June 1999), '69th annual report', Basel, www.bis.org.

Bank for International Settlements (November 2001), 'Recommendations for securities settlement systems', Basel: Committee on Payment and Settlement Systems of the central banks of the Group of Ten Countries, with the IOSCO Technical Committee (CPSS-IOSCO), www.bis.org.

Bank for International Settlements (November 2004), 'Recommendations for central counterparties', Basel: Committee on Payment and Settlement Systems of the central banks of the Group of Ten Countries, with the IOSCO Technical Committee (CPSS-IOSCO), www.bis.org.

Bank for International Settlements (December 2004), 'Triennial and semiannual surveys on positions in global over-the-counter (OTC) derivatives markets at end June 2004', Basel: BIS Monetary and Economic Department, www.bis.org.

Bank for International Settlements (June 2006), 'International convergence of capital measurement and capital standards: A revised framework', Comprehensive Version, Basel: Basel Committee on Banking Supervision, www.bis.org.

Bank for International Settlements (March 2007) 'New developments in clearing and settlement arrangements for OTC derivatives', Basel: The Committee on Payment and Settlement Systems of the Bank for International Settlements, www.bis.org.

Bank for International Settlements (13 November 2007), 'Triennial and semiannual surveys on positions in global over-the-counter (OTC) derivatives markets at end June 2007', Basel: BIS Monetary and Economic Department, www.bis.org.

Bank for International Settlements (November 2008), 'OTC derivatives market activity in the first half of 2008', Basel: BIS Monetary and Economic Department, www.bis.org.

Bank for International Settlements (20 July 2009), 'CPSS-IOSCO working group on the review of the "Recommendations for Central Counterparties"', Basel, CPSS-IOSCO press release, www.bis.org.

Bank for International Settlements (September 2009), 'The Joint Forum Report of Special Purpose Entities', Basel: Basel Committee on Banking Supervision, www.bis.org.

Bank for International Settlements (November 2009), 'OTC derivatives market activity in the first half of 2009', Basel: BIS Monetary and Economic Department, www.bis.org.

Bank for International Settlements (2 February 2010), 'Standards for payment, clearing and settlement systems: review by CPSS-IOSCO', Basel, CPSS-IOSCO press release, www.bis.org.

Bank for International Settlements (March 2010), 'International banking and financial market developments', *Basel Quarterly Review*, www.bis.org.

Bank for International Settlements (26 July 2010), 'The Group of Governors and Heads of Supervision reach broad agreement on Basel Committee capital and liquidity reform package', Basel Committee on Banking Supervision, Basel, press release plus Annex, www.bis.org.

Bank for International Settlements (12 September 2010), 'Group of Governors and Heads of Supervision announces higher global minimum capital standards', Basel Committee on Banking Supervision, Basel, press release plus Annex, www.bis.org.

Bank of England (1999), 'Central counterparty clearing houses and financial stability, *Financial Stability Review*, June, London.

Bank of England (April 2009a), 'Rethinking the financial network', Speech by Andrew Haldane, Executive Director for Financial Stability, at the Financial Student Association, Amsterdam, www.bankofengland.co.uk.

Bank of England (April 2009b), 'Payment systems oversight report 2008', Issue No. 5, London, www.bankofengland.co.uk.

Bank of England (8 May 2009), 'Small lessons from a big crisis', Remarks by Andrew Haldane, Executive Director for Financial Stability, at the Federal Reserve Bank of Chicago 45th Annual Conference, *Reforming financial regulation*, www.bankofengland.co.uk.

Bank Mees & Hope NV (1987) 'Annual report', Amsterdam.

Becker, Ursula (2002), *Kaffee Konzentration: Zur Entwicklung und Organisation des Hanseatischen Kaffeehandels*, Stuttgart: Franz Steiner Verlag.

Bernanke, Ben S. (1990), 'Clearing and settlement during the crash', *The Review of Financial Studies*, **3**(1), 133–151.

Binder, Jim (2008), 'Seven exchanges, one clearing house, intense competition', *Swiss Derivatives Review*, **37**, Summer, Zurich.

Black, Fischer and Scholes, Myron (1973), 'The pricing of options and corporate liabilities', *The Journal of Political Economy*, **81**(3) (May–June), Chicago: University of Chicago Press.

Board of Banking Supervision (18 July 1995), Report of the Board of Banking Supervision Inquiry into the circumstances of the collapse of Barings, London: HMSO.

BOTCC, By-Laws (Editions of 1925, 1930 and 1935), Chicago.

BOTCC, Board of Trade Clearing Corporation (1925), Certificate of Incorporation, Wilmington, Delaware.

BOTCC (2002–3), 'Trusting, Growing, Leading, Clearing: a History', Company brochure.

BOTCC (14 July 2003), Email from Dennis Dutterer, BOTCC President and CEO, to the CFTC, Chicago.

Boyle, James Ernest (1920), *Speculation and the Chicago Board of Trade*, New York: McMillan Co.

Boyle, James E. (1931a), 'Cottonseed Oil Exchanges', *The Annals of the American Academy of Political and Social Science*, **155**, Part 1, Philadelphia.

Boyle, James E. (1931b), 'The New York Burlap and Jute Exchange', *The Annals of the American Academy of Political and Social Science*, **155**, Part 1, Philadelphia.

Brady Commission (January 1988), 'Report of the Presidential Task Force on Market Mechanisms', named after Nicholas Brady, Chairman, Washington. DC, http://www.archive.org/details/reportofpresiden01unit.

Brockhaus Konversationslexikon, 14th edition 1892–95, Leipzig, FA Brockhaus.

Chicago Board of Trade (14 June 2003), Letter from Bernie Dan, CBOT president and CEO, to the CFTC, Chicago.

CCorp (2006), 'A History: Trusting, Growing, Leading, Clearing', Chicago: CCorp.

CCorp (20 December 2007), 'The Clearing Corporation announces restructuring and investment by global financial institutions focused on OTC derivatives clearing', press release, Chicago.

CCorp (9 July 2008), 'Testimony of the Clearing Corporation to the US Senate subcommittee on securities, insurance and investment; committee on banking, housing and urban affairs', Washington.

CCorp and DTCC (29 May 2008), 'The Clearing Corporation and The Depository Trust & Clearing Corporation announce Credit Default Swap (CDS) Clearing Facility linked to DTCC's Trade Information Warehouse', press release, Chicago and New York.

CCP12, The Global Association of Central Counterparties (April 2009), 'Central counterparty default management and the collapse of Lehman Brothers', www.ccp12.org.

C Czarnikow Ltd (15 September 1938), 'Weekly price current'.

CESR, the Committee of European Securities Regulators, (23 March 2009), 'The Lehman Brothers default: An assessment of the market impact', Paris, www.cesr.eu.

CFTC (1988), 'Final report on stock index futures and cash market activity during October 1987', Washington DC.

CFTC (11 March 2002), 'Summary report of the Commodity Futures Trading Commission on the Futures Industry Response to September 11th', Washington.

CFTC (15 October 2008), Written testimony before the House Committee on Agriculture, Walter Lukken, acting CFTC Chairman, Washington, DC.

CFTC (25 September 2009), 'Prepared remarks of Gary Gensler', CFTC Chairman, to an EU Commission conference on *OTC Derivatives Regulation,* Brussels, www.CFTC.gov.

CFTC (9 March 2010), Keynote address by Gary Gensler to Markit's *Outlook for OTC Derivatives Markets* conference, New York, www.CFTC.gov

CFTC (21 July 2010), 'CFTC releases list of areas of rule-making for over-the-counter derivatives', press release, Washington DC, www.CFTC.gov.

CFTC (16 September 2010), Gary Gensler, 'Remarks before the ISDA Regional Conference', New York, www.CFTC.gov.

CFTC (1 October 2010a). Commissioner O'Malia, 'Opening statement on Public Meeting Governance, Financial Resources, Interim Final Rule: Pre-Enactment Swaps', Washington DC, www. CFTC.gov.

CFTC (1 October, 2010b), Commissioners' statements on DCO governance, Press Room, Speeches & Testimony, Washington DC, www.CFTC.gov.

CFTC and SEC (30 September 2010), 'Findings regarding the market events of May 6, 2010', joint report, Washington DC, www.CFTC.gov.

Chalmin, Philippe (1990), *The Making of a Sugar Giant*, London: Harwood Academic.

Chancellor, Edward (1999), *Devil Take the Hindmost*, UK: MacMillan.

Chicago Journal of Commerce (30 July 1925), 'Pit clearing house plans hit obstacle'.

Chicago Journal of Commerce (26 August 1925), 'Board of trade to vote again on changing clearing methods'.

Chicago Mercantile Exchange (15 June 1921), 'Constitution, by-laws and clearing house rules'.

Clearnet SA (April 2000), *Clear News*, Issue 1, Paris.

CME Group (8 June 2006), 'Efficient clearing and settlement systems: The case for market-driven solutions', Speech of Craig Donohue, CEO of the CME, to FESE's 10th *European Financial Markets Convention*, Zurich.

CME Group (3 December 2009), 'CME Group announces dealer founding members for CDS initiative', Chicago, http://cmegroup.mediaroom.com/index.php?s=43&item=2968&pagetemplate=article, (accessed 20 December 2010).

CME Group (18 October 2010) 'CME Group begins clearing OTC interest rate swaps', news release; http://cmegroup.mediaroom.com/index.php?s=43&item=3073&pagetemplate=article (accessed 20 December 2010).

Commodity Futures Modernization Act, HR 5660, US law, 106th Congress (1999–2000).

Competition Commission (29 July 2005a), 'Notice of provisional findings made under rule 10.3 of the Competition Commission Rules of Procedure in respect of i) The anticipated acquisition of London Stock Exchange PLC by Deutsche Börse AG and ii) The anticipated acquisition of London Stock Exchange PLC by Euronext NV.

Competition Commission (29 July 2005b), 'CC considers LSE mergers would harm competition', news release 46/05, London.

Conant, Charles A. (1905), *Principles of Money and Banking*, Vol. II, New York and London: Harper & Brothers.

Counterparty Risk Management Policy Group II (CRMPG-II) (25 July 2005), 'Toward greater financial stability: a private sector perspective', New York.

Counterparty Risk Management Policy Group III (CRMPG-III) (6 August 2008), 'Containing systemic risk: The road to reform'. New York.

Cranston, Ross (2007), 'Law through practice: London and Liverpool commodity markets c. 1820–1975', LSE Law, Society and Economy Working papers 14/2007, London: London School of Economics, Law Department.

Czarnikow (5 December 1974 to 29 January 1976), *Czarnikow Weekly Review*, Editions numbered: 1209, 1211, 1213, 1217, 1250, 1259, 1264 and 1268. London.

De Lavergne, A. (1931), 'Commodity Exchange in France', *The Annals of the American Academy of Political and Social Science*, **155**, Part 1, Philadelphia.

Den Heijer, Henk (2002), *The VOC and the Exchange*, Euronext Amsterdam NV and Stichting VvdE with the Nederlandsch Economisch-Historisch Archief (NEHA), Amsterdam.

Deutsche Börse (February 2001), 'Verkaufsprospekt/Börsenzulassungsprospekt', Frankfurt, www.deutsche-boerse.com.

Deutsche Börse Group (2008), *The Global Derivatives Market: An Introduction*, Frankfurt, www.deutsche-boerse.com.

Deutsche Börse, MATIF, MONEP, SBF-Bourse de Paris and SWX-Swiss Exchange (17 September 1997), Frankfurt, Paris and Zurich Exchanges extend their alliance, joint press release, Frankfurt, Paris, Zurich.

Deutsche Bundesbank (January 2003), 'Role and importance of interest rate derivatives', Monthly Report, Frankfurt.

Dodd-Frank Wall Street Reform and Consumer Protection Act, HR 4173, US law, 111th Congress (2009–2010).

DTCC (1999), 'How we serve the financial industry'. Company brochure, New York.

DTCC (1 June 2006), 'Donald F Donahue elected President and CEO of DTCC', press release, New York, www.dtcc.com.

DTCC (2007), 'Putting customers first; Annual report 2006', New York, www.dtcc.com.

DTCC (11 October 2008), 'DTCC addresses misconceptions about the Credit Default Swap Market', press statement, New York, www.dtcc.com.

DTCC (22 October 2008), 'DTCC Trade Information Warehouse completes Credit Event Processing for Lehman Brothers', press release, New York, www.dtcc.com.

DTCC (29 October 2008), 'Delivering certainty, creating possibilities, managing risk', Presentation of CEO and Chairman Donald Donahue to the DTCC Executive Forum 2008, New York, www.dtcc.com.

DTCC (30 October 2008), DTCC successfully closes out Lehman Brothers bankruptcy, press release, New York, www.dtcc.com.

DTCC (31 October 2008), 'DTCC to provide CDS data from Trade Information Warehouse', press release, New York, www.dtcc.com.

DTCC (12 January 2009), 'DTCC to support all central counterparties for OTC credit derivatives', press release, New York, www.dtcc.com.

DTCC (23 March 2009), Remarks by Donald Donahue at the ISITC 15th annual industry forum in Boston, www.dtcc.com.

DTCC (29 April 2009), 'Proposed merger between LCH.Clearnet and DTCC not proceeding', press release, New York and London, www.dtcc.com.

DTCC (2009), 'Annual report 2008', New York, www.dtcc.com.

DTCC (2010), 'Making a difference', Annual Report 2009, New York, www.dtcc.com.

DTCC and LCH.Clearnet (22 October 2008), 'DTCC and LCH.Clearnet announce plans to merge and create world's leading clearing house', joint press release, New York and London, www.dtcc.com and www.lchclearnet.com.

Duffie, Darrell, Li, Ada, Lubke, Theo (January 2010), 'Policy perspectives on OTC derivatives market infrastructure', Staff Report no. 424, Federal Reserve Bank of New York, www.newyorkfed.org.

Duffie, Darrell and Zhu, Haoxiang (9 March 2009), 'Does a central clearing counterparty reduce counterparty risk?', Stanford University.

EACH (July 2008), 'Inter-CCP risk management standards', www.eachorg.eu.

EACH (August 2009), Comments on the European Commission communication, Enhance the resilience of OTC Derivatives Markets, of July 2009, www.eachorg.eu.

EACH, ECSDA, FESE (7 November 2006), 'European Code of Conduct for Clearing and Settlement', Brussels, published respectively by: the European Association of Central Counterparty Clearing Houses (EACH), the European Central Securities Depositories Association (ECSDA) and the Federation of European Securities Exchanges (FESE), www.eachorg.eu.

EACH, ECSDA, FESE (28 June 2007), 'Access and interoperability guideline, Brussels, www.eachorg.eu.

Eberhardt, Jörg and Mayrhofer, Thomas (2002), 'Die Entwicklung der Magdeburger Börse', in *Jahresbericht, Studentischer Börsenverein Magdeburg e V, 2001–2*. Magdeburg, Germany.

ECB (27 September 2001), 'The Eurosystem's policy line with regard to consolidation in central counterparty clearing', Frankfurt, www.ecb.eu.

ECB (2005) 'Integration of securities market infrastructures in the Euro Area', Schmiedel, Heiko and Schönenberger, Andreas, ECB Occasional Paper No. 33, Frankfurt, http://www.ecb.int/pub/pdf/scpops/ecbocp33.pdf (accessed 10 December 2010).

ECB (19 June 2008), 'Summary of the 18th meeting of the Contact Group on Euro Securities Infrastructures (COGESI), Frankfurt, www.ecb.eu.

ECB (18 December 2008), 'Decisions taken by the governing council of the ECB (in addition to decisions setting interest rates)', Frankfurt, www.ecb.eu.

ECB (August 2009), 'Credit default swaps and counterparty risk', Frankfurt, www.ecb.eu.

ECB (29 September 2010), 'Keeping the momentum for financial reform'. ECB President, Jean-Claude Trichet's keynote address at the *Eurofi Financial Forum* 2010, Brussels.

ECB and CESR (May 2009), 'Recommendations for securities settlement systems and recommendations for central counterparties in the European Union', [the ESCB-CESR standards], Frankfurt and Paris.

Ellison, Thomas (1886), *The Cotton Trade of Great Britain*, London: Effingham Wilson.

ELX Futures (14 October 2009), 'CFTC approves ELX "EFF" Rule', press release, New York, www.elxfutures.com.

EMCF (29 December 2009), 'Interoperability for CCPs: A way forward', www.euromcf.nl.

EMCF (2010), 'Clearing solutions for all to see, Annual report 2009', www.euromcf.nl.

Emery, Henry Crosby (1896), *Speculation on the Stock and Produce Exchanges of the United States*, Studies in History, Economics and Public Law, volume 7, number 2, New York. Also published as an Elibron Classics Replica Edition by Adamant Media in 2005.

Eurex Clearing (22 July 2008), 'Eurex clearing plans to build European CCP platform for clearing services in OTC derivatives', Frankfurt.

Eurex Clearing (24 July 2009), 'Eurex Credit Clear – the European OTC clearing solution for credit default swaps – to start on 30 July 2009', Frankfurt, www.eurexclearing.com.

EuroCCP (17 June 2009), 'EuroCCP proposes European Convention on interoperability', London.

EuroCCP (2010), 'Report and financial statement for the year ended 31 December 2009'.

EuroCCP (January 2010), 'Recommendations for reducing risks among interoperating CCPs: A discussion document', London, www.euroccp.co.uk.

Euroclear (20 July 2006), 'Sir Nigel Wicks to become Euroclear Chairman as of 1 August 2006', Brussels. Archived and dated 24 October 2006 under Media Releases on www.euroclear.com.

Euronext NV (2006), 'Notes to the consolidated financial statements: Registration document and annual report 2005'.

European Commission (May 1999), 'Financial services: Implementing the framework for financial markets – Action plan', Brussels, Com (1999) 232, 11.05.99. www.ec.europa.eu.

European Commission (May 2002), 'Clearing and settlement in the European Union. Main policy issues and future challenges, Brussels, COM(2002)257.

European Commission (28 April 2004), 'Clearing and settlement in the European Union – The way forward', Brussels: COM(2004)312, www.ec.europa.eu.

European Commission (30 June 2005), 'Securities trading, clearing, central counterparties and settlement in EU 25 – An overview of current arrangements', Brussels: London Economics commissioned by DG Competition, European Commission. www.ec.europa.eu.

European Commission (13 September 2005), 'Fund management – Regulation to facilitate competitiveness, growth and change', Brussels: Commissioner McCreevy at the 14th annual *ALFI-NICSA Europe-USA Investment Funds Forum*, Luxembourg, www.ec.europa.eu.

European Commission, Competition DG (May 2006), 'Competition in EU securities trading and post-trading: Issues paper'. Brussels: DG Competition, European Commission www.ec.europa.eu.

European Commission, Internal Market DG (May 2006), 'Draft working document on post-trading', plus Annex I, 'Analysis of studies examining European post-trading costs', Brussels.

European Commission (11 July 2006), 'Clearing and settlement: The way forward', Brussels, McCreevy remarks to the Economic and Monetary Affairs Committee of the European Parliament, www.ec.europa.eu.

European Commission (November 2006), 'Clearing and Settlement Code of Conduct', Brussels: McCreevy speech at press conference, 7 November 2006, www.ec.europa.eu.

European Commission (17 October 2008), 'Statement of Commissioner McCreevy on reviewing derivatives markets before the end of the year', Brussels, www.ec.europa.eu.

EU Commission (18 December 2008), 'Industry commitment to the European Commission regarding central counterparty clearing of credit default swaps in Europe', Brussels, www.ec.europa.eu.
EU Commission (17 February 2009) 'Letter to Commissioner McCreevy, from signatories of the industry commitment to the European Commission regarding central counterparty clearing of credit default swaps in Europe'. Brussels, www.ec.europa.eu.
EU Commission (3 July 2009), 'Ensuring efficient, safe and sound derivatives markets', Brussels, Communication COM 332 final; plus Commission Staff Working Paper Accompanying the Commission Communication, SEC (2009) 905 final, www.ec.europa.eu.
EU Commission (24 September 2009), 'Derivatives and risk allocation', Remarks of Commissioner McCreevy at the Derivatives Conference Speakers' Dinner before a Commission Derivatives Conference, Brussels, www.ec.europa.eu.
EU Commission (20 October 2009), 'Ensuring efficient, safe and sound derivatives markets: future policy actions', Brussels, Communication COM (2009) 563 final, www.ec.europa.eu.
EU Commission (20 October 2009), 'Financial services: Commission sets out future actions to strengthen the safety of derivatives markets', press release, IP/09/1546, Brussels, www.ec.europa.eu.
EU Commission (15 September 2010), 'Proposal for a regulation on OTC Derivatives, Central Counterparties and Trade Repositories', COM (2010) 484/5, Brussels, www.ec.europa.eu.
EU Council of Ministers (2 December 2008), 'Ecofin Council conclusions on clearing and settlement, Brussels, www.consilium.europa.eu/ueDocs/cms.../en/ecofin/104530.pdf.
European Commission Services (January 2010), 'Staff Working Document on possible further changes to the Capital Requirements Directive', Brussels, www.ec.europa.eu.
European Financial Services Round Table (December 2003), 'Securities clearing and settlement in Europe, Brussels: EFR, www.efr.be.
European Monetary Institute (1996), 'Payment systems in the European Union' [The Blue Book], Frankfurt.
European Securities Forum (15 June 2000), press release, London.
European Securities Forum (2 December 2000), 'EuroCCP: ESF's blueprint for a single pan-European central counterparty', London.
Falloon, William D. (1998), *Market maker: A sesquicentennial look at the Chicago Board of Trade*, Chicago: Board of Trade of the City of Chicago.
Federal Reserve Bank of New York (9 June 2008), 'Statement regarding June 9 meeting on over-the-counter derivatives', New York, www.newyorkfed.org.
Federal Reserve Bank of New York (10 October 2008), 'New York Fed to host meeting regarding Central Counterparty for CDS', press release, New York, www.newyorkfed.org.
Federal Reserve Bank of New York (31 October 2008), 'New York Fed welcomes further industry commitments on over-the-counter derivatives', New York, www.newyorkfed.org.
Federal Reserve Bank of New York (1 March 2010), 'New York Fed welcomes further industry commitments on over-the-counter derivatives', New York, www.newyorkfed.org.
Federal Reserve Bank of New York (8 September 2009), 'Market participants commit to expand central clearing for OTC derivatives', New York, www.newyorkfed.org.
Federal Reserve Bank of New York (24 September 2009), 'A global framework for regulatory cooperation on OTC derivative CCPs and trade repositories', press release, New York, www.newyorkfed.org.
Federal Reserve Board (7 April 2003), 'Interagency paper on sound practices to strengthen the resilience of the US financial system', Washington: Office of Comptroller of the Currency, SEC.
Federal Reserve System (Effective 4 March 2009), 'Ice US Trust LLC, New York, Order Approving Application for Membership', Washington DC, www.federalreserve.gov.
Federal Trade Commission (1920), 'Report of the Federal Trade Commission on the grain trade, Volume 5', Washington DC: Government Printing Office.
Felloni, Giuseppe and Laura, Guido (2004), *Genoa and the History of Finance: A series of firsts?* www.giuseppefelloni.it (accessed 3 December 2010).
FIA Global Task Force on Financial Integrity (June 1995), 'Recommendations for regulators, exchanges and clearinghouses, forming part of Financial Integrity Recommendations for Futures and Options Markets and Market Participants', Washington, DC: FIA.
Financial News (28 January 2008), 'Banks mull European derivatives exchange', London.
Financial Services Agency (21 January 2010), 'Development of institutional frameworks pertaining to financial and capital markets', Tokyo, www.fsa.go.jp/en/news/2010/20100122-3/01.pdf

Financial Services Authority and HM Treasury (December 2009), 'Reforming OTC derivative markets, A UK perspective', London, www.fsa.gov.uk/pubs/other/reform_otc_derivatives.pdf (acccessed 13 December 2010).
Financial Stability Forum (10 October 2008), 'Report of the Financial Stability Forum on enhancing market and institutional resilience: Follow up on implementation', Washington/Basel, www.financialstabilityboard.org.
Financial Times (13 February 1888), 'Mincing Lane in feeble form: A proposed innovation'.
Financial Times (FT.Com) (19 June 2003), 'CME and CBOT fight foreign rivals: Open warfare breaks out over plans of world's largest derivatives exchange to enter the US market'.
Financial Times (15 October 2003), 'Eurex sues its rivals in Chicago'.
Financial Times (7 January 2005), Letter to the Editor from Chris Tupker, Euroclear Chairman.
Financial Times (15 March 2005), 'Interview: Charles Carey, Chicago Board of Trade'.
Financial Times (5 July 2006), 'Teaching a gorilla to tap-dance', article by Richard Beales.
Financial Times (FT.Com) (17 October 2006), 'Merger bolsters Chicago's business profile'.
Financial Times (30 January 2009), 'Paris toughens regulation line with call for clearing system'.
Financial Times (FT.Com) (29 December 2009), 'Rolet urges safeguards on clearing houses'.
Financial Times (12 May 2010), 'Brussels warns on 'widely' varying clearing house rules'.
Financial Times (31 May 2010), 'Clearing reforms for Chile's Exchange', Buenos Aires.
Finextra (14 May 2010), 'S&P cuts NYSE Euronext rating on clearing plans; puts LCH.Clearnet on "creditwatch"'.
FSA, AFM, DNB, FINMA and SNB (12 February 2010), 'Communication of regulatory position on interoperability'.
Fukuyama, Francis (1992), *The End of History and the Last Man*, New York: Avon Books.
Futures Industry Magazine (September 2009), 'The Gensler Agenda, an interview with Will Acworth'. Washington DC: Futures Industry Association. www.futuresindustry.org/futures-industry.asp.
Geithner, Timothy (9 June 2008), 'Reducing systemic risk in a dynamic financial system', Remarks of New York Fed President Timothy Geithner at the Economic Club of New York, New York.
Gensler, Gary (18 November 2009), 'Testimony before the Senate Committee on Agriculture', Washington DC: CFTC, www.CFTC.gov.
Gensler, Gary (18 March 2010), 'OTC Derivatives Reform' to a meeting at Chatham House, London, Washington DC: CFTC, www.CFTC.gov.
Gidel, Susan Abbott (2000), '100 years of futures trading: From domestic agricultural to world financial', *Futures Industry Magazine*, December 1999/January 2000, Washington, DC: Futures Industry Association, www.futuresindustry.org/futures-industry.asp.
GAO (April 1990), 'Report to congressional committees: Clearance and settlement reform'. Washington DC. Appendices contain responses supplied by the CFTC, CME, NSCC, OCC and SEC.
Gelderblom, Oscar and Jonker, Joost (2005), 'Amsterdam as the cradle of modern futures and options trading, 1550 to 1650': in Goetzmann W.N. and Rouwenhorst K.G. (eds) *The Origins of Value: The financial innovations that created modern capital markets*, Oxford, UK: OUP.
Geljon, P.A. (1988), 'Termijnhandel in Nederland', published in *Termijnhandel en termijnmarkten*, Deventer, Kluwer.
Giovannini Group (November 2001), 'Cross-border clearing and settlement arrangements in the European Union', Brussels: European Commission, www.ec.europa.eu.
Giovannini Group (April 2003), 'Second report on EU clearing and settlement arrangements', Brussels: European Commission, www.ec.europa.eu.
Gowers, Andrew (21 December 2008), *Sunday Times*.
Greenspan, Alan (5 May 2005), 'Risk transfer and financial stability', remarks delivered via satellite to the Federal Reserve Bank of Chicago's forty-first Annual Conference on Bank Structure, Chicago.
G20 (2 April 2009), 'Declaration on Strengthening the Financial System', London, www.g20.org/Documents/g20_communique_020409.pdf.
G20 (25 September 2009), 'Leaders' statement: The Pittsburgh Summit', September 24–25 2009, Pittsburgh, www.pittsburghsummit.gov/mediacenter/129639.htm.
G30 (March 1989), 'Clearance and settlement systems in the world's securities markets', New York and London: Group of Thirty.
G30 (July 1993), Derivatives: Practices and principles, New York and London: Group of Thirty.

G30 (January 2003), Global clearing and settlement: A plan of action, New York and London: Group of Thirty.

Harding, John and Miller, Robert (21 November 1979), 'Financial futures in London?', London, report commissioned by ICCH.

Harris, Siebel (1911), 'The methods of marketing the grain crop', *The Annals of the American Academy of Political and Social Science*, **38**, Philadelphia.

Hay Davison, Ian (May 1988), 'The operation and regulation of the Hong Kong securities industry: Report of the Securities Review Committee', Hong Kong: Government Printer.

Hendricks, Darryll, Kambhu, John and Mosser, Patricia (May 2006), 'Systemic risk and the financial system', NewYork, background paper commissioned by the Federal Reserve Bank of New York.

HKEx, Hong Kong Exchanges and Clearing Ltd (January 2009), *Exchange*. A quarterly newsletter, Hong Kong, www.hkex.com.hk.

HM Treasury (February 1999), 'Financial Services and Markets Bill: Draft recognition requirements for investment exchanges and clearing houses', London.

House of Lords (2010), 'The future regulation of derivatives markets: Is the EU on the right track?' European Union Committee. Report with evidence published as HL Paper 93, 31 March 2010, London: the Stationery Office Ltd.

Hutcheson, John M. (1901), *Notes on the Sugar Industry*, Greenock, Scotland: John MacKelvie and Sons.

ICE (14 September 2006), 'IntercontinentalExchange enters into agreement to acquire New York Board of Trade', press release, Atlanta, www.theice.com.

ICE, The Clearing Corp (10 October 2008), 'Industry Group signs letter of intent to establish global central counterparty clearing for credit default swaps', joint press release, New York, www.theice.com.

ICE, The Clearing Corp (30 October 2008), 'IntercontinentalExchange, The Clearing Corporation and nine major dealers announced new developments in global CDS clearing solution. ICE to acquire The Clearing Corporation as clearing initiative advances', joint press release, New York, www.theice.com.

ICE (2 July 2009), June and second quarter results, New York/Atlanta, www.theice.com.

ICE (4 March, 5 March, 6 March, 10 March 2009 and 9 March 2010), News releases on CDS clearing, New York/Atlanta, www.theice.com.

ICE (4 October 2010), 'ICE reports record futures volume; $12.1 Trillion cleared in CDS: Totals from respective launches of ICE Trust and ICE Clear Europe to 30 September 2010', news release, Atlanta, www.theice.com.

IMF (September 2003), 'Global financial stability report. Chapter III Appendix: Case studies', Washington DC, www.imf.org.

IMF (April 2010), 'Global financial stability report. Chapter 3: Making over-the-counter derivatives safer: the role of central counterparties', Washington DC, www.imf.org.

International Commodities Clearing House (1988), *100 Years of ICCH*, London: ICCH.

ISDA (8 April 2009), 'ISDA announces successful implementation of "Big Bang" CDS protocol', New York, www.isda.org.

ISDA (2009), *ISDA 2009 Operations Benchmarking Surveys*, www.isda.org.

Janes, Hurford and Sayers, H.J. (1963), *The Story of Czarnikow*, London: Harley Publishing.

Jevons, William Stanley (1875), *Money and the Mechanism of Exchange*, London: Kegan Paul, Trench, Trübner & Co.

Jones, Lynton (April 2009), 'Issues affecting the OTC derivatives market and its importance to London', Bourse Consult, London.

JSCC (24 March 2010), 'Three year business plan' (FY2010-FY2012), Tokyo, http://www.jscc.co.jp/en/news/2010/3/Three-year%20Business%20Plan(FY2010~FY2012).pdf (accessed 10 December 2010).

JSCC, TSE, Japan Securities Depository Center study group (27 March 2009), 'Report on improvements of post-trade processing of OTC derivatives trades in Japan', Tokyo, www.tse.or.jp/english/news/200903/090330_a1.pdf (accessed 20 December 2010).

Kennedy, Paul (1988), *The Rise and Fall of the Great Powers*, London: Unwin Hyman.

Kenney, Dave (2006), *The Grain Merchants: An illustrated history of the Minneapolis Grain Exchange*, Afton, Minnesota: Afton Historical Society Press.

Kuprianov, Anatoli (1995), 'Derivatives debacles: Case studies of large losses in derivatives markets', *Economic Quarterly*, **81**(4), Fall, Federal Reserve Bank of Richmond.

Lacombe, Robert (1939), *La Bourse de Commerce du Havre (Marchés de Coton et de Café)*, Paris, Librarie du Recueil Sirey.
Lamfalussy Group (November 2000), 'Initial report of the committee of wise men on the regulation of European securities markets', Brussels: European Commission, http://ec.europa.eu/internal_market/securities/docs/lamfalussy/wisemen/initial-report-wise-men_en.pdf (accessed 10 December 2010).
Lamfalussy Group (February 2001), 'Final report of the committee of wise men on the regulation of European securities markets', Brussels: European Commission, http://ec.europa.eu/internal_market/securities/docs/lamfalussy/wisemen/final-report-wise-men_en.pdf (accessed 10 December 2010).
LCH (1991–2, 1992–3, 1993–4, 1994–5, 1995–6, 1996–7, 1998, 1999, 2000, 2001, 2002), Report and Accounts; and 'Interim Report for Half Year to 30 April 2003'.
LCH (October 1992), *Open House*, A journal published by LCH.
LCH and Clearnet SA (4 April 2000), 'Clearnet and LCH to create consolidated European clearing house', joint press release, London and Paris.
LCH and Clearnet (2003), 'Creating the central counterparty of choice', London and Paris.
LCH.Clearnet Group, Annual reports and consolidated financial statements: 2003, 2004, 2005, 2006, 2007, 2008, 2009, London, www.lchclearnet.com.
LCH.Clearnet Group (25 June 2003), 'An interview with David Hardy', London: LCH.Clearnet.
LCH.Clearnet Group (29 August 2006), 'Interim report for the half year to June 2006', London.
LCH.Clearnet Group (2007), 'Chairman's statement from the report and consolidated financial statements'.
LCH.Clearnet Group and Euronext NV (12 March 2007), 'LCH.Clearnet and Euronext announce repurchase by LCH.Clearnet of shares held by Euronext to more closely align customer and shareholder interests', joint announcement, www.lchclearnet.com.
LCH.Clearnet Group (9 August 2007), 'LCH.Clearnet requests interoperability links under Code of Conduct with Deutsche Börse and Borsa Italiana', press release, London, www.lchclearnet.com.
LCH.Clearnet Group (20 September 2007), 'LCH.Clearnet to implement Code of Conduct internally', press release, London, www.lchclearnet.com.
LCH.Clearnet Group (2008), 'Chief Executive's review, annual report and consolidated financial statements'.
LCH.Clearnet and Nymex (6 March 2008), 'Nymex and LCH.Clearnet announce historic clearing alliance', press release, New York and London.
LCH.Clearnet Group (29 April 2008), 'Results and announcements', press release.
LCH.Clearnet Group (8 October 2008), '$9 trillion Lehman OTC interest rate swap default successfully resolved', LCH.Clearnet Media Centre, London, www.lchclearnet.com.
LCH.Clearnet Group (31 October 2008), 'LCH.Clearnet and LIFFE agree new clearing arrangement', press release, London, www.lchclearnet.com.
LCH.Clearnet, Liffe, NYSE Euronext (22 December 2008), 'Liffe and LCH.Clearnet lead the way with the launch of Credit Default Swaps on Bclear', joint announcement, Amsterdam, Brussels, Lisbon, London, New York, Paris, www.lchclearnet.com.
LCH.Clearnet Group (2009) '2008 annual report and consolidated financial statements'.
LCH.Clearnet (3 February 2009), 'HSBC and JP Morgan become OTCDerivNet shareholders, further consolidating support for LCH.Clearnet's SwapClear service', press release, London, www.lchclearnet.com.
LCH.Clearnet SA (13 February 2009), 'LCH.Clearnet to launch Eurozone clearing of Credit Default Swaps', press release, Paris, www.lchclearnet.com.
LCH.Clearnet Group (29 September 2009), 'LCH.Clearnet to return up to €444 million to shareholders', London; LCH.Clearnet Group results and announcements, London, www.lchclearnet.com.
LCH.Clearnet Group with Euroclear (29 September 2009), 'LCH.Clearnet and Euroclear to jointly improve post-trade processing', joint announcement, London and Brussels, www.lchclearnet.com.
LCH.Clearnet (6 November 2009), 'LCH.Clearnet successfully realigns shareholder base', London. www.lchclearnet.com.
LCH.Clearnet (17 December 2009), 'LCH.Clearnet launches buy-side clearing for global OTC interest rate swaps', London, www.lchclearnet.com.
LCH.Clearnet Group (16 February 2010) '2009 annual report and consolidated financial statements'.
LCH.Clearnet Ltd and SIX x-clear AG (8 February 2010), Link agreement summary, London and Zurich, www.lchclearnet.com.

LCH.Clearnet Ltd (12 February 2010), 'Cross margining agreement review', London, Circular No 2581, www.lchclearnet.com.
LCH.Clearnet Group (12 May 2010), NYSE Euronext Clearing Services, Statement, London, www.lchclearnet.com.
LCH.Clearnet Group (9 September 2010), 'Notification: €130 bn of Spanish debt cleared in the first month', London, www.lchclearnet.com.
LCH.Clearnet Group (5 October 2010), 'LCH.Clearnet enhances CDS Clearing Service: Totals for the period from 31 March to 24 September 2010', press release, Paris, www.lchclearnet.com.
Levine, Allan (1987), *The Exchange: 100 Years of Trading Grain in Winnipeg*, Winnipeg: Peguis Publishers.
London Stock Exchange (23 July 2007), 'Proposed merger of London Stock Exchange Group plc and Borsa Italiana SpA'. Circular to shareholders and Notice of Extraordinary General Meeting, London.
LPCH (April 1888a), *Preliminary General Rules as to Membership*, London.
LPCH (April 1888b), *Preliminary Regulations for the Admission of Brokers authorised to deal with the London Produce Clearing House Ltd in Coffee Business for Future Delivery*, London.
LPCH (May 1888), *Regulations for Coffee Future Delivery Business*. London.
LPCH (July 1893), *Regulations for Future Delivery in Rio Coffee*, London.
LPCH, Annual Reports, 1888–1949.
LSE Group (18 January 2010), 'London Stock Exchange Group appoints new Director of Post Trade Services', press release, London, www.londonstockexchangegroup.com.
Lurie, Jonathan (1979), *The Chicago Board of Trade 1859–1905*, Urbana: University of Illinois Press.
Meier, Richard T and Sigrist, Tobias (2006), *Der helvetische Big Bang*, Zurich: Verlag Neue Zürcher Zeitung.
Melamed, Leo (June 1987), 'The way it was – An oral history', *Institutional Investor Magazine*.
Melamed, Leo (1988), 'Evolution of the International Monetary Market', *Cato Journal*, **8**(2), Fall.
Melamed, Leo (October 1988), 'Black Monday; What we know a year after the fact', Chicago: Chicago Enterprise.
Melamed, Leo, with Tamarkin, Bob (1996) *Escape to the Futures*, Chichester, UK: John Wiley & Sons, Ltd.
Merrill Lynch Europe Ltd (12 December 2008) 'London: Winning in a changing world – Review of the competitiveness of London's Financial Centre', Report commissioned by the Mayor of London, London, www.thecityuk.com.
Miller, Merton H. (May 1986) 'Financial innovation: The last twenty years and the next', Graduate School of Business, The University of Chicago, Selected Paper Number 63.
Minneapolis Chamber of Commerce (1902; 1915; 1917; 1920; 1922; 1926 and 1934), Rules and by-laws.
Minneapolis Tribune (24 July 1891), 'The grain clearing house'.
Minneapolis Tribune (3 September 1891), 'They don't want it: The Chamber of Commerce Clearing House Scheme dies a'bornin'.
Minneapolis Tribune (2 November 1891), 'A perfect clearing house: The one established by the Chamber of Commerce works like a charm'.
Miyamoto, Matao (1999). 'The Dojima Rice Exchange, the world's first commodity futures market', *Journal of Japanese Trade and Industry*, May/June.
Morris, Virginia B. and Goldstein, Stuart Z. (2009) *Guide to Clearance & Settlement: an introduction to DTCC*, New York: Lightbulb Press.
Moscow, Michael H. (4 April 2006), 'Remarks' to a Joint Conference of the European Central Bank and Chicago Fed on *Issues Related to Central Counterparty Clearing*, Frankfurt.
Moser, James T. (1994), 'Origins of the modern exchange clearinghouse', Working Paper Series, *Issues in Financial Regulation*, Federal Reserve Bank of Chicago, Chicago, USA.
Norman, Peter (2007), *Plumbers and Visionaries: Securities settlement and Europe's financial market*, Chichester, UK: John Wiley & Sons, Ltd.
NYSE Euronext (25 March 2008), 'Liffe to create LiffeClear', news release, Amsterdam, Brussels, Lisbon, London, Paris, New York, www.euronext.com.
NYSE Euronext (12 May 2010), 'NYSE Euronext announces European clearing strategy', Amsterdam, Brussels, Lisbon, London, New York and Paris, www.euronext.com.
NYSE Euronext and DTCC (18 June 2009), 'NYSE Euronext and DTCC to create Joint Venture for more efficient clearing of US Fixed Income Securities and Derivatives', joint press release, New York, www.dtcc.com.

NYSE Euronext and DTCC (13 October 2009), 'NYSE Euronext & DTCC finalize Joint Venture Agreement to create New York Portfolio Clearing', joint press release, New York, www.dtcc.com.

NYSE Group and Euronext NV (1 June 2006), 'NYSE Group and Euronext NV agree to a merger of equals', joint news release, New York and Paris.

Office of Fair Trading (30 June 2008), 'ICE Clear Europe Ltd: Application to become a recognised clearing house'; report submitted to the UK Treasury on 15 April 2008. OFT 1003: non-confidential report under section 303(3) of the Financial Services and Markets Act 2000, published as crown copyright.

Operations Management Group (OMG) (31 July 2008), 'Summary of OTC derivatives Commitments', New York. Further commitments covered in the book followed on 31 October 2008, 2 June 2009, 8 September 2009, 1 March 2010, www.newyorkfed.org.

The Options Clearing Corp (2010), 'Good News and New Opportunities', 2009 Annual Report, Chicago, www.optionsclearing.com.

Orbell, John (2004), 'Czarnikow, (Julius) Caesar (1838–1909)', *Oxford Dictionary of National Biography*, Oxford: Oxford University Press.

Paulson, Hank (2010) *On the Brink*, New York: Business Plus.

People's Bank of China (28 November 2009a), 'Speech of Governor Zhou Xiaochuan at the Opening Ceremony of the Shanghai Clearing House', http://www.pbc.gov.cn/publish/english/956/2010/20100524152218896622313/20100524152218896622313.html (accessed 20 December 2010).

People's Bank of China (28 November 2009b), 'Interbank Market Clearing House Co Ltd set up in Shanghai', News release, www.pbc.gov.cn/english (accessed 20 December 2010).

Poitras, Geoffrey (2000), *The Early History of Financial Economics, 1478–1776*, Cheltenham, UK: Edward Elgar.

Pozmanter, Murray (10 September 2009), 'Why competition really is the future'. Letter to the *Financial Times*.

President's Working Group on Financial Markets (14 November 2008), 'Policy objectives for the OTC derivatives market', Washington DC, www.ustreas.gov/press/releases/hp1272.htm.

PwC (7 November 2008), 'Unsettled trades – market update'. PwC communication regarding LBIE (in administration), London, www.pwc.co.uk.

Rees, Graham L. (1972), *Britain's Commodity Markets*, London: Paul Elek Books.

Reserve Bank of India (March 2010), 'Financial stability report', New Delhi.

Reuters News (17 July 2001), 'Banks see no pan-European share trade counterparty', London.

Reuters (14 April 2010), 'Firms reaped windfalls in Lehman auction: examiner', New York/Chicago: Reuters.

Reuters (28 April 2010), 'CFTC, SEC frown on bigger safety net for clearers', Washington DC.

Rodengen, Jeffrey l. (2008), *Past, Present and Futures: Chicago Mercantile Exchange*, Write Stuff Enterprises.

Roy, Siddhartha (2006), 'India's experiment with a new settlement system for its domestic foreign exchange market', http://www.ccilindia.com/RSCH_ATCL.html (accessed 9 December 2010).

Rufenacht, Charles (1955), *Le Café et les Principaux Marchés de Matieres Premieres*, Le Havre: Ste Commerciale Inter-Oceanique.

St Paul Daily Globe (3 September 1891), 'They voted it down'.

Sano, Zensaku and Iura, Sentaro (1931), 'Commodity exchanges in Japan', *The Annals of the American Academy of Political and Social Science*, **155**, Part 1, Philadelphia.

Santos, Joseph (2008), 'A history of futures trading in the United States, *EH Net Encyclopaedia*, Whaples, R. (ed.), http://eh.net/encyclopaedia/article/Santos.futures (accessed 3 December 2010).

SBF Paris Bourse MATIF (24 January 1997), 'MATIF opts for NSC for off-hours trading. Joint SBF Paris Bourse–MATIF subsidiary to manage index futures', press release, Paris.

SBF (1 June 1999), 'SBF Group restructures, specialising to meet international competition even more effectively', press release of ParisBourse SBF SA, Paris.

Schaede, Ulrike (1983), 'Forwards and futures in Tokugawa period Japan: A new perspective on the Dojima rice market', *Journal of Banking and Finance*, **13**, 487–513. Also in Smitka, Michael (ed.) (1998), *The Japanese Economy in the Tokugawa Era, 1600–1868*, New York and London: Garland Publishing.

Securities Commission (1 November 1990), 'Report on the enquiry into the trading in the five year government stock No 2 futures contract on the New Zealand Futures and Options Exchange in 1989', Wellington: New Zealand.

SEC (February 1988), 'The October 1987 market break', Washington DC.

SEC (28 December 1999), 'Government Securities Clearing Corporation; Notice of filing of proposed rule change relating to the formation and involvement in the European Securities Clearing Corporation'. *Federal Register*, **65**(3), Washington.

Securities Industry Association (May 2005), 'Organisation in the US Market for Clearing and Settlement', New York, Background note prepared by the Cross-Border Subcommittee of the SIA for the European Commission, www.ec.europa.eu.

Seifert, Werner with Voth, Hans-Joachim (2006), *Invasion der Heuschrecken*, Berlin: Econ Verlag.

SGX (20 September 2010), 'Singapore Exchange – First in Asia to clear OTC traded financial derivatives', Singapore, www.sgx.com (accessed 20 December 2010).

Shimoda, Tomoyuki (2006), 'Exchanges and CCPs: Communication, governance and risk management'. Presentation to the joint conference of the *European Central Bank and the Federal Reserve Bank of Chicago on the role of Central Counterparties (CCPs)*, 3–4 April 2006, Frankfurt.

Storry, Richard (1960), *A History of Modern Japan*, London: Penguin Books.

Swan, Edward (2000), *Building the Global Market: A 4000 year history of derivatives*, New York: Kluwer Law International.

Tamarkin Bob (1993), *The Merc*, New York: Harpercollins.

Teweles, Richard J., Harlow, Charles V. and Stone, Herbert L. (1974), *The Commodity Futures Game*, New York: McGraw-Hill.

The Times, London: Following editions are referred to: 12 February 1909; 21 April 1909; 1 January 1913; 31 January 1914; 5 February 1916, Law Report; 25 October 1921; 4 December 1969; 3 November 1971; 16 May 1972; 18 December 1974; 3 December 1979; 31 January 1981; 12 October 1981.

Thistlethwaite, Frank (1955), *The Great Experiment*, Cambridge: University Press.

Tupker, Chris (12 September 2008), Speaking at the 2008 *Eurofi Conference, EU Priorities and Proposals from the Financial Services Industry for the ECOFIN Council,* Nice.

US Department of Justice (November 1998), 'Antitrust Division versus American Stock Exchange, CBOE, Pacific Exchange and Philadelphia Exchange: Civil Action No. 00-CV-02174(EGS)', Washington DC.

US Department of Justice (11 September 2000), 'Justice Department files suit Challenging Anticompetitive Agreement among Options Exchanges', press release, Washington DC.

US Department of Justice (31 January 2008), 'Comments of the US Department of Justice in response to the Department of Treasury's request for comments on the Regulatory Structure Associated with Financial Institutions', Washington, DC, www.justice.gov/.../comments/229911.htm.

US Department of the Treasury (14 November 2008), 'PWG announces initiative to strengthen OTC derivatives oversight and infrastructure', press release, Washington DC, www.ustreas.gov/press/releases/hp1272.htm.

US Department of the Treasury (13 May 2009), 'Letter of Timothy Geithner to Senate Majority Leader Harry Reid and others', Washington DC.

US Department of the Treasury (17 June 2009), 'Financial regulatory reform: A new foundation'. Washington DC, www.ustreas.gov.

US Department of the Treasury (10 July 2009), Timothy Geithner, US Treasury Secretary, before the House Financial Services and Agriculture Committees joint hearing on regulation of OTC derivatives.

US Department of the Treasury (11 August 2009), 'Administration's regulatory reform agenda reaches new milestone: Final piece of legislative language delivered to Capitol Hill', Washington DC, www.ustreas.gov.

US House of Representatives Committee on Oversight and Government Reform (7 October 2008), 'Hearing on the AIG bailout'. Washington, DC, http://oversight.house.gov.

Valukas, Anton R. (2010), 'Examiner Report re Lehman Brothers Holdings Inc. to the US Bankruptcy Court Southern District of New York'. Volume 5, Section III.B,3,(h) CME Avoidance Analysis. Published in redacted form 12 March 2010 and unredacted 14 April 2010, Chicago and New York: Jenner & Block LLP.

Various authors (1911), The Exchanges of Minneapolis, Duluth, Kansas City, Mo., Omaha, Buffalo, Philadelphia, Milwaukee and Toledo, *The Annals of the American Academy of Political and Social Science*, **38**, Philadelphia.

Vega, Joseph de la (1996), *Confusión des Confusiones*, Marketplace Book edition, New York: John Wiley & Sons Inc.

Weber, Max (1988), 'Die Börse', in *Gesammelte Aufsätze zur Soziologie und Sozialpolitik*, Tübingen, Germany: Marianne Weber; also available at http://www.zeno.org/Soziologie/M/Weber,+Max/Schriften+zur+Soziologie+und+Sozialpolitik/Die+Börse/II.+Der+Börsenverkehr (accessed 3 December 2010).
White House (15 November 2008), *Declaration of the Summit on Financial Markets and the World Economy*. Washington, www.iasplus.com/crunch/0811g20declaration.pdf.
Winnipeg Grain and Produce Exchange Clearing Association (March 1901), 'Clearing Association, Agreement and Subscription List'.
Winnipeg Grain and Produce Exchange Clearing Association (28 June 1901), 'Certificate of Incorporation'.
Winnipeg Grain and Produce Exchange Clearing Association (12 July 1921), 'Nature of Organisation and Historical'.
Wood, Duncan (15 April 2010), 'LCH.Clearnet CEO calls rival "reckless" as Fannie, Freddie clearing battle heats up', *Risk Magazine*, London.
World Federation of Exchanges (2010) *WFE 2009 Market Highlights*, www.world-exchanges.org (accessed 20 December 2010).

ADDITIONAL READING

Boland, Vincent (2009), 'Banking: The first chapter', *FT Weekend Magazine*, 18–19 April 2009.
Coste, René (1959), *Les Cafiérs et les Cafés dans le Monde*, Paris, Editions Larose.
Deutsche Börse Group (2009), *The Global Derivatives Market: A Blueprint for Market Safety and Integrity*, Frankfurt, www.deutsche-boerse.com.
Hasenpusch, Tina P. (2009), *Clearing Services for Global Markets*, Cambridge University Press.
LCH (2002), *Market Protection*, London, London Clearing House Ltd.
Lee, Ruben (January 2010), *The Governance of Financial Market Infrastructure*, Oxford Finance Group, www.oxfordfinancegroup.com.
Leick, Gwendolyn (2002), *Mesopotamia. The Invention of the City*, London: Penguin Books.
Tett, Gillian (2009), *Fool's Gold*, London, Little Brown.
Young, Patrick L. [editor] (2004), *An Intangible Commodity*, Swiss Futures & Options Association.

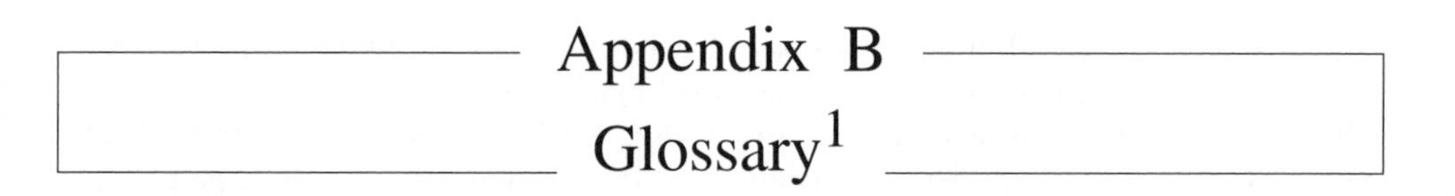

Appendix B Glossary[1]

Algorithmic trading (also **automated** or **algo trading)** The use of computers to make trading decisions with the computer algorithm deciding such features as the timing, price or quantity of the order, and often initiating the order without human intervention. See also **high-frequency trading**, which has grown rapidly on the back of the increased speeds and capabilities of algorithmic processing.

Arbitrage The exploitation of price differences in connected markets.

Back office The part of a firm that is responsible for post-trade activities.

Back testing An ex-post comparison of observed outcomes compared with expected outcomes.

Bilateral collateral agreement An agreement that defines the terms or rules under which collateral is posted or transferred between counterparties to a non-cleared OTC derivatives contract.

Central Counterparty (CCP) An entity that interposes itself between counterparties to contracts traded in one or more financial markets, becoming the buyer to every seller and the seller to every buyer, with the aim of ensuring that trades are completed if one or more counterparties defaults.

Central counterparty CCP link An arrangement between two or more CCPs that provides clearing of trades between the participants of the CCPs involved, without obliging participants of one CCP to become members of the other CCPs.

Central securities depository (CSD) An infrastructure that holds or controls the holding of physical or dematerialised financial instruments belonging to all, or a large proportion, of the investors in a particular securities market. The CSD effects the centralised transfer of ownership of such securities by entries on its books and records.

Clearing In securities markets, the process of establishing settlement positions, including the calculation of net positions, and the process of checking that securities, cash or both are available for the settlement of obligations. In the case of derivatives, it has come to refer to the process of daily marking to market, netting and daily settlement of positions leading to the establishment of final delivery positions in cash, commodities or securities. May be summed up as the process used for managing the risk of open positions.

Clearing house A central entity (or central processing mechanism) through which financial institutions agree to exchange transfer instructions for funds, commodities or securities. As

[1] This glossary has been compiled from several sources. It includes selected items from the glossary of the CPSS-IOSCO 'Recommendations for CCPs', published in November 2004 by the Bank for International Settlements, which are reproduced by permission of the BIS. It has also drawn on glossaries in the European Commission's 'Staff Working Document' accompanying its proposals for a 'Regulation on OTC Derivatives, CCPs and Trade Repositories' of September 2010; the EU Commission's Communication, 'Ensuring efficient, safe and sound derivatives markets' of July 2009; the ESCB-CESR 'Recommendations for securities settlement systems and central counterparties in the European Union' of May 2009 and the author's book *Plumbers and Visionaries* of December 2007. The author is grateful to Rory Cunningham for his advice on the selection.

this book demonstrates, clearing houses have acted increasingly as central counterparties for their participants, and in the process have assumed significant financial risks.

Clearing member A member of a clearing house: that is, an entity that contracts directly with a clearing house and thereby benefits from the clearing house's counterparty credit protection. In a CCP context, a general clearing member (GCM) clears its own trades, for its customers and for non-clearing members, the latter being participants of the trading venue where the GCM trades but which do not have direct access to the CCP. There are also direct and individual clearing members, whose roles can vary from CCP to CCP, but generally clear on their own behalf and on behalf of their customers.

Code of Conduct Agreement brokered by the European Commission and signed on 7 November 2006 by the chief executives of European equities trading and post-trade companies with the main aim of offering market participants the freedom to choose their preferred provider of services separately at each layer of the transaction chain, comprising trading, clearing and settlement. The code has failed in its main aim of enabling market participants to choose separately their trading, clearing and settlement venues thereby overcoming the barriers to cross-border equities trading between EU member states.

Collateral An asset or third-party commitment that is used by the collateral provider to secure an obligation vis-a-vis the collateral taker. Collateral is used by a clearing house or other taker to protect itself should the clearing member or client fail. See also **Margin**.

Collateral management service A centralised service that may handle any of a variety of collateral-related functions for a client firm, including valuation of collateral, confirmation of valuations with counterparties, optimisation of collateral usage and transfer of collateral.

Complete clearing Term used to describe the method of clearing houses that functioned as the buyer to every seller and seller to every buyer in the early years after the technique was introduced in the US in the late 19th century. Now known as CCP clearing.

Confirmation A document identifying the details of a trade and any governing legal documentation, as agreed by both parties. The confirmation document serves as the final record of the trade. See also **Verification**.

Counterparty A party to a trade.

Credit event An event that may trigger the exercise of a CDS contract. Credit events include failure to pay interest or principal when due, bankruptcy or restructuring.

Cross-border trade A trade between counterparties located in different countries.

Cross-margining agreement An agreement between two CCPs which makes it possible to limit the margin requirements for institutions participating in both CCPs by considering the positions and collateral of such participants as one portfolio.

Default The failure to satisfy an obligation on time in accordance with the terms and rules of the system. A failure to pay or deliver on the due date, breach of agreement and the opening of insolvency proceedings can constitute events of default. Default is usually distinguished from a failed transaction, which can arise for reasons that are technical or temporary.

Default fund A fund composed of assets typically contributed by a CCP's participants that may be used by the CCP in certain circumstances to cover losses and liquidity pressures resulting from defaults by the CCP's participants. Also known as clearing fund.

Default waterfall A pre-specified sequence in which the instruments for safeguarding the CCP are to be used in the event of a clearing member's default, including **Margin**, **Default fund** and other resources, such as insurance or parental guarantees.

Delivery The final transfer of a security or financial instrument.

Delivery versus Payment (DvP) A procedure that links the transfer of securities or other financial instruments and the payment of funds in such a way that the delivery of the assets occurs if, and only if, payment occurs.

Derivative A financial contract, the value of which depends on the value of one or more underlying reference assets, rates or indices. Derivatives contracts include forwards, futures, options, swaps or combinations of these.

Directive A European Union law applied with binding force throughout the EU but where it is left to the member state to decide the form and methods necessary to achieve the desired result in national laws through a process of transposition.

Discount Price expressed as the number of percentage points below par: for example, a discount price of 3% equals a price of 97 when par is 100.

EMIR (European Markets Infrastructure Regulation) Working title of EU legislation proposed by the European Commission in September 2010 to regulate CCPs, the OTC derivatives market and trade repositories.

Equity Ownership interest in a corporation in the form of common stock or preferred stock. The securities representing ownership of the stake can be quoted or listed shares traded on a stock exchange, unquoted or unlisted shares and other forms of equity. Equities form the risk-bearing part of the company's capital. They usually produce income in the form of dividends.

Euro The European single currency: usually expressed in lower case as 'euro' or by the symbol €.

Eurosystem Comprises the ECB and the central banks of those countries that have adopted the euro. Not to be confused with the ESCB (European System of Central Banks), which comprises the ECB and central banks of all EU member states. The Eurosystem and ESCB coexist as long as there are EU member states outside the euro area.

Exposure The amount of funds at risk. In other words, the amount that may be lost in an investment.

Fail or failed transaction A failure to settle a transaction on the contractual settlement date, usually because of technical or temporary asset-delivery difficulties. Fail is qualitatively different from default.

Final maturity Repayment in full of a debt security, investment trust or a preferred stock issue, at stated maturity.

Final settlement The discharge of an obligation by a transfer of funds and/or a transfer of securities or commodities that become irrevocable and unconditional.

Financial resources In the context of a **default waterfall**, the combination of resources that a CCP maintains for use in the event of a default by a participant. Financial resources generally comprise collateral (including margin) posted by participants to meet various CCP requirements, a default fund, as well as a CCP's capital and retained earnings. The CCP might also have contingent claims on non-defaulting participants, parent organisations or insurers.

Financial Services Action Plan (FSAP) EU programme, comprising 42 measures, drawn up in 1999 with the aim of creating a single European market for financial services. The single market is still work in progress as this book goes to press.

Fixed income security An investment that provides a return in the form of fixed periodic payments and eventual return of principal at maturity. Unlike a variable income security, where payments change based on some underlying measure such as short-term interest rates, fixed income securities payments are known in advance.

Front office A firm's trading unit and other areas that are responsible for developing and managing relationships with counterparties.
Fungibility In the context of derivatives markets, contracts that can be offset. Only fungible contracts can be used to close open positions.
Futures contract A legal agreement to buy or sell a standard quantity of a specified asset for delivery at a fixed future date at a price agreed today.
Governance Procedures through which the objectives of a legal entity are set, the means of achieving them are identified and the performance of the entity is measured. This refers, in particular, to the set of relationships between the entity's owners, board of directors, management, users, regulators and other stakeholders that influence these outcomes.
Group of Seven (G7) The US, Japan, Germany, France, UK, Canada and Italy. The G7 group of leading industrialised countries was the main forum for attempts to coordinate economic policy between 1987 and 2008.
Group of 10 (G10) Belgium, Canada, France, Germany, Italy, Japan, the Netherlands, Sweden, Switzerland, UK and US. Confusingly made up of 11 countries, the G10 was established in the 1960s to make resources available to the IMF, in case of need, through the General Arrangements to Borrow (GAB). As its members were, and still are, financially important, it has acted as a forum for financial policy cooperation.
Group of Twenty (G20) The G7 countries plus: Argentina, Australia, Brazil, China, India, Indonesia, Mexico, Russia, Saudi Arabia, South Africa, Republic of Korea, Turkey plus the EU. Took over the international economic policy coordination role from the G7 in November 2008, after the financial hurricane of September–October that year.
Group of Thirty (G30) An eminent financial think tank.
Haircut The difference between the market value of an asset and the value that it can collateralise. A collateral taker applies haircuts in order to protect itself against losses caused by declines in the market value of assets that it holds in case it has to liquidate them.
Hedge A position established in one market in an attempt to offset exposure to the risk of an equal but opposite obligation or position in another market.
Hedging The act of taking a position in a derivatives contract to insure against future price fluctuations.
High-frequency trading (HFT) The execution of computerised trading strategies that enable financial assets to be bought and sold in milliseconds (one-thousandth of a second) or microseconds (one millionth of a second) and which are held for extremely short periods. Using algorithms, computers execute thousands of trades in the blink of an eye. Concerns about HFT came to the fore after the 'Flash Crash' of 6 May 2010 when the Dow Jones Industrial Average plunged by nearly 1000 points in 20 minutes.
Horizontal integration Where clearing and settlement activities are separately owned and controlled from trading activity but where one or all of these three activities are integrated with those of other providers according to function.
Initial public offering (IPO) The first time a company makes its shares available for sale to the public.
International Central Securities Depository (ICSD) An entity that settles trades in international securities and cross-border transactions in various domestic securities. Like CSDs, ICSDs hold and administer securities or other financial assets, are involved with the issuance of new securities and enable transactions to be processed by book entry. Europe's two large ICSDs – Euroclear Bank and Clearstream Banking Luxembourg – were set up in 1968 and 1970 respectively to settle Eurobonds.

International securities identification number (ISIN) A 12-digit security identification code. Its registration and maintenance authority is ANNA, the Association of National Numbering Agencies.
Interoperability Where one infrastructure service provider creates a business relationship with another infrastructure service provider, horizontally or, less typically, with another layer of the capital market, to provide cross-system execution of services such as clearing and settlement. Interoperability requires technical compatibility between systems, but can only take effect where commercial agreements have been concluded between the schemes concerned.
Interoperable systems Two or more systems whose operators have entered into an arrangement – including links – between themselves that involves cross-system execution of trades.
Intraday credit Credit extended for a period of less than one business day, sometimes by a central bank.
Investment Services Directive (ISD) European Union law of 1993 that was intended to create a single capital market for Europe but had a limited impact only.
Issuer The entity, which is obligated on a security or other financial instrument: for example, a corporation or government having the authority to issue and sell a security on the primary market.
Issue price Initial issue price of a financial instrument.
Margin An asset (or third-party commitment) that is accepted by a counterparty to ensure performance on actual or potential obligations to it or to cover market movements on unsettled transactions.
Margin categories include

- **Initial margin** The returnable deposit paid to the clearing house by the counterparty when entering into transactions on the markets cleared. Initial margin is the estimate of the worst case loss on a contract or portfolio over an assumed close-out period for the position held under normal market conditions in the event of the counterparty's default.
- **Variation margin** Funds that are paid by (or received by) a counterparty to settle any losses (gains) resulting from marking open positions to market. In some markets the term is also used to describe the posting of collateral by a counterparty to cover a mark-to-market deficit.

Margin call A process whereby counterparties are required to supply additional securities or cash in cases where collateral value falls below a certain level.
Markets in Financial Instruments Directive (MiFID) European Union legislation that took effect in November 2007. MiFID comprehensively revised the 1993 **Investment Services Directive** (ISD), with the aim of further integrating and boosting competition in EU financial markets.
Marking to market The practice of revaluing open positions in financial instruments at current market prices and the calculation of any gains or losses that have occurred since the last valuation.
Matching The process for comparing trade or settlement details provided by counterparties in written or electronic form to ensure that the two agree with respect to the terms of the transaction.
Moral hazard The incentive for persons involved in financial institutions to engage in imprudent risks because of the existence or expectation of government protection or insurance.

Multilateral netting Netting on a multilateral basis by summing each participant's bilateral net positions with the other participants to arrive at a multilateral net position. Such netting is often conducted through a central counterparty, but can also be done by other entities.
Netting An agreed offsetting of obligations or positions, for example, by participants in a CCP. Netting reduces the gross risk exposures of the CCP and its members. It can also cut sharply a clearing member's transaction costs of closing out or settling trades, reduce the complexity of its back office and the risk of failed deliveries. In securities clearing, netting reduces a large number of gross positions or obligations to a smaller number of net obligations or positions and can sharply reduce settlement volumes.
Notional amount The reference amount on which a derivative contract is written.
Novation A process through which the original obligation between a buyer and seller is discharged through the substitution of a new party, for example a CCP, as seller to buyer and buyer to seller, creating two new contracts.
Open interest The total number of open derivative contracts on a specific underlying. Open interest is registered on the books of a CCP.
Option A contract that gives the holder the right, but not the obligation, to buy or sell a specified asset at an agreed price on or before an agreed-to date in the future. The right to buy an asset is known as a call option. The right to sell is known as a put option.
Over-the-counter (OTC) market Market outside organised exchanges in which trades are conducted through a telephone or computer network connecting the market participants, until recently, usually without a CCP.
Oversight Typically carried out by a central bank, oversight of financial infrastructures promotes the objectives of safety and efficiency by monitoring existing and planned service providers by assessing them against applicable standards and principles and, where necessary, inducing change.
Plain vanilla transactions Generally a type of derivative trade with simple, common terms that can be processed electronically. Transactions with unusual or less common features are often referred to as exotic, structured or bespoke.
Position The stance an investor takes vis-a-vis the market. An investor's position is said to be long or short when he or she buys or sells a financial instrument. In futures or options markets, a short position is an open sold position. A short seller is someone who sells a cash asset not previously owned. Often also used to refer to an investor's or intermediary's overall portfolio of securities and/or derivatives.
Premium Price expressed as the number of percentage points above par: for example, a premium of 3% equals a price of 103 where par is 100.
Principal A party to a transaction that acts on its own behalf. In acting as a principal, a firm is buying or selling, or lending or borrowing securities from its own account.
Proprietary trading or 'prop trading' When a firm trades financial instruments with its own money to profit from the market rather than with its customers' money to earn commissions from processing trades.
Reference entity A corporate, sovereign or any other form of legal entity that has incurred debt, on which a CDS is written.
Regulation In the context of the European Union, a uniform EU law applied with binding force throughout the EU that does not need transposition into national laws.
Regulator A government agency, or a self-regulatory body, that sets the rules for the regulation of a market, its participants and infrastructure, as well as the relationship between the different parties in the market.

Repo or sale and repurchase agreement Contract to sell and subsequently repurchase securities at a specified date and price. It involves a cash loan against a guarantee in securities, with a firm commitment that the seller will repurchase the securities and reimburse the cash at an agreed price and date. At the initiation of the transaction, the seller is the securities provider and the buyer is the cash lender. At the maturity of the transaction, remuneration – the accrued interest – is usually paid to the cash lender.
Risks Categories include

- **Counterparty credit risk** The risk that a counterparty will not settle an obligation for full value, either when due or at any time afterwards. Counterparty credit risk includes replacement cost risk and principal risk.
- **Custody risk** The risk of loss on securities in safekeeping (custody) as a result of the custodian's insolvency, negligence, misuse of assets, fraud, poor administration or inadequate record keeping.
- **Investment risk** The risk of loss faced, for example by a CCP, when it invests its own resources or cash margin posted by its participants in obligations with market, credit and liquidity risks.
- **Legal risk** The risk that a party will suffer a loss because laws or regulations do not support contractual rules (e.g., of a CCP) or the property rights and other interests held (e.g., through a CCP). Legal risk also arises if the application of laws and regulations is unclear.
- **Liquidity risk** The risk that a counterparty will not settle an obligation for full value when due, but on some unspecified date thereafter, thereby preventing the entity from fulfilling its own obligations as they fall due (e.g., intra-day).
- **Market risk** The risk of losses from movements in market prices.
- **Operational risk** The risk that deficiencies in information systems or internal controls, human errors, management failures or external events such as natural disasters or terrorist attacks will result in unexpected losses.
- **Principal risk** The risk that the seller of an asset delivers it but does not receive payment or that the buyer of an asset makes payment but does not receive delivery. In such an event, the full principal value of the asset or funds transferred is at risk.
- **Replacement cost risk** The risk that a counterparty to a trade for completion at a future date will default before final settlement. The resulting exposure is the cost of replacing the original transaction at current market prices. Also known as 'pre-settlement risk'.
- **Settlement bank risk** The risk that a CCP's settlement bank could fail, creating credit losses and liquidity pressures for the CCP and its participants.
- **Settlement risk** The general term used for the risk that settlement in a funds or securities transfer system will not take place as expected. This risk may comprise both credit and liquidity risk.
- **Systemic risk** The risk that the inability of one institution to meet its obligations when due will cause other institutions to be unable to meet their obligations when due. Such a failure may cause significant liquidity or credit problems and, as a result, might threaten the stability of, or confidence in, markets.

Security An instrument that signifies an ownership position in a corporation, a credit relationship with a corporation or governmental body, or other rights to ownership.
Securities lending and borrowing The lending of securities in exchange for a fee. Can involve transferring full ownership of securities with or without a guarantee or a firm commitment that the seller will repurchase the securities at an agreed price and date.

Segregated account An account used for the segregation of a client's assets.
Segregation A method of protecting a client's assets by holding them separately from those of the custodian, charged with safekeeping the assets, or from those of other clients.
Settlement The completion of a transaction wherein the seller transfers securities or commodities to the buyer and the buyer transfers cash to the seller.
Settlement bank A bank that is used to effect cash settlements between a CCP and its participants.
Settlement interval The amount of time in securities settlement that elapses between the trade date and the settlement date. Typically measured relative to the trade date: for example, if three days elapse, the settlement interval is T+3.
Settlement price Price used by a CCP as the basis for margin calculations. May be an official market closing price or the price of the asset as defined by CCP rules.
Side Half of a trade cleared by a CCP when it acts as the buyer to every seller and the seller to every buyer. Every trade registered with the CCP has two sides – a buy side and a sell side. CCPs often measure the volume of trades cleared in terms of sides.
Silo The result of exclusive vertical integration of infrastructure service providers, often in one corporate entity. A silo can encompass all elements of the transaction chain from trading, through central counterparty clearing to settlement. Often described as a vertical silo.
Straight Through Processing (STP) The automated end-to-end processing of trades, including, where relevant, the confirmation, matching, generation and clearing and settlement of transactions without the need for manual intervention in re-keying or reformatting data.
Stress testing The estimation of credit and liquidity exposures that would result from the realisation of extreme price changes.
Swap A form of derivative contract created when two counterparties agree to exchange one stream of cash flows against another on a notional principal amount of two financial instruments. There are several types of swap with very different risk profiles. Interest rate swaps (IRS) are an important hedging instrument and are the most common. There are also credit default swaps (CDS), equity swaps, commodity swaps and foreign exchange swaps.
Target2-Securities (T2S) Securities settlement service being developed by the ECB for the eurozone and other European countries, with launch scheduled for 2014. T2S will be fully owned and operated by the Eurosystem.
Trade repository A centralised registry that maintains an electronic database of open OTC derivative contracts.
Underlying The financial instrument, security or commodity on which a derivatives contract is based.
Verification The process of comparing and, if necessary, reconciling discrepancies in the transaction or settlement details which is commonly handled at or close to the point of trade. Verification covers issues such as price, quantity and settlement date of the trade and is preliminary to, rather than part of, clearing and settlement.

Appendix C
Abbreviations of Company, Industry Group and Regulators' Names

ACCC Adler, Coleman Clearing Corporation
ACP Autorité de contrôle prudential (France)
AFM Autoriteit Financiële Markten (Netherlands)
ALK Amsterdamsche Liquidatiekas
Amex American Stock Exchange
AMF Autorité des Marchés Financiers (France)
ASX Australian Securities Exchange
BaFin Bundesanstalt für Finanzdienstleistungsaufsicht (Germany)
BCC Banque Centrale de Compensation (France)
BIS Bank for International Settlements
BOTCC Board of Trade Clearing Corporation
Cb Commission bancaire (France)
CBOE Chicago Board Options Exchange
CBOT Chicago Board of Trade
CCIFP Chambre de Compensation des Instruments Financiers de Paris
CCIL Clearing Corporation of India
CC&G Cassa di Compensazione e Garanzia (Italy)
CCorp The Clearing Corporation
CEA Commodity Exchange Authority
CECEI Comité des Établissements de Crédit et des Entreprises d'Investissement (France)
Cesame The (EU Commission's) Clearing and Settlement Advisory and Monitoring Expert Group
CESR Committee of European Securities Regulators
CFTC Commodity Futures Trading Commission
CLAM Caisse de Liquidation des Affaires en Marchandises (of Paris)
CME Chicago Mercantile Exchange, now part of the CME Group
COGESI European Central Bank's Contact Group on Euro Securities Infrastructures
CPSS Committee on Payment and Settlement Systems
CRMPG Counterparty Risk Management Policy Group
CSFI Centre for the Study of Financial Innovation
DG Comp European Commission directorate general for enforcing EU competition law
DG Markt European Commission directorate general for the Internal Market
DKV Deutscher Kassenverein
DNB Dutch National Bank or De Nederlandsche Bank

DoJ	US Department of Justice
DTB	Deutsche Terminbörse
DTC	Depository Trust Company
DTCC	Depository Trust and Clearing Corporation
EACH	European Association of Central Counterparty Clearing Houses
ECB	European Central Bank
ECOFIN	The formation of the EU Council of Ministers comprising economic and finance ministers from all member states
ECON	European Parliament's economic and monetary affairs committee
ECSDA	The European Central Securities Depositories Association
EMCC	Emerging Markets Clearing Corporation
EMCF	European Multilateral Clearing Facility NV
ESCB	European System of Central Banks
ESF	European Securities Forum
ESIUG	European Securities Industry Users' Group
ESMA	European Securities and Markets Authority
ESRB	European Systemic Risk Board
EuroCCP	European Central Counterparty Ltd
FDIC	Federal Deposit Insurance Corporation
FESE	Federation of European Securities Exchanges
FGC	Futures Guarantee Corporation (of Hong Kong)
FIA	Futures Industry Association (of the US)
FICC	Fixed Income Clearing Corporation
FINMA	Swiss Financial Market Supervisory Authority
FOA	Futures and Options Association (of the UK)
FSA	Financial Services Agency (of Japan)
FSA	Financial Services Authority (of the UK)
FSB	Financial Stability Board
FSF	Financial Stability Forum
FSOC	Financial Security Oversight Council
FSSCC	Financial Services Sector Coordinating Council (for Critical Infrastructure Protection and Homeland Security)
FTC	Federal Trade Commission
GAO	General Accounting Office
GNMA	Government National Mortgage Association
GSCC	Government Securities Clearing Corporation
HKFE	Hong Kong Futures Exchange
HKEx	Hong Kong Exchanges and Clearing Ltd
HKMEx	Hong Kong Mercantile Exchange
HKSCC	Hong Kong Securities Clearing Company
ICC	Intermarket Clearing Corporation (US)
ICCH	International Commodities Clearing House (UK)
ICE	IntercontinentalExchange
IDCG	International Derivatives Clearing Group (US)
IDCH	International Derivatives Clearinghouse (US)
IMF	International Monetary Fund
IMM	International Monetary Market (US)

IOSCO	International Organisation of Securities Commissions
IPE	International Petroleum Exchange (UK)
ISB	Inter Sociétés de Bourse (of Paris)
ISDA	International Swaps and Derivatives Association
ISE	International Securities Exchange (US)
ITC	International Tin Council
JSCC	Japan Securities Clearing Corp
KLCCH	Kuala Lumpur Commodity Clearing House
KRX	Korea Exchange
LBH	Lehman Brothers Holdings
LBI	Lehman Brothers Inc.
LBIE	Lehman Brothers International Europe
LBSA	Lehman Brothers Securities Asia
LBSF	Lehman Brothers Special Financing Inc.
LCE	London Commodity Exchange
LCH	London Clearing House
LPCH	London Produce Clearing House
LIFFE	London International Financial Futures Exchange
LME	London Metal Exchange
LSE	London Stock Exchange
Ltd	LCH.Clearnet Ltd
LTOM	London Traded Options Market
MATIF	Marché à Terme d'Instruments Financiers (France)
MBSCC	Mortgage-Backed Securities Clearing Corporation
MICEX	Moscow Interbank Currency Exchange
MONEP	Marché des Options Négociables de Paris
NASD	National Association of Securities Dealers (US)
NCC	National Clearing Centre (of Russia)
NMS	National Market System (US)
NSCC	National Securities Clearing Corporation (of the US)
NSCCL	National Securities Clearing Corporation Ltd (of India)
NYBOT	New York Board of Trade
NYMEX	New York Mercantile Exchange
NYPC	New York Portfolio Clearing
NYSE	New York Stock Exchange
NZFOE	New Zealand Futures and Options Exchange
OCC	Options Clearing Corporation
OFT	Office of Fair Trading (of the UK)
OMG	Operations Management Group (of OTC dealers)
OSE	Osaka Securities Exchange
PwC	PricewaterhouseCoopers UK
SA	LCH.Clearnet SA
SEC	Securities and Exchange Commission
SEHK	Stock Exchange of Hong Kong
SFC	Securities and Futures Commission (of Hong Kong)
SFE	Sydney Futures Exchange
SFOA	Swiss Futures and Options Association

SGX Singapore Exchange Ltd
SIFMA Securities Industry Financial Markets Association
SIMEX Singapore International Monetary Exchange
SNB Swiss National Bank
SOFFEX Swiss Options and Financial Futures Exchange
TSB Trustee Savings Bank
UDT United Dominions Trust
VOC Verenigde Oost-Indische Compagnie (Dutch East India Company)
WFE World Federation of Exchanges

Index